THE MYOCARDIUM:
FAILURE AND INFARCTION

Adapted from
Hospital Practice

Illustrated by
Bunji Tagawa

Albert Miller
(charts and graphs)

Carol Woike

and the following contributing artists
Joan Dworkin, Gaetano Di Palma, Robin Ingle, Alan D. Iselin,
Enid Kotschnig, Irwin Kuperberg, Adele Spiegler

Photographs by
**Lester Bergman, Dan Bernstein, Jon Brenneis, James B.
Caulfield, M.D.** *(Massachusetts General Hospital)*, **and Arthur Leipzig**

*(For specific illustration credits
and data sources, see page 409.)*

Designed by
Robert S. Herald

THE MYOCARDIUM: FAILURE AND INFARCTION

Edited by
Eugene Braunwald, M.D.

Hersey Professor of the Theory and Practice of Physic,
Harvard Medical School,
and Physician-in-Chief,
Peter Bent Brigham Hospital, Boston

with the collaboration of
Amy Selwyn
Senior Editor, Hospital Practice

HP Publishing Co., Inc. • Publishers • New York

To Dr. Theodore Cooper
who, as Director of the National Heart and Lung Institute,
has provided the creative leadership so necessary for the
advances in cardiovascular science described herein

Table of Contents

Section VI

CONSEQUENCES OF MYOCARDIAL INFARCTION

Section VII

TREATMENT OF MYOCARDIAL INFARCTION

Contributing Authors

WALTER H. ABELMANN Professor of Medicine, Boston City Hospital, Harvard Medical School; Head, Cardiovascular Division, Thorndike Memorial Laboratory.

W. GERALD AUSTEN Professor of Surgery, Harvard Medical School; Chief, General Surgical Services, Massachusetts General Hospital, Boston.

J. THOMAS BIGGER, JR. Associate Professor of Medicine and Pharmacology, Columbia University College of Physicians and Surgeons; Director, Cardiac Intensive Care Unit, Columbia-Presbyterian Hospital, New York City.

WILLIAM C. BIRTWELL Associate Professor of Surgery (Biomedical Engineering), School of Medicine, State University of New York at Stony Brook.

SIDNEY BLUMENTHAL Professor of Pediatric Cardiology and Associate Dean for Continuing Education, University of Miami School of Medicine.

EUGENE BRAUNWALD Hersey Professor of the Theory and Practice of Physic (Medicine), Harvard Medical School; Physician-in-Chief, Peter Bent Brigham Hospital, Boston.

MORTIMER J. BUCKLEY Associate Professor of Surgery, Harvard Medical School; Associate Visiting Surgeon, Massachusetts General Hospital, Boston.

CHARLES A. CHIDSEY III Associate Professor of Medicine and Pharmacology and Head, Division of Clinical Pharmacology, University of Colorado Medical Center, Denver.

ROBERT E. DAVIES Benjamin Franklin Professor of Molecular Biology and Chairman, Department of Animal Biology, University of Pennsylvania School of Veterinary Medicine, Philadelphia.

JAMES O. DAVIS Professor and Chairman, Department of Physiology, University of Missouri School of Medicine, Columbia.

HAROLD T. DODGE Professor of Medicine, Co-director, Division of Cardiology, and Director, Cardiovascular Research and Training Center, University of Washington School of Medicine, Seattle.

DONALD B. EFFLER Head, Department of Thoracic-Cardiovascular Surgery, Cleveland Clinic Foundation.

ALFRED P. FISHMAN Professor of Medicine and Director, Cardiovascular-Pulmonary Division, University of Pennsylvania School of Medicine, Philadelphia.

MEYER FRIEDMAN Director, Harold Brunn Institute, Mount Zion Hospital and Medical Center, San Francisco.

JOSEPH L. GOLDSTEIN Head, Division of Medical Genetics and Assistant Professor of Internal Medicine, University of Texas Southwestern Medical School, Dallas.

DONALD C. HARRISON — William G. Irwin Professor of Cardiology and Chief of Cardiology, Stanford University School of Medicine and Stanford University Hospital.

HERMAN K. HELLERSTEIN — Associate Professor of Medicine, Case Western Reserve University; Associate Physician, University Hospitals of Cleveland.

MARY JANE JESSE — Berenson Professor of Pediatric Cardiology and Director, Center for the Study of Atherosclerosis in Childhood, University of Miami School of Medicine.

ARNOLD M. KATZ — Philip J. and Harriet L. Goodhart Professor of Medicine (Cardiology), Mount Sinai School of Medicine of The City University of New York.

THOMAS KILLIP — Roland Harriman Professor of Cardiovascular Medicine, Department of Medicine, Division of Cardiology, the New York Hospital – Cornell Medical Center, New York City.

GLENN A. LANGER — Professor of Medicine and Physiology, University of California, Los Angeles, School of Medicine.

JOHN H. LARAGH — Professor of Clinical Medicine, Columbia-Presbyterian Medical Center, New York City.

PETER R. MAROKO — Assistant Professor of Medicine, Harvard Medical School; Associate in Medicine, Peter Bent Brigham Hospital, Boston.

ELDRED D. MUNDTH — Associate Professor of Surgery, Harvard Medical School; Assistant Surgeon, Massachusetts General Hospital, Boston.

J. FRASER MUSTARD — Professor of Pathology, Faculty of Medicine, McMaster University, Hamilton, Ontario.

OGLESBY PAUL — Professor of Medicine, Northwestern University Medical School; Attending Physician, Northwestern Memorial Hospital; Medical Director, Northwestern University Medical Associates, Evanston; Former President, American Heart Association.

JOSEPH K. PERLOFF — Professor of Medicine and Pediatrics, and Chief, Section of Cardiology, University of Pennsylvania School of Medicine, Philadelphia.

PETER E. POOL — Associate Clinical Professor of Medicine, University of California, San Diego; Director of Cardiology, Encinitas Hospital, San Diego.

WILLIAM C. ROBERTS — Chief, Section of Pathology, National Heart and Lung Institute, National Institutes of Health, Bethesda; Clinical Professor of Pathology and Medicine (Cardiology), Georgetown University, Washington, D.C.

RAY H. ROSENMAN — Associate Director, Harold Brunn Institute; Associate Chief, Department of Medicine, Mount Zion Hospital and Medical Center, San Francisco.

JOHN ROSS, JR. — Professor of Medicine and Head, Cardiology Division, Department of Medicine, University of California, San Diego.

ABRAHAM M. RUDOLPH — Neider Professor of Pediatrics and Professor of Physiology, Senior Staff Member, Cardiovascular Research Institute, University of California, San Francisco Medical Center.

WILLIAM C. SHELDON — Department of Cardiovascular Disease and the Cardiac Laboratory, Cleveland Clinic Foundation.

SOL SHERRY — Professor and Chairman, Department of Medicine, Temple University School of Medicine; Director, Temple University's Specialized Center of Thrombosis Research; Physician-in-Chief, Temple University Hospital, Philadelphia.

NORMAN E. SHUMWAY — Professor of Cardiovascular Surgery and Chief, Cardiovascular Surgery Division, Stanford University School of Medicine.

BURTON E. SOBEL — Associate Professor of Medicine and Director, Cardiovascular Division, Barnes Hospital and Washington University School of Medicine, St. Louis.

EDMUND H. SONNENBLICK — Associate Professor of Medicine, Harvard Medical School; Director of Cardiovascular Research, Department of Medicine, Peter Bent Brigham Hospital, Boston.

HARRY S. SOROFF — Professor and Chairman, Department of Surgery, School of Medicine, State University of New York at Stony Brook.

JEREMIAH STAMLER — Professor and Chairman, Department of Community Health and Preventive Medicine and Harry W. Dingman Professor of Cardiology, Northwestern University Medical School, Chicago.

ROBERT W. WISSLER — Donald N. Pritzker Professor of Pathology and Director, Specialized Center of Research in Atherosclerosis, University of Chicago.

Introduction

In the final analysis, life ceases when the heart fails to deliver sufficient oxygenated blood to sustain the viability of the metabolizing tissues. As usually defined, however, heart failure is the state in which an abnormality of cardiac function is responsible for the inability of the heart to pump blood at a rate commensurate with the requirements of these tissues. Even within this more restricted definition, heart failure is clearly the most important cause of death in our society today, and, for more than a quarter of a century, cardiovascular disease has been responsible for close to 50 percent of all deaths in this country. A large fraction of these result from myocardial infarction, in which ischemic damage of heart muscle results in a reduction in the quantity of the remaining normal contractile apparatus.

The purpose of this volume is to present many of the "growing points" of contemporary knowledge concerning the mechanisms of normal cardiac contraction, the alteration of these mechanisms which occur in heart failure, the physiologic and clinical responses of the patient to impaired cardiac function, and the etiology and consequences of myocardial ischemia, as well as the treatment of myocardial infarction and failure. Emphasis is placed on new concepts and principles rather than on practical details. While an effort was made to select topics and authors so that consideration would be given to the leading theories relevant to each major topic, it should be emphasized that the goal of this volume is not to provide a complete textbook, covering every important aspect of the field. Rather, it is the hope that the contents will serve to excite, stimulate, and acquaint the reader with some of the potentially most promising areas in this critically important, rapidly moving area of medicine.

A brief comment concerning the preparation of this volume is in order because the methods used differed considerably from the usual. Each of the chapters first appeared as an individual paper in HOSPITAL PRACTICE between April 1970 and October 1973. All of the articles were revised and brought up to date for inclusion in this volume. In drafting their presentations, the authors had the collaboration of a most capable medical writer, Amy Selwyn, a Senior Editor of HOSPITAL PRACTICE. The presentation of the material, both verbal and graphic, involved collaboration between the authors and David Fisher, Executive Editor of HOSPITAL PRACTICE, Gertrude Halpern, Managing Editor, and Robert Herald, Art Director. The talented scientific illustrators who contributed to the work are credited by name on the page facing the title page.

In addition to the above, I would like to acknowledge my indebtedness to Herb Cornell, Director of the Book Division of the HP Publishing Co., Inc., for his supervision of the publishing and production of the book, to his assistants Katherine Bloch and Angel Kuchinski, and to my secretary, Caryn Sandrew, for her efforts on behalf of this project.

In order to understand the underlying derangement of the myocardium that occurs in heart failure, it is essential first to come to grips with the basic contractile process. The ultrastructural components of the cardiac cell, as viewed by the high-resolution electron microscope, are considered first, and the fundamental biochemical and biophysical basis of the contraction of the normal and failing heart are then discussed. Although the biochemical defects responsible for all forms of heart failure have not been identified with certainty, there is increasing evidence that an abnormality related to excitation-contraction coupling is involved in many instances. This is one of the most exciting medical developments of the past decade.

Building upon this background, attention is directed to the mechanisms of salt and water retention in heart failure, to disturbances of the autonomic nervous system in heart failure, and to such other important topics as the unique features of heart failure during infancy, the proper application and interpretation of bedside techniques in the recognition of heart failure, and the latest concepts dealing with fundamental mechanisms of action of drugs such as cardiac glycosides and the newer diuretics and antiarrhythmic agents.

Elucidation of the etiology of coronary atherosclerosis is now one of the most important questions facing biomedical science. The spontaneous development of arteriosclerosis is a pathologic process limited almost entirely to the human species, and it now appears that it has plagued us since antiquity; examination of ancient Egyptian mummies has revealed clear-cut evidence of its presence. However, the association of coronary occlusion and myocardial infarction was established only about 100 years ago, and the clinical-pathologic correlation, allowing establishment of the diagnosis during life, was worked out even more recently, i.e., at the beginning of this century.

It is not clear whether myocardial infarction reached its current high incidence during the last few decades or is just being recognized more readily than heretofore. Probably both factors are involved to some extent. The development of more sensitive and reliable techniques for the detection of coronary atherosclerosis, of myocardial ischemia, and of frank necrosis, both pre- and postmortem, unquestionably allows the detection of a larger fraction of patients with acute myocardial infarction and related syndromes. At the same time, it is difficult to avoid incriminating the increasing emotional pressures, the accelerating pace and mobility, the higher caloric intake, and the reduction of physical labor as being responsible, in some measure, for what may be considered appropriately an "epidemic of the affluent." In any event, arteriosclerotic coronary artery disease may now be considered the greatest scourge of Western man; its impact on our society is so profound in terms of the number of premature deaths, the even greater number of living, afflicted, and disabled patients, and the personal suffering and economic loss which it causes that, by comparison, it dwarfs all of the other critical medical and societal problems that face us in this turbulent era.

Following the recognition of acute myocardial infarction as a clinical-pathologic entity, treatment consisted of strict rest, presumably to let the scar heal in order to prevent myocardial rupture. I recall the debate that raged early in my training over Dr. Samuel Levine's then heretical suggestion of "armchair treatment" of this condition. The first modern milestone in the management of patients with acute myocardial infarction came approximately a decade ago with the introduction of the coronary care unit, and it soon became clear that the inhospital mortality could be reduced by half, largely as a consequence of the detection, immediate treatment, and prevention of primary arrhythmias. Only a small dent, however, has been made in the *overall* mortality from acute myocardial infarction, for two reasons. First, the outcome in the patient with cardiogenic shock, or so-called "myocardial power failure," has not been materially affected. Second, and even more important, it is now recognized that the number of patients with acute myocardial infarction who succumb in the hospital may be likened to the tip of an iceberg. A much larger number of patients die relatively suddenly, before they can reach the hospital. Management of these patients poses a far more difficult problem. Thus, now that the first flush of enthusiasm over the success of the coronary care unit has faded, many thoughtful physicians are again beginning to feel frustrated, since further progress in the control of this condition appears to be far more difficult to achieve.

It is unlikely that a single solution to the enormous problem of acute myocardial infarction—i.e., a single mode of treatment that will abolish the problem in the manner that penicillin provided a definitive treatment for pneumococcal pneumonia or appendectomy for appendicitis—will be forthcoming in the foreseeable future. I believe it is more likely that genuine control of this disease process will require a multipronged attack involving many strategies. These are likely to include but will probably not be limited to the following:

• Retardation of the development of arteriosclerosis by diet and/or drugs in the population at large.

• Detection, surveillance, and prompt treatment of patients at more than usual risk for the development of arteriosclerosis; these patients include not only those with elevated blood lipids, hypertension, the cigarette smoking habit, and elevated blood sugar, but, as is becoming increasingly evident, those with certain behavioral and attitudinal responses to psychologic stress.

• Streamlining the medical care delivery system so that patients who have developed, who are developing, or even those who are very likely to develop an acute myocardial infarction can receive specialized care without delay. This will require logistic efforts of major proportions as well as intensive and extensive public education.

• Resolution of coronary thrombi by thrombolytic agents.

• Reduction by various biochemical, physiological, and mechanical techniques of the quantity of myocardium infarcted following an occlusion.

• Encouragement of the development of coronary collaterals.

• Surgical bypass of obstructed or obstructing lesions along with the resection, in some instances, of irreversibly damaged tissue.

• When all else fails, temporary or even permanent mechanical support of the circulation.

A number of these promising preventive and therapeutic measures are already clearly in view, while others are just appearing on the horizon; most are discussed in this volume.

Three chapters deal with various aspects of direct coronary revascularization, an operation which may well prove to be among the most remarkable achievements in the history of cardiovascular surgery. Commencing with the pioneering work of Claude Beck in the 1930's, cardiovascular surgeons have developed a large number of procedures designed to augment the flow of blood to the ischemic myocardium. Perhaps the very number and diversity of procedures speak most eloquently for their inadequacy. The questionable efficacy of epicardial abrasion, gastropexy, and internal mammary implantation, the high risk of coronary endarterectomy, and the frequent technical problems arising from patch grafts are well known and have been repeatedly aired.

However, with autogenous saphenous vein bypass grafts, pioneered by Johnson, Flemma, Lepley, and by Favaloro, Effler, Groves, and their respective associates, we may be dealing with a procedure of qualitatively greater import. It is clear that this operation: 1) delivers substantial quantities of blood to previously ischemic myocardium through a graft that often remains patent for at least four to five years, 2) can be accomplished by a skilled, experienced surgical team with a relatively low mortality (less than three percent in properly selected patients), and 3) results in relief of angina pectoris in a large majority of patients. Already the procedure is being extended from patients with incapacitating angina to those with: 1) impending and acute myocardial infarction, 2) cardiogenic shock, and 3) minimal symptoms but anatomically favorable lesions.

I share the excitement of many others that at long last here may be a form of therapy that can, under appropriate circumstances, favorably alter the course of the disease in many patients with arteriosclerotic coronary artery disease. Accompanying this optimism, however, is an uneasiness that by simple common consent, rather than by rational analysis of data, we may be adopting for general use a form of therapy that has yet to prove its effectiveness in a rigidly controlled clinical trial. Is our disappointment with previous treatment failures and our overwhelming desire to solve this most serious of all medical problems propelling us headlong into the position where it will be considered poor medical practice to withhold this form of therapy from almost any patient with coronary artery disease? Will the physician who does not urge coronary arteriography in every person who might have coronary sclerosis be subject to criticism, even though the long-term effectiveness of direct revascularization has not yet been demonstrated?

Many questions must be answered. First and foremost: How do the survival rates and symptoms compare in closely-matched groups of operated and nonoperated patients? How does operation affect the incidence of myocardial infarction, congestive heart failure, arrhythmias, angina, and other symptoms? What are the long-term changes in the interposed venous segment? What is the long-term patency rate of the graft? What is the rate of development of arteriosclerotic disease in the coronary vessels distal to the anastomosis when they are exposed to systemic pressure and are no longer "protected" by a more proximal stenosis? What are the effects of bypass surgery on the contractile activity of previously ischemic myocardium? How do the clinical effects of revascularization compare with vigorous dietary and antilipemic treatment, particularly in patients with relatively mild disease?

That the answers to such questions must be sought among many different groups of patients compounds the problem, of course. The effects of the operation will have to be analyzed in patients by sex, age, arterial pressure, number of previous infarcts, extent of myocardial dysfunction, etc. Obviously, this will be a difficult task, but it is one that will have to be carried out and completed, hopefully sooner rather than later.

Not long ago, heart failure and myocardial infarction were subjects of primary interest to the physician caring for adult patients, and of little concern to other specialists or to non-clinicians. This volume demonstrates how radically that picture has changed. Electronmicroscopists, cellular physiologists, geneticists, lipid chemists, electrophysiologists, pharmacologists, pathologists, hemodynamicists, pediatricians, surgeons, bioengineers, psychiatrists, hematologists, and epidemiologists have all contributed to the identification and beginning solution of these important problems and the contributions from these and other disciplines will undoubtedly continue.

This volume comes at a critical time. If we liken the conquest of heart failure and myocardial infarction to the climbing of a mountain, then we might say that we have now assessed its height, assembled the team at the base, and have even climbed a small portion of the way up. Now we are on the first plateau and the terrain ahead looms steeper and rougher. It is a good time to regroup and reassess the rest of the climb from this new vantage point and plan the strategy of the ascent. One can only hope that our endurance and supplies will enable us to make it to the summit.

EUGENE BRAUNWALD, M.D.

Boston, Massachusetts
January, 1974

Section One
Cardiac Contraction Mechanisms

Myocardial Ultrastructure in the Normal and Failing Heart

EDMUND H. SONNENBLICK

Harvard Medical School

The performance of the heart as a pump is primarily dependent on the contractile activity of the myocardium; the contraction of the myocardium in turn reflects the summated and integrated working of its individual contractile elements – the *sarcomeres*. This premise is the rationale for examining the ultrastructure of the heart in relation to the continuum of cardiac function, a continuum that extends from normal performance to advanced failure.

Starting from this premise, this chapter will discuss, in order, the structural and functional components of the cardiac cell, the mechanisms through which the phenomena observable in the sarcomere become relevant to myocardial behavior, and the relationships between derangements at the ultrastructural level and the development of cardiac failure.

Ultrastructure consists of those morphologic features that are adequately observable with the resolution and magnification of the electron microscope. Even with the light microscope, the myocardium is composed of numerous interconnecting and branching *cells*, or *fibers*, each 5μ to 10μ in diameter and 50μ to 75μ in length. Covering the fibers externally is the *sarcolemma*, a membrane that sets the cell off from the extracellular fluid and serves to carry electrical activity across the surface of the cell.

At their ends, the widely branching cardiac fibers are joined by modified cell surface membranes, called *intercalated discs*. These serve the purpose of holding the cells together, provide a site for passage of molecules between cells, and provide a pathway of low electrical resistance between the cells. Thus, a "functional syncytium" is created.

Located centrally within the cardiac fiber is the nucleus. Longitudinally, the fibers contain irregular rodlike structures or *fibrils*. The electron microscope shows that the fibrils run the length of the fiber and are composed along their length of regular, repeating structures – the sarcomeres, the ultimate units of contraction in heart as well as skeletal muscle. The sarcomeres give the fibrils their striped or striated appearance. Sarcomeres, in turn, are composed of two sets of rodlike filaments, thicker ones composed of aggregates of *myosin* molecules, thinner ones of aggregates of *actin*. Interactions between actin and myosin at specific sites along the filaments produce contraction of the myocardium. Other regulatory proteins have been localized to the thin actin filament, including the complex of *tropomyosin* and *troponin*, whose role will be discussed later.

Activation of the contractile system is mediated by two membranous systems that may be defined structurally (see Chapter 4, "Calcium Metabolism in the Normal and Failing Heart," by Chidsey). These are the sarcolemma and its tubular invaginations deep into the cell, called *transverse tubules* or the *T system*, and the *sarcoplasmic reticulum*, which is composed of a fine network of tubules within the cell, surrounding the myofibrils. It should be emphasized that the T tubules do not actually open up into the fiber, although the sarcoplasmic reticulum abuts on both the sarcolemma and T system to form specialized terminals or *junctions*.

During activation, electrical activity is carried across the sarcolemma, generated primarily by a flux of Na^+ and K^+ and transmitted deep into the cell by the T system. At the same time, a minute amount of calcium is transmitted across these membranes into the cell. Larger amounts of calcium, which can trigger contraction by permitting force-generating interaction between actin and myosin, are stored in the sarcoplasmic reticulum. Recent evidence suggests that during activation a small amount of calcium, crossing the surface membrane into the cell, can release larger amounts of calcium, which are stored in the sarcoplasmic

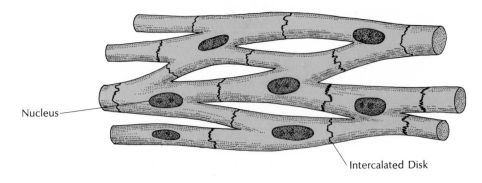

Nucleus

Intercalated Disk

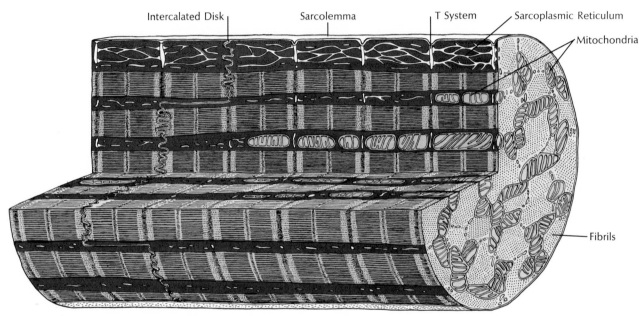

Intercalated Disk | Sarcolemma | T System | Sarcoplasmic Reticulum

Mitochondria

Fibrils

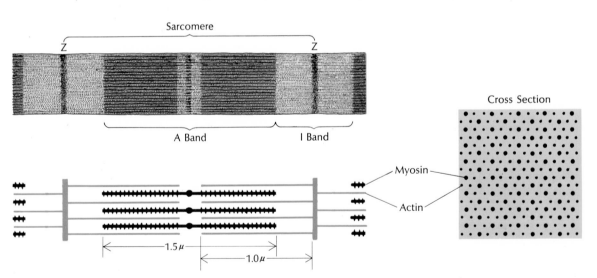

Sarcomere

Z   Z

A Band   I Band

Cross Section

Myosin

Actin

1.5μ

1.0μ

Myocardial structure, as seen under the light and electron microscopes, is schematized. Top drawing shows section of myocardium as it would appear under light microscope, with interconnecting fibers or cells attached end-to-end and delimited by modified cell membranes called intercalated disks. Ultrastructural schematization (center drawing) illustrates the division of the fiber longitudinally into rodlike fibrils, in turn composed of sarcomeres, the basic contractile units. Within the sarcomeres, thick filaments of myosin, confined to the central dark A band, alternate with thin filaments of actin which extend from the Z lines (delimiting the sarcomere) through the I band and into the A band where they overlap the myosin filaments. These landmarks are seen in detail drawings (bottom). On activation a repetitive interaction between the sites shown displaces the filaments inward so that the sarcomere and hence the whole muscle shortens, with maximum overlap at 2.2μ. Also depicted are the membranous systems: the T system that carries electrical activity into the cells and the sarcoplasmic reticulum that releases calcium to activate the contractile machinery. Like the intercalated disks, these are specialized extensions of the superficial sarcolemma. Note also the rich mitochondrial content, typical of "red" muscle, which is highly dependent on aerobic metabolism.*

reticulum. This mechanism is termed "regenerative calcium release." This calcium in turn activates the contractile system of the sarcomeres (see Chapter 2, "Contractile Proteins in the Normal and Failing Myocardium," by Katz). Subsequently, the sarcoplasmic reticulum reabsorbs this calcium, leading to inactivation of the cell. The exact biochemical details of this morphologic system are currently a subject of active study.

The energy for contraction in heart muscle is derived primarily from aerobic metabolism that occurs within mitochrondria. These oblong bodies exist in plethora between the fibrils and exhibit a platelike or lamellar internal structure. Aerobic enzymes are arranged along these lamellae. Glycolytic enzymes, a minor source of high-energy phosphate production in heart muscle, are localized to the cytoplasm.

The contractile machinery, comprised of fibrils and their constituent sarcomeres, makes up only about 50% of the myocardial fiber. This is an appreciably lower percentage of contractile protein than is found in skeletal muscle, where upwards of 80% to 90% of total mass is contractile fibers. This difference reflects mainly the greater amount of mitochrondria in heart muscle.

Under the electron microscope, the outstanding topographic feature of the sarcomere is its banded appearance — alternating bands of dark and light repeating from sarcomere to sarcomere. Alternations in the repetitive banding of the sarcomere reflect the relative disposition and overlap of the two sets of protein filaments that interact to produce the force of contraction.

At both ends of the sarcomere, there are thin dark lines that are called Z lines. The Z lines provide insertion points for the thin actin filaments from the two abutting sarcomeres. While the detailed structure of the Z line is still not fully clarified and varies somewhat from muscle to muscle, it has the general appearance of a straw mat into which the thin actin filaments are interwoven. The thin filament itself is composed of two chains of actin molecules associated with elongated molecules of tropomyosin. Another protein complex, troponin, is located periodically along the actin chains in association with tropo-

myosin and serves to inhibit the enzymatic inactivation of actin with myosin (see Chapter 2 by Katz).

At the center of the sarcomere is a broader dark area, the A band, composed of the thicker myosin filaments. Between the dark Z lines and the dark A band are two lighter zones, the I bands. Thin filaments extend inward from the Z lines through the I bands and end near the center of the A band. The thick filaments run the length of the A band. Thus in the lateral portions of the A band there is an overlap of thick and thin — myosin and actin — filaments. In longer sarcomeres, a relatively lighter zone, which is termed the H zone, appears at the central portion of the A bands. The H zone represents that portion of the A band where only thick filaments are present.

The thick filaments are composed of aggregates of myosin molecules that have an elongated portion and a globular end. These molecules of myosin are arranged so that their long portions are parallel and the globular portions project outward. As H. E. Huxley has shown, these periodic projections are directed away from the center of the thick filament at intervals of 400 angstroms, leaving a bare area in the center. Moreover, this globular head contains an enzyme that splits ATP (ATPase) and can interact with actin to form a "cross bridge" for generation of force and shortening. At the center of the A band, the thick filaments are connected by fixed bridges that hold them in relative position and create a darkened area of cross banding called the M line. At rest, troponin, which is located periodically along the actin filament in association with tropomyosin, inhibits the interaction of these thick filament projections with the actin filament. When calcium is available to interact with troponin, this inhibition ceases and bridges are formed between myosin and actin. A change in the shape of the globular portion of the myosin head is thought to occur, producing relative motion between the two sets of filaments. An enzyme in the myosin portion of the bridge for splitting ATP is also activated, and ATP is broken down to ADP and phosphate. With motion, the bridge is broken only to be remade further along the filament. ATP is apparently reformed after the bridge moves and is detached, ready

for a repetition of the same cycle. In this repetitive fashion and through such bridge formations, contraction is generated. The force that will be generated by the interaction of the actin and myosin filaments will be determined then by the number of cross bridges that are formed. This, in turn, will depend on two major factors: the relative degree of overlap of the filaments and the amount of "activating" calcium available to permit an interaction to occur.

Because the degree of overlap of filaments determines to a considerable extent the degree of interaction, the normal lengths of the filaments are extremely important in visualizing the process. The thick myosin filaments are approximately 1.5μ in length; the thin actin filaments, extending from the Z line from either direction, measure about 1.0μ. Present evidence strongly suggests that the absolute length of the filaments remains constant during the resting period and in the course of contraction. When the cell is activated, however, a repetitive interaction occurs between sites along these filaments. This interaction effectively pulls the thin filaments inward toward the center of the A band, shortening the sarcomere and hence the muscle. This process gives us the "sliding model" for muscle contraction, clearly established for skeletal muscle and now well documented for the myocardium as well.

The contractile force or actively developed tension of heart muscle, as in other muscles, depends on its initial length when other conditions remain constant. This phenomenon has been studied in isolated segments of heart muscle held at various lengths. When the resting or unstimulated muscle is stretched, an initial force or resting tension (preload) is required to hold it at that length. When stimulated at that fixed length, the activated muscle will develop a contractile force related to that length. This relation of developed force and initial length is termed the length-active tension curve (see page 6). The curve for actively developed tension can be shifted upward (e.g., by epinephrine, digitalis glycosides, or augmented bath calcium) or downward (e.g., barbiturates, decreased bath calcium) so that the tension developed at any given length is altered.

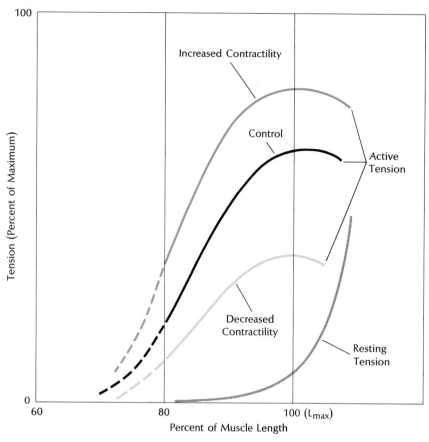

The relationship of initial length and developed tension is termed the length-active tension curve. The resting tension curve rises abruptly once L_{max}, the length at which maximal actively developed tension occurs, is reached. The active tension curve can be shifted upward by augmenting contractility (e.g., adding bath calcium or catecholamine) or downward (e.g., toxic "failure"). Whether upward or downward, the shift in the active tension curve is symmetrical.

This shift in the developed tension curve relative to muscle length characterizes a change in contractility of the muscle.

Let us now relate these events to the ultrastructure of heart muscle, and specifically to the sarcomere and its length. Once the length-tension curve is determined, the muscle can be held at a known length, fixed with glutaraldehyde, sectioned, and viewed under the electron microscope. In heart muscle, sarcomere length changes directly with initial muscle length along the rising portion of the length-active tension curve, where significant resting tension exists. At shorter muscle lengths, buckling of the muscle and its fibers occurs since non activated sarcomeres do not shorten further. The precise relations between absolute sarcomere length and actively developed tension have best been demonstrated in skeletal muscle fibers by A. H. Huxley and associates.

In skeletal muscle fibers, active tension is maximal and *constant* between a sarcomere length of 2.2μ and 2.0μ. Recalling the 1.0μ length of the actin filaments and the 0.2μ area in the center of thick filament devoid of projections for cross bridge formation, such a range of sarcomere lengths would provide for an optimal overlap of thick and thin filaments. The skeletal fiber is much more distensible than heart muscle, and when it is stretched beyond the length where developed tension is maximal, its sarcomeres are elongated further. H zones appear in the center of the sarcomeres; the developed tension falls in direct proportion to the decreasing overlap of thick and thin filaments and the resulting decrease of the number of force-generating cross bridges within the A band. Tension approaches zero when a sarcomere length of 3.5μ is reached. This figure is interesting since it can also be obtained by adding

the lengths of the thin filaments (1.0μ each) and the thick filament (1.5μ). Thus, if overlap between thick and thin filaments is removed, active tension cannot be developed.

At sarcomere lengths less than 2.0μ, thin filaments move into the opposite half of the sarcomere and actively developed tension falls. Why this fall occurs when there is still a major overlap of filaments is not completely understood. It may result from any or all of the following: restoring forces that resist penetration of the thin filament into the opposite portion of the sarcomere; inactivation of bridges due to shortening per se; or lateral displacement of the filaments, since volume of the sarcomere remains constant. The importance of restoring forces at shorter sarcomere lengths in cardiac muscle is only now being appreciated.

In cardiac muscle, sarcomere length can also be correlated with muscle length and developed tension, although not with the precision possible in skeletal fibers. At L_{max}, defined as the muscle length where force of contraction is greatest, sarcomere length averages 2.2μ. As sarcomere and muscle length is decreased, developed tension falls. At muscle length 10% shorter than L_{max}, actively developed force will have fallen nearly 50%. This occurs despite the fact that myofilament overlap in the resting muscle is still optimal. Part of the decline in developed tension between sarcomere lengths of 2.2μ and 2.0μ may reflect the much greater compliance of heart muscle during contraction as compared with skeletal muscle. Accordingly, the sarcomeres of heart muscle probably shorten during isometric contraction, when overall muscle length is still fixed. This translation of myofilaments during isometric contraction produces a greater fall in active tension development than might have been anticipated, since the overlap of myofilaments should still be optimal. At shorter muscle lengths, force continues to fall but buckling of the fiber exists and sarcomeres, which shorten during contraction, elongate during relaxation. This phenomenon may relate to the resting force noted previously; it is seen progressively as sarcomere lengths of 1.9μ or less are reached.

When the muscle length is extended

to L_{max}, actively developed tension does not continue to rise, although resting tension increases precipitously. In cardiac muscle, the sarcomeres resist further elongation beyond L_{max} and are rarely found to exceed 2.4μ to 2.5μ in length. Thus, the usual dissociation of thick and thin filaments in long sarcomeres of skeletal muscle may not be seen, and H zones are difficult to perceive in heart muscle. If the muscle is forcibly stretched beyond L_{max}, sarcomere length no longer increases directly with muscle length. When the muscle is stretched 20% beyond L_{max}, sarcomere length may only be 10% longer than that at L_{max}. The result of this dissociation of sarcomere length and muscle length in overstretched heart muscle is a distortion in the interrelations of fibrils. This distortion, termed "slippage," is seen even acutely in isolated segments of muscle and will be discussed later in the context of chronic dilatation of the intact heart.

To understand the import of sarcomere structures in cardiac perform-ance, it is necessary to turn to some of the kinetics governing the functioning of the heart as a pump. A necessary starting point is Starling's law of the heart, which in its simplest form stipulates that the heart will pump out the blood that is returned to it from the venous system on a beat-to-beat basis, and that both the initial size of the heart (prior to contraction) and the volume of blood ejected will be determined primarily by the volume of blood returned to it from the circulation. This may be exemplified with figures derived from experiments with the intact dog's heart. If the initial or end-diastolic ventricular volume is 40 cc, the output with contraction, or stroke volume, will be about 25 cc, or about 60% of the initial volume. If the dog then lies down, causing a sudden increase in venous return that raises the end-diastolic volume to 50 cc, the following contraction will eject 30 cc of blood. The stroke volume (output per beat) is determined directly by the end-diastolic volume (volume just prior to contraction). The ratio of the stroke volume to the end-diastolic volume (ejection fraction) remains essentially constant. Of course, these relations are also affected by the load against which the heart is pumping, i.e., the pressure (afterload), and by the "contractility" of the ventricle at that moment. In contrast to the Starling phenomenon, which depends on alterations in end-diastolic volume or resting fiber length (preload), a change in contractility is defined as a change in function that alters stroke volume and/or pressure development and is not dependent on a change in diastolic volume.

As venous return and ventricular end-diastolic volume rise, so does ventricular end-diastolic pressure. The phenomenon takes place in both the right and left sides of the heart, providing a balance between the two sides of the circulation. An inevitable result otherwise would be the displacement of excessive systemic blood into the pulmonary vascular bed, with attendant pulmonary edema, or the total

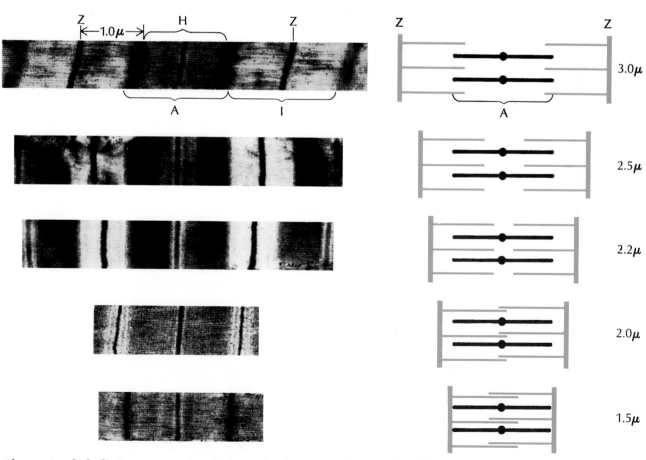

The way in which altering sarcomere length changes band pattern is shown in actual frog sartorius muscle sarcomeres (left) and in correlated diagrams. The sarcomere at 2.2μ is at L_{max} at which length maximum contractile force is produced.

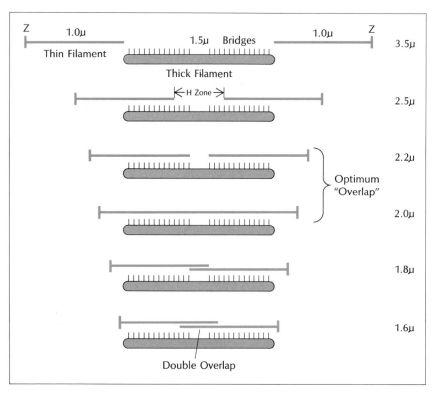

The diagram above shows the theoretically possible relationships among sarcomere length, filament overlap, and contractile force.

depletion of the pulmonary vascular volume.

Starling's law of the heart is based on the fact that the heart is a muscle and, more precisely, a muscle that pumps. Certain characteristics, such as the length-tension curve, pertain to all muscles. In the intact heart, the length-passive tension curve of isolated heart muscle is reflected in the relation between the end-diastolic volume and end-diastolic pressure. Because the heart normally doesn't operate at L_{max} but at a point somewhat lower, i.e., on the ascending limb of the length-active tension curve, an increase in the passive tension will augment the force of contraction, increase the extent to which the muscle can shorten with a given load, and cause more blood to be ejected. This accounts for the change in the output of the heart that corresponds to increased initial size, and, of course, also provides the heart with reserve capacity and with the ability to compensate in certain situations.

Other mechanical and geometric considerations must be kept in mind. First is the LaPlace relation which states that the tension in the wall of a sphere is directly related to the pressure in and the radius of the cavity, and inversely related to the thickness of the wall. Thus, if the end-diastolic volume is increased, the tension generated in the wall in systole must be higher to develop the same pressure to open the aortic valve and eject blood. As tension in the wall is increased, a decrease in the extent of shortening during systole will occur. Because of geometric considerations, the same stroke volume could still be ejected with decreased shortening as the ventricle enlarges. However, if an increased stroke volume is to be produced in direct relation to the increased end-diastolic volume, the extent of shortening must be restored despite the increased tension load. Accordingly, one must move up the length-active tension curve of the muscle fibers in the wall of the heart.

How, then, does the Starling relation work and what sets its limits? In the intact heart, as in isolated cardiac muscle, there is a direct relation between sarcomere length and fiber length. When diastolic filling pressure is augmented, myocardial fiber lengths in the wall of the heart are lengthened. In canine hearts, sarcomere lengths in the wall of the heart have been cor-

related with diastolic filling pressure. At normal filling pressures in the left ventricle, ranging from 6 mm Hg to 8 mm Hg, diastolic sarcomere lengths range between 2.05μ and 2.15μ; at zero filling pressure, sarcomere length shortens to 1.90μ. At the normal upper limit of filling pressure in the left ventricle, which ranges from 12 mm Hg to 15 mm Hg, sarcomere length approaches 2.2μ in the midwall of the heart. Thus, the normal left ventricle functions with diastolic sarcomere lengths just shorter than the apex of the length-active tension curve. During normal systole, with an ejection fraction of 55%, midwall sarcomeres shorten to about 1.8μ. This shortening of the activated sarcomere explains the extent of ventricular emptying. Moreover, with potentiated contraction, further shortening of sarcomeres in the ventricular wall has been observed and here, too, the augmented emptying is accounted for by the extent of shortening of the sarcomere. Thus the ventricle is designed so that the upper limit of normal filling pressure is achieved at the optimal length of the heart's basic contractile unit — the sarcomere. The sarcomere length below 2.2μ provides the reserve for the Starling mechanism, while the normal ventricle operates on the most advantageous portion of the sarcomere length-tension curve.

With further acute distension of the ventricle beyond its normal limits, filling pressure rises very rapidly for relatively small increments in volume. Although additional small increments in sarcomere length beyond 2.2μ are observed, sarcomeres do not elongate as might be anticipated from the acute change in volume; here "slippage" may also be occurring.

Why does the Starling curve reach a limit? Here again one can relate physiologic events to the length-tension curve for muscle. As one ascends the length-tension curve, a point (L_{max}) is reached where further stretching of the muscle will not result in increased developed tension. Therefore, the sarcomeres and the whole muscle will not shorten as much and the heart will not expel more blood despite increased filling pressures and augmented diastolic volume. In an attempt to compensate for the deficit in output, the heart will continue to get larger. Moreover, as diastolic volume is augmented, filling pressure rises more abruptly for lesser increments in volume. The individual with the failing heart may no longer operate on the ascending limb of the length-active tension curve but, rather, near its apex. Here he has lost the ability to generate increased tension by augmenting end-diastolic volume. With increased venous return, filling pressure in the ventricles will continue to rise without further augmentation of cardiac output.

Now let us turn to some of the problems confronted if cardiac dilatation supervenes either as a consequence of myocardial weakness and/or overload. In the normal heart, wall tension falls during the course of ejection as the volume decreases substantially. In the wall of the dilated heart, tension remains elevated since initial volume is augmented, and does not decrease markedly in systole since stroke volume is reduced. In this sense, dilatation and decreased stroke volume place an added tension load on the sarcomere, which may already be pushed to the apex of its length-tension curve. If the end-diastolic size is increased, the tension must rise to maintain output. However, when the muscle begins to become overstretched, contractile force and extent of shortening cannot increase further. In terms of the length-tension curve, we are now approaching the descending limb. In functional terms, the heart must continue to dilate as a compensatory mechanism. Cardiac function gets progressively worse, further dilatation supervenes, and the heart loses its ability to maintain a steady state. This is one of the critical ways in which cardiac failure can be related directly back to sarcomere length.

In both acute and chronic dilatation of the left ventricle, there is an increase in sarcomere length. In the heart chronically dilated secondary to volume overloading, the compliance of the ventricle is commonly altered so that the heart holds a larger blood volume in diastole for a given filling pressure. Thus, the curve relating filling pressure to diastolic volume is shifted to the right. When studied in animal models, sarcomere lengths are found to be at the peak of the length-active tension curve, i.e., around 2.2μ or 2.25μ. Notably, very long sarcomeres do not occur in the chroni-

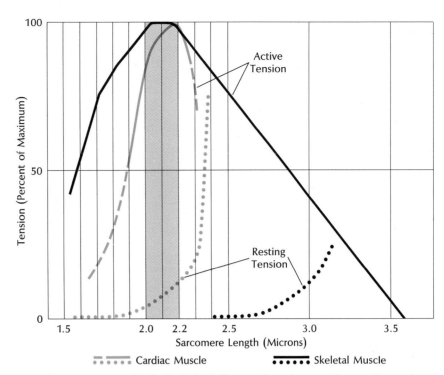

Length-tension curves for both skeletal fibers and cardiac muscle are shown above. Cardiac muscle has considerable resting tension compared to most skeletal muscle; moreover, the range of sarcomere lengths for cardiac muscle is smaller and the curve at shorter sarcomere lengths falls more abruptly.

cally dilated left ventricle. Thin filaments are not withdrawn from the sarcomeres and accordingly H zones are not seen. However, there is no reserve capacity since any further lengthening would place the heart on the descending limb of the length-active tension curve. At the same time, the volume in the left ventricle is somewhat larger than can be explained by simple elongation of sarcomeres. Two or more possibilities exist to explain such a finding. Sarcomeres may be added in series as hypertrophy ensues; alternatively, some element of "slippage" may have occurred with chronic dilatation. As noted for isolated segments of muscle,

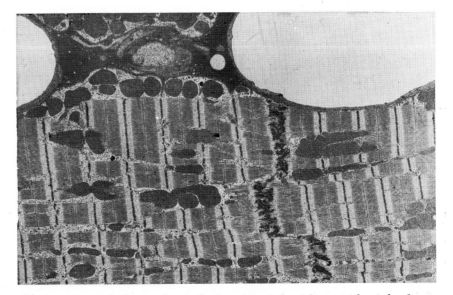

Electronmicrograph shows a longitudinal section of the right ventricle of dog heart. The repetitious pattern of the sarcomeres "in register" is readily visible, as are such features as the intercalated disks (jagged lines) and the numerous mitochondria.

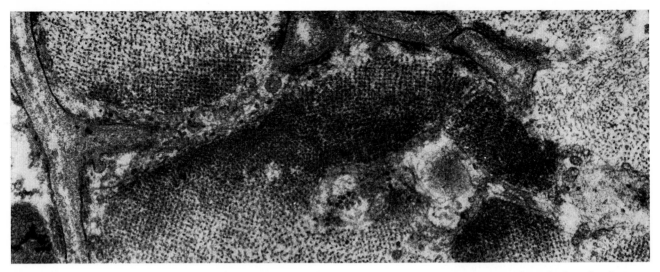

The Z line, which appears as a darkened orthogonally patterned area running horizontally through this electronmicrograph, is a prominent feature of a section cut through the I band of two sarcomeres. Actin filaments are seen on both sides of the Z line.

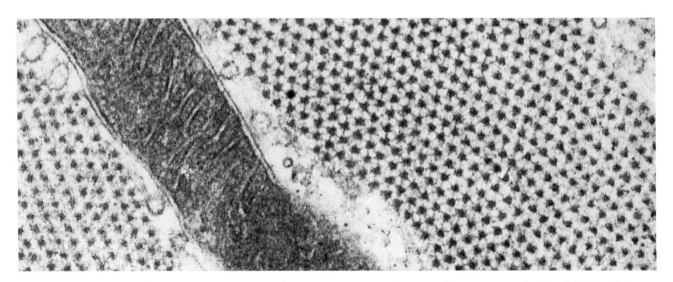

In this electronmicrograph of a transverse section made across the center of the A band, only the thick myosin filaments are seen. No thin actin filaments are to be found. Bridges between many of the thick filaments are clearly visualized.

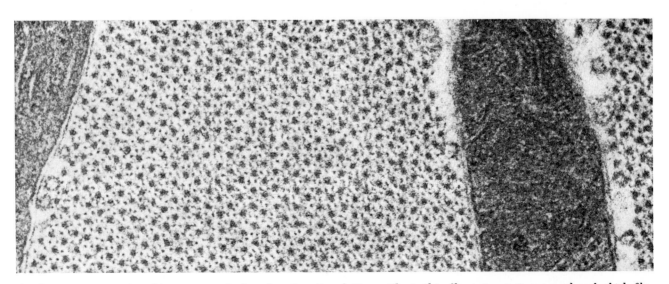

Another transverse section, this one across the lateral portion of the A band, shows both thick and thin filaments. The hexagonal lattice, with six thin filaments rotating around each thick filament, can be discerned. Parts of two mitochondria also appear.

sarcomere and muscle length become partially dissociated in overstretched tissue with distortion of the fibrils. Normally, in heart cells, the sarcomeres along parallel fibrils are arranged so that the Z lines of the sarcomeres line up—much as though they were freight cars in a railroad yard with trains on parallel tracks and with the cars of each train so aligned that all their couplings were exactly opposite one another.

When heart muscle is significantly overstretched, the fibrils begin to lose this register and start to show an irregular zig-zag pattern. Accordingly, one cell can become longer than its serial components by allowing one portion to slide in one direction, another in the other. This "slippage" could be an important factor in chronic failure and ventricular dilatation. While the sarcomere is limited in its ability to stretch, the cell apparently can become longer through distortions in register. Clinically, the result may be a permanently deformed cell that may underlie the large dilated ventricle with filling pressures less than the observed volume might predict. In chronic dilatation, enlargement of the heart beyond the size that could be predicted from an increased sarcomere length has been shown. "Slippage" has been noted in such hearts and remains a plausible, although unproven, explanation for the disparity.

In the chronically dilated right ventricle in the dog, sarcomeres elongated beyond 2.2μ to as much as 2.4μ and 2.5μ have been observed. It is not known whether this reflects a greater distensibility of the fibers in this thinner wall; further study is warranted. At any rate, when ventricular volume is increased beyond optimal sarcomere length, increased diastolic tension will not be rewarded with increased pumping capacity. Without increased developed tension in the wall, increased volume will lower the ejection fraction (i.e., the ratio of stroke volume to end-diastalic volume). This might be termed an important functional lesion in chronic dilatation. At this stage, all the heart can do to make up for the deficit in output is to dilate further.

It should be emphasized that cardiac dilatation is not the cause per se of myocardial failure; rather, it is an

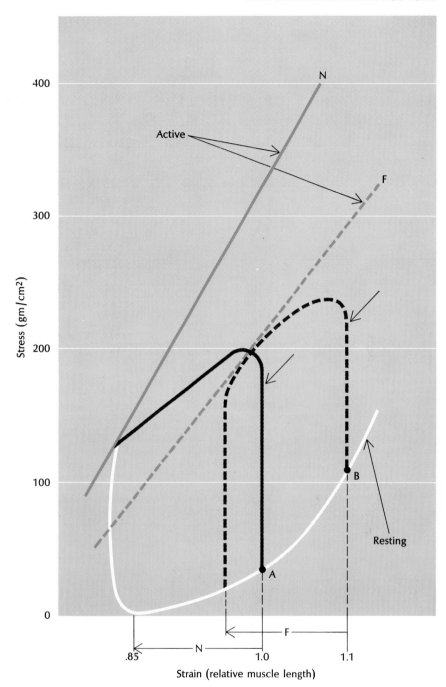

The curves represent the relationships between stress (force in the ventricular wall) and strain (change of length for the shortening muscle). The lowest curve shows the relationship between the resting force on the muscle and initial muscle length. The upper curves (N for normal and F for failing) depict the maximum forces generated by an activated muscle as a function of length. At point A, normal muscle begins contracting from the resting curve. Force development proceeds until arrow, when shortening or, in the intact heart, ejection of blood occurs. Force rises slightly beyond this point and then begins to fall as the ventricle gets smaller. Ultimately, relaxation takes place as the shortening curve approaches the normal isometric tension curve. Point B marks the start of shortening for the failing ventricular muscle. The muscle is longer to begin with in compensation for depressed function, represented by the movement of dashed-line curve to the right. At any given length, less force can be generated by the failing muscle. After ejection (arrow) there is some fall in stress within the wall, but it is less than in the normal heart. Line N can now be compared with line F and the point is made that failing ventricular muscle has a larger load and shortens to a lesser degree. Hence the failing muscle has a depressed curve relating stress development to length and an abnormally large stress load during systole, thus further limiting the extent of muscle shortening.

initial compensation for primary depression of myocardial contractility and/or a volume overload. However, we have noted that rapid overstretch of normal heart muscle studied in vitro can lead to disruption of cell membranes and subsequent cellular necrosis. It may be theorized that such a loss of cells in overstretched myocardium may further worsen the situation and provide a basis for "patchy fibrosis" as a superimposed pathologic process.

When a child's heart is overloaded, the child is able to handle that overload because the reserves intended to last a lifetime are virtually intact. But with the passage of time, function deteriorates and superimposed loads become ever more burdensome. In the absence of valvular heart disease or damage secondary to ischemia, one may live until 90 before load exceeds function. Failure is not a dilated heart. On the contrary, the dilated heart is the compensation for the occurrence of myocardial failure, but as dilatation progresses, the function of the dilated heart fails.

What are some of the initial factors leading to deterioration of myocardial performance and what ultrastructural changes, if any, are associated with these phenomena? First it should be recognized that functional abnormalities may not be reflected by any obvious structural changes. In hypertrophy of the myocardium, myofibrils appear larger in diameter, leading to an enlargement of cells rather than an increase in their number. Nuclei enlarge considerably while mitochondria increase in number, so that the ratio of mitochondrial mass to myofibrillar mass remains about the same.

In the presence of ischemia attendant on loss of coronary blood flow, changes in the activation system, in

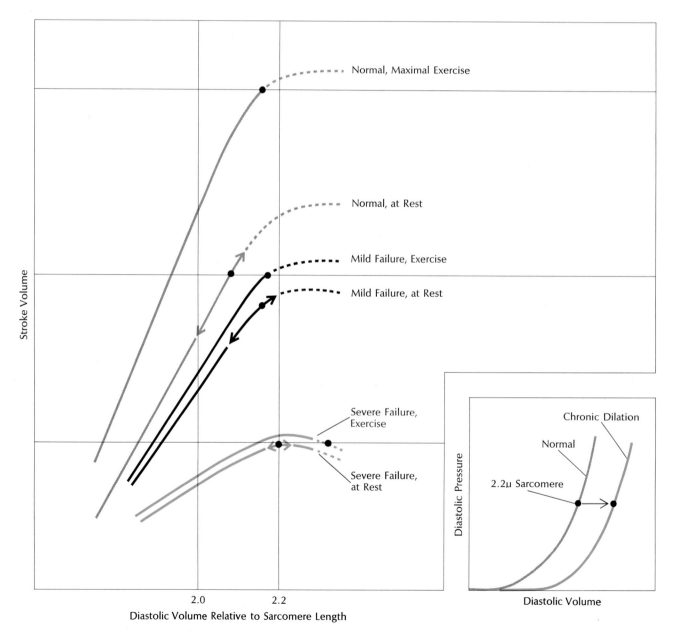

Curves show the relationship between stroke volume and diastolic volume, which in turn is related to sarcomere length, in normal hearts and in hearts with mild and severe failure, at rest and during exercise. In severe failure, further augmentation of diastolic volume can no longer increase stroke volume. Arrows along slope indicate diastolic reserve.

the mitochondria, and in the sarcomeres occur in the course of time. However, loss of contractile function precedes these apparent structural changes, and in the early stages the structure may appear normal.

In examining the surface membranes as ischemia is prolonged, disruptions and breaks may be seen. The possibility exists that these disruptions increase membrane permeability so that normal gradients for electrolytes cannot be maintained. At the same time, elements of the activation mechanism – the T system – become dilated. The reason for this is not clear, but it is possible that the metabolic inadequacies resulting from ischemia could lead to breakdown of bits and pieces of the cell. Lysosomes, which are localized membrane-contained packets of lytic enzymes within the cell, are disrupted, contributing to the destruction of membranes. In turn, this may increase osmotic pressure, allowing fluid to enter and dilate the cell.

Even greater morphologic damage is seen in the mitochondria subsequent to ischemia. Vacuolation occurs and water droplets appear inside the mitochondria. They lose their normal crystalline structure, become loosely packed, swell, and tend to dissolve. These events, which take place under the influence of hypoxia, may also be observed in tissue from animals with severe congestive failure. However, it is important to distinguish between structural and biochemical damage.

In fact, although the mitochondria may appear to be extremely ragged and disrupted, there may be little evidence that their function is seriously compromised until quite late. Further, some of the ischemic changes in the appearance of the mitochondria may also be artifactual and occur as a result of fixation methods. This is especially true in the fixation of tissue that is already compromised.

With prolonged ischemia, the sarcomeres begin to manifest contraction bands in which some of the myofibrils contract and then do not relax. Thus, areas are seen in which the sarcomeres are jammed together and their distribution becomes irregular in relation to their length. This process of contracture may be associated with damage to the cell surface membrane so that activating calcium cannot be excluded from the sarcomeres and persistence of cross bridges remains. What is quite remarkable in the picture of ischemic changes is their early total reversibility. If blood flow is restored within 30 or even 45 minutes of interruption, most of the changes – disruption of surface membranes; swollen, vacuolated mitochondria; sarcomere irregularities – may disappear. Even the mitochondria, which may take a long time to recover morphologically, seem to regain their functional integrity very rapidly. This reversibility serves to warn us that great caution is needed in seeking to relate what is seen to deficits in function of the organ. The history of

medicine and medical research is replete with situations in which investigators have found an abnormality and considered it responsible for the disorder being studied. In fact, the abnormality may be merely an associated event or a result of the disease process and not causative. Relative to ultrastructure, artifacts of fixation must also be considered. On the other hand, some morphologic or biochemical alteration so slight as to be overlooked or ignored may be of much greater significance. Before one can make meaningful correlations of cause and effect, an evaluation system must be established in which the generalized effects of cellular disorders and possible specific events can be weighed. However, studies of myocardial ultrastructure have not yet progressed to the stage where such a system can be defined.

A promising start has been made in elucidating the ultrastructural landmarks of contractility. But there are still important gaps. More knowledge about the force-generating sites on the contractile protein filaments is needed. Further, added attention must focus on the system that controls activation and relaxation, and its contribution to cardiac contractility. Ultrastructural studies may also afford a means of understanding the role of the right ventricle in relationship to both function and failure. It appears that the techniques that will make it possible to acquire this information are now available.

Contractile Proteins in Normal and Failing Myocardium

ARNOLD M. KATZ

Mount Sinai School of Medicine

When the service was finished, the king would know how many of the fellowship had sworn to undertake the quest of the [Holy Grail] and they were counted and found to number a hundred and fifty. . . . And at sunrise they all parted company with each other, and every Knight took the way he best liked.

> King Arthur. Tales of the Round Table
> by Andrew Lang

As the quest of the Holy Grail captured the imagination of the Knights of the Round Table, so the search for a biochemical defect in the failing heart has attracted the attention of the modern cardiologist. Unlike the legendary search, which led to the destruction of King Arthur and his court, the current efforts to identify biochemical alterations in the failing heart have both broadened our knowledge of cardiac function and expanded the fellowship of those who endeavor to understand the biochemical basis of cardiac contraction. The goal, however, remains elusive. While a number of metabolic alterations have been identified in the failing, hemodynamically overloaded heart, it remains to be demonstrated which of these are secondary to other biochemical sequelae of heart failure, which represent compensatory mechanisms that aid these hearts in meeting the hemodynamic overload, and which, if any, is the primary defect responsible for heart failure.

Since cardiac contraction, and hence the pumping action of the heart, depends on a complex series of interactions by the cardiac contractile proteins, evidence that an alteration in their structure or function might underlie development or progression of heart failure has long been sought. The identification of any alteration in the heart's contractile proteins must, of course, be preceded by knowledge of their normal behavior. For this reason, this chapter will begin with a description of these proteins, first as individual entities, then in terms of their interactions. Finally, specific mechanical properties of the living muscle will be related tentatively to particular contractile protein interactions.

From a physiologic standpoint, the chief mechanisms regulating contractile force in the heart are intrinsic to the muscle cell, whereas in skeletal muscle regulation is extrinsic and governed by the central nervous system. Mechanical performance in skeletal muscle is thus altered by variations in the number of contractile units activated via individual motor neurons; when the situation requires, the number of activated units is readily increased. Also, in skeletal muscle rapid trains of stimuli reaching the muscle fiber by way of its motor nerve can enhance tension by causing summation of individual contractile responses, or, in a fully developed response, a tetanic contraction. In the heart these do not apply. Functionally (although not anatomically) a syncytium, the heart responds to stimuli in an all-or-none manner. Fractional activation is normally impossible. In addition, the heart remains refractory to effective stimulation until the contractile response has ended, so that summation of contractions and tetanic contractions are impossible. Moreover, while development of tension is related to initial length (preload), both types of muscle normally operate at or near the peak of their length-tension curves. Changes in rest length seem to be of greatest significance for short-term adjustments in cardiac function. Denied the adaptive responses of skeletal muscle to extrinsic control, the heart must depend on alterations in the biochemical and biophysical properties of the muscle itself. Changes in contractility – defined here as changes in mechanical performance not dependent on resting length or end-diastolic volume – thus reflect changes in the physical and chemical interactions of the

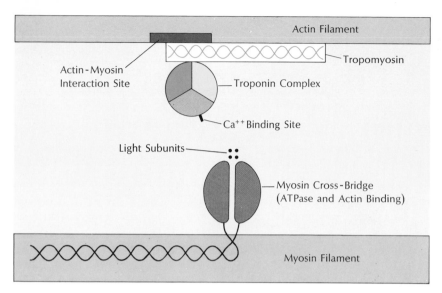

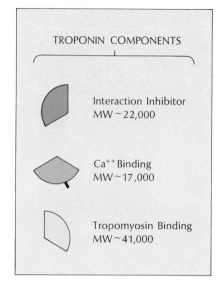

Schematic diagram of the contractile proteins of muscle indicates the relative positions of myosin and actin, the primary contractile proteins, and the modulatory proteins, tropomyosin and troponin, which serve to control muscle activity. According to recent work, the light myosin subunits may determine the maximum rate of energy release during contraction. Three discrete proteins have been identified within the troponin complex. One apparently serves as calcium receptor, one acts to inhibit the actin-myosin interaction that results in contraction, while the third binds the troponin complex to tropomyosin.

contractile proteins in the myocardium.

Biochemically, the cardiac contractile proteins appear to differ less from those in skeletal muscle than was once believed. Quantitative differences are evident (for example, only one third to one half as much cardiac myosin is recovered per gram of muscle tissue), but major aspects of function are essentially the same. Indeed, the large body of knowledge gained from studies of skeletal muscle proteins (chiefly the "fast" skeletal muscle of rabbits) has made the cardiac con-

tractile proteins and their behavior easier to understand. It still remains true, however, that our knowledge of the contractile proteins in either cardiac or skeletal muscle is far from complete. What seems a firm fact today may well be only a part of the story tomorrow. Troponin, most recently identified of the major components of the contractile machinery, illustrates this point. Initially troponin was thought to be a single globular protein serving as receptor for the calcium released to the contractile ap-

paratus in the final stages of excitation-contraction coupling; it is now clear that troponin is a complex of at least three proteins (see below). Furthermore, myosin, the chief constituent of the thick filaments of the sarcomere, is now known to contain several low-molecular weight subunits that appear to determine both the rate of ATP hydrolysis in vitro and shortening velocity in the living muscle. Cumulative experience, beginning with early studies of skeletal muscle proteins more than a century ago, should have taught us to expect no less.

In the 1860's, when Kühne first isolated myosin by extracting skeletal muscle with solutions containing high concentrations of neutral salts, it was assumed that myosin was the only protein present. This notion persisted for decades despite considerable study of myosin preparations. The presence of a second protein in ordinary myosin preparations was not seriously considered until 1941 when Szent-Györgyi and coworkers observed that the myosin obtained by prolonged extraction of muscle mince differed in behavior from myosin obtained by a brief extraction procedure. More detailed analysis of these preparations by Straub and coworkers in 1942 led to identification of actin as a discrete protein, present in myosin prepared by prolonged salt extraction. Subse-

Major and Minor Mechanisms Regulating Muscular Performance

	Skeletal Muscle	Cardiac Muscle
Ability to summate individual contractile events (partial and complete tetanus)	Minor	Absent
Ability to vary number of active motor units	Major	Absent
Ability to undergo length-dependent changes in contractile properties (length-tension or Frank-Starling relationship)	Usually Minor	Major in beat-to-beat regulation Minor in sustained circulatory changes
Ability to change intrinsic contractile properties (contractility)	Minor	Major in sustained circulatory changes Minor in beat-to-beat regulation

quently, the supposedly pure actins prepared in a number of laboratories were found to contain additional constituents. One of these was identified as *tropomyosin* around 1962. This third protein had been isolated in 1948 by Bailey, though its functional role in muscle was unrecognized until 1964, when several groups of investigators, including our own, found this to be a "modulatory protein," capable of influencing the interactions between actin and myosin. Not long afterwards work in our laboratory indicated the presence of additional proteins in actin preparations that formed Ca^{++}-sensitive actomyosins (see below). It soon became apparent that this additional protein material was *troponin*, another modulatory protein isolated and named around the same time (1965) by Ebashi and coworkers.

As we look back now, it is apparent that Kühne's original myosin preparations must have contained all of these proteins. Evidence that there may be additional components of the contractile machinery has since been obtained; our discussion here, however, will be centered on these four, since their activity can be directly related to important features of cardiac muscle contractility.

It is well established that myosin is the major constituent of the thick filament of muscle sarcomere, whereas actin and the tropomyosin-troponin complex are located on the thin filament (see Chapter 1, "Myocardial Ultrastructure in the Normal and Failing Heart," by Sonnenblick).

Structurally, cardiac myosin (like

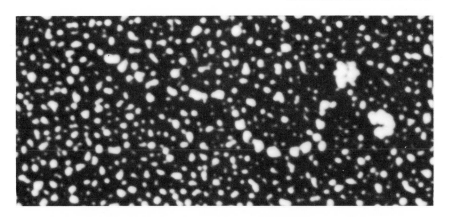

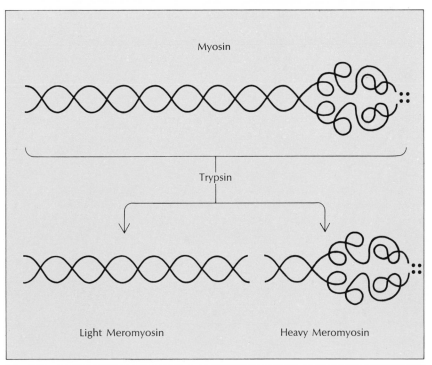

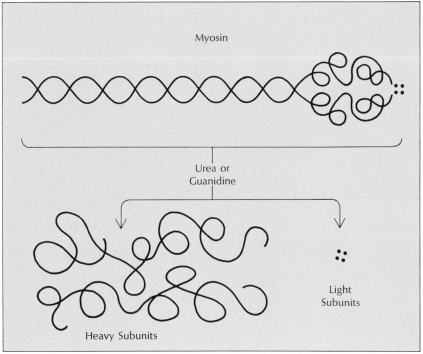

The elongated structure of the myosin molecule and the paired globular or "head" region are clearly seen in electron micrograph by Slayter and Lowey (Proc Natl Acad Sci 58:1614, 1967). The paired globular protein contributes the cross-bridge of the thick filament. Diagrams schematize some of the fragmentation procedures used to analyze myosin substructure. Proteolytic digestion yields heavy and light meromyosin, the former possessing the ATPase activity and actin-binding properties of native myosin. However, release of true subunits requires disruption of hydrogen-bonded structures and is achieved with concentrated urea or guanidine. Light subunits thus released have been linked with specific functional characteristics of heart muscle.

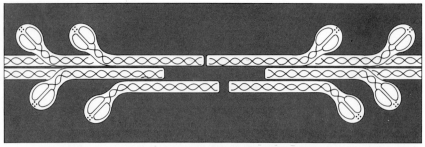

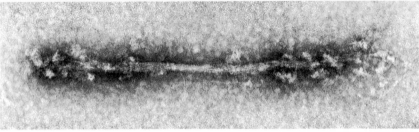

In electron micrograph (original magnification x145,000) by H. E. Huxley of synthetic myosin filament (analogous to thick filament of muscle), oppositely oriented projections extend from a central bare area (J Mol Biol 7:281, 1963). Contraction occurs when these projections, the myosin cross-bridges, interact with actin. The orientation of myosin molecules within this filament is schematized in the drawing at top.

skeletal myosin) is an elongated molecule with a globular enlargement at one end, resembling a tadpole. The globular head end is attached to a long tail that exists as a "coiled coil"– two parallel α-helices wound around each other. According to current estimates the molecular weight of both cardiac and skeletal myosin is in the range of 450,000.

Given the large size of the myosin molecule, it was reasonable to assume that it might contain several subunits; indeed, myosin subunits have been identified and linked with specific functional characteristics of heart muscle, as will be discussed shortly. I am not referring here to the heavy and light meromyosins produced by treatment of the myosin molecule with a proteolytic enzyme such as trypsin. These meromyosins represent fragments obtained by breakage of polypeptide chains. Although often referred to as myosin subunits, they really are not, since by definition the term subunit refers to a discrete polypeptide chain attached to other such chains by hydrogen bonds, disulfide bridges, or other nonpeptide intramolecular bonds.

Proteolytic digestion did, however, provide the first useful means of degrading skeletal myosin and analyzing its components. The more rapidly sedimenting heavy meromyosin exhibits the principal properties of native myosin: hydrolysis of adenosine triphosphate (ATP), the chief energy source for contraction, and binding with actin. Light meromyosin, which retains the solubility characteristics of native myosin, possesses neither ATPase nor actin-binding activity. Both heavy and light meromyosins can be obtained from cardiac myosin, although the conditions for proteolytic cleavage differ significantly from those used to release meromyosins from skeletal myosin.

When purified myosin preparations from either cardiac or skeletal muscle are allowed to aggregate in vitro, one can see structures analogous to the thick filament as visualized by electron microscopy.

The core of the thick filament corresponds to the interwoven tails of the myosin molecules (light meromyosin moiety). Projections oriented in opposite directions at both sides of a bare area in the center of the thick filament – the cross-bridges – correspond to the heavy meromyosin moiety that hydrolyzes ATP and interacts with actin on the thin filament to produce muscular contraction. Evidence supplied by electron microscopy of purified myosin shows distinct pairing in the globular or head region of the myosin molecule, each portion representing one of the paired "heads" of the cross-bridge

of the thick filament of muscle.

Efforts to produce true myosin subunits at first met with little success. Early reports indicated that agents such as urea or guanidine – capable of disrupting hydrogen-bonded structures – released low-molecular weight fragments from skeletal myosin, but these studies were not pursued. Within the past few years there has been renewed interest in identifying and characterizing myosin subunits. There is now reason to believe that the nature of certain myosin subunits may be a major determinant of the level of enzymatic activity responsible for release of energy for the contractile process and, therefore, in the regulation of contractile performance in intact muscle.

A variety of means, in addition to the guanidine and urea, can be employed to fragment myosin without hydrolysis of peptide bonds. Among these are alkali treatment, acetylation, and succinylation. Use of these methods in skeletal myosin from "fast" muscles releases a heavy myosin subunit and three or four lighter subunits. The heavy subunit can be further dissociated, for example, by concentrated guanidine, into two polypeptide chains (each with a molecular weight of approximately 210,000). Light and heavy subunits are obtainable by similar means from cardiac as well as skeletal muscle. Although the light subunits of cardiac myosin differ electrophoretically from those of "fast" skeletal muscle, they are similar to those of "slow" skeletal muscle.

Biochemically, "fast" and "slow" skeletal muscles differ in a critical respect: As we and others have shown, ATPase activity of fast muscle myosin is high whereas ATPase activity of slow muscle myosin is low, reflecting different rates of chemical energy utilization during the contractile process. Of more pertinence to our present discussion is that ATPase activity of cardiac myosin is relatively low, and is indeed quite comparable to that of slow skeletal myosin. The lower ATPase activity of cardiac myosin is associated with a correspondingly lower maximal rate of energy utilization in the living muscle. This has considerable physiologic significance, because in order for the heart's contractile activity to be maintained continuously it is essential that the rates of ATP production and utilization be balanced. Hence, the lower rate of energy liberation by cardiac myosin facilitates the maintenance of this balance.

To put these observations in perspective, a key difference between fast and slow skeletal muscle must be brought to mind: In nature, fast skeletal muscle, which is usually white in color, is generally found where contractile response must be rapid but not prolonged; thus, in the European rabbit, back and hind leg muscles – which are fast – are used for short bursts of activity (a run into its burrow to escape danger). Fast muscle is also found in the flight muscles of birds that use their wings only for brief flights, such as the chicken, whose breast is "white meat." On the other hand, slow skeletal muscle, which like cardiac muscle is red in color, is adapted for prolonged activity. Thus, there is slow muscle in the back and hind legs of the European hare, which eludes pursuit by sustained running, and in flight muscles of birds that fly long distances, such as the duck and the goose, whose breast is "dark meat."

In view of the electrophoretic differences between the light subunits of cardiac myosin and fast skeletal myosin – and the similarities of the cardiac subunits and those of slow skeletal myosin – could the nature of the myosin light subunits be a factor determining the level of myosin ATPase activity? To establish that myosin light subunits do play such a role would require an experiment in which light and heavy subunits from two dissimilar systems were isolated and recombined. Measurement of ATPase activity of hybrid myosins should then provide the answer. While this has been difficult because of the lability of the peptide chains on dissociation, there is now some evidence that the light subunits confer the level of ATPase activity that is characteristic of a given myosin. This observation, as we shall see, may be of importance in understanding the response of the heart to chronic hemodynamic overloading.

Studies of skeletal actin, which appear to apply equally to cardiac actin, have shown that this is a globular protein having a molecular weight of approximately 47,000. Actin can exist in either of two states: monomeric

globular (G) actin, stable in solutions of low ionic strength, can be polymerized to yield fibrous (F) actin by adding any of a number of salts to the solution. Depolymerization occurs when ionic strength of solutions containing F-actin is reduced. Apparently the effect of the salts is non-specific; polymerization is induced by screening negative charges on the G-actin molecule that ordinarily prevent interactions between monomers.

Under ordinary conditions, for G-actin to polymerize, both a bound nucleotide (usually ATP) and a bound divalent cation (either Ca^{++} or Mg^{++}) must also be present. Apparently both are loosely bound at or near a single site on the G-actin molecule. When polymerization takes place, the actin-bound ATP is hydrolyzed and the resulting ADP as well as the divalent cation become tightly bound to the F-actin polymer. Depolymerization of F-actin must take place in solutions containing free ATP, otherwise a G-actin–containing ATP will not reappear. Studies with ring-labeled nucleotide indicate that depolymerization involves an ADP-ATP exchange rather than rephosphorylation of actin-bound ADP. Under special conditions, actin preparations can be shown to be capable of ATP hydrolysis. This occurs at high temperatures, for example when both G-actin and F-actin are present and rapid cycles of polymerization and depolymerization are taking place. Physiologically, however, actin should probably not be considered an ATPase.

The question is whether any of these interesting chemical reactions are of importance in muscular contraction. As noted, recovery of actin-bound ATP after depolymerization appears to require exchange of free ATP for bound ADP; however, significant in-

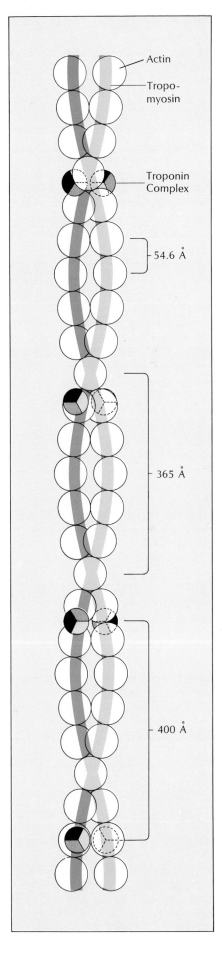

Schematized view of thin filament of muscle shows location of elongated tropomyosin molecules between twin chains of actin. Longitudinal spacing of the troponin complex, which is bound to tropomyosin, occurs at a periodicity of approximately 400 Å. The modulatory proteins, tropomyosin and the troponin complex, thus lie in the grooves of twisted double-stranded actin filament. The latter, the F-actin polymer, consists of two rows of G-actin monomers, 54.6 Å in diameter, with an internode distance of 365 Å.

Actin

Tropo-myosin

Troponin Complex

54.6 Å

365 Å

400 Å

corporation of free ATP into actin is not observed in muscular contraction, either in vivo or in various in vitro systems. In addition, the polymerization-depolymerization cycle can be demonstrated to occur when actin devoid of both bound nucleotide and cation is stabilized in solutions containing high concentrations of sucrose. Thus it cannot now be shown that actin-bound nucleotide plays a role in muscular contraction; instead, actin-bound ATP and cation may serve principally to stabilize certain conformational characteristics of the G-actin molecule.

The physiologic role of actin relates to its interaction with myosin, which initiates contraction through the sliding filament mechanism. Chemically, this is expressed in part as an activation by actin of myosin ATPase activity. Thus, actin converts myosin ATPase of low activity into the highly active actomyosin ATPase. At the same time that actin enhances myosin ATPase activity, physicochemical changes in the actomyosin complex take place that appear to be analogous to contraction in the living muscle. These changes – superprecipitation – will be discussed below. Also, the properties of actin-myosin interaction, and their significance in intact muscle, will be considered more fully as we proceed.

Let us focus now, however, on the third of the individual contractile proteins – tropomyosin. As already noted, for a long time after its discovery, tropomyosin had no known function. As with other contractile proteins, the molecular weight of tropomyosin has been periodically reevaluated. It now seems clear that tropomyosin has a molecular weight of 70,000, being composed of two subunits, each having a molecular weight of around 35,000. Like the light meromyosin "tail" of the myosin molecule, tropomyosin is in a coiled-coil conformation; in the case of tropomyosin, however, use of structure-disrupting agents does not cause dissociation of the subunits unless a disulfide bridge is first reduced. Structurally, cardiac and skeletal tropomyosins appear to be virtually identical.

Coexistence of tropomyosin and actin in a single structure within the myofibril was strongly suggested by the stoichiometric binding between the two. Once they were both localized to the thin filament, the elongated tropomyosin molecule was shown to lie in a groove between two actin monomers. Optical measurements on tropomyosin preparations show a 400Å periodicity also seen in the thin myofilament. The significance of this finding was unclear until work was under way with troponin in in vitro systems. Labeled troponin was found to bind to tropomyosin crystals with a linear periodicity of approximately 400 Å. Thus the 400 Å periodicity, long recognized in intact muscle, apparently represents the spacing of the troponin complex along tropomyosin in the thin filament.

I refer to the troponin complex, since, as already indicated, troponin probably represents three discrete proteins. One component of the troponin complex has a high-affinity calcium-binding site and is now believed to be the *calcium receptor* of the contractile apparatus. The second troponin component is an *interaction inhibitor*, which serves, along with tropomyosin, to inhibit the primary interaction between actin and myosin. The third component of the troponin complex is a *tropomyosin-binding protein*, which binds the troponin complex to tropomyosin. Before discussing in more detail what is known of troponin function, something further should be said about interactions of the contractile proteins, more specifically actin-myosin systems in the presence and absence of the tropomyosin-troponin complex under various experimental conditions.

Study of actomyosin preparations reconstituted by combining purified myosin and actin has shown that both energy liberation and contraction, the essential biochemical features of the contractile process (except for its control by calcium), can be explained by a series of interactions in this two-protein system. Thus, reconstituted actomyosin incubated with ATP and Mg^{++} manifests ATPase activity and undergoes physicochemical changes analogous to contraction in intact muscle. The types of intervention that promote or inhibit these interactions between actin and myosin are numerous and complicated. For example, increasing the concentration of any of several salts – i.e., increasing ionic strength of the solution – will dissociate actin and myosin and thus inhibit ATPase activity, giving rise to a situation analogous to diastole (rest). Conversely, actin and myosin reassociate to give a state analogous to systole (contraction) in which ATPase – and thus the rate of chemical energy liberation – is high.

Actually, changes in actomyosin ATPase activity reflect quite complex phenomena. As noted above, ATPase activity of actomyosin can be inhibited by agents causing actin and myosin to be dissociated: Among these dissociating agents is ATP itself. Yet ATP also causes contraction, and when actomyosin preparations are incubated at low ATP concentrations, ATPase activity tends to be high. The dissociating effect of ATP, manifest as a decrease in ATPase activity, only appears when ATP concentration is high. When actomyosins are incubated at high ATP concentrations, therefore, the ATP initially causes dissociation of actin and myosin. As time passes, however, and myosin ATPase slowly hydrolyzes ATP, a critical ATP concentration is reached where the two proteins reassociate, ATPase activity increases, and contraction occurs. This explains the well-recognized, if confusing, dual action of ATP.

With these considerations in mind, ATPase activity can be used as an index of the extent and rate of interaction between actin and myosin and to relate the effects of various interventions in vitro to alterations of contractile behavior in living muscle. Physicochemical changes already referred to can also be shown to reflect the state of interaction between actin and myosin. Although these might be studied with actomyosin in solution, it must be remembered that in living muscle actomyosin exists as an insoluble gel; thus, to examine certain properties of the contractile proteins it is necessary to employ the more complex and heterogeneous actomyosin gels. As usually prepared, the gel exists as irregular flocks that form a loose pellet after low-speed centrifugation. If ATP in low concentrations is added, the flocks shrink so that a reduced volume of precipitate is collected after centrifugation, this process being called *superprecipitation*. The changes can also be followed by recording transmission of light through actomyosin gels; as a rule superprecipitation is associated with an increase in turbidity and hence in optical density; dissociation by ATP is recorded as a decrease in turbidity. The optical measurement of superprecipitation is complex, however, depending to a significant extent on the geometry of the spectrophotometer used to measure turbidity.

Thus the two-protein combination of actin and myosin possesses the salient contractile properties of the myofibril. Yet something must be missing, since in living muscle the contractile process is now generally believed to be initiated when calcium is released in the final stages in excitation-contraction coupling, whereas reconstituted actomyosin preparations of the type we have been discussing are calcium-insensitive. However, when actomyosin is prepared by prolonged extraction of muscle with salt solutions, the resulting *natural actomyosin* (as opposed to *reconstituted actomyosin* made by combining individually purified actin and myosin) *is* sensitive to Ca^{++} at low concentrations. In fact, it was this finding that led to a search for a calcium-sensitizing factor that is lost in purification of actin and myosin. At one point this calcium-sensitizing factor was thought to be tropomyosin, but it is now apparent that the sensitization of actomyosin to calcium requires all of the troponin components in addition to tropomyosin. Tropomyosin alone can act to inhibit the actin-myosin interactions but in a manner that is insensitive to Ca^{++}. Chemically, this inhibition is manifested as a depression of Mg^{++}-activated ATPase activity, physically, as a delay in onset of superprecipitation. In terms of physiologic control, these inhibitory actions are critically influenced by the calcium-binding component of troponin, since only with its addition does the system become calcium-sensitive.

When comparisons were made of purified cardiac and skeletal troponin several years ago, the former appeared to show lower calcium affinity. However, this type of study has been repeated with the more purified preparations now available; there is a good probability that the reported difference in calcium affinity reflects damage to the cardiac protein during extraction

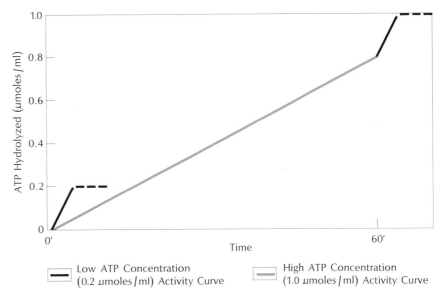

High ATPase activity is seen in actomyosin preparations incubated at low ATP concentrations, whereas low ATPase activity occurs at high ATP concentrations, as indicated above. When initial ATP concentration is high, actin and myosin dissociate, but with time, myosin ATPase activity reduces ATP concentration of medium to a point at which the two proteins reassociate; high ATPase activity is then seen and contraction occurs.

and purification. (As noted earlier, labile proteins are more difficult to isolate from cardiac than from skeletal muscle.) However, a significant difference in strontium-binding by cardiac and skeletal troponins, demonstrated by Ebashi and coworkers, suggests that the troponins of cardiac and skeletal muscle are structurally dissimilar.

To calculate the total amount of calcium needed to activate the contractile machinery fully, starting from a calcium level at which there is no actin-myosin interaction, two factors must be considered: the calcium required for binding to the contractile proteins and the calcium required to increase the concentration of free calcium in intracellular fluid. The first can be determined by estimating the number of calcium-binding sites of the contractile proteins, either by direct measurement of the amount of Ca^{++} bound to "natural" actomyosins in relation to the actomyosin content of the myocardium, or by calculating the amount of troponin in a given amount of heart muscle. By either method, the amount of calcium required to activate all actin-myosin interactions appears to be in the range of 50 μmoles/kg wet weight of mammalian ventricle. To achieve maximal systolic force — where virtually all troponin sites would be bound to Ca^{++}— an additional 10 μmoles/kg wet weight are needed to raise tissue water Ca^{++} concentrations from 10^{-7} M, the diastolic level, to 10^{-5} M, the systolic level.

Thus at least 60 μmoles Ca^{++}/kg wet weight of muscle must be released during excitation-contraction coupling to achieve a maximal contraction in heart muscle. This total does not take into account the calcium that may be bound to other myocardial cell ele-

Calcium Requirement for Cardiac Contraction (Approximate)	
1. To bind to cardiac troponin	50 μmoles/kg
2. To raise tissue Ca^{++} from 10^{-7} M to 10^{-5} M	10 μmoles/kg
3. To bind to other structures (e.g., mitochondria)	unknown
Minimal total calcium to be released during systole . . .	60 μmoles/kg

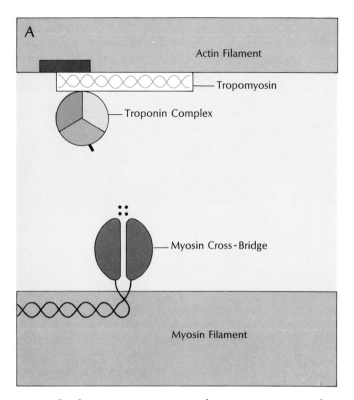

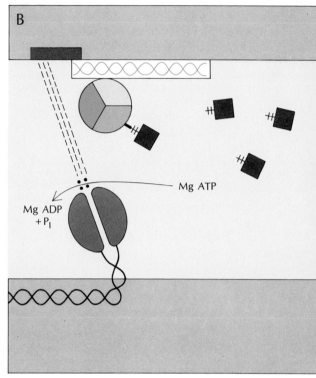

In postulated sequence of events resulting in contraction and relaxation of cardiac muscle, interaction between myosin and actin is inhibited during diastole (A) by the modulatory proteins, *tropomyosin and troponin. At onset of systole (B), binding of calcium to one component of the troponin complex overcomes the inhibition and initiates the actin-myosin interactions primary to*

ments, for example the mitochondria, as free Ca^{++} is increased in the cell.

From what has been said it should be apparent that tropomyosin and the troponin complex are not contractile proteins as such; they do not participate directly in contraction. More correctly, they should be referred to as *modulatory proteins* since their principal role is to modulate the actin-myosin interactions that are primary in contractions. Specific features of these interactions should be underscored: Provided calcium is present at levels that saturate the calcium-binding component of troponin, there is no inhibitory effect on actin-myosin interaction by the modulatory proteins. However, when calcium is removed from its binding site on troponin, for example by a calcium chelator, there is marked inhibition of actin-myosin interaction. When calcium is again added and rebinds to troponin, the inhibitory action of the troponin-tropomyosin complex is reversed.

Thus, the action of Ca^{++} that initiates contraction results not from an activation of the contractile process as such, but from reversal of a pre-existing inhibition. To be sure, inter-

actions of the modulatory proteins may well prove more complex than outlined here; any conclusions drawn must be considered tentative at best. Nonetheless, a framework can now be developed to explain the normal sequence of events in the heart's contractile machinery that results in contraction.

The important question raised at the outset was whether changes in the cardiac contractile proteins might be responsible for the impairment in myocardial function associated with heart failure. Reports by several investigators have documented a decrease in contractile force—manifested as a depression in development of muscle tension and in velocity of muscle shortening—in myocardium isolated from hypertrophied and failing hearts. In biochemical studies, enzymatic properties of cardiac contractile proteins have been compared in normal and pathologic states. The most significant observation has been a decrease in myosin AT Pase in failing ventricles; however, not all studies are consistent on this point. Abnormalities in the physicochemical interactions between actin and myosin have

also been reported, but again there is disagreement as to the findings.

Before discussing the functional significance of the reported decline in myosin AT Pase activity in the failing heart, it will be useful to review briefly the possible relationship between the biochemical and biophysical properties of the contractile proteins and their expression in the living muscle as specific features of the mechanics of contraction. As of now, the extent to which changes in myocardial performance in intact muscle reflect changes in the contractile proteins is not clear. One of the problems is that the properties of the contractile proteins in intact muscle cannot be studied directly or measured by present techniques. The contractile state of muscle — and changes in contractility — can be measured only indirectly, in terms of muscle mechanics. This complexity must be kept in mind when efforts are made to use mechanical measurements of cardiac contraction to assess myocardial function under clinical conditions. Moreover, in attempting to relate specific aspects of mechanical performance of heart muscle to the contractile proteins and their

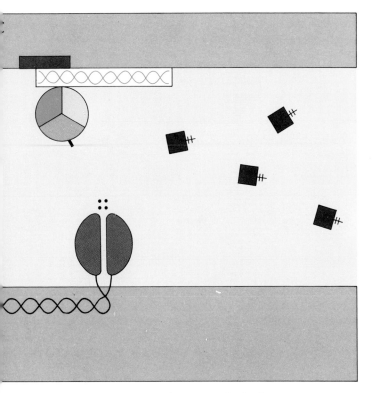

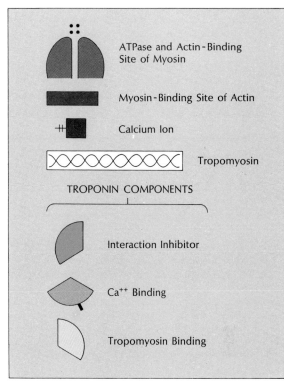

ATPase and Actin-Binding
Site of Myosin

Myosin-Binding Site of Actin

Calcium Ion

Tropomyosin

TROPONIN COMPONENTS

Interaction Inhibitor

Ca^{++} Binding

Tropomyosin Binding

contraction; with removal of calcium from the binding site, actin-myosin interaction is again inhibited and the muscle relaxes (C). Role of calcium in initiating contraction thus appears to involve

reversal of a preexisting inhibition rather than activation of the contractile process. The exact molecular changes in this Ca^{++}-mediated process of excitation-contraction coupling are not known.

interactions, we must also consider that the concepts worked out in skeletal muscle do not appear to be entirely applicable to the heart.

The mechanical features of muscle contraction are often expressed in terms of the relation of tension development (P) to shortening velocity (V); a plot expressing V as a function of P normally takes the form of a rectangular hyperbola, the force-velocity curve. Studies in skeletal muscle established that in freely shortening muscle, velocity is maximal (V_{max}) at zero load; conversely, tension is maximal (P_o) when muscle shortening cannot occur, as during an isometric tetanic contraction. Thus, P_o of skeletal muscle can be determined directly, V_{max} is obtained by extrapolation – by applying the equation for a rectangular hyperbola to measurements of muscle shortening at intermediate loads. In cardiac muscle, however, both must be determined by extrapolation since the heart is incapable of tetanic contraction.

In his classic formulations of skeletal muscle contraction some 30 years ago, A. V. Hill proposed that the inverse relationship between force and

velocity could be explained if "active points" in the molecular machinery – the sites in muscle that generate tension and effect shortening – existed in one of two states. In the first, corresponding to P_o, all active points are engaged in generating and holding tension. In the second, corresponding to V_{max}, active points are in a free state, able to take part in the conversion of chemical to mechanical energy that results in muscle shortening. At any moment, Hill theorized, the distribution of active points between the two states would be determined by the load borne by the muscle. If the ends of a muscle are fixed so that no shortening can occur, all active points will be in the combined state and maximal tension would develop. On that basis, maximal tension would be determined by the *number* of active points. At the other extreme, with all active points in the free state and none holding tension, both shortening velocity and the rate of energy release required to effect shortening would be at the maximal level. Thus both V_{max} and the maximal rate of energy release would be limited by the *rate of turnover* of active points in muscle.

In other words, what Hill's insight told him was that quite different properties of muscle apparently determine maximal tension and maximal shortening velocity. Developments in the past decade have confirmed his prediction. Hill's term "active point" has since been replaced by actin-myosin interaction; force-velocity relationships can thus be viewed in terms of the *number* of active interactions between myosin cross-bridges of the thick filament and sites of actin in thin filament, and of the *rate* of chemical turnover of interaction sites.

There is considerable evidence that the number of active sites, expressed per unit of cross-sectional area of muscle, does determine the amount of tension developed by the contractile element of muscle. The number of active sites is clearly affected by changes in sarcomere length. For example, in muscle stretched to lengths beyond the peak of the length-tension curve, there is decreasing overlap of thick and thin muscle filaments; as a result, as sarcomere length increases, active tension decreases. Along this descending limb of the length-tension curve, decreasing overlap between thick and

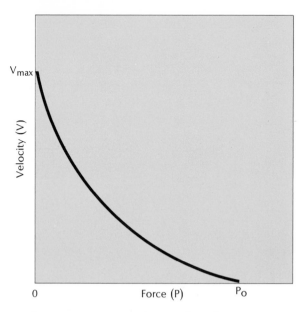

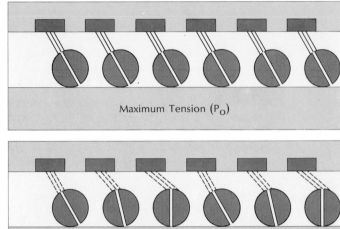

Representation of force-velocity relationship of active muscle (left) shows maximal shortening velocity (V_{max}) in muscle at zero load. Maximal tension (P_o) occurs when shortening is prevented, as during isometric contraction. According to current theory, tension is maximal when all actin-myosin interaction points are in the combined state (upper right); in contrast, velocity is maximal when tension is zero and all active points are free to participate in chemical reactions that lead to shortening (lower right).

thin filaments caused by further stretching of muscle should be accompanied by a decline in maximal tension, which is indeed what was found by Gordon, A. F. Huxley, and Julian. However, if V_{max} is determined by a different property of the contractile machinery, as we suggest, it should remain unchanged, which was found to be so by these investigators.

But consider how the situation differs in cardiac muscle: Normally the myocardium functions on the ascending limb of the length-tension curve, and when it is stimulated to contract, the developed force becomes progressively reduced during systole because of sarcomere shortening. Even during an isometric contraction, some loss of force accompanies the contractile element shortening that occurs by extension of the series elasticity of heart muscle. Moreover, in heart muscle, a significant part of resting tension is maintained by noncontractile structures; the attenuating effects of

series elasticity and the contribution to resting tension of the parallel elastic component must be kept in mind in interpreting force measurements in the heart. As contraction proceeds, a significant fraction of the initial tension appears to be transferred from the parallel elasticity to the myofilaments. For these reasons total external systolic force represents only an approximation of actual force development by the heart's contractile proteins.

Now let us turn to shortening velocity. If, as suggested, maximal shortening velocity reflects the rate at which active sites convert chemical to mechanical energy, V_{max} should be independent of both the number of active sites and their rate of activation. In other words, even a single active site should cause a muscle to shorten at its maximal rate if the site were in fact exposed to zero load, as A. F. Huxley has suggested. However, because of elastic forces and internal viscosities, truly unloaded shortening of active muscle, cardiac or skeletal, is unlikely to occur.

Force-velocity measurements to estimate V_{max} and P_o for heart muscle are subject to error for another reason. Because the active state is slow in onset, the number of active actin-myosin interactions increases continuously during the period of contraction. Esti-

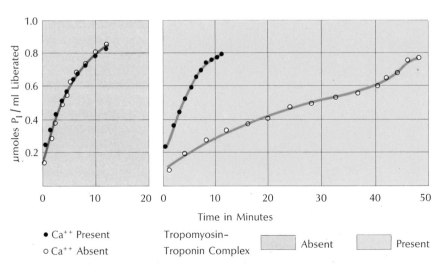

Calcium's role as "derepressor" acting via an inhibition of the modulatory proteins is suggested by this experiment. In absence of troponin-tropomyosin complex (left), ATPase (ordinate) is high, whether Ca^{++} is present or not; when the modulatory proteins are added to medium, rapid enzymatic activity occurs only if Ca^{++} is present (right).

mates of V_{max} made by extrapolation of force-velocity are thus influenced by time-dependent as well as length-dependent changes in the number of active sites. To add another factor, parallel elasticity of cardiac muscle, which accounts in part for the high resting tension, may also contribute to measured shortening velocity and the "series elasticity" now appears to change during the slow cardiac contraction. It is for these reasons that values for P_o and V_{max} reported for the heart do not have the same important biochemical significance that they do in skeletal muscle.

A point to keep in mind in reference to the heart is that important changes in contractile properties occur without alterations in sarcomere length; these represent the changes in contractility described at the beginning of this chapter. The explanation for these length-independent changes appears to be in the chemistry of contractile proteins; specifically, changes in P_o may be brought about by changes in the amount of Ca^{++} available for binding to troponin (see Chapter 4, "Calcium Metabolism in the Normal and Failing Heart," by Chidsey). Factors acting to decrease the number of troponin molecules receiving Ca^{++} during systole should be expected to reduce maximal tension; on the other hand, an increase in the amount of calcium delivered to the contractile machinery should make possible increased maximal tension by increasing the number of active force-generating sites.

From what has been said of the action of Ca^{++} in initiating contraction it now appears likely that its role is limited to control of actin-myosin interactions through an "on-off switch" mechanism. With the binding of Ca^{++}

Whereas the maximal tension a muscle can develop is controlled by the number of actin-myosin interactions, maximal shortening velocity appears dependent only on the rate of chemical turnover of interaction sites. Thus, reduced contractility could be due to a decrease in the number of sites ($-P_o$) or in their rate of interaction ($-V_{max}$). The former could result from a reduction in the quantum of Ca^{++} released during excitation-contraction coupling, the latter from a change in the properties of myosin light subunits that appear to determine enzymatic activity.

Normal

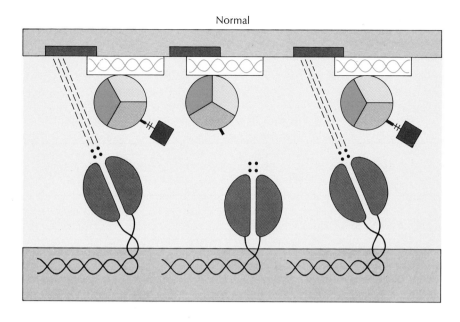

Reduced Contractility ($-P_o$)

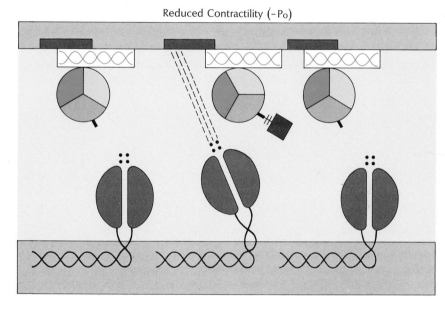

Reduced Contractility ($-V_{max}$)

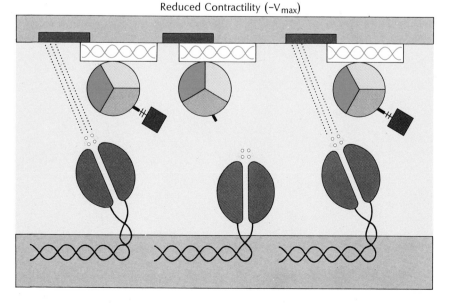

to troponin, the tropomyosin-troponin complex can no longer inhibit actin-myosin interactions and the latter are fully expressed. Therefore changes in the rate of development of tension in the contractile element (dP/dt) appear to be determined by alterations in the rate at which Ca^{++} is bound to troponin. For example, an increase in the rate of Ca^{++} binding should, in theory, cause an increase in dP/dt. (In this reference, as elsewhere in this chapter, it must be remembered that P represents force, not pressure.) However, the many uncertainties described above make it impossible to relate the rate of tension development directly to the rate of Ca^{++} delivery to troponin.

If these formulations prove correct, enhanced myocardial contractility that results from augmentation of maximal tension may be said to result from an increase in the amount of Ca^{++} delivered to the heart's contractile proteins; concomitant elevation in dP/dt indicates that the rate of Ca^{++} delivery is also increased. On the other hand, if the amount and/or the rate of calcium delivery are reduced – as is suggested to occur in heart failure – this could explain a decline in maximal tension or in the maximal rate of tension development. Such a change, of course, would result from changes in the Ca^{++} delivery systems of excitation-contraction coupling, rather than from changes in the contractile proteins themselves (see Chapter 4 by Chidsey).

Since maximal shortening velocity appears to reflect a different parameter of muscle function, one might expect that it is related to a different property of muscle chemistry. Such, in fact, appears to be the case: Recent studies by a number of groups, working independently, have documented a close relationship between V_{max} and myosin ATPase activity. Moreover, these findings can be related to differences in myosin enzymatic activity already referred to: V_{max} is significantly higher in fast skeletal muscle, which has relatively high myosin ATPase activity, than in slow skeletal muscle, which has relatively low myosin ATPase activity. A comparison of myosin ATPase activity of muscles differing over a 100-fold range in V_{max} (in a meticulous study by Bárány and coworkers) showed an excellent correlation between enzymatic activity and maximal shortening velocity.

More recently this relationship was substantiated in studies of cross-innervated fast and slow skeletal muscle: V_{max} and myosin ATPase activity were altered in a parallel manner depending on the nature of the motor nerve. On this basis, if myosin ATPase activity is determined by the properties of the myosin light subunits, as suggested earlier, it follows that maximal shortening velocity as well may be so determined. A change in V_{max} thus may reflect a primary modification of the myosin molecule, evident in vitro as a change in myosin ATPase activity.

Since it seems clear that the chemistry of the myosin-ATP interaction governs the maximal velocity at which muscle can shorten, then interventions that alter V_{max} can be presumed to act primarily on the hydrolytic site of myosin (whereas interventions altering P_o or dP/dt should be acting on those systems responsible for delivery of Ca^{++} to the contractile proteins, or on the Ca^{++} receptor of troponin). Our story of the nature and role of the cardiac contractile proteins would be more complete if this were known to be the case. But it is not. For example, if cardiac glycosides enhance myocardial contractility in part by augmenting V_{max}, as has been reported, evidence should be obtainable of an increased rate of energy turnover by the heart's contractile proteins. Although there have been conflicting reports on this point, in my view the weight of evidence is negative;

Close correlation of maximal shortening velocity of muscle and myosin ATPase activity has been documented for both fast and slow muscle in a variety of animals (graph is based on work by Bárány et al). In studies of cross-innervated fast and slow muscle, V_{max} and myosin ATPase activity have been shown to undergo parallel alterations.

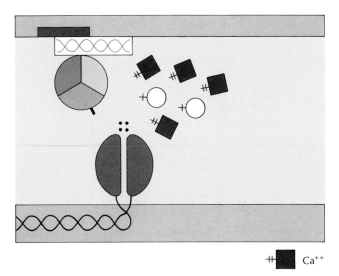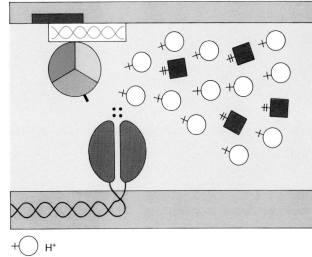

$+\!+\!\blacksquare$ Ca^{++} $+\!\bigcirc$ H$^+$

Experiments showing significant reduction of Ca^{++} binding to troponin by increased hydrogen ion concentration suggest that a fall in pH in ischemic myocardium (right) may play a part in depressing its contractility after coronary occlusion.

cardiac glycosides have no appreciable influence on the ATPase activity of myosin alone, myosin plus actin, or the "complete" actin-myosin-troponin-tropomyosin system. Significantly, one substance that has a definite action on cardiac contractile proteins in studies in vitro is hydrogen ion; the action is to inhibit binding of Ca^{++} to troponin. A decrease in intramyocardial pH, such as probably occurs in the ischemic myocardium, may thus be directly responsible for depressed contractility after coronary artery occlusion.

To extend this line of reasoning, variations in either the amount or rate of Ca^{++} delivered to muscle should be without effect on V_{max}. However, a Ca^{++}-dependent shift in V_{max} has been reported by several investigators, again on the basis of extrapolations of force-velocity data. Direct examination of the effect on V_{max} of variations in delivery of Ca^{++} to the contractile proteins, on the other hand, indicates that V_{max} is independent of the amount of Ca^{++} that is bound to troponin as long as the conditions at the time of study dissociate fully the thick and thin filaments.

Thus we are left with ambiguities and a number of unanswered questions. One conclusion that seems warranted at present is that estimates of V_{max} based on extrapolations from force-velocity data should probably be considered among empirical indices of myocardial function rather than as direct measurements of specific properties of the contractile process.

In terms of the quest set forth at the outset, can we consider the reported fall in myosin ATPase activity in the failing heart to represent a "defect" responsible for the clinical deterioration? Such a conclusion, while reasonable, must be weighed against the possibility that a fall in myosin ATPase activity represents instead a compensatory mechanism that allows the heart to function under conditions of hemodynamic overloading. Thus, it becomes important to ask whether a decrease in myosin ATPase activity (and, presumably, V_{max}) could help the left ventricle adapt to the demands of an abnormality like aortic stenosis. Recent studies of the energetics of contraction in fast and slow muscles appear to provide an affirmative answer. Thus, in slow muscle, in which both myosin ATPase

activity and V_{max} are low, the development and maintenance of tension have been found to be more efficient than in fast muscle. In the heart, in which the overall rate of energy utilization cannot exceed the rate of energy production, a reduction in myosin ATPase activity under conditions of hemodynamic overloading would be of considerable value in preserving cellular energy levels, albeit at the cost of a reduction in speed of contraction. For this reason, although the evidence on this subject remains incomplete, a decline in myosin ATPase activity in the overloaded heart, possibly due to the synthesis of a new myosin light subunit, might represent a compensatory mechanism that permits the organism to survive, though at a lower level of function.

As in the legend of the Round Table, therefore, the object of this quest remains elusive. Yet as more investigative "Knights" set out, each taking a slightly different road in the search for greater understanding of cardiac function in health and disease, the fellowship becomes stronger, and additional light is cast on the critical problems of cardiac function.

Biochemical Processes in Cardiac Function

ROBERT E. DAVIES

University of Pennsylvania

The mechanical events within the heart's ultimate unit, the sarcomere, through which contractile force is generated, were the starting point for the portion of this book on cardiac failure. It is a logical next step to consider the biochemical mediators and processes that provide the energy, the environment, and the control mechanisms for these mechanical events.

Heart muscle, like all other muscles and indeed like most energy-producing or -utilizing tissues, uses a single energy source, adenosine triphosphate (ATP). Because the heart is an aerobic tissue, ATP production in the heart is largely the result of oxidative phosphorylation. This is in contrast to skeletal muscle, which, when working rapidly, obtains most of its ATP from anaerobic glycolysis, a mechanism employed by the myocardium only for short periods.

In oxidative phosphorylation, two compounds are joined to form ATP. These are an inorganic phosphate and adenosine diphosphate (ADP). When ATP is cleaved to re-form ADP and inorganic phosphate, about 10,000 calories (10 kilocalories or nutritional calories) are released for each gram molecule of ATP or inorganic phosphate. Although the amount of ATP involved in a working contraction is very small – perhaps 0.5 to 1.0 micromoles per gram of muscle – and the total ATP content of the body is quite modest, it is broken down and reused so rapidly that an amount comparable to the whole weight of the body is used each day. This is possible because of the remarkable efficiency with which ATP is produced.

Although quantitatively the most important fuels used by the heart to manufacture ATP are the fatty acids, it can also use glucose or its storage-form polymer, glycogen. If the heart starts with glycogen, it first breaks it down to glucose phosphate. This compound is in turn metabo-

lized through various steps to fructose diphosphate and to the phosphoglyceric acids, thence to pyruvate. These steps, which have the effect of activating the substrates themselves, require ATP. If the starting point is glucose, two molecules of ATP are required for each unit of glucose; with glycogen, only one ATP molecule is needed. However, four molecules of ATP are then produced as each molecule of glucose is metabolized to lactic acid.

Once the substrates are activated, ATP can be produced. In the heart, the most important mechanism, oxidative phosphorylation, is initiated by the pyruvate entering the citric acid (Krebs) cycle where it is oxidized to acetyl coenzyme A and then through a series of intermediate steps involving the successive oxidation of the carbons of pyruvate to carbon dioxide. The hydrogens of the pyruvic acid and other intermediates are transported through the electron transport facilities of the cytochrome system of enzymes so that they reduce oxygen to water. As the electrons move along the cytochromes, three ATP molecules are formed for every oxygen atom reduced. This, then, is the most important energy-producing system in oxidative metabolism, with the net effect being the production of 38 molecules of ATP for the oxidation of each molecule of glucose.

Fats can use the Krebs cycle even more efficiently than carbohydrates. Nonesterified fatty acids are broken down, two carbons at a time, to make acetyl coenzyme A, which enters directly into the Krebs cycle where oxidation metabolism results in the manufacture of large amounts of ATP. In fact, for equivalent weights of material, more ATP is produced from fat than from carbohydrate.

The above, of course, represents an extremely abbreviated description of the biochemical pathways involved in ATP production. Those readers desiring more detail will

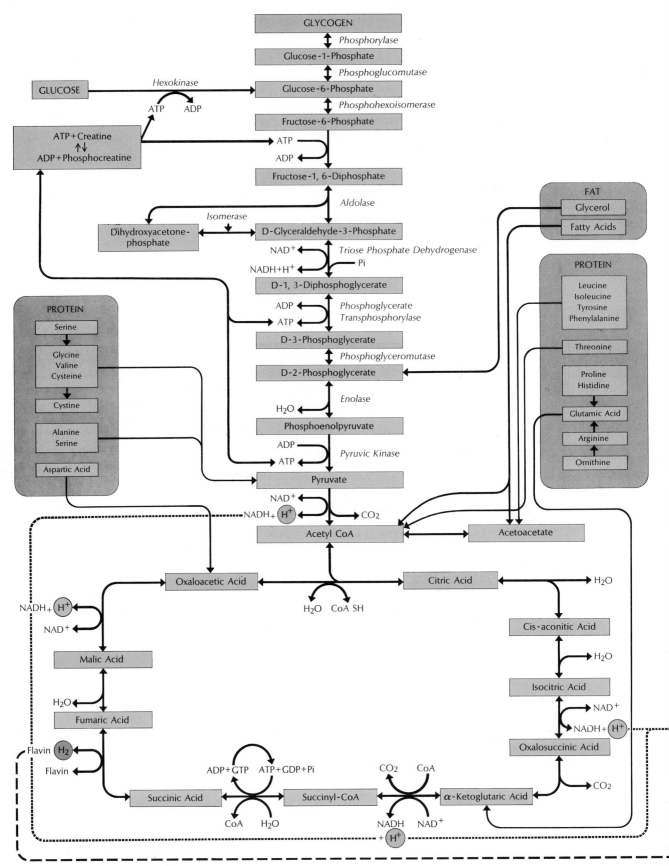

Shown diagramatically are the pathways for production of ATP from foodstuffs, most commonly fats or carbohydrates (glucose or glycogen); proteins may also be used in starvation. Initial steps

involve activation of the substrates. The carbohydrates are metabolized to pyruvate, which enters the citric acid (Krebs) cycle and is oxidized to acetyl coenzyme A. Fatty acids are also me-

find it in the figure at left and below.

Before the utilization of ATP in cardiac contraction as well as in the heart's anabolic processes is discussed, it may be useful to recall some of the morphologic characteristics of the myocardial cell and to relate these to its metabolic activity. The enzymatic systems required for anaerobic glycolysis exist either free in the sarcoplasm or rather loosely bound to the sarcoplasmic reticulum. Some of the enzymes needed for fatty acid oxidation are also free in the sarcoplasm. However, when one turns to oxidative phosphorylation, the focus of attention immediately becomes the mitochondria or, as they are often called in heart muscle, the sarcosomes. All of the enzymes required in the citric acid cycle, the cytochrome enzymes required for electron transport, and the substances involved in the reduction of oxygen are located in the mitochondria. It is here that oxidative phosphorylation takes place. All that is required from outside are the substrates carried in the coronary blood, oxygen, and the fatty acids and glucose from food. Glycogen is made within the heart from circulating glucose, and most glucose is converted to the storage form before being utilized for ATP production. The fatty acids reach the heart attached to circulating proteins as free (unesterified) fatty acids that are transported into the myocardium and then used directly for ATP synthesis. Incidentally, proteins may be degraded enzymatically to liberate amino acids, which can participate in the citric acid cycle after removal of their amino groups by transamination. However, except in cases of starvation, protein is not a major source of muscle energy.

For the ATP produced in the mitochondria to function as a source of energy for contraction it must traverse the distance between the site of production and the site of contractile activity, that is to say, from the mitochondria to the filaments within the sarcomeres. While the details of this transport have not been entirely elucidated, it seems certain that simple diffusion is rapid enough and quantitatively sufficient to meet the needs of the heart.

The thick filaments of the sarcomere are assemblages of myosin molecules that are composed of two peptide chains, each of which can be cleaved into two parts, light meromyosin (LMM) and heavy meromyosin (HMM). An isolated myosin molecule would give something of the appearance of a tadpole with two heads and two tails, the tails made up of two long intertwined threadlike chains of LMM and the two heads of HMM. There are also some light separate subunits (see Chapter 2, "Contractile Proteins in the Normal and Failing Myocardium," by Katz). The light meromyosin appears to be essentially structural in function. The heavy meromyosin is an enzyme, in fact an ATPase, capable of breaking ATP down to ADP and inorganic phosphate.

This breakdown of ATP by heavy meromyosin occurs only when the muscle is actively contracting. Besides magnesium, which is always present, two requirements govern this selectivity. To operate enzymatically in situ, HMM requires the presence of both calcium and actin, the latter being — with tropomyosin and troponin — the structural protein that makes up the thin filaments of the sarcomere. Tro-

pomyosin probably binds troponin periodically to actin, and troponin is now known to be the protein to which calcium binds.

The sequence of events appears to start with the activation of the heart by the pacemaking impulse, the biochemical nature of which will be described subsequently. After activation, some calcium enters from outside, but most of it comes from stores within the cisternae of the sarcoplasmic reticulum. It diffuses through the sarcoplasm and attaches to the troponin on the thin filament and, in the overlap region of the thick and thin filaments, causes the heavy meromyosin—ATPase to break down ATP to ADP and inorganic phosphate. The energy thus released results in the sliding of the thin filaments over the thick filaments, producing the development of force and shortening of the muscle. The actual point at which the ATP is used is at the head end of the myosin molecule, which under the electron microscope can be seen to be the crossbridge or site of action of the myosin filament.

Considerable progress has been made in elucidating the mechanism that accounts for the sliding of the thin over the thick filaments. It has been demonstrated that the crossbridges must act cyclically. At rest, they are not linked with the thin filaments, but during activity links are established. X-ray films taken by Dr. Hugh Huxley and by other investigators have helped clarify this process. A comparison of the length of the crossbridges with the distance moved by the actin filaments shows that when the sarcomere shortens, an individual crossbridge must interact cyclically several times to produce con-

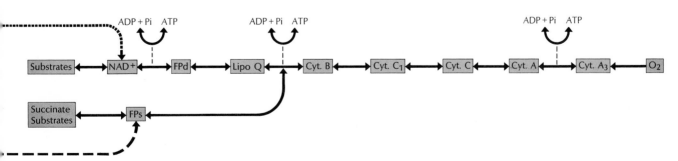

tabolized to acetyl coenzyme A. Within the Krebs cycle, carbons are successively oxidized to carbon dioxide and oxidative phosphorylation is initiated. The electrons from the hydrogens of the intermediates are transported through the electron transport facilities of the cytochrome enzymes where, except for the succinate, three ATP molecules are formed for every half O_2 reduced.

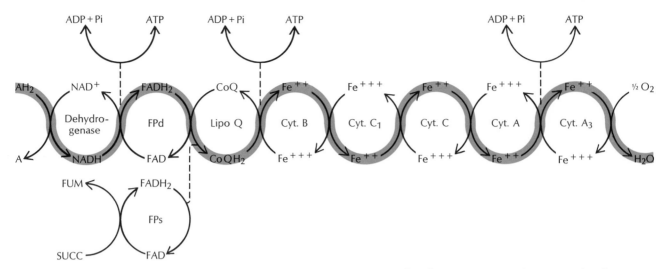

In detailed representation of the electron transport facilities provided by the cytochrome system of enzymes, one can see the specific sites of production of each of the two or three molecules of ATP produced for every atom of oxygen reduced to water. Reduction occurs as hydrogen electrons from pyruvic acid and other intermediates are transported through the system.

tinuous movement. The number of interactions involving any individual crossbridge varies with the amount of work done and the distance the muscle shortens.

Several theories have been advanced with regard to the manner in which the crossbridge interactions may occur. It has been suggested that the crossbridges could move either like rowboat oars sweeping to-and-fro or they could act like a rubber band or a helical spring, reaching out to make contact with the actin, then contracting to pull it along into overlap with the myosin filaments. The mechanism for force generation in striated muscle proposed by A. F. Huxley and R. M. Simmons in 1971 could fit either of these possibilities.

It should be made clear that there is a good deal about this interaction that remains to be proved or clarified. Thus, the nature of the sites on the actin and myosin that link with each other has not been defined chemically. What is clear is that in the natural situation, the thick and thin filaments remain separate from one another in the presence of magnesium, troponin, and A T P until calcium is presented to the system. With the influx of calcium, the filaments become linked with each other.

More is said about the role of calcium in cardiac contractility in Chapter 2 by Katz and in Chapter 4 by Chidsey. However, the role of magnesium also requires comment. A great deal is still not known, but what does seem to be clear is that magnesium is needed in all reactions in biochemistry that involve organic phosphate molecules. The evidence is occasionally indirect, since with some available techniques magnesium cannot be used and manganese must serve as a model. The evidence suggests that magnesium acts as a glue to hold the organic phosphate to the enzymatic protein. The generally accepted view is that magnesium is required to hold the A T P in place. It is known that in the absence of magnesium, the linkage of actin and myosin does not take place. Whether or not there is any movement of magnesium during these interactions is not known.

Although calcium appears to diffuse into the sarcoplasm and to the region of the contractile proteins spontaneously, without the expenditure of energy, work is needed, and therefore A T P must be utilized, to pump it back to the sarcoplasmic reticulum. This active transport is highly efficient, with two calcium ions pumped out for every molecule of A T P broken down in the process. Quantitatively, the total energy needed for activation-relaxation is relatively small, involving no more than about one fifth of the total A T P required in a normal working contraction. However, this fraction is dependent on the total amount of work being done. If a muscle is very lightly loaded, the work needed to move calcium may take a major share of the muscle's total usage of A T P. If a muscle is heavily loaded – a condition that generally applies to cardiac muscle, which must work with a high degree of efficiency – the energy requirements of the contractile process take by far the major portion of the total energy.

The energy requirements of active transport mechanisms, those required for moving not only calcium but also sodium, potassium, and other ions that cross the sarcolemma, are, then, relatively minor. Nevertheless, it is important to keep in mind that the contractile processes do not account for the total energy requirements of the heart. Some energy is used in the activation process, some in transport mechanisms, and some in the general metabolism of the muscle, the process of resynthesizing the contractile proteins themselves. In this regard, it should be noted that the turnover time for contractile proteins is about 20 to 30 days, so obviously some work must be contributed to synthetic processes for replacement of these proteins. However, this remains considerably less than the energy requirements of continuous cardiac contraction.

In this discussion of active transport, mention has been made of the movement of both potassium and sodium ions. Both are involved specifically in activation of heart muscle, and they also take part in the electrical processes by which the action potential is moved from the nerves along the surface of the cell, the sarcolemma, and down inside the cell to the sarcoplasm and sarcomere via the membranes of the transverse T-system. In this process, the calcium is released from the sarcoplasmic reticulum and may be replaced by potassium. The importance of potassium is suggested by experiments in isolated systems that indicate myosin and actin are incapable of normal function in the absence of the potassium. Probably the potassium is needed as a general univalent ion to maintain the ionic strength within the cell. The role of potassium, of course, must be considered in relationship to sodium. As far as is known, every mammalian cell contains a sodium pump. In general, a cell that can be activated contains high internal concentrations of potassium; when the cell is stimulated or activated, a small amount of sodium enters the cell and a commensurate amount of potassium is released from the cell. This causes the depolarization of the electrical potential that can be measured along the surface of the cell in the form of electrocardiographic potentials. As this depolarization propagates, passing along the Purkinje fibers, different parts of the heart are activated to contract sequentially.

With the entry into the cell of small quantities of ionic sodium, there is a loss of some potassium to the extracellular environment. The movement of the sodium into the cell and of the potassium in either direction does not require energy. This can be explained on the basis of both concentration gradients and the electrical milieu. The inside of the cell has large quantities of positively charged K but is electrically negative. The outside of the cell is electrically positive, with small quantities of K. Effectively, the K in the cell is at electrochemical equilibrium with its environment and the K ions can move in and out without utilizing energy. Similarly, the sodium can move into the cell, with its electronegative status and low sodium concentration, without using energy. But to be removed from the cell into an electrically positive, high-sodium-concentration external milieu, an active mechanism is required – the so-called sodium pump – and this involves the contribution of energy by A T P. The precise mechanism by which the sodium pump in the cardiac muscle cell works has not been determined, and several theories have been

advanced to explain the action. It has been possible to isolate enzymes, A T Pases, from the cell membranes, and interestingly these enzymes are optimally activated by the concentration of sodium found inside the cell and the concentration of potassium found outside the cell. Moreover, these enzymes are directional or vector enzymes that move ions from one side of the cell membrane to the other with great efficiency. In fact, the energy utilization involving these enzymes can approach 100% of thermodynamic efficiency, which makes for a very remarkable transduction of energy from A T P into the osmotic separation of Na and K ions.

In discussing the sodium pump, it is interesting in the context of a discussion of cardiac failure to note that cardiac glycosides, such as digitalis, work in part at least by inhibition of this mechanism (see Chapter 13, "The Mechanism of Action of Digitalis," by Langer).

Similar lack of precision characterizes our knowledge of the role played by such neurohumoral agents as norepinephrine in the regulation of cardiac contraction. In general, it is known that for skeletal muscle, a single impulse suffices for complete activation of the muscle, but in cardiac muscle this is not true. The amount, extent, and velocity of the contraction can be affected by neurohumoral agents. Norepinephrine, for example, can increase the amplitude of cardiac contraction and thereby the total force that the heart can develop. This may be accomplished through increased liberation of calcium, but there could be an additional direct effect of the norepinephrine on the contractile mechanism, an effect that may result from stimulating the A T Pase of heavy meromyosin to act at higher speed. It has been discovered recently that there is a close correlation between the maximum rate at which an unloaded skeletal muscle can contract and the amount of A T Pase activity that can be detected in the cell in association with the actomyosin system. One may assume therefore that as the velocity of contraction of the heart increases so does the rate of A T P turnover and that this sequence is the result of norepinephrine activity.

Now that some of the major components of the biochemical systems involved in myocardial function have been discussed, it is possible to put some of these pieces together in an effort to present a unified picture of our knowledge and of the still significant gaps in that knowledge.

Starting from a resting cardiac muscle, the initial event is the pacemaking action potential transmitted

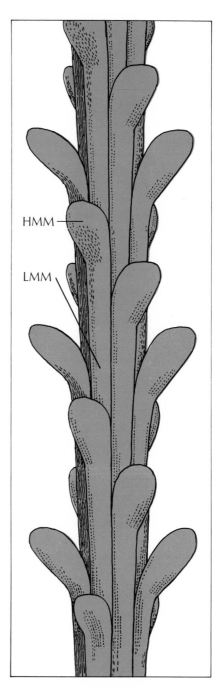

HMM

LMM

The arrangement of myosin molecules in the thick filament is schematized. Each molecule is shown with its long shaft of light meromyosin and a head of enzymatically active heavy meromyosin.

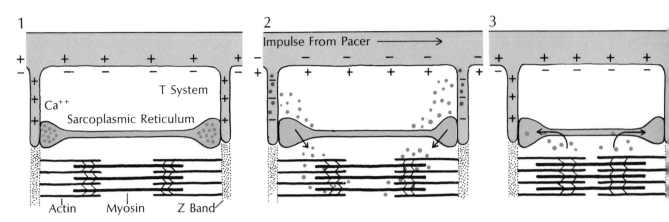

1   2   3

Impulse From Pacer ⟶

T System
Ca⁺⁺
Sarcoplasmic Reticulum

Actin   Myosin   Z Band

The role of calcium in initiating sarcomere contraction is well established. Subsequent to an impulse from the pacemaker, there is an influx of sodium and an efflux of potassium from the cell.

The resultant depolarization (— to +) triggers the release of calcium within the cell and the entry of extracellular calcium into the sarcoplasm. When the calcium concentration in the

along the surface of the sarcolemma, and thence by electrical depolarization deep into the muscle cells. This potential triggers the release of calcium from the sarcoplasmic reticulum. The calcium ions are diffused to the region of the sarcomeres. The ATPase in the head of the myosin filament is activated and in the presence of calcium, magnesium, actin, and troponin, ATP is cleaved. The breakdown produces the energy that allows the muscle to shorten by the sliding of the actin filaments over the myosin. This sliding in turn permits the links to re-form, break, re-form again, break again, etc. — up to and past the point at which the overlap between thick and thin filaments is sufficient to involve all of the active sites or crossbridges of the myosin.

Eventually, the calcium that is bound temporarily to the troponin dissociates and diffuses back to the sarcoplasmic reticulum, where it is bound and pumped, by a mechanism requiring ATP, back into the cisternae. Removal of calcium from the contractile machinery results in relaxation. Here, ATP has been broken down to ADP, which can be rapidly regenerated to ATP by reaction with phosphorylcreatine. This regeneration acts to restore the muscle energy immediately. Fur-

ther restoration is accomplished by oxidative phosphorylation involving acetyl coenzyme A derived primarily from fatty acids but also from glycogen.

This whole process is carefully controlled by a feedback mechanism governed essentially by the rate at which the heart is working. If it is working very hard and the heart rate is consequently increased, the metabolic process is speeded up to assure adequate restoration of ATP. This feedback can be accounted for by the role of one of the breakdown products of the reaction, ADP, which is in itself an activator of oxidative phosphorylation. When ADP is presented to the mitochondria, it causes an increase in electron transport and consequently increased oxidation and respiration. The cells use oxygen at an enhanced rate and the synthesis of ATP is speeded. In this way, the ADP is removed from the system and the respiration is able to return to its normal level.

The glycolytic pathways serve as backup systems for the restoration of ATP. These pathways can function in several ways, both aerobically and anaerobically, and their relative importance varies between cardiac and skeletal muscle. One of the aerobic pathways involves the enzyme, myo-

kinase, which turns two molecules of ADP into one molecule of adenosine monophosphate (AMP) and one molecule of ATP. This AMP turns on glycolysis. In addition to this action, calcium and epinephrine are able to activate the phosphorylases, and these enzymes can break down glycogen. Once again, we are dealing with a self-regulating process. The glycogen breakdown causes formation of more ATP, some of which is made from AMP. The effective removal of AMP turns off the phosphorylases and reduces glycolysis so that the muscle returns to a resting state. Of course, in applying the term resting state to cardiac muscle, one must recognize that the heart's activity is continuous. In contrast to the skeletal muscle, which can go from nearly complete rest to a very high rate of activity, the heart muscle goes from relative rest to intense activity, that is, the level required to maintain the body's basal metabolic activity, in response to the changes in the body's requirements for oxygen and nutrients in the blood. If the oxygen available to the heart does not allow restoration of ATP by normal oxidative processes, the processes of anaerobic glycolysis provide some energy.

These restorative processes and the

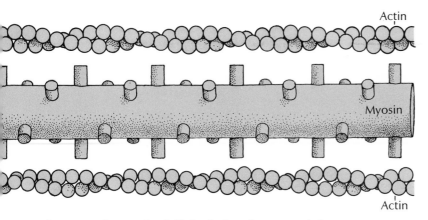

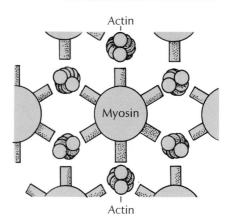

sarcoplasm rises above a threshold level, the calcium may link actin and myosin filaments within the sarcomere, and thus contraction takes place. The active removal of the calcium from *the sarcoplasm results in relaxation. Schematized on this page are longitudinal and cross-sectional views of actin and myosin filaments, with HMM periodically forming crossbridges.*

feedback mechanisms that govern them are all basically short-term mechanisms to cope with constantly changing demands upon the heart. There are other, longer-term compensatory mechanisms, notably those that produce cardiac hypertrophy. The heart, like any other muscle, will grow if used at high rates for prolonged periods. More muscle mass will be laid down; under some conditions the heart muscle can double its mass in only a few days of intense activity. This will increase the total work that can be done but the increase will not be proportional to the increased mass. The amount of force that can be developed per gram of hypertrophied muscle is less than that per gram of original muscle. All evidence is that this loss relates more to morphologic changes than to biochemical derangements. Goldspink and a number of other investigators have shown that when skeletal muscle hypertrophy occurs, there is no increase in the number of fibers but there *is* an increase in the number of fibrils, with some of the fibrils becoming rather large. These enlarged fibrils tend to have less contractile protein per gram of muscle than normal fibrils. The increase is in extra-myofibrillar space. Thus, although the

molecules of actin and myosin are individually as effective as in the nonhypertrophied heart, their concentration is less and they therefore appear less efficient on a per gram basis.

One must be very cautious in interpreting the changes of hypertrophy, particularly in relationship to cardiac failure. At this time, there is really no solid evidence that there are any major differences in the physiologic properties of the contractile proteins in the failing heart. Some investigators have claimed that there is a depression in myofibrillar ATPase activity. However, these findings are very difficult to interpret, largely because the failing heart rapidly becomes damaged, and this damage may very well include autolytic destruction of the contractile proteins. Therefore, when one isolates these proteins and finds them less effective enzymatically, one may really be observing changes that are a consequence of failure, rather than changes that are contributory to failure.

The same critical outlook is appropriate in evaluating findings that the carnitine-dependent system, a system that is necessary for the entry of free fatty acids into the mitochondria, is severely depressed in the experimentally failing heart. Once again,

one can not exclude the possibility that the abnormal conditions created by heart failure and by the ischemia that has induced failure have resulted in the breakdown of a delicately balanced system.

In all cases studied to date, any biochemical changes seem to follow failure rather than to participate in its causation (see Chapter 5, "The Biochemical Basis of Heart Failure," by Pool). Most of the changes seen in the failing heart can be induced in normal hearts subjected, for example, to prolonged anaerobiosis. These changes certainly do not constitute evidence that basic mechanisms such as those that govern respiration and oxidative phosphorylation are any different in the heart just going into failure than in the normal heart. This is not to say that we can exclude changes such as defects in the processes involving release and resorption of calcium as being possibly involved in the pathogenesis of cardiac failure. But thus far our techniques have almost all looked at the biochemical status in heart failure after the fact, and therefore they tell us very little about any biochemical lesions that might precede the clinical manifestations of heart failure.

Calcium Metabolism in the Normal and Failing Heart

CHARLES A. CHIDSEY III

University of Colorado

In the search for a specific biochemical lesion to account for the pathophysiologic changes in heart failure (and a variety of potential defects have been considered) the evidence points increasingly to an abnormality in calcium metabolism as the most likely possibility. That the presence of calcium has an important bearing on myocardial function has of course long been known. Ringer's observation that heart muscle would contract only if calcium was present in the medium was made in 1883; the ability of calcium directly to stimulate the contraction of muscle has been known since the studies of Heilbrunn and coworkers more than 30 years ago. The critical role of calcium in mediating excitation-contraction coupling has since been amply documented; moreover, recent observations indicate that calcium is essential at several points in the sequence of muscle activation and relaxation (see Chapter 2, "Contractile Proteins in the Normal and Failing Myocardium," by Katz). Currently, interest is focused both on delineating further the mechanism of action of calcium as it affects normal myocardial function and on clarifying the relationship between calcium metabolism and the development of cardiac failure.

A principal question in research on heart failure is whether a deficit in available calcium or an alteration in its intracellular distribution, or both, may underlie the observed impairment of myocardial function. Proof of depressed intrinsic myocardial contractility in heart failure came initially through observations of cardiac muscle removed from patients with valvular heart disease undergoing surgery. These studies were carried out at the National Heart Institute in association with the research group led by Braunwald. Left ventricular papillary muscles, obtained from patients undergoing valve replacements, showed an inability to develop increased tension as resting muscle length was increased. Extension of these studies to laboratory animals permitted more definitive observations: Assessment of contractile state either in terms of length/active tension or force/velocity relationships confirmed a decrease in muscle function in cardiac failure.

Then studies were carried out in cats in which right heart failure was induced by means of pulmonary artery constriction. Papillary muscles were examined in terms of the force of isometric contraction at any given muscle length, as well as the extent and velocity of muscle-fiber shortening when various loads were applied. In muscles from failing hearts, active developed tension was below normal at all muscle lengths along the length/tension curve; maximum velocity of shortening and maximum rate of tension development were also reduced. When procedures that ordinarily would augment isometric tension were introduced — for example, post-extrasystolic potentiation by means of paired electrical stimulation or an increase in the frequency of contraction — peak tension and the rate of tension development were increased but still did not reach even basal levels observed in isolated normal muscle. Further studies of the mechanics of myocardial function in intact animals corroborated that in the presence of heart failure the intrinsic contractile state of the myocardium and its individual fibers is significantly depressed. For a time such mechanisms as ventricular dilatation and hypertrophy and increased sympathetic stimulation can maintain circulatory compensation in the presence of reduced intrinsic contractility. Thus, although there is a demonstrable reduction in the intrinsic velocity of shortening of muscle fibers, isometric force development may be decreased only minimally. But as compensatory mechanisms fail, the intrinsic contractile state of each unit of myocardium is further depressed and a marked decrease occurs in maximal isometric force.

It was logical to ask whether the defective myocardial

contractility seen in heart failure might relate to a defect in myocardial energy production. This possibility was essentially ruled out in a series of studies that were initiated in my laboratory and that showed normal coupling of electron transport and oxidative phosphorylation in mitochondria isolated from failing hearts; mitochondrial storage of the high-energy phosphate compounds, adenosine triphosphate (ATP) and creatine phosphate (CP), was also normal. However, an impairment in utilization of stored energy for the mechanical work of muscle still remains a possibility. Studies initiated by Albert and Gordon have clearly shown a deficiency in activity of myofibrillar ATPase, the enzyme of the contractile proteins that controls release of energy from ATP for contraction.

Some investigators have questioned whether the reported decrease in enzyme activity is likely to be of significance. Indeed, unless an enzyme is rate-limiting in a series of reactions, which may not be the case here, even a substantial reduction in its activity may be of little import. However, several findings in reference to myofibrillar ATPase activity suggest the relevance of these findings to heart failure. For example, in studies in rats, Albert observed a gradual reduction with aging in myofibrillar ATPase activity associated with reduced myocardial contractility. Others have found that skeletal muscles intended for "fast" activity, for instance the gastrocnemius, show higher myofibrillar ATPase activity than do "slow" muscles supplying chiefly strength. On this basis, the relationship of depressed myofibrillar ATPase activity to heart failure may warrant further investigation (see Chapter 2 by Katz).

When early workers linked the presence of calcium to the process of muscle contraction, not much was yet known of the contractile proteins and their interactions. Once they were identified and characterized by electron microscopy, their function in excitation-contraction coupling could be delineated better in biochemical terms. As Weber and others showed, a biochemical representation of contraction could be produced with a preparation that included the contractile proteins myosin and actin, ATP as energy source, and magnesium, on

which the reaction was dependent. Contractile activity – shown by hydrolysis of ATP and superprecipitation of the actomyosin complex – would occur, however, only when calcium was present to bind with contractile protein and activate ATPase. Moreover, there was a direct relationship between the calcium concentration of the medium and the extent of ATP hydrolysis and actomyosin precipitation. Variations of this type of experiment were performed by a number of investigators; invariably, calcium proved to be the trigger initiating muscle contraction.

However, subsequent work with more-highly purified myosin and actin yielded puzzling results: Contractile activity could be produced by addition of ATP and magnesium alone. Was calcium then dispensable? Matters were clarified when it was realized that the purification process had removed the regulatory proteins tropomyosin and troponin, which had been unknown at the time of the original experiments. As Ebashi and colleagues demonstrated, in preparations containing all four proteins plus ATP and magnesium, contractile activity would occur only in the presence of calcium. However, interaction between myosin and actin to activate contraction was not directly stimulated by calcium. Rather, by binding with troponin, calcium effectively altered its inhibition of the interaction between actin and myosin. Thus, in relation to the contractile proteins, calcium serves as a de-repressor, preventing troponin from impeding the interaction between actin and myosin that would otherwise occur (see Chapter 2 by Katz).

Obviously, calcium's role must be considered also in relation to the electrophysiologic events coupling muscle excitation to contraction, beginning with the arrival of the impulse and the depolarization of the sarcolemmal membrane surrounding the muscle cell. When Heilbrunn first linked calcium to excitation-contraction coupling, he suggested that depolarization somehow resulted in entry of calcium at the cell surface in sufficient quantity to initiate a response. However, the speed of muscle contraction following depolarization made this unlikely; it was soon real-

ized that no chemical agent could diffuse into the interior of the muscle fiber rapidly enough to account for its activation. Relating the electrophysiologic events to the anatomic components of the contractile apparatus as defined by electron microscopy established the sequence of events as it is understood today. Following spread of the action potential across the sarcolemma, the signal is transmitted to the interior of the cell via the invaginations of the sarcolemma, comprising the transverse tubular system, and thence to the longitudinal tubular membrane system, comprising the sarcoplasmic reticulum. Calcium sequestered in the sarcoplasmic reticulum is released in the immediate vicinity of the myofilaments composed of the contractile and regulatory proteins. Once there, it binds with troponin and initiates muscle contraction; with recapture of calcium by the sarcoplasmic reticulum, the muscle relaxes. Observations with the electron microscope made evident how the process is facilitated by the close proximity of the sarcoplasmic reticulum to the myofibrils. In addition, biochemical studies documented the capacity of muscle fragments derived from sarcoplasmic reticulum for active calcium uptake.

In actuality, well before sarcoplasmic reticulum per se was characterized, fractionation of muscle cells had yielded a microsomal fraction – called grana – that proved remarkably potent as a calcium pump, capable of accumulating calcium from surrounding medium against high electrochemical gradients. When experiments similar to those cited earlier were performed, preparations containing contractile proteins, ATP, magnesium, and calcium ceased to show contractile activity as soon as this microsomal fraction was added. Later, when sarcoplasmic reticulum was identified as a major constituent of muscle microsomal fractions, there seemed little doubt of its similarity to grana.

It should be stressed that the findings in relation to calcium and the contractile process described thus far derived chiefly from studies of skeletal muscle. Although it was not explicitly stated, it was generally assumed that the model for excitation-contraction coupling arrived at for skeletal muscle could be applied with relatively minor modification to heart muscle.

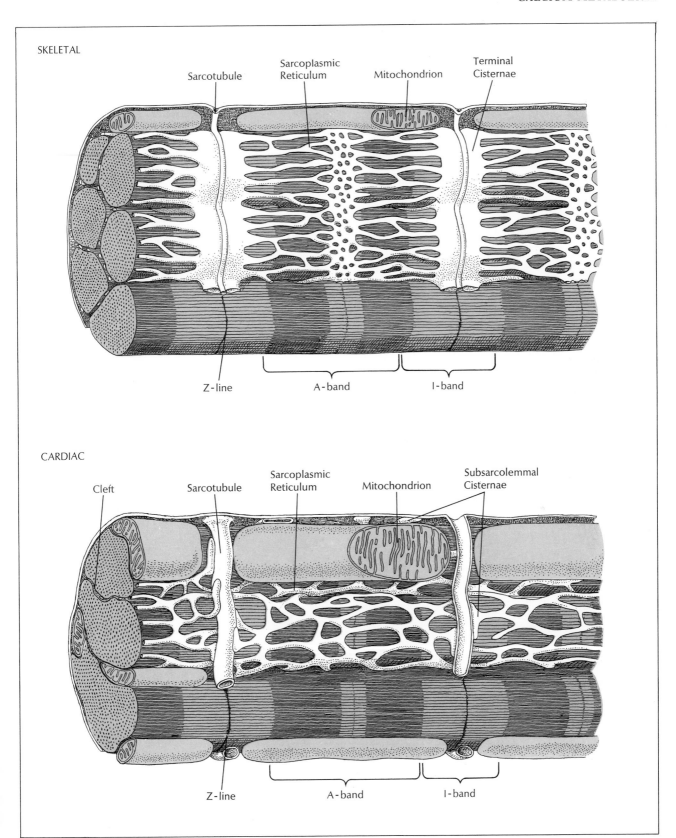

SKELETAL

Sarcotubule   Sarcoplasmic Reticulum   Mitochondrion   Terminal Cisternae

Z-line   A-band   I-band

CARDIAC

Cleft   Sarcotubule   Sarcoplasmic Reticulum   Mitochondrion   Subsarcolemmal Cisternae

Z-line   A-band   I-band

Studies at the ultrastructural level have established significant differences between skeletal and cardiac muscle in organization and structure of subcellular organelles, as illustrated above. In skeletal muscle (top) discrete myofibrils of uniform size are each enclosed by sarcoplasmic reticulum; a slender sarcotubule is in continuity with the cell membrane and associated terminal cisternae are located at the Z-line bounding each sarcomere. In cardiac muscle (lower drawing), the sarcoplasmic reticulum is simpler in pattern and the skeletal muscle abundance of reticulum in the region where contractile proteins interact (A-band) is absent. Sarcotubules are wider and there are subsarcolemmal cisternae rather than the skeletal muscle counterpart, the terminal cisternae. Cardiac muscle is richer in mitochondria, reflecting heart's dependence on oxidative metabolism.

While in its essentials the contraction-relaxation process in the two muscle types is the same, critical differences are now recognized. These differences may have special meaning in terms of our thesis that a deficit or maldistribution in intracellular calcium may be of importance in development of heart failure.

Before comparisons were made with the electron microscope, electrophysiologic studies pointed up characteristic distinctions: for one thing cardiac muscle cannot be tetanized as can skeletal muscle. Unlike skeletal muscle, cardiac muscle has significant resting tension. Also, onset of contraction following membrane excitation is significantly slower in cardiac muscle, as is the onset of relaxation.

Observations at the ultrastructural level shed more light on these findings. In representative studies, such as those by Fawcett and coworkers on cat myocardium, ventricular muscle has been analyzed with respect to organization of contractile apparatus as well as structure and location of subcellular organelles. Not unexpectedly, a cardinal feature of heart muscle is a greater representation of mitochondria, reflecting dependence of the heart on aerobic metabolism. Mitochondria in cardiac muscle are both larger and more numerous than in skeletal muscle; in contrast, the sarcomeres containing the contractile apparatus comprise a smaller proportion of the myocardial cell. In comparison with skeletal muscle cells, the sarcoplasmic reticulum is sparsely distributed and underdeveloped.

When one considers the relationship of the sarcolemma to the internal membrane system in skeletal muscle, the importance of these differences becomes more apparent. In skeletal muscle the longitudinal tubules of the sarcoplasmic reticulum are confluent with transverse elements of larger caliber, the terminal cisternae. The latter occur as pairs, one pair on either side of the so-called Z-line bounding each sarcomere; between each pair of terminal cisternae is a slender sarcotubule in continuity with the sarcolemma. The combination of the sarcotubule of the sarcolemma and the two associated terminal cisternae of the sarcoplasmic reticulum comprise what is called the triad of skeletal muscle. The sarcotubules provide for spread of electrical activity from the surface of the muscle fiber into the interior; the terminal cisternae and contiguous sarcotubules assure release and recapture of calcium in the contraction-relaxation cycle.

By contrast, in cardiac muscle the ultrastructural organization is quite different. Sarcotubules are much wider in diameter; the pairs of transverse cisternae are absent. Absent too is the region of abundant lateral anastomosis of sarcotubules in the middle of the A-band of the sarcomere, where myosin and actin filaments interact. Instead, the sarcoplasmic reticulum of cardiac muscle is a simpler network of tubules of more uniform size. Myofibrils are not individually enclosed by the sarcoplasmic reticulum. Rather, the sarcoplasmic reticulum is more diffusely and sparsely spread over the myofilament mass. A further feature of cardiac muscle is the presence of local subsarcolemmal cisternae. Physiologically these may be the counterpart of the terminal cisternae of skeletal muscle, although more limited in size and content.

The suggestion from these ultrastructural observations is that delivery of calcium to the contractile apparatus from intracellular binding sites may not be as efficient in cardiac as in skeletal muscle; in this connection the earlier finding of slower activation and relaxation of cardiac muscle takes on fresh meaning. It is known, of course, that neither cardiac nor skeletal muscle is completely dependent on intracellular calcium stores. With depolarization and membrane excitation, calcium as well as sodium rapidly enters the muscle cell; presumably in both types of muscle this calcium becomes available for use by the contractile apparatus. This calcium may not be utilized directly for activation, but may be bound temporarily to the sarcoplasmic reticulum where it will be released to activate a subsequent contraction. In skeletal muscle, however, the calcium entering from outside the cell may be considered relatively superfluous since there is ample calcium within, awaiting release by the sarcoplasmic reticulum. Thus, the difference here between cardiac and skeletal muscle would appear to be the size of the calcium pool stored in the sarcoplasmic reticulum. Because this calcium pool is smaller in cardiac muscle, extracellular calcium is apparently indispensable, even under normal conditions. In support of this point, skeletal muscle will contract in the absence of calcium in an external medium for a considerable period, whereas, as already noted, cardiac muscle contraction ceases almost im-

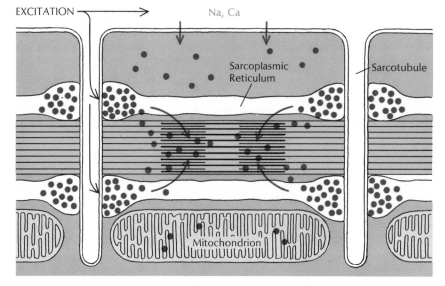

EXCITATION   Na, Ca

Sarcoplasmic Reticulum   Sarcotubule

Mitochondrion

Excitation of cardiac or skeletal muscle cell prompts rapid inflow of both calcium and sodium across the cell membrane and release of calcium sequestered in intracellular binding sites, chiefly in the sarcoplasmic reticulum, for delivery to the contractile apparatus. The simpler pattern of sarcoplasmic reticulum and its relative paucity in cardiac muscle suggest that the delivery of calcium for muscle activation may be less efficient in the heart than is true of the same process in skeletal muscle.

mediately when extracellular calcium is withdrawn.

It seems evident, therefore, that the delivery of calcium to the contractile proteins from the intracellular sites is limited in capacity and dependent on extracellular calcium. If the intracellular store is only just sufficient – as comparisons with skeletal muscle suggest – then a reduction in the release of calcium from the sarcoplasmic reticulum and its extensions might seriously limit contractile function.

In studies over the past few years we have been exploring the possibility that an abnormality of this nature might explain the muscle dysfunction associated with heart failure. As a beginning, however, more information was needed about another group of organelles that may also play a role in intracellular calcium regulation and hence cardiac contractility, the mitochondria. Needless to say, mitochondria have been studied chiefly for their role in energy production; in converting energy from oxidation of metabolites to high-energy phosphates, they provide the A T P required for the contractile process (see Chapter 3, "Biochemical Processes in Cardiac Function," by Davies and Chapter 5, "The Biochemical Basis of Heart Failure," by Pool). In addition, mitochondria can concentrate large amounts of calcium within their structures when incubated in vitro in the presence of A T P. Given the relative abundance of mitochondria in cardiac muscle – and the paucity of sarcoplasmic reticulum – it seemed to us worth examining the potential importance of both subcellular organelles in the intact myocardium in relation to intracellular calcium storage.

In these experiments, in which rabbit hearts were perfused with a balanced salt solution, the effect of varying the concentration of calcium in the perfusate was studied, as shown in the figure at right. Calcium concentrations varied from values below the usual physiologic levels to values considerably above these levels. The purpose was to magnify the response in order to illuminate perhaps more subtle effects occurring under normal conditions. Mitochondrial and microsomal fractions were derived from the hearts by a rapid isolation and fractionation procedure; calcium uptake was measured in rela-

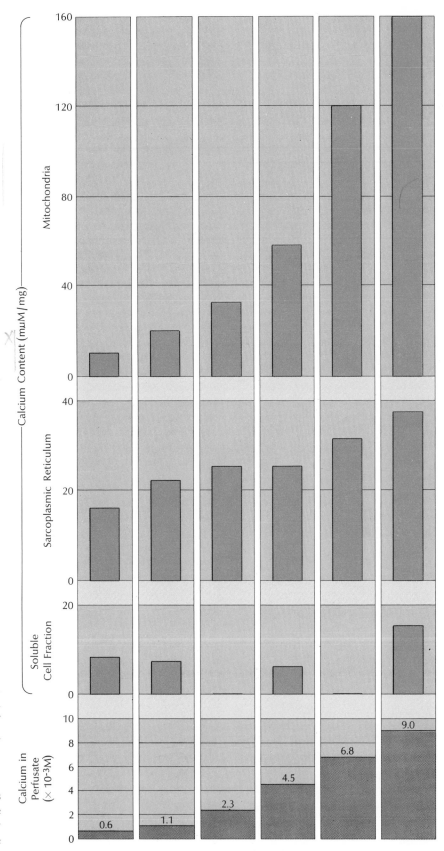

Following perfusion of isolated rabbit hearts with solutions containing calcium in varying concentrations, mitochondrial calcium content is increased in direct relation to the extracellular calcium concentration of the perfusate, as can be seen in graph. This is in contrast to uptake by the sarcoplasmic reticulum and by the soluble cell fraction. Such findings support the possibility that the mitochondria participate in intracellular calcium regulation, buffering the myoplasm against abnormal rises in calcium concentration.

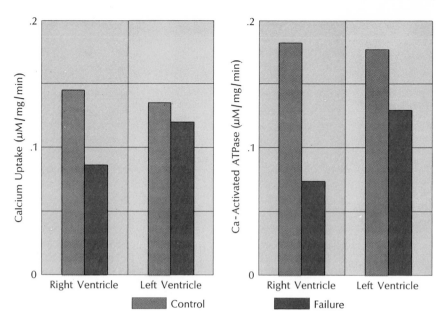

In microsomes prepared from failing right ventricles of calves with induced heart failure, both calcium uptake and calcium-activated ATPase activity were significantly reduced from normal values. Calcium-activated ATPase activity was measured by the rate of inorganic phosphate liberated in an aliquot of protein-free filtrate. Values for calcium uptake and ATPase activity of the left ventricles were also somewhat lower, but not significantly so, than in left ventricles of control animals. Since both calcium uptake and calcium-activated ATPase activity were reduced, it was concluded that the change in uptake was not due to uncoupling of the calcium pump.

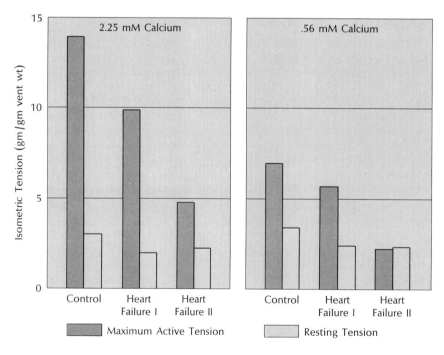

In studies of rabbits with heart failure, evidence of depressed myocardial contractility was obtained in isolated hearts perfused with calcium at either normal or low concentrations. Maximum active tension, determined with a force transducer, was markedly reduced relative to ventricular weight in the failing heart; greater depression was seen in animals with more advanced heart failure (II). In control preparations, maximum active tension was clearly influenced by the calcium concentration of the perfusate; in contrast, resting tension was not significantly affected.

tion to each change in perfusate calcium.

Total intracellular calcium showed only a modest increase until the perfusate calcium was increased beyond 4.5 mM. In contrast, the relative change in mitochondrial calcium over the range of extracellular calcium concentrations used was far greater. As calcium in the perfusate was increased from 0.56 to 9.0 mM, mitochondrial calcium increased progressively with each increment, rising from 10.7 to 163.6 mμM/mg mitochondrial protein. On the other hand, the sarcoplasmic reticulum proved to have a relatively limited capacity to increase its calcium content. Uptake was altered only at the highest calcium concentrations in the perfusate; changing the calcium concentration from 0.56 to 9.0 mM increased uptake from 16.6 to only 37.7 mμM/mg microsomal protein.

These observations cast a somewhat different light upon intracellular regulation of calcium flux by the sarcoplasmic reticulum. Although the sarcoplasmic reticulum may be responsible for rapid changes in the supply of free calcium for the contraction-relaxation cycle, it apparently is unable to take up an excess that may accumulate in the myoplasm as the result of increased entry. Rather, this role may be played by the mitochondria; perhaps in addition to their other functions, the mitochondria act to buffer the myoplasm against abnormal increases in calcium concentration.

For the mitochondria to play a part in calcium exchange they must of course have an effective release mechanism, although so far there are no data to suggest its nature. Without a release mechanism of some kind one cannot account for the lower calcium content of mitochondrial fractions that we found when extracellular calcium concentration was reduced. Even with an effective release mechanism, however, it seems doubtful that the rate of release from the mitochondria could be rapid enough to allow them a primary role in normal excitation-contraction coupling.

Considering the acknowledged importance of calcium in the functioning of the myocardial cell, relatively little is known about the process of calcium transport. Uptake of calcium by the sarcoplasmic reticulum is an energy-dependent process involving A T P, but the mechanism of calcium release from the sarcoplasmic reticulum is less clear-cut. Movement of calcium across the cell membrane is also not well understood. Entry of calcium occurs, probably by passive diffusion, at the onset of contraction when the sarcolemmal membrane is depolarized (see Chapter 13, "The Mechanism of Action of Digitalis," by Langer). Removal of calcium appears to be a more complex process. Normally, with muscle at rest, intracellular calcium concentration is in the range of 10^{-7}, while in extracellular fluid it is 10^{-3}; this a greater difference than that for any other cation across biologic membranes. Given the large gradient between intracellular and extracellular fluid calcium concentration, outflow across the sarcolemmal membrane may well be dependent on a calcium pump; attempts to demonstrate an active, energy-requiring process have been unsuccessful. It is of interest that red cells have been shown to contain a calcium-stimulated enzyme system causing A T P hydrolysis that could be appropriate for the

purpose; thus far its involvement has not been demonstrated in muscle, either skeletal or cardiac.

In our view it is not possible from the available evidence to estimate exactly how much of the calcium utilized for excitation-contraction derives from intracellular vs extracellular sites. It is probable that the major share of calcium for excitation-contraction coupling is provided by the sarcoplasmic reticulum and its extensions; on this basis calcium metabolism in heart muscle has been studied mostly in terms of uptake and release by the sarcoplasmic reticulum. Initial experiments with fragments of sarcoplasmic reticulum from skeletal muscle, already referred to, demonstrated active uptake of calcium from the surrounding medium; calcium uptake and muscle relaxation could be closely correlated using in vitro contraction systems. Indeed, on this basis sarcoplasmic reticulum came to be known as the "relaxing factor." When cardiac muscle came under study, it was uncertain that the same term could be applied. Initially, investigators had less success in isolating cardiac

muscle sarcoplasmic reticulum capable of active calcium uptake. With further work, however, active uptake was demonstrated in sarcoplasmic reticular preparations. The uptake mechanism was dependent on A T P, which was hydrolyzed by a calcium-activated A T Pase in the sarcoplasmic reticular preparations. From this point, several investigators, using a variety of experimental preparations, sought to determine how calcium uptake might be affected in heart failure.

A suitable animal was needed to test the hypothesis that an abnormality of sarcoplasmic reticulum might be present in chronic heart failure. Fortunately, local circumstances suggested a logical choice. In Colorado, cows grazing at high altitudes are naturally vulnerable to a condition known as brisket disease — a type of congestive failure in which edema is confined chiefly to the brisket, or breast region, rather than the lower limbs, as in human patients. Under conditions of low-oxygen tension prevailing at high altitudes the arteries in the pulmonary vascular bed of these animals tend to constrict and impede blood flow to the

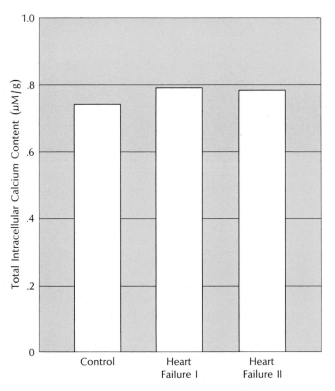

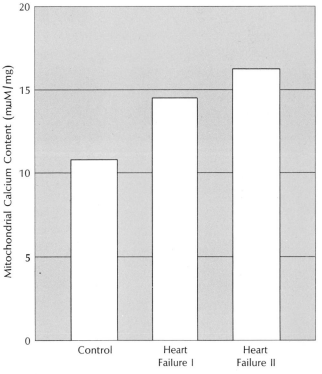

In the failing rabbit heart, perfusion with calcium-containing solutions brought little change in total intracellular calcium regardless of the severity of heart failure; however, mitochondrial calcium content was significantly increased in the failing heart, more so in the advanced heart failure group (II). In other determinations, made immediately after removal of the hearts, total intracellular calcium was unchanged whereas mitochondrial calcium was again increased, suggesting that augmented affinity of binding in mitochondria, relative to the sarcoplasmic reticulum, could reduce the calcium available for contraction.

lungs, resulting in an inordinate increase in pulmonary artery pressure. With progressive pulmonary hypertension there is progressive narrowing of blood vessels. In actuality, full-blown brisket disease is usually limited to animals grazing at very high altitudes (10,000 feet or higher). In my laboratory, in studies carried on in collaboration with Joseph Suko and John Vogel, its equivalent could be readily produced in calves at the altitude of Denver (5,200 feet) by ligating the right pulmonary artery in newborn calves. In other animals, including man, this would have had little effect on pulmonary artery pressure, but the calves responded with progressive pulmonary hypertension and right ventricular hypertrophy. Within six to eight weeks all were in heart failure, shown clinically by persistent distention of the external jugular veins, edema of the brisket area, ascites, and hydrothorax. Hemodynamic measurements performed just prior to sacrifice documented the presence of advanced heart failure. At this point the animals were sacrificed, the hearts removed, and mitochondria and sarcoplasmic reticular preparations were made. The sarcoplasmic reticular preparations were incubated in vitro with radioactive calcium and ATP and the rate of calcium uptake and associated ATP hydrolysis by the sarcoplasmic reticular ATPase was measured. Sodium oxalate was used in these studies in order to trap the radioactive calcium that had been transported into the vesicular structure of the sarcoplasmic reticulum by precipitation as the relatively insoluble calcium oxalate. Thus, we measured calcium uptake by these vesicles in contrast to calcium binding, which is of a lower order of magnitude and is measured by techniques to be discussed later.

In control sarcoplasmic reticular preparations, calcium uptake was seen to increase rapidly at a linear rate until essentially all of the calcium in the incubation medium had been removed. Calcium-activated ATPase activity followed a similar pattern. Both calcium uptake and calcium-activated ATPase activity were reduced significantly to approximately 50% of the control value in sarcoplasmic reticular preparations from failing right ventricles of these animals. Thus,

again, there was no evidence that reduced uptake was due to uncoupling of the calcium pump.

What is of most interest is that abnormal calcium uptake was consistently demonstrated only in sarcoplasmic reticular preparations of the failing *right* ventricle. The sarcoplasmic reticulum prepared from the nonfailing left ventricles of these same animals had normal function in regard to calcium uptake and ATPase activity.

Mitochondria incubated under the same conditions proved unable to take up calcium at rates similar to the sarcoplasmic reticulum; uptake was nonlinear and by 10 minutes had not reached a maximum as it had in the sarcoplasmic reticulum. Therefore, it seemed unlikely that the mitochondria, which are known to contaminate in part the sarcoplasmic reticular preparations, were contributing significantly to calcium uptake in the sarcoplasmic reticulum. Furthermore, inhibitors of mitochondrial function, such as sodium azide, had little effect when added to either the control or failure sarcoplasmic reticular preparations, although they totally blocked calcium uptake by the mitochondria. Since these were in vitro studies, it could not be concluded with certainty that the same reduced function of the sarcoplasmic reticulum would be present necessarily in the intact myocardial cell of the failing heart. Nonetheless, it is tempting to consider the implications if this were the case. Since uptake of calcium by the sarcoplasmic reticulum initiates relaxation of cardiac muscle, logically the relaxation process might be most affected. Inadequate reduction of intracellular calcium could result in delayed or incomplete relaxation that would interfere importantly with the mechanical performance of the heart. On the other hand, it has been suggested that muscle relaxation cannot be directly related to calcium uptake as measured by the method of calcium uptake described (with oxalate), since relaxation occurs so much more rapidly than calcium uptake. Obviously one can draw only relative conclusions from studies such as this; nonetheless, the findings have provided insight into sarcoplasmic reticular function on which to base further work. If, as has been suggested, calcium uptake by the

sarcoplasmic reticulum occurs in two phases – initial rapid binding by the sarcoplasmic reticular membrane followed by slower movement into the vesicle – then this has to be taken into account. Relaxation of cardiac muscle has been linked with this rapid-binding phase but at the present time one cannot be certain of the relationship. More information should be forthcoming with further use of a relatively new technique for measuring rapid calcium binding by the vesicular membrane. The method (developed by Ebashi and coworkers) utilizes a dye, murexide – which binds calcium in solution at pH 7.0 – and dual-beam spectrophotometry for measurement. The rate of calcium accumulation by the sarcoplasmic reticulum is indicated by changes in light transmission and a shift in the absorption maximum.

In studies using this technique, Harigaya and Schwartz studied the kinetics of calcium binding by sarcoplasmic reticulum obtained from rabbit cardiac and skeletal muscle.

When preparations obtained from failing human heart muscle were analyzed, the calcium-binding pattern differed from that in normal heart muscle – characteristically the rate of calcium uptake by the sarcoplasmic reticulum was slowed and release of accumulated calcium was delayed. However, as the investigators noted, rabbit and human heart muscle might not be quite comparable, and the control data were from rabbits and the failure data were from man.

As investigation by our group proceeded, we approached the relationship of myocardial calcium metabolism and heart failure another way, in studies carried out with Dr. Yoshihisa Ito and Dr. Suko. The experimental preparation differed from that in our earlier study in that chronic heart failure was developed in rabbits in which aortic insufficiency had been induced by passing a catheter retrograde across the aortic valve into the left ventricular cavity and perforating the valve cusps thereby.

Within six weeks all animals had developed evidence of heart failure. Cardiac hypertrophy, pulmonary congestion, and edema were found when the animals were sacrificed. The hearts were removed immediately at the time of sacrifice for in vitro per-

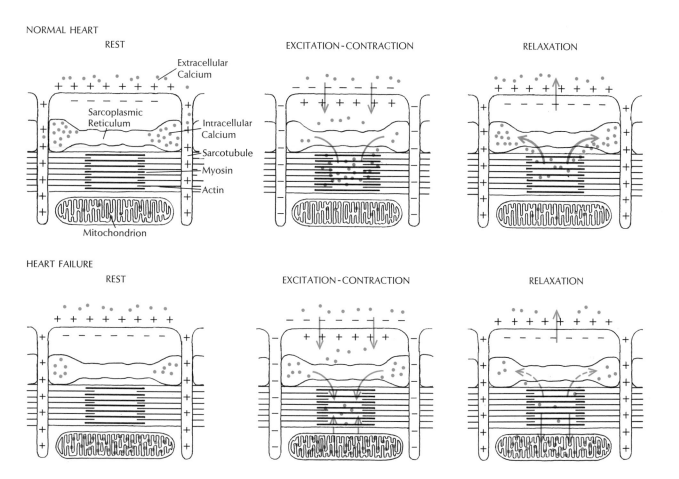

NORMAL HEART

REST • EXCITATION-CONTRACTION • RELAXATION

HEART FAILURE

REST • EXCITATION-CONTRACTION • RELAXATION

In the normal heart at rest, extracellular calcium is concentrated in the region of the sarcolemmal membrane and its invaginations (sarcotubular system); intracellular calcium sequestered chiefly in the sarcoplasmic reticulum is awaiting delivery to the contractile apparatus. With excitation of the cell membrane and depolarization, there is rapid entry of extracellular calcium; spread of electrical activity via the sarcotubules causes release of intracellular calcium and activation of contraction. For muscle to relax, intracellular calcium must be recaptured by the sarcoplasmic reticulum; efflux of calcium across the cell membrane probably also occurs. In contrast, according to the sequence of events postu-

lated to occur in heart failure, ineffective calcium pumping by the sarcoplasmic reticulum may alter the normal relaxation process, making the mitochondria the dominant calcium uptake mechanism and a source of activator calcium for contraction. If so, in resting muscle relatively little calcium would be available for release from the sarcoplasmic reticulum to activate contraction. While the mitochondria may contain an ample amount, it is likely to be released slowly; thus, with depolarization a diminished amount of calcium might be supplied to the contractile proteins. Whether the depressed myocardial contractility characteristic of heart failure develops on this basis remains to be determined.

fusion studies. The appearance of the lung was used to judge the severity of heart failure: cases with edema demonstrable only on compression of the cut lung surface were rated as grade I, those with spontaneous exudation of fluid on cutting the lung and hemorrhagic areas throughout were rated as grade II. In preparing the hearts for perfusion, the aortic insufficiency was overcome by exerting tension on a cone-shaped silicone stopper positioned by catheter against the base of the heart.

During perfusion the contractile state of each heart was measured by connecting it to a Statham force trans-ducer placed at the apex of the left ventricle, the position of which was adjusted to the position of the transducer until maximum isometric tension was achieved. As we were to learn, depression of muscle function and severity of heart failure are likely to be closely correlated. Perfusion was with a buffered salt solution as used earlier. Calcium concentration in the perfusate was purposely varied between two different levels during these experiments – at a "normal" (2.25 mM) or low (0.56 mM) concentration, each used for a 30-minute period (see graph on page 42). If a derangement in calcium metabolism were present, perhaps it would become more apparent under the latter conditions.

As things worked out, with either normal or low calcium concentration in the perfusate, myocardial contractility was markedly impaired: In grade II cases, maximum active tension was reduced to about 35% of control values; tension was reduced both as an absolute value and relative to ventricular weight. In grade I cases, active tension relative to ventricular weight was reduced during both normal or low calcium perfusion but total active tension was not. When these findings were related to the severity

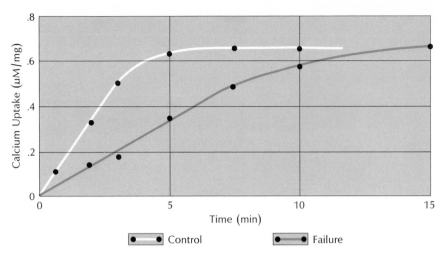

Uptake of calcium by sarcoplasmic reticular preparations can be studied in vitro. As shown in graph, the uptake of calcium from surrounding medium is slowed markedly in preparations derived from failing hearts incubated at 25° C in the presence of calcium, ATP, magnesium, potassium, and oxalate.

of heart failure, greater depression of myocardial contractility was shown in animals with more advanced failure.

A key aspect of the study was to determine myocardial calcium concentration. If calcium metabolism is impaired in heart failure, as the evidence suggested, perhaps this would be reflected in a diminished cellular content of calcium or in altered intracellular distribution. When measurements were made, total intracellular calcium proved to be about the same in failing and control hearts after perfusion. However, *mitochondrial* calcium was markedly increased (from a mean of 10.9 mμM/mg mitochondrial protein in control preparations to 14.6 in cases of grade I severity and 16.3 in grade II cases).

The findings in reference to mitochondrial calcium took on more significance when related to those in muscle tissue obtained promptly after death from rabbits with and without heart failure. Again, total myocardial calcium was virtually unchanged in failing hearts, whereas mitochondrial calcium was increased. Thus, when the artificial conditions of perfusion and an in vitro system were eliminated, heart failure was still associated with a significant alteration in intracellular calcium distribution.

What accounted for the increment in mitochondrial calcium? Two possibilities suggested themselves: an increased affinity for calcium in mitochondria of the failing myocardial cell, or a decreased affinity for calcium in other calcium storage sites. Of course we were reminded of the depressed calcium uptake of sarcoplasmic reticu-

lum obtained from failing hearts. From our earlier experiments in rabbits we knew, too, that mitochondria in the intact heart are capable of large increases in calcium uptake when extracellular calcium concentration is increased. Taking these findings together, was it possible that the mitochondrial increase was the consequence of an excess of available calcium, resulting from ineffective calcium pumping by the sarcoplasmic reticulum? Thus far one can only tentatively suggest that this might be the case, and what the effects might be if it were. Conceivably, if the sarcoplasmic reticulum can no longer maintain myoplasmic calcium concentration low enough for muscle relaxation, the mitochondria might become the dominant uptake mechanism and a source of activator calcium for muscle contraction. However, given the slow rate of calcium uptake by the mitochondria, it seems likely that the rate of release would be slow as well. As a result, following depolarization, a diminished quantity of calcium might be delivered for muscle activation. Might this help to explain the depressed myocardial contractility characteristic of heart failure? As of now we do not know.

In more recent studies, calcium uptake by sarcoplasmic reticulum from these rabbits with experimentally induced heart failure was studied in more detail. This time, again, while the *amount* of calcium taken up was the same in failing and normal hearts, the *rate* of uptake in the failing heart was definitely slower. Reviewing the evidence, then, heart failure does seem to be associated with an abnormality of calcium pumping by the sarcoplasmic reticulum. In addition, we were able to show that addition of cardiac glycoside, either in vivo or in vitro, did not reverse the depressed function of the sarcoplasmic reticulum.

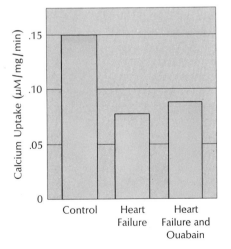

In sarcoplasmic reticular fractions prepared from failing hearts, addition of the cardiac glycoside ouabain to the reaction mixture did not significantly raise calcium uptake. Glycoside concentrations ranging from 10⁻⁷ to 10⁻⁴M were utilized; incubation was at 25°C.

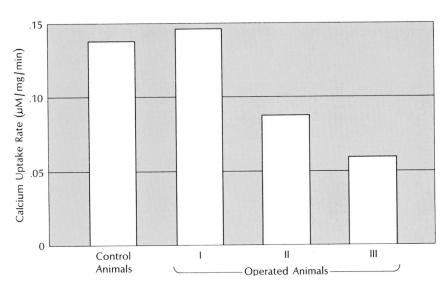

A critical question of course is whether the abnormality occurs in advance of heart failure or as a consequence. We attempted to approach it by closely following the changes in calcium metabolism as heart failure progresses. Rabbits in which aortic insufficiency was induced were sacrificed after varying intervals. In animals sacrificed at two weeks, sarcoplasmic reticulum showed normal calcium pumping; at four weeks — before there were objective signs of heart failure — calcium uptake was already significantly reduced. As expected, by six weeks, when all animals were in failure, there was a marked impairment in calcium pumping. Thus it seems clear that an alteration in calcium metabolism may appear very early in the course of heart failure, but proof is not yet in hand that it definitely precedes it.

These relationships may be better understood as the nature of the abnormality is more completely delineated. Obviously, further biochemical studies are required to define the alteration in sarcoplasmic reticulum at the molecular level. In addition, the implications of these alterations of sarcoplasmic reticular function at the level of the mechanics of the intact cell require further definition in the failing heart. Is relaxation delayed or incomplete, leading to increased diastolic compliance and thereby reduced myocardial contractility? What evidence is there that the reduced rate of force development and total developed force of the failing heart are the myocardial cells' reflection of a reduced rate of activator calcium release from the sarcoplasmic reticulum? These and other related questions will provide further challenge to cardiologists willing to probe the problem of heart failure at the molecular level.

As shown in graph at top, progressive alterations in calcium metabolism were seen in rabbits sacrificed 2 to 6 weeks after chronic heart failure was induced by experimental aortic insufficiency. In animals sacrificed at 2 weeks (Group I) the rate of calcium uptake by sarcoplasmic reticulum was within normal limits. At 4 weeks (Group II) — before clear signs of failure were present — calcium pumping was already significantly reduced and the degree of impairment increased as failure progressed (Group III). In this study, severity of heart failure was judged by the degree of pulmonary edema observed at sacrifice as quantified by lung weight (graph at center). As is shown, lung weight related to body weight was essentially the same in Groups I and II, whereas a marked increase is apparent in Group III. Left ventricular weight related to body weight gave evidence of increasing cardiac hypertrophy as failure advanced (bottom).

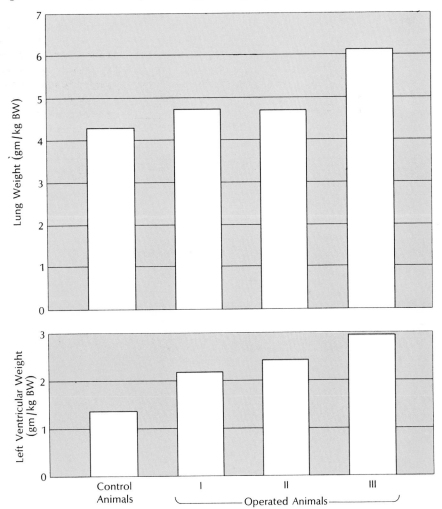

The Biochemical Basis of
Heart Failure

PETER E. POOL

University of California, San Diego

In congestive heart failure a depression in intrinsic myocardial function has impaired the capacity of the heart to pump blood at a rate commensurate with body requirements. There are now definitive ways of documenting the depressed contractile state of the failing ventricle (see Chapter 7, "Hemodynamic Aspects of Cardiac Failure," by Dodge and Chapter 23, "Hemodynamic Changes in Acute Myocardial Infarction," by Ross); however, the mechanism for this depressed state has yet to be delineated. By implication, biochemical derangement of some kind must underlie the defective physiologic performance of the heart; failure to identify and characterize the basic abnormality has surely not been from lack of effort on the part of many investigators. With better techniques for quantifying the function of the heart as muscle tissue, the concept that a single biochemical defect underlies the onset of heart failure seems in several ways less tenable than it once did. In actual fact the cause more probably involves a failure of integration of several basic mechanisms, some of which may still be unsuspected, although most are beginning to be defined.

An important accomplishment of investigations to date has been to pinpoint several biochemical processes that can be safely discounted as individual causal factors in heart failure; thus concerted attention can now be directed at the more promising possibilities. In recent years, research has focused on possible defects in cardiac energy metabolism, in protein synthesis, and in the excitation-contraction coupling process that governs the contractility of the myocardium. We are now much closer to an overview of the complex interactions that constitute the process of hypertrophy and heart failure.

An important feature of muscle cell function in the heart, or elsewhere, is the process whereby chemical energy supplied to the contractile apparatus is changed into the mechanical work of myocardial contraction (see Chapter 3, "Biochemical Processes in Cardiac Function," by Davies). It seemed logical, therefore, that evidence for a biochemical abnormality in failing heart muscle be sought first in the area of myocardial energy metabolism. To be sure, any of several metabolic functions might be involved. There might be a defect in conversion of substrates taken up by the myocardium from the coronary capillary bed into the key energy sources for contraction – the high-energy phosphates, adenosine triphosphate (ATP) and creatine phosphate (CP). Or the defect might not be in energy production but in energy storage, whereby steady-state concentrations of high-energy phosphate compounds are maintained by the cell for use by the contractile apparatus. Alternatively, the defect might be in energy utilization – the rate and efficiency of conversion of chemical energy into the mechanical energy of cardiac muscle function.

There is little to suggest any diminution in myocardial extraction of oxidizable substrates such as glucose, lactate, or fatty acids in association with congestive heart failure. Indeed, coronary sinus catheterization studies both in animals and in patients with congestive heart failure, in particular those of Bing, had clearly shown normal extraction values. However, some early reports suggested that a defect in either energy production or storage might be the underlying biochemical lesion in heart failure. This was the inference drawn from the characteristic changes in myocardial energetics seen when the heart is deprived of oxygen by hypoxia or ischemia. Alterations immediately occur in the provision of energy to the myocardium, the earliest being a curtailment of the process of oxidative phosphorylation whereby both ATP and, indirectly, CP are made available to the myocardium. In severe hypoxia there is relative failure to resynthesize ATP after it is used, producing increasing concentrations of inorganic phosphate and adenosine diphosphate (ADP); the latter two compounds together play an important role in activating compensatory pathways of metabolism.

These and other changes in myocardial energetics were observed to occur in close temporal relationship to the familiar mechanical and electrical changes in the myocardium associated with hypoxic or ischemic states. Hence it was tempting to ascribe functional alterations such as diminished cardiac work performance or arrhythmias to the decrease in energy stores, presumably because of decreased energy production. In fact this became an accepted view, even before definitive studies could be done to prove its validity. But while there could well be both a causal and temporal relationship of the observed changes in myocardial energetics and the early damaging effects of hypoxia and ischemia it was also possible that factors other than energy provision were responsible. The several phases of energy metabolism as well as alternative possibilities would have to be carefully explored.

In evaluating energy production, evidence was sought of impairment of mitochondrial function in the heart, since it is in the mitochondria that the energy of substrate oxidation is converted by oxidative phosphorylation into the terminal-bond energy of ATP and CP (see Chapter 3 by Davies). As electrons derived from substrate oxidation flow down the electron transport chain, sufficient energy is liberated to generate ATP. In normal mitochondria the relation of the number of atoms of inorganic phosphate (P) esterified with ADP to form ATP to the number of atoms of oxygen consumed in the process (P/O ratio) is 3:1; a lower ratio indicates mitochondrial damage. In all tissues, including myocardium, rates of electron transport and of oxidative phosphorylation are normally tightly coupled; a blockade of oxygen uptake will halt phosphorylation and vice versa. If the substrate for phosphorylation, ADP, is absent, oxygen utilization will cease, provided the processes are tightly coupled in the normal fashion. The ratio of oxygen uptake by mitochondrial preparations in the presence of ADP, compared with its uptake in the absence of ADP, expresses the extent to which the processes are completely coupled. This respiratory control ratio, as it is called, is normally in excess of 4:1; again, a lower ratio indicates mitochondrial damage.

By these measurements, impairment in mitochondrial function was

reported in animal experiments in which left ventricular hypertrophy and failure had been induced by aortic constriction. For example, mitochondria isolated from guinea pigs showed a reduction in P/O and respiratory control ratios. Similar findings were obtained in mitochondria isolated from the dog, along with a diminished myocardial concentration of malic acid dehydrogenase. Reduced concentrations of this and other mitochondrial enzymes were reported in postmortem specimens from patients who died of heart failure.

But there were also differing reports: Mitochondrial function was found to be entirely normal in the guinea pig heart with failure produced by aortic constriction and in the dog with failure secondary to pulmonic stenosis and tricuspid regurgitation. It was puzzling that such divergent results could obtain under apparently similar experimental conditions; it was also evident that whatever the findings in experimental heart failure in animals they might well not apply in man. In the clinical setting cardiac failure usually has a relatively slow onset whereas even in chronic failure preparations in animals, failure develops relatively rapidly. Surely an explosive series of cellular events occurs along with the rapid development of ventricular hypertrophy following such acute interventions; this in itself might result in disorders of mitochondrial function. For more information it would be necessary to examine human mitochondrial function and morphology and the content of high-energy phosphate compounds in human myocardial tissue.

Such a study was among the first in a series conducted at the National Heart and Lung Institute in the mid-1960's and continued at other institutions.

The first human study, like later ones, employed myocardial tissue obtained at the time of cardiac operations from patients with heart failure. This provided an opportunity to measure the functional capacity of mitochondria from the viable human heart (in postmortem tissue variable degrees of autolysis may be present). Mitochondria were isolated from papillary muscle specimens removed from the left ventricle at the time of mitral valve replacement where this

muscle might interfere with the function of the implanted valve. Determinations of oxidative phosphorlylation and oxygen consumption were then made with these mitochondria. Myocardial biopsy specimens were also analyzed for content of high-energy phosphate compounds.

The patients all had symptoms of markedly reduced cardiac reserve and were in functional classes III and IV by the New York Heart Association criteria. Despite the fact that cardiovascular function was limited, oxidative phosphorylation was not affected. Both P/O ratios and the respiratory control ratio confirmed the functional integrity of the organelles. The findings were also supported by other measurements of mitochondrial function. Moreover, examination of mitochondrial ultrastructure failed to reveal any structural alterations. And measurement of high-energy phosphate compounds in the myocardial biopsy specimens showed essentially the same ATP and CP levels whether obtained from patients with or without congestive heart failure.

It is now apparent that the process of developing hypertrophy and, under continued stress, the onset of congestive heart failure are attended by major alterations in mitochondrial function involving degeneration of some of these organelles and enhanced activity by others. This enhanced activity is marked by increased incorporation of amino acids into mitochondrial protein. Other mitochondrial functions that involve the exchange of ions, especially calcium, have been shown to be altered by the development of heart failure (see Chapter 4, "Calcium Metabolism in the Normal and Failing Heart," by Chidsey). However, in none of these investigations is there clear evidence that the energy-producing functions of the myocardium are deficient, and it is clear that it is possible to induce heart failure in the presence of normal mitochondrial function, thus indicating that mitochondrial deterioration does not necessarily play a causative role in congestive heart failure.

There seemed little question that the defect was not in energy production. If a defect in energy metabolism was responsible for defective ventricular function, would it prove to be at the level of myocardial energy stor-

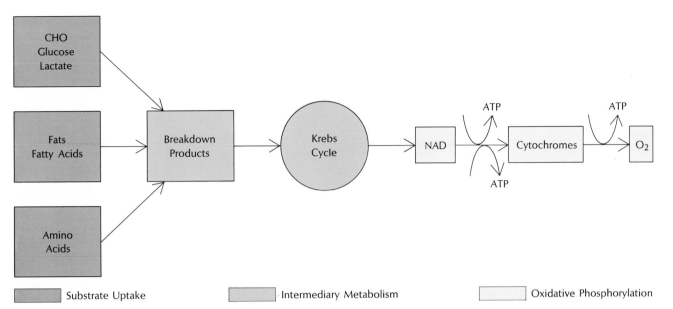

Because of their preeminence in cardiac metabolism, among the first biochemical processes studied for their possible impairment in cardiac failure were those of energy production, i.e., substrate uptake, intermediary metabolism, and/or oxidative phosphoryla- tion (diagrammed above). It was reasoned that defects in these processes would be reflected in abnormalities of substrate utiliza- tion, oxidative phosphorylation, or oxygen consumption. The re- sults of relevant studies are summarized graphically below.

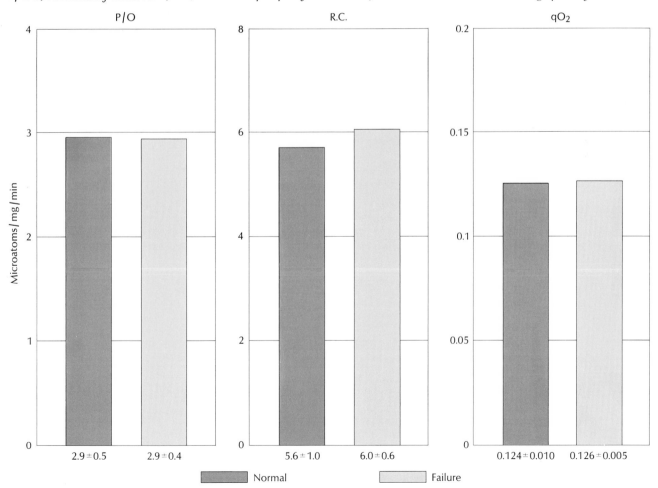

If there were impairment of oxidative phosphorylation in heart failure, it should be reflected in abnormality of mitochondrial processes as shown by μM of ADP phosphorylated per $\mu atom$ of oxygen consumed (P/O), by ratio of oxygen consumed in the pre- sence of ADP to O_2 consumed in the absence of ADP (R.C.), or in consumption of $\mu atoms$ of O_2 per mg of mitochondrial protein per minute (qO_2). As shown in studies using glutamate as sub- strate and cat heart mitochondria at $25°C$ as the experimental preparation, there is no significant difference in efficiency of oxi- dative phosphorylation between normal and failing heart muscle.

age? The possibility that an alteration in the heart's store of high-energy phosphates could be related to heart failure was actually first suggested in the 1930's when the ATPase activity of myosin was first discovered. The possibility grew stronger when it was demonstrated a few years ago that ATP is the immediate source of energy for muscle contraction. If an alteration of the heart's high-energy phosphate stores were involved in heart failure it should show up as a depression in the steady-state levels of ATP or of CP, which acts as an auxiliary energy store and provides for continuous replenishment of ATP.

Several workers found evidence for a depletion of high-energy phosphate stores in both acute and chronic heart failure, but others did not. However, the finding that high-energy phosphate stores were depleted did not necessarily warrant the assumption that the two were causally related. To clarify the question we wanted to determine whether it was possible to produce a distinct diminution in cardiac performance at a time when myocardial energy stores were not detectably altered. The experiments were done in dogs with heart failure induced by hypoxia. Bilateral adrenalectomies were performed and the animals subsequently treated with hexamethonium and propranolol; this was to ensure that activation of the heart via direct neural stimulation or circulating neurohumors would not affect the results. Biopsy samples were taken before the experiment, during induction of hypoxia, after onset of early heart failure, and later, as myocardial performance further deteriorated.

Myocardial concentrations of ATP were maintained even in the presence of severe hypoxia and myocardial failure; there was a small depression in average CP concentration in early failure in two-thirds of cases, but this did not occur in the others. Thus, hypoxic inhibition of myocardial function was clearly not initiated by a fall in total ATP levels. When CP levels became depressed, it was not until after the contractile state of the left ventricle had begun to decline. Similar results were obtained in other experiments, also in dogs, with acutely induced ischemic heart failure.

To be sure, the possibility remained that a small, discrete store of energy necessary for some vital cellular function was preferentially depleted. Meerson has suggested that decreased levels of high-energy phosphate compounds might be the common denominator in the stimulus to hypertrophy resulting from a number of diverse causes. However, the sum of available evidence did dissociate the onset of congestive heart failure from alterations in total energy stores.

Thus, it was time to consider the third possibility — a disturbance of energy utilization in the contractile process. This could occur if the contractile proteins themselves were altered; indeed this was once believed to be the basic biochemical abnormality in congestive heart failure. Cardiac myosin isolated from dogs in congestive failure reportedly differed in molecular weight from cardiac myosin from normal dogs. However, further studies by a number of workers have failed to reveal abnormalities in any of the contractile proteins, whether in physical structure, chemical composition, or any other property that could be considered.

A defect in energy utilization might entail either inefficient conversion of chemical energy into mechanical work, or efficient conversion at an abnormal rate. To determine this we evaluated the efficiency of energy conversion in right ventricular papillary muscles isolated from cats with experimental right ventricular failure secondary to pulmonary artery constriction. Energy production was interrupted so as not to influence the result; glycolysis was inhibited by exposure of muscles to iodoacetic acid; oxidative phosphorylation was inhibited by exposing the muscles to Krebs solution previously equilibrated with 95% N_2 and 5% CO_2. Utilization of energy stores was determined both in the basal, noncontracting state and when muscles were stimulated to contract under isometric conditions.

The contractile function of these muscles was severely depressed and the amount of energy used was reduced in proportion to the reduction in contractile element work. Thus, the efficiency with which chemical energy was converted into mechanical work was not impaired.

The possibility remained that the rate of energy transduction might be altered, and this was explored by measuring the ATPase activity of myofibrils isolated from normal and failing hearts. Release of energy from ATP in the contractile process is controlled by a specific ATPase within the myofibril, which splits the terminal phosphate bond of ATP and thereby liberates its energy. The rate of energy release from ATP appears to be related to activity of this enzyme, although no clear-cut evidence exists that the rate of ATPase activity in vitro necessarily parallels that in

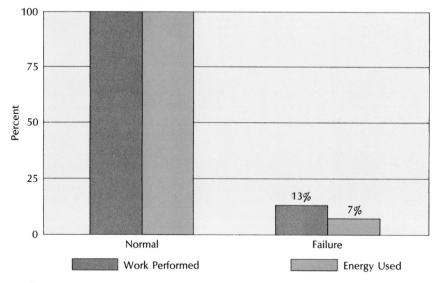

Inefficiency in energy conversion could not be demonstrated in failing cat heart muscle stimulated to contract and perform work. Although such muscles could perform only 13% of the mechanical work of muscles from normal animals, to do so they utilized only 7% as much energy in the form of high-energy phosphates.

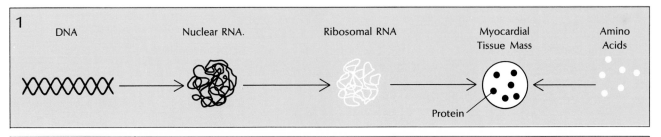

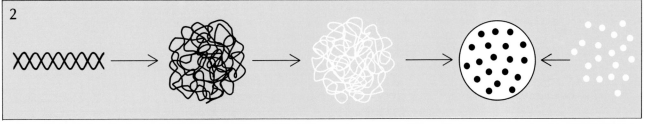

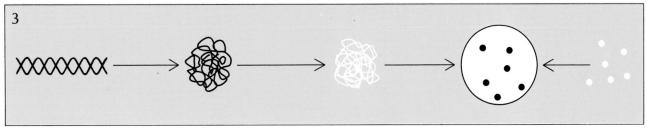

If normal protein synthesis (1) were disrupted in heart failure, defects might occur at the stage of DNA-directed RNA synthesis or in synthesis of proteins from amino acids as invoked in the ribosomes by mRNA. In cardiac hypertrophy (2) an increase is observed in RNA and there is increased incorporation of amino acids into proteins, producing a greater myocardial tissue mass but no increase in nuclear DNA. When failure (3) ensues, there is a relative diminution in these processes, but it is not known whether a switching-off of protein synthesis partly accounts for the failure state or is merely a concomitant phenomenon.

vivo. Since the unloaded velocity of muscle contraction (V_{max}) is known to be depressed in heart failure, this suggested that AT Pase activity of the contractile proteins might also be reduced. However, studies in this connection had given confusing results. In our experiments, either right ventricular hypertrophy or failure was produced by graded pulmonary artery stenosis in the cat and AT Pase activity of myofibrils isolated from these hearts was compared with that isolated from the ventricles of normal cats. Mechanical properties of papillary muscles from the right ventricles were also examined.

A severe experimental failure was associated with a significant depression (by an average of 39%) in myofibrillar AT Pase activity. In the presence of hypertrophy without overt hemodynamic failure, AT Pase activity was also reduced but to a lesser degree. The reduction in AT Pase could be correlated generally with the depression of intrinsic contractility both in hypertrophy and in heart failure.

Was the reduction in AT Pase activity related directly to depression of the contractile state? That is still a key question. There also remains the possibility that depression of AT Pase activity in congestive failure may be related not to alterations in cardiac contractility but to some other abnormality induced by the heart failure state. Indeed, more recently these observations of decreased myofibrillar AT Pase activity have been confirmed by others. In addition, other AT Pase activities such as those associated with the sarcolemma and sarcoplasmic reticulum have also been found to be depressed in the presence of heart failure. These findings may indicate a role for altered ion transport in heart failure as well as provide additional evidence for alterations in protein metabolism and function since AT Pase activity resides in proteins.

One conclusion seems clear: The weight of evidence to date points away from any causal relationship between primary defects in the process of energy metabolism — whether in energy production, storage, or utili-

zation — and development of the congestive heart failure state. True, aspects of energy metabolism may be altered or stressed in the presence of congestive failure, and in severe heart failure some structures such as the mitochondria may undergo degeneration. It seems most likely, however, that any changes in total energy metabolism that accompany the heart failure state are not causal.

As noted earlier, another focus of investigation has been on the role of protein synthesis, a continuous process in the normal myocardium that assures a sufficiency of proteins both for energy metabolism and for the renewal of cell structure and function. Moreover, protein synthesis is essential to the process of compensatory hypertrophy, which results from stress and precedes heart failure. In the experimental animal the stress imposed by an acutely increased load on the heart consistently leads to an activation of protein synthesis. This is the response of the myocardium to an increase in load per unit mass; it continues until some equalization of this

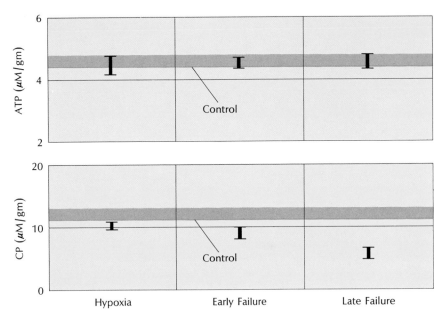

Despite profound mechanical changes resulting from hypoxia-induced heart failure in dogs, levels of myocardial energy stores as measured in biopsy specimens remained essentially normal. There was no diminution whatever in average concentration of ATP; creatine phosphate concentration did decline in some animals in late failure but was never significantly below control values in early failure stage.

load is brought about by an increase in myocardial mass. Protein synthesis then returns to normal but usually only for a time. Associated with persistence of the abnormal load and advancing heart failure, several investigators have observed a decrease in the synthesis of protein, manifest as a decrease in myosin and other A T Pase activities, a decrease in the amount or activity of other myocardial enzymes, and a diminution in resynthesis of contractile proteins including actin, myosin, and tropomyosin.

A number of studies have shown that any of the three critical phases in protein synthesis can be altered in the hypertrophied and failing myocardium. The effect may be at the stage of replication, the process of D N A-directed D N A synthesis; it may be at the stage of transcription, when R N A polynucleotides are synthesized on the D N A template; or in the final process of translation, whereby the genetic code, now in the form of nucleotides of R N A, is translated into the synthesis of proteins from amino acids.

In experimental cardiac hypertrophy and failure the total myocardial content of D N A and R N A is increased. The increase in R N A content exceeds the increase in myocardial mass, the net result being an increase in myocardial R N A concentration. In contrast, myocardial D N A content is increased more or less in proportion to the increase in myocardial size; thus myocardial D N A concentration is unchanged.

The myocardial cell does not seem to proliferate during hypertrophy; instead it increases in size. The observed increase in total myocardial D N A content implies an increase in the D N A content of each myocardial cell. However, when Meerson and coworkers measured D N A content in individual cells in the hypertrophied myocardium they showed that virtually the entire increase in D N A content within the myocardium during hypertrophy occurs in connective tissue cells in the myocardium rather than in cardiac muscle cells themselves. Thus, there was no increase in nuclear D N A synthesis in the myocardial cell during hypertrophy and no increase in the number of nuclei; instead each unit of DNA in the hypertrophied myocardial cell served a greatly expanded cell volume. Others have since confirmed these findings.

An augmentation in the process of transcription is also characteristic of myocardial hypertrophy. Several studies in this connection have made use of the properties of actinomycin D, which specifically blocks R N A

polymerase, the critical enzyme by which R N A polynucleotides are synthesized on the D N A template. Thus, in experimental coarctation of the aorta, myocardial hypertrophy can be prevented by administration of actinomycin D, and in the absence of an activation of protein synthesis heart failure ensues rapidly. The fact that in the absence of acute stress actinomycin D does not immediately inhibit protein synthesis indicates that the already synthesized R N A is capable of continuing protein synthesis for some time; in the acutely stressed heart, however, an increased synthesis of ribosomal R N A is required. In accord with this observation, Meerson and colleagues demonstrated an increase in the number of nucleoli per nucleus in cells in the hypertrophied heart; the nucleoli are centers of ribosomal activity and reflect an increase in this activity. Moroz, as well as Fanberg and Posner, observed increased protein synthesis in the microsomal fraction of acutely stressed hearts, as well as increased yields of microsomal and soluble R N A, while Nair and coworkers reported an increase in R N A polymerase activity in cardiac hypertrophy.

An activation in protein synthesis at the translation phase would be indicated by increased incorporation of amino acids into protein, accomplished by increased amounts of new ribosomal and messenger R N A available to the cell. This has been precisely the finding in animals as well as in isolated heart preparations subjected to an acute ventricular overload. An interesting observation of Meerson has been that the increase in amino acid incorporation is confined to the early stages of acute overload; in heart failure occurring some months after experimentally produced coarctation of the aorta, incorporation of amino acids was decreased. He postulated that the decreased incorporation could explain the failure of cellular structure to be renewed during the stress of hyperfunction and thus could contribute to the heart failure state. The stimulus responsible for the initiation of these alterations in protein metabolism also remains to be elucidated. Lesch, Gorlin, and Sonnenblick have shown that increased tension applied to rabbit papillary muscles increases the uptake of amino acids. Meerson has suggested that a distintegration of cell structures caused by a lack of energy supplies, or, alternatively, alterations in cyclic A M P levels may affect protein synthesis. Finally, Tolnai and Beznak have described an increase in activity of hydrolases (the destructive enzymes released by lysosomes) in association with hypertrophy.

Taken together these findings leave no doubt that acute stress on the myocardium activates all stages of protein synthesis. There is proliferation of D N A, albeit confined to myocardial connective tissue cells. There is an increase in synthesis of new R N A of all types and, as a result, increased incorporation of amino acids into protein. However, activation of these processes is associated primarily with the stage of hypertrophy preceding clinical heart failure. The diminution in these same processes that occurs with heart failure may or may not be causally related to the onset of the congestive failure state. The requisite experiments to determine whether a turning off of protein synthesis is at least partly responsible for the heart failure state have not yet been done. More work is needed to learn whether there may be specific defects in protein synthesis that would not be identifiable when one examines the overall process. Moreover, it is still not known whether the diminution in protein synthesis shown in animals also occurs in man with chronic low output failure of the clinically common type.

Thus, while changes in energy metabolism and in protein synthesis may ultimately contribute to the process of heart failure, evidence so far suggests they do not play the primary causative role. A third possibility, however, and one that is currently arousing special interest, is that the defect may be in excitation-contraction coupling, the sequence of events leading from electrical depolarization of heart muscle to contraction of the sarcomere. If such a defect did exist it would be expected to involve uptake and release of calcium by the sarcoplasmic reticulum or cell membrane, since the presence of calcium is indispensable for utilization of A T P in the contractile process (see Chapter 2, "Contractile Proteins in the Normal and Failing Myocardium," by Katz). Studies in this area have been facilitated since

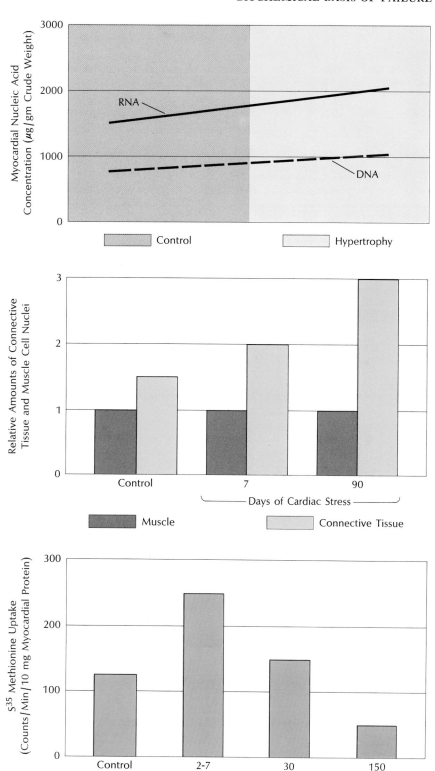

Comparison of myocardial RNA and DNA concentrations in dogs with experimental aortic stenosis and in normal animals revealed marked increases in concentrations of both nucleic acids in animals with hypertrophied left ventricles (top). Increases of up to 33% were observed in the experimental group, although the RNA/DNA ratio remained similar in both. Measurement of DNA content in individual cells in the hypertrophied myocardium disclosed that virtually the entire increase in DNA content was in connective tissue cells in the myocardium rather than in cardiac muscle cells (center). Whereas uptake of amino acid (S³⁵ methionine) by myocardial protein is significantly increased during the stage of acute overload resulting in cardiac hyperfunction and hypertrophy, it shows a decrease as cardiac failure supervenes (data from Meerson).

55

it became feasible to obtain relatively pure preparations of sarcoplasmic reticulum and to make accurate measurements of calcium uptake and release, utilizing either radioactive calcium or a dye reaction measured by spectrophotometry. These studies are extensively reviewed in Chapter 4 by Chidsey.

If a defect does exist in excitation-contraction coupling, the question again is whether it precedes heart failure and causes it or merely accompanies it. It may seem logical to suggest causation because of evidence that contractility of the heart is regulated by changes in calcium flux and because pharmacologic alteration of contractility will be reflected in corresponding variations in calcium flux. Surely the depression in contractility found in heart failure could be due to depression of these mechanisms. A key laboratory experiment would be to see whether one can create heart failure without alterations in the excitation-contraction coupling process, as was done in the studies of energy metabolism.

Unfortunately, the really definitive experiments cannot be done until more practical ways are found to examine the fluxes of calcium as they occur in living tissue. Nonetheless, the area of excitation-contraction coupling now appears the most promising for further investigation, perhaps because we still know relatively little about it. Whether a defect here will prove to be the specific biochemical lesion that has long been sought, or one of several underlying the heart failure state, will have to be demonstrated in the future. In the past few years our understanding of the biochemical processes involved in heart failure has expanded enormously. Perhaps the most consistent pattern that has developed is a confirmation of the overview provided by Meerson, who described the changing processes of hypertrophy and heart failure. Unfortunately, the specific biochemical signals responsible for these changes have not yet been revealed, and thus the search continues for a single outstanding biochemical abnormality. The likelihood is, however, that a constellation of biochemical abnormalities rather than a single defect will be found to underlie the congestive heart failure state.

Section Two

Physiologic Mechanisms in Heart Failure

The Autonomic Nervous System in Heart Failure

EUGENE BRAUNWALD

Harvard University

From the time that William Harvey discovered the prime function of the heart to be that of a pump, physiologists and clinicians have marveled at the remarkable ability of this organ to modify its performance according to the needs of the peripheral tissues. Radical alterations in heart rate and cardiac output are accomplished with ease, and in a matter of seconds. Efforts to understand better the mechanisms whereby the heart controls propulsion of blood through the circulatory system to meet changing conditions have occupied generations of researchers in the field of cardiovascular disease. Over the years this question has been explored at many levels: in isolated heart muscle, in whole heart, in heart-lung preparations, and in intact animals. More recently, refinement of investigative techniques has permitted more direct study of myocardial function in man.

A fact basic to regulation of myocardial function is that while heart muscle resembles other striated muscle structurally and biochemically, it differs from it in an important way. When called upon to increase contractile activity it does not do so by modifying the number of contractile units that play a role, as is the case with skeletal muscle. The magnitude of contractile response is controlled instead by the length of the muscle fibers at the time of activation, ventricular end-diastolic volume and filling pressure being the chief expressions of fiber length and tension (see Chapter 1, "Myocardial Ultrastructure in the Normal and Failing Heart," by Sonnenblick, and Chapter 2, "Contractile Proteins in the Normal and Failing Myocardium," by Katz).

But this control mechanism, despite its key role, is not the only one that regulates the heart's performance. There is a second crucial mechanism, whereby changes in activity of the autonomic nervous system (consisting of the sympathetic and parasympathetic systems) can directly alter ventricular function at any given level of end-dias-tolic volume or pressure. Indeed, Starling himself, noted for elucidating the first intrinsic mechanism governing heart action, recognized the importance of neurohumoral adjustments in adapting ventricular function to the body's requirements. As he observed in a paper published in 1920:

"No understanding of the circulatory reactions of the body is possible unless we start first with the fundamental properties of the heart muscle itself and then find out how they are modified, protected, and controlled under the influence of mechanisms — nervous, chemical, and mechanical — which under normal conditions play upon the heart."

All four heart chambers are richly endowed with sympathetic nerves that serve as a link between the brain and contracting heart muscle. Nerve terminals storing the sympathetic neurotransmitter norepinephrine are found throughout the heart wherever their presence could count: in the sinoatrial and atrioventricular nodes, in the Purkinje system, in the atrial and ventricular myocardia. At these sites the neurotransmitter acts principally to stimulate the heart's beta-adrenergic receptors, as can be confirmed experimentally by infusion of a beta-adrenergic stimulant such as isoproterenol. The responses elicited are similar to those produced naturally by norepinephrine release from sympathetic nerve endings.

The heart, like other organs innervated by sympathetic nerves, can readily extract norepinephrine from the blood stream, and for a long time it was assumed that the heart's norepinephrine stores were derived primarily from the blood. Within the past few years it has been demonstrated experimentally, both in canine and guinea pig heart preparations, that the heart itself and its constituent sympathetic nerve endings can synthesize the neurotransmitter from its precursor amino acid tyrosine and need not be dependent on extraction from the blood to maintain its stores. Indeed, it now appears that fully 90% of the norepinephrine present in the heart is manufactured there. In this sense one can think of the heart as an endocrine gland that synthesizes and releases a hormone, norepinephrine, as needed to allow the circulation to respond appropriately to changing metabolic demands of body tissues.

Norepinephrine acting on the sinoatrial node increases the rate of diastolic depolarization and thus speeds the heart rate. Norepinephrine acting on the atrioventricular node increases the velocity of conduction and diminishes the refractory period during which the A V node is unresponsive to stimuli coming from the atrium. By increasing the excitability of nonautomatic tissue, norepinephrine can also induce ventricular tachycardia and

other arrhythmias. Most important of all from the point of view of normal cardiovascular function – as well as its maintenance in disease states – norepinephrine can significantly improve myocardial contractility.

Animal experiments a decade ago by Sarnoff and coworkers demonstrated that either electrical stellate ganglion stimulation or norepinephrine infusion augments the strength of atrial contraction and thus the atrial contribution to ventricular filling. Even more pertinent to the discussion to follow, they also showed that either nerve stimulation or neurotransmitter infusion markedly increases external stroke work and power produced by the ventricle at any given mean atrial pressure and at any end-diastolic pressure or fiber length.

The interest of our research group has focused on the importance of the sympathetic nervous system, particularly as it affects ventricular function, in normal circulatory regulation in man. A special concern also has been

to assess the importance of the sympathetic nervous system in maintaining circulatory adequacy when the myocardium is depressed, or when an increased hemodynamic burden is placed on the heart because of an imbalance between cardiac output and the perfusion requirements of peripheral tissues.

An intriguing early experiment in our laboratories indicated the potential importance of the adrenergic nervous system in patients undergoing thoracotomy. Measurement of the effects of direct electrical stimulation of the sympathetic nerves with use of a myocardial strain gauge arch showed a consistent and significant increase in the force of ventricular contraction, although the length of segment of myocardium to which the strain gauge was sewn remained constant.

It seemed clear that stimulation of nervous pathways in the sympathetic nervous system could result in profound augmentation of the contractile state of the human myocardium. However, it could not be concluded from such stimulation experiments that the ordinary activity of the adrenergic nervous system has a significant effect on myocardial function in intact man.

Thus, several initial studies by our group were aimed at establishing normal parameters by evaluating the role of the sympathetic nervous system in

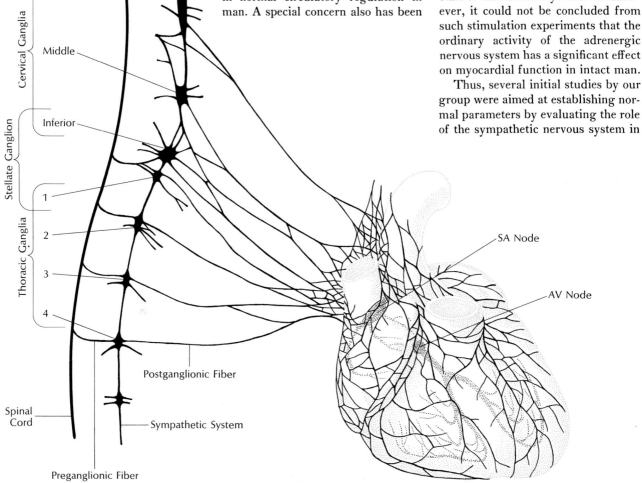

Sympathetic pathways to and in the heart are shown above. All four chambers are richly endowed with sympathetic nerves, with heavy concentrations in the regions of the SA and AV nodes. The atria appear to be more densely innervated than the ventricles.

exercise. Other investigators as well were suggesting that sympathetic activity could be important in mediating cardiovascular response to exercise, since many changes in cardiac performance during exercise resemble those resulting from stimulation of sympathetic pathways.

In one study we attempted to define the relationship of changes in heart rate, sympathetic activity, and ventricular dimensions in the cardiovascular response to mild exercise (performed on a bicycle ergometer in the supine position). Subjects were a group of patients being reevaluated some months after cardiac surgery. At the time of the exercise test they had only trivial abnormalities in cardiac function, so their responses might be considered analogous to those of normal subjects under similar conditions.

Dimensions of the left and/or right ventricle were obtained by measuring the distances between radiopaque markers (placed during cardiac surgery) on sequential frames of cineradiograms exposed at 30 frames per second; intraventricular pressure was simultaneously determined. The cineradiographic technique also permitted analysis of myocardial force-velocity relations, an analysis predicated on the fact that throughout active contraction the position of the force-velocity curve of the myocardium is determined by muscle length and contractile state. Thus, if the force-velocity relation is always examined at the same muscle length, this relation will define the contractile state of the myocardium.

The patients first performed light exercise as instructed; after a rest period, they repeated the exercise while the right atrium was electrically stimulated to keep the heart rate constant. The contribution of the sympathetic nervous system was assessed by administering the adrenergic-blocking agent propranolol before the exercise. (The availability of drugs that selectively block activity of the adrenergic nervous system has made it far easier to estimate the role of this system in maintenance of myocardial function in man.)

During the first exercise period there was a decrease in ventricular end-diastolic dimensions; during exercise at a constant heart rate these

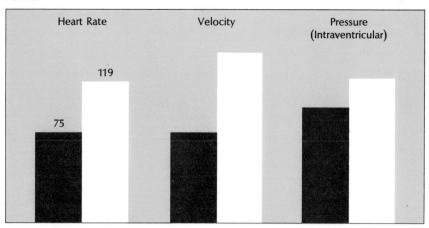

Normal

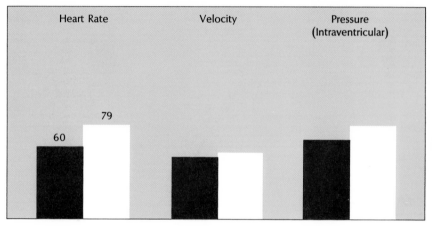

β Blocked

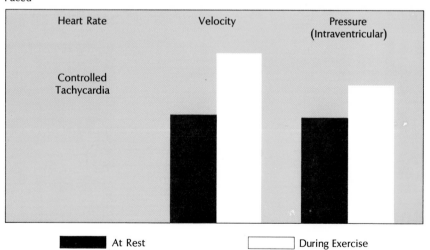

Paced

The effect of exercise on various cardiac parameters in normal individuals was measured under various conditions. The straightforward response to exercise is graphed (top) and shows increases in heart rate, velocity of fiber shortening, and intraventricular pressure. The most marked increase was that in velocity, reflecting an effect of exercise on myocardial contractility. All effects were minimized when propranolol was administered to block beta-adrenergic response (center). Next, controlled tachycardia was induced by means of electrical pacing, with heart rates at rest being set at levels close to those observed in the individuals during normal exercise. It was found that the tachycardia by itself did not produce upward shifts in velocity of the same magnitude as those associated with exercise-induced tachycardia. It was concluded that the increase in heart rate characteristic of exercise contributes to enhanced ventricular performance but is not as great a factor as is increased sympathetic activity.

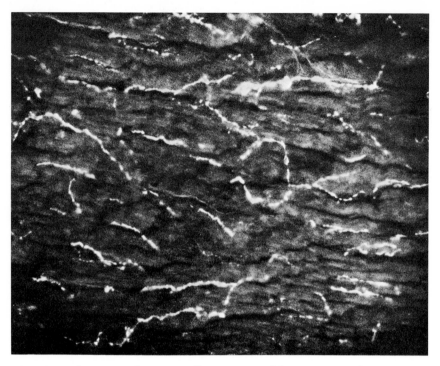

The rich supply of sympathetic nerve fibers in a normal heart is seen in this fluorescent preparation of calf right ventricle. Photograph is from studies by Jacobowitz, Chidsey, and Vogel, courtesy Dr. David Jacobowitz, University of Pennsylvania.

dimensions increased. However, the most striking alteration was in the contractile state of the myocardium, as shown by the increased velocity of muscle fiber shortening regardless of intraventricular pressure and dimensions. For example, during the first exercise period – when cardiac response was allowed to occur spontaneously – velocity per isolength of muscle fiber increased by an average of 80%; at the same time cardiac output increased by only 36%. Thus the performance of the ventricle had improved, but clearly not as much as contractility.

The relative roles of both the alterations in heart rate and sympathetic activity were also investigated with the subjects at rest but with induced tachycardia. The force-velocity relationship was shifted as before, but to a relatively small extent in comparison with that produced by exercise. Moreover, since greater shifts in force-velocity relationships occurred when exercise was performed at a constant rate, it would appear that the increase in heart rate in spontaneous exercise is a contributory but not the chief factor affecting the contractile state of the myocardium.

On the other hand, in the experiments with propranolol it was shown that adrenergic blockade almost completely prevented the exercise-induced shift in force-velocity relationships. The small residual increases in contractility that occurred with propranolol could be attributed to the elevation in heart rate that still occurred despite the block, since, when heart rate was also controlled, even these small shifts were abolished. Without adrenergic blockade, there was clearly an improvement during exercise in the contractile state of the myocardium, primarily because of increased sympathetic activity, which allowed the ventricle to eject blood more rapidly in order to meet increased metabolic requirements.

One interesting finding in these studies was that ventricular dimensions were reduced less during exercise than when a similar increase in heart rate was induced at rest. At any given heart rate, ventricular end-diastolic and end-systolic dimensions as well as stroke volume were all larger during exercise than at rest. Thus it can be seen that the Starling mechanism does in fact participate in the adaptation of the heart to exercise, even with an actively functioning sympathetic nervous system.

More information on the role of sympathetic activity in mediating cardiovascular response to exercise was sought in another study of healthy volunteers and patients with mild-to-moderate heart disease, who performed exercise on a motor-driven treadmill at varying speeds and inclines. Responses with and without adrenergic blockade with propranolol were determined at both submaximal and maximal exercise levels in healthy subjects and at submaximal levels in those with heart disease.

With adrenergic blockade, exercise at both levels invariably caused lesser increases in heart rate, cardiac output, mean arterial pressure, and left ventricular minute work. However, the fact that increases occurred despite adrenergic blockade confirmed that sympathetic nervous stimulation of the heart is not the only mechanism whereby heart rate and cardiac output are augmented during exercise.

In other experiments, sympathetic blockade produced with use of guanethidine again caused depression of the circulation during exercise. During a predrug exercise period, exertion resulting in a four-to-fivefold increase in oxygen consumption brought average increases above resting values of 68% in heart rate, 17% in stroke volume, 96% in cardiac output, and 129% in left ventricular minute work. After administration of both guanethidine and atropine, identical levels of exercise produced average increases above resting values of only 28% in heart rate, 1% in stroke volume, 30% in cardiac output, and 5% in left ventricular minute work. Blockade of the parasympathetic nervous system alone with use of atropine did not interfere with the circulatory response to exercise, whereas when only the sympathetic system was blocked with guanethidine, cardiac output, mean arterial pressure, and left ventricular work during exercise were significantly lower than during the predrug exercise period.

With these data in hand on the normal role of the sympathetic system in modulating cardiovascular function, the next logical step was to attempt to determine how the system might act to maintain myocardial function in patients whose cardiovascular reserve is reduced by failure. If for no other reason, the widespread clinical use of adrenergic-blocking drugs in such patients gave immediate practical importance to evaluation of sympathetic activity. We hoped these studies might also increase understanding of basic mechanisms that operate in heart failure.

A number of findings over the years had indicated that cardiovascular sympathetic nervous system function is altered in the clinical syndrome of congestive failure. The tachycardia, diaphoresis, peripheral vascular constriction, and suppression of urine formation in patients with heart failure had all been considered evidence of increased sympathetic nervous activity (see Chapter 9, "The Clinical Manifestations of Cardiac Failure in Adults," by Perloff).

More direct evidence was obtained in a study in which subhypotensive doses of guanethidine were used to interfere with the activity of the sympathetic system in patients with heart failure. The 10 patients studied had inactive rheumatic valvular or primary myocardial disease. All had signs or symptoms of right- and/or left-sided congestive failure at the time of investigation. Manifestations of failure were increased in the five patients with more severe disease (functional classes III or IV by the New York Heart Association criteria). All showed an increase in dyspnea, orthopnea, and body weight; venous pressure and sodium excretion were also

increased. In the five with less severe disease, congestive failure did not worsen with administration of the blocking agent.

Thus the sympathetic nervous system did appear to play a compensatory role in the circulatory adjustment of patients to heart failure. The findings also suggested a need for caution in the clinical use of adrenergic-blocking agents to treat patients with limited cardiac reserve.

More evidence for such a role was obtained by measurements of the concentration of norepinephrine in arterial blood. With sympathetic activity, a portion of the norepinephrine released from nerve terminals spills over into the bloodstream; determining the plasma norepinephrine concentration therefore provides a crude index to the level of sympathetic activity. Sensitive fluorometric techniques now available allow accurate measurement of norepinephrine levels not only in blood but in urine and tissue as well.

In normal subjects, moderate muscular exercise was associated with only a slight increase in arterial norepinephrine (from a mean of $0.28\mu g/L$ to $0.46\mu g/L$). In patients with congestive heart failure, mean norepinephrine values were higher to begin with ($0.63\mu g/L$) and increased to far higher values with exercise (to $1.73\mu g/L$). Interestingly, resting and exercise levels in patients who

had heart disease but were not in failure proved to be similar to those in normal subjects.

The elevated resting levels in patients with heart failure – and the excessive increase during exercise – evidently reflected an increased response of the sympathetic nervous system. The conviction grew that this increased response plays a useful supportive role in such patients.

Measurements of 24-hour urinary norepinephrine excretion were also made in a sizable group of subjects including 13 normal individuals, 30 patients with congestive failure, and 14 with heart disease but no failure. Norepinephrine excretion averaged $22\mu g/day$ in the normal subjects; it was significantly elevated in patients with heart failure, averaging $46\mu g/day$ in patients in functional class III and $58\mu g/day$ in patients in class IV. Again there was little or no difference between normal subjects and those with heart disease but no failure.

Given this evidence of hyperactivity of the sympathetic system in heart failure, we wondered if cardiac stores of the neurotransmitter would be elevated. Accordingly, cardiac norepinephrine concentration was measured spectrofluorometrically in biopsy specimens of atrial tissue obtained from patients undergoing open cardiac operations. The group included 34 patients who had not experienced failure prior to surgery and 49 who had. Un-

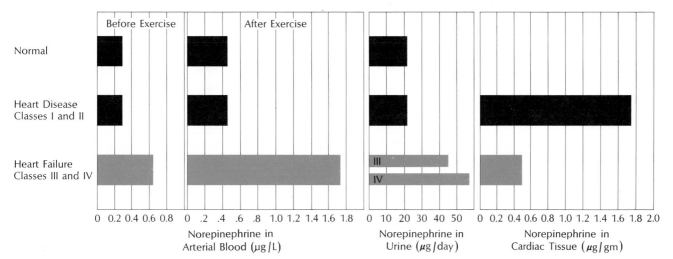

By using sensitive fluorometric techniques, it is possible to measure response to sympathetic activity as reflected in norepinephrine release to the circulation, its levels in the urine, and the amounts stored in heart tissue. The data presented here indicate that patients in heart failure have a higher level of sympathetic activity than either normal individuals or heart disease patients not in failure. At the same time, the failure patients showed a severe reduction in their cardiac norepinephrine stores (as studied in atrial appendage biopsies taken at surgery). Patients are classified by the criteria of the New York Heart Association.

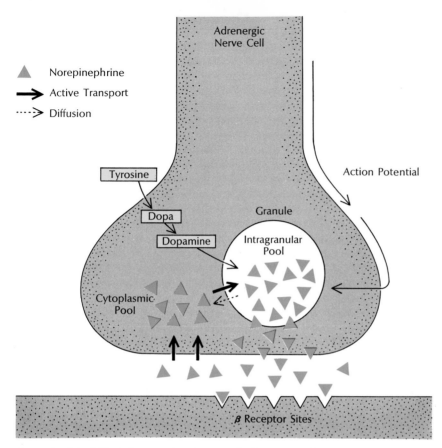

Approximately 90% of the norepinephrine in the heart is synthesized locally. The synthesis of norepinephrine from circulating tyrosine is schematized above, with the neurotransmitter stored either in granules or in the cytoplasm. In response to an action potential, the granules release norepinephrine, which leaves the nerve cell, attaches to myocardial beta-adrenergic receptor sites, and stimulates contraction.

expectedly, the norepinephrine concentration was significantly reduced in the patients with heart failure; it averaged $0.49\mu g/gm$ of tissue in patients who had been in failure as against $1.77\mu g/gm$ in those who had not. Extremely low values were found in some patients with failure — norepinephrine concentrations of less than 10% of the average normal level.

Concentrations of the neurotransmitter were also measured in papillary muscles removed from the left ventricles of patients undergoing mitral valve replacement; these levels were markedly depressed in patients with mitral regurgitation who had been in severe left ventricular failure. Comparison of norepinephrine concentrations in ventricular and atrial tissues in individual patients showed a significant positive correlation.

The observed reduction in cardiac norepinephrine concentration might have been sufficient to impair adrenergic function, provided it was true depletion. Conceivably, the amount of

norepinephrine per unit weight of tissue could be reduced merely because the presence of hypertrophied myocardium or fibrous tissue diluted a fixed number of normal nerve endings. This was one of several questions most readily studied in animal models of heart failure. Three mammalian species with chronic heart failure produced by different interventions were included so as to approximate, if possible, the several forms of heart failure encountered clinically. In the guinea pig, primary left heart failure was induced by constriction of the ascending aorta; in the dog, primary right heart failure was induced by surgery to create pulmonary stenosis and tricuspid insufficiency; in the cat, right ventricular hypertrophy with and without heart failure was induced by different degrees of pulmonary artery constriction.

In all three animal species, heart failure was associated with profound depletion in cardiac norepinephrine

concentration. The depletion was evident in both right and left ventricles no matter which ventricle carried the primary hemodynamic burden. In the experimental animal, the total content of cardiac norepinephrine (as well as its concentration) can be readily determined; this value was also markedly depressed in animals with heart failure. In dogs with heart failure, reduction of the norepinephrine stores in the heart was sufficient to abolish the contractile response of isolated papillary muscle to the sympathomimetic amine tyramine, which causes release of norepinephrine. In other words, true depletion of cardiac norepinephrine appears to occur in failure rather than the dilution of a normal complement by enlargement of the heart.

The time required after onset of heart failure for depletion of neurotransmitter stores was determined in the guinea pig. The concentration was found to be normal one day after aortic constriction but by the fifth day it had decreased to 22% of normal values. By that time substantial ventricular hypertrophy had already occurred. Values remained depressed for the 65 days during which the experiment was continued. Norepinephrine stores were also measured in guinea pig kidney to determine whether the depletion involved adrenergic nerves in other organs. There was no consistent change in renal stores for the failure group as a whole, providing further evidence that the norepinephrine depletion was limited to cardiac tissue.

The next task was to attempt to define the mechanism by which the depletion occurs. Defects of synthesis, uptake, and binding of norepinephrine or increased neurotransmitter turnover could all have been potential causes, and these possibilities were all investigated. From the evidence it appeared that a serious defect in both norepinephrine synthesis and neuronal binding exists in the failing heart.

The defect in binding of norepinephrine was observed by measuring the norepinephrine retained in the hearts and kidneys of guinea pigs after infusion of *l*-norepinephrine. In normal animals, ventricular and renal concentrations rose to peak values at the completion of the infusion; the concentrations declined over the ensuing three hours to values approaching control levels. In contrast, in animals with heart failure the same dose of neurotransmitter produced smaller increments in norepinephrine concentration and lower peak values. When tracer quantities of tritium-labeled *dl*-norepinephrine were injected, similar results were obtained. An hour later the left ventricles of the normal guinea pigs contained twice as much of the labeled norepinephrine as did those with heart failure.

It was reasoned that the altered capacity to retain administered neurotransmitter might be due to either a reduction in the total number of nerves in the myocardium or a diminution in the number of intraneuronal binding sites, or both. The subcellular distribution of administered radioactive norepinephrine was evaluated in the norepinephrine-depleted failing dog heart; the similarity of distribution in the normal and failing heart pointed to a reduction in the number of nerve endings.

Net turnover rates were measured by administering a tracer dose of radioactive norepinephrine to guinea pigs and following the specific activity for 72 hours. In both normal and failing animals the decline in specific activity was complex and exhibited two exponential components (compatible with the occurrence of a multi-compartmental distribution of norepinephrine, as suggested also by other investigators). Absolute levels of specific activity and rates of norepinephrine disappearance were essentially the same in normal animals and in those with heart failure, indicating similar net turnover rates. But if smaller increments in norepinephrine levels after infusion in the failing animals could not be explained in terms of more rapid net turnover of neurotransmitter, this more strongly suggested that an abnormality of uptake and/or binding was at least partly responsible for the depletion. In view of the smaller norepinephrine stores, the presence of normal net turnover rates also suggested that the rate of formation might actually be reduced.

More direct evidence of a defect in neurotransmitter synthesis was obtained in enzyme studies in dogs with induced right heart failure and severe cardiac norepinephrine depletion. It has been known for some years

that biosynthesis of norepinephrine proceeds through a series of steps from tyrosine to dopa to the immediate precursor dopamine. More recently it was learned that tyrosine hydroxylase, which catalyzes the first of these reactions (tyrosine to dopa), is the rate-limiting enzyme in synthesis of the neurotransmitter. Tyrosine hydroxylase activity in the right ventricle was markedly reduced in the affected dogs. Furthermore, there was a highly significant positive correlation when norepinephrine concentration and enzyme activity were related to each other in individual chambers of normal and failing hearts. Thus it appeared highly likely that the reduction of enzyme concentration was responsible for the cardiac neurotransmitter depletion in heart failure. What caused the reduced enzyme activity and depleted norepinephrine stores remains a puzzle.

The biochemical abnormality did not seem to play a primary role. It

seemed more likely that the reduced enzyme activity and depletion of norepinephrine occurred secondarily, perhaps as a result of a prolonged intensive barrage of sympathetic activity serving to bolster activity of the failing heart. Among findings suggesting that this is so is the fact that patients in whom overall activity of the sympathetic nervous system seems most intense, as reflected in elevated blood and urinary norepinephrine levels, have shown the most striking reductions in neurotransmitter stores. However, at present the mechanism ultimately responsible for the reduction in enzyme activity and norepinephrine synthesis remains to be elucidated. What can be said about the effects of the profound depletion of cardiac neurotransmitter on heart function? Could this be the basis for the intrinsic weakness of failing heart muscle?

It had been shown experimentally in cats that congestive heart failure

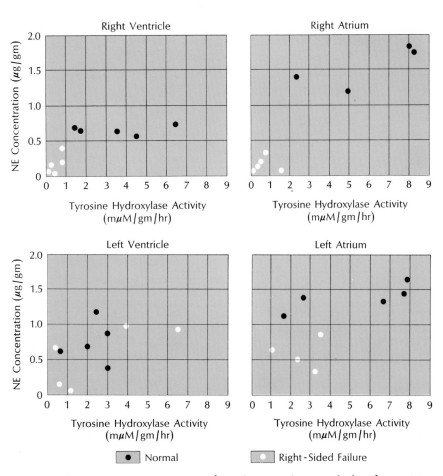

Norepinephrine concentration is expressed as a function of tyrosine hydroxylase activity in dogs with normal hearts and with right heart failure. In animals with right-sided failure, there is severe norepinephrine depletion in the affected right heart chambers.

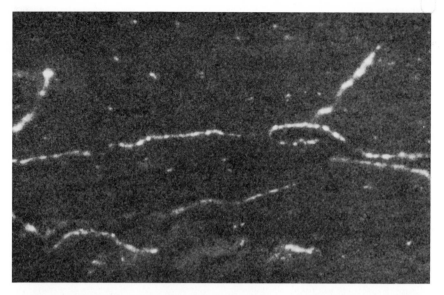

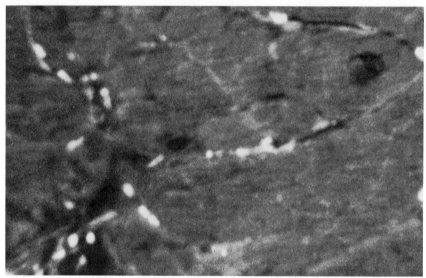

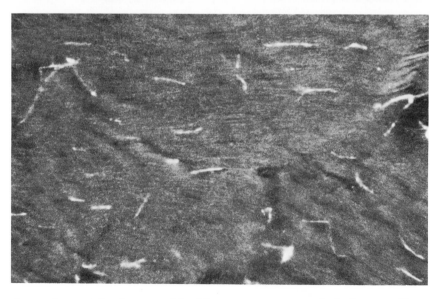

Steer right ventricle when normal (top) has an extensive network of adrenergic fibers; when right heart failure is induced (center), fluorescent fibers are largely depleted, but after recovery from failure (bottom), the sympathetic pathways to the affected chamber are substantially reestablished (Jacobowitz, Chidsey, and Vogel).

is associated with marked depression of the contractile state of cardiac muscle, reflected in a downward shift of the force-velocity curve and a reduction in the speed of contraction. The ventricles from which these failing muscles were removed had been found depleted of cardiac norepinephrine. But the question remained whether the cardiac norepinephrine depletion as such was responsible for the depression of contractile performance in the failing heart. To find the answer it was necessary to examine the contractile state of cardiac muscle depleted of norepinephrine by a mechanism other than heart failure. The method selected entailed total chronic extrinsic denervation by means of mediastinal neural ablation (an operative procedure developed by Dr. Theodore Cooper); the cat papillary muscle was selected since extrinsic cardiac denervation had already proved feasible in this species. These experiments were also aided by newer methods for extending quantitative analysis of the mechanical properties of skeletal muscle to isolated preparations of myocardium.

Findings were compared in muscles obtained from normal animals and from those depleted of norepinephrine by cardiac denervation or by treatment with reserpine. The contractile state of the norepinephrine-depleted myocardium proved well within normal limits, whether depletion was achieved pharmacologically or with use of cardiac denervation. There was little difference in the three groups in terms of resting and active length-tension curves or force-velocity relations, or in augmentation of isometric tension achieved by paired electrical stimulation or by increasing the frequency of contraction in stepwise increments. It seemed evident then that the cardiac norepinephrine depletion that occurs in congestive heart failure is not responsible for the depression of failing heart muscle. Apparently cardiac stores of norepinephrine are not fundamental to maintaining the intrinsic contractile state of the myocardium. However, other findings indicate that cardiac norepinephrine depletion may seriously impair adrenergic function by interfering with release and transmission of neurotransmitter. For example, in one pertinent study the norepinephrine concentration in heart muscle was related to its ability to augment tension on stimulation with the norepinephrine-releasing sympathetic amine tyramine. The muscles were obtained from patients undergoing cardiac surgery. There was a significant correlation between norepinephrine concentration and maximum tension. Only muscles with higher concentrations could increase active tension further in response to tyramine, indicating impaired release in muscles having significantly reduced stores of neurotransmitter.

Another pertinent finding is that norepinephrine-depleted muscle from the failing heart remains at least normally responsive to exogenous norepinephrine. When the inotropic effect of l-norepinephrine was compared in heart muscle of normal cats and cats with pulmonary artery constriction, all muscles responded to exogenous norepinephrine with a normal and, in some instances, even a supernormal increase in tension. This observation, coupled with the knowledge that circulating norepinephrine concentration is markedly increased in heart failure, strengthens the proposal that the circulating catecholamines may for a time play an important role in maintaining the contractile function of the failing heart. However, with progres-

sive heart failure and increasing dependence on sympathetic activity, the circulating catecholamines may no longer be able to provide sufficient support. Gradually, as the cardiac norepinephrine stores become seriously depleted, there develops a relative deficiency of sympathetic function, which in turn adversely affects contractile function. If at this point a drug such as a beta-adrenergic receptor blocker that prevents circulating catecholamine from stimulating the myocardium is administered, the patient's condition may be aggravated rather than improved.

The suggestion that there may be significant interference with transmission of sympathetic impulses as heart failure advances is based on experiments in dogs subjected to graded electrical stimulation of sympathetic nerves. Chronotropic and inotropic responses were compared in normal dogs and in dogs with right heart failure and cardiac norepinephrine depletion. Increments in heart rate and in ventricular contractile force were sharply reduced in the dogs with heart failure. In these same experiments it was shown that the heart muscle of dogs with heart failure continued to respond to exogenously administered norepinephrine.

Thus, while the norepinephrine de-

pletion of congestive failure does not impair cardiac performance by altering the basic contractile state of the heart, it may indeed impair it by interfering with the augmentation in contractility that normally is readily provided by the sympathetic nervous system. From studies to date, a key defect seems to be a drastic decrease in the quantity of neurotransmitter released per nerve impulse. The reduction in maximal response to sympathetic stimulation seen in animals with experimental failure suggests that even an abnormal increase in the impulse traffic along the cardiac sympathetic nerves does not substantially augment the contractile state of the myocardium. In this way, a critical mechanism for improving contractile force of the failing heart may go awry, unfortunately at the very time when it is sorely needed to prevent intensification of the heart failure.

While the discussion up to this point has been confined to a consideration of the sympathetic division of the autonomic nervous system, recent research has focused attention on the parasympathetic division. Actually, our understanding of the latter precedes that of the former. The Nobel prize winning studies of Otto Loewi at the beginning of this century not only provided proof for the release of

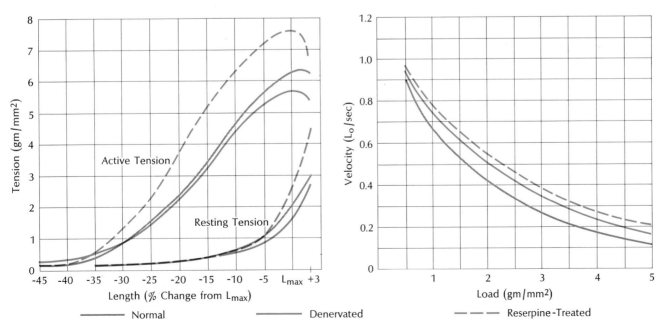

Normal ————— Denervated ————— Reserpine-Treated – – – –

No significant changes from normal values were observed in the length-tension relationships in cat papillary muscles when norepinephrine supplies were essentially eliminated by either cardiac denervation or treatment with reserpine (left). Similarly, normal curves were elicited in norepinephrine-depleted muscles in terms of the force-velocity relationships (graph at right). Velocity in this context is the velocity of shortening of the muscle fibers and serves as an index of cardiac contractility.

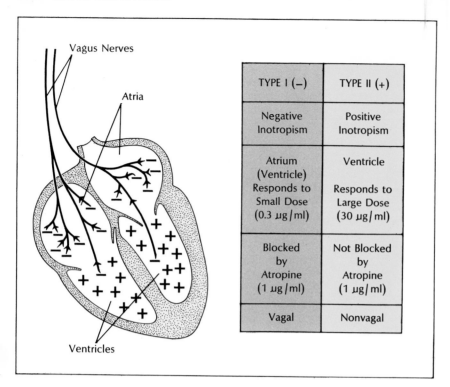

TYPE I (−)	TYPE II (+)
Negative Inotropism	Positive Inotropism
Atrium (Ventricle) Responds to Small Dose (0.3 μg/ml)	Ventricle Responds to Large Dose (30 μg/ml)
Blocked by Atropine (1 μg/ml)	Not Blocked by Atropine (1 μg/ml)
Vagal	Nonvagal

Schematic above shows two types of cholinergic receptor sites in the heart. Dose responses are to acetylcholine (adapted from Buccino et al by permission of the American Heart Association).

an active substance during stimulation of the vagus nerve of the perfused frog heart, and thus laid the groundwork for modern concepts of neurohumoral transmission, but they gave early indication of the complexities of vagal control of the heart. Loewi's observations could not be immediately corroborated by other investigators because of technical difficulties arising from inadvertent stimulation of sympathetic fibers in the mixed vagosympathetic trunk; in some instances stimulation of this trunk produced cardiac inhibition and at other times acceleration. The intimate anatomical association of sympathetic and parasympathetic fibers innervating the heart and the complex interactions between adrenergic and cholinergic mechanisms have caused the subject of the parasympathetic control of the heart to be clouded by conflicting observations. For many years the parasympathetic system was considered to be of little if any importance in the control of cardiac function. However, an ever increasing number of histological and physiological studies now indicate the existence and physiological importance of the terminal parasympathetic innervation of

the myocardium, the specialized conduction fibers, and the coronary vessels.

In the last decade, evidence has been obtained which indicates that the terminal innervation of the ventricles as well as the atria includes parasympathetic nerve fibers. The demonstration of ganglia within the ventricular myocardium suggested the presence of parasympathetic nerve fibers, and the vagal nature of these ganglia was supported by their persistence after total surgical cardiac denervation and cardiac transplantation. Although it is now clear that parasympathetic fibers are present throughout the ventricles, their density is considerably sparser in these chambers than in the atria. Furthermore, the vagal trunks receive abundant sympathetic fibers from the stellate ganglia via the ansa subclavia and actually are mixed parasympathetic-sympathetic trunks. Activation of the parasympathetic nerves results in release of acetylcholine from postganglionic nerve endings.

Cholinergic interventions produce their action upon the heart by a variety of mechanisms. The inhibitory actions appear to be closely related to their ability to decrease the duration

of the action potential and subsequent cellular influx of ionic calcium (see Chapter 2, "Contractile Proteins in the Normal and Failing Myocardium," by Katz). In addition, acetylcholine reduces adenyl cyclase activity and adenosine 3':5'-cyclic phosphate (cyclic AMP) accumulation of broken cell preparations from mammalian atria and ventricles. Since cyclic AMP is a powerful stimulant of cardiac contractility, its reduction would be expected to reduce contractility. On the other hand, under special conditions, for example after atropine administration, cholinergic interventions may cause stimulatory effects. There is now abundant evidence to indicate that acetylcholine releases norepinephrine from depots in the heart that are located predominantly in postganglionic adrenergic nerve fibers.

Cholinergic and sympathetic influences interact synergistically and antagonistically in their actions upon the heart. It appears that under conditions involving a high level of sympathetic tone, the vagal center in the medulla is inhibited by higher centers in the hypothalamus. In addition, cholinergic and sympathetic mechanisms interact at the receptor level; the inhibitory actions of acetylcholine on automaticity and contractility of atrial tissue predominate over the excitatory actions of catecholamines.

Although an inhibitory effect of the vagi upon *ventricular* contractility has been questioned for many years, recent investigations by Levy and his associates have clearly indicated that stimulation of the vagosympathetic trunk produces a negative inotropic effect on the ventricle. In addition, there is now convincing evidence that stimulation of parasympathetic nerve fibers produces distinct vasodilatation in the coronary vascular bed.

Parasympathetic nerve fibers in the vagosympathetic trunk form a portion of the efferent limb of a number of cardiovascular reflexes. Depending upon the type of stimulus and the afferent receptor stimulated, vagal inhibitory influences on heart rate or contractility, or both, may be activated, whereas under opposite circumstances tonic vagal restraint may be withdrawn. Studies in our laboratory have shown that in conscious human subjects and dogs at rest, the predominant mechanism of reflex slowing as a consequence of arterial pressure elevation is through parasympathetic activation, and most of the immediate cardiac acceleration during exercise is by means of withdrawal of parasympathetic restraint.

Recently, a new technique has been devised by Bristow, Smyth, and co-workers for evaluating the sensitivity of the baroreceptor reflex to pharmacologically induced acute elevations in arterial pressure. Since the reflex bradycardia observed with activation of this reflex has been shown to be unaffected by prior beta-adrenergic receptor blockade but is abolished by atropine, this technique appears also to be a sensitive test for evaluating the parasympathetic control of the heart under a variety of conditions and disease states. We have demonstrated, in a group of conscious, unsedated patients with chronically implanted carotid sinus nerve stimulators, that the reflex bradycardia induced by direct stimulation of this nerve is not attenuated by propranolol but is abolished by atropine administration. In order to evaluate the influence of background autonomic activity on this reflex, it was reevaluated with the patients standing and during moderate treadmill exercise. While standing up did not alter the response, the prolongation of the R-R interval observed under stimulation of the carotid sinus nerves during treadmill exercise was strikingly reduced in subjects who had not received atropine.

Recent studies in our laboratories have indicated a profound blunting of this vagally mediated component of the baroreceptor reflex in conscious human subjects with various heart diseases and in conscious dogs with cardiac hypertrophy or failure, or both. The slope of the regression line, relating the prolongation of the R-R interval to this rise in systolic arterial pressure during the transient elevation of arterial pressure induced by an intravenous injection of l-phenylephrine, was a small fraction of the normal in human subjects and dogs with cardiac disease. The difference between the normal response and the response in heart failure was not altered by propranolol, whereas reflex slowing was abolished by atropine. The extent of this dysfunction of the baroreceptor reflex arc appeared to be a function of the severity of the cardiac abnormality, since the dogs with hypertrophy but without overt heart failure had less reduction of sensitivity than those with overt heart failure.

Furthermore, the increases in resting heart rate induced by administering atropine after propranolol were found to be substantially less in patients with heart disease than in normal individuals. Similarly, atropine produced much less tachycardia in conscious dogs with experimental heart failure than in normal healthy dogs. These findings were interpreted as showing a reduced degree of parasympathetic restraint on the sinoatrial node. Another study noted an absence of tachycardia after atropine administration and less reflex bradycardia during acutely induced hypertension in patients with chronic Chagas' disease of the heart, compared to patients with a variety of other cardiomyopathies. The results of all of these studies, then, point to a prominent defect in cardiac control by the parasympathetic as well as the sympathetic system in patients with heart disease. The mechanisms responsible for this defect have not been clearly established.

Regardless of the precise mechanism responsible for the observed defect in parasympathetic function, it is interesting to speculate on its possible functional relevance. The ability to alter heart rate constitutes an extremely important mechanism by which the cardiac output is adjusted. Indeed, under normal circumstances, changes in heart rate account in large measure for changes in cardiac output, alterations in stroke volume playing a far less important part. Only when the ability to vary ventricular rate is impaired, as in atrioventricular block or during electrical stimulation at a constant rate or after surgical denervation, are changes in cardiac output mediated primarily by alterations in stroke volume. In patients with impaired cardiac reserve, the ability of stroke volume to rise is, of course, limited, and when this limitation is combined with defective control of heart rate, it may contribute importantly to the inability to raise cardiac output appropriately.

There is now substantial evidence that the ventricular myocardium also possesses a parasympathetic innervation, which, when activated, whether directly or by reflex, reduces myocardial contractility. If the demonstrated impaired function of parasympathetic control involves not only the fibers innervating the sinoatrial node but also the ventricles, it might be responsible for additional loss of the fine control of cardiac activity provided the normal heart by the autonomic nervous system.

In conclusion, the impairment in parasympathetic cardiovascular regulation, when coupled with the loss of sympathetic nervous system control associated with cardiac norepinephrine depletion, limits the ability to augment cardiac output either by elevating stroke volume or heart rate. These derangements of the autonomic nervous system may well play critical roles in the limited cardiac response to exercise characteristic of heart failure.

7

Hemodynamic Aspects of Cardiac Failure

HAROLD T. DODGE

University of Washington

The heart may be unable to pump an adequate supply of blood to meet the metabolic needs of the body because of impaired myocardial performance or because of a mechanical defect that imposes an excessive workload, or, quite often, a combination of myocardial and mechanical factors. Through various adaptive mechanisms, primarily chamber hypertrophy and/or dilatation, cardiac output may be maintained despite advancing heart disease. When these mechanisms are no longer adequate to maintain cardiac output at a level that satisfies body requirements, the clinical syndrome of congestive heart failure develops (see Chapter 9, "The Clinical Manifestations of Cardiac Failure in Adults," by Perloff).

For rational management of not only heart failure but also the disorders preceding it, it may be critically important to evaluate precisely cardiac performance as affected by the mechanical and (or) myocardial factors present. However, until recently there were no satisfactory techniques available for quantifying the necessary data. Clinically, it is often obvious that a patient is developing signs of cardiac dilatation or hypertrophy as compensation for decreased myocardial contractility or increased mechanical loads. But it may be difficult to determine when in the course of heart disease the compensatory mechanisms have become inadequate to prevent congestive failure. Conventional pressure and flow measurements give valuable information but they frequently tell relatively little about the effectiveness of the heart as a muscle and as a pulsatile pump. More precise means have been developed for defining the changes in ventricular anatomy and function that occur with disease. Within the past several years techniques utilizing angiocardiography have made such measurements possible. Their use has greatly increased our understanding of the hemodynamic adjustments in chronic heart disease, in particular those leading to left ventricular failure. They have also made possible more definitive evaluation and improved management of patients.

In our initial work in this field, conducted before 1956, we attempted, through studies in postmortem hearts distended with known amounts of contrast material (barium sulfate paste), to establish a method for quantifying changes in left ventricular volume in man by use of biplane angiocardiography. The preparation was suspended over the angiocardiographic unit and biplane x-rays were made on the hearts as they were rotated into differing positions with respect to the x-ray tubes and films. Volumes calculated from biplane films of the opacified left ventricle were compared with the known volumes. In addition, the effects of position and rotation on projections of the left ventricle were studied by use of clay models patterned on opacified left ventricular chambers.

In this and subsequent investigations it was assumed that the left ventricle could best be represented as an ellipsoid, since earlier work by several investigators had shown that total heart volume calculated from an ellipsoid geometric reference figure gave results tallying closely with directly measured heart volume. The method we have used is based on measurement of chamber area and maximal chamber length.

The margins of the projected image are traced, and each respective diameter (D) is derived from its respective planimetered area (A) and its maximum length (L_m) as follows:

$$\frac{D}{2} = \frac{2A}{\pi L_m}$$

Left ventricular volumes (V) are then calculated using the formula for the volume of an ellipsoid:

$$V = \frac{4}{3} \pi \frac{D_a}{2} \times \frac{D_l}{2} \times \frac{L_m}{2}$$

where D_a and D_l are the respective diameters in the anteroposterior and lateral views calculated by the first equation and L_m is the longest measured length whether on the anteroposterior or lateral roentgenogram. All measurements are corrected for nonparallel x-ray beam distortion (by means of a correction factor derived from the distance of the estimated center of mass of the opacified left ventricular chamber to the x-ray tubes and films). Calculated volumes are corrected by a regression equation:

$$V' = 0.928V - 3.8 \text{ ml}$$

in which V' is the adjusted volume and V the volume calculated by the previous equation. The regression equation was determined from the studies of postmortem hearts distended with known volumes of contrast medium.

With the autopsy studies as a foundation, experiments were performed in a small group of patients with and without heart disease. Left ventricular volume was related to left ventricular filling pressure. Clinically, an increase in left ventricular filling pressure has been considered a reliable early sign of left ventricular weakness. However, animal studies suggested an increase in end-diastolic volume to be a more consistent indicator. Observations among these patients—later amply confirmed in more detailed investigations of larger groups—indicated that in man with chronic heart disease there are marked patient-to-patient differences in end-diastolic volume for a given filling pressure. These studies indicated that changes in left ventricular volume are likely to be a more sensitive index than changes in filling pressure of left ventricular dysfunction and incipient heart failure.

In collaboration with Dr. J. Ward Kennedy and others, we established normal values for left ventricular volumes through angiocardiagraphic studies of 22 adults who had no evidence of heart disease. Between 40 and 60 cc of contrast material were rapidly injected into either the pulmonary artery, left ventricle, or left atrium, and six films per second were taken during the phase of ventricular opacification. The mean for left ventricular end-diastolic volume proved to be 70 ± 20 ml per square meter of body surface area; thus volume in an average-sized adult would be in the range of 120 to 130 ml. Mean end-systolic volume was found to be 24 ± 10 ml/m²; mean stroke volume was 45 ± 13 ml/m². The ratio of stroke volume to end-

diastolic volume, or the systolic ejection fraction, showed a narrow range of variation, with a mean of 0.67 ± 0.08.

As part of this study, normal values were also established for left ventricular wall thickness and muscle mass, using an angiocardiographic technique for calculating ventricular mass also worked out in our laboratories. Again, our aim was to devise a quantitative method for use in determining normal values and then to use it to elucidate the changes occurring with advancing heart disease and failure. In observations on normal subjects, mean left ventricular wall thickness during diastole was 8.9 mm for women and 11.9 mm for men; mean left ventricu-

lar mass was 76 gm/m² for women and 99 gm/m² for men.

With the method we have used, left ventricular mass is considered to include the weight of the free wall of the left ventricle and the entire thickness of the interventricular septum. A segment of free left ventricular wall as visualized on the anteroposterior film is selected and its area determined by planimetry. Average thickness is obtained by dividing segment area by segment length. To determine left ventricular weight the following method is used: First, left ventricular chamber volumes are calculated by use of the formula for the volume of the ellipsoid as cited above. Volume of chamber plus muscle wall

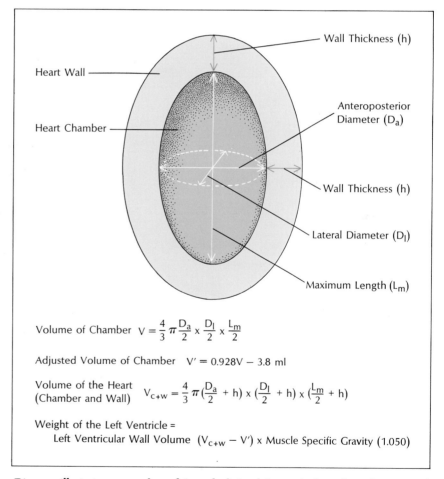

Volume of Chamber $V = \dfrac{4}{3}\pi \dfrac{D_a}{2} \times \dfrac{D_l}{2} \times \dfrac{L_m}{2}$

Adjusted Volume of Chamber $V' = 0.928V - 3.8 \text{ ml}$

Volume of the Heart (Chamber and Wall) $V_{c+w} = \dfrac{4}{3}\pi \left(\dfrac{D_a}{2} + h\right) \times \left(\dfrac{D_l}{2} + h\right) \times \left(\dfrac{L_m}{2} + h\right)$

Weight of the Left Ventricle = Left Ventricular Wall Volume $(V_{c+w} - V') \times$ Muscle Specific Gravity (1.050)

Diagram illustrates approach used for calculating left ventricular volume by means of quantitative angiocardiography. Margins of projected image of left ventricular chamber are traced and maximum length is measured in anteroposterior and lateral views. Minor axes are derived from the planimetered areas of the chamber in both views; all dimensions are corrected for distortion from nonparallel x-rays. Left ventricular volumes are calculated using the formula for the volume of an ellipsoid since (with regression-equation adjustment) this has given results that tally closely with directly measured ventricular volume. To determine left ventricular mass, volume of the ventricular chamber is subtracted from volume of chamber plus wall; multiplying wall volume by the specific gravity of cardiac muscle converts volume to heart weight or mass.

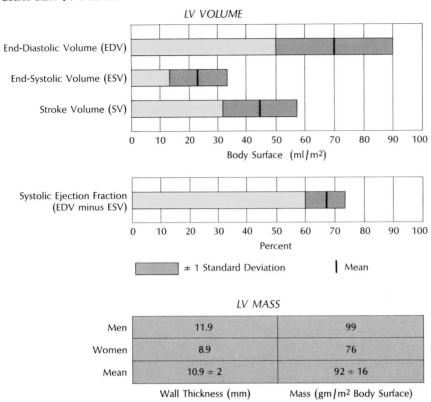

LV VOLUME

End-Diastolic Volume (EDV)

End-Systolic Volume (ESV)

Stroke Volume (SV)

0 10 20 30 40 50 60 70 80 90 100

Body Surface (ml/m²)

Systolic Ejection Fraction
(EDV minus ESV)

0 10 20 30 40 50 60 70 80 90 100

Percent

± 1 Standard Deviation | Mean

LV MASS

	Wall Thickness (mm)	Mass (gm/m² Body Surface)
Men	11.9	99
Women	8.9	76
Mean	10.9 ± 2	92 ± 16

Use of quantitative angiocardiography and cardiac catheterization, in a group of adults demonstrated to be free of heart disease, to determine values for left ventricular volume gave the mean and ± 1 standard deviation shown by the darker color in the bars of top graph. Normal values for left ventricular wall thickness and mass are given in table.

(V_{c+w}) is determined according to the equation:

$$V_{c+w} = \frac{4}{3}\pi\left(\frac{D_a}{2} + h\right) \times \left(\frac{D_1}{2} + h\right) \times \left(\frac{L_m}{2} + h\right)$$

where h equals wall thickness, and D_a, D_1, and L_m are axes, as previously defined.

The volume of muscle mass was computed by subtracting the volume of the chamber, V', from the volume of chamber plus wall, V_{c+w}. The weight of muscle was determined as the product of muscle volume and 1.050, which is the specific gravity of heart muscle.

This method was also developed and tested in studies on postmortem hearts. In these hearts, with left ventricular weights ranging from 121 to 453 gm, the left ventricles were distended with known volumes of contrast material and biplane x-ray films taken, and chamber volume and ventricular mass were calculated as described above. The calculated values agreed closely with the directly measured ventricular weights.

In several patients, this method was further tested by comparing left ventricular mass as calculated from angiocardiograms performed up to 15 months prior to death with left ventricular weight as determined at postmortem examination. There was good correlation between calculated and measured values for ventricular weight in all but one subject, in whom left ventricular mass was misjudged because right ventricular hypertrophy led to an overestimation of left ventricular wall thickness. It was concluded that this technique for determining left ventricular mass would also be subject to error if there were pericardial effusion, since the left ventricular wall would appear abnormally thickened, or if the left heart border were obscured by a pleural effusion, or if a ventricular aneurysm involved the free wall of the left ventricle. With these exceptions, it appeared that determinations of ventricular mass, along with determinations of ventricular dimensions and volume, could provide information currently available in no other way on hemodynamic changes in heart failure.

When these techniques were applied in groups of patients with various types of chronic heart disease, the hemodynamic changes differed substantially according to type of heart disease, that is, whether it was due primarily to myocardial or mechanical factors, and, if mechanical, whether the problem was one of volume or pressure overload on the heart. The findings served to document the truly remarkable hemodynamic adjustments that can be made by a diseased heart before clinically evident heart failure supervenes. They also helped to define the limits of compensation achievable through such mechanisms as dilatation and hypertrophy. In a sense both dilatation and hypertrophy may be viewed as early manifestations of cardiac decompensation; once they appear, the heart already has a diminished capacity to handle further increases in mechanical load or further decreases in myocardial contractility.

Among patients with chronic volume overload — that is, with aortic or mitral valve insufficiency — both the left ventricular end-diastolic and end-systolic volumes are significantly increased in proportion to regurgitant and stroke volumes. The more severe the valvular insufficiency, the larger the stroke volume. As much as 300 ml of blood may be ejected with each heart beat, or four to five times more than the normal stroke volume; this appears to be the upper limit possible, but clearly the heart can adjust to such chronic volume loads at least for a while. Left ventricular minute outputs as large as 25 to 30 liters are observed in such patients.

Significantly, in most patients with valvular insufficiency, the systolic ejection fraction is similar to that seen in patients without heart disease: approximately two thirds of the end-diastolic volume is ejected during systole. The appropriate level of diastolic volume for a given stroke volume can be estimated from the systolic ejection fraction. With stroke volumes of 250 to 300 ml, the end-diastolic volume is appropriately enlarged to values in excess of 400 ml. The primary means of augmenting stroke volume is by dilatation of the ventricular chamber as predicted by the Frank-Starling hypothesis (see Chapter 1, "Myocardial Ultrastructure in the Normal and

Failing Heart," by Sonnenblick). Although the wall thickness of the ventricle remains essentially normal, overall mass of ventricular muscle is increased along with the ventricular dilation. Ventricular dilation of more than mild degree appears not to occur until very late in patients with chronic heart disease in the absence of ventricular hypertrophy, i.e., without muscle mass increase.

With chronic pressure overload on the heart, as in aortic stenosis, the systolic ejection fraction and end-diastolic volume remain essentially normal until very late in the course of the disease. The left ventricle functions with work loads that are as much as two to three times normal. The chief hemodynamic adjustment here is hypertrophy of the chamber walls with a demonstrable increase in both wall thickness and the mass of ventricular muscle. In this instance, too, the heart can withstand great demands, but there are definite upper limits of adaptation. Weight of the hypertrophied left ventricle rarely exceeds 900 gm and such massive hypertrophy occurs with aortic valve insufficiency or when there is both a pressure and volume overload.

In earlier acute experiments performed in animals, hemodynamic adjustment to pressure overloads was shown to involve dilatation of the heart and a reduction in ejection fraction, which is in disagreement with the findings described above in patients with chronic heart disease. Since the earlier findings were obtained in acute experiments they were evidently not applicable to patients with chronic heart disease. The differences observed appear to be related to development of hypertrophy in response to pressure loads in the course of chronic heart disease.

Additional clinical investigations brought out significant contrasts in hemodynamic response to myocardial disease as against mechanical problems due either to volume or pressure overloads. For example, patients with myocardial disease usually have an increased left ventricular diastolic volume; however, the left ventricle is inappropriately dilated with respect to stroke volume so that the systolic ejection fraction is reduced and the end-systolic, or residual, volume increased. Left ventricular end-diastolic

volume is increased in some patients to above 500 ml, again some five times the normal value. The systolic ejection fraction in patients studied to date has been as low as 0.08. This low value, indicating excessive left ventricular dilatation relative to stroke volume, is one of the hemodynamic hallmarks of chronic myocardial disease.

Values for the systolic ejection fraction of less than 0.5 are generally considered abnormal and indicative of inappropriate ventricular dilatation to compensate for myocardial disease. As in valvular disease with volume overloads, the heart maintains stroke volume primarily through the mechanism of dilatation. Overall weight of the left ventricle is also increased, but

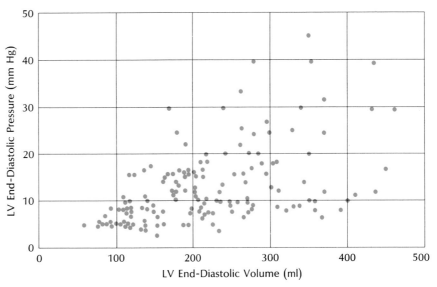

When data from 160 patients with chronic heart disease are plotted by relating left ventricular end-diastolic volume and end-diastolic pressure, the wide range of volumes at any given level of filling pressure is clearly seen. Only when volumes are in excess of 400 ml is the end-diastolic pressure likely to be consistently elevated; volumes three to four times normal may occur with normal diastolic pressure. There are also patients with elevated filling pressures and normal or only slightly enlarged volumes.

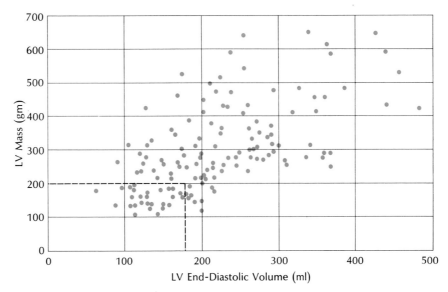

In chronic heart disease left ventricular dilatation is associated with ventricular hypertrophy whether or not there is an increased level of pressure-volume work. Actually, ventricular dilatation of more than a mild degree does not seem to occur in the absence of ventricular hypertrophy, as shown here when left ventricular mass is plotted against end-diastolic volume in 144 patients with various types of heart disease. Normal limits of volume and mass are indicated by dashed lines at lower left.

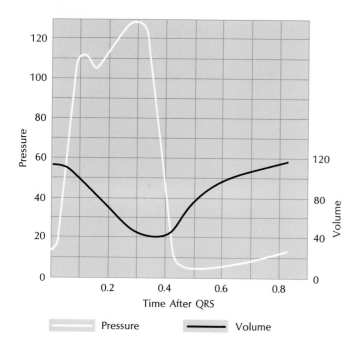

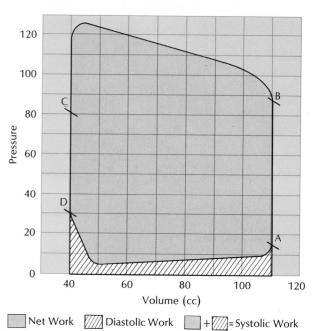

▭ Net Work	▨ Diastolic Work	▨ + ▨ = Systolic Work

Left ventricular pressure and volume curves are related with respect to time (panel at left) to construct a pressure-volume curve (panel at right). Systolic pressure-volume work is determined from the systolic pressure-volume relationships. Work expended in distending the diastolic left ventricle is determined from pressure-volume relations during diastole. At A above, mitral valve closes; B, aortic valve opens; C, aortic valve closes; D, mitral valve opens. Mitral valve opens at elevated ventricular diastolic pressure because of elevated left atrial pressure due to mitral valve stenosis.

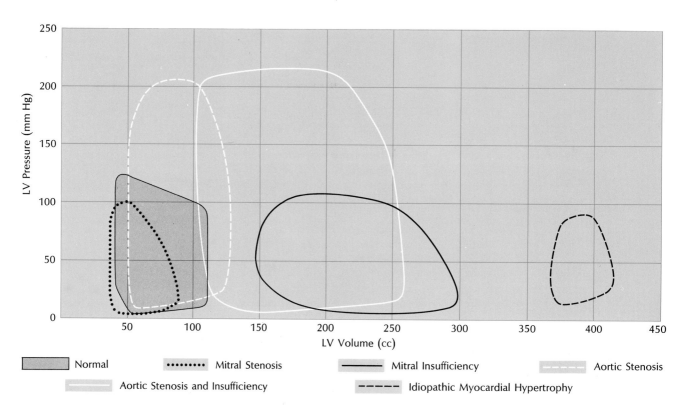

▨ Normal	••••••• Mitral Stenosis	───── Mitral Insufficiency	────── Aortic Stenosis
═════ Aortic Stenosis and Insufficiency		─ ─ ─ ─ Idiopathic Myocardial Hypertrophy	

In left ventricular pressure-volume curves from patients with different varieties of heart disease, height of each curve is determined by systolic pressure and width by stroke volume. The two smallest curves — one from a patient with mitral stenosis, the other from a patient with primary cardiomyopathy — indicate similar stroke volumes; however, in the latter the dilated left ventricle is functioning at an inappropriately large volume and ejection fraction is low. Mitral insufficiency curve demonstrates volume overload by the large excursion along the volume axis and the absence of an isovolumic contraction period. Shape of the aortic stenosis curve shows the effect of pressure overload. Aortic stenosis and insufficiency curve demonstrates influence of pressure and volume overload, with the large area subtended by the curve and accordingly large pressure-volume work value.

with wall thickness remaining essentially normal.

The relationship of stroke volume and end-diastolic volume as expressed by the systolic ejection fraction appears to provide a means for evaluating myocardial performance in the presence of mechanical defects that impose a chronic pressure or volume overload on the left ventricle. A depressed ejection fraction indicates the presence of depressed myocardial performance in addition to the mechanical defect.

In many of the patients studied, elevations of ventricular end-diastolic pressure were present whether ventricular failure resulted from an increased mechanical load or from myocardial disease. In addition there are large patient-to-patient differences in left-ventricular pressure-volume relationships. Diastolic volumes three to four times normal are seen with diastolic pressures within the normal range. This is particularly observed in patients with long-standing ventricular dilatation from volume overloads resulting from aortic or mitral valve insufficiency or from chronic left ventricular myocardial disease. Accordingly, chronic ventricular dilatation is often associated with changes in the elastic properties of the left ventricle, so that the ventricle is more distensible and functions at a large volume with an essentially normal level of filling pressure (see Chapter 1 by Sonnenblick). Decreased ventricular distensibility is often observed in conditions associated with ventricular hypertrophy and increased left ventricular wall thickness as occurs in response to pressure overloads. Under these conditions there may be striking elevation of ventricular diastolic pressure in the presence of normal diastolic volume. An elevated left ventricular filling pressure with a normal or only slightly enlarged diastolic volume also occurs with ischemic heart disease. Ventricular distensibility and its influence on ventricular filling pressure and pulmonary venous pressure are important in considering the pathophysiology of heart failure because many of the symptoms of left ventricular failure are related to pulmonary venous hypertension.

Through the kinds of measurements described, what is obtained essentially is an analysis of the perform-

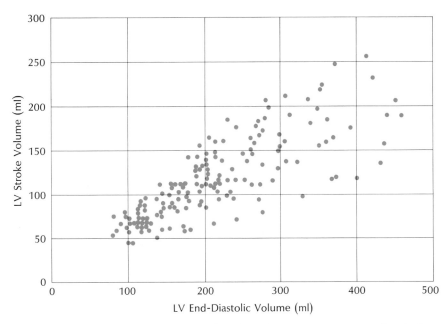

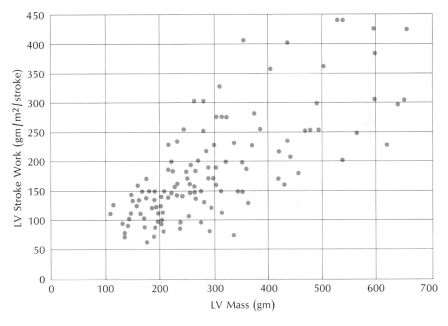

When stroke volume was related to end-diastolic volume in 165 patients with valvular disorders, largest volumes were found in those with greater degrees of aortic or mitral insufficiency (see graph above). These conditions are associated with volume overload. Plotting the left ventricular mass against the level of stroke work (see graph below) also gave a positive correlation.

ance of the heart as a pump, in terms of the size or volume of the pump, its weight or mass, the amount of blood ejected per beat, and so on. More information on pump performance can be obtained when these measurements are related to those of chamber pressure. Ventricular volume and pressure may be related to each other over an entire cardiac cycle to construct a pressure-volume curve. This is a closed loop with the timing of valve opening and closing indicated therein;

height and width of the curve are determined by the systolic pressure and stroke volume respectively (see graph 74, bottom)

The area subtended by the systolic portion of the curve provides a measure of left ventricular systolic stroke work; the area subtended by the diastolic limb provides a measure of diastolic work performed in distending the ventricle during diastole. Net work is the difference between the two; considering the left ventricle as a pump, net work is the difference between work output of and work input to the ventricular chamber.

Diastolic work may be viewed as energy supplied in priming the pump; with left ventricular failure and a rise in diastolic pressure there is an increase in diastolic work relative to systolic work and thus a decrease in net work. Values for diastolic work may be three to four times above normal under these conditions. In the absence of valvular insufficiency this work is largely generated by the left atrium and the right ventricle; it is the physiologic basis, at least in part, for right ventricular failure seen in patients with left ventricular failure.

Largest values for work expended in filling the diastolic left ventricle are seen in patients with aortic and mitral valve insufficiency, in whom ventricular stroke volume and filling pressure may be greatly increased. Under these conditions a considerable portion of the work of ventricular filling for a given heartbeat comes from energy supplied by the left ventricle in the preceding beat. This work is performed by blood returning to the left ventricle as a consequence of the regurgitant flow.

Pump performance can be further evaluated by relating ventricular work to ventricular chamber volume. This appeared to be a useful approach to the evaluation of ventricular myocardial performance on the basis of acute studies in animals; however, it has proven less useful in patients with chronic heart disease, particularly when the increased ventricular work results from a pressure overload – since then the principal compensatory mechanism is not dilatation but hypertrophy of the ventricle. For this reason, in analyzing ventricular performance in terms of left ventricular work, it may be better to do so relative to left ventricular weight, that is, to express performance as work per unit of weight of left ventricular muscle. With such an analysis myocardial disease is characterized by low work values relative to mass. Unfortunately, such an expression is not responsive to acute changes of work load and would be expected to give false estimates of ventricular performance under such conditions. The illustra-

tion on page 75 shows the relationship between left ventricular stroke work and left ventricular muscle mass in 165 patients with valvular heart disease.

Another way to analyze pump performance is in terms of left ventricular power, referring to the rate at which the ventricle performs its work. In these calculations, power is computed as instantaneous pressure multiplied by the instantaneous velocity of ejection of blood from the left ventricle, the latter determined from the left ventricular volume curve. Ventricular power studies further show the extent of hemodynamic adaptation possible in chronic heart disease: Whereas in normal resting subjects peak power values are in the range of 500 to 600 grammeters per second, values up to four times higher are seen in patients with chronic heart disease.

Experience to date suggests that measurement of ventricular power output may prove the most informative of the methods thus far available for evaluating ventricular function on the basis of pump performance. This is because it includes an expression of

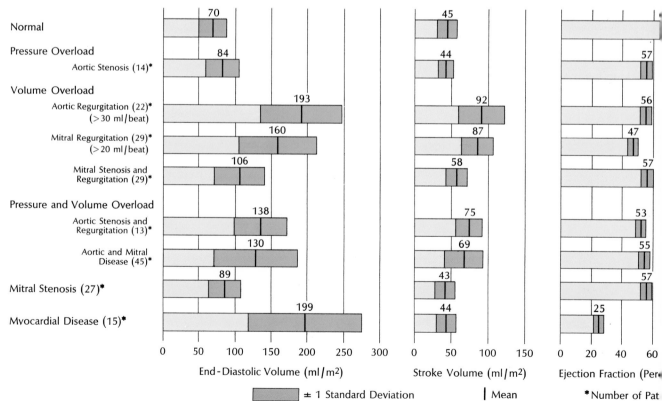

As indicated in graph comparing hemodynamic findings in normal subjects and in patients with various types of heart disease, chamber volumes in valvular disorders associated with pressure overload are similar to those for the normal left ventricle. With volume overload there is dilatation of the left ventricle, the extent of dilatation being proportional to the stroke volume. In most patients with valvular disease approximately two thirds of the end-diastolic volume is ejected with systole, as in normals.

pressure, volume, and also time. It is known from experiments on isolated heart muscle that time-related functions should be taken into account in assessing muscle function. This appears true also for evaluating heart function in the intact animal and man. As with other hemodynamic variables, when the ventricle is considered as a pump, the volume or mass at which power is measured needs to be considered if one is to use power as an index of myocardial performance. This is shown in an illustration on page 78 where power adjusted for end-diastolic volume is related to ejection fraction, the stroke volume adjusted for end-diastolic volume. As shown, in general, patients with a depressed ejection fraction also have depressed power values per unit of end-diastolic volume. The use of cine-angiocardiographic techniques, which provide rapid rates of filming and of high-fidelity pressure recordings, is important in analyzing time-related variables, as must be done in computing ventricular power output.

The use of computer technology has greatly facilitated calculations with

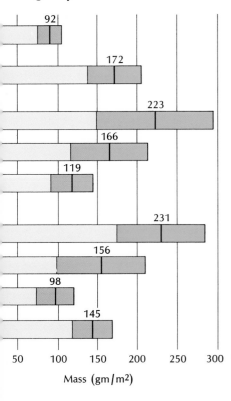

In the cases shown a reduced ejection fraction indicates disproportionate ventricular dilatation and suggests myocardial as well as valvular disease is present.

all the current angiocardiographic techniques for assessing left ventricular function. This is particularly important in analyzing data when fast filming rates are used, because of the large amount of data to be analyzed and calculated. Methods have also been developed for computing left ventricular chamber volumes from angiocardiograms filmed in a single plane, which reduces the amount of data to be analyzed and the cost of x-ray equipment and film. The overestimation of volumes when calculated from films taken in the single anteroposterior or right anterior oblique projection is greater than when calculated from biplane films, but when calculated values are adjusted by appropriate regression equations, volumes calculated by the single plane methods are generally comparable to those calculated by the biplane methods.

Other new approaches to quantifying hemodynamic changes in chronic heart disease are also coming into use, notably the analysis of ventricular performance in terms of wall stress and strain. The aim here is to provide a measurement of heart muscle performance in contrast to measurement of heart pump performance when one looks at the ventricle as a whole. In stress/strain analysis one is looking at the performance of the heart in terms of forces acting directly on the heart muscle during contraction, this being the stress expression. The strain expression refers to the distance the heart muscle is able to contract against a given force. Because of the relationship of wall forces to chamber pressure and chamber dimensions, chamber forces increase as the ventricle dilates. For a given chamber pressure, a dilated left ventricle has greater wall force than does a left ventricle of normal size. This stress/strain analysis will usually reveal increased stress or force per unit area in patients with chronic heart disease compensated chiefly by ventricular dilatation.

Wall force per unit area is also a function of wall thickness. In chronic heart disease associated with ventricular hypertrophy and increased wall thickness – for example, in pressure overload defects such as aortic valve stenosis – the increased wall thickness

tends to maintain wall stress within normal limits.

From stress/strain relationships within the wall of the heart one can calculate work per unit of myocardium – work being the product of stress and strain, or force times distance. In patients with myocardial disease the work per unit of myocardium is reduced relative to normal.

If in addition to the stress/strain analysis one looks at the wall data as a time-related function, in terms of rate of contraction, one can determine the force-velocity relationships within the wall of the heart. Indeed the stress/strain observations with respect to time have become the basis for applying the force-velocity information previously obtained in isolated heart muscle preparations to the heart of the intact experimental animal and the heart of intact man (see Chapter 1 by Sonnenblick).

With the kind of quantitative data obtainable by these techniques for assessing heart pump and muscle performance, it has become feasible to apply them increasingly to the clinical evaluation of patients with chronic heart disease. For example, in a patient with valvular heart disease, a comparison of stroke volume and end-diastolic volume by means of the systolic ejection fraction helps to determine the appropriateness of left ventricular dilatation for the mechanical load placed on the left ventricle by the valvular lesion. A low ejection fraction indicates excessive dilatation of the left ventricle relative to the mechanical load and is therefore evidence for myocardial disease. Myocardial performance can be evaluated more directly and independently of the mechanical load by analysis of wall stress, strain, and velocity relationships; depressed myocardial function results in low myocardial segment work, power, and velocity of contraction.

In a patient with valvular insufficiency, volumetric and peripheral blood flow measurements may be combined to calculate the mechanics of overload and the extent of valvular insufficiency. Granted that such detailed studies may not always be necessary to arrive at clinical decisions, with more complex problems it may be important to obtain a quantitative

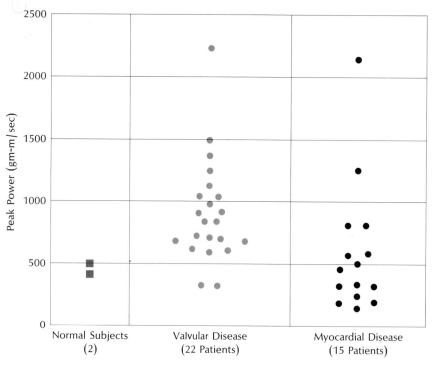

In ventricular power studies, power is computed as instantaneous pressure multiplied by instantaneous velocity of ejection of blood as determined from the LV volume curve. Peak power values up to four and five times higher than the normal range are seen in patients with valvular disease. In myocardial disease, ventricular power is often depressed. Myocardial disease here is based on a depressed ejection fraction. Some of the patients classified as having myocardial disease also had valvular heart disease with pressure and/or volume overloads, accounting for some of their high peak power values.

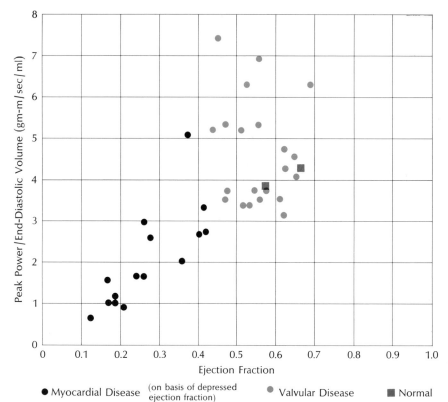

Calculation of ventricular power in relation to end-diastolic volume shows that patients with depressed values for peak power with respect to end-diastolic volume also usually have low stroke volumes relative to end-diastolic volume (low ejection fraction).

assessment of the severity of the mechanical defect.

When there is insufficiency both of aortic and mitral valves, the angiocardiographic techniques combined with a measure of effective cardiac output or forward flow provide a measure of the overall valvular insufficiency but do not permit a separate evaluation of the degree of insufficiency at the mitral and aortic valves. From visual observation of the x-ray images, the severity of leakage through the individual valves is estimated. This information is of value in determining the necessity for correcting individual valve defects.

In a patient with myocardial disease plus a mechanical problem resulting in a pressure or volume overload, the key question can be whether or not, given the possibly increased risk due to the presence of myocardial disease, one should attempt surgery of a potentially correctable mechanical problem. These techniques for evaluating ventricular function permit complex clinical decisions to be made more readily. One can arrive at an index of the severity of myocardial disease and the severity of the mechanical problem and plan accordingly.

This is far from an academic issue, since often more than one kind of heart disease is present. A patient with coronary disease and heart failure may in addition have mitral valve insufficiency as a consequence of papillary muscle dysfunction, or an area of the ventricle that is akinetic, dyskinetic, or aneurysmal. The mechanical defects are amenable to surgery, but the risk of surgery and ultimate benefit to be derived from surgery are likely to be influenced by the level of the myocardial performance and the severity of the mechanical defects, which can be independently evaluated by these newer techniques.

It is also anticipated that with use of these techniques it may prove possible to identify in advance those patients in whom progressive ventricular dilatation or hypertrophy will prove reversible once the mechanical problem is corrected. There is no way of making such a prediction at present, but approaches are now available for learning the answers that were not available even a few years ago.

8

Mechanisms of Salt and Water Retention in Cardiac Failure

JAMES O. DAVIS

University of Missouri

The mechanisms whereby sodium is retained and concomitant edema is produced have been shown to be multifactorial. The interrelationships among many of these factors are illustrated opposite. It has proved convenient to classify the primary elements involved in sodium retention as if they were three discrete factors. In this classification, factor I is reduction in glomerular filtration rate (G F R); factor II is the influence of the hormone aldosterone and of the renin-angiotensin system intimately associated with this adrenocortical sodium-retaining agent; factor III is an additional sodium-retaining factor, or factors, which probably includes a hormone but whose exact nature is still not defined. Indeed, future research may lead to fractionation of factor III into several factors.

The order in which these three factors are listed reflects to a large degree the sequence in which it was discovered that they are important in the retention of salt and water in cardiac failure. It has been generally recognized for decades that decreased cardiac output from the failing myocardium leads to reductions in both renal blood flow (R B F) and G F R. Aldosterone was discovered in 1953 and has been the subject of intensive research since then. Attempts to isolate and characterize factor III have been a major area of concentration for many investigators in recent years.

A reduction in G F R was not only first in chronology of discovery but, clearly, is a very important determinant of sodium retention during acute heart failure. In the patient developing congestive heart failure, an acute reduction in cardiac output leads to a decrease in G F R and this mechanism is extremely effective in decreasing salt and water excretion for the first 24 to 48 hours. Also, a reduction in G F R probably makes a contribution to the signal leading to increased aldosterone secretion via the renin-angiotensin system by decreasing the sodium load to the macula densa.

In chronic heart failure, however, a high plasma level of aldosterone is one of the essential and most important factors leading to sodium retention and edema formation.

The discovery of aldosterone in 1953 followed closely upon the recognition that fecal excretory patterns of patients with congestive heart failure commonly are characterized by low sodium and high potassium concentrations. Shortly thereafter it was found that urinary aldosterone excretion is increased in patients with failure and that its secretion by the adrenals is elevated. In normal individuals, the daily secretion of aldosterone ranges from $50\mu g$ to $200\mu g$. In patients with cardiac failure, aldosterone secretion varies from normal to 25 to 50 times normal and reaches 4 to 5 mg daily in individuals with severe congestive failure. It should be noted that meaningful measurements of aldosterone production can be made only in the presence of normal sodium ingestion since a low sodium intake is itself provocative of aldosterone hypersecretion.

As noted above, the most severe cases of congestive failure are likely to be accompanied by the greatest enhancement of aldosterone secretion and, in general, there is a direct correlation between the level of aldosterone elaboration and the severity of failure. However, the correlation is probably closer still between severity of disease and the peripheral plasma level of the hormone. This is a particularly important parameter since it reflects both of the mechanisms that are operative in aldosterone metabolism, namely, increased secretion by the adrenals and decreased destruction by the liver.

Two basic methods are available for measuring the rate of inactivation or catabolism of aldosterone. In one method, tritiated aldosterone is given intravenously as a constant infusion in an attempt to achieve a constant plasma level

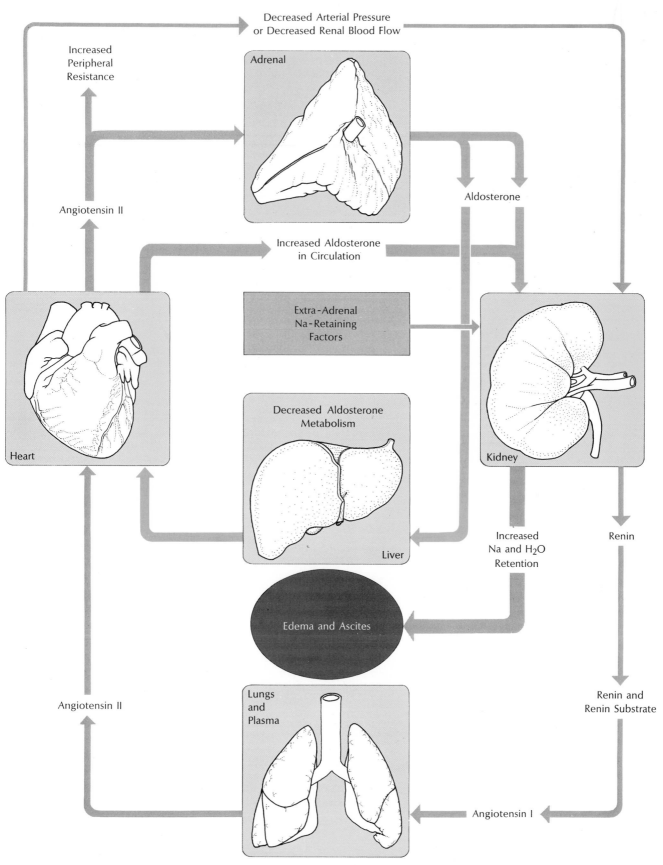

This schematic representation of factors leading to salt and water retention in congestive failure is arranged with the starting point at the cardiac defect that results in decreased renal perfusion pressure and renal plasma flow. This triggers renin release and activates the angiotensin-aldosterone system. In addition to direct effects on the kidney, alterations are present in circulatory dynamics in the liver and the periphery. The role of extra-adrenal Na-retaining factors is also indicated.

of aldosterone-H³. While the infusion proceeds, the plasma level of the steroid hormone is measured at intervals. If the plasma level remains steady, one can deduce that the rate of catabolism or destruction equals the rate of infusion. A decline in the plasma level of aldosterone-H³ indicates a rate of destruction greater than that of infusion while, of course, any increase in plasma level reflects a rate of destruction smaller than that of infusion.

Catabolism can also be gauged by measuring the biologic half-life of the hormone. After either tritiated or C¹⁴-labeled aldosterone is injected intravenously, the rate of destruction can be plotted in terms of the decline in counts per minute of the radioactivity per milliliter of plasma. Normally, in man, it takes 34 minutes for half of the radioactivity in cpm/ml of plasma to disappear from plasma. In individuals in cardiac failure, the biologic half-life of aldosterone is likely to be substantially prolonged and may, for example, be as long as 68 minutes, indicating a catabolic rate of one half normal. Under these circumstances, the decreased rate of aldosterone destruction leads to a rise in the plasma level of the hormone.

The liver is the major site (85% to 90%) for destruction of aldosterone. If one removes the liver from an experimental animal, aldosterone catabolism becomes negligible. Further, by various studies it has been established that the primary determinant of aldosterone destruction by the liver is the rate of hepatic blood flow. Thus, the decline in hepatic blood flow, which of course is secondary to a reduction in cardiac output, can be pinpointed as the major cause of decreased hepatic destruction of aldosterone in the failure patient.

Just as altered cardiac hemodynamics appear to provide the major explanation for reduced catabolism of aldosterone, so do they account for the more important component leading to hyperaldosteronemia in cardiac failure, increased adrenal secretion of the hormone. One of the most characteristic hemodynamic changes in cardiac failure is decreased renal blood flow, again secondary to reduced cardiac output (see page 81). There is evidence to suggest that in some way this decreased renal blood flow or some closely associated functional change is translated by the juxtaglomerular (JG) cells of the kidney (see page 83) into a signal for increased renin release; these changes initiate a sequence of biochemical events (to be discussed later) that eventuates in aldosterone hypersecretion.

Investigators in the field are still far from clear on the nature of the signal perceived by the JG cells. There are two principal theories that, with variations, currently predominate in our thinking. The first is the baroreceptor hypothesis. This holds that the renal afferent arterioles, which contain the highly differentiated JG cells, respond to a decrease in stretch consequent to reduced perfusion pressure and renal blood flow by releasing renin. Important to this hypothesis is the idea first suggested by John Peters at Yale University School of Medicine that a decrease in cardiac output in cardiac failure leads to a decrease in arterial filling. This decrease in arterial filling might be sensed by the JG cells as a decrease in the stretch of the renal afferent arterioles.

A second theoretical schema of the events leading to increased renin release is the so-called macula densa hypothesis. The macula densa is the first portion of the distal tubule and, anatomically, it lies in close approximation with the JG cells of the renal afferent arteriole. It has been postu-

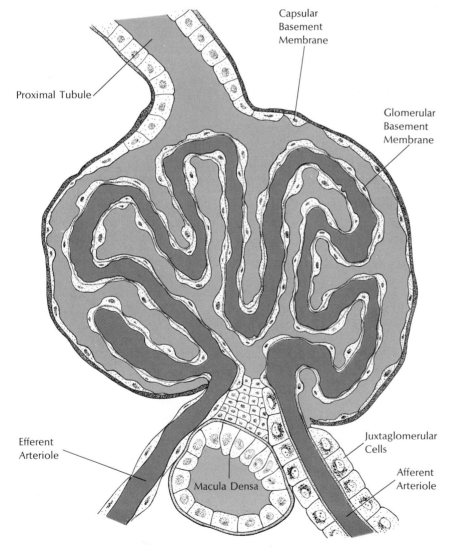

Proximal Tubule

Capsular Basement Membrane

Glomerular Basement Membrane

Efferent Arteriole

Juxtaglomerular Cells

Macula Densa

Afferent Arteriole

In this drawing of juxtaglomerular (JG) cells and the macula densa, one sees the anatomic relationships critical to many of the pathophysiologic events involved in the retention of sodium and water in congestive heart failure. Note the relationship of the JG cells to the lumen of the afferent arteriole into which they secrete renin and the proximity of the macula densa to the JG cells, suggesting its role in signaling renin release.

lated that the signal is a decrease in the sodium load passing the macula densa that activates it to trigger release of renin by the J G cells, perhaps by the mediation of a local hormone. Much of the support for this concept comes from the morphologic observations that establish not only the proximity of the macula densa to the J G complex but also the presence of projections of macula densa cells toward the J G cells.

As is suggested above, the underlying premise of the macula densa hypothesis is that a decreased sodium load reaches the structure. Accordingly, such a decrease in macula densa sodium might occur in cardiac failure before the aldosterone-secretion pathways are initiated. The intermediate mechanism here could be the decreased G F R previously identified as factor I. An acute reduction in G F R is frequently associated with a marked decrease in the renal excretion of sodium. Experimentally, it takes only two to five minutes to induce sodium retention by clamping the aorta and thereby reducing G F R. The precise mechanism whereby a reduction in G F R leads to more complete proximal reabsorption of sodium is unknown. Recent evidence points to the importance of physical factors that occur in association with the decrease in G F R; it has been suggested that increased postglomerular capillary colloid osmotic pressure increases the passive reabsorption of sodium by the proximal tubule. Whatever the mechanism, one may visualize a sequence of events initiated by failure-induced reduction of cardiac output that produces, in turn, a decrease in filtration rate, a reduction in the filtered sodium load, and a decrease in sodium load reaching the macula densa.

However, the above explanation for the events leading to sodium retention is inadequate to explain what occurs in chronic congestive heart failure in the absence of a demonstrable decline in G F R. Under these circumstances, it seems likely that the decreased stretch mechanism in the renal afferent arterioles is operative. It is quite possible that both the baroreceptor and macula densa mechanisms operate in tandem. A secondary mechanism is mediated through the increase in activity of the sympathetic nervous system that occurs in heart failure

Baroreceptor Hypothesis

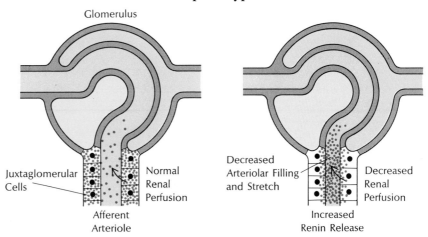

Glomerulus

Juxtaglomerular Cells

Normal Renal Perfusion

Afferent Arteriole

Decreased Arteriolar Filling and Stretch

Decreased Renal Perfusion

Increased Renin Release

Although the exact nature of the "signal" that causes the JG cells to release renin is not fully understood, two theories with variations provide the most widely accepted explanations. The baroreceptor theory postulates that the decreased renal perfusion occurs in association with a known marked reduction of renal blood flow in heart failure and results in incomplete filling at the level of the renal arterioles. This leads to decreased "stretch" in the JG cells and provides the signal for renin elaboration. An alternate hypothesis, the macula densa theory, suggests that as a result of reduced glomerular filtration, the sodium load reaching the distal tubule is reduced. This reduction is sensed by the macula densa, which is in close proximity to the JG cells and, possibly through the action of a local hormone (double arrow), signals them to secrete renin.

Macula Densa Hypothesis

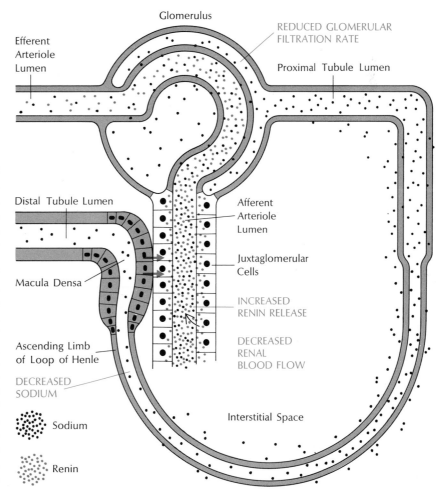

Glomerulus

REDUCED GLOMERULAR FILTRATION RATE

Efferent Arteriole Lumen

Proximal Tubule Lumen

Distal Tubule Lumen

Afferent Arteriole Lumen

Juxtaglomerular Cells

Macula Densa

INCREASED RENIN RELEASE

DECREASED RENAL BLOOD FLOW

Ascending Limb of Loop of Henle

DECREASED SODIUM

Interstitial Space

Sodium

Renin

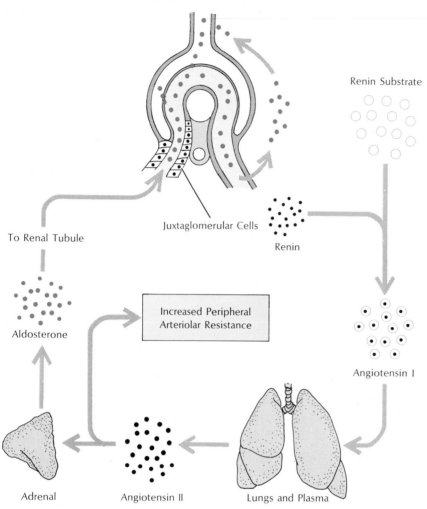

Renin Substrate

Juxtaglomerular Cells

To Renal Tubule

Renin

Aldosterone

Increased Peripheral Arteriolar Resistance

Angiotensin I

Adrenal

Angiotensin II

Lungs and Plasma

The biochemical pathway from renin to aldosterone is depicted above. After renin is released into the circulation by the JG cells it acts enzymatically upon renin substrate (angiotensinogen) to produce angiotensin I. This is converted, somewhat in the plasma but mostly in the lungs, to angiotensin II. Not only does the angiotensin II act upon the adrenal cortex to cause secretion of aldosterone but it also acts upon the peripheral arterioles to increase peripheral resistance. Thus, two of the mechanisms that help to maintain the circulation — increased resistance and aldosterone-mediated sodium and water retention — are called into play.

(see Chapter 6, "The Autonomic Nervous System in Heart Failure," by Braunwald); the renal sympathetic nerves end in the J G cells and heightened sympathetic activity stimulates the J G cells to release renin. Also, the plasma level of norepinephrine is elevated in patients with congestive failure; as a consequence of the overactivity of the sympathetic nervous system, a portion of the norepinephrine released from nerve terminals spills over into the bloodstream. Norepinephrine acts through a variety of mechanisms to increase renin release, including a direct action on the J G cells.

Whatever the precise complex of mechanisms in renin release is, clearly events leading to sodium retention are initiated by secretion of renin by the J G cells. Renin is secreted into the lumen of the renal afferent arterioles and thence enters the general circulation where the renin levels in peripheral plasma become elevated. The enzymatic nature of renin has been known for years and recent studies have provided estimates that it has a molecular weight of around 40,000.

Once in the peripheral plasma, renin encounters another protein, a liver-derived substance generally known as renin substrate (an α-2 globulin) but also called angiotensinogen, indicating its role as the precursor of angiotensin. Studies of the active component in the α-2 globulin show that the substrate needed for the action of renin is a tetradecapeptide. The formation of angiotensin I by the action of renin on renin substrate takes place in the plasma. The conversion of the decapeptide angiotensin I to the octapeptide angiotensin II also occurs to some extent in plasma but the reaction is slow. In fact, until recently it was believed that this was the exclusive site for this conversion. However, since 1967 it has been shown that the conversion in peripheral plasma is secondary in importance to the conversion of angiotensin I to angiotensin II that occurs in the lungs. About 50% of the angiotensin I entering the right heart is converted to angiotensin II in a single passage through the lungs.

From the evolutionary point of view, conversion in the lungs is an elegant mechanism. From this site, angiotensin II can circulate rapidly before being inactivated and be available to the zona glomerulosa of the adrenal cortex where it directly stimulates aldosterone secretion. Of course, such stimulation is not the sole physiologic capability of angiotensin II. Indeed, from its discovery in 1940 until its relationship to aldosterone was established in 1960, interest in angiotensin centered on its vasopressor qualities. One can speculate that the two roles are not unrelated. Angiotensin could also act upon peripheral arterioles to increase peripheral resistance, and, indeed, there is recent evidence (from Johnson and Davis) that this occurs. These workers gave an angiotensin II antagonist, 1-sarcosine-8-alanine-angiotensin II, intravenously to dogs with thoracic caval constriction (a model for low-output heart failure) to investigate the role of angiotensin II in the maintenance of arterial pressure. The antagonist produced a striking fall in arterial pressure and aldosterone secretion, in spite of an accompanying increase in plasma renin activity. These results suggest an important role for angiotensin II in the maintenance of arterial pressure in heart failure by its action on specific receptor sites in arteriolar smooth muscle and in the adrenal cortex. Therefore, by raising peripheral resistance in the presence of a decreased cardiac output (flow), angiotensin could provide a compensatory mechanism to increase organ perfusion pressure in the failure patient.

Carrying this conjecture a step further, one can construct a scheme in which angiotensin II increases aldosterone secretion within 15 to 30 minutes and is available for its pressor function through action on the peripheral arterioles. Obviously, both of these activities can be viewed as compensatory mechanisms directed toward maintaining the circulation in the face of compromised blood flow to the peripheral tissues. Unfortunately, both of these compensatory mechanisms may be inadequate and a state of frank congestive heart failure may ensue.

One question raised by these considerations is why the patient in heart failure does not overrespond and become hypertensive. The answer is not completely understood. However, clinical experiments by Laragh at Columbia University and in my former laboratory in Bethesda in 1962 demonstrated that both the failure patient and the animal with experimentally induced failure are less sensitive to angiotensin than the normal individual. Administration of angiotensin II intravenously to either experimental animals or patients with cardiac failure gave a reduced pressor response. From the above mentioned studies with the angiotensin II antagonist, it now appears that available receptor sites in arteriolar smooth muscle in cardiac failure are so "saturated" with angiotensin II (because of the high endogenous level of the peptide) that exogenously given angiotensin II is less effective.

It is possible that another homeostatic mechanism that controls the metabolism of renin is operating at an abnormal level in heart failure. It will be recalled that one of the most important intermediate reactions of a patient in cardiac failure is the development of a high plasma level of renin as well as aldosterone. It will be remembered that the high level of aldosterone appears in many cases to be a function of decreased liver metabolism as well as of increased secretion. The question, then, is whether or not some parallel phenomenon might be involved in the elevation of plasma renin. Our experimental studies have revealed that in low-output failure, which is the predominant form of congestive failure, the hepatic clearance

of renin was normal, while in high-output failure, removal of renin by the liver was reduced. Further experimentation on the inactivation of renin by the liver has demonstrated that in acute hemorrhage and in sodium depletion, both potent stimulators of renin release, the hepatic clearance of renin was markedly depressed and this depression contributed substantially to elevated levels of plasma renin. In a sense, the failure to find reduced

hepatic clearance of renin in experimental low-output failure is surprising in view of the greatly reduced hepatic blood flow. There is apparently some compensatory mechanism operating to improve the liver's efficiency in extracting and clearing the renin available to it from its compromised blood supply.

Having discussed various aspects of the metabolism of aldosterone, renin, and the angiotensins, we can

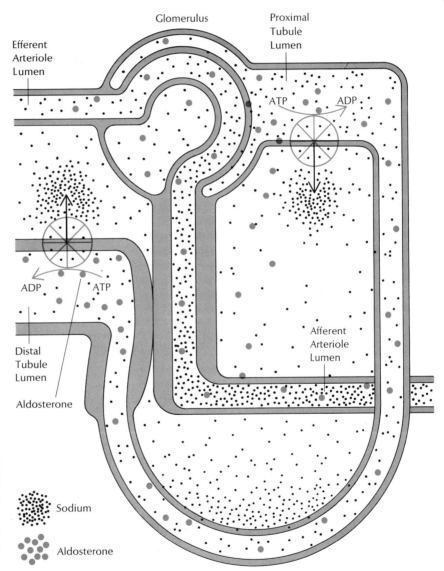

Aldosterone's ability to cause reabsorption of sodium from the distal tubule is believed to be a function of its ability to enhance the reduction of ATP to ADP and inorganic phosphate, with consequent energy production. This energy is required to translocate sodium from the luminal side of the tubule to the interstitial space. The sodium is able to diffuse passively from the distal tubule lumen down a concentration gradient into the cells of the distal tubule. However, passage from the cell interior to the interstitial space must be achieved against gradients both in Na concentration and in electrical charge, and active sodium pumping occurs. Sodium retention occurs as the fraction of sodium reabsorbed from the glomerulus is increased above the normal level of 99%. A similar active transport mechanism is believed to exist in the proximal tubule but aldosterone does not appear to influence proximal sodium reabsorption.

now turn to the direct interaction between aldosterone and its target structure, the renal tubule, and the resultant end product, edema. The result of this interaction is enhanced sodium transport and increased passive reabsorption of water. What sites and actions lead to these end results?

The early evidence suggested that aldosterone acts at two different sites in the renal tubule. The data for an action in the distal nephron is convincing, and the results indicate that the primary influence of the hormone is to enhance the active transport of the sodium ion. Recent observations have failed to confirm the earlier impression that aldosterone acts on the proximal tubule to promote sodium reabsorption. Rather, it now appears that physical factors in the postglomerular circulation operate to influence the passive reabsorption of sodium by the proximal tubule. The high filtration fraction in heart failure indicates that postglomerular capillary colloid osmotic pressure is elevated. Thus, an elevation in osmotic pressure would favor the passive movement of sodium and water across the proximal tubular epithelium, and recent evidence suggests that this passive reabsorption is effected through paracellular channels which are present between the cells of the proximal tubule.

The so-called sodium pump mechanism is thought to occur at the interstitial side of the tubule cell. Before the sodium ion reaches this site it must be provided to the luminal side of the renal tubular cell. This is done through passive filtration of the ion through the glomerular membrane and movement down the renal tubular system to the luminal side of the distal tubule cell. The concentration of sodium in proximal renal tubular fluid is essentially the same as in plasma (neglecting the Donnan effect), that is to say, about 140 mEq/l. The sodium concentration in the renal tubular cell is much lower, on the order of 30 mEq/l. Thus, there is passive diffusion of sodium down the concentration gradient from the lumen into the interior of the tubular cell. However, to be moved into the interstitial fluid, the sodium ion must overcome gradients in both concentration and electrical potential. For this, energy is required and, of course, one important source of en-

ergy comes from hydrolysis of ATP. A prominent theory is that aldosterone catalyzes an initial reaction that is part of a series of enzymatic reactions that promote the formation of ATP and, thereby, energy is derived for active sodium transport.

It has been demonstrated that without the participation of aldosterone (i.e., in an adrenalectomized animal) sodium balance is well maintained if sodium intake is high. Under such circumstances, 99% of the filtered sodium is reabsorbed and 1% excreted. By the addition of aldosterone, sodium excretion decreases transiently and sodium reabsorption approaches 99.9%. Thus, the increase in fractional sodium reabsorption required for net sodium retention to occur is extremely small. This increase appears to be achieved by bolstering the active sodium pumping mechanism. At least, this is currently the most widely held view; there are some dissenters. Leaf and his associates at Harvard Medical School have suggested that another mechanism may be enhancement of the entry of the sodium ion into the luminal side of the cell. There is, however, agreement that aldosterone, whether by providing energy for active transport or by increasing permeability, facilitates the translocation of sodium from lumen to interstitium through the cells of the distal parts of the nephron. The resultant increased tubular reabsorption of sodium is followed passively by water.

In addition to promoting sodium retention, aldosterone also increases potassium excretion. The classic view of these changes has been that sodium and potassium are involved in an exchange process across the cells of the distal tubule and to a lesser extent in other parts of the renal tubular system. There is, of course, evidence that exchange or a closely analogous phenomenon occurs in the ionic fluxes in myocardial cells described in other chapters of this book. Recently, however, Giebisch at Yale University has concluded on the basis of his studies that potassium is passively secreted by the distal tubule cells. This finding requires some modification of the concept of a simple ion exchange mechanism, as held previously.

This recent evidence is very suggestive and helps to make certain find-

ings understandable, findings that emerged from earlier studies performed in our laboratory and by other investigative groups. Typical of these researches are those done on adrenalectomized animals, which were used because their renal tubules are for some reason more sensitive to aldosterone than are those of the normal animals. If aldosterone is given intravenously to an adrenalectomized animal, a marked reduction in sodium excretion occurs and becomes maximal within three to four hours. Simultaneous studies of potassium excretion revealed that kaliuresis actually precedes the onset of sodium retention. This observation certainly suggests that the processes involved are not simply an exchange between the two cations.

The response of the kidneys in chronic situations is more complex and involves an important difference between normal individuals and patients in heart failure. If one starts with a normal human subject in sodium balance and ingesting an average amount of dietary sodium, 100 mEq/day, and if the subject receives a large daily dose of aldosterone (e.g., 0.5 to 1.0 mg per day in oil), there will be a marked reduction in sodium excretion that lasts from three to five days. But after five days, the subject "escapes" from the sodium-retaining action of aldosterone; sodium excretion returns to normal and a new equilibrium state is established at a higher level of total body sodium. Also, plasma sodium concentration increases from a normal level of 142 mEq/l to 150-152 mEq/l.

In this normal subject, the retention of sodium is initially accompanied by increased potassium excretion. However, while escape from sodium retention occurs, the increased excretion of potassium continues and one witnesses a fall in plasma potassium to levels reflecting a hypokalemic metabolic alkalosis. In the patient in heart failure, however, the escape phenomenon for sodium fails to occur. The patient continues to retain sodium, but potassium excretion is essentially normal and no hypokalemia results. One explanation that has been advanced to explain this difference in response is that the heart failure patient reabsorbs sodium almost completely in the proximal tubule and that little sodium reaches the distal tubule for exchange with potassium. However, recent observations from different laboratories suggest that the final concentrations of sodium and potassium in urine are achieved by actions at different sites in the distal nephron. So the older explanation for normo-kalemia in heart failure now appears to be too simple. It should also be emphasized that recent micropuncture experiments performed by Knox and Schneider at the University of Missouri gave convincing evidence that increased fractional reabsorption of sodium also occurs in the distal tubule in experimental high-output heart failure. Similar conclusions on distal sodium reabsorption were reached by Levinsky and associates at Boston University from studies in dogs with thoracic caval constriction, a model for low-output heart failure.

The question of why the normal subject escapes from the sodium-retaining action of aldosterone brings us to the discussion of factor III, the so-called sodium-retaining factor or factors. This factor can be exemplified in the dog with a large arteriovenous (AV) fistula; these animals are not in cardiac failure and sodium balance is normal. If one administers a large dose of aldosterone to such an animal, the dog starts retaining sodium in much the same manner as a normal subject, but escape from the sodium-retaining action of aldosterone fails to occur (see graphs). The consequence is that the animal continues to retain sodium and water, becomes increasingly edematous, and dies of pulmonary edema within a few weeks. With regard to potassium excretion, the AV fistula dog does not excrete excessive amounts of this ion or develop kaliuresis or hypokalemia. These findings are essentially the same as those seen in patients with cardiac failure.

When we first observed these phenomena in 1953, deoxycorticosterone was used as the mineralocorticoid rather than aldosterone. With further study and elaboration of this concept (1964), we designated the agent that makes the renal tubules more responsive as an *extra-adrenal sodium-retaining factor*. This is a purely descriptive term and we did not know then, nor do we know at the time of this writing, whether we are dealing

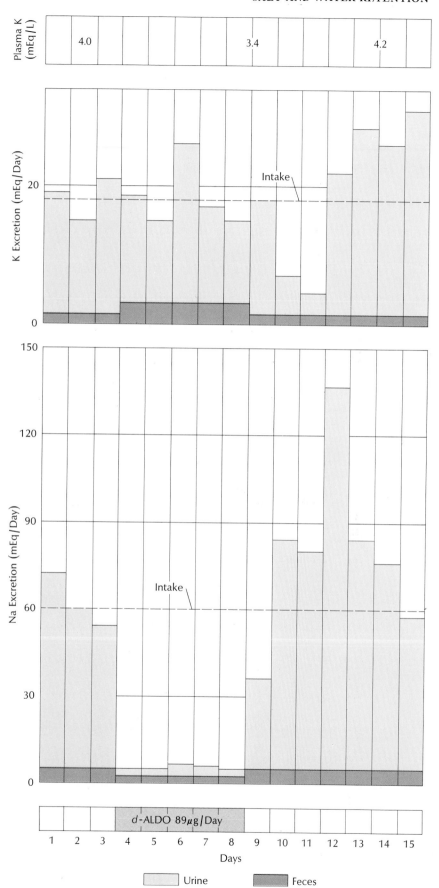

The effects of aldosterone infusion on a dog with an AV fistula are plotted above. Sodium retention is marked and prolonged while the effects on potassium parameters are much less pronounced, with only a short-lived reduction in plasma concentration.

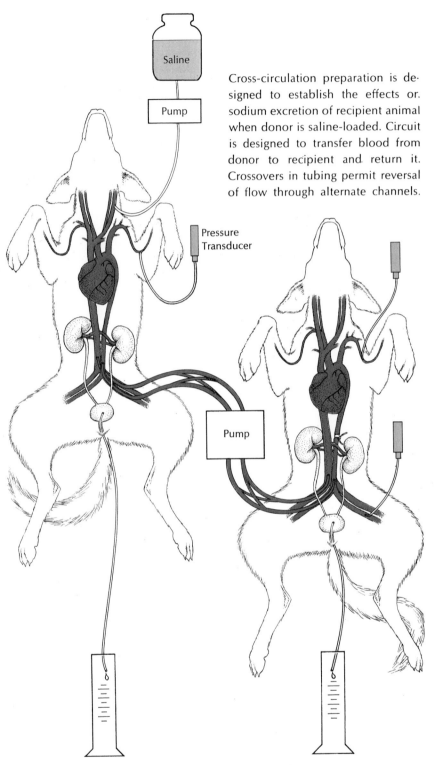

Cross-circulation preparation is designed to establish the effects or sodium excretion of recipient animal when donor is saline-loaded. Circuit is designed to transfer blood from donor to recipient and return it. Crossovers in tubing permit reversal of flow through alternate channels.

The preparation described and illustrated above was used in establishing the humoral nature of a natriuretic factor (factor III) that may be involved in the pathogenesis of congestive cardiac failure. With this preparation and with precautions taken to eliminate the influences of altered glomerular filtration rate and of aldosterone, it was shown that saline loading of a donor dog resulted in enhancement of the sodium excretion of the recipient animal. While experiments such as this seem to establish the humoral nature of factor III, there are still considerable gaps in knowledge as to the precise role of this hormone. One hypothesis now under intensive investigation is that under physiologic conditions, the hormone might be activated by a salt load in order to increase natriuresis, while in heart failure the hormone might become less available. Under such circumstances it would be the relative lack of the factor III hormone that contributes to the sodium and fluid retention seen in cardiac failure.

with a factor (or group of factors) that promotes sodium transport, or with one that acts on the renal tubules to produce rejection of sodium. In other words, the sodium retention induced by this factor could be either the result of a high level of a sodium-retaining factor or lack of a natriuretic factor. Indeed, there is now evidence from several laboratories for the existence of a salt-losing factor.

In cross-circulation experiments, we have been able to demonstrate that if a saline load is administered to one dog of a pair, the second dog is induced to excrete large amounts of salt. The experimental design for this study is shown at the left. These experiments, done with a number of controls designed to eliminate the roles of aldosterone and of the G F R, establish the humoral nature of factor III. More recently, several workers have attempted to purify factor III and there are suggestions that a humoral agent which is protein or peptide in nature may be involved. But there is obviously a great deal more work to be done before the nature of factor III is completely clarified, and that work is progressing currently in many laboratories. A major focus of our cross-circulation study was to test out the possibility that factor III is a hormone. Under physiologic conditions it might be activated by a salt load, whereas in heart failure something might happen to make the hormone less available and salt retention ensue.

Several possible loci for secretion of this humoral agent have been suggested. In our early cross-circulation experiments, in which the saline-loaded donor was bilaterally nephrectomized, a much smaller increase in sodium excretion occurred in the recipient than when the kidneys of the donor animals were intact. These observations suggest a renal origin for the natriuretic factor. In this regard, it should be mentioned that certain prostaglandins are present in high concentrations in the renal medulla and that both PGA_2 and PGE_2 are natriuretic. There is also recent evidence that sodium loading activates the renal kallikrein system. It is evident, therefore, that the so-called factor III may include several different humoral agents.

Early in the discussion it was noted that the renal sympathetic nerves are well situated morphologically to influence the J G complex and to trigger the renin-angiotensin-aldosterone mechanism. Moreover, there is a good correlation among physical activity, increased norepinephrine release, and increased renin secretion. In this sense, the sympathetic nerves, by influencing renin release, do play a role in sodium retention. The fact that physical activity is related to the extent to which this neural influence is brought into play is one of several reasons for restricting activity in patients with cardiac insufficiency.

At least one other such argument is worthy of mention. It has been pointed out that the liver is the principal site of the catabolism of aldosterone and that this catabolism is reduced as a result of the decreased hepatic blood flow sequential to reduced cardiac output in failure. In congestive heart failure, the patient is extremely sensitive to activity and exercise so far as hepatic blood flow is concerned. With intense physical activity, hepatic flow falls to as low as 10% to 15% of normal. This certainly results in a marked decrease in aldosterone breakdown. The effects might be disastrous in terms of elevation of the plasma level of aldosterone and exacerbation of sodium retention.

There are still many gaps to be filled before we can talk in terms of a unified concept of the mechanisms of salt and water retention in congestive heart failure. It is clear, however, that aldosterone and the renin-angiotensin system are very active participants in these mechanisms and that one other factor is important, the so-called extra-adrenal sodium-retaining factor or factors. At the same time one should not minimize the significance of decreased G F R, particularly in acute situations when sudden drops in filtration rate occur and exert their effects over a period of a day or two. In chronic congestive failure, however, aldosterone and the extra-adrenal factors must be assigned the prime responsibility of sodium retention and edema.

Section Three

Clinical Manifestations of Heart Failure

The Clinical Manifestations of Cardiac Failure in Adults

JOSEPH K. PERLOFF

University of Pennsylvania

It is important that the physician have a clear understanding of both the clinical manifestations of cardiac failure and the many disease states responsible for its presence. For the purposes of this discussion, I shall concentrate on the clinical manifestations that are common to heart failure per se regardless of its genesis. It is useful to point out that these manifestations differ substantially in adults and infants (see Chapter 10, "Cardiac Failure in Children: A Hemodynamic Overview," by Rudolph), so that each age group deserves separate attention. The following remarks will relate to heart failure in the adult.

When we use the term "heart failure" we mean that cardiac performance is inadequate for tissue requirements; under these circumstances the heart can be said to have "failed" in its prime mission as a pump. When the heart begins to fail, a number of compensatory mechanisms come into play (see Chapter 7, "Hemodynamic Aspects of Cardiac Failure," by Dodge and Chapter 6, "The Autonomic Nervous System in Heart Failure," by Braunwald), and these, for a time, can permit adequate cardiac performance. But when they, too, become inoperative or inadequate, certain symptoms and signs develop that represent the features upon which the clinical recognition of heart failure is based. These symptoms and signs are best considered in an orderly sequence, namely, the clinical history, the physical appearance, the arterial pulse, the jugular venous pulse, the precordial movements, auscultation, the electrocardiogram, and the chest x-ray. The information derived from such an evaluation does not directly depend upon sophisticated diagnostic techniques, but instead is available to the physician in his office or at the bedside. Each step in the sequence should be explored in depth, while at the same time each part should be related to the whole so that a complete, harmonious picture emerges.

Considerations in the History

Dyspnea, i.e., subjective difficulty in breathing, is a common early symptom of heart failure and is generally a direct consequence of a rise in pulmonary venous pressure caused by failure of the left heart. This rise in pressure results in pulmonary congestion, which causes the lungs to stiffen or become less compliant; in addition, there may be an increase in airway resistance. The net effect is an increase in the work of breathing that manifests itself symptomatically as breathlessness.

The many different patterns of dyspnea are, of course, both interesting in themselves and important for the clinician to recognize. Dyspnea may initially express itself as insomnia or nocturnal restlessness, which can readily be misinterpreted. Cardiac dyspnea is characterized by rapid, shallow breathing, which must be distinguished from the "hyperventilatory" dyspnea of anxiety. The dyspnea of anxiety may result from fear of nonexistent heart disease or from concern over a cardiac disorder that though present is too mild to cause symptoms of any sort. The breathlessness of anxiety is not rapid and shallow; instead the patient takes deep sighing breaths and complains that no matter how deeply he inhales, his air hunger is not satisfied. It is axiomatic that in many anxious patients, hyperventilatory dyspnea coexists with true cardiac dyspnea.

Another important distinction is between *effort* dyspnea and dyspnea at rest. In the early stages of heart failure, dyspnea is provoked only by effort, subsiding entirely at rest. It is understandable that the less the cardiac reserve, the less the effort required to cause dyspnea. The relationship between breathlessness and the amount of effort required to provoke it has been used in the symptomatic classification of cardiac patients by the New York Heart Association (see table on page 95).

Still another characteristic of dyspnea is its relationship

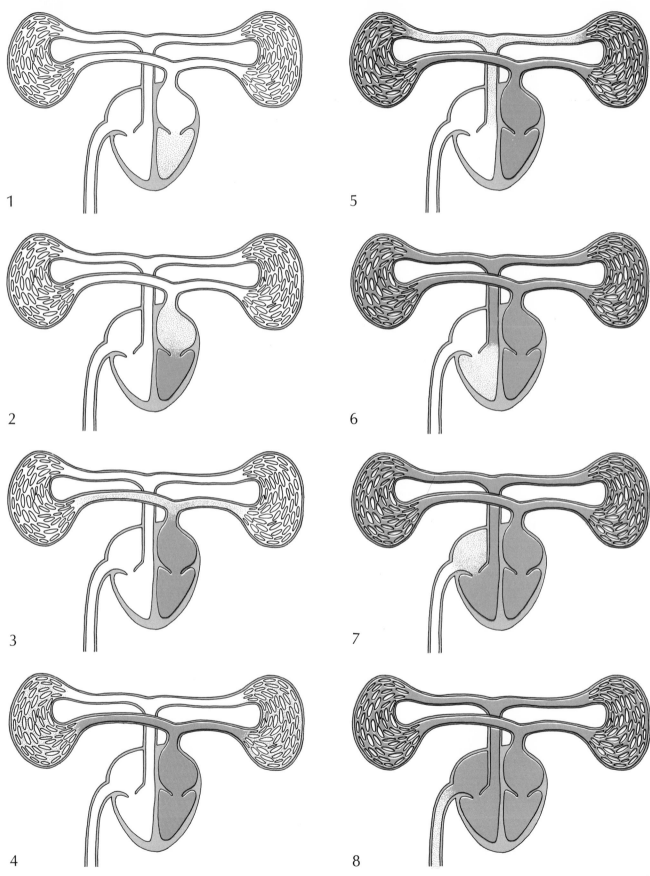

1

2

3

4

5

6

7

8

From left heart failure to pulmonary edema and dyspnea (1-4): Increased pressure (light color) in left ventricle during diastole is transmitted retrograde to the pulmonary veins and capillaries, producing stiffening and congestion of lungs.

From left heart failure to right ventricular failure and generalized edema (5-8): Pressure rise in pulmonary capillary bed is transmitted to pulmonary artery and right heart, producing congestion in venae cavae and venous side of systemic circulation.

to position. A well-known pattern in this regard is orthopnea, a term applied when dyspnea manifests itself or worsens in the recumbent position. The work of breathing is greater when patients with decreased lung compliance (stiff, congested lungs) lie flat; this tendency is aggravated not only by the increase in venous return that attends recumbency but also by elevations of the diaphragm that exist in patients with ascites and hepatomegaly.

An interesting aspect of positional dyspnea is its occasional relationship not simply to recumbency as such but to recumbency on the left side (left lateral decubitus dyspnea). Patients complain of breathlessness when they turn on their left side; such complaints may be ignored by the physician in his search for the more recognized pattern of orthopnea. The mechanism of left lateral decubitus dyspnea is not established, but it is known that certain individuals experience hypotension and a presumed fall in coronary arterial perfusion in this position. Accordingly, not only dyspnea but ischemic pain may result from turning on the left side.

Paroxysmal nocturnal dyspnea is still another form of recumbent breathlessness that occurs typically after prolonged recumbency; typically, the patient retires and falls asleep only to awaken in the night acutely short of breath. At least partial relief follows assumption of an upright position, usually sitting. Paroxysmal nocturnal dyspnea results from the increase in blood volume that occurs with resorption of the dependent edema accumulated during the day. The inadequate left ventricle cannot handle the increased volume load; the ensuing rise in pulmonary venous pressure causes congestion and stiffening of the lungs and acute recumbent dyspnea.

Closely akin to the paroxysmal dyspnea described above is acute pulmonary edema. Fluid initially leaves the alveolar capillaries because of an increase in hydrostatic pressure and capillary permeability. The essential cause of this type of pulmonary edema is the rise in pulmonary venous pressure associated with left heart failure. When fluid enters the alveoli, gas exchange is compromised; this deficit coexists with the handicap of stiff, congested lungs. Acute pulmonary

Functional Classification of Cardiac Patients

This functional classification, originally developed by the New York Heart Association, is based on the patient's ability to perform physical activities.

CLASS I: No limitation. Ordinary physical activity does not cause undue fatigue, dyspnea, palpitation, or angina.

CLASS II: Slight limitation of physical activity. Such patients will be comfortable at rest. Ordinary physical activity will result in fatigue, palpitation, dyspnea, or angina.

CLASS III: Marked limitation of physical activity. Less than ordinary activity will lead to symptoms. Patients are comfortable at rest.

CLASS IV: Inability to carry on any physical activity without discomfort. Symptoms of congestive failure or angina will be present even at rest. With any physical activity, increased discomfort is experienced.

edema can develop in susceptible individuals at night or during the day, either "spontaneously" or after physiologic stress such as effort, excitement, etc. The dyspnea is often accompanied by pink, frothy sputum.

Cheyne-Stokes respiration – i.e., periods of hyperpnea alternating with apnea – is yet another respiratory pattern that may occur with cardiac failure. This breathing pattern is relatively common in elderly individuals with left ventricular failure, especially when they have been given barbiturate sedatives. Occasionally the hyperpneic phase of Cheyne-Stokes respiration is mistaken for paroxysmal nocturnal dyspnea, which in fact may coexist.

At this point, I would like to comment briefly on "angina with decubi-

tus," i.e., nocturnal angina that is a manifestation of heart failure and that at times merges with the complaint of nocturnal dyspnea. The pattern is often unmistakable. A patient with typical effort angina finds that the frequency of pain decreases during the day only to be replaced by troublesome nocturnal pain that seriously disturbs his sleep. The essential provoking mechanism is similar to that of nocturnal dyspnea, but now the response of the left ventricle to the increase in volume load (resorption of diurnal edema) is chiefly pain instead of breathlessness. Relief from nocturnal angina is not accomplished with nitroglycerine but instead by treatment for heart failure that is the immediate cause.

Cough is an important and often

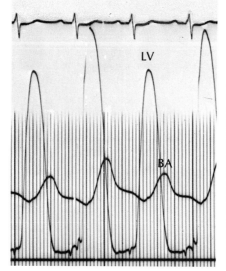

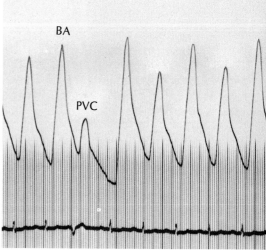

A classic strong-weak-strong-weak pattern is apparent in both brachial and left ventricular pulse pressures in tracings at left; patient had aortic stenosis. Other tracing shows that a premature ventricular contraction may precipitate or exaggerate pulsus alternans, facilitating detection of this sign of left ventricular failure.

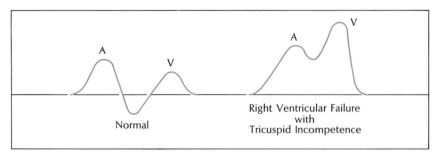

Normal

Right Ventricular Failure
with
Tricuspid Incompetence

Normally the A wave of the jugular venous pulse is greater than the V; in right ventricular failure accompanied by tricuspid incompetence, the descending limb of the A wave is attenuated and the V wave increases, as shown at right above.

neglected symptom of left ventricular failure and is closely related to dyspnea. Patients may complain of an annoying dry, hacking cough – cough with effort, cough with emotional stress, cough at night. Nocturnal cough – which can occur with or without overt nocturnal dyspnea – may seriously interfere with sleep and result in insomnia and fatigue. It should also be borne in mind that cough may reflect recurrent pulmonary emboli to which individuals with cardiac failure are especially prone; such cough may be unaccompanied by pleuritic pain or hemoptysis.

The problem of hemoptysis itself should be touched on in a discussion of heart failure. The pink, frothy sputum of acute pulmonary edema results from an intra-alveolar mixture of fluid, red cells, and air. In addition, in mitral stenosis, high left atrial and pulmonary venous pressures are transmitted into submucosal bronchial veins, which may dilate and rupture, producing copious hemoptysis, a dramatic event described as "pulmonary apoplexy." Still another form of hemoptysis is that which results from pulmonary embolism, to which patients with congestive heart failure – especially the edematous cardiac at bedrest – are susceptible.

Just as *pulmonary* edema is a manifestation of *left* heart failure, *systemic* edema is a manifestation of *right* heart failure. Systemic edema can be subtle, and at its inception may require careful comparisons of daily weights for confirmation. It is useful to ask patients to record their basal nude weights each morning before breakfast, a maneuver that requires no more than a flat bathroom scale. Basal body weights obtained in this

manner normally change relatively little from day to day, so that subtle but real weight gains due to fluid retention are readily detected. This form of occult edema precedes the dependent pitting edema of feet and ankles. Dependent pedal edema simply means that the gravitational effects of the upright position result in sufficient hydrostatic pressure to express fluid from the intravascular compartment into the extravascular tissues.

Patients become aware of dependent pedal edema, especially if marked. Lesser degrees of edema can be inferred by asking patients if at the end of the day they notice pitting depressions on the feet or legs when shoes or constricting garters are removed. If dependent edema exists, patients should be advised to avoid the tourniquet effect of garters, which interfere with venous return and aggravate pedal edema. Dependent edema may also develop in individuals confined to bed, but under these circumstances the dependent portion of the body is the sacrum rather than the legs. Patients are seldom aware of presacral edema, which must be specifically sought during the physical examination.

The ultimate in edema accumulation is anasarca – generalized massive edema including genitalia, thorax, arms, and occasionally face. Ascites is usually accompanied by edema but occasionally exists with comparatively

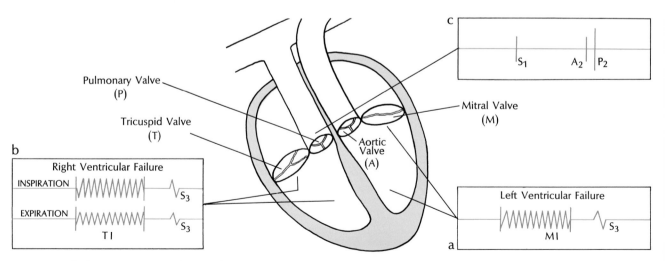

Diagrammed above are some of the auscultatory changes associated with cardiac failure. A pathologic third heart sound will be heard (at the apex) during mid-diastole; combined with a slight increase in heart rate, it produces a gallop rhythm. If the apposition of the mitral leaflets is altered by changes in left ventricular geometry, the holosystolic murmur of mitral incompe- *tence (MI) may be heard (a). Similarly, right ventricular failure may lead to tricuspid incompetence (TI) and produce a lower left sternal edge holosystolic murmur that increases with inspiration and decreases with expiration (b). The rise in pulmonary venous and pulmonary arterial pressures (see illustrations on page 94) may intensify the sound of pulmonary valve closure (c).*

little peripheral edema. Ascites that is disproportionate to the degree of edema is likely to occur with tricuspid stenosis or constrictive pericarditis.

Ascites, like other forms of edema, can sometimes be suspected from the history. A male, for instance, may become aware of an increase in girth requiring a looser belt or purchase of a larger size; a female with ascites may be aware that her girdle no longer fits comfortably. Massive ascites may aggravate orthopnea by forcing the diaphragm upward in the recumbent position. It should be pointed out that aggravation of dyspnea or orthopnea may stem not only from abdominal fluid (ascites) but also from large pleural effusions that compress the lungs. The presence of pleural effusions cannot be inferred from the history but must be established by physical signs and x-rays.

Another important area in the history relates to gastrointestinal symptoms. Hepatic pain (right upper quadrant or epigastric) results from acute distension of Glisson's capsule as a result of the hepatomegaly of right ventricular failure. The pain may occur at rest or after effort, when a rise in systemic venous pressure further distends the liver. Edema of the bowel may accompany the venous congestion of right ventricular failure and may alter gastrointestinal function, resulting in anorexia, nausea, abdominal distension, and a sense of fullness after meals. It should not be forgotten that nausea, anorexia, and emesis may also be due to cardiac drugs such as digitalis glycosides.

Certain symptoms reflected in the history stem from variations in renal clearance. Oliguria tends to occur during the day in the ambulant patient in failure. The opposite is the case at night, i.e., there is a tendency for diuresis with recumbency. Nocturia can be frequent and annoying, interfering with sleep and contributing to the fatigue that is commonly present in patients with heart failure.

Diaphoresis, especially evident as inappropriate sweating, reflects the increased adrenergic activity of heart failure (see Chapter 6 by Braunwald). It has to be emphasized that this diaphoresis must be distinguished from that of fever, which is not a feature of heart failure in adults. If fever actually exists, an alternative expla-

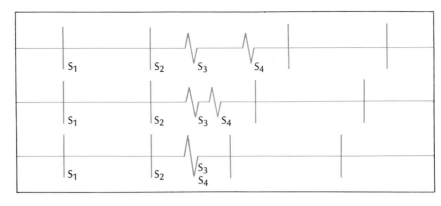

With a fast heart rate or long PR interval, the third and fourth heart sounds may summate to produce a summation sound or a summation gallop rhythm.

nation such as pulmonary embolism, thrombophlebitis, or infection must be sought.

Fatigue as a symptom associated with heart failure may – as noted above–result from insomnia, nocturia, nocturnal dyspnea, nocturnal cough, etc. However, fatigue may be a direct consequence of the failure itself. A low cardiac output accounts for this; such fatigue can appear during effort, can occur at rest, and generally worsens as the day goes on. In addition, the *catabolic* effect of chronic cardiac failure often manifests itself as weakness and real weight loss despite intermittent reaccumulation of edema.

Physical Examination

I would like to address myself in turn to the patient's physical appearance, the examination of the chest and abdomen, the arterial pulse, the jugular venous pulse, precordial movement, and cardiac auscultation.

Physical appearance: A previously healthy individual with the recent rapid development of serious congestive heart failure appears acutely ill, with dyspnea, orthopnea, and diaphoresis; if the failure is promptly relieved, the patient then appears relatively normal. In contrast, the individual with serious *chronic* cardiac failure suffers the consequences of a protracted catabolic disease and appears chronically ill and wasted.

The appearance of the skin itself is important. The dusky discoloration of cyanosis results from an increase in tissue extraction of oxygen from systemic capillaries as a compensatory mechanism for the low cardiac output

of heart failure. This form of cyanosis is "peripheral" since the systemic arterial O_2 content is normal. Another compensatory mechanism involves redistribution of blood from skin to more vital tissues so that skin temperature falls. Finally, the exaggerated adrenergic discharge that is part of heart failure causes sweating. The combined effects of these several influences result in dusky, cold, sweaty skin.

Peripheral edema was mentioned in detail earlier. Suffice it to say at this point that the appearance of edema should be specifically sought on physical examination, especially around the malleoli, dorsum of the feet, pretibial areas, and sacrum.

An interesting though uncommon aspect of the physical appearance is jaundice. Jaundice in heart failure is an occasional consequence of either abnormal liver function associated with hepatic congestion or the release of bilirubin from an area of hemorrhagic pulmonary infarction.

Examination of the chest: The traditional items of interest in this area are rales, wheezing, and pleural effusion. Intra-alveolar fluid produces fine rales; fluid within the lumens of bronchioles and bronchi produce coarser rales; interstitial edema produces no rales at all despite overt dsypnea. Wheezing results from narrowing of the lumens of airways by edema of their walls. It is a point of interest that the rales of heart failure can be bilateral, or unilateral on the right; unilateral left-sided rales suggest pulmonary emboli rather than heart failure per se. Similarly, pleural effusions in congestive heart failure can be bilateral, or unilateral on the right, but are seldom in the left chest alone.

The abdomen: Four items are of importance – hepatomegaly, hepatic pulsations, ascites, and splenomegaly. The liver may not only be large but also tender because of acute distension of Glisson's capsule. It is important to remember that emphysema with low diaphragms may result in a palpable liver that is low but not large and not tender. Furthermore, in the true hepatomegaly of right heart failure the liver may exhibit phasic pulsations synchronous with those of the right atrium. In essence the wave form of the right atrial pulse is transmitted to the liver so that both A wave and V wave may be palpable in the hepatic pulse. In addition, bimanual palpation sometimes detects systolic expansion of the liver. Attention should then be directed to the flank dullness of ascites as well as to the enlarged spleen of congestive splenomegaly.

The physical signs of cardiac failure cited thus far usually present in much the same form regardless of the cause of failure. However, the signs described below vary considerably depending upon the presence of certain forms of coexisting heart disease such as acquired valvular disease, congenital heart disease, etc. I will emphasize the essentials common to cardiac failure as such and will not discuss the modifications and physical signs caused by coexisting valvular or congenital disorders.

The arterial pulse: An increase in the pulse rate in heart failure is in part a response to adrenergic activity (see Chapter 6 by Braunwald). In addition to a faster resting rate, there tends to be excessive acceleration with exercise and delayed return to resting levels; this is so because an increase in cardiac output in response to effort is largely achieved by more beats per minute rather than by an increase in stroke volume.

Pulsus alternans is a subtle but reliable sign of left ventricular failure. Palpation is more useful than the blood pressure cuff since the palpating finger can be trained to detect not only the alternation in pulse pressure from beat to beat but also the alternation in the rate of pressure development, i.e., the varying rates of rise of the arterial pulse. These variations can

occur on alternate beats – the strong-weak-strong-weak of classic pulsus alternans (see page 95) – or can occur with a rather random distribution. The normal tendency for peripheral amplification of the femoral pulse makes alternation especially apparent at that site. As a rule the brachial pulse is quite satisfactory. Since there is a strong tendency for a premature ventricular contraction to precipitate or exaggerate pulsus alternans, special attention should be paid to the beats immediately following the premature contraction (see lower right page 95).

The abnormal response of the arterial pulse to Valsalva's maneuver is a manifestation of cardiac failure that can be recognized by careful palpation. Normally, straining against a closed glottis causes a decrease in pulse pressure and an increase in pulse rate; immediately after release from straining the pulse pressure increases (overshoot) and the rate slows. In cardiac failure, straining causes little or no change in pulse pressure or rate, and release is not followed by an increase in pulse pressure or by reflex slowing.

The jugular venous pulse: Careful observation of the jugular venous pulse is a convenient and more reliable means of estimating the venous pressure than manometric determination via a needle in an antecubital vein. The clinician can readily train himself to assess both the height and wave form of the venous pulses in the neck.

The superficial jugular vein is a useful index of mean right atrial pressure, but occasionally venospasm collapses the vein despite a high right atrial pressure. The A and V waves both rise as the mean right atrial pressure rises; when right ventricular failure is accompanied by tricuspid incompetence, the descending limb of the A wave is attenuated and the V wave increases (see page 96). Occasionally, right heart failure manifests itself by an alternation in the jugular venous A wave. At times, systemic venous pressure is sufficiently high to dilate peripheral veins such as those on the dorsum of the hands or beneath the tongue.

The hepato-jugular reflux should be mentioned in connection with the jugular venous pulse of right ventricular

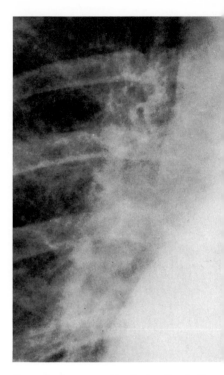

X-ray findings are often instructive in the assessment of cardiac failure. On this page, the right superior pulmonary vein as it emerges from hilus has obliterated

failure. Normally, compression of the liver or abdomen results in an increased venous return that is immediately translated into an increase in forward flow by a healthy right ventricle; the jugular venous pulse rises transiently if at all. With right ventricular failure, a similar maneuver results in a *persistent* rise in jugular venous pressure. (Note: The abdominal pressure must be applied firmly but *gradually*, otherwise the patient will respond by straining, which in itself will raise the jugular venous pressure.)

Precordial palpation: An increase in heart size is a common manifestation of congestive heart failure. Estimates of cardiac dimensions are more accurately achieved by palpation rather than percussion. Identification of the left ventricular impulse determines the lateral border of the heart unless pericardial effusion coexists. Dilatation of the left ventricle in cardiac failure results in displacement of the impulse to the left. (Note: The left ventricular impulse is identified as an apical zone of anterior displacement with medial retraction; examination in a partial left lateral po-

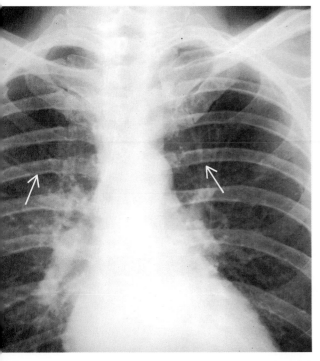
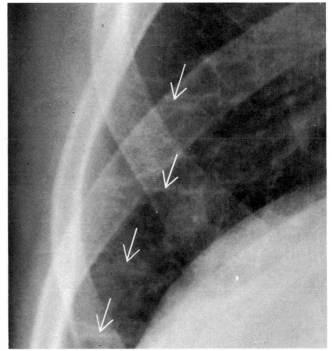

the normal angle between right upper pulmonary vein and the right pulmonary artery, straightening the lateral hilar shadow. Center, bilateral prominence of superior pulmonary veins produces the so-called antler effect (arrows). Right, close attention to the details of x-ray films may reveal the presence of Kerley lines (B type) such as those indicated above (arrows). These fine horizontal densities are caused by a thickening of interlobular septa that results from an increase in pulmonary venous pressure.

sition materially assists in locating and characterizing this impulse.) In addition to systolic movement, mid-diastolic distension of the left ventricle can sometimes be palpated as the failing chamber receives blood during the passive filling phase of the cardiac cycle. With right ventricular failure, one can occasionally palpate a right ventricular impulse along the lower left sternal edge or in the sub-xyphoid area.

Auscultation: Gallop rhythm has long been a hallmark of ventricular failure. It is important to emphasize that the gallop rhythm associated with heart failure results from the presence of a pathologic third heart sound (see illustration at bottom of page 96). Third heart sounds occur during the passive filling phase of the cardiac cycle (mid-diastole). These sounds are heard in most normal children, but there is a strong tendency for third heart sounds to be absent in healthy adults, especially after age 40. Ventricular failure results in the re-appearance of the third heart sound, which is then pathologic. The combination of first heart sound, second heart sound, and third heart sound

together with a slight increase in heart rate produces the classic cadence of a gallop rhythm.

The fourth heart sound – which occurs during the atrial contribution to ventricular filling (presystole) – is not in itself a sign of failure but usually reflects a decrease in ventricular compliance (distensibility) associated with ischemic heart disease or systemic hypertension. Should a patient with a fourth heart sound develop ventricular failure, a third heart sound might then appear and result in a "quadruple gallop rhythm," i.e., first sound, second sound, third sound, fourth sound. With a fast heart rate and/or long PR interval, the third and fourth heart sounds summate and accordingly amplify (see page 97).

It is worth emphasizing that third and fourth heart sounds are typically soft low-frequency events best detected by lightly touching the bell of the stethoscope to the skin. Left-sided third and fourth sounds are generated within the left ventricular cavity and are elicited by placing the bell precisely over the left ventricular impulse.

Four other auscultatory points

should be made. As the left ventricle fails, the pulmonary venous and pulmonary arterial pressures rise and the sound of pulmonary valve closure becomes louder (see page 96). Left ventricular failure, by changing the geometry of the ventricle, interferes with apposition of the mitral leaflets, resulting in the apical holosystolic murmur of mitral incompetence. Similarly, right ventricular failure may cause tricuspid incompetence, which produces a lower left sternal edge holosystolic murmur. The tricuspid murmur can further be identified by its tendency to appear or increase with inspiration and decrease with expiration. However, with advanced right ventricular failure, that chamber may be incapable of increasing its stroke volume and regurgitant flow during inspiration, so the typical inspiratory increase may not occur. Finally, attention should be paid to alternation of heart sounds and murmurs as manifestations of heart failure. Aortic systolic murmurs are especially likely to alternate with left ventricular failure. In addition, the first, second, third, and fourth heart sound may alternate.

The Electrocardiogram

The electrocardiogram is of undisputed value in the evaluation of the etiology of heart disease but not in assessing the presence or degree of heart failure. Electrical alternans, i.e., alternation of the P wave, the QRS, or the T wave is not a sign of heart failure as opposed to mechanical alternans. Even total electrical alternans of the P, QRS, and T wave is a manifestation of pericardial effusion rather than heart failure.

The X-ray

Plain film radiography is an invaluable adjunct in the clinical assessment of congestive heart failure. The size and shape of the cardiac silhouette vary according to the etiology of the underlying heart disease, but the roentgen appearance of the lungs forms a common denominator that reflects heart failure per se. Careful attention to proper technique of film exposure is vital in providing fine details that are necessary for accurate interpretation.

Pulmonary edema: There are two forms of pulmonary edema, namely, interstitial and intra-alveolar edema. Interstitial pulmonary edema is the commoner and may be mistaken for poor film technique because it presents as generalized clouding or haziness of the lung fields all the way to the periphery. Vascular markings lose their sharp outline; edema surrounding bronchi results in distinctive, peribronchial cuffing, which should be sought by identifying end-on bronchi, especially in the inner third of the lung fields. Intra-alveolar edema results in radiodensities that are most prominent in the inner and middle zones of the lung, causing the characteristic "butterfly" appearance, with the heart as the body of the butterfly and the edema the wings. Intra-alveolar edema is essentially perihilar and bilaterally symmetrical.

Veins: Another important aspect of the chest x-ray is the appearance of the pulmonary and systemic veins. As pulmonary venous pressure rises, there is a tendency for the superior pulmonary veins to dilate and become prominent while the arteries and veins to the lower lobes constrict and become less prominent. The bilateral prominence of the superior pulmonary veins has been likened to the appearance of "antlers," an apt analogy (illustrated on page 99).

Distension of the right superior pulmonary vein as it emerges from the hilus causes straightening of the lateral hilar shadow, i.e., obliteration of the normal angle between the right upper pulmonary vein and the right pulmonary artery (page 98). In addition, the normally clear angle between the right pulmonary artery and the right atrial silhouette becomes clouded.

A rise in systemic venous pressure (right heart failure) results in prominence of the superior vena cava and azygous veins. The superior cava forms a vertical density at the right base; the azygous vein forms a pear-shaped density in the first right intercostal space as the dilated vessel courses forward to join the superior vena cava.

Kerley lines: Two types of Kerley lines are recognized – B lines (more distinctive) and A lines (a less common term). Kerley B lines are linear densities caused by thickening of the interlobular septa due to an increase in pulmonary venous pressure, especially in mitral stenosis but occasionally in left ventricular failure alone (page 99). These densities are represented by fine horizontal lines in the costophrenic angles and are most readily seen when properly exposed films are taken in full inspiration. Kerley A lines are less distinctive linear zones of peribronchial edema extending peripherally from the hilus.

Hydrothorax: Three types of chest effusions are important in congestive heart failure, namely, effusions into the free pleural space, loculated effusions into interlobular spaces, and subpleural effusions. Pleural effusions generally reflect biventricular failure and are seldom present with left ventricular failure alone. It is a point of interest that the pleural effusions of congestive heart failure may be right-sided or bilateral but rarely isolated to the left chest.

Free pleural fluid causes blunting of the costophrenic angles. The blunting can be seen in the posteroanterior film but is most easily detected in the lateral projection. Effusions in the interlobular spaces may simulate tumors and have been designated "vanishing tumors of the lung." The densities are ovoid, band-shaped, or wedge-shaped and are best seen in the oblique projections. They may persist after other signs of congestive heart failure have disappeared. Subpleural effusions, especially in the diaphragmatic subpleural space, are difficult to recognize and may be overlooked even when large. These subpleural effusions simulate elevations of the diaphragm and should be suspected in the presence of unexplained unilateral diaphragmatic elevation in patients with congestive heart failure.

Pulmonary emboli: Since patients with congestive heart failure are prone to pulmonary embolism, this complication should always be considered when x-rays are interpreted. Emboli may cast single or multiple shadows chiefly in the lower lobes, especially the right lower lobe. Roentgen features of heart failure commonly coexist.

In summary, certain clinical manifestations are common to cardiac failure per se irrespective of etiology. The purpose here has been to emphasize these manifestations as they present in the adult. Accordingly, attention has been devoted to clinical expressions of heart failure as manifested in the history, physical signs, and x-ray. The clinician should examine each of these areas in depth while relating each to the whole so that a complete, harmonious picture is established.

10

Cardiac Failure in Children: A Hemodynamic Overview

ABRAHAM M. RUDOLPH

University of California, San Francisco

When at any time of life the heart fails to provide an output adequate for the body's needs the reasons are to be found in a continuum of hemodynamic change. Either alteration in the heart compromises its ability to meet its circulatory responsibilities, or a new hemodynamic situation uncovers an existing flaw. The most radical changes happen at birth and continue with lessening intensity through the first year of life. It is in this period that up to 90% of heart failure in children occurs.

The principal source of an infant heart's pathologic disadvantage is to be found in congenital cardiac anomalies that may be nondetrimental when fetal circulatory mechanisms are operative but compromise some sequential flow patterns that take effect after birth. Prompt diagnosis and intervention may be required to save the infant's life. The appropriateness of treatment selected depends on an understanding of how the defects affect the hemodynamic situation and in what way they make themselves known.

Elimination of the placental circulation at birth removes a large, low-resistance circuit from the infant's systemic circulation and results in an immediate and dramatic increase in total systemic vascular resistance. At the same time, expansion of the lungs with air results in a marked decrease in the resistance of the blood vessels there and the establishment of a pulmonary circulation to maintain an adequate oxygen supply to the body. There is a three- to tenfold rise in pulmonary blood flow within the first few minutes after birth. While the direct physical effect of inflated alveoli helps dilate pulmonary vessels, the more important physiologic mediator appears to be the radically increased oxygen content in the blood and in the alveoli, to which pulmonary vessels appear extremely responsive. Also worth noting is the possible involvement of the kallikrein-kinin system. Bradykinin, a potent dilator of pulmonary vessels, is capable of constricting the umbilical artery and ductus arteriosus. These three physiologic events are all of importance in postnatal adjustments of the circulation. Elevated levels of bradykinin and its precursors have been noted in umbilical-cord and systemic blood of newborn experimental animals. The process may be partially triggered by pO_2 changes.

At the same time, umbilical venous flow to the lower body having been terminated, the amount of blood returning to the right atrium is reduced and that returning from the lungs to the left atrium is increased. The resulting raised differential of left over right atrial pressure functionally closes the flap of the foramen ovale. Simultaneously, increased pO_2 of aortic blood mediates the constriction of the muscle of the ductus arteriosus and the functional closure of that structure within 10 to 15 hours after birth; anatomic closure due to fibrosis or thrombosis is completed several days or weeks later.

With further expansion of alveoli and greater oxygenation of the blood, pulmonary vascular resistance continues to decrease and pulmonary blood flow to increase during the first few days of life.

During the first six to eight weeks the pulmonary circulation continues to undergo changes. Arterioles lose a great deal of smooth muscle component and dilate, and pulmonary arterial pressure, having fallen below systemic pressure, further declines to near-adult levels. Recognition of these shifting relationships is of prime importance in interpreting the hemodynamic implications of congenital heart lesions that produce communications between pulmonary and systemic circuits.

The factors now determining continued hemodynamic change are, first, the size of the communication defects and, second, the relationship between systemic and pulmonary vascular resistances. If the defect is very large, pressures between these two circuits continue to be equalized and the distribution of blood will continue, as in the fetus, to be determined by the relative resistances between the two circulations rather than by the sequence of normal adult flow. This presents no immediate problem at birth because pulmonary vascular resistance is still relatively high and there is not yet significant flow in either direction across a persistent patent ductus arteriosus or ventricular septal defect. However, as pulmonary resistance undergoes its normal maturational decrease, with dilation of arterioles and disappearance of smooth muscle, there is an increase of blood flow into the pulmonary circulation, and the demands of the handicapped systemic circulation are preempted by flow through the defect.

This increase of blood flow through the lungs results, of course, in increased pulmonary venous return to the left atrium and left ventricle. As pointed out by Frank and Starling, the ventricular action is directly related to the volume of blood that expands it in preparation for its systolic contraction. The left ventricle, its distension progressively increased by the growing volume of blood returning from the lungs, now increases its stroke volume. As pulmonary resistance continues to fall during the first few weeks of life, the systemic circulation may become further disadvantaged. A greater and greater load is placed on the left ventricle as it labors against the mounting volume and seeks vainly to satisfy the deprived systemic requirements. Progressive increase in end-diastolic pressure and volume results. As long as the ventricle can maintain this increased stroke volume no symptoms will occur, but eventually the organ is overextended and cardiac failure, predominantly left-sided, will follow.

This mechanism of left ventricular failure, which must be seen in relation to the postnatal decrease in pulmonary vascular resistance, explains the phenomena associated with all congenital heart lesions that establish a large communication between the ventricles or great vessels — truncus arteriosus communis, aortopulmonary fenestration, transposition with large ventricular septal defect, and the like. Much depends on the size of the

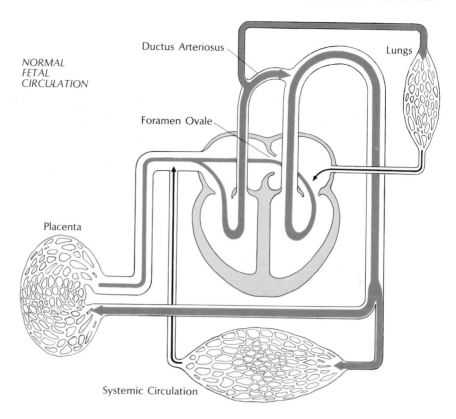

NORMAL FETAL CIRCULATION

Ductus Arteriosus

Lungs

Foramen Ovale

Placenta

Systemic Circulation

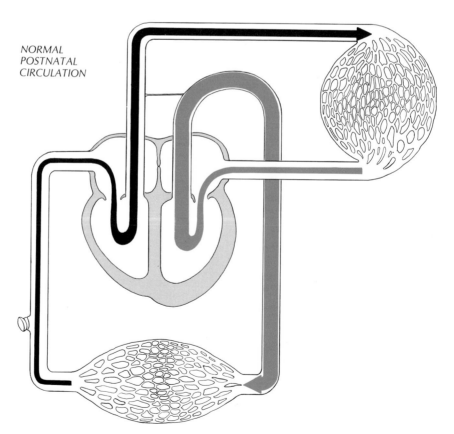

NORMAL POSTNATAL CIRCULATION

In these drawings of fetal and postnatal circulations, and in those that follow, magnitude of flow is indicated by width of vessel, magnitude of pressure by thickness of arrow (arterial blood, red; venous, black). Emphasis here is on placental and pulmonary circulatory adjustments at birth when elimination of low-resistance placental circulation increases systemic vascular resistance while pulmonary vascular resistance is decreased.

defect. When it is small enough to allow differential pressures between right and left circuits, the process described above — preferential flow to the decreasingly resistant pulmonary vascular bed — is attenuated and there is an important purchase of time. The somewhat less extreme volume load on the left ventricle stimulates adaptive mechanisms that allow it to cope. It is almost certain that sympatheticoadrenal responses participate in this; it has been well shown that when the sympatheticoadrenal system is blocked in such circumstances, cardiac failure occurs much more rapidly. A second adaptive mechanism brought into play is left ventricular hypertrophy, a phenomenon that requires time to develop.

During this period of stress any additional summons on cardiac output can precipitate cardiac failure in an infant who otherwise shows no clinical signs or symptoms relating to a cardiac defect. The development of physiologic anemia may not be important in a normal 2-to-3-month-old infant, but in one with a left-to-right shunt it may trigger heart failure. Any infection that demands increased cardiac output may do the same.

The importance of the relationship between pulmonary and systemic vascular resistances in the development of heart failure in infancy is dramatically illustrated in certain instances where pulmonary vascular resistance is circumstantially prevented from decreasing. That is why this type of heart failure is less common at high altitudes, where lower atmospheric oxygen delays the fall in pulmonary resistance. Similarly, infants with pulmonary diseases that cause hypoventilation, and thus lowered alveolar pO_2, may also demonstrate a delay in the pulmonary vascular maturational changes and thus may not develop heart failure until the pulmonary disease is cured.

For some reason yet to be elaborated, cardiac failure is rare in infants with atrial septal defect. Before birth, the right atrial pressure is higher than the left. But after birth, with normal maturation, decreased pulmonary resistance, and decreased right ventricular pressure, the atrial pressures are first equalized and then reversed.

When a large atrial septal defect is present, the left and right atrial pressures tend to equalize. It was generally held for many years that since the right ventricular muscle was as thick as that of the left ventricle in the fetal and immediate postnatal period, there was very little left-to-right shunt in newborn infants with even very large atrial septal defects. It was thought that if the two ventricles were of equal weight they had a similar compliance, and that it was necessary for the right ventricular muscle to thin out relative to the left before a large shunt could develop.

By ventricular compliance we refer to the amount of pressure required to produce a certain volume change in the ventricle. It has long been held that a hypertrophied ventricle has a low compliance and thus requires a relatively higher filling pressure to produce given volume changes. This hypothesis would suggest that greater end-diastolic, or filling, pressures would be found in individuals with pulmonic or aortic stenosis and consequently hypertrophied right ventricles. Nevertheless, it is well known that even in severe right ventricular hypertrophy with pulmonic stenosis there may be normal end-diastolic pressure and apparently normal stroke volume. On the other hand, it is probable that when hypertrophy has been present for some time decreased compliance is brought about more by increased fibrous and supporting tissues than by any muscular change.

It is now known, however, that large left-to-right shunts can occur within a few days after birth in infants with large atrial septal defects. This may be explained not on the basis of a change in right ventricular muscle but rather on the fall in pulmonary and rise in systemic vascular resistance. If the left and right ventricles are subjected to the same filling pressure, then end-diastolic volumes would be similar. Since, however, during systole the right ventricle is eject-

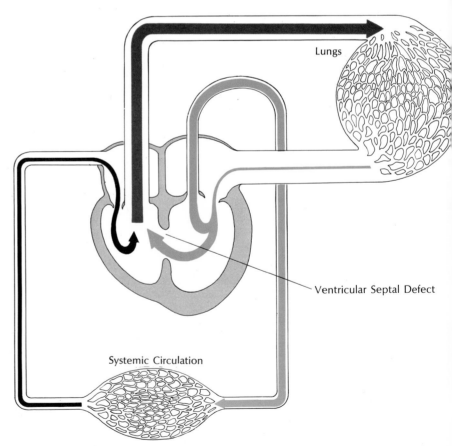

A large ventricular septal defect can predispose the infant to left heart failure. The maturational decrease in pulmonary vascular resistance causes increased flow into the lungs at the expense of the systemic circulation. Venous return to the left heart rises, enhancing stroke volume. The load on the left ventricle progressively increases as a concomitant of the effort to satisfy systemic needs.

ing against a lower outflow resistance, due to the drop in pulmonary vascular resistance, it would empty to a greater extent, viz., its end-systolic volume would be smaller. In diastole there would be a greater volume directed to the right ventricle because it would have a lower end-systolic volume and pressure than the left. The greater the decline in pulmonary vascular resistance, the greater will be the left-to-right shunt.

The rarity of cardiac failure in infants with large atrial septal defects is thus probably related to the fact that the development of the shunt is dependent on the fall in pulmonary vascular resistance and pulmonary artery pressure, and the large increase in volume handled by the ventricle is ejected at a low pressure.

When it comes to congenital defects of an obstructive nature, the main cause of heart failure is related to the increased systolic pressure re-

quired to effect flow across the obstructed segment. If there has not been time for a compensating hypertrophy to develop, the increased end-systolic volume will dilate the ventricle. An increase in end-diastolic pressure and volume will then occur, with the same consequences of over-extension and failure as occur with shunt lesions. It is for this reason that in patients with coarctation of the aorta or aortic stenosis heart failure is so common soon after birth, for it is at this time that a major overload of pressure is applied to the left ventricle, before it has had an opportunity to develop an adaptive hypertrophy. Should the lesion be small enough to permit time for adaptive growth, heart failure would be unusual until late childhood or adult life.

The elevation of left ventricular end-diastolic pressure, either in left-sided obstructive lesions or large left-to-right shunt lesions at the ventricular

or ductal levels, results in an increase in left atrial and pulmonary venous pressure. When this pressure reaches the point where exudation of fluid through pulmonary capillaries exceeds the amount that can be removed by lymphatic drainage, pulmonary edema develops. The critical pressure level at which this occurs appears to be considerably lower in the infant than in the adult. In an adult, pulmonary edema is usually manifested only when left atrial pressure exceeds about 25 mm Hg, but in infants it is not unusual to see clinical evidence of pulmonary edema with pressures as low as 15 mm Hg. The difference may be related to the greater capillary permeability of the infant lung or to a slower lymphatic drainage. At any rate, pulmonary edema is associated with increased rate and depth of breathing – and this is by far the most common presenting sign of heart failure in the infant, inasmuch as the vast majority of the defects that produce heart failure in infancy are associated with left-sided failure. It is not unusual, in cases where no local murmurs can be detected, for a misdiagnosis of pulmonary disease to be made initially. Commonly, the picture is one of increased respiratory effort, with decreased pO_2, mild cyanosis, and slightly elevated pCO_2.

So far we have discussed the mechanisms involved in the more common left-sided disorders. When left-sided failure persists for some time, right-sided failure usually develops. However, right-sided failure may be primary, as in the case of severe pulmonic stenosis or preductal coarctation of the aorta with patent ductus.

It is of much interest that the infant with right-sided failure does not commonly present with gross edema, as does the adult. Rather, the main and earliest feature is hepatomegaly. Although some increase in right atrial and venous pressure does occur, it does not reach the levels associated with right heart failure in adults. The reasons are not entirely clear. Possibly, the infant venous system is more compliant than that of the adult, so that a greater relative volume of blood can be accommodated in the liver and in the rest of the venous system without as much increase in pressure. Evidence of venous

Frank failure will not supervene as long as the left ventricle can maintain the increased stroke volume. However, eventually the increase in muscle mass and other compensatory mechanisms will no longer yield increased cardiac output and failure will result. Left and right ventricular enlargement will occur; pulmonary vein pressure will be elevated and pulmonary edema develop. Some impairment of oxygenation may result from edema.

Causes of Cardiac Failure in Infancy

DISTURBANCES IN CIRCULATORY DEVELOPMENT

A. *High-volume loads*

  1. Left-to-right shunt

    a. Aortopulmonary: patent ductus arteriosus, aortopulmonary fenestration, truncus arteriosus communis

    b. Ventricular: ventricular septal defect, atrioventricularis communis (both alone or with transposition of the great arteries), double outlet right ventricle

    c. Pulmonary to systemic venous: atrial septal defect, total anomalous pulmonary venous connection

  2. Peripheral arteriovenous fistula

    a. Cerebral

    b. Hepatic

  3. Valvar regurgitation

    a. Mitral

    b. Tricuspid

    c. Absent pulmonary valve

B. *Obstructive lesions*

  1. Outflow obstruction

    a. Left: coarctation of aorta, hypoplastic aorta, aortic stenosis

    b. Right: pulmonary stenosis or atresia

  2. Inflow obstruction

    a. Left: mitral atresia, cor triatriatum, stenosis of pulmonary veins, total anomalous pulmonary venous connection with obstructed common pulmonary vein

    b. Right: tricuspid atresia with small foramen ovale

C. *Inadequate systemic perfusion*

  1. Hypoplastic left heart with constricted ductus arteriosus

DISTURBANCES IN MYOCARDIAL FUNCTION

A. *Congenital:* anomalous origin left coronary artery, endocardial fibroelastosis

B. *Metabolic:* glycogen storage disease, hypocalcemia, hypoglycemia

C. *Infection:* viral myocarditis

DISTURBANCES IN CARDIAC RHYTHM

A. *Supraventricular tachycardias*

B. *Congenital complete heart block*

DISTURBANCES IN MYOCARDIAL OXYGEN SUPPLY

A. *Severe anemia*

B. *Severe hypoxemia and acidemia*

DISTURBANCES IN CARDIAC FILLING

A. *Pericardial effusion*

B. *Tension pneumothorax*

---

congestion is not usually apparent in infants, partly because the short neck and skin folds make it difficult to observe neck veins.

With right-sided failure there is, in infants as in adults, increased sodium retention and consequent diffuse edema (see Chapter 8, "The Mechanisms of Salt and Water Retention in Cardiac Failure," by Davis). This edema is rarely severe; one reason for this is that infant tissue can probably accommodate added fluid more readily than adult tissue can. More important is the fact that since right-sided failure in infants most commonly follows left-sided failure, the infant is usually quite ill with respiratory distress before the chronic edema so often seen in adults has time to develop. When it does develop, the pattern of distribution is different from that in the adult, no doubt because of the infant's horizontal posture. Edema tends to occur in dependent areas, such as the sacrum, and is frequently first seen around the eyes. This distribution is similar to that seen in renal disease. But the infant behaves much like the adult with regard to sodium excretion and one of the early signs of heart failure is increased perspiration, especially about the face 'and head and particularly while feeding.

There are, of course, other reasons for heart failure in infants and children, and chief among these is myocardial disease. The mechanism of failure here is related to the inability of the myocardium in such situations to expel an adequate stroke volume. End-systolic and diastolic volumes then increase together with end-diastolic pressure, producing the same developments that have been described in shunt and obstructive lesions. In infancy the condition is most usually related to Coxsackie infection or to subendocardial fibroelastosis. In older children, myocardial disease may also be associated with Coxsackie infection or with influenza and other viral diseases; fibroelastosis may also present for the first time in older children, and in these cases it is not known whether the lesion has been present from birth or occurred as a later development. A very common cause of heart failure in children above the age of one year, however, is still rheumatic fever, despite the decline in its severity in the past two decades. Most such cases of heart failure are seen during the acute attack, but in older children and adolescents the failure may be related to valvular involvement such as aortic or mitral insufficiency.

Note should be made that the arrhythmias are a not infrequent cause of heart failure in the infant, supraventricular tachycardia being chief among them. The longer the episode of arrhythmia, the greater the incidence of heart failure; when supraventricular tachycardia persists longer than 24 hours there is almost always some degree of heart failure. Also, arrhythmias are important in precipitating heart failure in myocardial disease and other conditions; for example, in a child with rheumatic heart disease and mitral insufficiency there may be no sign of failure until the occurrence of supraventricular tachycardia, atrial flutter, or fibrillation.

An effort has been made in the foregoing to relate the changing nature of the physiologic disturbances to the clinical consequences of congenital heart lesions. But a great deal more study of fetal and infant circulation is necessary. In the meantime, so far as treatment is concerned, the clinician must rely on existing methods of improving myocardial contractility, decreasing sodium retention or increasing its elimination, and general support. When successful, such treatment buys important time for adaptive cardiac mechanisms to assert themselves or for corrective surgery. It may be useful here to comment on some problems of management.

The mainstay of improving myocardial contractility is, of course, digitalization (see Chapter 13, "The Mechanism of Action of Digitalis," by Langer). A number of digitalis preparations are at hand, but no advantage of one over the other has been shown in the treatment of infants, and it is therefore advisable that physicians become thoroughly familiar with one or two of them rather than range over the wide variety. I prefer digoxin, deeming it advantageous in infants to use a rapidly absorbed and rapidly excreted drug. The dosage schedule is quite variable and the drug may be given intravenously, intramuscularly, or orally, although intravenous administration should be reserved for true emergencies. It should be stressed that the dosage of any digitalis preparation should be the minimum adequate to produce clinical improvement without producing toxicity. While general guidelines are incorporated in the table on page 108, individuals vary in their response and sensitivity, and it is essential to observe them closely.

The toxic effects of digoxin in infants and young children are almost invariably cardiac arrhythmias or varying degrees of heart block. Because of the relatively high frequency of such conduction disturbances, repeated E C G monitoring is advised. It is very unusual to see vomiting or gastrointestinal upset, as in adults with digitalis toxicity.

Special care must be taken with the very small or premature infant, who is quite vulnerable. Equal precaution is indicated for patients with acute myocarditis, who often develop toxic effects even with very small doses of digitalis. It is the author's practice to obtain E C G tracings for such patients two to three hours after each dose during the first two days of digitalization. Once the patient is on an established maintenance dose, the E C G need be checked only occasionally unless infection or complicating symptoms develop.

Diuretics have become an important tool in recent years in the treatment of cardiac failure in infants, particularly in acute conditions (see Chapter 14, "Diuretics in the Treatment of Congestive Heart Failure," by Laragh). It is extremely important when treating infants to obtain a baseline sample of blood for electrolyte analysis, so that the effects of diuretics on electrolyte balance can be evaluated. The mercurials have been largely replaced by ethacrynic acid or furosemide, the effect of which is frequently striking. The recommended dose of each is 1 mg/kg, ethacrynic acid administered intravenously and furosemide given intramuscularly; this dose may be repeated at intervals of about four hours. It has been my practice to switch from ethacrynic acid to chlorothiazide after severe symptoms of pulmonary edema abate, usually after 24 hours. With a chronic regimen of four days of chlorothiazide followed by three days off there is rarely any need for potassium supplementation, inasmuch as the infants have a good potas-

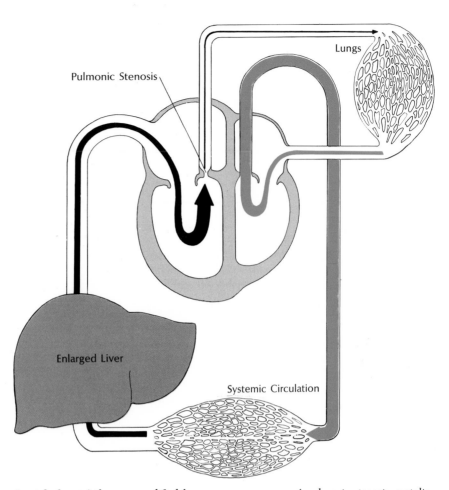

In right heart failure, exemplified here as a consequence of pulmonic stenosis, systolic pressure in the right ventricle is increased by the outflow obstruction and the ventricle becomes enlarged. Right atrial and venous pressures increase with venous congestion, the earliest manifestation of which is often hepatomegaly.

sium intake in milk and fruit juices. Nevertheless, intermittent checks of serum potassium levels should be performed.

Other supportive therapy includes oxygen administration, often necessary to overcome the impaired oxygenation occasioned by the presence of edematous fluid in the alveoli. Usually, 40% oxygen is all that is necessary in infant cardiac failure; higher levels should be avoided because of the hazard of damage to the respiratory epithelium. In addition, when the infant is extremely restless and distressed, it is often advantageous to use morphine at subcutaneous doses of 0.05 mg/kg.

When cardiac failure is manifested solely through the development of an arrhythmia, treatment will depend largely on the type. Digitalis is almost always effective against supraventricular tachycardia, the most com-

mon arrhythmia in infancy. If it is not effective, administering propranolol in addition may help relieve the tachycardia and revert the heart to sinus rhythm. When distress persists despite such treatment, external countershock should be tried; it has been effective in supraventricular tachycardia as well as in ventricular arrhythmias. Digitalis is sometimes ineffective in terminating recurrent arrhythmia, and in such instances propranolol may be added. If both are not effective, quinidine may be used. But quinidine sulfate can be a dangerous drug, particularly in infants, and it should be started cautiously, with careful observation by the electrocardiograph. It is my practice to start with a dose of 1 mg/kg, increasing this slowly every three hours, with E C G observation an hour after each dose, until the recommended dosage level of 4 mg/kg is reached. Should

Digoxin Dosage in Infants and Children*

Total Digitalizing Dose: First 24 Hours

Age of Child	Micro-grams/kg	Route
Prematures	25-50	Oral
Birth to 2 Years	60-80	Oral
Over 2 Years†	40-60	Oral

Schedule: Give ⅓ or ¼ of total dose stat followed by ⅓ or ¼ at 6-8 hour intervals. It is desirable to check on ECG 3-4 hours after each dose (midway between doses).

† *Usual maximum in children over 2 years is 2.5 mg.*

Maintenance dose: ¼ to ⅓ of digitalizing dose.

Intramuscular administration: usually about ¾ of oral dose.

* *Average requirements.*

there occur any prolongation of the QRS interval to greater than 50% of the resting level, there should be no further increase in quinidine dosage.

In older children with arrhythmias it is advisable to begin treatment with digitalis. If this is not effective, propranolol or, if necessary, quinidine can be tried. Patients with chronic rheumatic carditis and chronic atrial arrhythmias who do not respond to digitalis or quinidine may react favorably to external countershock.

Steroids have markedly decreased the mortality in acute rheumatic carditis and are definitely indicated in the presence of cardiomegaly or other evidences of heart failure. The dose that usually is adequate is 2 mg/kg/day, but this can be doubled if the condition is severe and the patient slow in responding. After the first week, it is suggested that steroids be given every other day, instead of daily, until evidence of acute carditis has disappeared.

The treatment of acute myocarditis associated with viral infections is mainly supportive. Extreme caution, watching carefully for the possible development of ventricular arrhythmias or heart block, is necessary in using digitalis, because these patients are frequently susceptible to digitalis toxicity. The usual support with diuretics and oxygen is recommended.

Catecholamines can provide important treatment for infants whose cardiac failure is associated with large shunts (see Chapter 6, "The Autonomic Nervous System in Heart Failure," by Braunwald). Experimental animals in which large left-to-right shunts were produced were found to be much less able to tolerate these shunts when the sympathetic system was blocked, and they went rapidly into failure. With continuous catecholamine infusion their tolerance of the shunt was considerably strengthened. Further, judging from urine assays, there is evidence of increased catecholamine release in infants with heart disease.

These findings have been applied in the treatment of infants with heart failure due to left-to-right shunts who do not respond to digitalis or diuretics. Epinephrine was first used; it appeared to increase myocardial contractility and overcome symptoms of cardiac failure. More recently it has been shown that the effect of catecholamine is largely related to beta-adrenergic stimulation, and isoproterenol has been used selectively in these circumstances.

Catecholamine infusion should be considered if digitalis and diuretics produce no response within 12 to 15 hours. It is important to bear in mind that epinephrine or isoproterenol will increase the heart rate. Since there is risk of inducing ventricular tachycardia with these drugs, it has been my practice to reduce the dosage at any evidence of arrhythmia or if the heart rate goes above 180 to 200 beats per minute. The ventricular ectopic beats present during the acute failure episode often disappear as contractility improves. In patients who are being prepared for surgery the infusion is often valuable as a preoperative measure; it may be continued during surgery and for 4 to 6 hours afterwards. In others, it may be continued for periods of 24 to 48 hours after the acute episode has passed, after which the rate of administration is tapered off.

The indications to proceed with surgical management depend to some extent on the circumstances. If extreme cardiac failure can be managed medically, it is often best to wait until the acute episode has passed. In obstructive lesions, once there has been severe failure, it is best to proceed to surgery at once because of the danger of subsequent attacks. In infants with left-to-right shunt lesions, whose cardiac failure has been precipitated by some intercurrent infection or incident, the decision for surgical interference is best deferred until after medical management and subsequent assessment of the lesion by cardiac catheterization. When failure is associated with a patent ductus arteriosus, surgical correction should almost certainly be undertaken after the failure has been medically improved. When there is difficulty in managing heart failure in the patient with a large ventricular septal defect, and if there is no evidence that an intercurrent lesion precipitated the failure episode, banding of the pulmonary artery generally is indicated. This will result in increased outflow resistance of the right ventricle, thereby decreasing the left-to-right shunt, the venous return to the left ventricle, and the left ventricle volume overload. Recently, however, the risks of direct closure of the ventricular septal defect in infancy have decreased; this may soon become the procedure of choice.

It is important to stress that a full evaluation is imperative for the infant with congenital heart disease who has had an episode of heart failure. It is not advisable to allow such an infant to continue without a positive diagnosis. The evaluation will usually involve cardiac catheterization, which can be delayed until after recovery from the acute episode if the patient is responding well. But if response to medical management is inadequate, catheterization should be undertaken immediately. With care, these diagnostic studies can be done with minimal risk. If it has been necessary to resort to the use of isoproterenol, it is helpful to continue its administration during the procedure. Anesthetic agents that decrease myocardial contractility, such as fluothane, should not be used. It is preferable to use no general anesthetic, and one should attempt to prevent arrhythmias by avoiding unnecessary manipulation of the catheter.

When better answers to the problems of treatment of infant heart failure appear, they will arise out of increased knowledge of normal and impaired hemodynamics in the fetus and child. We need to know much more about how congenital defects influence pulmonary circulation and the ductus arteriosus in fetal life and how such developments bear on postnatal adaptation. The mechanisms that mediate the transition from fetal to postnatal circulation still elude us. When we know why and how oxygen dilates the pulmonary vessels and constricts the ductus arteriosus, and when we have a clearer insight into the relationship between pO_2 and ductal resistance, we will make great strides in managing those infants whose adaptation to the terms of extrafetal life requires control over these factors.

The Cardiomyopathies

WALTER H. ABELMANN
Harvard University

There was a time when many if not most episodes of heart failure were attributed to myocarditis. With wider recognition of other forms of heart disease and realization that usually there was no evidence of inflammatory changes, the diagnosis was less often employed and fell into general disregard. A whole generation of physicians grew up duly warned about myocarditis as a condition widely overdiagnosed and overreported. The possibility of its presence was seldom considered even when it would have been entirely logical to do so.

Today a more balanced view would apply. Both inflammatory and noninflammatory cardiomyopathies are more often correctly identified than not. However, it is also quite likely that their true incidence and prevalence in this country are considerably greater than is generally realized. This would seem to apply to the cardiomyopathies as a group. In this chapter, "cardiomyopathy" is defined as disease that attacks primarily the heart muscle and spares, or only minimally involves, other structures: pericardium, coronary vessels, or heart valves. Cardiomyopathies due to a known infectious or toxic agent, or associated with a known systemic disease, have been labeled "secondary cardiomyopathies." Disease of heart muscle of unknown cause and not associated with systemic disease is known as "primary cardiomyopathy."

In many regions outside the U.S. and western Europe, cardiomyopathy is a major cause of disability and death. A survey in Jamaica attributed 15% of heart failure in patients past the age of 35 to cardiomyopathy; in Uganda endomyocardial fibrosis was identified in 11% of patients with clinical heart disease; in northwest Brazil cardiomyopathy accounts for fully 30% of heart disease.

By contrast, in the U.S. fewer than 1% of deaths due to heart disease can be attributed to cardiomyopathy. However, any data on disease incidence, prevalence, and mortality always stand in important relationship to recognition. Also, where a recognizable disease is extremely prevalent the presence of another, less clinically striking, disease of the same organ system may be difficult to discern. Could the high prevalence of arteriosclerotic heart disease in this country tend to prevent identification of noncoronary forms of myocardial disease? There is good reason to believe so. When cardiomyopathy is diligently sought for it is often found. For example, when Saphir examined multiple blocks from both atria and ventricles, inflammatory lesions of the myocardium were recognized in up to 9.3% of autopsy specimens. Formerly, at our hospital fewer than 1% of our cardiac consultations were for cardiomyopathy, but in the latest tally the figure was 5%; much of the increase may have been due to improved identification. During life, cardiomyopathy may be missed because the disease is often clinically silent. In part this is because lesions may be focal rather than diffuse, affecting but a fraction of heart muscle, and unless they produce disturbances of conduction or major arrhythmias their functional effect is likely to be negligible. On the other hand, serious arrhythmias, cardiac arrest, or cardiac failure may be the first overt manifestations of cardiomyopathy. At least in some cases these might be prevented or treated more successfully if the preceding subclinical process had been recognized.

For many clinicians the diagnosis of cardiomyopathy remains one of exclusion. But a more direct approach is possible and probably should be more generally applied, considering the tendency still to assume that any nonvalvular or noncongenital cardiac disorder is probably coronary in origin.

Although no one manifestation is clearly diagnostic of cardiomyopathy, a constellation of certain signs should prompt suspicion, or even a presumptive diagnosis: cardiomyopathy is more common in men, particularly young men, who do physical work. The victim is usually totally asymptomatic when the first abnormality – left, right, or combined ventricular hypertrophy or enlargement – is seen on a routine chest x-ray or electrocardiogram. Or an otherwise healthy individual may begin to complain of occasional palpitation, dizziness, or syncope, and an electrocardiogram may reveal a transient arrhythmia or conduction abnormality. There may be an episode of mild heart failure with spontaneous recovery and no recurrence for a considerable time. These signs in an individual without pain, heart murmur, or history of lung disease or hypertension are quite likely due to cardiomyopathy.

Occasionally the focus of myocardial damage is large enough to yield an electrocardiographic picture indistinguishable from an old myocardial infarction. In chronic cardiomyopathies the electrocardiogram may show absent R waves in precordial leads or suggest apical or subendocardial infarction. More often the E C G changes are quite nonspecific; the same changes in the QRS complex, ST segments, and T waves are often seen in other conditions.

Moreover, the pathologist using standard procedures will as a rule be unable to identify lesions of specific diagnostic value. The lesions may be focal or diffuse, associated with mononuclear or polymorphonuclear infiltrates, fibrosis, hypertrophy, and, more rarely, with granulomas. Histologic examination of heart tissue rarely permits an etiologic diagnosis, and myocardial biopsy has only occasionally been helpful. To compound the difficulty, while it is now believed that many cases are probably associated with some toxic or infectious agent, in only a small minority of clinical cases can a known factor be incriminated.

		HYPERTROPHIC	OBSTRUCTIVE	CONGESTIVE
MORPHOLOGIC		Left or biventricular hypertrophy	Hypertrophy of ventricular septum and anterior mitral valve leaflet obstruct left ventricular outflow tract	Biventricular dilatation
HEMODYNAMIC	Cardiac Output	Normal	Normal or ↓	↓↓
	Stroke Volume	Normal	Normal or ↓	↓↓
	Ventricular Filling Pressure	Normal or ↑	Normal or ↑	↑↑
	Other Findings		Aortic systolic pressure gradient May have mitral regurgitation (mm Hg) 200 150 --LV BA 100 50 0 LV (Left ventricular) BA (Brachial arterial)	May have mitral or tricuspid regurgitation Wide arteriovenous O₂ differen Decreased ejection fraction

Recently fresh interest has developed in using newer techniques including electron microscopy, histochemistry, and immunology to learn more about the etiology and pathophysiology of cardiomyopathies. In part this reflects a growing suspicion that early acute forms of cardiomyopathy may possibly pave the way for the development of a chronic disorder inflicting significant morbidity and mortality.

One of the puzzles about cardiomyopathies has been that the principal morphologically recognizable responses of the myocardium to disease and injury are much fewer than are the recognized myocardial diseases. That makes it reasonable to assume that the myocardial abnormalities may represent unitary responses — perhaps operating through a common pathway. And even if the determinants of myocardial injury were better understood one would still have to explain not only how injury occurs but why. About 5% of systemic blood flow perfuses the coronary vascular bed, making a total of some 360 liters daily that perfuse the myocardial capillaries in an average sedentary man (more in a physically active individual). Accordingly, any potentially damaging agent entering the bloodstream, even if transiently, reaches the myocardium and could attack the myocardial interstitium. This includes a variety of agents such as infectious organisms, toxins, drugs, and abnormal metabolic products. However, potentially noxious substances are also likely to be removed promptly because of the high vascularity of the heart and its network of lymphatic channels. The responsiveness of coronary vessels to increased metabolic demands also has a protective effect; at times of increased need these vessels automatically dilate to increase coronary blood flow and oxygen delivery to the myocardium. Thus, even when the partial pressure of oxygen falls to a comparatively low level, myocardial oxygenation is maintained throughout wide ranges of the activity of the normal heart. The heart's priority call on both blood flow and oxygen may in part account for the relative rarity of clinically or pathologically demonstrable myocardial disease in systemic infections and general toxic states.

Although generalizations must be stated cautiously because of the multiplicity of disorders included, certain shared features in reference to the course of cardiomyopathy are worth noting. For example, in acute myocarditis — regardless of etiology — the stage of maximal tissue injury is usually also the stage of maximal clinical evidence of myocardial disease, although quite typically the myocardial damage exceeds any clinical manifestations. In most instances the episode of disease is followed by complete recovery, but in fatal cases death is likely to occur early, usually at the height of illness. The course may be so rapid as to preclude development of congestive failure. Occasionally, acute myocarditis may present as forward failure with severe arterial hypotension and progress to fulminating cardiac shock, carrying the gravest prognosis.

In chronic cardiomyopathy a long asymptomatic course generally precedes the first evidence of disease. In chronic cardiomyopathy that is characterized chiefly by hypertrophy of cardiac muscle, the asymptomatic stage may be prolonged for years or it may be interrupted by embolic episodes secondary to mural thrombosis or by sudden death. The last is more likely in obstructive cardiomyopathy, in which ejection of blood is impeded by muscular narrowing of either ventricular outflow tract.

Recent studies by several investigators have identified four distinct hemodynamic patterns, each characteristic of a type of cardiomyopathy, thereby elucidating its pathophysiology. One of these patterns is virtually normal, in terms of cardiac output and stroke volume and either normal or mildly-to-moderately elevated left ventricular filling pressures. This pattern is generally seen in chronic cardiomyopathies presenting as cardiomegaly of unknown etiology, with x-ray and E.C.G evidence of left ventricular hypertrophy, with or without arrhythmias, embolic episodes, or intermittent left ventricular failure. A second, obstructive, pattern is seen in massive cardiac hypertrophy, involving especially the ventricular septum, resulting in obstruction of the left ventricular outflow tract. This hypertrophic obstructive cardiomyopathy is also known as idiopathic hypertrophic subaortic stenosis. Recently, it has been recognized that the obstruction of the left ventricular outflow tract is due in part to anterior displacement of the anterior leaflet of the mitral valve during the latter part of systole, to the point of making contact with the hypertrophied interventricular septum.

This same abnormality can be detected by means of echocardiography, an increasingly valuable noninvasive diagnostic technique. The degree of obstruction may vary from time to time and even from beat to beat. A

RESTRICTIVE

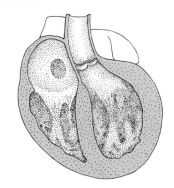

Stiffening of ventricular walls by infiltration or deposits (e.g., amyloid)

Normal or ↓

Normal or ↓

 ↑

Characteristic ventricular pressure tracings resemble constrictive pericarditis: early diastolic dip.

End-diastolic plateau

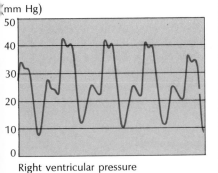

Right ventricular pressure

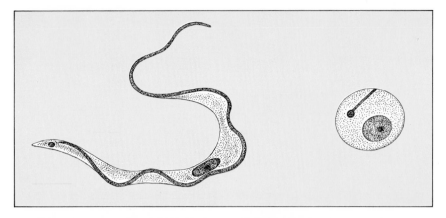

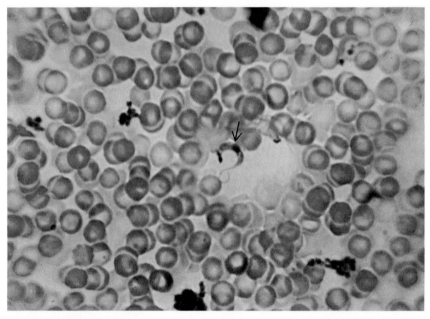

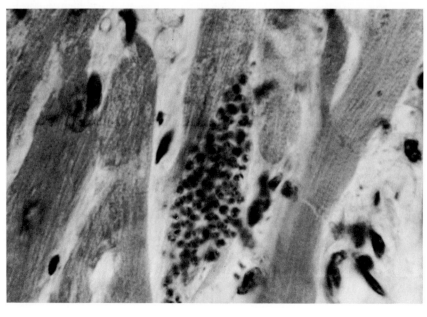

Experimental model of chronic Chagas' disease was developed by inoculating mice with Trypanosoma cruzi; the blood and intracellular leishmanial forms are shown in drawings. Parasitemia appears during second week; peripheral blood smear was made 30 days after inoculation (one organism can be seen). An aggregate of leishmanial forms in the myocardium (pseudocyst) is shown in the lower photo, made at 49 days postinoculation.

decrease in left ventricular volume, such as accompanies upright posture or the Valsalva maneuver, tends to increase obstruction; whereas an increase in left ventricular volume, as in the supine position or in congestive heart failure, decreases obstruction. This obstructive syndrome can be differentiated from that of fixed valvular or subvalvular obstruction, which it resembles clinically, by the phenomenon of postextrasystolic accentuation: The increased contractile force resulting from postextrasystolic potentiation increases the degree of obstruction; thus the post extrasystolic beat is characterized by a pulse pressure that is more narrow than the pulse pressure of the normal beats. Muscular obstruction is also increased by use of inotropic agents such as digitalis glycosides or isoproterenol and diminished by beta-adrenergic blocking agents such as propranolol. Idiopathic hypertrophic subaortic stenosis is often familial, and examination of a patient's family may lead to early detection of other cases.

A third, or restrictive, hemodynamic pattern is relatively rare and is typical of diffuse infiltrative or degenerative myocardial disease, such as may be caused by amyloidosis or by myocardial fibrosis, especially when the endocardium is also involved. Here, cardiac output may be normal or diminished, but left and also right ventricular filling pressures are elevated. Ventricular pressure tracings show a characteristic early diastolic dip, followed by an elevated end-diastolic plateau. This reflects a decreased compliance of the ventricle that limits diastolic filling. This pattern resembles that seen in constrictive pericarditis.

The fourth, or congestive, hemodynamic pattern is usually one of biventricular failure; findings include a combination of low cardiac output, small stroke volume, a wide arteriovenous oxygen difference, and a significant increase in both left and right atrial and ventricular end-diastolic pressures. Response to exercise is poor; ventricular filling pressures tend to increase but cardiac output does not increase proportionately; O_2 extraction increases and arteriovenous oxygen difference widens even further. This is the hemodynamic pattern most often seen clinically in both acute and chronic cardiomyopathies, since these cases frequently come to light only with onset of heart failure.

Certain noticeable variations in prevalence of cardiomyopathy among different patient groups have yet to be satisfactorily explained. Search for cardiomyopathy at an inner city general hospital, as I have done, and you will find it regularly. Search a community hospital in the suburbs, where the general health level is better, and you will find it only rarely. Myocardial lesions and diseases are also known to occur more frequently among the chronically ill and debilitated. These observations have led to speculation that either infection or malnutrition may be the responsible factors in cases not otherwise explained. To be sure, the suggestion that infection may be an important cause of myocardial disease is hardly new. There is scarcely any known infectious agent – bacterial, rickettsial, spirochetal, viral, or parasitic – that has not been associated with myocardial lesions. Most recently, Coxsackie B viruses have been implicated in acute myocarditis, first mainly among newborn infants, then also in older children and adults. Nutritional disorders including dysproteinemias and iron deficiency anemia have also been incriminated; even the lack of a single dietary constituent such as thiamine can be solely responsible for myocardial disease.

However, knowing that a given substance or the lack of it is capable of producing heart muscle injury is not the same as proving it responsible in a particular case. Thus far the chief evidence has been indirect. For instance, following clinical outbreaks of illness caused by certain influenza and Coxsackie viruses more acute myocarditis has been recorded, and routine E C G's show a higher incidence of abnormalities. It is logical to suggest that the excess myocardial disease is due to the predominant virus or viruses, but it is difficult to be certain. Demonstrating neutralizing antibodies in the blood against a given virus or recovering virus by culturing throat or intestinal washings does not establish cause and effect within the heart muscle.

Work by several investigators strongly suggests that development of myocardial disease, and its severity

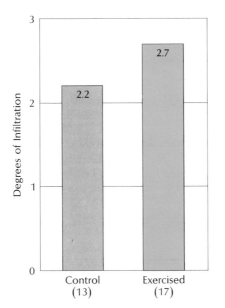

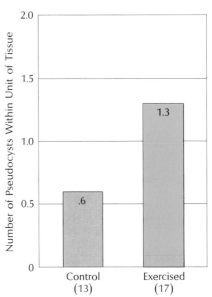

Effects of forced exercise (by swimming) on acute myocarditis were studied in T. cruzi-*infected mice; as graphs indicate, infiltration and encystation were more extensive in exercised than control mice. The number of animals in each group is indicated in parenthesis. Myocardial section from exercised mouse (below left) shows more pronounced infiltration and necrosis at 50 days postinoculation than does control (right); two foci of leishmanial forms of* T. cruzi *can be seen (arrows).*

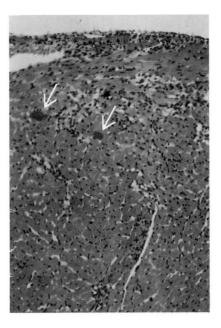

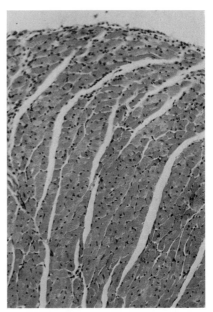

once it develops, depends on a combination of factors. For example, the myocardial lesions of acute experimental Chagas' disease – myocarditis due to *Trypanosoma cruzi* – are more severe and extensive if nutritional deficiency accompanies the parasitic infection. When Yaeger and Miller carefully studied the course of the disease in rats they found that in animals also rendered thiamine deficient, lesions were more extensive and parasites more numerous. Similar effects were seen in infected animals made deficient in pantothenate, pyridoxine, or lysine. In other work, J. M. Pearce found that the severity of experimental myocarditis induced by virus infection could be markedly increased by subjecting the animals to anoxia. Pearce also found that whereas myocarditis could be induced by intravenous injection of *Streptococcus pyogenes* toxin, the incidence was far greater if the animals were also inoculated intratesticularly with virus III. Conceivably, bacterial infections of the respiratory tract, by their com-

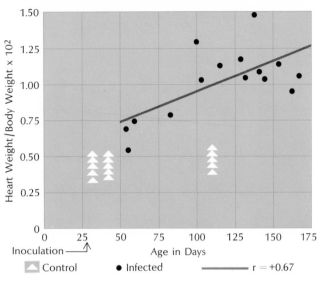

With the passage of time, the mean heart weight/body weight ratios of T. cruzi-infected mice became significantly greater than those of noninfected controls, as is shown by the graph at left.

As the graph at right demonstrates, exercise as such has an additive effect on heart weight. This additive effect becomes much more pronounced when infection is present.

bined toxic and anoxic effects, may increase the incidence of myocarditis from underlying viral infections.

In our laboratory, we have studied experimental Chagas' disease, a model of cardiomyopathy that closely resembles a human disease of considerable clinical importance in several areas of the world. In Central and South America alone an estimated seven million are presently infected with Chagas' disease; another 20 million are considered at risk. There are no effective specific measures for in-

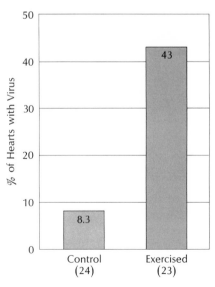

Virus replication is augmented by exercise in experimental Coxsackie A myocarditis, as shown by recovery of virus from hearts of exercised, infected animals sacrificed four and nine days after inoculation.

terrupting the course of the disease; only palliative means are available to control advancing heart failure.

Other workers have focused on the acute stages of Chagas' disease; our intent was to develop a model paralleling all stages of the human disease, presenting in sequence the inflammatory lesions of acute, subacute, and chronic myocarditis, the later stages of myocardial fibrosis and necrosis, and progressive development of cardiac hypertrophy, dilatation, and heart failure. By this means we sought to learn more about the pathophysiology of the disease and to examine the possible effects of several factors implicated as modifiers of myocardial disease in man.

The model was developed by producing a relatively mild disease in mice by inoculating them at around one month of age with a Colombian T. cruzi strain. Infection could be demonstrated in all inoculated animals by examination of the peripheral blood for trypanosomes; parasitemia appeared during the second week after inoculation, reached its peak during the fifth week, and had largely subsided by 12 weeks thereafter. During the acute parasitemic phase the animals appeared healthy, grew normally, and maintained their weights. Beginning with the third month, their fur became ruffled and sparse, and body weight fell significantly below that of noninfected controls; muscle

wasting and weakness became increasingly evident. After subsidence of the acute parasitemic phase, gross dilatation of cardiac chambers was more often seen; myocardial infiltrates became progressively more widespread and foci of degeneration more severe. Acute infiltrative and necrotic lesions continued to appear and increased in intensity and distribution until more than a year after inoculation.

The effects of forced exercise – swimming at a 33° C water temperature an hour a day five times a week – were studied during the acute and subacute phases. Ratios of heart weight to body weight were determined in infected animals. During both acute and subacute phases the combination of myocarditis and exercise produced significantly greater cardiac hypertrophy and a greater death rate than either factor alone. On microscopic examination the enlarged hearts of the infected "swimmers" showed more diffuse cellular infiltrates and more severe necrosis than those of control animals. Thus in both the acute and subacute phases of the disease the level of the animals' activity appeared to be a determinant not only of heart weight but also of the extent of parasitic invasion and the inflammatory response of the host.

Moreover, although the disease-enhancing effects of forced exercise were maximal when imposed during the acute phase of the disease, they were also seen when exercise preceded the acute infection. Among mice made to swim the 300 minutes weekly starting eight weeks before inoculation and for another eight weeks during infection, 9 of 12 died during the acute phase. Individual hearts from infected exercised animals – especially those that died early – were remarkable for the severity and diffuseness of myocardial infiltration and necrosis, and for the abundance of parasitic aggregates.

Significantly, around the same time, in experiments with Coxsackie A viral myocarditis, we showed that virus replication in the mouse heart was augmented by physical exercise. This effect has since been confirmed for Coxsackie B viruses by our former collaborator Martin Lerner, now at Wayne State University. Through such experiments it has been quite firmly established, for both parasitic and viral myocarditis, that exercise has a deleterious effect, clearly favoring the invading organism over the host. In this context perhaps the observed decrease in spontaneous physical activity in animals infected with Chagas' disease was adaptive in exerting a protective effect on the heart.

In any case, the findings relative to exercise may have immediate clinical pertinence. The practice of early mobilization and activity of patients with heart disease, which began with increased awareness of the dangers of prolonged bed rest following myocardial infarction, has often been extended to include patients with other heart diseases, often without differentiation of the underlying cause. The animal findings suggest the possibility that an acute inflammatory process in the heart may subside sooner if the organ is rested. Until there is evidence to the contrary, probably all inflammatory heart lesions should be treated by limitation of activity.

We also sought to assess the possible role of immune responses in the progression from acute to chronic phases in myocardial disease. Animals infected with *T. cruzi* were treated with cyclophosphamide. This immunosuppressive drug modified significantly the acute disease – but not as anticipated. Parasitemia increased, myocarditis was exacerbated, mortality rose. Intracardiac thrombosis appeared with striking frequency.

Earlier observers had found the use of corticosteroids associated with increased mortality in acute Chagasic myocarditis; similar findings have also been reported in experimental Coxsackie myocarditis. Rather than support the view that immune processes per se are the cause of heart damage in myocarditis, evidence of this kind suggests that these processes appear to benefit the host. Even with the limited data available, caution would seem indicated in the use of immunosuppressive agents and corticosteroids in patients with proved infectious myocarditis. Corticosteroids should probably be limited to the treatment of severe, life-threatening myocarditis associated with collagen diseases such as acute rheumatic fever and lupus erythematosus or granulomatous diseases such as sarcoid.

A key question about myocardial diseases as a group is the relation between acute inflammatory forms of disease and chronic cardiomyopathy. It has been postulated that chronic cardiomyopathy may be a late stage of an episode of acute myocarditis that has perhaps occurred in the distant past; the theory has been that the chronic disease could result from a hyperimmune response to the earlier infection or perhaps an autoimmune response to components of myocardial tissue released by necrosis. The possibility of a relationship will no doubt remain very much alive as long as most cases of chronic cardiomyopathy remain etiologically unexplained.

Only recently Lerner and coworkers reported intriguing findings in mice that had experimental myocarditis induced with Coxsackie B virus. Well after the acute stage of disease had passed there was a chronic phase marked by myocardial fibrosis and hypertrophy. Thus there now is a chronic cardiomyopathy that seems to be a sequel to acute myocarditis, but if this occurs in man as well as mice remains to be seen.

Also unknown is the role of alcohol in development of cardiomyopathy. In our studies of Chagasic myocarditis, inoculated, ethanol-fed mice had a more severe and lethal form of disease than those fed isocalorically with sucrose. Clinically, it is well known that cardiomyopathy develops with undue frequency among chronic alcoholics, and the term alcoholic cardiomyopathy is well entrenched in the medical literature. Is there reason to postulate an etiologic role for alcohol in cardiomyopathy? Several studies suggest that alcohol is toxic to heart muscle. Ventricular function is impaired, both in man and animals, with high concentrations of alcohol in the blood, and withdrawal of alcohol improves cardiac performance in patients with abnormal myocardial function. But what has not been shown is that alcohol as such can produce hypertrophy, fibrosis, congestive heart failure, and other abnormalities characteristic of chronic cardiopathy. Identical findings are seen in individuals who never drink.

Interestingly, a few years ago a distinctive form of cardiomyopathy associated with excessive ingestion of

---

Classification of Cardiomyopathies

(after Mattingly)

Disorders responsive to specific therapy in color

INFLAMMATORY	METABOLIC	NEUROMUSCULAR
Bacterial	Nutritional	Muscular dystrophies
Viral	Hormonal	Friedreich's ataxia
Parasitic	Electrolyte	
Nonspecific	Thiamine deficiency	IDIOPATHIC
Hypersensitivity	Thyrotoxicosis	Idiopathic hypertrophy
Brucellosis		Idiopathic hypertrophic
Tuberculosis	INFILTRATIVE	subaortic stenosis
Psittacosis	Amyloidosis	Familial cardiomyopathy
Rickettsial	Glycogen storage	Alcoholic cardiomyopathy
Toxoplasmosis	disease	Endomyocardial fibrosis
Lupus erythema-	Hemochromatosis	Postpartum cardiomy-
tosus	Neoplastic disease	opathy

a specific alcoholic beverage – beer – was traced not to the beer itself but to cobalt salts added to enhance its appearance. The disease was marked by sudden onset of rapidly progressive right heart failure, massive cardiac enlargement, and quite frequently a quick death. Within a short period there was a 48-case outbreak in Quebec, with 20 fatalities, and one of 40 in Omaha, with 16 fatalities.

Pathologists viewing histologic material were struck by the nature and severity of the myocardial lesions, unlike any previously seen in chronic alcoholic patients. In Canada, an expert committee of the health ministry first ruled out a number of toxic agents (arsenic, pesticides, magnesium, phosphorus, and radium included). Cobalt was implicated on the basis of thyroid pathology. It seems that cobalt was being used as an additive to maintain the "head" of draught beer; the same was true in Omaha. In both cities the outbreak occurred shortly after the cobalt-containing additive was first used; it ended when the practice was discontinued.

Subsequently, the investigators succeeded in partially reproducing the pathologic changes and the fatal disease in animals by administering cobalt, but any precise relationship of the cobalt to the disease entity in humans was not established. It was postulated that the cobalt effect was not one of direct injury to the heart but that, perhaps through enzyme interference, cobalt might be exaggerating a thiamine deficiency caused by the high alcohol intake.

However, with mounting interest in the cardiomyopathies it has become apparent that only rarely is a single agent likely to inflict sufficient muscle injury so as to make cardiac impairment clinically evident. More typically a multiplicity of factors seem to impinge on the heart and tax its reserve. It is surely more than coincidence that the populations of those regions where cardiomyopathy is most common are also exposed to many other stresses – severe nutritional deficiency, various infectious diseases, anemia due to parasitic infestation, hot and humid environment. In these areas cardiomyopathy often

becomes manifest for the first time in women during pregnancy; not uncommonly these women develop signs of heart failure that then subside and do not reappear until the next pregnancy.

All of these conditions – pregnancy, infection, nutritional deficiency, extremes of temperature and humidity – share a common feature. They are likely to impose demands for increased cardiac output and work. Under normal circumstances the heart has more than adequate reserves to enable it to meet changing physiologic requirements, and when it is impaired or damaged by disease it may still perform normally at rest but be liable to failure when its workload is increased. The same situation will apply whether the damage results from interference with myocardial perfusion or inflammatory and necrotic processes in the myocardium. Whatever the individual or immediate cause, it is the relationship of reserve capacity to cardiac load that determines the level at which heart failure will occur, or whether it occurs at all. The more compromised the reserve capacity, the lower the threshold at which heart failure occurs. Actually, in the various forms of cardiomyopathy, heart failure, if it occurs, is usually a late event, though it is unlikely unless there is severe and diffuse myocardial involvement. There can be significant underlying damage and compensatory hypertrophy before signs of serious dysfunction appear.

Whereas heart failure in chronic cardiomyopathy is most often biventricular, in acute myocarditis it is likely to affect predominantly the right ventricle, for reasons not yet clear. This is one of the observations we have been attempting to follow up by studies of the distensibility or compliance of both ventricles in the experimental model of Chagasic myocarditis. In the normal animal the thinner-walled right ventricle is already more distensible than the left for a given amount of pressure. In the presence of myocarditis both ventricles, but especially the right, become more distensible. Evidently the thinner-walled right ventricle is weakened more than the left by the inflammatory process.

As a rule, the heart failure of cardiomyopathy responds to standard regimens including diuresis, sodium restriction, and digitalis. However, it should be noted that there appears to be an increased likelihood of digitalis toxicity, especially in acute myocarditis. For this reason it is advisable to use short-acting glycosides such as ouabain or digoxin in submaximal doses, to digitalize slowly, and to monitor the electrocardiogram. Given the likelihood of toxicity, use of digitalis is not advised in acute myocarditis in the absence of heart failure.

According to some reports, clinical response to digitalis is likely to be inadequate in chronic cardiomyopathy when biventricular failure occurs. We have not found this to be the case. In studies of the effect of ouabain on right and left ventricular function in such patients, in our laboratory and elsewhere, positive inotropic action has been demonstrated with few exceptions, the latter mainly in cases of restrictive myocardial disease.

From what has been said earlier there appear to be sound reasons for recommending restriction of bodily activity and even bed rest in the presence of heart failure. In this connection it is worth recalling the clinical studies of George Burch and associates in New Orleans, which showed that intractable myocardial failure often responds favorably to prolonged bed rest. A climatically controlled environment, where the high heat and humidity of New Orleans could not add to the cardiac workload, was also of benefit.

Needless to say, it would be preferable to prevent progression of the myocardial disease to the stage of clinical failure. For this reason it is important to identify and, if possible, control the contributory causes – perhaps a systemic disease, obesity, or some environmental stress – that can both precipitate and perpetuate heart failure. It is hoped that more systematic application of available methodology, not only laboratory techniques for delineating etiologic factors but epidemiologic approaches to prevalence and incidence patterns, will increase our knowledge of the cardiomyopathies and improve their control.

Chronic Cor Pulmonale

ALFRED P. FISHMAN

University of Pennsylvania

In parts of the world having an unusually high incidence of bronchitic infection, cor pulmonale is a common type of circulatory ailment. For example, in regions of England and India, particularly those in which dust, smog, and smoke are always in the air, cor pulmonale may account for up to one fourth of patients hospitalized for heart failure. This figure may be even higher in certain parts of the United States, such as Arizona, where patients with respiratory disorders tend to congregate. Unfortunately, reliable estimates or comparisons of incidence are not possible because of inadequate recognition and reporting of the cardiac disorder. Nonetheless, cor pulmonale does seem to constitute a substantial fraction of heart disease (at least 6% to 7% in the U. S.) and its incidence seems destined to increase as chronic pulmonary disease becomes more prevalent.

To keep matters in perspective, it should be added at once that chronic pulmonary disorders are more apt to cause breathlessness than to strain the right ventricle to the stage of cor pulmonale. Indeed, not only does the right heart remain normal in size in the great majority of patients with diffuse pulmonary disease but it may even be unusually small, as it is in the severer types of emphysema (Burrows, 1966). On the other hand, the type of pulmonary disorder most commonly associated with cor pulmonale, i.e., chronic bronchitis, is remarkable in that dyspnea is not a prominent feature.

A brief list of initiating disorders that may culminate in cor pulmonale is on page 123. Rarely, as in massive conglomerate fibrosis, multiple pulmonary emboli, or "primary pulmonary hypertension," does the evolution of cor pulmonale depend simply on curtailment of the pulmonary vascular bed and on mechanical obstruction to blood flow. Instead, whether cardiac problems are apt to arise in patients with pulmonary disorders depends chiefly on the state of the arterial blood, particularly hypoxemia. Because of the preeminent role of hypoxemia, the present discussion of cor pulmonale will begin by focusing on disorders of the ventilatory apparatus that impair aeration of the blood and their circulatory sequelae.

Normally, the lungs maintain delicate balance in alveolar-capillary gas exchange so that the gaseous composition of arterial blood remains remarkably constant over a wide range of metabolic requirements. The basis for this stability is the precise adjustment of the alveolar ventilation to the changing metabolic needs of body tissues; arterial blood oxygen and carbon dioxide tensions are thus maintained within narrow normal limits, at approximately 95 mm Hg and 40 mm Hg, respectively. When the balance is upset in the direction of alveolar hypoventilation, the arterial carbon dioxide tension is automatically raised and the oxygen tension automatically lowered.

Alveolar Hypoventilation: General and Net

For several reasons the arterial pCO_2 is the more frequently used index of alveolar ventilation. Alveolar ventilation and alveolar pCO_2 are related in a straightforward mathematical way, and alveolar and arterial pCO_2 are usually almost identical. This close relationship does not apply between alveolar and arterial pO_2 (the latter being invariably lower). Moreover, chemical control of respiration is tied much more closely to changes in arterial pCO_2 than to the arterial pO_2. In practice, an arterial pCO_2 in excess of 45 mm Hg is accepted as evidence of alveolar hypoventilation; a decrease in pO_2 regularly accompanies the increase in pCO_2.

These principles apply clinically to alveolar hypoventilation in either of its distinctly different forms – *general* or *net*. In the *general* form, the lungs are normal but inadequately ventilated. They may be pictured as a bellows that fails to perform well because of either an inadequate drive from the respiratory centers in the brain or deformity of its walls, which limits its excursions by virtue of the work or energy that has to be spent in breathing. Practi-

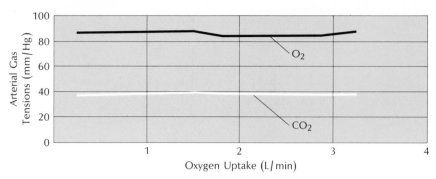

As oxygen uptake increased during exercise, arterial oxygen and carbon dioxide tensions remained remarkably constant over a wide range of metabolic requirements.

cally the entire gas-exchanging portion of the lungs shares in the hypoventilation, although there may be regional differences in degree related to normal variations in the mechanical properties of different parts of the lung. Since there is no clinical evidence of pulmonary disease, the alveolar hypoventilation often goes unrecognized for a long time unless the existence of predisposing factors is appreciated and the possibility of alveolar hypoventilation is investigated by determining arterial blood gas tensions.

The *net* form of alveolar hypoventilation occurs more commonly. Total ventilation may be normal or excessive, but exchange between alveolar gases and pulmonary capillary blood is deficient. Imbalances between alveolar ventilation and blood flow exist throughout the lungs; regions of hypoventilation are interspersed with regions of hyperventilation. Although such intermingling may suffice to maintain CO_2 tensions at normal levels, hyperventilated alveoli cannot compensate fully for hypoventilated alveoli with respect to maintaining normal oxygen tensions. Therefore, in *net* alveolar hypoventilation, it is not unusual to find a stage of arterial hypoxemia preceding the stage of CO_2 retention. In contrast, in *general* alveolar hypoventilation, arterial hypoxemia and hypercapnia are associated from the start.

To return to cor pulmonale, the prerequisite for its development is pulmonary hypertension. Although other forms of cardiac overload, such as inordinate venous return to the heart or tachycardia, may be taxing, cor pulmonale is not apt to develop unless pulmonary arterial blood pressure is also high.

Alveolar hypoventilation is the most common cause of pulmonary hypertension and cor pulmonale. The cardiorespiratory effects of alveolar hypoventilation, whether net or general, are directly attributable to the abnormalities in blood gases that are produced. That the circulatory load is attributable to hypoxemia rather than to hypercapnia is supported by the occurrence of pulmonary hypertension and enlargement of the right ventricle in natives living at high altitudes (for example, Morococha, Peru, altitude 14,900 ft.) where hypoxemia is not associated with hypercapnia. It should be noted that at high altitudes, despite chronic unremitting hypoxia from birth, only the right ventricle hypertrophies; the left ventricle remains normal in size. The mechanism responsible for the hypoxia-induced pulmonary arterial constriction is still somewhat of a puzzle. However, there is little doubt that both intra- and extrapulmonary influences are involved: The release of histamine by mast cells within the lungs may mediate the intrapulmonary response to hypoxia whereas the sympathetic nervous system contributes the extrapulmonary (lesser) component to the vasoconstrictor response. The pressor

NORMAL   GENERAL HYPOVENTILATION   NET HYPOVENTILATION

Lung
Upper $\frac{VA}{Q}$ >1 $\frac{VA}{Q}$ =1 $\frac{VA}{Q}$ <1

Middle   =1   <1   =1

Lower   =1   <1   >1

Alveolus

Capillary

○ $\frac{VA}{Q}$ = $\frac{\text{Alveolar Ventilation}}{\text{Capillary Blood Flow}}$ ●

In the normal lung, the ventilation-perfusion ratio (VA/Q) mostly averages one, except for the apices, which are hypoperfused with respect to the alveolar ventilation. In general hypoventilation, though the lung may be normal, most of it is underventilated due to inadequate "bellows" component of breathing. In net hypoventilation, abnormalities in arterial blood gases, i.e., low arterial oxygen tension and high arterial carbon dioxide tension, are caused by mismatching of alveolar ventilation and pulmonary capillary blood flow as intrinsic pulmonary disease distorts ventilation-perfusion relationships.

response is exaggerated if muscular pulmonary vessels are hypertrophied (as in the fetus or at high altitude) or if the extent and distensibility of the pulmonary vascular bed is restricted by disease.

In patients prone to pulmonary hypertension and development of cor pulmonale, the hypertension often first appears during a bout of acute hypoxia concurrent with bronchopulmonary infection. At first, pulmonary hypertension is associated with a normal or even increased cardiac output and with normal filling pressures in the right ventricle. But, as it is prolonged or becomes more severe, abnormally high filling pressures may develop and the cardiac output may fall, i.e., the right heart fails. During right heart failure, the pulmonary arterial pressure increases further, reaching levels of twice or three times normal. End-diastolic pressures in the right ventricle are high (greater than 10 mm Hg), systemic veins are congested, and cardiac output fails to increase normally during exercise despite the high filling pressures in the right side of the heart.

An important concept in reference to cor pulmonale is that while by definition the right heart must be enlarged, right ventricular failure is a complication and not an essential feature for the diagnosis. Its counterpart on the left side of the circulation is hypertensive heart disease before the onset of left ventricular failure. Inevitably, cor pulmonale is preceded by pulmonary hypertension, usually an acute exacerbation superimposed on a modest, sustained pulmonary arterial hypertension. Unfortunately, because there are no certain clinical indices of pulmonary hypertension, cor pulmonale is often recognized only after right ventricular dilatation has progressed to the point of failure. Some uncertainty still exists concerning the extent of involvement of the left heart in cor pulmonale. Experience at high altitude, where hypoxia is unremitting and pulmonary arterial pressures are consistently higher than at sea level, suggests that left ventricular dysfunction in patients with cor pulmonale is probably due to independent disease of the left ventricle, e.g., coronary atherosclerosis.

The effect of CO_2 on the pulmonary circulation appears to be by way of

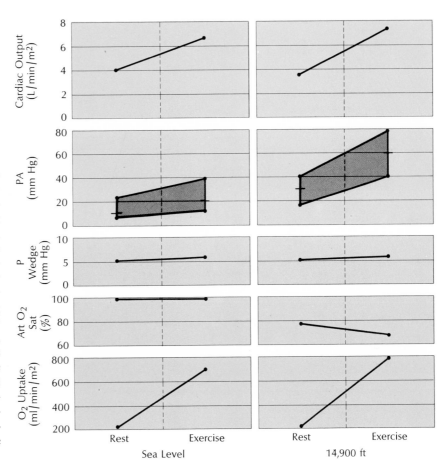

Circulatory load leading to cor pulmonale is attributable primarily to hypoxemia, as indicated by high pulmonary artery pressures in healthy subjects living under chronic hypoxic conditions at high altitudes.

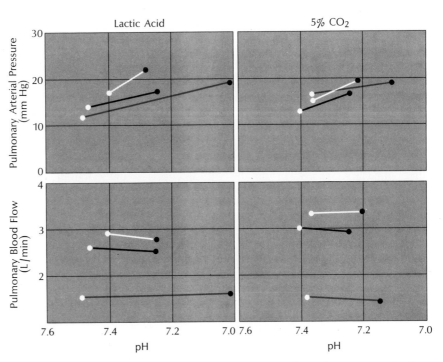

Pulmonary effects of carbon dioxide appear to result from the acidosis generated rather than from direct molecular action, as suggested by similarities in blood flow and arterial pressure values when three animals were infused with lactic acid or breathed 5% CO_2.

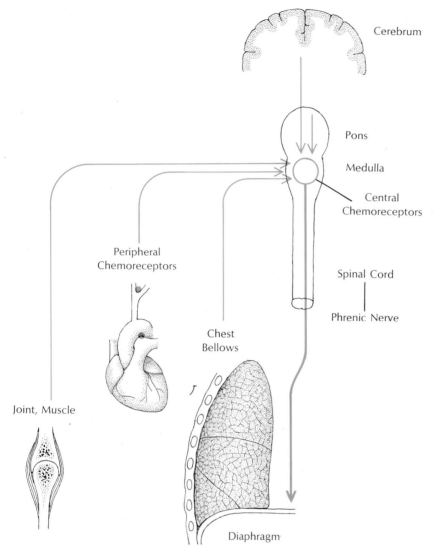

Cerebrum

Pons

Medulla

Central
Chemoreceptors

Peripheral
Chemoreceptors

Spinal Cord

Phrenic Nerve

Chest
Bellows

Joint, Muscle

Diaphragm

Cor pulmonale may occur despite normal lungs in patients with general alveolar hypoventilation if there is interference with the normal regulation of ventilation and the genesis of ventilatory drive from the respiratory center in brain, as shown schematically here. Inadequate ventilatory drive may be functional in origin (due primarily to carbon dioxide retention) or be caused by anatomic damage of several kinds.

As CO_2 is retained and CO_2 tensions become elevated in both blood and tissues, the stage is set in two ways for further CO_2 retention: first, a blunting of responsiveness of the respiratory center to the CO_2 stimulus; second, bicarbonate retention by the kidney. In turn, both of these developments promote further CO_2 retention. Moreover, not only the hypercapnia resulting from the primary disorder of the lungs or ventilatory apparatus but also the hypercapnia of metabolic alkalosis may contribute to functional respiratory depression. Spontaneous fluctuations in ventilation are common once alveolar hypoventilation exists, and blood gas composition fluctuates accordingly, particularly during sleep.

Pulmonary Hypertension

Failure to recognize that alveolar hypoventilation is the chief cause of cor pulmonale can be critical, since unless ventilation is improved other therapeutic measures are likely to be ineffective. This is not to say that alveolar hypoventilation is the only underlying mechanism or that its correction should be the sole aim in therapy. Pulmonary hypertension does occur, although rarely, because of anatomical restriction of the pulmonary vascular bed. However, it is much more common for these two mechanisms to coexist, and even in patients with extensive anatomical restriction of the pulmonary vascular bed, pulmonary hypertension sufficient to strain the right heart seldom occurs without some degree of alveolar hypoventilation. Since the alveolar hypoventilation is generally more reversible than the mechanical influences, it becomes a logical target for treatment.

In the normal individual the pulmonary circulation is a capacious, highly distensible system working at very low pressure, part of a coordinated system by which the lungs accomplish their task of oxygenating the blood. A cardiac output of five to six liters per minute at rest is easily accommodated with pulmonary arterial pressures of only 20 to 28 mm Hg in systole, and 8 to 12 mm Hg in diastole. A threefold increase in blood flow, such as occurs during moderate exercise, is associated with only slight

the acidosis that it generates rather than by a direct molecular action on the pulmonary vessels. In the hypoxemic patient, hypercapniac acidosis acts synergistically to augment the degree of pulmonary arterial hypertension; conversely, alkalosis may blunt the pressor response to hypoxia. It should be noted that acidosis, per se, must be severe to elicit a marked pulmonary hypertensive response.

In contrast to its adjunctive role in regulating the pulmonary circulation, CO_2 is the major regulator of the cerebral circulation. Hypercapnia evokes cerebral vasodilatation and increases cerebrospinal fluid pressure; acute and sudden increases in CO_2

tension cause anesthetic effects, eliciting clinical manifestations that range from weakness and irritability to confusion and narcosis. When severe hypoxemia and hypercapnia coexist, it may be impossible to distinguish between their separate neurologic effects. Then priority in treatment has to be directed towards restoring tolerable levels of hypoxia, since nervous tissue may quickly suffer irreversible damage if oxygenation remains inadequate. Indeed, relieving hypercapnia without ensuring adequate oxygenation may exaggerate cerebral hypoxia, since the vasodilator effect of the CO_2 enhances oxygen delivery to the tissues of the brain.

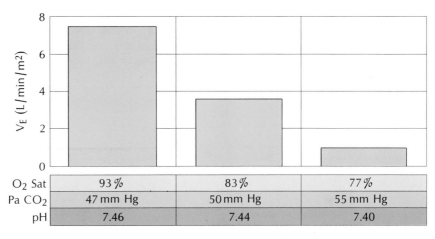

V_E (L/min/m²)		
O₂ Sat	93 %	83 %	77 %
Pa CO₂	47 mm Hg	50 mm Hg	55 mm Hg
pH	7.46	7.44	7.40

Wide spontaneous variations in ventilation and blood gas composition in patient with alveolar hypoventilation are typical in both net and general forms of this disorder.

increments in pulmonary arterial pressures. The large reserve capacity of the lungs permits near-normal pressure-flow relationships to be maintained in the pulmonary vascular bed with as little as one third of normal lung remaining; even patients who have had a pneumonectomy can accommodate a two- to threefold increment in pulmonary blood flow without overtaxing the right heart, as long as the patient's remaining lung is free of fibrosis, emphysema, or pulmonary vascular changes.

Nonetheless, with sufficient restriction in the extent and distensibility of the vascular bed, even modest increments in blood flow may elicit considerable pulmonary hypertension. Sufficient restriction could occur, for example, as a result of extensive pulmonary resection, or from arteriosclerotic narrowing or occlusion of pulmonary arteries and small vessels, or from pulmonary emboli or thrombosis. Alternatively, increased resistance to pulmonary blood flow may occur indirectly as a consequence of changes in adjacent parenchymal disease, of pulmonary edema, or from extrapulmonary distortion and compression accompanying severe musculoskeletal deformity of the thorax.

Clinical Recognition

The diagnosis of cor pulmonale is apt to be overlooked unless each patient having the proper initiating mechanism is considered as a potential candidate. In practice, the greatest difficulty is encountered in the elderly bronchitic, who is resigned to cough, sputum, and breathlessness as part of aging and "smoker's cough," thereby unintentionally misdirecting the examiner to the diagnosis of "arteriosclerotic heart disease."

Right ventricular enlargement is difficult to prove clinically. Indeed, even a retrospective evaluation of clinical data after the enlargement has been found at autopsy often fails to disclose convincing clinical evidence. Part of the difficulty stems from the dislocation and distortion of the heart produced by pulmonary and thoracic disease. Such geometric rearrangements affect not only the clinical manifestations but the x-ray and electrocardiographic evidence as well.

Of much greater practical importance than establishing that the patient has chronic cor pulmonale is the recognition that a patient with certain underlying disorders is a candidate for right ventricular failure if the initiating mechanism is aggravated or if a complication, such as the hypoxia of an acute respiratory infection, should supervene. However, once the proper initiating mechanisms exist, a combination of signs and symptoms may strongly suggest, albeit not prove, that the patient does indeed have cor pulmonale: a systolic thrust is detected to the left of the sternum or in the epigastrium; the heart is not very large; the observation that the pulmonary component of the second sound is louder than the aortic component in the pulmonary area – particularly if the second sound is palpable there – raises the prospect of pulmonary hypertension. A ventricular gallop rhythm in the absence of orthopnea suggests that the right, rather than the left, ventricle may be primarily affected.

Although considerable reliance continues to be placed on the x-ray and on the electrocardiogram for the diagnosis of cor pulmonale, unfortunately neither the x-ray nor the electrocardiogram has proved to be a sensitive indicator for detecting enlargement of the right ventricle. By x-ray, the characteristic features are those of antecedent severe pulmonary hypertension, i.e., a loss of normal pulmonary arterial convexity in the cardiac silhouette in conjunction with prominent proximal and attenuated distal pulmonary arterial branches; signs of the initiating pulmonary disorder, coupled with conventional evidences of right ventricular enlargement. These features are most distinctive when considerable pulmonary hypertension has lasted a long time.

The electrocardiogram often is inconclusive. The most convincing evidence for right ventricular enlargement usually is found in the patient with severe unremitting pulmonary hypertension, such as diffuse obliterative pulmonary vascular disease. On the other hand, in chronic obstructive lung disease, which is much more common, telltale changes are unusual not only because of the hyperinflated lungs but also because pulmonary arterial pressures are usually only

---

Etiologic Bases for Cor Pulmonale

Disorders of the Lungs and Airways

Chronic obstructive lung disease (COLD)

Diffuse pulmonary interstitial infiltrates, granulomata, or fibrosis

Disorders of the Chest Bellows and Inadequate Ventilatory Drive

Kyphoscoliosis, neuromuscular incompetence, marked obesity, idiopathic alveolar hypoventilation

Disorders of the Pulmonary Arterial Tree

Multiple pulmonary emboli, primary pulmonary hypertension

Evolution of Cardiorespiratory Failure in Kyphoscoliosis

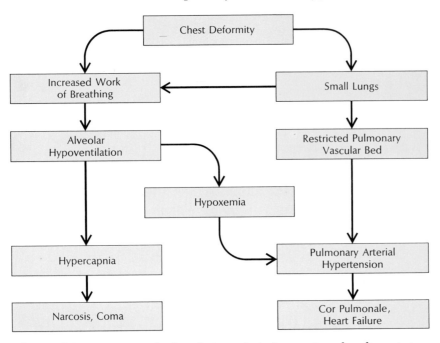

Thoracic deformity in severe kyphoscoliosis results in hypoxemia and cardiorespiratory failure both through restricted ventilatory capacity imposed by reduced lung volume and increased work of breathing due to abnormal elastic resistance of chest.

the right heart has failed, i.e., when jugular venous pressures are high and tricuspid insufficiency, hepatic congestion, and peripheral edema are present. Although the heart may return to normal size after recovery from the episode of heart failure, the patient will remain a candidate for right heart failure as long as the initiating disorder persists.

Kyphoscoliosis

Skeletal deformities that restrict the thoracic cage are likely to be associated with the development of cor pulmonale only when substantial alveolar hypoventilation is also present. For example, pectus excavatum does not cause either alveolar hypoventilation or cor pulmonale. Also, ankylosing spondylitis causes no more than mild alveolar hypoventilation; the levels of hypercapnia and hypoxemia are slight and pulmonary hypertension is exceedingly rare. On the other hand, such disorders as muscular dystrophy, poliomyelitis, or severe kyphoscoliotic deformity of the thoracic spine are all associated with alveolar hypoventilation, pulmonary hypertension, and cor pulmonale. In these conditions, of course, *general* alveolar hypoventilation is the type involved since the act of breathing and not an abnormality of the lungs is the responsible factor.

Kyphoscoliotic subjects have traditionally been short-lived. Our studies have shed some light on the cardiac and pulmonary mechanisms that are involved. The sequence of events that predisposes to death in circulatory and respiratory failure is illustrated above left. The pivotal role in this sequence is played by alveolar hypoventilation. The thoracic deformity in kyphoscoliosis – chiefly dwarfing and distortion of the thoracic cage – leads to alveolar hypoventilation in two ways. First, there is an absolute reduction in ventilatory capacity imposed by reduced lung volumes and mechanically disadvantaged thoracic muscles. The degree of hypoxemia and hypercapnia can be directly correlated with the decrease in vital capacity. Second, the abnormal elastic resistance of the chest wall (compliance may be reduced to 25% of normal) markedly increases the mechanical work of breathing.

mildly elevated until a complication, such as an acute respiratory infection or pulmonary embolus, elevates pulmonary arterial pressure. Three conclusions may be drawn about using electrocardiograms for diagnosing cor pulmonale: 1) unequivocal patterns of right ventricular hypertrophy are uncommon; 2) if a characteristic pattern is present, the degree of right ventricular enlargement is severe; and 3) in the course of chronic obstructive lung disease, serial changes in the electrocardiogram, rather than particular patterns, may provide clues to the detection of cor pulmonale.

As noted, the diagnosis of cor pulmonale is often appreciated only after

Two separate indices of ventilatory drive may be used as shown in this figure. Simultaneous record of phrenic nerve activity and tidal volume allows distinction between an inadequate nervous output to the diaphragm vs a refractory chest bellows in the genesis of general alveolar hypoventilation.

Any increase in tidal volume requires inordinate increments in mechanical work on the part of the chest. In some mysterious way automatic adjustments occur in the regulation of breathing, resulting in a ventilatory pattern of shallow breaths and rapid frequency, thereby reducing the effort and energy cost of breathing. One unfortunate consequence of this adaptation is an augmented dead space ventilation at the expense of alveolar ventilation.

Severe thoracic deformity, particularly when associated with dwarfing, not only sets the stage for chronic alveolar hypoventilation but has other consequences as well. Gas exchange in the small (childlike) lungs of the kyphoscoliotic may be barely adequate for adult metabolic requirements at rest. During exercise arterial blood gases become markedly abnormal as the lungs fail to aerate the blood adequately. Moreover, the mechanically disadvantaged chest is metabolically costly to operate and is incapable of the free and easy motion characterizing the large, effortless tidal volumes of normal subjects during exercise.

The pulmonary circulation not only shares in the compression and distortion but is embedded in a fleshy lung, which further limits its distensibility. Our studies comparing the pulmonary circulation in kyphoscoliotic patients before and after development of alveolar hypoventilation provide insight into the role of blood gas disturbances in evolution of cor pulmonale. Individuals with normal or near-normal systemic arterial oxygen tensions generally had normal resting pulmonary artery pressures; as a group, those with lowest arterial oxygen tensions also showed the largest increments in mean pulmonary artery pressure in response to increase in pulmonary blood flow. When alveolar hypoventilation occurs in such patients, either as a consequence of progressive deformity or as a result of bronchitis or pneumonia, it may further compromise gas exchange, thereby triggering the development of cor pulmonale.

An important contributing element to sudden death in the kyphoscoliotic subject with CO_2 retention may be the measures taken to make the patient comfortable and to improve oxygenation. At one time, it was not uncommon for such a patient to be treated with oxygen for cyanosis and with sedatives for restlessness (due to hypercapnia). Unfortunately, both of these measures may effect calamitous increases in the degree of hypercapnia – sedatives by depressing further the sensitivity of the respiratory centers in the brain to carbon dioxide; oxygen by abolishing the hypoxic drive to ventilation from the peripheral chemoreceptors. A similar sequence may complicate other neuromuscular disorders that lead to general alveolar hypoventilation through their effect on ventilatory mechanisms. Muscular dystrophy and poliomyelitis are examples, although in polio not only the muscles but the respiratory center and nerves may be irreparably damaged.

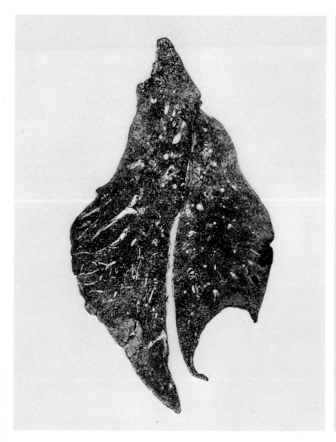

Compression of the lungs in severe kyphoscoliotic deformity of the thoracic spine results in a marked reduction in lung size and an altered external contour, as is evident in the whole-lung section shown at left, which was prepared from the lungs of a patient with kyphoscoliosis. Whole-lung section from a normal lung is shown at right for comparison.

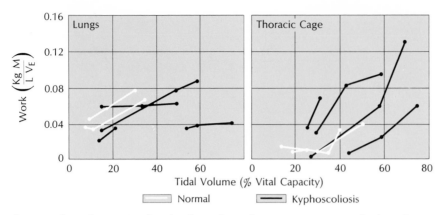

In cor pulmonale associated with a limited ventilatory apparatus, e.g., kyphoscoliosis, any increase in tidal volume requires inordinate increments in mechanical work.

Extreme Obesity

The Pickwickian syndrome, leading to heart failure in certain cases of extreme obesity, is apparently also a consequence of severe general alveolar hypoventilation associated with an abnormal breathing pattern. The characteristic somnolence and lethargy apparently can be related to carbon dioxide retention; the heart failure is due largely to hypoxia. In such individuals the accumulated body fat appears to limit the performance of the ventilatory apparatus much as if a structural deformity were present. In many, but not all, patients loss of weight restores alveolar ventilation to normal and reverses the syndrome.

It is particularly puzzling that not all equally obese individuals develop alveolar hypoventilation and its consequences. Nor is the occurrence of alveolar hypoventilation only related to the degree of obesity. Indeed, the most obese man ever seen here – his weight was in excess of 600 pounds – showed no evidence of alveolar hypo-

ventilation. Why some obese people develop blood gas disturbances whereas others do not is not yet clear. Possibly, alveolar hypoventilation occurs only when the extreme obesity coexists with a congenitally poor ventilatory response to chemical stimuli such as hypoxia or hypercapnia. Such poverty of response might occur in normal individuals and be of no clinical significance but become important in patients whose mechanical performance of the chest is impaired by obesity.

It should be noted in passing that the cor pulmonale of obesity is unusual in that the left as well as the right ventricle may enlarge appreciably and even fail. Presumably the left ventricular hypertrophy and dilatation are consequences of the distinctive hemodynamic load that obesity generates: the circulating blood volume and cardiac output increase considerably as an adaptation to the metabolic needs of the large body mass. In addition, the left ventricle may be

taxed by systemic hypertension, which occurs more often in very obese subjects than the general population.

Our discussion of cor pulmonale in disorders associated with general alveolar hypoventilation would be incomplete without further mention of individuals whose lungs are normal but receive an inadequate ventilatory drive from respiratory centers in the brain. Such patients can breathe quite normally if asked, but have an inadequate inner drive to do so; hence arterial hypoxemia and CO_2 retention develop. (The respiratory depression is of course likely to be compounded by CO_2 retention from any other cause, such as chronic lung disease, the administration of sedatives, prolonged vomiting, or metabolic alkalosis following the administration of potent chloruretic agents such as ethacrynic acid.) By blunting sensitivity of the respiratory centers to the CO_2 stimulus, CO_2 retention effectively neutralizes the chief mechanism for preventing accumulation of CO_2. In such patients the importance of the hypoxic drive to ventilation is increased; hence use of oxygen therapy must be carefully regulated.

Anatomical damage to the respiratory centers causing general alveolar hypoventilation can result from localized lesions of the type seen in bulbar poliomyelitis or following cerebral vascular thrombosis. Or the injury may take the form of diffuse and nonspecific inflammatory lesions such as are seen at autopsy in patients with "dead" respiratory centers from unknown cause. Interestingly, study of a few of these "idiopathic" cases has pointed to an earlier bout with encephalitis that may have left residual brain damage. Severe hypoxia functionally depresses, and may produce anatomical damage to, the brain. It seems reasonable that some instances of unexplained respiratory depression could be caused either by an undetected inflammatory process or by hypoxic damage to the brain. In any case, experience has shown that arterial blood gases usually can be promptly restored to normal in such patients by means of voluntary or mechanical hyperventilation, an important consideration in management.

The disorders in which alveolar hypoventilation results from intrinsic bronchopulmonary disease are of the

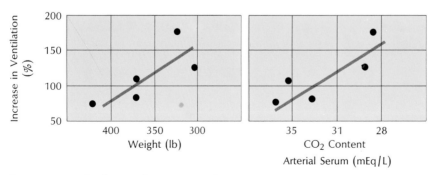

Restoration of alveolar ventilation to normal can reverse sequence leading to cor pulmonale, seen in effects of weight reduction in patient with cardiorespiratory failure due to extreme obesity.

greatest concern clinically, because of the number of persons affected. Since pulmonary hypertension elicited by net, as well as general, alveolar hypoventilation arises mainly from hypoxia and acidosis, it follows that in these patients too, restoration of arterial blood gases towards normal may prevent or reverse the cardiopulmonary effects. As has been said, an essential first step is to suspect the presence of cor pulmonale in a patient with an appropriate pulmonary disorder. This can sometimes be difficult, for example in the elderly patient who has had a productive cough for years and who might be suffering either from cor pulmonale or from arteriosclerotic coronary artery disease. If there is clinical evidence of hypoxemia and hypercapnia (such as the combination of cyanosis, warm hands, clouding of the sensorium or somnolence, and suffusion of the conjunctivae), particularly if the patient is not orthopneic and blood gas determinations show corresponding abnormalities, the likelihood of pulmonary hypertension and cor pulmonale is enhanced.

Spectrum of Bronchopulmonary Disorders

To help identify the patient with bronchopulmonary disease who is vulnerable to cor pulmonale, it is important to recognize that only certain bronchopulmonary diseases are likely to be associated with sufficient alveolar hypoventilation to cause right heart strain. In addition, rational therapy depends on appreciating critical individual differences. Practically speaking, it is useful to think in terms of a spectrum of disorders.

At one end of the spectrum are forms of lung disease in which the predominant problem is airway obstruction, for example, cystic fibrosis of the pancreas, asthma, and bronchitis. Although cystic fibrosis is rather uncommon compared to bronchitis, the extensive bronchial obstruction that characterizes this disorder is responsible for the high incidence of cor pulmonale as a cause of death. It serves as a useful example of what bronchial obstruction, per se, can do. Overdistention of the alveolar-containing parts of the lung is secondary to the obstruction; the alveolar walls are dilated but intact. But, because of the

plugged airways, the balance between alveolar hypoventilation and perfusion is so deranged that hypoxemia and CO_2 retention are all too likely to occur even at rest. Life may be threatened by the circulatory sequelae of the hypoxemia and the respiratory consequences of hypercapnia.

At the other end of the bronchopulmonary spectrum is emphysema, a heterogeneous group of disorders in which the dominant feature is destruction of lung tissue, and airway obstruction is either absent or slight. The experimental prototype is the state produced by inhalation of papain; the closest clinical analog is paracinar emphysema, of which diffuse bullous disease may be a severe form. The characteristic features are increased pulmonary distensibility, decreased recoil force, reduction in the diffusing capacity of the lungs, and a combination of increased radiolucency and attenuation in pulmonary vasculature. Here both alveolar ventilation and circulation are impaired proportionally, as though sections of lung had been amputated. Since there is no imbalance between the remaining gas-exchanging portions of the lungs, the patient's arterial blood gases are virtually normal even though he is dyspneic. As long as he pays the penalty of increased work in breathing, his lungs continue to fulfill their purpose in gas exchange.

Although the two ends of the spectrum represent important clinical disorders and do serve to illustrate the "pure" consequences of bronchial obstruction and parenchymal rarefaction, respectively, the most common clinical disorders are in the middle of the spectrum, i.e., a combination of airway obstruction and alveolar destruction. This is the heterogeneous group of "chronic obstructive lung diseases" (COLD). This group ranges in composition from the "pink puffer" to the "blue bloater." The "pink puffer" spends his life breathlessly preoccupied with the act of breathing. He even defers eating for the sake of breathing. As the result of unremitting respiratory effort, his arterial blood gases remain near normal, thereby avoiding pulmonary hypertension and cor pulmonale. During an upper respiratory infection he may become indistinguishable from the "blue bloater": he may die hypoxemic and

hypercapniac. On the other hand, proper treatment usually restores him to his breathless, pink state.

The "blue bloater" suffers the consequences of mismatched alveolar gas and blood secondary to predominantly bronchial obstruction (net alveolar hypoventilation). He is cyanotic and lethargic; rarely as breathless as the "pink puffer," he is prepared to pause to eat and, indeed, is often somewhat overweight. It is critically important to appreciate the important pathogenic role of bronchitis in the "blue bloater" with cor pulmonale so that treatment can be aimed at relieving bronchial obstruction and correcting blood gas abnormalities.

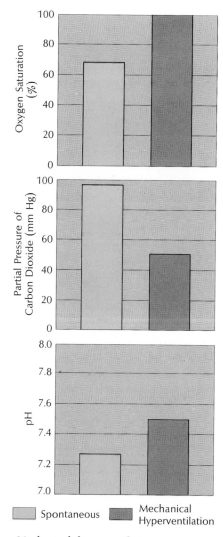

Mechanical hyperventilation restores arterial blood gases to normal in patient in whom alveolar hypoventilation and heart failure resulted from impaired sensitivity of respiratory center.

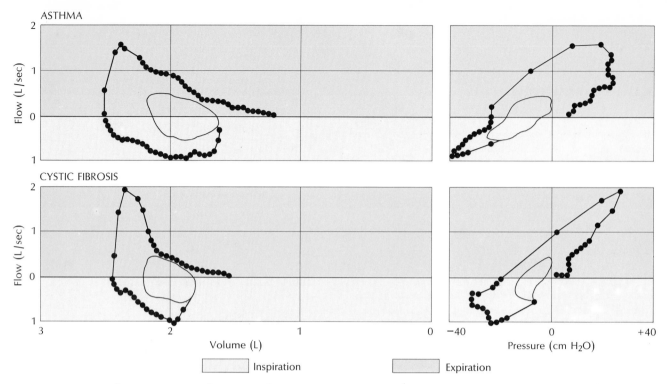

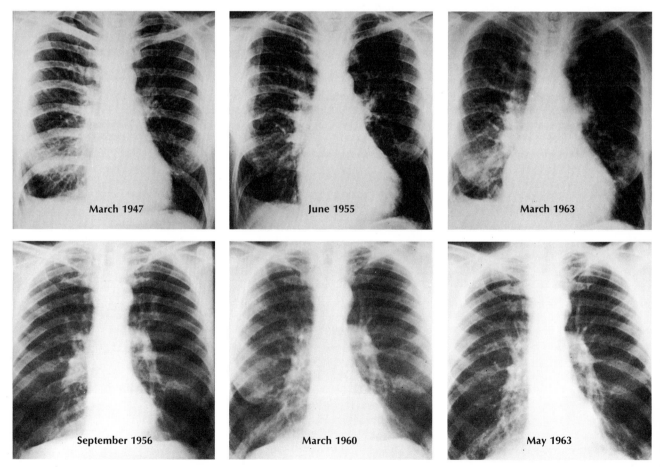

Two instances of obstructive airway diseases predisposing to severe hypoxemia are shown above. Rates of airflow are related to lung volume (left panels) and to the transpulmonary pressures that generated them (right panels). The inner small loops represent tidal breathing. Throughout controlled vital capacity maneuver (large loops with dots) flow rates are reduced.

When the predominant problem in lung disease is airway obstruction, impaired alveolar-blood gas exchange may lead inexorably to cor pulmonale and cardiomegaly, as seen in x-rays (top) of patient with chronic bronchitis. Conversely, in the one with emphysema, blood gases may remain normal and pulmonary hypertension and cor pulmonale may be avoided over a long period.

The Sites of Airway Obstruction

Of some help for the proper understanding and treatment of airway obstruction would be a clear picture of the sites of obstruction. Attempts are being made to provide this information using physiological methods since postmortem studies can only be suggestive. Our group undertook to make this distinction for asthma vs cystic fibrosis using the interrelationships of transpulmonary pressure, lung volume, and rates of airflow as originated by Fry and Hyatt. At the higher lung volumes, patients with cystic fibrosis were shown to be capable of achieving surprisingly high levels of ventilation whereas, despite strenuous efforts, asthmatic patients were unable to improve their ventilatory performance. The results supported the anatomical observations that asthma affects primarily the small airways whereas cystic fibrosis affects the large and the small airways. Collapse of the large airways during coughing was observed in some patients with cystic fibrosis and in some with COLD, accounting for the ineffectiveness of the cough in mobilizing bronchial secretions in such patients. This expiratory collapse also emphasized the desirability of postural drainage as a therapeutic measure since it does not involve an increase in expiratory pressures.

Macklem and coworkers, using a combination of anatomical and physiological techniques to partition airway resistance, demonstrated how conventional tests of pulmonary function may fail to disclose obstructive changes in the small airways. They showed that while extensive disease of the small airways did not appreciably lower airway resistance, the distribution of inspired air was distinctly abnormal. They concluded that plugging, inflammation, and distortion of small bronchial walls could derange ventilation-perfusion relationships sufficiently to produce abnormal blood gases long before clinical disability occurred or abnormalities were seen in tests of ventilatory performance. These observations may be relevant to the pathogenesis of cor pulmonale since they may account for the sudden appearance in the clinic of a "blue bloater" with remarkably ab-

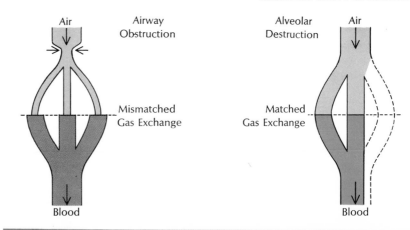

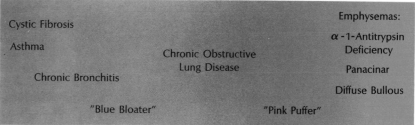

This spectrum of bronchopulmonary disease suggests that patients in whom airway obstruction predominates are more vulnerable than those with emphysema to the circulatory sequelae that eventuate in cor pulmonale. In the airway-obstructed group, the hypoxia and hypercapnia resulting from a deranged balance between ventilation and perfusion may lead to cor pulmonale. In the emphysema group, ventilation and perfusion are impaired proportionately and blood gases remain normal or near-normal.

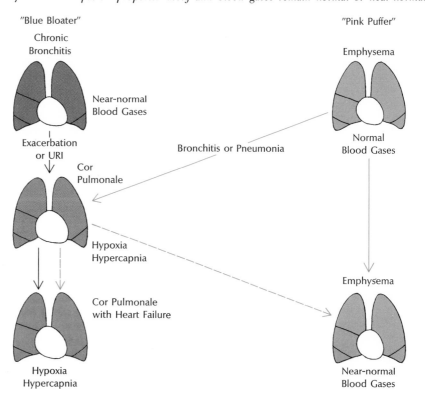

A "pink puffer" may spend his life huffing and puffing without becoming hypoxemic or developing cor pulmonale (frames at right). An episode of bronchitis or pneumonia may precipitate cor pulmonale and he will go on either to heart failure or revert to his "pink puffer" state. On the other hand, the "blue bloater" (chronic bronchitis) is hypoxemic even when he is free of an acute exacerbation and may be toppled into cor pulmonale and heart failure by a mild upper respiratory infection (panel at left).

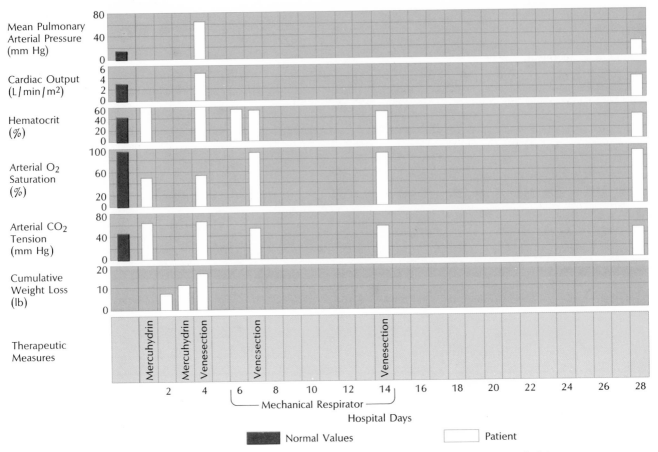

Cardiopulmonary changes with various therapeutic measures are shown in a patient with cor pulmonale associated with kyphoscoliosis; in such patients, accumulated body fat apparently limits ventilatory apparatus as if structural deformity were present. As can be seen, marked improvement in blood gas composition occurred with weight loss and the use of mechanical respiration.

normal blood gases, even though there is little antecedent history of respiratory difficulty except for "smoker's cough."

Workers trying to clarify the pathogenesis of chronic obstructive lung disease have sporadically directed their attention to genetic influences. Our own studies on parents of children with cystic fibrosis, as well as on the coincidence of Marfan's syndrome and bullous disease of the lungs, were inconclusive because of the difficulty in obtaining sufficient numbers of comparable subjects for study. Much more convincing is the recent evidence that some cases of paracinar emphysema may involve a genetically determined enzyme defect (alpha-1-antitrypsin deficiency) that produces rarefaction of lung tissues. Although this fresh insight has reawakened interest in the predisposing pathogenic mechanisms for chronic obstructive lung disease, it seems unlikely that the bulk of instances of this disorder will be explicable on this

basis. Nonetheless, it is clear that genetic predisposition may determine whether the noxious effects of smoking and air pollutants reach clinical status in any particular individual.

Pathologists are now attempting to relate pulmonary structure to function, examining whole-lung sections from patients with destructive emphysema and with bronchitic airway obstruction. Broad differences in pathology are found, but they are not enough to account for the variability in expression of bronchopulmonary disease. Part of the problem is that although elaborate techniques are being utilized to study distribution of airways and alveoli, far fewer studies have been or are being done on blood supply to the lung. Moreover, because of the great expanse of lung tissue, it is difficult to relate blood supply to air supply at the level of the alveoli and capillaries, where mismatching becomes a problem. It must be admitted that we really have little understand-

ing as yet of why mismatching occurs.

In diseases marked by gross distortion of the pulmonary parenchyma, cor pulmonale is unusual unless ventilation-perfusion relationships are severely upset. Most commonly, large fibrotic masses act to reduce or eliminate both ventilation and circulation to a region, rather than serving to derange the balance between the two. As noted earlier, cardiac complications are uncommon in uncomplicated silicosis or tuberculosis. On the other hand, pulmonary hypertension and cor pulmonale are not uncommon when silicosis or tuberculosis are compounded by extensive fibrotic distortion, shrunken lobes, and bronchial obstruction. The likelihood of cor pulmonale is further increased by chronic pleurisy, fibrothorax, or excisional surgeries. In such cases a combination of anatomical restriction of the vascular bed and disturbances in alveolar-capillary gas exchange is usually involved in pathogenesis of pulmonary hypertension.

Medical Management

One reason that this chapter has emphasized recognition and differentiation of the various etiologies of cor pulmonale is that effective management depends on a clear understanding of the disorder and of its pathogenesis. Relief of alveolar hypoventilation of either the net or general type is usually remarkably successful in restoring the circulation to normal. Most often, the patient comes to the physician because of a combination of hypoxemia, hypercapnia, and right heart failure that has been precipitated by a bout of upper respiratory infection. The trick in treatment is to sustain the patient for the days or weeks that are required to restore the patient to his preinfection state. Meanwhile, blood gases have to be reverted towards normal.

An element of confusion has been introduced by the fact that mechanical measures to improve alveolar ventilation vary considerably from one clinic to another. But, in general, simple measures suffice if the candidate for cor pulmonale is kept under close medical surveillance and is treated promptly, at the first signs of upper respiratory infection, with proper antibiotics, hydration, and bronchodilators. Corticosteroids are rarely indicated unless there is a strong asthmatic component in the bronchial disorder. When hypoxia and hypercapnia become threatening, mechanical aids to respiration are usually needed. They are then part of a respiratory care program involving not only assisted ventilation but also full medical management including antibiotics and proper bronchopulmonary toilet.

If right failure does develop, it often does so insidiously: edema of the ankles and legs increases gradually over days or weeks; polycythemia and cyanosis grow more marked; tachycardia becomes persistent; the blood volume expands; the conjunctivae, like the veins and tissues, are congested. However, right heart failure may also begin suddenly during a bout of respiratory infection that critically compromises gas exchange. Although standard therapy for heart failure (low salt regimen, digitalis, diuretics) should be used as needed, priority in treatment should be given to restoring the blood gases to acceptable levels by arresting bronchopulmonary infection. Eliminating the infection invariably involves the proper choice of antibiotics. This choice is of utmost concern. One of the penicillins or tetracycline, singly or in combination, generally proves to be the mainstay of antibiotic treatment. Many other antibiotics have their advocates. However, caution must be used in selecting antibiotics simply on the basis of sensitivities to cultured organisms because some of the newer antibiotics may exert undesirable side effects on the underlying disorder, e.g., neuromuscular blockade. Measures to decrease the circulating blood volume are more than ordinarily important if polycythemia is present. Nonetheless, management of the circulatory symptoms is destined to defeat unless the upper respiratory infection is brought under control.

Diuretics must be selected and used with more care than usual in order to avoid intensifying respiratory depression by metabolic alkalosis (see Chapter 14, "Diuretics in the Treatment of Congestive Heart Failure," by Laragh). For example, potent diuretics such as ethacrynic acid tend to aggravate ventilatory insufficiency by lessening the stimulatory effect of CO_2 on the respiratory centers. The associated hypochloremia also makes it difficult to promote renal excretion of bicarbonate. It is easier to avoid this complication by using chlorothiazide or mercurial diuretics, which are less potent even though they, too, cause concomitant potassium and chloride loss in urine. The regular administration of potassium chloride during the course of diuretic therapy may help to avoid bicarbonate excess and hypokalemia. Furosemide is an effective agent, not only promoting bicarbonate and chloride excretion but also improving alveolar ventilation. However, like ethacrynic acid, it is prone to cause appreciable metabolic alkalosis because of its diuretic potency.

Vigorous therapy directed chiefly at the pulmonary disorder often provides dramatic relief both of impaired gas exchange and the complications brought on by heart failure. In moderate-to-severe cases, it may take two weeks to a month for arterial oxygen saturation at rest to return to normal and CO_2 tensions to approach normal. Values for blood volume, hematocrit, cardiac output, and pulmonary arterial pressure also often return to prefailure, even completely normal, levels. In some clinics, the hematocrit has proved to be a useful clue to the surreptitious recurrence of hypoxemia, either at rest or during the exertion of daily life. Phlebotomies of 300 to 400 ml are then used as needed to restore blood volume and hematocrit to near-normal levels.

Particularly noteworthy is the role of exposure to air pollutants, including smoke and fog, in the pathogenesis of chronic bronchitis and in predisposing to cor pulmonale. It is, indeed, pointless to establish a time-consuming regimen for managing bronchial infection unless the patient is removed from exposure to air pollutants, not only occupational pollutants but also those from the inhalation of cigarette smoke.

As we stated earlier, heart failure is a complication of cor pulmonale that may be avoided if the underlying pulmonary or ventilatory disorder is recognized and controlled. Nonetheless, it is reassuring that along with the antecedent pulmonary hypertension and cor pulmonale, the cardiac complications are reversible if treated adequately and in time.

Treatment of Heart Failure

The Mechanism of Action of Digitalis

GLENN A. LANGER

University of California, Los Angeles

Nearly two centuries have passed since Withering first used and described the effects of digitalis in 1784. But it has been only recently that physicians employing the cardiac glycosides have been able to do so on other than an empiric basis. Perhaps this fact, more than any other, explains why even now the problems of digitalis toxicity are not uncommon and present many practitioners with complex clinical situations in the course of treating cardiac failure.

The unprecedentedly long lag between employment and understanding is in no way a reflection of lack of interest by either clinical or laboratory investigators in the mechanism of action of the digitalis glycosides. Rather, it is a function of the fact that until we had the technical capacity to visualize the ultrastructure of the myocardial cell (see Chapter 1, "Myocardial Ultrastructure in the Normal and Failing Heart," by Sonnenblick), use isotopic tracers, and refine biochemical methods, it was difficult to formulate plausible working hypotheses regarding the contractile processes of the heart muscle. We therefore necessarily lacked the means to comprehend the role that digitalis played in enhancing contractility.

More specifically, understanding of the mechanism of action of digitalis must be based on detailed knowledge of the ionic fluxes that accompany and mediate cardiac contraction. The ions most pertinently involved in these fluxes are calcium, sodium, potassium, and, probably — although here our knowledge is limited — chloride.

In the normal resting cardiac fiber (or cell), the potential across the sarcolemma is on the order of 80 to 90 mv, with the inside of the cell negative in relationship to the outside. For the cell to be fully activated, depolarization takes place so that the membrane resting potential of -80 to -90 is altered to $+15$ or $+20$ at the peak of excitation (see Chapter 26, "Antiarrhythmic Drugs in Ischemic Heart Disease," by Bigger). When fully achieved, this alteration in electrical relationship is termed regenerative depolarization and results in the change in charge required for the development of a full action potential so that contraction occurs.

The current required for depolarization is carried by the positively charged sodium ion. Upon excitation, there is a rapid influx of sodium ions across the sarcolemma and probably the transverse tubular system (T system). The depolarization of the cell triggers the release of ionic calcium from as yet undefined regions of the cell membrane to the region of the sarcomeres. The function of calcium in facilitating cardiac contraction is discussed in Chapter 2, "Contractile Proteins in the Normal and Failing Myocardium," by Katz and in Chapter 3, "Biochemical Processes in Cardiac Function," by Davies. Briefly, calcium appears to interact with troponin, which is also an inhibitor of actin-myosin coupling. This interaction leads to the stimulation of myofibrillar ATPase, resulting in an abolition of troponin inhibition and in a link between the two sets of filaments, permitting them to couple, slide in relationship to each other, and cause contraction of the sarcomere.

It should be emphasized that the source of coupling calcium in mammalian heart muscle is very different from the source in skeletal muscle. A significant fraction of this calcium is superficially located in heart muscle and is probably not derived from intracellular sarcoplasmic cisternae. Recent laboratory studies indicate that fixed negative charges located in the basement membrane or the sarcolemma and within the transverse tubular system bind the large amounts of calcium important in coupling excitation to contraction.

The intimate relationship between sodium and calcium ions in cardiac muscle was first suggested more than 50 years ago by Daly and Clarke, who observed that reduction of the external concentration of sodium, which bathes the sarcolemma, increases the contractile response, that is, the tension developed by the myocardial fiber. Studies in our laboratory since 1963 have further defined this relationship. It is now quite clear that the decrease in external sodium results in an increased uptake of calcium ions and in an enhanced rate of tension development, which can be expressed as the maximum change of force with respect to time or maximal dP/dt.

The reasons for this interrelationship are not entirely clear, but it appears that there is an area on or within the sarcolemma where sodium and calcium compete for receptor or carrier sites or where the removal of sodium makes the membrane more permeable to calcium. This area may be the basement membrane mentioned above.

Regardless of the specific mechanism, it is the reduction of sodium that permits the increased calcium uptake with each excitation, and it is the increased calcium uptake that allows for increased coupling of calcium at the troponin sites on the myofilaments and the augmentation of tension necessary for contraction.

In connection with the fact that the reduction of sodium from the area of the sarcolemma results in increasing calcium within the cell, it is pertinent

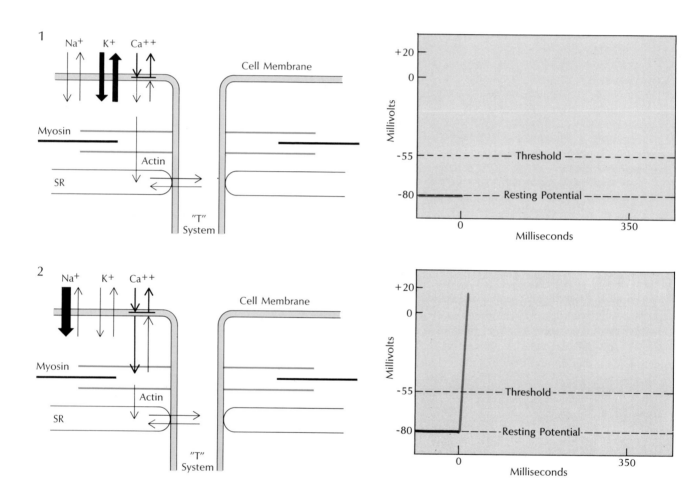

Correlation of ionic movements with cardiac electrical cycle: (1) Prior to excitation Na+ permeability is low, K+ relatively high and inward Ca movement very small. The membrane potential (–80 mv) is determined predominantly by the K+ diffusion potential. Note that extracellular Ca++ is depicted to be in equilibrium with Ca++ bound to sites on the cell membrane. (2) Excitation occurs with a large increase in Na+ permeability with a small net movement (10-15 μM Na+/Kg) Na+ into the cell in the course of the depolarization spike. K+ permeability begins to decrease and Ca++ begins to move inward from the sites on the membrane. (3) Na+ permeability starts to decrease and K+ permeability decreases further as the plateau of the action potential is entered. Inward Ca++ movement rises rapidly permitting actin-myosin interaction and force development. (4) K+ permeability rises and K+ moves outward. Na+ permeability falls toward resting levels. Inward Ca++ movement declines and sequestration at SR and juxtamembrane areas rises — leading to relaxation. (5) Permeabilities have returned to rest levels but Na+ is being extruded and K+ taken up in the active transport process mediated by the Na+-K+ pump.

to note recently reported studies by Baker, Blaustein, Hodgkin, and Steinhardt in England. These investigators employed a system in which an essentially isolated membrane was derived from a squid axon and found that either reduction of the sodium in the medium perfusing the outside of the membrane or enhancement of the sodium inside the membrane produced a greatly increased calcium influx. It may well be that this property is common to all excitable membranes, including those of cardiac muscle cells.

Having established in broad outline the movements of the sodium and calcium ions, it is appropriate to turn to those of potassium. The potassium ion is important in providing to the cardiac action potential certain of its unique and functionally vital characteristics. In many cell depolarization phenomena, influx of sodium is followed by an efflux of potassium. Since potassium as well as sodium is positively charged, the discharge of potassium by the cell is necessary to repolarize the cell and prepare it for its next action potential. In nerve cells and skeletal muscle, the efflux of potassium follows very rapidly upon the influx of sodium. In these cells, the return of the membrane to resting potential may take only a few milliseconds, as in a nerve cell, or from 10 to 15 msec, as in skeletal muscle. But in cardiac muscle, the duration of the action potential extends to from 200

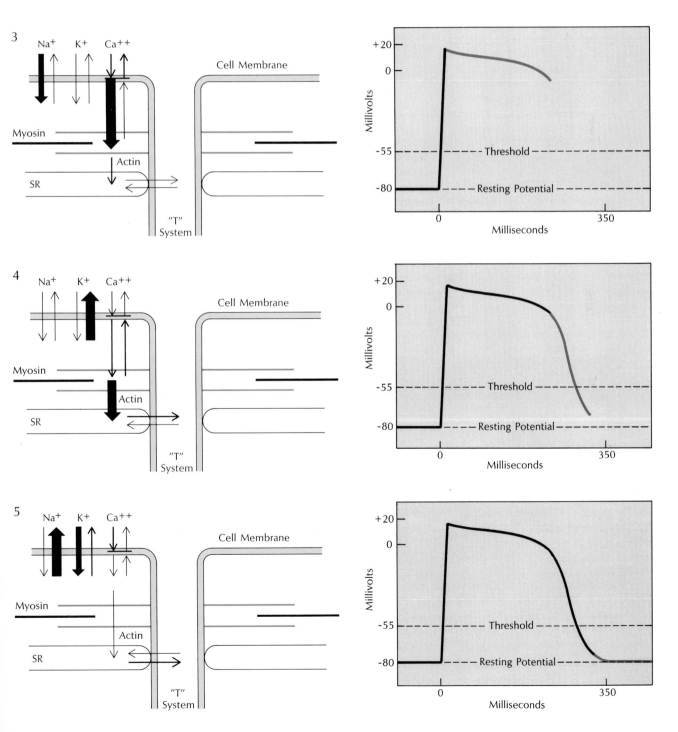

to 300 msec. The delay is achieved by a retardation of the efflux of potassium and this is the basis for the extended refractory period in cardiac contraction.

One must keep in mind that at the end of the action potential the cardiac fiber is relatively rich in sodium and poor in potassium. At this point, active sodium and potassium pumping is required to restore the cell to its steady-state ionic composition before the occurrence of the next action potential. These temporal relationships are important because they suggest the existence of rather precise feedback mechanisms to control the sodium pump and to determine its timing and activity with regard to the expulsion of sodium and to the reestablishment of the internal potassium concentration. They are also central to this discussion because many of the toxic effects of the digitalis glycosides are believed to be related specifically to this system.

Mention having been made of the sodium pump, it would now be appropriate to describe this physiologic mechanism as well as another ionic "pump" functioning within the myocardial cell, that which removes the calcium in order to permit uncoupling of the actomyosin and relaxation of the contractile elements of the heart.

At rest, calcium concentration about the myofilaments is less than 10^{-7} molar. Full activation is achieved when calcium concentration rises to approximately 10^{-6} or perhaps a bit higher. This 10- to 15-fold increase in concentration is achieved by release of the calcium from the surface membrane sites of the cell. Release from the lateral cisternae may be considerably less in cardiac as compared with skeletal muscle, as discussed previously. For relaxation to occur, the calcium concentration must be dropped below the threshold level for coupling, and this is achieved by an active process in which energy is expended to move calcium against a major concentration gradient; this is the so-called calcium pump. Present evidence indicates that this pump is a function of the sarcoplasmic reticulum, and for it to operate the S R must first bind the calcium at specific sites. From these the calcium is translocated into the sarcoplasmic reticulum by a process utilizing approximately 15% to 20% of the energy derived from oxidative metabolism within the myocardial fiber.

As the relaxation process proceeds, the cell is simultaneously repolarized so that, as noted above, it is now in a sodium-rich and potassium-poor state. Before the next action potential can be instituted, active pumping of sodium by means of a sodium pump localized on the sarcolemma must take place if the cell is to stay in a steady state with regard to its sodium and potassium concentrations. One might interject parenthetically here that little can be said definitely about the major anion involved in these fluxes, chloride. It is quite well established that some chloride translocation takes place during the course of the action potential. However, the characteristics of this translocation, whether active or passive, remain very much in dispute at this time, so that any attempt to describe the processes is likely to be more confusing than enlightening.

To return to sodium, it should be noted that for sodium to be removed from the cell, both a concentration gradient and an electrical gradient must be countered since the cell has been repolarized and is now negative internally as compared with externally. Thus energy is required if the sodium cation is to be pumped from the cell and the original ionic concentrations of the cell reestablished. The energy requirement is relatively small, probably less than 5% of the total utilized by the cell in a heart beating at 70 to 80 beats a minute. Despite the quantitatively low requirement, we now know that this energy has a high priority in terms of the overall cellular metabolism. This is physiologically imperative since if the sodium pump were turned off, sodium would rapidly build up within the cell, and it would become inexcitable in the course of about three hours. In

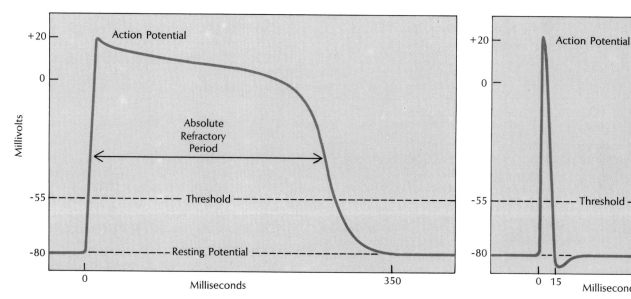

Difference in electrical patterns between cardiac (left) and skeletal muscle (for which delayed potassium efflux in the former is responsible) results in the so-called absolute refractory period during which the heart muscle cell cannot be restimulated.

other words, the sodium and potassium outside-to-inside ratios would arrive at a point at which an inward sodium flux across the cell membrane would no longer be possible, regenerative depolarization would be prevented, and the heart would stop.

Up to now, we have been sketching the movements of the ionic constituents required by the myocardial cell in the performance of its contractile function. We have done so in order to lay the groundwork for a discussion of the effects of the inotropic digitalis glycosides. Before turning to this, the main burden of this chapter, let me correlate portions of the previous discussion by describing the mechanical events that are mediated. In order to function, the cardiac muscle must develop an active force that has both a rate of development and a duration. To define our terms a little more precisely, the rate of development of force is related directly to the rate of development of the active state, i.e., of the instantaneous rate of development of the active processes leading to the full development of active tension. In terms of the ionic fluxes, the more calcium delivered to the myofilament the greater the intensity of the active state (see Chapter 2 by Katz), and the longer the calcium remains at the myofilament the greater the duration of the active state. The intensity of the active state is proportional to the maximum rate of force development (or maximum dP/dt), and the duration of the active state is essentially equal to the time to peak tension (T P T) in cardiac muscle.

The question whether digitalis glycosides act entirely through their effect on active ionic movements, rather than by any direct action upon the contractile proteins, is still somewhat subject to debate. Some investigators, notably Morales, have suggested a direct influence on actomyosin. However, the work of A. M. Katz indicates no such effect and I believe the evidence strongly suggests that the inotropic properties of digitalis are a result of its ability to alter ionic movements. In our own studies, we have been unable to demonstrate a significant increment of force development by the cardiac glycosides without demonstrating their inhibiting effects upon active sodium pumping.

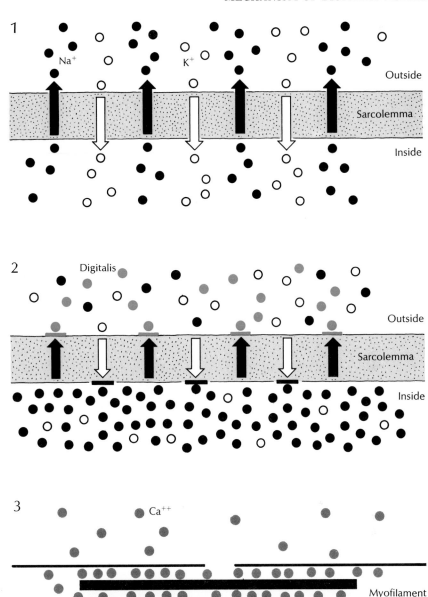

The action of digitalis is schematized. In the undigitalized heart (1), the necessary removal of sodium from the cell is accomplished by an active transport mechanism, utilizing ATP hydrolyzed by an ATPase. Digitalis (2) appears to interfere with the ATPase, thus inhibiting the sodium pump. This would allow Na to accumulate at the inner surface of membrane. Such an accumulation is proposed to augment the influx of calcium into the area of the myofilament with each excitation, thus potentiating contractility (3).

It is certainly well established from the work of Skou and of Glynn and his associates that the digitalis glycosides significantly affect active sodium transport. The effect is inhibitory, as has been shown not only in cardiac muscle but also in nerve, red-blood cells, and skeletal muscle. The inhibition occurs by a mechanism not yet completely defined, through interaction of the digitalis glycosides and the sodium-potassium-activated A T Pase. This is the enzyme directly controlling the hydrolysis of the A T P involved in production of energy for sodium transport. Not unexpectedly, the sodium-potassium A T Pase is concentrated about the sarcolemma.

The effect of the digitalis glycosides in an actively beating cardiac muscle is a decrease in the process of sodium pumping. They thereby produce an increment in internal sodium. This is

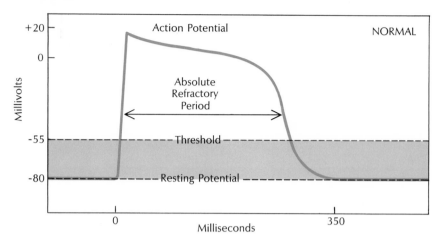

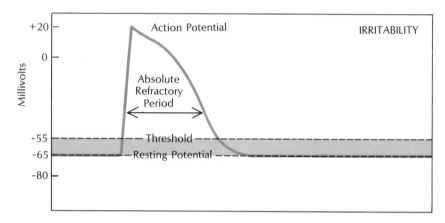

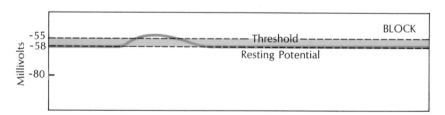

When digitalis is administered into the toxic range, potassium is lost from the cell in excessive quantity. The resting potential of the cell decreases (becomes less negative) to a point closer to the threshold for firing, and the action potential shortens. Muscle irritability is produced. In addition, as the resting potential continues to decrease another phase may be reached where, though the threshold is closer, it is harder to elicit a regenerative action potential. The cell becomes inexcitable and heart block may ensue.

probably the primary effect of a therapeutically effective dose of digitalis. It will be recalled that the diminution of sodium from an area of the cell membrane achieved by either translocating it to the outside or by allowing it to accumulate inside the cell will permit augmentation of the calcium influx. Studies in our laboratory support the hypothesis that the primary action of the digitalis glycosides is inhibition of the sodium pump, so that there is an increment of internal sodium concentration in-

side the myocardial fiber. Following directly upon this enhancement of sodium, there is an increment in the calcium that is transmitted with each excitation to the interior of the cell. This, in turn, results in increased actomyosin coupling and in a mechanical enhancement of the maximal dP/dt. This of course is the classical result of administration of digitalis.

In this context, the movements of the potassium ion, which with regard to the glycosides are well known, are in reality secondary to the inhibition

of active sodium transport. As sodium accumulates within the cell, potassium ions are depleted in order to maintain the cell in an isosmotic state. Although this depletion of potassium is not directly related to the inotropic effect of digitalis, it becomes extremely important when one discusses the toxic effects of digitalis excess such as the production of arrhythmias or block.

In our laboratory, we have been unable to separate the ability of the digitalis glycosides to inhibit the sodium pump from their ability to produce a positive inotropic effect. Moreover, we have been able to show that digitalis does not act upon all sodium transport in the fiber but only on a portion of it. In terms that are scientifically inexact but do convey the idea, digitalis would appear to produce a "compartmentalization" of the sodium, so that a fraction of the sodium is transferred with each action potential to a very slowly exchanging area of the cell. Unless we can demonstrate this compartmentalization of sodium, we cannot demonstrate the concomitant enhancement of calcium influx.

By way of further elaboration of the circumstances under which digitalis acts, the experiments described by Moran in 1967 can be cited. He found that the action of the digitalis glycosides is greatly influenced by the rate at which the myocardium is stimulated. When myocardial tissues were placed in a bath with a therapeutic dose of digitalis, the action of digitalis was inhibited unless the muscle was stimulated to contract. On the other hand, stimulation of the muscle speeded the action of digitalis. The rate of development of the inotropic action of digitalis was directly proportional to the rate of stimulation of the muscle. This can be explained on the basis of the sodium pump. In the quiescent muscle, there is almost no sodium transport to be inhibited and consequently digitalis' inotropic action is proportionally curtailed.

In our studies we have been able to quantify the amount of ionic inhibition required to develop a maximal inotropic effect. If one utilizes a drug such as ouabain, which requires a half hour to demonstrate its full inotropic effect, and one has a heart beating at 80 times a minute, a sodium transport inhibition of only 1% is required to produce the ionic disequilibrium for maximum inotropic effect.

This 1% inhibition of sodium pumping is sufficient to result in a secondary potassium loss. The net potassium loss is in the vicinity of 1 to 1.5 mM out of a total tissue concentration of 85 to 90 mM, again somewhere in the vicinity of 1%. The effect of this magnitude of potassium loss on the electrophysiologic characteristics of the myocardial cell is small. However, if one extrapolates to a situation in which there is increased administration of the digitalis glycoside into the toxic range, sodium transport is impaired to a greater degree and with this impairment there is a proportionally increased net potassium loss. Now it must be kept in mind that the resting potential of the sarcolemma is almost entirely dependent on the intracellular to extracellular potassium ratio. Therefore, as intracellular potassium concentration falls, the membrane resting potential drops too; it becomes less negative. Through a certain range, the cell is coming closer and closer to its threshold for regenerative depolarization. Rather than the cell having to go a distance of, say, 40 mv to fire, it may now have to go only 15 or 20 mv. The shorter the distance between resting potential and depolarization threshold, the more irritable the cell.

We can now look to see what this might mean if a myocardial cell with pacemaker activity — a Purkinje fiber cell for example — is depleted of potassium. Normally a Purkinje fiber cell has a firing rate of 35 to 40 times a minute, well below that of sinus depolarization. This differential makes possible the maintenance of a normal sinus rhythm. One must also keep in mind that digitalis exerts a vagal effect on the sinus that is bradycardic. So on one hand we have the Purkinje fiber cell losing potassium and having its resting potential come closer and closer to the threshold for firing; on the other hand, the sinus rate is being slowed. In addition, digitalis enhances the rate of phase 4 depolarization in Purkinje cells. Clearly, the conditions for the establishment of an ectopic arrhythmia are being developed.

However, this is not the whole story. The effects of potassium loss and sodium enhancement within the cell are biphasic. As we lower the resting potential closer and closer to the threshold for regenerative depolarization, the cell becomes less excitable rather than more so. This seeming paradox can be explained on the basis of sodium fluxes. The lower (more positive) the membrane resting potential becomes the more difficult it becomes to develop a sodium current across the membrane. In other words, the ability of the cell to establish a regenerative depolarization is increasingly compromised (see Chapter 26 by Bigger). Thus, the cell enters a phase where it becomes less rather than more excitable and eventually inexcitable. When this happens in the region of the A-V node, for example, digitalis toxicity can result in partial or complete A-V block. The ability of digitalis glycosides to disturb A-V conduction is, of course, well known.

We can now turn to several areas in which our knowledge is at best extremely sketchy. The first of these can be formulated as a question: Why does digitalis act as it does? The evidence that digitalis in some way interferes with ATPase hydrolysis of the ATP required to provide energy for the sodium pump has already been presented. How does digitalis do this? There are only two pieces of evidence that can be offered with any degree of confidence as partial answers to this question. The first, derived from the studies of Keynes, is that digitalis acts only on the external surface of cell membranes. There appears to be an asymmetry of the membrane with respect to the sites of digitalis activity, with the molecular acceptor sites for digitalis activity located only on the outside. Since it is well established that increasing potassium concentrations on the outside of the membrane result in the inhibition of glycoside action, one can hypothesize that it is the ability of the digitalis glycosides to attach to specific sites on the external surface of the myocardial cell membrane that gives them their ability to inhibit the action of the sodium-potassium-activated ATPase.

A second area in which our knowledge is extremely tentative has relevance to a clinically very familiar and very puzzling phenomenon — the great difference in individual reactions to the cardiac glycosides. This marked variability may be the human counterpart to a species-to-species variability observed in animal experiments. It has been shown, for example, that rats are notoriously resistant to the inotropic effects of digitalis and fail in large measure to bind the glycosides to their myocardial cell membranes. The explanation for the fact that in some patients the therapeutic dose of digitalis is several times the usually required dose may well lie in a diminished ability to bind the glycosides.

Throughout this discussion of the mechanism of action of the digitalis glycosides, stress has been laid upon the primary effect that these drugs have upon ionic fluxes. Certainly the clinical implications of this emphasis should not be ignored. For example, the concomitant administration of digitalis and the diuretic agents, particularly the more potent kaliuretic agents such as ethacrynic acid and furosemide, must be undertaken with an awareness that a diminished serum potassium, which is to say a diminished potassium at the external surface of the cardiac-muscle-cell membrane, increases sensitivity to the glycoside. In any patient being treated with digitalis glycosides, close surveillance of electrolyte balance must be a first priority.

Finally, a word of caution should be offered with regard to all that has gone before in this chapter. What has been presented is one point of view, a working hypothesis with a reasonable chance of explaining many key elements in basic glycoside action. Other points of view have recently been presented in a comprehensive study by Lee and Klaus. Perhaps by the time of the 200th anniversary of the first clinical use of digitalis, the knowledge required to place the use of the glycosides on a fully scientific basis will have been achieved.

Diuretics in the Treatment of Congestive Heart Failure

JOHN H. LARAGH

Columbia University

As with so many aspects of cardiac failure, the basic "lesion" in congestive heart failure is a consequence of inappropriate compensation. The sequence, of course, begins with degenerative changes in the myocardium leading to incompetence of the cardiac pump. It can then be traced to decreased mean arterial pressure generated during cardiac contraction, which provides the energy for glomerular filtration and delivery of blood to the kidney. In a manner not yet fully understood, this reduction of renal blood flow is associated with a signal to the kidney to conserve sodium, and this conservation underlies the fluid retention that produces congestion in the lungs, liver, abdomen, and peripheral tissues. The signal for the kidney to retain sodium involves renal vasoconstriction with reduced filtration and reduced sodium supply to the distal macula densa. Either of these reductions operates in turn to stimulate renin release and aldosterone secretion (see Chapter 8, "The Mechanisms of Salt and Water Retention in Cardiac Failure," by Davis). Thus, ultimately, the compensation reaction produces congestion, which results in further impairment of the already compromised cardiac performance.

As long as one keeps in mind that the original failure is myocardial, it is clinically quite pragmatic to regard congestive heart failure as a disease whose major determinant is the kidney. Equally, diuretics can be discussed as the key to any regimen for the management of congestive heart failure. Not that a theoretical basis is needed for assigning such primacy to the diuretics. Every clinician must be aware of the revolutionary improvement in our ability to manage and to understand disorders characterized by abnormal fluid accumulation and/or elevated blood pressure that has resulted from the development of effective oral diuretic agents, starting with the introduction of chlorothiazide in 1958. Now, physicians treating congestive heart failure have available at least five different classes of diuretic agents (see pages 146 and 147), each of which is capable of selectively interfering in a different way with the active transport mechanisms involved in tubular reabsorption and thereby promoting natriuresis and diuresis.

Renal Transport Mechanisms

A brief review of the mechanisms of salt and water transport in the kidney will form the basis for discussion of the selective action of different diuretics. The glomerular filtration rate in man is approximately 100 ml/min, with the resulting filtrate containing concentrations of sodium and other electrolytes equal to those found in plasma. Tubular reabsorption returns at least 99% of the filtrate to the circulation, the remaining 1% being excreted. Normally, about 70% of the filtrate is returned to the circulation by the proximal tubule in the form of an isotonic solution containing equivalent amounts of sodium and water. In other words, there is no dilution or concentration in conjunction with reabsorption from the proximal tubule, and water absorption in this region is secondary to activation of sodium reabsorption. The permeability of the proximal tubular membrane to water permits passive isotonic reabsorption of water first into the interstitium and from there into the circulation. Two qualitatively different transport processes operate in the proximal tubule. By one mechanism, actively reabsorbed sodium is accompanied by chloride and isosmotic amounts of water. By the other, sodium is reabsorbed in exchange for the hydrogen ions generated within the proximal tubular cells by the hydration of CO_2 – a reaction catalyzed by the enzyme carbonic anhydrase. The hydrogen ions elaborated into proximal tubular fluid in exchange for sodium combine there with filtered bicarbonate ions to form CO_2 and H_2O, a reaction facilitated by the presence of carbonic anhydrase in the proximal tubular cells. The reabsorbed sodium ions are returned to the peritubular blood along with an amount of newly generated HCO_3 equivalent to approximately 90% of the bicarbonate that was filtered at the glomerulus.

The other major changes in composition occur distally in the nephron, where the remaining 30% of the filtrate is acted upon. The next reabsorption site is the renal medullary portion of the ascending limb of the loop of Henle. This portion of the nephron is impermeable to water. So, although active sodium reabsorption takes place, returning anywhere from 15% to 30% of the filtered sodium to the body, an equal amount of water is not removed. Fluid remaining in the lumen becomes dilute in terms of concentration of sodium, chloride, and other electrolytes. Conversely, fluid on the interstitial side of the nephron, in the renal medulla, becomes hypertonic to plasma, generating the driving force for the eventual production of concentrated urine when the filtrate passes by again in the collecting ducts. The process of dilution continues as the dilute tubular fluid passes back into the renal cortex and as sodium reabsorption continues without equivalent water movement in the next portion of the nephron, still within the ascending limb of the loop of Henle. The passage of fluid through the distal convolution and the collecting duct then continues without osmotic equilibration with the hypertonic medullary interstitium, unless the kidney is under stress to retain water mediated by antidiuretic hormone (ADH), which acts to increase the water permeability of the descending limb and collecting ducts. ADH activity can result in a concentrated urine with approximately a 1,200 milliosmolal concentration of solutes, about four times the osmolality of plasma. In this way, small volumes of water with high concentrations of sodium are excreted. On the other hand, under stress of water ingestion, dilution can occur that will produce urine with one sixth or less of the normal osmolality. Thus, large volumes of water with low concentrations of sodium are excreted.

Essentially, all diuretic agents function by affecting the processes of tubular reabsorption either directly or by inhibiting those hormones that regulate these processes. Because different agents affect different steps in the sequence, the physician has not

Salt and Water Transport and Reabsorption
Water Diuresis

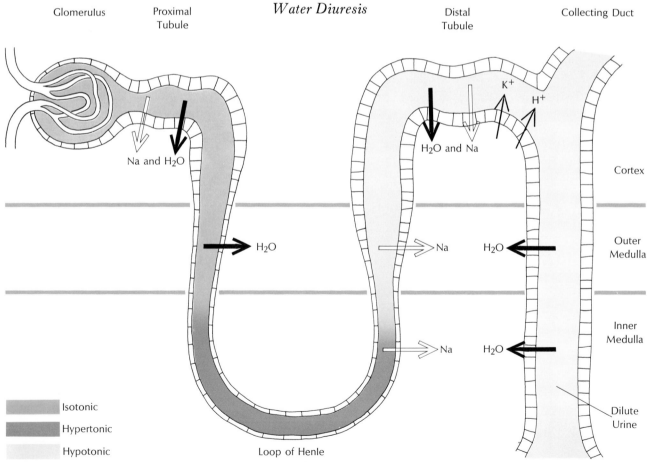

Schematic representation shows the movement of water and electrolytes in the nephron. Indicated are sites at which both water and ionic constituents are reabsorbed, resulting in essentially isotonic tubular fluid; sites where water alone is reabsorbed, producing concentration and hypertonicity; and sites where electrolytes are reabsorbed without water, resulting in dilute or hypotonic fluid. These differences are of particular relevance in relation to the sites of action of diuretics (see facing page).

only a choice that may be governed by definable physiologic needs but also the opportunity to design a diuretic regimen that is rationally tailored to specific clinical problems. This will be discussed in terms of the specific diuretic agents now available. First, however, let us return to the concept that congestive heart failure represents an inappropriate compensation in response to derangement of the normal interactions between the heart and the kidney.

The obvious premise is that the initial fluid overload in congestive failure results from the failure of the heart as a pump, a failure that relates back to a basically mechanical defect, albeit one that probably has a biochemical basis, i.e., faulty performance by muscle fibrils. Cardiac output is reduced as is delivery of blood to the kidneys. This, in turn, reduces the kidney's capacity to excrete salt and therefore leads to the accumulation of water and to congestion, which then increases the demands on a cardiac pump that, to start with, lacked the ability to handle even normal demands.

Physical and Hormonal Factors in Renal Sodium Excretion

The first question to be asked is why the reduction of blood flow in the kidney should lead to retention of salt and water. There is evidence suggesting that the kidney's functional incompetence is not simply the product of underperfusion. It has been shown that the renal tubules are actually hyperactive, that they reabsorb proportionally more of the filtered sodium than the normal kidney. In a sense, the kidney is responding as if there were a shortage of electrolytes in the circulation. It is not altogether clear why this should be so, but it now appears that changes in intrarenal physical factors in the postglomerular circulation, especially a reduced hydrostatic pressure and an increased oncotic pressure, work to promote increased sodium reabsorption in the proximal tubules.

Over and above this, the reduced effective blood volume or reduced arterial "filling" consequent to poor cardiac pumping induces an increased renin secretion by the kidneys. This is induced either by a baroreceptor signal at the afferent arterioles or by a reduced delivery of sodium to the distal tubular macula densa cells, which may have a natriastat that modulates renin secretion by the adjacent juxtaglomerular cells of the afferent arterioles.

Sites of Action of Different Diuretics

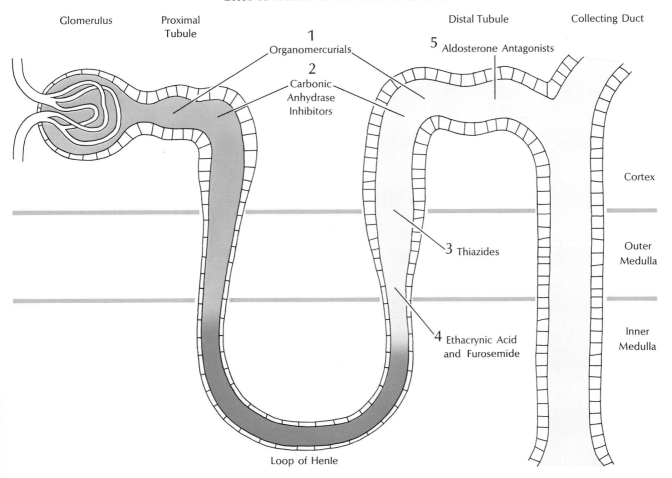

The mercurials (1) act in proximal or distal tubule to inhibit isosmotic reabsorption. Carbonic anhydrase inhibitors (2) act there also, blocking acidification and preventing H-Na exchange and Na reabsorption. Thiazides (3) act in ascending limb of loop of Henle and in distal cortical convolutions to interfere with dilution. Ethacrynic acid and furosemide (4) also interfere with dilution and also block Na transport, depressing concentration. Aldosterone antagonists (5) interfere with Na retention and K excretion.

Organomercurials

METHOD OF ADMINISTRATION: *Parenteral.*
SITE OF ACTION: *Proximal and/or distal tubule.*
METHOD OF ACTION: *Decrease isosmotic reabsorption.*
SHORTCOMINGS: *Route of administration.*

Anti–Carbonic Anhydrase Sulfonamides

METHOD OF ADMINISTRATION: *Oral.*
SITE OF ACTION: *All along nephron, primarily in proximal tubule.*
METHOD OF ACTION: *Enzymatic blockade to prevent hydrogen ion secretion by kidney and inhibit acidification of urine. They thus prevent reabsorption of sodium, which usually results from exchange of sodium ions in tubular urine and hydrogen ions.*
SHORTCOMINGS: *Rapid development of tolerance.*

Thiazides

METHOD OF ADMINISTRATION: *Oral.*
SITE OF ACTION: *Within ascending limb loop of Henle and distal convoluted tubu*
METHOD OF ACTION: *Interfere with dilut of urine and thereby prevent the reabso tion of sodium and other electrolytes distal cortical convolutions, resulting inhibition of free water formation and e hanced excretion of Na, Cl, K, and oth ions.*
SHORTCOMINGS: *Kaliuresis may lead hypokalemia; some tendency to devel refractoriness.*

By whichever mechanism angiotensin via renin generation elicits the secretion of aldosterone, aldosterone in turn further amplifies sodium reabsorption (see Chapter 8 by Davis). However, the retained sodium continues to "leak" from the effective circulation into the edema spaces so that a signal for inexorable and continued sodium excretion persists, leading to the congested and edematous state.

The Basis for Diuretic Therapy

How can this vicious cycle of cardiac incompetence, decreased output and perfusion, salt conservation, fluid congestion, and exacerbated cardiac incompetence be broken? Certainly one could rationally concentrate on the underlying pathophysiologic flaw by seeking to increase cardiac contractility and output. And indeed this is what is done, wherever possible, with digitalis and other inotropic drugs (see Chapter 13, "The Mechanism

of Action of Digitalis," by Langer). However, we have learned in the past dozen years that in patients whose cardiac failure is clinically manifested most conspicuously by edema, more consistent and often more dramatic results can be achieved by addressing our therapeutic attentions to the kidney disturbance. Thus the remarkably successful role played by diuretics.

Depending on the taxonomic criteria one uses, the different diuretic agents now available for the management of congestive heart failure and other edematous states can be subdivided in varied ways (see above). Based on differences in their physiologic effects, they fall into five different groups: the organomercurials; the sulfonamide-carbonic anhydrase inhibitors; the chloruretic sulfonamide compounds, among which the thiazides were the first, and remain the foremost, representatives; ethacrynic acid and furosemide; and the potassium-retaining diuretics, no-

tably aldosterone antagonists (see below). For each of these groups, current concepts of their site and mode of action will be discussed, thus laying the groundwork for a subsequent discussion of the rational design of diuretic regimens.

Organomercurials

From the discovery of their diuretic potential in the early 1900's for close to half a century, the organomercurials served as the only available and effective compounds for removal of excess body fluid. This property of the mercurials was happened upon by physicians using them in the treatment of syphilis and observing the profound diuretic effect on some patients. The organomercurials remain among the most effective of diuretic agents, but their use is, of course, severely limited by the need for parenteral administration. In terms of the site of action, there is still no clear

uretic Agents

Ethacrynic Acid

Furosemide

METHOD OF ADMINISTRATION: *Oral.*

E OF ACTION: *Loop of Henle and distal involuted tubule.*

THOD OF ACTION: *Similar to thiazides; ability in addition to block sodium nsport in loop of Henle, therefore de-ssing urinary concentrating as well as nary diluting activity. Effects are there-e highly potentiated in relationship to izides.*

RTCOMINGS: *"Violence" of action may d to rebound on cessation of administra-n, with consequent fluid retention.*

Aldosterone Antagonists

Spironolactone

Triamterene

MK-870

METHOD OF ADMINISTRATION: *Oral.*
SITE OF ACTION: *Distal renal tubule.*
METHOD OF ACTION: *Compete with aldos-terone for receptor sites, thereby prevent-ing aldosterone-catalyzed Na-K exchange and excessive potassium loss.*

SHORTCOMINGS: *Less potent as natriuretic agents than thiazides, ethacrynic acid, and furosemide (see text).*

---

evidence as to whether the mercurials act by distal tubular blockade or by proximal tubular blockade, but it has been established that at either site they function primarily by inhibition of an isosmotic reabsorptive process. Mercurial agents do not significantly inhibit either urinary concentrating or diluting mechanisms.

Carbonic Anhydrase Inhibitors

The discovery of the diuretic value of carbonic anhydrase inhibitors in one sense ushered in the new age of diuretic therapy. These drugs were harbingers of the far more important things to come only a year or so after. Once again, progress came in the form of fortuitous fallout from an-other branch of chemotherapy. It was noted that patients with congestive heart disease receiving sulfanilamide for pneumonia often had impressive diureses. It was known that sulfanila-mide is a carbonic anhydrase inhibi-

tor and that the process of hydrogen ion secretion by the kidney was de-pendent on the carbonic anhydrase system. From these premises, it was decided to seek sulfonamide com-pounds more specifically tailored for their carbonic anhydrase inhibition, and these were developed. Although the carbonic anhydrase inhibitor diu-retic drugs are still in use, their role has been somewhat limited by the rapid development of tolerance to them. They are generally effective for a day or two and then lose their po-tency in the person being treated. For this reason, the carbonic anhydrase inhibitors are best used intermittently and as adjuvants to other diuretics. Used in this way they can produce striking diuresis in refractory patients.

The mode and site of action has been suggested above in the observa-tion that the carbonic anhydrase in-hibitors act by blocking an enzyme system that is necessary for the secre-tion of hydrogen ions by the kidney.

These drugs act all along the nephron, primarily in the proximal tubule, by inhibiting the acidification of the urine. This serves to produce natri-uresis and diuresis because the secre-tion of hydrogen ions into the tubular urine is accomplished by an exchange with sodium ions, which are then re-absorbed. By blocking acidification, sodium reabsorption is prevented.

Thiazides (Chloruretic Sulfonamides)

If the discovery of the carbonic an-hydrase inhibitors was the forerunner of the revolution in management of congestive heart failure, then that revolution came into full force with the discovery and introduction of chlorothiazide. Here at last was an oral drug that could produce a potent diuresis. Nor were any problems of refractoriness apparent with chloro-thiazide. Now, of course, there are probably a score or more thiazide drugs on the market. Basically, none of these analogs differ significantly from chlorothiazide. One may need a different number of milligrams of one analog to achieve an equipotent dose with another, and there may be some differences in duration of action, but essentially all of the thiazides are closely similar in their therapeutic capacity.

The sites of action of the thiazides have been quite well pinpointed in the proximal tubule as well as in the more cortical diluting segment of the distal tubule. These drugs do not interfere with urinary concentration. The result includes the inhibition of free water formation and the excre-tion of not only sodium and water but also of chloride, potassium, and other ions. The kaliuretic effect of the thia-zides constitutes one of the problems in their use. Before discussing this, however, let us turn to the newer com-pounds, ethacrynic acid and furosem-ide, which resemble the thiazides in terms of their diuretic and electrolytic effects but are more powerful.

Ethacrynic Acid and Furosemide

Quantitatively, both of these newer agents exert a much greater effect than the thiazides, probably because, in addition to their thiazide-like inter-ference with diluting mechanisms in

147

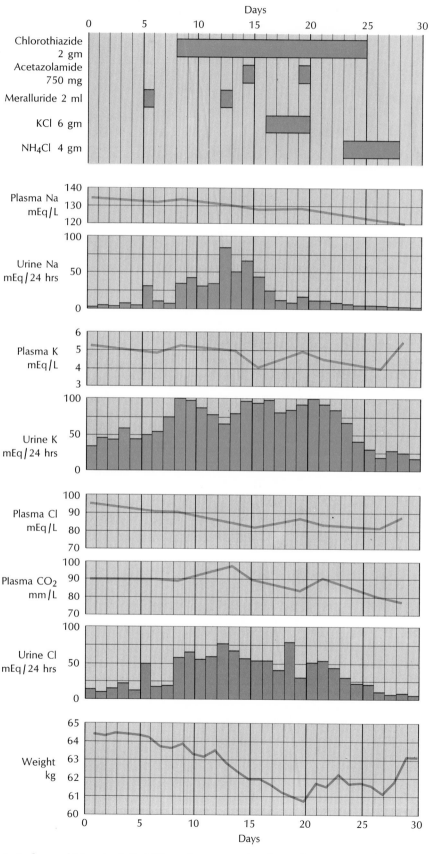

the distal cortical tubules, they also block sodium transport in the loop or early ascending limb. Therefore, they depress urinary concentrating as well as urinary diluting activity. For this reason, the potent agents are often referred to as "loop diuretics."

Aldosterone Antagonists

The two basic effects of the adrenal hormone aldosterone on electrolytes are the promotion of sodium retention and potassium excretion. It is this combination that tends to make the aldosterone antagonists ideal diuretics in a clinical context, where the physician is most likely to be seeking sodium excretion and potassium retention. Three pharmacologic agents have proved capable of effective aldosterone antagonism – spironolactone, the most widely used; triamterene; and amiloride (M K-870). The last is the most powerful of the three but, although widely used abroad, it has not received Food and Drug Administration approval for clinical use. All three of these agents act by competing for receptor sites at the distal renal tubule where the aldosterone-catalyzed exchange between sodium and potassium ions takes place. These compounds are thus especially valuable in correcting potassium loss produced by the thiazides or other diuretic species. Spironolactone is a true competitive inhibitor of endogenous aldosterone and has no action in the absence of this hormone. On the other hand, triamterene and amiloride can block the aldosterone-directed transport mechanism even in the absence of the hormone and therefore have the properties of a noncompetitive inhibitor. This means that the latter two drugs can still be effective even when endogenous aldosterone secretion is enormous.

In an important sense, spironolactone and other diuretics in its class approach the ideal in their mode of action and effects. It is true that they are not as powerful acutely as the thiazides or ethacrynic acid and furosemide as natriuretic agents. This is because aldosterone has only a minor influence on the total bulk of electrolyte reabsorption by the tubule. But practically, a minor effect steadily maintained for enough time is a major effect. By administering spironolactone

A single case history is plotted. The patient, a man in advanced congestive failure, was essentially nonresponsive to the organomercurials but showed striking diuresis when thiazides were introduced. Salt supplementation corrected a mild hypochloremic alkalosis. Addition of meralluride or acetazolamide to the regimen potentiated the natriuresis but there was a gradual diminution of the natriuretic response to the thiazides.

over, say, three or four weeks, one may actually induce a greater sodium and water loss than with more powerful natriuretic agents – even with ethacrynic acid or furosemide. With these latter two drugs there is a tendency in the patient to develop resistance and on cessation of the drug, a rebound to the violence of its action. The consequent fluid retention may annul the diuretic benefits. Something can be said, therefore, for gradual, smooth diuresis, and in many cases the physician's or patient's impatience to see tangible results quickly may cause an inappropriate turning away from the aldosterone antagonists as the first diuretic to be tried.

What is an ideal diuretic regimen? Obviously there is no single answer to this question. What should be stressed is the fact that different classes of diuretics act at least in part on different sites in the renal tubules, thus affecting qualitatively different transport mechanisms. By taking advantage of this selectivity, the clinician may choose a particular diuretic to correct any particular derangement in the blood electrolytes of the patient. There are many practical illustrations of combined use of diuretics to achieve maximum efficacy. In fact, the only two classes that cannot be used effectively in combination are the organomercurials and the carbonic anhydrase inhibitors, since the latter may block the effects of the mercurials by preventing acidification of the urine.

In designing a regimen, one must also take into account the fact that with thiazides, ethacrynic acid, and furosemide there is a tendency to develop some degree of refractoriness. These drugs tend to be most powerful in the first few days of administration, then to lose some efficacy.

This is one of the reasons why many of us have advocated intermittent programs in which "resting periods" are allowed. Not only will this provide recovery time for the drug action but it also will permit restoration of the electrolyte imbalance that commonly occurs with diuretics. For example, if a patient is receiving thiazides there will be some potassium loss and therefore some danger of hypokalemia. If, on the other hand, a three-day period of taking the drug followed by three days of rest is prescribed, the patient may replenish his

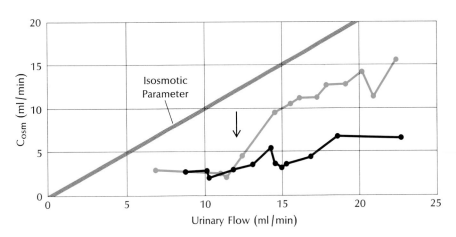

Data from a normal subject support the concept that two diuretics administered on different days act at different sites in the renal tubule. Both chlorothiazide (red line) and meralluride (black line) increased the urine volume to the same extent but chlorothiazide caused greater increment in total solute excretion. It thus acts more distally, preventing selective solute reabsorption at the site where free water is made available. Arrow indicates the time of administration of either one of the drugs during similarly maintained water diureses. The individual points represent consecutive ten-minute periods during which urine was collected.

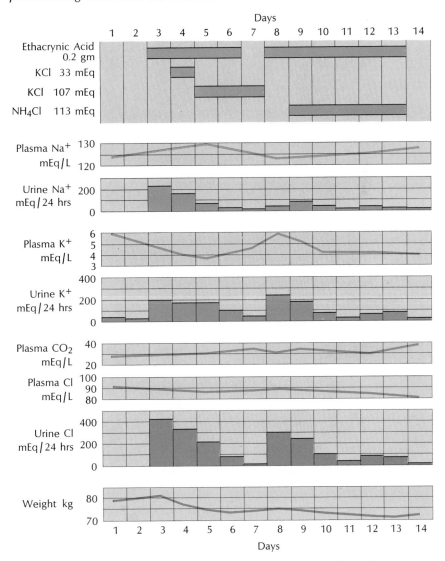

On prolonged ethacrynic acid regimen, natriuresis in failure patient declined on continuous, was restored on intermittent therapy. Diuresis also tended to correct hyponatremia.

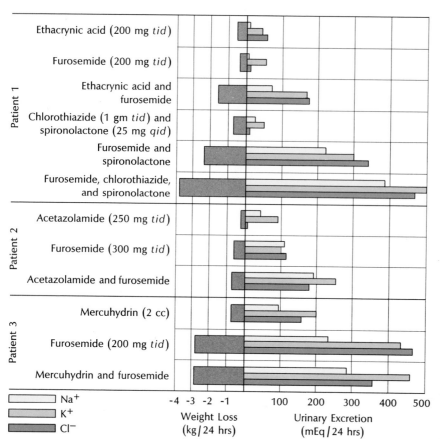

The effects of ethacrynic acid and furosemide, used alone, together, or in combination with other diuretic agents, are shown in three different patients with refractory edema.

potassium from natural food sources such as fruit and meat, which are abundant in ionic potassium.

The two main arguments against intermittent therapy are that such regimens are inconvenient for the patient and the physician, an argument which I think can be dismissed out of hand, and that a smooth, even diuretic effect is lost. It is true that with intermittent regimens, the patient's weight may fluctuate to a greater extent, climbing during the off periods, then dropping sharply when the drug is reintroduced. And I would agree that this is not as desirable as a daily blockade, but on balance I believe the advantages of intermittent therapy outweigh the disadvantages.

One major exception to this evaluation would apply to the aldosterone antagonists. These can be effective only on a continuous basis, since one must strive for high enough blood levels to create a chronic blockade of potassium loss. For this reason we are beginning to feel increasingly that to treat any difficult patient, the best approach is to start with spironolactone

or triamterene, then add one of the thiazides or ethacrynic acid or furosemide intermittently. In this way one can maintain an even baseline effect while preventing potassium depletion.

In many patients, of course, thiazides alone will do the diuretic job when administered on an intermittent basis. If we start with thiazides and they prove inadequate, our next step is to add an aldosterone antagonist, which we give chronically while using the thiazides intermittently. If this still fails to produce adequate diuresis, we substitute one of the two more powerful agents, ethacrynic acid or furosemide, for the thiazide. In rare cases, with very sick patients, none of these regimens may be effective. As a last resort in such cases we give volume expanders such as hypertonic mannitol (two liters of a 10% solution given slowly over ten hours while watching cardiac function) or albumin together with cortisone. The purpose of these maneuvers is to correct the poor forward delivery from the heart and consequent underperfusion of the arterial tree that may occur

in serious congestive heart failure. By increasing the perfusion of the kidney, the physician may provide a more favorable environment for the action of the diuretics and thereby increase their efficacy. Cortisone and particularly those glucocorticoid analogs with less sodium-retaining action seem to make a specific contribution to the enhancement of renal blood flow. Aminophylline may also be useful for this. Obviously, such combined approaches should not be used on an outpatient basis and, in fact, by definition, are appropriate only to a desperately ill, hospitalized individual.

Dangers of Potassium Replacement

It should be noted that in describing these various regimens, no mention is made of using potassium supplementation in the form of potassium salts. We have never advocated such supplementation for ambulatory patients because the amounts of potassium chloride required for correction can be dangerous by virtue of toxicity to the heart and because of their tendency to cause ileal ulceration. We believe hyperkalemia is far more threatening to the cardiac patient than hypokalemia. Potassium salts are far more potent physiologic and pharmacologic agents than is generally recognized, even by those who are aware that these salts can be and have been used to induce cardiac arrest. Accordingly, potassium supplementation is best carried out only as a hospital procedure under close supervision.

The best approach to potassium depletion involves 1) intermittent therapy with a kaliuretic diuretic and 2) use of baseline therapy with an aldosterone antagonist. This is because potassium depletion is most likely to occur in more severely ill patients who exhibit marked secondary aldsteronism. Indeed, our studies indicate that even the most potent loop diuretics will not induce any potassium loss in either adrenalectomized or spironolactone treated patients. Accordingly, if time is allowed for restoration of effective plasma volume, or when possible dietary salt is liberalized, the diuretic induced aldosterone response will abate. If intermittent therapy does not eliminate the problem, therapy with spironolactone, triamterene, or amiloride is indicated.

A look at the present and the future in any review of a field as rapidly developing as that of diuretic therapy must be concerned with the physiologic implications as well as with the therapeutic criteria. It is significant, therefore, that in the more than a dozen years in which oral diuretics have been available, we have used these agents not only for their primary purposes, the dissipation of edema and the control of hypertension, but also as an extremely valuable tool for the dissection of renal tubular transport mechanisms. Many of the facts cited to explain the sites and mechanisms of action of the various classes of diuretics have actually been learned from observing these drugs in action and then reasoning backwards. We have also made a substantial beginning toward understanding the intrarenal transport mechanisms for regulation of sodium reabsorption at a perhaps more basic level, that is to say, in terms of control by signals arising extrarenally. The effects of chlorothiazide and other diuretics on the release of renin and on aldosterone secretion might also involve extrarenal signals. Solution of the problem of how diuretic-induced depletion of electrolytes and fluid triggers increased renin and then aldosterone secretion could, for example, go a long way toward unraveling the delicately entwined mechanisms for sodium and blood pressure homeostasis.

These are but examples of the type of problem that can be productively approached through close study of the roles played by diuretics. We are in the particularly happy position of being able to pursue such studies while providing our patients with the immense and often lifesaving benefits of the very agents through which increased knowledge will come.

Section Five

Atherosclerosis and the Etiology of Myocardial Infarction

Development of the Atherosclerotic Plaque

ROBERT W. WISSLER

University of Chicago

The goal of defining the most important events in formation of an atherosclerotic plaque has been sought by many investigators ever since it was recognized that most coronary heart disease is a clinical consequence of advancing atherosclerosis. Most workers have taken as their premise that lipid deposition within the arterial wall is the definitive step in the sequence that results in a fully formed plaque. Some have held the view that an event such as accumulation of collagen and fibrin precedes the lipid and in some way alters the intimal surface of the vessel wall so that lipid is more readily deposited. Typically, an advanced "complicated" plaque consists of a lipid-filled necrotic center, a fibrous cap enclosing the lesion, and often calcification at the base.

Examining a small lesion that is presumably at an early stage reveals few of the complex changes that occur during its progression. However, when lesions of varying degrees of severity are studied histopathologically, the most common "pure" lesion is most often seen to consist predominantly of small accumulations of lipid, with little accumulation of collagen, fibrin, elastin, or mucopolysaccharides. This has been our experience in a large consecutive series of human autopsies; the other components appear to develop primarily in reaction to the presence of lipid in the intimal and inner medial layers of the artery wall.

But if lipid deposition is a primary event in pathogenesis, it must be considered in reference to the hyperlipidemia that is also associated with atherosclerosis. Epidemiologic studies strongly support a relationship between excessive dietary cholesterol, saturated fats, and calories, and development of hyperlipidemia and atherosclerosis along with its clinical effects (see Chapter 19, "Genetic Aspects of Hyperlipidemia in Coronary Heart Disease," by Goldstein and Chapter 20, "The Primary Prevention of Coronary Heart Disease," by Stamler). Lipid elevation has also been linked to hereditary atherosclerosis; in patients with familial hyperlipidemia, the likelihood of premature severe coronary disease is markedly increased.

Animal experiments show that almost every species develops atherosclerosis once sustained elevation of blood lipids has been accomplished. However, acknowledging an important relationship between hyperlipidemia and atherosclerosis still requires us to explain how an excess in serum lipid results in lipid deposition in the artery wall, and how in turn the latter is related to clinical atherosclerosis.

Using standard staining techniques, a histopathologist can easily separate the several tissue components in a developing plaque and assess their relative contribution. Even when the disease consists of a small, fatty streak, lipid is seen not only within cells of both the intima and inner media of the vessel wall but also in association with elastin and other fiber proteins that may become more prominent as the lesion advances. Thus, in viewing the pathogenesis of atherosclerosis, one must take into account factors causing influx of lipid into the vessel wall and also those causing it to be deposited preferentially in certain locations.

Although there are still many unknowns, new insight into the mechanisms involved has been gained through looking at atherosclerosis from a somewhat different vantage point – in terms of the cellular basis of plaque development. Our studies in this connection and related work by others will form the basis of the discussion that follows.

It should be made clear before we proceed that the presence of lipid per se in the arterial wall is not necessarily a very serious pathologic process. Deposition of lipid in small amounts – the so-called *fatty streaks* – is a natural phenomenon commencing early in life in virtually all human populations and animal species regardless of the diet consumed. As documented by McGill and others, the

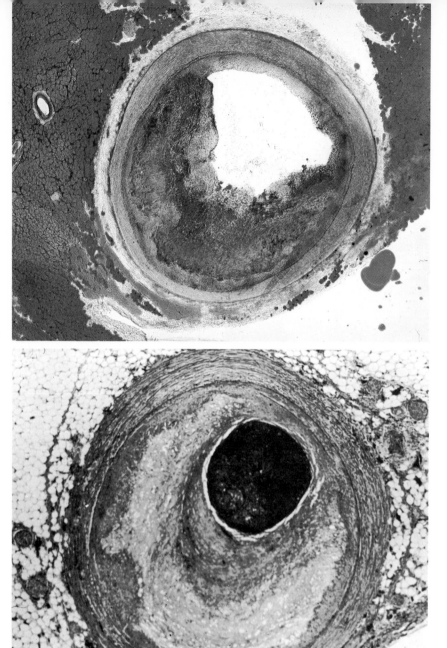

At top is section of severely atherosclerotic coronary artery from fairly young man; intima and media show remarkable deposition of lipid substances that stain red with oil red O stain. Only a small fibrous cap is present in this soft plaque. The surrounding oil red O–positive adipose tissue is usually present in the epicardium and serves as control for the stain. Lower photo shows an atherosclerotic plaque in left coronary artery of an elderly male, with a superimposed occlusive thrombus.

search laboratories today, since only when this advanced stage is reached does the disease process emerge above the clinical horizon, so to speak, as acute myocardial infarction or some other form of clinical manifestation. Aortic atherosclerosis often tends to progress more rapidly than coronary atherosclerosis, for reasons not well understood, but it is apparent that in either case the clinical consequences derive from the chemical nature of the lesion as well as its location. In a coronary artery a fully developed plaque containing a lipid-filled necrotic center and fibrous cap may well have sufficient mass to cause almost complete occlusion of the lumen. It is usually at this stenotic stage that the narrowed lumen is likely to be finally occluded by a thrombus. Given the size of the aorta, the mass of a plaque may be of less significance but its capacity to weaken the vessel wall still has serious import and aneurysms may form.

In both locations there is the danger that rupture of the fibrous cap of the lesion followed by ulceration will result in formation of mural thrombi composed mainly of platelets and fibrin; thrombosis may then contribute to vessel narrowing or occlusion or lead to embolization by thombus fragments. Emboli may also arise from release of atheromatous debris from the ulcerated plaque.

Research during the past decade has centered interest on a critical interplay between factors in the vessel lumen that facilitate diffusion of serum lipids into the artery wall and factors within the wall itself responsible for lipid entrapment and accumulation.

In turning first to factors within the lumen, it is logical to focus on the serum lipoproteins because of their essential role in lipid transport. Evidence from many studies in man and several species of animals has established the concept that lipid enters the artery wall by means of diffusion from the lumen of the serum lipoproteins. The several lipoprotein complexes normally present in the blood differ in the type and amount of lipid carried, but regardless of lipid content, their size and configuration must be consistent with easy passage into the artery wall for arterial deposition to occur (see illustration on page 160).

As Gofman perceptively observed,

sequence usually begins within the first decade, when the presence of minimal fatty streaking is often readily apparent. Fatty streak development usually advances very little during the second decade, or even in the third, in populations *not* predisposed to atherosclerosis. In those that are, the process accelerates rapidly in many members, especially males, in the third decade; lipid accumulation increases and there is some fibrous protein deposition surrounding the fatty streaks. In these same populations development of true atheromatous

plaques – containing lipids, increased collagen, and mucopolysaccharides, as well as fibrin and sometimes red blood cells – is often well under way by the fourth and fifth decades. By this time, lipid, originally the predominant or sole constituent, is only one of several components of the lesion.

What are the reasons for *progression* in some populations and some individuals from the stage of fatty streak formation to abnormal accumulation of lipid and formation of a complicated plaque? This is one of the major problems being studied in re-on the basis of the physical dimensions of components of the artery wall, delineated by electron microscopy, probably all but one of the lipid-carrying molecules in the blood should be capable of entry. The largest of the lipoproteins—the chylomicrons—are probably barred because the intercellular spaces and vacuoles of the endothelium, as well as the dimensions of the internal elastic membrane, are too small to allow passage. By the same token there is only slight impediment to entry of the other three major lipoprotein complexes — very low-density, low-density, and high-density lipoproteins.

These designations, applied to lipoproteins separated by ultracentrifugation, reflect the varying amounts of lipid and protein present in each complex and hence their molecular density. In addition to their lipid and protein content, lipoproteins also vary in electrical charge and thus are separable by electrophoresis into pre-beta lipoprotein (very low density), beta lipoprotein (low density), and alpha lipoprotein (high density). Goldstein discusses the subject further in Chapter 19.

Thus it appears that these three lipoprotein fractions do enter the artery wall with relative ease, as Gofman predicted. However, only one of the three — low-density (L D) lipoprotein — is likely to accumulate therein. Apparently certain properties of L D lipoprotein, not yet fully understood,

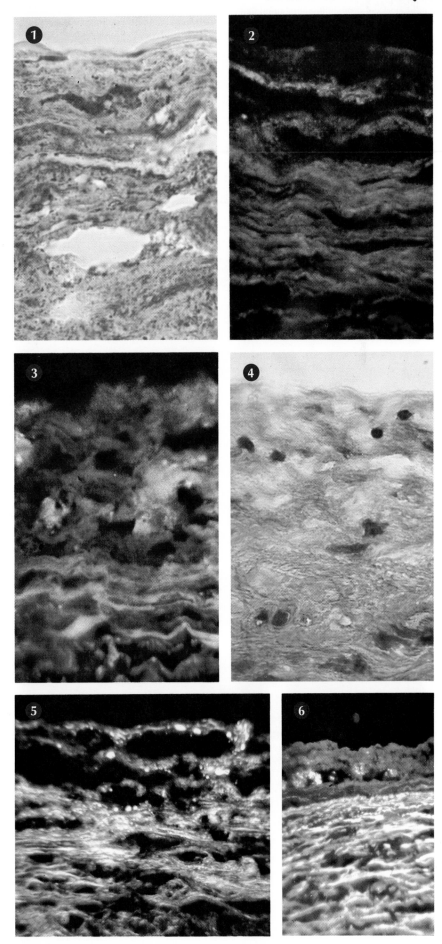

In micrographs (with Kao and Knieriem) at right, fatty streak of human aorta is shown stained with oil red O stain (1) and displays lipid localized in slightly thickened intima. In photo 2, made with nearby section, fluorescein-labeled antibodies to low-density lipoproteins are responsible for the green streaks. Middle: an early atherosclerotic lesion is stained (3) with fluorescein-labeled antibody to fibrin and (4) with Mallory-picro fuchsin, which stains fibrin red. Interstitial fibrin deposition in small clumps is apparent; some are deep in media. Fluorescein-labeled antihuman myosin was used in 5 and stains fibrous plaque from abdominal aorta bright green; subsequent phosphine 3R staining for fat indicates that lipid droplets (white) are located in myosin-containing arterial cells. Fluorescein antihuman myosin was also used in 6, showing hyperplastic intima of thoracic aorta from 29-year-old woman.

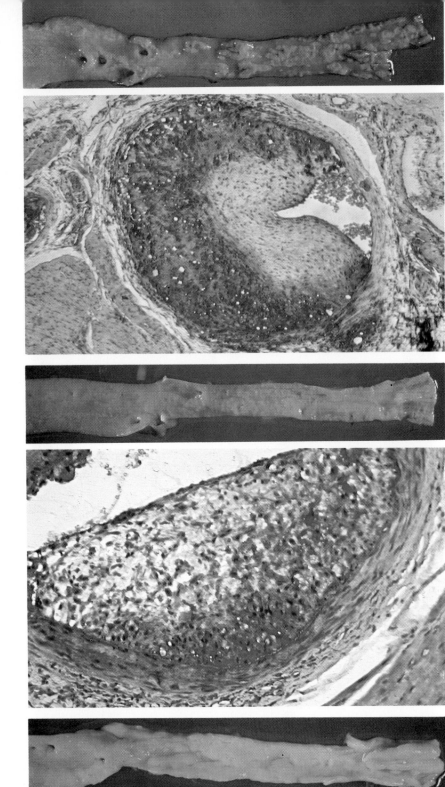

account for this selective trapping. What is known is that among the four major serum lipoprotein complexes, LD lipoprotein is the chief carrier of cholesterol; hence when LD lipoprotein accumulates in the vessel wall, it is logical that cholesterol accumulates with it.

The possibility that physicochemical differences among the lipoproteins might have physiologic or pathologic significance, or both, was initially raised in the early 1950's by Gofman, Kunkel, and others. In recent years, a number of experimental observations have been providing confirmation. To be sure, the likelihood that LD lipoprotein or any macromolecule can enter the artery wall so that abnormal deposition becomes possible hinges on multiple factors related to the permeability of the vessel's endothelium. For example, as studies by Mustard and coworkers have shown, platelet agglutination at the injury site and release of platelet constituents (vasoactive amines) are probably major factors in increasing permeability to serum proteins, so that entry occurs at a faster rate (see Chapter 17, "Platelets and Thrombosis in Acute Myocardial Infarction," by Mustard). Hemodynamic forces are also important in determining the point in the artery wall where lipid deposition will occur. According to several investigators, localization of atherosclerotic plaques at specified sites in the vessel wall can be related to disturbance in blood flow in the same area, leading to increased tension on the artery wall. In addition, Dr. Seymour Glagov at the University of Chicago has demonstrated that with increased peripheral resistance there is increased arterial wall tension, which in turn is associated with a general acceleration in the

Variable appearance of lesions in aortas and coronary arteries of rhesus monkeys fed different atherogenic diets are shown at left. At top, gross aorta and microscopic coronary views from coconut oil+butter+cholesterol–fed animal: lipid deposition, intimal proliferation, and luminal narrowing are marked. Center, from butter+cholesterol–fed monkey: lesions are lipid-rich but have less fibrosis. Bottom, from peanut oil+cholesterol–fed animal: advanced plaque has thick fibrous coat. Use of trichrome stain would reveal abundant collagen and some new elastin in lesion.

atherosclerotic process. This may be related to increased permeability of the endothelium to plasma molecules, in particular L D lipoprotein.

Evidence of several types has confirmed that L D lipoprotein, alone among the serum lipoproteins, is selectively bound to the arterial intimal and medial components. Among the first in this hemisphere to study the question (in the early 1960's) was Tracy in our laboratory, who applied immunologic procedures to identify serum lipoprotein constituents in extracts of atherosclerotic human aortas. Up to about that time, it had been assumed that while there might be considerable lipid deposition in the artery wall, it was unlikely that lipoprotein could be specifically identified as such. In Tracy's studies, sequestration of L D lipoprotein in the aortic intima was clearly demonstrated and the lipoprotein antigen appeared to be bound to acid mucopolysaccharide.

Subsequently a number of investigators have applied immunohistochemical techniques to analysis of atherosclerotic lesions, utilizing preparations of antisera against the protein moiety (apoprotein) of L D lipoprotein. In studies by Kayden and later by Watts and others, L D lipoprotein was demonstrated in lesions stained with fluorescein-labeled antibody; Watts also utilized ferritin-labeled antibody in confirming that material in the lipid droplets in the cells of the artery contained the same antigenic groupings as L D lipoprotein. Utilizing the latter technique with electron microscopy, he also demonstrated the presence of lipoprotein within cells of the lesion as well as in interstitial tissue.

In an autopsy study combining an immunohistochemical approach and light microscopy, Kao and I attempted to correlate histologic evidence of deposition of lipid and other plasma constituents in human aortic lesions with their location as revealed microscopically. For this study rabbit antisera were prepared against high-density (H D) and L D lipoproteins, albumin, gamma globulin, and fibrinogen.

In tissue sections treated with fluorescein-labeled anti-H D lipoprotein antibody there was usually slight and inconsistent staining of diseased intima. In contrast, sections stained with anti–L D lipoprotein antibody showed pronounced fluorescence in the same areas where substantial lipid deposition was present. The latter was revealed by oil red O staining of adjacent sections. In lesions treated with antifibrinogen gamma globulin there was also intense staining, indicating fibrin deposition in almost all aortic sections containing L D lipoprotein in substantial amounts. Significantly, however, the staining pattern did not indicate localization of fibrin in the same areas where lipid and lipoprotein were concentrated. In some cases, labeled antibody to fibrinogen focally stained the fibrous cap of an atheroma; in others, the center of more advanced lesions. More often a fleck-like staining pattern prevailed in several areas of the thickened diseased intima and sometimes interstitially in the media as well. In none of the sections examined was there convincing evidence that fibrin accumulation represented recent or partially organized thrombi.

These findings have an important bearing on the thesis that deposition of fibrin as a component of mural thrombi plays an essential role in development and progression of the atherosclerotic plaque. According to the observed pattern of fibrinogen (fibrin) deposition, there is little to suggest that this is the case. Rather, the appearance of fibrin interstitially in the intima and even deeper in the media suggests that there may be a mechanism to convert fibrinogen to fibrin within the artery wall. Studies by Stolzner et al in our laboratory suggest platelets or platelet fragments may enter the wall and activate this mechanism. On the other hand, there is no question that a fully developed plaque may be highly thrombogenic once its fibrous cap is ruptured. Not only are the plaque contents often rich in phospholipid, which contributes to tissue thromboplastic activity, but plaque rupture increases the extent of platelet accumulation at the site because of the platelet-agglutinating effect of collagen.

In Kao's study, the youngest patients were newborn infants, the oldest a woman of 94. In all, tissue sections were obtained at autopsy from close to 30 aortas, and more than 50 diseased areas were sampled, representing lesions of varying severity as well as ostensibly normal tissue. In the

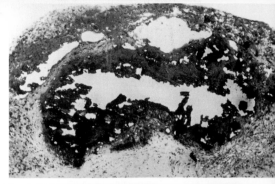

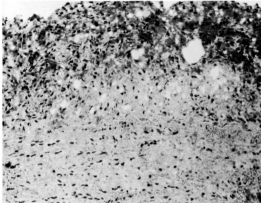

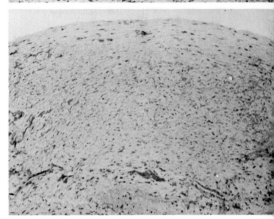

Views of atheromatous lesions in the abdominal aorta are shown in monkeys whose coronary lesions are shown on opposite page, in same order of dietary groups.

newborn, aortic tissue showed no evidence of L D lipoprotein localization in the intima or inner media, but traces were present in these locations in the aortas of two infants 4 and 12 months old, both with congenital heart disease. By the second decade, L D lipoprotein deposition was demonstrable in the fatty streaks of most patients; the few exceptions showed little or no fatty streak development, and the grossly normal areas of these slightly diseased vessels showed no demonstrable L D lipoprotein.

Among older patients, grossly normal and abnormal aortas both showed specific L D lipoprotein staining throughout the intima, which was usually significantly thickened whether or not there were focal lesions. L D

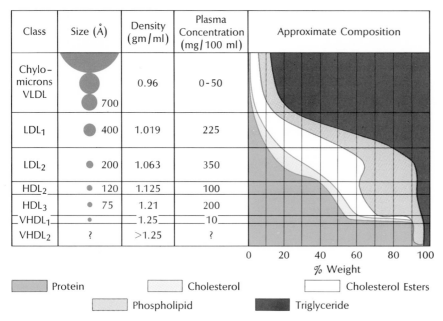

Class	Size (Å)	Density (gm/ml)	Plasma Concentration (mg/100 ml)	Approximate Composition
Chylo-microns VLDL	700	0.96	0 - 50	
LDL₁	400	1.019	225	
LDL₂	200	1.063	350	
HDL₂	120	1.125	100	
HDL₃	75	1.21	200	
VHDL₁		1.25	10	
VHDL₂	?	>1.25	?	

0   20   40   60   80   100
% Weight

■ Protein   □ Cholesterol   □ Cholesterol Esters
□ Phospholipid   ■ Triglyceride

Some properties of human serum lipoproteins are summarized in diagram developed by Scanu on the basis of data from several sources. Only the largest class, the chylomicrons, are barred by size from passing through the endothelium into the arterial wall.

lipoprotein deposition was also evident in fatty plaques with fibrous caps, as it was either in advanced lesions associated with ulceration or with thrombosis.

There was, however, a major difference in these lesions as compared with those in an earlier stage of atherosclerosis. In the lesions in the younger individuals the intensity of fluorescence in tissue stained for L D lipoprotein and the staining pattern of adjacent tissue treated with oil red O for fat corresponded closely. In advanced lesions in older persons, on the other hand, the presence of L D lipoprotein was limited chiefly to the periphery and base of the lesions. The necrotic center of these severe plaques often showed little correlation between the findings in fluorescent-stained tissue and adjacent sections stained with oil red O. This observation supports the likely possibility, to be considered later at greater length, that in the older lesions breakdown of L D lipoprotein molecules may have occurred, leaving behind cholesterol and its esters, which are less metabolizable.

Let us turn now to the factors in the artery wall related to entrapment of L D lipoprotein. By intent, wall structure and function will be considered in cellular terms, in view of recent research identifying a specific cell type in the artery wall as of prime

importance in the pathogenesis of atherosclerosis. In brief, the evidence indicates that this cell population – having the characteristics of smooth muscle cells and situated normally in the media of the arterial wall – is the principal intracellular location for lipid deposition and accumulation associated with atherosclerosis. Moreover, this same cell, which contains contractile protein, appears to be largely responsible for production of other major extracellular components of the plaque, including the fiber proteins and acid mucopolysaccharides, which also probably play a major part in the localization of lipid.

Atherosclerosis has for many years been accepted as a disorder of intimal function, and indeed intimal cell proliferation associated with tissue thickening and fibrosis are among the hallmarks of a developing plaque. It should be stressed, however, that in the human atherosclerotic lesion, at all stages, there is likely to be lipid accumulation in preexisting medial cells as well as in the intima.

Although medial lipid accumulation has rarely been emphasized by others, we have quite regularly observed it. This may be explained in part by the methods we have used to prepare fat stains – from free-floating sections or **from Carbowax-embedded sections** that are relatively thick. In these prep-

arations, sudanophilic lesions appear more vivid to the eye than they otherwise would. Consistently, lipid-containing medial cells have shown reactivity with specific antibody to L D lipoprotein. Earlier, in studying atherosclerosis from human autopsies, in rats, and in cebus monkeys, we had noted the accumulation of lipid in superficial medial cells as well as intimal plaques, and, more recently, in the rhesus monkey, intracellular medial lipid had also been identified in developing atheromatous lesions.

What relation have these findings to the intimal changes typical of atherosclerosis? It now appears that much of the intimal thickening and collagen formation may derive from cells normally present in the media that proliferate and then migrate to the intima in response to lipid deposition. Once there, their further proliferation contributes both to intimal thickening and fibrous encapsulation of the lesion. Alternatively, medial cells damaged by the presence of excess lipid may contribute to central necrosis of the atheromatous plaque.

Many histology textbooks describe two cell types, smooth muscle cells and fibroblasts, in the media of medium-sized and large arteries. On the other hand, according to most electron microscopists, normally there are no cells resembling the usual tissue fibroblasts in the media of mammalian arteries. Virtually always, smooth muscle cells are the only type present. In comparative studies of aortic media in man and several mammalian species, Wolinsky and Glagov in our department identified a basic structural unit of the media including the smooth muscle cell that is largely responsible for the maintenance of a lamellar architecture, with orderly arranged elastica. Associated with these cells they found elastin lamellae and collagen fibers and a fine elastin net. Among their pertinent observations was that in all mammals studied, the number of medial lamellar units appears to be limited to about 29, unless the medial vasa vasorum are present.

In man, the relative absence of penetrating vasa vasorum in the coronary arteries and the abdominal aorta means that both the intima and media depend for oxygenation on diffusion of oxygen from the lumen. Thus any interference with delivery of oxygen to this avascular zone might seriously impair tissue respiration. (This will be discussed more extensively later.)

Electron microscopic studies (see below) have confirmed the distinctive features of medial cell ultrastructure: Classically it is an elongated cell with a centrally located nucleus often having wrinkled contours; within the cytoplasm are longitudinally arranged myofilaments typical of a smooth muscle cell. There is a clearly defined plasma membrane containing numerous micropinocytotic vesicles and, coating the interstitial face of the plasma membrane, a basement membrane, the latter closely associated with collagen and elastin fibers. It was findings such as these—along with the absence of any other major cell type in arterial media—that prompted speculation that the smooth muscle cell characteristic of the media might be responsible for production of the

several components of connective tissue normally found there. On this account it has been referred to as the "multifunctional medial mesenchymal cell." As a corollary it is suggested that a proliferation in these cells along with a shift in their location and an alteration in the relative proportion and arrangement of components of the medial smooth muscle cell might be of utmost importance in the development of atherosclerosis.

Admittedly, until very recently the evidence linking the arterial medial cell to formation of the fiber proteins and the ground substance in atherosclerosis has been largely circumstantial. The fact that the smooth muscle cell appears to represent the sole cell type in the media is scarcely proof that collagen, elastin, or other components are products of this cell. Presumably, collagen could be produced by widely dispersed and inapparent fibroblasts, although there have been no reports

supporting a fibroblastic origin of arterial medial collagen. Elastic tissue fibers are produced elsewhere in the body where apparently there are no smooth muscle cells. However, this really does not weaken our case; after all, keratin is formed by cells of two different germ layers, the ectoderm and endoderm, and osteoid and cartilage are often formed far from the usual precursor cells. As for acid polysaccharides, they are known to occur in many sites characterized by an abundance of smooth muscle, for example, the umbilical cord, the wall of the uterus, and the intestine. On balance, although we do not know if the arterial medial cell is responsible for the several properties assigned to it, it seems reasonable to assume that it may be, and recent work in tissue culture supports this assumption.

Actually, one of the first observations of a possible association of smooth muscle cells and atherosclero-

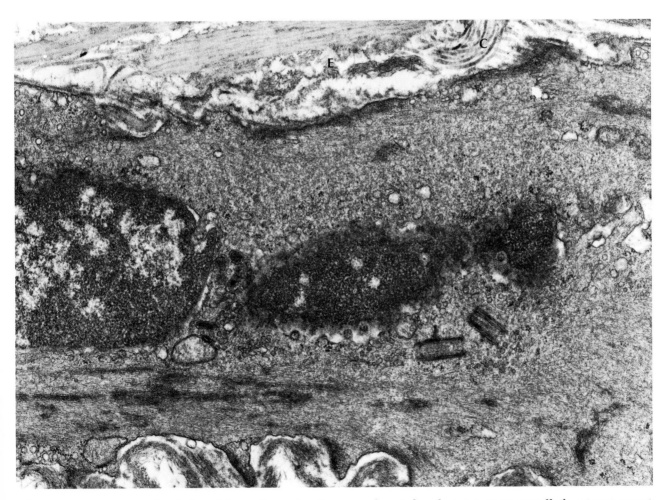

Electron microscopic view of typical medial smooth muscle cell, from study by Rose Jones, is from abdominal aorta of a rhesus monkey fed corn oil + 2% cholesterol for one month. Noteworthy are elongated nucleus, prominent microfibrils, micropinocytotic vesicles, basement membrane, and the closely associated elastin (E) and collagen (C) fibers. Magnification is x40,000.

161

Composition of the 'Table-Prepared' Human Diets Fed to Rhesus Monkeys

Ingredients*	Daily Portion (gm)	
	Average American Diet	Prudent American Diet
Nonfat dry milk	11.0	10.0
Eggs (hard boiled)	10.0	0
Roast beef (lean)	15.0	5.0
Beef fat	2.4	0
Roast pork (lean)	7.0	3.0
Pork fat	1.6	0
Salmon (can)	3.0	6.0
Baked chicken	6.0	18.0
Turkey	0	8.0
Liver (beef)	2.0	0
Cheese (American)	2.4	0
Cottage cheese	0	3.0
Bread (white)	36.0	36.0
Potato (baked)	20.0	20.0
Carrots (cooked)	20.0	20.0
Lettuce (raw)	10.0	10.0
Dry cereal	4.0	0
Banana	20.0	20.0
Apple (raw)	20.0	20.0
Pound cake	8.0	0
Orange juice	24.0	24.0
Sugar	18.0	9.0
Cottonseed oil	1.8	0
Margarine (saturated)	4.4	0
Margarine (unsaturated)	0	3.0
Corn oil	0	7.0
Butter	9	0
Lard	2	0
Bacon (fried)	3	0
Total grams	260.6	222.0
Daily calories/monkey	560	360

* Selected by Dr. Dorothea Turner, Chief Medical Nutritionist of the University of Chicago Hospitals and Clinics, based on U.S. food consumption tables and, for prudent diet, on recommendations of several national groups studying diet and heart disease.

sis was made in 1950 by the Canadian investigator Altschul, who on the basis of conventional staining called attention to the presence of "smooth muscle–containing" cells, presumably of medial origin, in proliferative intimal lesions. At that time most investigators favored the view that the predominant cells in the lesion were most likely fibroblasts or macrophages; not until almost a decade later were Altschul's conclusions substantiated by electron microscopy. Parker, and later Buck, did so in the same species studied by Altschul (the rabbit), and others made similar observations in the rat. Beginning about 1960 Haust, Movat,

and More, and later many others, identified smooth muscle cells — or myointimal cells as they came to be called — as a common electron microscopic finding in human lesions.

More recently, immunohistochemical techniques have been applied in confirming the presence of smooth muscle cells as the principal cell type in human atheromata. With this approach, muscle cells are identified by their characteristic proteins, myosin and actomyosin, and by other features not shared by such cells as lymphocytes or fibroblasts. In our laboratory, Knieriem and coworkers utilized fluorescence microscopy to study aortic

lesions in human autopsy specimens showing varying degrees of atherosclerosis. Later these studies were extended to bovine atherosclerosis. In tissue showing histologic evidence of intimal hyperplasia (our classification for the smallest lesions), bright fluorescence clearly indicated the presence of contractile protein. Smooth muscle cells were also readily identified in both intima and media of fatty streaks; however, as the lesion progressed toward formation of an atheroma with central necrosis, intact smooth muscle cells were seldom seen within the body of the plaque although they were still prominent at its margins. Many of these findings were soon confirmed by Becker and Murphy.

In part because of the relative absence of typical smooth muscle cells in advanced atherosclerosis, especially when the cells assumed a foamy appearance owing to the accumulation of huge numbers of lipid droplets, some doubt has been raised about the cellular nature of the plaque. Indeed, some investigators consider it unlikely that smooth muscle cells have particular significance either in early or advanced atherosclerosis. For example, many workers have described undifferentiated foam cells in both human and in experimental arterial lesions. Both Geer and Still have maintained that many of the foam cells observed in atherosclerotic lesions are probably derived from a blood monocyte or lymphocyte, or both, rather than from the medial cell. On the other hand, meticulous ultrastructural studies by Imai and coworkers have indicated that the smooth muscle–containing medial cell of the artery wall can undergo all of the transformation necessary to explain the various appearances seen in atherosclerosis. Obviously, if alterations in a particular cell play a key role in atherogenesis, its precise identification is a crucial matter. Given both the electron microscopic and immunohistochemical findings, there seems little question that the medial smooth muscle cell has a predominant part to play in the development of both the early and later stages. In advanced lesions, the less frequent occurrence of typical smooth muscle cells is explainable by intervening significant changes in the structure and/or metabolism of these cells. It is our thesis that this may indeed be what occurs, and that the changes result from the damaging action of accumulated L D lipoprotein.

As already noted, the presence of L D lipoprotein in the arterial wall is characteristic of atherosclerosis. But can its presence be demonstrated in cells that are identified as smooth muscle cells? In the studies by Knieriem et al, fluorescence microscopy of lesions showing intimal hyperplasia indicated L D lipoprotein deposition within cells throughout the thickened intima. This was in the sections adjacent to those where the same cells were shown to contain myosin and actomyosin. In fatty streaks and small cellular plaques, there also appeared to be predominantly intracellular lipoprotein deposition in myosin- or actomyosin-containing cells as well as slight traces of fluorescence extracelularly. But at later stages the fluorescence pattern proved similar to that already cited in reference to the contractile proteins: The necrotic centers of atheromatous plaques showed little immunohistochemical evidence of L D lipoprotein deposition either inside or outside the cells, while at the periphery and base, intense fluorescence indicated appreciable L D lipoprotein deposition.

Several other notable observations were made in these studies. For example, in the smallest lesions, in which both myosin and L D lipoprotein were easily identified, lipids often could not be detected by either oil red 0 or phosphine 3R fat stains – suggesting that trapping of L D lipoprotein within these cells may represent the earliest change in development of an atherosclerotic lesion from which later changes derive. In fatty streaks there was moderate lipid deposition, both intracellular and extracellular; in more advanced lesions there was a disproportionate increase in extracellular lipid.

The relative absence of L D lipoprotein could be accounted for if, by the later stages of plaque development, protein and lipid had split apart – in which case most of the stainable lipid in the necrotic center of the lesion no longer would show evidence of specific apoprotein binding.

On the basis of findings such as those described, it seems plausible to suggest that progression of atherosclerosis to the point of central necro-

sis and fibrous encapsulation entails substantial damage to a significant proportion of the medial cells in the affected portion of the artery wall, damage directly related to the accumulation followed by the breakdown of L D lipoprotein. Once damaged, many of the affected cells apparently go on to die – hence the necrotic center of the atheromatous plaque. Cells near the border of dead and dying arterial tissue are somehow stimulated to proliferate so that they contribute further to intimal thickening and fibrosis.

This, then, is the dual role we postulate for medial smooth muscle cells; but to prove our case is another matter. If damage and necrosis of these cells is related to the presence of L D lipoprotein, which of its constituents are so difficult to metabolize that their accumulation causes cell injury? If proliferation and migration of medial cells is largely responsible for the intimal thickening of atherosclerosis, what stimulates the proliferation and migration? If the medial cell is truly multifunctional and responsible for producing at least four major components – collagen, elastin, myosin, and mucopolysaccharides – then the presence of intimal thickening, glycoprotein accumulation, and severe fibroplasia in many of the advanced lesions suggests that under certain conditions there is a diversion of synthetic processes resulting in increased synthesis of collagen and mucopolysaccharides. Is this at the expense of myosin and

elastin formation? If indeed this is what occurs, then what mechanisms stimulate the cell to convert to more abundant formation of collagen and/ or mucopolysaccharides?

These are important questions. What kinds of studies are likely to provide meaningful answers? It goes without saying that definitive information concerning the development of human atherosclerosis is difficult to achieve for many reasons. One is the gradual progression of lesions and the variety of both endogenous and exogenous factors that might play a contributory role. Nor, in living subjects, can one know precisely when the atherosclerotic process was initiated or estimate its severity prior to the appearance of clinical complications. A suitable experimental model of the disease is essential. Animals such as the rabbit, the rat, the chicken, and the dog have all served as valuable experimental subjects; however, we believe that a much more satisfactory model is the rhesus monkey. Both in their early and later stages, atherosclerotic lesions in the rhesus monkey closely resemble those seen in humans; moreover, complex lesions characterized by central necrosis, severe fibroplasia, stenosis, ulceration, thrombosis, and calcification also occur as they do in human atherosclerosis. And so do the "clinical" complications of coronary occlusion, myocardial infarction, ischemic gangrene, etc. A particular advantage is that observations can begin at an essentially disease-free base-

Results of Feeding Experiments in Monkeys

Measurements Made	Dietary Group	
	Average American	Prudent American
Terminal serum cholesterol	383	199
Terminal total serum lipids	1,029	549
Gross surface area of aorta involved (%)	54	9
Microscopic severity of aortic atherosclerosis	21	5
Microscopic incidence of aortic atherosclerosis	46	15
Microscopic severity of coronary atherosclerosis	9	2
Microscopic incidence of coronary atherosclerosis	27	6

line, since spontaneous atherosclerosis is rare.

In our series of rhesus studies we began by slightly altering the relatively simple dietary approach developed by Taylor, Cox, and colleagues, who found that hypercholesterolemia and atherosclerosis could readily be produced in these animals merely by supplementing the standard low-fat commercial primate ration with 25% butter fat and 2% crystalline cholesterol. On this regimen many of their animals developed severe atherosclerosis and, in general, its severity correlated positively with the degree of hypercholesterolemia and the duration of fat feeding.

We found that the rhesus atherosclerotic process could be markedly accelerated by using a 50:50 mixture of coconut oil and butter fat to supplement the cholesterol-enriched primate ration. We had predicted this very intense atherogenicity of coconut oil from studies we had carried out in cebus monkeys using this highly saturated lipid, which, when fed as the sole food fat, had resulted in unusually high blood cholesterol levels and particularly severe proliferation of arterial intima. Similar results had been reported in other species by Malmros in Sweden. In almost all of the rhesus monkeys we have studied, very high blood lipid levels resulted from feeding the diet containing coconut oil,

butter, and cholesterol. After nine months on the diet (when the animals were autopsied) the severity of damage was evident both in terms of surface area involved and the nature of typical lesions. The explanation that suggested itself was that some element in coconut oil had acted to stimulate cell proliferation and to irritate the artery wall, but if so, its nature still eludes us. However, on the basis of these observations we were prompted to explore the effects of long-term feeding of other food fats. Here, too, there were paradoxical findings. For example, when rhesus monkeys were maintained for a year on a standard primate diet containing 2% cholesterol, and supplemented either with butter, corn oil, or peanut oil, remarkable differences were evident in the nature and degree of aortic involvement discovered at autopsy. Butter-fed monkeys, who had manifested the greatest rise in serum fats, typically developed a "soft," lipid-rich atheroma; lipid deposition was often prominent throughout almost the entire thickness of the intima as well as in preexisting medial cells. In animals fed corn oil, there was little intimal thickening and little evidence of lipid extending into medial cells. The most notable findings were in animals fed peanut oil; although serum lipid levels were increased less than with corn oil, the atherosclerotic lesions were very

severe. In theory, the unsaturated state of peanut oil should have provided protection, but clearly it had not done so.

Prior to these studies other investigators, on the basis of experiments in rats and other species, had also called attention to the special atherogenicity of peanut oil. The rhesus monkey studies provided strong confirmation and documented the distinctive features of the lesion, which in this species is characterized by relatively minor lipid deposition — except deep within the plaque — but there are prominent intimal cell proliferation and accumulation of collagen. Recently we extended these studies to the coronary arteries of rhesus monkeys, and again found peanut oil to be far more atherogenic than we would have predicted on the basis of its lipid and fatty acid content. It is of interest that although coconut oil also produces very severe intimal cell proliferation, the lesions are generally quite dissimilar: with coconut oil there is usually an abundance of lipid in the intima and relatively little collagen deposition. The dissimilarity is presumably related to differences in chemical composition of the fats. As noted, the responsible element in coconut oil remains unknown. There is evidence relating the atherogenicity of peanut oil, at least in part, to its content of arachidic and behenic fatty acids. This had been learned in studies conducted by David Kritchevsky of the Wistar Institute that we have been able to help with. The findings also suggest that some of the atherogenicity of peanut oil may relate to the arrangement of fatty acids in triglycerides.

Needless to say, we can only speculate on the implications of these findings to the clinical situation in man; given the artificial conditions of the experiments, there may be no direct applicability. On the other hand, reference must be made to other recent experiments in our laboratory in which rhesus monkeys have been maintained for two years on a "typical" or "average" American diet, "table-prepared" and then mixed into a paste for feeding to the animals. This diet, developed for us by Dorothea Turner, the chief medical nutritionist of the University of Chicago Hospitals and Clinics, was tested in a comparative study in which other monkeys

Tissue cultures grown from primary explants of rhesus monkey aorta are used to study interaction of lipoprotein and arterial medial cells. Electron micrograph below (Fisher-Dzoga and Jones) shows two smooth muscle cells raised in such a culture; characteristics are similar to those of cell shown on page 161 (x40,000).

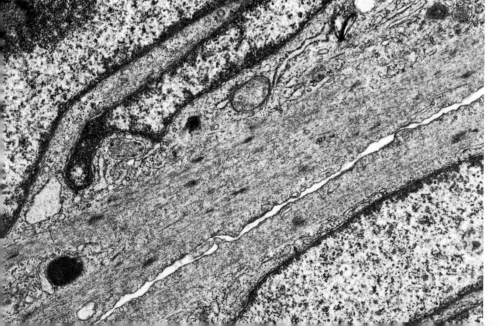

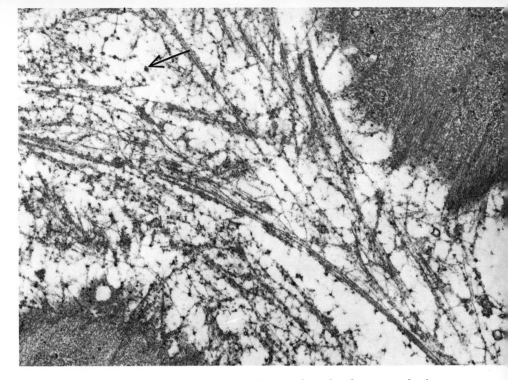

Treatment with ruthenium red demonstrates acid mucopolysaccharide in ground substance of medial cell cultured from primary explant of rhesus thoracic aorta (x40,000). Numerous electron-dense granules can be seen in the extracellular spaces (arrow).

were fed the "prudent" diet recommended by the American Heart Association – designed to reduce intake of saturated food fats, calories, and cholesterol. In limited quantities the typical diet resulted in definite elevations of blood lipids and produced atheromatous plaques in most animals. Lesions often contained a necrotic center with most of the lipid contained in the intimal part of the plaque; in deeper areas lipid was also evident in preexisting medial cells. In contrast, in animals on the prudent diet, little serum cholesterol elevation and virtually no atheromatous change were seen. These studies offer a direct experimental demonstration, perhaps the first realistic one on record, that an ordinary American diet results in the kind of arterial disease that may increase the likelihood of heart attacks. They also support the view that a table-prepared diet limited in calories, cholesterol, and saturated fats can inhibit atherosclerosis. The actual dietary intake of basic food elements of these two groups of monkeys is seen in the table on page 162.

Curiously, when some monkeys were fed the typical diet *ad libitum*, the atherosclerotic process was not accelerated (as we had thought it might be). Instead, levels of serum cholesterol and total lipids remained low, and there was little or no discernible atherosclerosis. Also curiously, these animals gained little weight in spite of the quantities of food eaten, and, in fact, a number of them sickened and died before the two years were up.

Thus far, careful histopathologic examination of tissue sections has not clarified the reasons for this apparently toxic reaction; it is difficult even to suggest an explanation. We are on somewhat firmer ground in discussing the observations in reference to limited feeding of the typical diet. As part of the study, we compared the reaction of normal aortic media to lipoprotein fractions obtained from monkeys fed either an average or prudent diet, preparing the fractions by ultracentrifugation and injecting them (using surgical approaches) into the media of recipient animals. H D lipoprotein, regardless of the source, disappeared rapidly and had little effect on the artery wall. L D lipoprotein from monkeys on an average diet appeared to be retained longer in the vessel wall

than L D protein from animals on the prudent diet regimen; more cell damage was evident at the ultrastructural level as well. The subnatant defatted protein derived from either group of animals had little effect on the artery wall, suggesting that the lipid portion of the lipoprotein complex may have been responsible for the damage seen.

Is it the L D lipoprotein itself or the lipid that it carries into arterial medial cells that is more important in development or progression of atherosclerosis? From the immunohistochemical evidence cited earlier, it appears that intracellular localization of L D lipoprotein may be the first change leading to plaque formation, but a number of investigators have questioned whether the intact L D lipoprotein molecule actually enters the cell. Recent studies by Hollander and coworkers with radioactively labeled L D lipoprotein are, however, consistent with the view that the substance does make its way through the intima and into the lesion. Even so, it is uncertain whether the principal trapping of lipoprotein or lipid that initiates cell injury takes place inside medial cells or on their outer surface, or occurs extracellularly because of lipoprotein and/ or lipid accumulation on fiber proteins. Other recent work by Kramsch of Hollander's group has shown binding of elastin to cholesterol and probably also to L D lipoprotein.

On the basis of our own studies, we have leaned toward the view that intracellular localization of L D lipoprotein in preexisting medial cells is the triggering mechanism leading either to proliferation and migration of these cells and more active collagen synthesis, or to cell injury and death. Whether this is true or not, it is clearly important to define the cellular and molecular mechanisms whereby L D lipoprotein is bound to or gains entry to the cell and the factors that govern its retention in the artery wall. To this end we have recently been utilizing a tissue culture system for observing the interaction of lipoprotein and arterial medial cells. In these studies Dr. Katti Fisher-Dzoga and others in our group have utilized cultured cells derived from primary explants of arterial media obtained from rhesus monkey aortas, according to the method developed in our laboratory. Small disc explants (2 mm in diameter) are punched out of the aorta after it has been stripped free of adventitia and intima; the explants are then placed in plastic tissue-culture flasks containing Eagle's medium supplemented with 10% calf or rabbit serum. Cell growth from the explants starts in a monolayer within 5 to 10 days; thereafter, the "laminated" growth pattern closely resembles that seen in vivo. Assurance that characteristic smooth muscle cells are being

---

Role of the Medial Cell in Atherogenesis

1. Takes up lipid (low-density lipo-protein) in situ

2. Is prone to injury by constituents of lipoprotein

3. May contribute to the fibrous cap by:

   A) Proliferation and/or migration

   B) Converting to collagen forma-tion

4. Cell injury and death contribute to atheroma with plaque ulcera-tion and thrombosis

---

cultured has been provided both by studies employing immunohistochem-istry and electron microscopy.

Thus far, our system has been used chiefly to look for clues explaining cell proliferation in response to L D lipo-protein, and we have learned that it is greatly increased in cultures treated with serum from hyperlipemic mon-keys as against those treated with nor-mal monkey serum. Moreover, when individual lipoprotein fractions derived from whole hyperlipemic serum were employed, there was no doubt that the L D fraction was responsible for the marked increases in cell prolifera-tion. Since the stimulating effect might have been due to the higher amount of cholesterol included in the hyperlipemic monkey diet, this possi-bility was checked also by equalizing the cholesterol level of the culture media. The greater growth stimula-tion was still apparent with the hyper-lipemic serum, implicating some fac-tor other than its cholesterol content.

Additional evidence concerning the functional characteristics of the smooth muscle cell has been reported by Rus-sell Ross and coworkers, who showed that cultured smooth muscle cells are capable of producing both collagen and elastin, as judged by incorpora-tion of radioactive precursors. Utiliz-ing electron microscopy, and ruthe-nium red as an indicator, Rose Jones in our laboratory has also produced evidence for acid mucopolysaccharide production by cultured cells.

Of course such observations increase the temptation to assume that altered function of smooth muscle cells must have an active part in atherosclerosis, but there is still much to be learned in reference to the role of this cell and its relation to L D lipoprotein deposi-tion. An important observation made by Lazzarini-Robertson, when he was studying the metabolism of labeled lipid in an arterial cell culture system, was that reducing the oxygen content of cells (by exposing them to a gas phase containing $<5\%$ O_2) increased uptake of extracellular lipids. If this situation were to apply in vivo, the presence of tissue hypoxia could result in self-perpetuating growth of the atherosclerotic plaque: lipoprotein uptake would increase because of hy-poxia, increasing the metabolic re-quirements of the affected cells, which, in turn, would aggravate the hypoxia and further increase the lipo-protein uptake.

This possibility should be consid-ered in reference to a finding cited earlier – that in man (as in other large mammals) the intima and inner me-dia of many arteries including the abdominal aorta lack penetrating vasa vasorum and therefore are dependent on diffusion of oxygen from the lumen. Calculating on the basis of respiratory rate of arterial tissue and the diffusion coefficient of oxygen, a maximal wall thickness of about 1.0 mm is compat-ible with diffusion of oxygen adequate for tissue needs. Normally, wall thick-ness is in this range, but what if thick-ness is increased by cell proliferation and fibrosis while factors such as L D lipoprotein deposition interfere with oxygen delivery to deeper layers of the avascular zone? A key factor in the progression and severity of athero-sclerosis may well be the vulnerability of cells in the arterial media to injury because their oxygen supply has been diminished. By the same token, in-creasing cellular oxygenation, if it were feasible, might prevent or con-trol development of atherosclerosis.

I say this in part on the basis of observations in our laboratory by Dr. Vesselinovitch, utilizing rabbits with severe arterial lesions induced by a highly atherogenic diet. When the animals were shifted to a low-choles-terol ration, serum cholesterol levels were substantially reduced and there was little disease or atherosclerotic damage. However, when some of the rabbits were also intermittently ex-posed to ambient hyperoxia (100% oxygen) serum cholesterol levels went down still more, and in several of the animals the atherosclerotic process was apparently not only arrested but remarkably reversed. When either es-trogen or a cholesterol-lowering drug was added to the regimen, improve-ment was even more pronounced.

We have also begun reversal ex-periments in monkeys with lesions in-duced by various food fats, thus far confining ourselves primarily to die-tary manipulation alone. Preliminary findings suggest that substantial re-versal is possible; moreover, the results are in line with the striking reversal results in rhesus monkeys reported by Armstrong, Warner, and Connor. It is encouraging that approaches to re-versal as well as prevention of ad-vanced atherosclerosis are within the realm of possibility. And if there are many answers that are still needed in reference to the fundamental mecha-nisms underlying the development of the atherosclerotic plaque, recent work has at least directed us to some of the right questions.

Prevention of Atherosclerosis:
A Pediatric Problem

SIDNEY BLUMENTHAL *and* MARY JANE JESSE

University of Miami

"It was surprising to find that many children under the age of three had fatty streaks in the aorta, and furthermore that every person beyond the age of three had some degree of fatty streaking." In this comment at an international pediatric conference in the spring of 1959, pathologist Russell L. Holman alerted physicians concerned with the care of children to a possibility few would have considered: that progressive atherosclerosis and such clinical sequelae as coronary disease may derive from alterations in the arterial vasculature having their onset during childhood.

If Holman's suggestion that atherosclerosis is "basically a pediatric disease" is viewed with less skepticism today, the relevance of these early vessel changes to later clinical events is still not generally appreciated. The logic – indeed, the necessity – of trying to prevent or control atherosclerosis nearer to the period in life when the process appears to begin also deserves greater appreciation. In truth, even a modest program of primary prevention directed principally at children and young adults might accomplish more than present efforts to control the end results of atherosclerosis severe enough to compromise the coronary circulation.

The sobering facts about coronary heart disease that make a prophylactic approach essential are well known, but deserve restatement here in the light of our context. The absence of advance warning in many cases (probably one third) of acute myocardial infarction is critically important, especially since sudden and unexpected death is often the first clinical sign that coronary disease is present. Analysis of fatal cases of acute infarction has established that about half the deaths occur within two hours of onset of symptoms and at least 60% of deaths occur within 24 hours.

Clearly the chief hope for a significant reduction in total morbidity and mortality must come through measures to control the underlying atherosclerotic process. Accordingly, as investigators have focused on trying to identify potential victims prior to an acute event, it has become apparent that coronary heart disease occurs with increased frequency in association with certain risk factors. Three in particular – hyperlipidemia, hypertension, and cigarette smoking – have been implicated in large-scale population studies as having the closest correlation with coronary heart disease (see Chapter 19, "Genetic Aspects of Hyperlipidemia in Coronary Heart Disease," by Goldstein and Chapter 20, "The Primary Prevention of Coronary Heart Disease," by Stamler); when the three are combined, vulnerability is greatly increased. (Epidemiologic data obtained in the National Cooperative Pooling Project documented that for middle-aged men with hyperlipidemia [serum cholesterol > 250 mg/100 ml] and hypertension [diastolic pressure > 90 mm Hg], who are also cigarette smokers, the risk of a "first coronary event" was eight times higher than for men without these traits. In the presence of two of the three factors there was a fourfold increase in risk. The Framingham study findings indicate an even greater liability imposed by multiple risk factors.)

To some investigators the epidemiologic findings suggest a primary pathogenetic role of these risk factors in atherosclerosis; on this basis, it is concluded that inter-

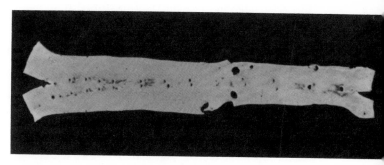

Fatty streaks, such as may represent the initial change leading to atherosclerosis, are revealed by fat staining in aortic specimen from 13-year-old accident victim. This and subsequent pathologic views are from Dr. Henry C. McGill, University of Texas.

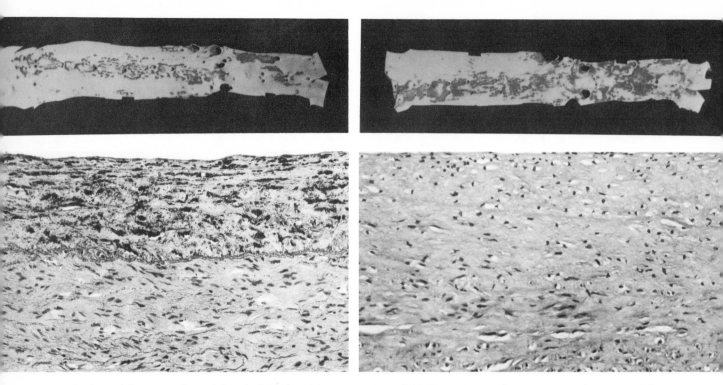

By late adolescence substantial aortic lipid deposition was typical finding in studies by McGill et al, as in specimen (top left) from 19-year-old male and its related microscopic section (bottom left). Increasing involvement is seen in young adults; specimen (top right) is from a 26-year-old male. Its paired section (bottom right) shows abundant fat, diluted by connective tissue.

vention to control them should reduce the likelihood that atherosclerosis will progress to the point of precipitating clinical heart disease. Thus far, primary prevention efforts have been confined largely to adults in middle life or beyond, and as yet there has been little conclusive evidence that such intervention has much of an impact on overall incidence of atherosclerosis or its complications. This may reflect, however, not the nature of the relationship between coronary risk factors and symptomatic disease so much as the timing of the intervention: attempts to modify risk factors may have started too late. Earlier intervention may well offer the possibility of influencing the process before irreparable damage has occurred. This is suggested by histopathologic evidence indicating that for a considerable period early in development of atherosclerosis, changes in the arterial vasculature are potentially reversible. Indeed, this period may extend for a number of years, beginning during childhood or adolescence and continuing into the third decade of life. Accordingly, the opportunity to retard progression of atherosclerosis should be greatest if preventive efforts are concentrated on the pediatric and young adult age groups. Our recent work along these lines will be discussed later in some detail.

Current concepts concerning the natural history of atherosclerosis derive quite directly from the landmark studies begun by Holman et al more than 20 years ago and continued after his death (in 1960) by McGill, Strong, and Geer. In the studies by this group, unselected aortic specimens analyzed for lipid content in a large autopsy series in New Orleans (some 1,200 cases) showed lipid deposition (fatty streaks) in the intimal portion of the artery wall in virtually all individuals past the early childhood years. The aorta rather than another artery was utilized since it offered the largest endothelial surface for direct examination. Lipid deposition, initially restricted to the aortic ring and arch, soon appeared in the descending thoracic and abdominal aorta. In the first decade, usually only limited intimal surface area was affected (about 10% by age 10); during the second, more of the intimal surface became involved, but throughout this period lipid deposits appeared capable of resorption. Starting in the third decade, the lesion took on quite a different appearance, becoming surrounded by fibrous connective tissue and penetrated by blood vessels. Not only had the character of the lesion changed but reversibility seemed less likely. At a later stage, when lesions were complicated by increasing accumulation of lipid and connective tissue, calcification, and necrosis, there appeared to be almost no possibility of regression.

Subsequently, similar observations were made in reference to the coronary arteries, except that lipid accumulation appeared to begin somewhat later – early in the second decade – and evidently was preceded by a prior stage identified microscopically as "musculoelastic thickening" of the coronary intima. As in the aorta, fatty streaks at first involved a relatively small surface area and appeared capable of regression. Again, however, with the passage of time the character of the lesion changed; what had begun as a simple lipid deposit had formed into a raised fibrous plaque protruding into the lumen. With increasing age of the subjects, typical plaques showed varying degrees of necrosis, hemorrhage into the lesion, and ulcer-

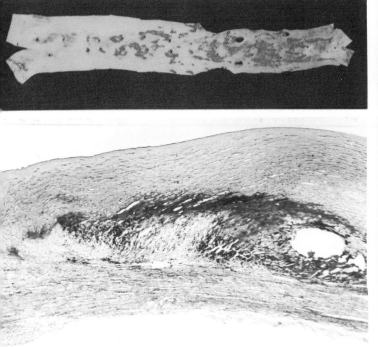

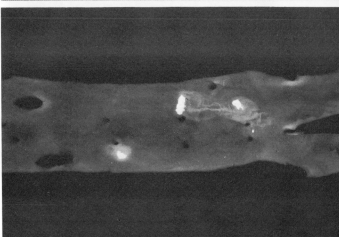

At age 35 fatty streaks in abdominal segment are still more extensive, as in gross specimen (top left); fibrous plaque in lower aorta is also evident. Section (bottom left) of large fibrous plaque

and muscular plaque overlying intimal lipid is from specimen of abdominal aorta (top right), from 38-year-old man. X-ray of same specimen demonstrates calcification in the fibrous plaques.

ation, changes that appeared to facilitate mural thrombus formation.

Through these observations McGill and his colleagues concluded that development of coronary fatty streaks, fibrous plaques, and complicated lesions generally followed a predictable time sequence, occurring in the second, third, and fourth decades respectively. These changes in the arterial vasculature have since been documented by a number of other groups. The implication is clear that they represent successive stages in development of atherosclerosis. Obviously the type of longitudinal study that could prove the case cannot be conducted, but several observations provide support: Pathologists examining coronary arteries are often unable to make a sharp distinction histologically between fatty streaks and fibrous plaques, suggesting a gradual transition from one to the other. Moreover, fatty streaks and fibrous plaques are usually found in approximately the same locations within the major branches of the coronary arteries.

What of the fact that arterial fatty streaks are also present in populations having a relatively low incidence of coronary heart disease? Does this

mean that they may *not* represent an early stage in pathogenesis of atherosclerosis? The pathologists cooperating in the International Atherosclerosis Project demonstrated the presence of intimal fatty streaking in children and adolescents of some 14 countries (in all, more than 23,000 sets of coronary arteries and aortas were examined). By intent, several countries (in Central America and Africa) were included because of their relatively low incidence of coronary disease. As in U.S. populations, fatty streaking of coronary arteries is generally well in evidence by the middle of the second decade. But the resemblance usually stops there. Fibrous plaques and complicated lesions vary in prevalence and extent with the incidence of clinical coronary disease. Their occurrence rate is high only in populations having high morbidity and mortality from coronary heart disease.

These findings suggest that the fatty streaks vary greatly in their potential: Under some circumstances they may be an early change leading to fibrous plaque formation; under other circumstances they are not. Among others favoring this view were the pathologists testifying before the

National Heart and Lung Institute (NHLI) Task Force on Atherosclerosis. Considering both the human and animal evidence they were agreed on three possibilities: that fatty streaks may regress, remain static, or progress to form fibrous plaques. Whether conversion occurs appears to depend largely on the amount of lipid in the streaks; necrosis of lipid-containing cells with release of lipid into the extracellular space stimulates connective tissue formation and increases fibrosis. Factors such as hemorrhage from vessels at the base of the lesion and mural thrombosis also increase the mass of a fibrous plaque, but the predominant role appears to be played by continuous accumulation of lipid (chiefly cholesterol) from the blood. Dietary patterns that act to increase serum lipid levels have been implicated in atherogenesis on this basis as well as on the basis of epidemiologic studies.

The undeniable importance of environmental factors in development of atherosclerosis should not lead us to overlook or downgrade the genetic component in atherosclerosis. Pathologic studies both here and abroad have consistently revealed both a gen-

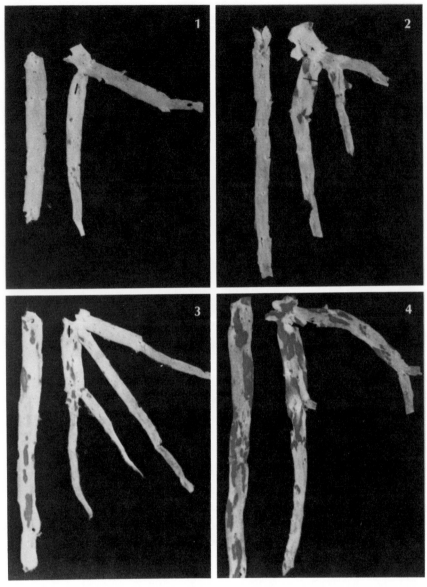

Whereas coronary arteries of 18-year-old female accident victim (1) show minimal lipid deposition, fatty streaks are extensive in all branches of specimen from youth of 20 who died of cerebral aneurysm (2). Greater fat accumulation is seen in vessels of 22-year-old woman (3) and still more in those of 30-year-old man (4), both accident victims.

structure, or end-organ response to stress. But while more detailed information is needed, the role of inherited factors is supported by a number of familial and experimental studies.

A number of recent familial aggregation studies have documented a greatly increased risk of coronary disease in first-degree relatives of coronary disease victims. In perhaps the most complete such study to date, Slack and coworkers in London found the risk of death from ischemic heart disease among first-degree male relatives of male victims aged 55 or younger to be five times that of the general population; among male and female relatives of female victims aged 65 or younger, there was a sevenfold increase in risk. Familial aggregation of any trait can of course reflect sharing of environmental factors as well as genes, including dietary and life-style patterns. Recent animal studies, in which environmental influence can be more precisely controlled, have shed light on this important area.

For example, Clarkson and Lofland found striking differences among squirrel monkeys in response to an atherogenic diet containing an excess of cholesterol. Some monkeys developed marked hypercholesterolemia; others on the same regimen showed little change from normal levels, and still others had intermediate levels. The finding of "hypo-responders" and "hyper-responders" suggested there was a high degree of genetic control over plasma cholesterol levels, a hypothesis borne out when the investigators performed selective breeding experiments. Progeny of hypo-responders and hyper-responders lived under identical conditions and after weaning consumed the same atherogenic diet. All animals with two parents who were hyper-responders proved to be hyper-responders as well; a similar pattern applied to the hypo-responders.

Among monkeys fed an atherogenic diet for some 30 months, plasma cholesterol levels correlated closely with development of atherosclerotic lesions. In hyper-responsive animals, lesions generally covered nearly all the intimal surface and often were complicated by hemorrhage, calcification, or aneurysms. Minimal, if any, changes were seen in hypo-responding animals. The genetic mechanisms underlying hyper-responsiveness remain

eral trend in reference to age-related changes in the arterial vasculature and remarkable variation: many individuals live to an advanced age free of clinical coronary disease and show minimal atherosclerosis at autopsy; others show severe changes while still relatively young. (Among American combat casualties in Vietnam, McNamara et al found some degree of coronary atherosclerosis in 45% of the men and gross evidence of severe coronary disease in 5%, a high proportion considering their mean age was 22.)

Taken together, both pathologic and epidemiologic findings tell us that

atherosclerosis severe enough to cause premature heart disease results from multiple factors acting in individuals whose susceptibility appears to be genetically determined. By the same token, others living under similar conditions are evidently protected, possibly on a genetic basis, against even minimal atherosclerosis as an accompaniment of the aging process. In theory, any of several facets of the atherosclerotic process could reflect faulty genetic control, among them metabolism of serum lipoproteins or lipids affecting their deposition in the vessel wall, abnormalities in vascular

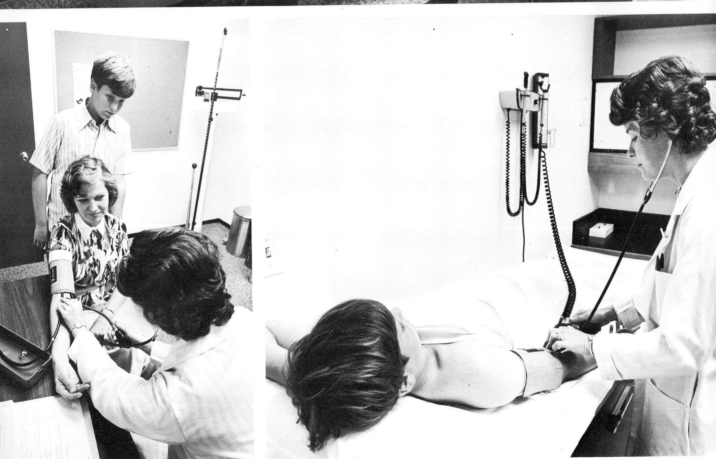

In University of Miami project to identify children at high risk of premature atherosclerosis, intake process begins with interview of affected parent (in this case the father) and other family members. Later, while mother's blood pressure is checked, son learns what to expect when his turn comes. Blood pressure and lipid measurements are also taken regularly in control families.

unclear, as do the reasons why hypo-responders appeared able to attain homeostasis so readily. Our concern, needless to say, is whether hyper-responsiveness of a similar type occurs in humans. If so, as the experimenters suggested, "early identification of susceptible individuals might be both possible and feasible."

It is now recognized, of course, that there are several distinct forms of familial hyperlipidemia in humans, each related to an abnormality – usually an inborn metabolic error – involving one of several serum lipoprotein complexes responsible for lipid transport in the circulation. The predominant lipid constituent in a given lipoprotein determines which lipid will be present in abnormal concentration (see Chapter 19 by Goldstein).

Thus in type I hyperlipoproteinemia, triglyceride levels are elevated either because of heavy fat intake or because a defect delays clearance of chylomicrons containing triglycerides as their chief component. In type II hyperlipoproteinemia, the serum lipid greatly in excess is cholesterol, the chief component of low-density lipoprotein (LDL). In type III, in which the problem seems to arise in the conversion of very low-density lipoprotein (VLDL) to LDL, both triglyceride and cholesterol levels are increased. In type IV – associated with abnormal accumulation of VLDL evidently resulting either from overproduction or delayed clearance from plasma – triglyceride but not cholesterol levels are affected. Type V, characterized by an increase in both chylomicron and VLDL levels, most often occurs as a secondary result of another disease, although occasionally the defect is inherited.

In classifying hyperlipidemias according to their lipoprotein pattern, Fredrickson, Levy et al at NHLI focused attention on familial type II hyperlipoproteinemia, which imposes a formidable risk of premature coronary disease. Among homozygous victims (familial type II is transmitted as a simple mendelian dominant with essentially complete expression) the atherosclerotic process is so accelerated that acute infarction may occur in childhood or early adolescence. Heterozygotes often remain asymptomatic for many years despite significant elevation in serum cholesterol. Their vulnerability to premature heart

disease is reflected in a few simple statistics: In a representative British study including persons both homozygous and heterozygous for type II, acute infarction struck in the males at a mean age of 43.8, and 75% were dead by age 60.

Like the other hyperlipoproteinemias, type II may also result from disorders influencing lipid metabolism, such as liver disease, nephrotic syndrome, and hypothyroidism. Such possible causes must naturally be ruled out. Among the genetically determined hyperlipidemias, however, type II hyperlipoproteinemia is clearly the most common; according to Levy, this type accounts for almost half the familial hyperlipidemia cases identified and studied by the NHLI group. Up to now, also, type II is the one genetically determined hyperlipidemia for which a specific mode of inheritance has been delineated.

At the clinical level, an important question is how often is familial atherosclerosis attributable to familial type II hyperlipoproteinemia (or to types III or IV, since both also appear to predispose to coronary heart disease, although to a lesser extent). The

relative importance of genetic hyperlipoproteinemia in the overall problem of coronary atherosclerosis also is far from certain. Evidence suggests that it represents a small but important fraction, but more solid information is needed.

Regardless of their number, affected individuals – particularly those at very high risk because of type II hyperlipoproteinemia – should be identified early in life so that any possibility of altering the course of their illness can be exploited.

Adults heterozygous for type II hyperlipoproteinemia have been treated by a number of investigators who report differing results. A dietary regimen low in cholesterol and high in unsaturated fats usually causes a 10% to 25% reduction in serum cholesterol concentration. Such a diet should be instituted in all patients with type II hyperlipoproteinemia. Lipid-lowering drugs (cholestyramine, nicotinic acid, etc.) usually are required, but should be individualized according to the patient's status. Significant lowering of cholesterol can be anticipated following management with diet and drugs. In the homozygote a combination of

Widow and two daughters of heart disease victim (dead at 36) look on as clinic director Pedro L. Ferrer completes periodic physical examination of son. At right, one of the girls is being prepared for electrocardiography. Aim of the battery of tests, performed

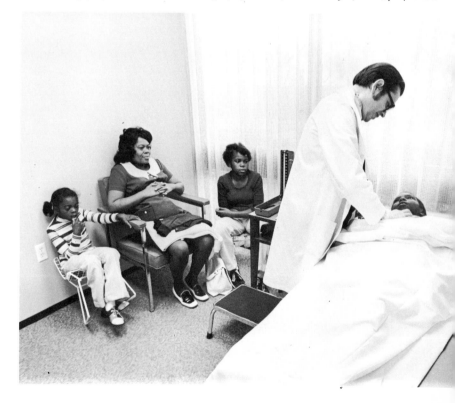

diet and drug therapy is essential.

Given these results in adults, it has been suggested that a similar approach be applied in children with type II hyperlipoproteinemia. Indeed, diet therapy essentially from birth has been implemented on a research basis in children diagnosed by cord blood analysis as having type II hyperlipoproteinemia. Reportedly, serum cholesterol levels have been effectively lowered in several cases; in the remainder, a drug-diet combination has been introduced once it was clear that diet alone would not work. My reasons for seriously questioning this approach will become evident as I focus now on details of our effort to apply primary prevention in children predisposed to hyperlipidemia or other traits increasing their vulnerability to atherosclerosis and coronary disease.

These studies are under way at our Specialized Center of Research in Atherosclerosis (SCOR), one of several such units under NHLI sponsorship directed toward identifying individuals at high risk of coronary heart disease in the hope that its clinical manifestations may be prevented or at least delayed. Other ongoing NHLI projects involve screening of children to determine whether risk factors associated with coronary heart disease in the adult are detectable during childhood. In two such programs, schoolchildren in Muscatine, Iowa, and Rochester, Minnesota, are being tested to establish the prevalence of hyperlipidemia and hypertension, and those with abnormalities are referred for further evaluation and possible therapy.

Our approach has been to study children considered prone to atherosclerosis and coronary disease on the basis of family history, on the assumption that this would provide a higher yield of "positive" cases for prospective study, and to follow up closely if dietary or medical intervention seems indicated. Accordingly, we have focused on families in which one parent has had a documented myocardial infarction by age 50, the cutoff age selected to ensure clearly premature disease. (The term premature has been variously defined by different investigators to include victims up to ages 60 or 65.) Our hypothesis, alluded to earlier, is that the impact of risk factors such as hyperlipidemia and hypertension in development of atherosclerosis is, at all ages, under genetic influence. In an infarction victim stricken by age 50 or younger it is assumed that there is a potent genetic component.

With identification of an affected family (referrals are made by interested physicians in our region), all progeny are evaluated in reference to a detailed family history and physical examination as well as to blood lipid concentrations and lipoprotein patterns, blood pressure, glucose tolerance, and several other parameters. The aim is to determine whether these children differ initially, or over time, from children of parents without identifiable coronary disease. The latter are usually neighbors invited to participate by an affected family, presumably similar in socioeconomic background and life-style.

To date, 94 families with 243 progeny have been enrolled and plans call for 500 progeny to be followed for at least a five-year period. (Thus far the youngest child has been four months old; most have been in the 6-to-15 age range, as would be expected with parents between ages 30 and 50.) The routine includes examination of each child three times during the first month and at regular intervals thereafter; the several initial visits are partly to permit repetition of quality control measurements in reference to serum lipid values and to tell us whether biologic variation in lipid levels over time, as seen in adults, occurs in children also. (It does.)

Analysis of data has been completed for 54 of the 94 families enrolled. In 27 of these families, a parent had experienced a premature myocardial infarction; the other 27 families were matched controls. The 70 children of case families had significantly higher cholesterol levels than the 67 control children. Eleven of the case children (15%) had cholesterol levels greater than 230 mg%, while the control children all had levels below 230 mg%. We consider this difference significant. Seven case children had cholesterol levels above 250 mg%, including four who had levels above 300 mg%. The families of these seven children had histories of type II hyperlipidemia, but there were no differences between them and the other

at each clinic visit, is to determine whether progeny of parents who have suffered acute myocardial infarction early in life may have increased vulnerability to coronary disease and whether it may be detectable before clinical manifestations are apparent.

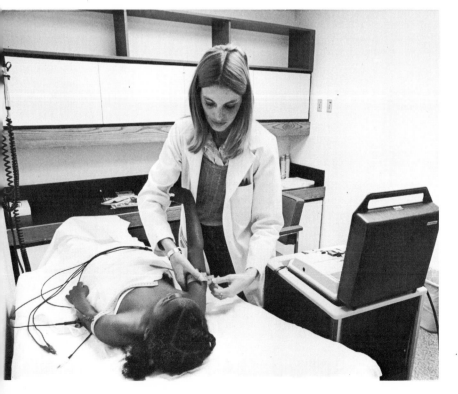

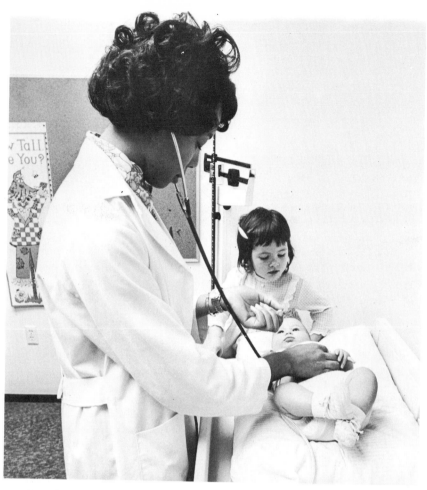

To date this four-month-old infant is the youngest individual enrolled in the Miami study; most of the children in both affected and control families have been in the 6-to-15 age range, as would be expected with parents between the ages of 30 and 50.

children in other parameters, including blood pressure and triglycerides.

Such findings, of course, should be considered in reference to normal cholesterol values for children; within the past few years, cross-sectional studies by several groups have provided some information on this point. Mean cholesterol concentration is in the range of 65 mg/100 ml in the neonate and increases to 160 or 170 mg/100 ml in the first two years. It has been reported that cholesterol levels remain stable until about age 20, but it appears from our study data that age trends are apparent between 2 and 14 years. The NHLI sponsored screening programs, involving large numbers of children (some 5,000 in Iowa alone), are yielding generally similar results, confirming a normal evolution of lipid levels. At about 20 years of age, a slow rise in serum cholesterol

begins and it continues through the fifth decade.

Our identification of both normal and abnormal values in progeny of infarction victims bears comment in relation to the Framingham study data on adults. Among middle-aged men having a first acute heart attack over a 12-year study period about 55% had manifested hyperlipidemia (cholesterol > 250 mg/100 ml) at intake. Other prospective studies involving adult populations have come up with similar findings – some subjects destined to have a coronary attack manifest hyperlipidemia or other risk factors, while in others predisposing traits may be absent. As our project proceeds, a multivariate statistical analysis of the type used in evaluating coronary risk factors in adults is to be applied to the children under study. Conceivably, some fresh insights may be gained as to the im-

portance of hyperlipidemia in relation to other known risk factors, or perhaps families with premature coronary disease may prove distinguishable in ways now unknown to us.

Meanwhile, there is the important question of intervention in children showing abnormal blood lipid patterns. Actually it is a two-edged question – not only *whether* to intervene but *when*. As already noted, treatment to control hyperlipidemia starting in the neonatal period is advocated by some. In our view it would seem more prudent to delay initiating treatment – either with drugs or diet – until an infant has been followed for at least a year. Given a moderate elevation (serum cholesterol in the range of 250 to 300) we would tend to delay therapy until after the second year, and at that time intervene actively to normalize blood lipid levels. Diet alone should be given a fair trial first, with drug treatment added later if control is not achieved.

This degree of caution seems indicated, since not enough is really known about possible undesired results of either drug or diet regimens in infants and young children. Even a remote possibility of adverse effects on growth and development – and this has been suggested – should keep us on guard against overdoing either form of therapy.

Something must be said about cord blood analysis in detection of hyperlipidemia, particularly its suggested use among routine tests performed at birth. While it is possible to diagnose hyperlipidemia by cord blood sampling – and we have done so on several occasions – there are still uncertainties as to the range of normal and abnormal values for specific lipoprotein fractions. In particular, high levels of high-density lipoproteins (HDL) occur in cord blood samples, contributing to the amount of total cholesterol measured. To make the diagnosis of type II hyperlipoproteinemia from cord blood determinations one must determine the level of LDL, in addition to the total cholesterol. Thus the presence of type II hyperlipoproteinemia or other defects may not always be accurately reflected. For this reason we currently advise against routine testing of cord blood or including analysis of serum samples for possible hyperlipidemia among the measurements generally performed in the course of early infancy. On the other hand, an infant presumably at high risk of hyperlipidemia according to family history should have his status clarified, perhaps not immediately after birth but surely sometime during the first year. (A fasting blood specimen showing significant elevation of cholesterol and triglycerides within the normal range, or slightly elevated, may be presumed indicative of type II hyperlipoproteinemia. To establish a familial basis, secondary causes must be excluded and other family members examined.)

Clearly an important implication of recent work in this area is that pediatricians generally must become more alert to the possibility of identifying individuals at risk of coronary disease later in life through predisposing traits evident in childhood. Of course, doing so means reorienting family history–taking to include questions about premature myocardial infarction or the presence of risk factors such as hyperlipidemia, hypertension, or diabetes. In practice this is rarely done because most pediatricians (like other physicians) have not yet begun to think of atherosclerosis as a disorder having its origins in childhood. This is not to suggest that all children be viewed as potential victims; the stress should be on selecting children at risk and identifying those among them with demonstrable abnormalities for potential therapy.

While most of our discussion of coronary risk factors has been in terms of hyperlipidemia, the prospect of detecting and dealing with essential hypertension early in life also warrants consideration. It is now clear that elevation in either systolic or diastolic pressure, or both, may promote atherogenesis and coronary disease. As is true of hyperlipidemia, there appears to be no blood pressure threshold; rather, blood pressure elevation operates as a continuous variable, correlating directly with coronary morbidity and mortality at any age. Long ago clinicians suspected a strong familial influence affecting blood pressure, and population studies have provided ample confirmation. Presumably a multifactorial inheritance pattern is involved, although this aspect has not been well defined.

Depending on how early in life this influence is expressed, a predisposition to blood pressure elevation might be identifiable in childhood, long before hypertension or its clinical consequences become evident. Actually, until recently there have been few studies of blood pressure in children, in part because it was assumed that it could not be measured reliably Among others, Moss and Adams, and Kass, Zinner, et al in their study of offspring of mothers initially seen because of bacteriuria during pregnancy have shown that valid determinations can be obtained in children. Investigators Kass, Zinner, et al tested some 720 children when they were 2 to 14 years of age. On the basis of cross-sectional data they identified a familial influence, and hypoth-

Measurement of serum lipid concentration and lipoprotein analysis are to be performed on blood sample drawn from study participant. Preliminary data show higher mean cholesterol levels in children of affected parents but also a wide range of lipid patterns.

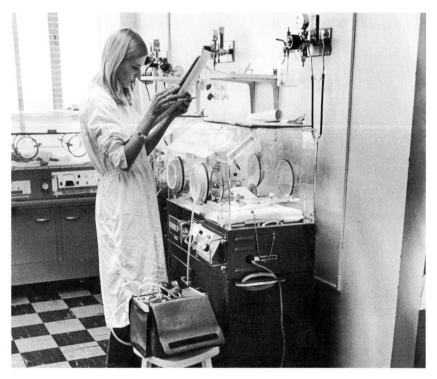

Cord blood analysis is undertaken to determine blood lipid patterns of neonates whose mothers have chronic hypertension, as part of Miami research project to identify progeny who may be at increased risk of premature cardiovascular disease.

esized that each individual's blood pressure may become channelized relatively early. They suggested that if pressures are low in childhood they tend to stay low, whereas pressures at or above the upper limit of normal to begin with are likely to remain high. We are in the process of testing this hypothesis by a longitudinal study.

If this hypothesis is proved true, then the process resulting in stable hypertension, and its effects on development of atherosclerosis, also has its roots early in life. Valid testing of this thesis requires longitudinal investigations to ascertain how blood pressure levels change over time. We recently launched such a study, as part of our SCOR project, in children considered at risk because of maternal essential hypertension. The mothers are being identified through our obstetric service and their offspring tested at regular intervals from birth onward. Repeated measurements also are being made in older siblings to see how they compare. As part of our research program we are also attempting to trace blood pressure patterns in early life by testing the newborns' parents and siblings in 100 families with maternal hypertension and 400 families without hypertension. There will thus be 500 pregnant women followed from their third trimester as well as their newborn infants and the remainder of the family, all followed longitudinally.

Through both projects we are trying to learn more about the range of normal blood pressure in children, which has not been well delineated, and to determine whether a blood pressure "track" for each individual is indeed established early in life, as the cross-sectional studies suggest. If so, how early? And could a child tending toward high blood pressure be moved off his track with appropriate treatment? If this seems a possibility, how soon should treatment be begun?

According to prospective studies in adult men, overall morbidity and mortality due to vascular disease are reduced by effective treatment of moderately elevated blood pressure. However, there is still little firm evidence that lowering blood pressure influences the occurrence or outcome of acute myocardial infarction. (Most of the gain appears to be in reference to cerebrovascular disease.) Perhaps the reason is that treatment of hypertension is usually begun in middle life or beyond. By then coronary vascular structure may have been so altered by persistent elevation of blood pressure that little can be done to stem the disease process.

Would intervention earlier in life make a difference? If incipient hypertension is identifiable in the early school years, that would seem the proper time to initiate appropriate medical therapy, at least for a trial period. Conceivably, a limited period of treatment in the initial stages of hypertension might eliminate the necessity of prolonged treatment later. This is only a suggestion, of course, for we still have much to learn of the natural course of hypertension, not only how – or if – it is usually initiated in early life but what factors act to sustain it.

In any case, a change in thinking in regard to hypertension is surely in order. The possibility of identifying children prone to hypertension should be kept in mind by the pediatrician; a mother may not think to tell her child's physician that she is under treatment for hypertension. Or she may not know what her blood pressure is, whether her husband is hypertensive, or what his blood pressure is. The physician should encourage her to obtain answers to these questions. As with hyperlipidemia, the aim should be to identify children who may be vulnerable, so that they can be evaluated and indications for treatment considered.

It must be more than evident by now that in our approach to primary prevention of coronary disease the position we have taken is that, given available information, the main thrust of such efforts should be directed at individuals believed to be at increased risk of progressive atherosclerosis and its sequelae. Doing otherwise, in our view, presupposes greater knowledge of the causes of atherosclerosis than we now have. Population studies relating incidence of coronary disease to serum lipid levels have led others to suggest that by controlling hyperlipidemia in the *general* population through dietary means, morbidity and mortality caused by heart disease could be decreased. As a corollary, some have suggested that prevention of hyperlipidemia might be accomplished if children were placed on a lipid-lowering dietary regimen early in life.

The major changes in national food habits required might well be justified if there were firm proof that reducing serum lipid levels at any age, by whatever means, could influence progression of atherosclerosis. But in fact we do not know whether modifying blood lipid levels by diet or drugs (or more effective control of hypertension) does retard the atherosclerotic process and either prevent or delay clinical coronary disease.

As the NHLI Task Force report concluded, "It is not known whether measures resulting in reduction of serum lipid and lipoprotein concentrations will also result in a lowering of the rate of occurrence of atherosclerotic clinical disease, either in individuals with normal serum levels or in individuals with elevated levels. Nor is it certain what kinds of diets are most effective in lowering levels of serum cholesterol, i.e., diets low in cholesterol and saturated fats, diets with reduced fat content, or diets high in polyunsaturated fats. Possible toxicity of prolonged use of such diets remains to be studied, especially during fetal development and in children."

Given the uncertainties, identification and treatment beginning early in life of individuals vulnerable to coronary disease seems to us quite appropriate, since the potential risks imposed may be well worth taking. As we learn more of the relation of risk factors to development of atherosclerosis and symptomatic coronary disease, involving the entire population in a preventive program along similar lines may appear more justified than it does to us today.

Platelets and Thrombosis in Acute Myocardial Infarction

J. FRASER MUSTARD

McMaster University

The relationship among platelets, thrombosis, and atherosclerosis in the development of myocardial infarction is still not fully understood. There is little doubt that most patients with myocardial infarction have fairly extensive atherosclerosis in their main coronary arteries. However, there is less evidence that occlusive thrombosis in the main coronary arteries causes most myocardial infarcts. This is particularly true for sudden deaths attributable to myocardial ischemia. Most studies of these cases of sudden death have failed to show evidence of occlusive thrombosis (see Chapter 18, "Coronary Artery Pathology in Fatal Ischemic Heart Disease," by Roberts). The reasons for our failure to define the relationship between thrombosis and myocardial infarction include 1) the problems involved in carrying out a careful, systematic, objective evaluation of the coronary arteries in postmortem studies, 2) the problem of establishing whether a lesion found at postmortem is a primary cause or occurred as a secondary event, 3) our lack of appreciation of the nature of the response of blood to injury (thrombosis), 4) our incomplete knowledge of the effect of disturbances in the microcirculation on myocardial functions, and 5) our incomplete knowledge about the process of atherosclerosis.

In this chapter an attempt will be made to relate what we now know about the process of thrombosis to the problem of myocardial infarction. The first section will deal with how blood responds to injury, the second with the question of thrombosis and myocardial injury, and the third with the relation of thrombosis to atherosclerosis.

The initial events in the response of blood to vessel injury were quite accurately described some 90 years ago, when Bizzozero showed that injury of a vessel in the mesentery of a guinea pig was quickly followed by accumulation of a mass of platelets and some white blood cells at the injury site. In drawings of the thrombus structure he showed platelets adherent to the vessel wall and to each other; no fibrin was depicted. The studies of Welch and of Eberth and Schimmelbusch not long afterward confirmed and extended the findings of Bizzozero. A fresh thrombus formed in response to injury was composed almost entirely of platelets and was later transformed into a fibrin mass. Curiously, after this work, and despite classic reviews by Welch, Aschoff, and others, interest centered chiefly on the blood coagulation mechanism, and the belief grew that arterial thrombosis is essentially a problem related to blood coagulation, with thrombi formed primarily from the deposits of fibrin produced from its precursor fibrinogen.

Unfortunately, the terms "thrombus" and "blood clot" are still used as synonyms, although clearly initiation of arterial thrombosis is largely independent of coagulation processes. (In contrast, venous thrombi have a larger coagulation component.) One reason why the misconception arose and persisted may have been that for a long time the role of platelets was not fully appreciated and they were little studied. More recently, detailed studies by electron microscopy of the structure of arterial thrombi, platelets, and the vessel wall have both confirmed the findings of the early workers and added new ones.

Thrombosis

When a blood vessel is injured sufficiently to expose the subendothelial structures, platelets instantly accumulate at the injury site, and within a few minutes a thrombus is formed consisting of densely packed platelets and some white cells, with a fibrin net around them. After a few hours, as the platelets begin undergoing degenerative changes and separate from each other, fibrin formation increases until, by 24 hours, the platelet mass has been largely replaced by fibrin. As seen in the electron micro-

1

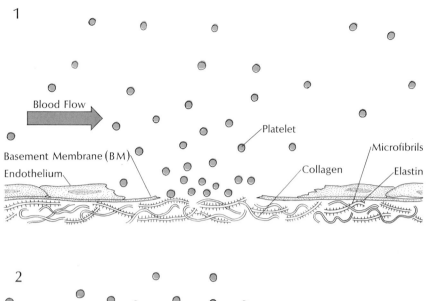

Blood Flow

Platelet

Microfibrils

Basement Membrane (BM)

Collagen

Elastin

Endothelium

2

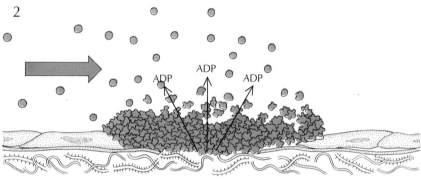

ADP

ADP

ADP

3

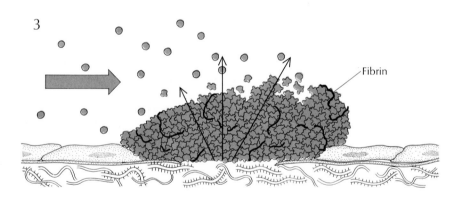

Fibrin

scope at this time, the lesion consists chiefly of fibrin with platelet debris interspersed among the fibrin strands. (In contrast, a clot would consist of a network of fibrin containing trapped red cells.) It should be pointed out that when flow is arrested by an occlusive thrombus in an artery, the blood distal and proximal to the occlusion may clot. This component of the thrombus would have the appearance of a blood clot. Within the first few hours the thrombus is invaded by polymorphonuclear leukocytes and mononuclear cells, which phagocytose cellular debris and intact platelets. After two or three days the amount of fibrin is markedly reduced and mononuclear cells are present in increasing numbers in the thrombus. By four to seven days the thrombus is covered with endothelium and contains numerous elongated cells, probably young smooth muscle cells. By the end of the first week, when the amount of fibrin is further reduced, there is evidence of collagen and elastin formation. By two weeks or so the initial platelet mass has organized into a fibrous thickening of the arterial intima, rich in collagen, smooth muscle cells, and elastic fibers.

While this is the characteristic pattern of organization of many thrombi, in some circumstances other features may be dominant. Some of the lesions may be rich in lipid and may include foam cells derived from mononuclear cells that have phagocytosed platelets. In other lesions, deposits of calcium are found.

A thrombus examined early in its evolution – even only a few hours after it begins to form – bears little

4

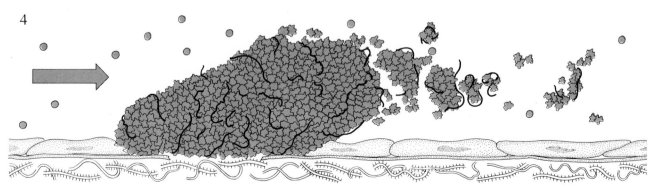

Thrombus formation begins with vessel injury, loss of endothelium, and platelet adherence to exposed BM, collagen, and microfibrils (1). ADP release fosters platelet shape change and aggregation (2). As mass grows, thrombin generation causes fibrin formation and more ADP release (3). Thrombus keeps growing unless interfering factors cause breakup of platelet-fibrin mass (4).

resemblance to the original platelet-rich mass. In considering the relation of thrombosis to atherosclerosis and its complications, one should therefore begin by considering the nature of the platelet response to vessel wall injury, a major stimulus for thrombus formation. Platelets appear to interact principally with collagen, basement membrane, and the microfibrils associated with elastin; up to now the mechanism of interaction with the vessel wall constituents has not been well defined. The epsilon amino groups of collagen are believed to be involved in the adherence of platelets to collagen, and an enzyme on the surface of the platelets (glucosyl transferase) may take part in the interaction. What is clear is that when platelets adhere to the vessel wall constituents, they are induced to discharge several major constituents including adenine nucleotides, serotonin, an antiheparin factor (platelet factor 4), and lysosomal enzymes.

In addition, platelets release a cationic protein having a similar effect on mast cells to that released from leukocytes. Some of the factors that are released from platelets are probably not important in the formation of a thrombus but, as will be discussed later, may be important in causing injury to the vessel wall.

The discharge of the contents of platelet granules is similar to that of other cells and appears to have at least two components: the release of the amine storage granule contents – adenosine triphosphate (ATP), adenosine diphosphate (ADP), serotonin – and the release of the lysosomal granule contents. As with many other secretory cells, cylic adenosine monophosphate (AMP) plays a part in the reaction and if the platelet cyclic AMP level is increased, the release reaction is inhibited.

It is well established that a key substance released by platelets is ADP, since this causes platelets flowing past the injury site to adhere to each other and to platelets already adherent to the vessel wall. This property of ADP was identified a decade or so ago by Gaardner et al in Norway; their experiments showed that ADP concentrations as low as 1 μM could cause platelets to adhere to each other. Although ADP for this reaction could be derived from injured cells in the vessel wall and from damaged red

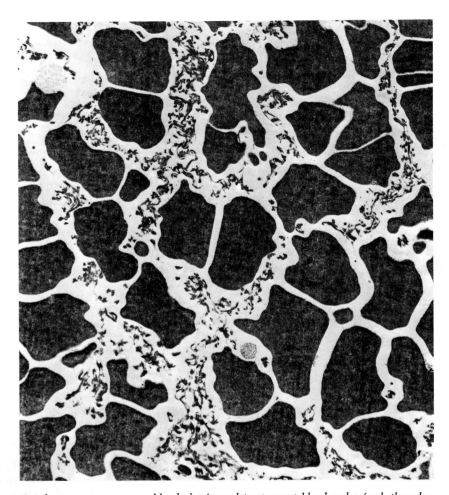

On electron microscopy, a blood clot formed in stagnant blood and a fresh thrombus formed in flowing blood are readily distinguished, since the former consists of a network of fibrin containing trapped red cells, as can be seen in photo reproduced above, while the latter is initially a platelet-rich mass that is soon replaced by fibrin.

blood cells in the area, ADP released by platelets is the principal source.

The mechanism whereby ADP causes platelet aggregation involves an alteration of platelet shape from a characteristic disc form to a more rounded one with pseudopods. As with the release of platelet constituents, the biochemistry is still not well defined, but divalent cations, chiefly calcium, and fibrinogen are required. If platelets lack glucose or are unable to use it, they become unresponsive to ADP; hence metabolic energy must be involved. A platelet contractile protein resembling actomyosin may also be important; it has been suggested that the normal disc shape of platelets represents a contracted state and that the interaction of ADP with a receptor on the platelet surface induces the swelling and pseudopod formation necessary for adherence and aggregation.

Recent work has shown that a

number of substances involved in inflammatory and immunologic reactions, among them antigen-antibody complexes, endotoxin, some viruses, and bacteria, may cause intravascular platelet aggregation. These intravascular masses may be important in the development of vessel injury and its clinical complications as well as causing a form of disseminated intravascular thrombosis. It appears that platelet aggregation caused by these intravascular stimuli also occurs through the release of platelet ADP. There are therefore two routes by which platelet aggregates can be induced to form: through the exposure of vessel wall stimuli as a result of vessel injury and through the effects of intravascular stimuli.

It must be stressed that neither release of platelet constituents leading to aggregation nor adherence of platelets to each other or to an injured

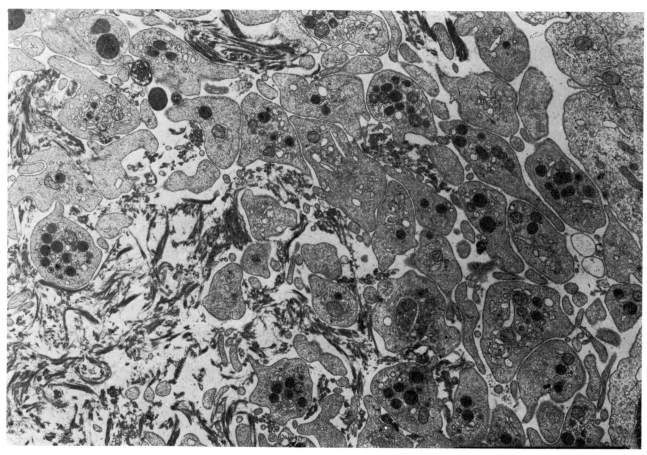

Initially composed chiefly of densely packed platelets, a fresh arterial thrombus (above) changes rapidly within first few hours as platelets undergo degenerative changes and fibrin formation increases (original electron micrograph x6,800). By 24 hours (below, original electron micrograph x2,600) the platelets have largely disintegrated and there is more fibrin present.

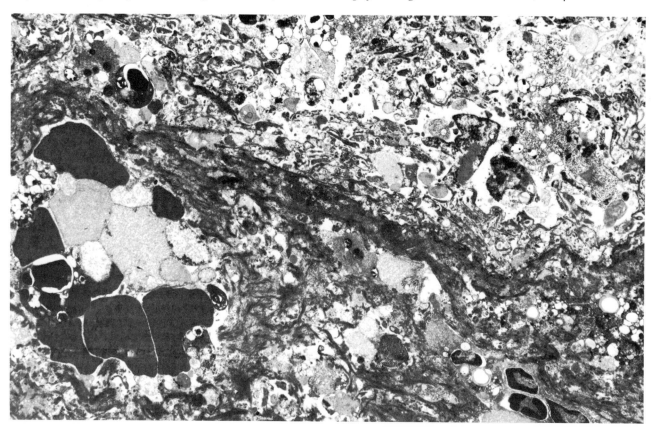

vessel wall is dependent upon coagulation. There is no doubt, however, that coagulation, although not required for the early stages of formation of arterial thrombi, significantly influences their growth and stability.

This is readily seen when A D P or thrombin is injected into experimental animals. Following an A D P infusion, platelet aggregates immediately form in the circulation but promptly break up when the infusion is stopped. If thrombin is infused, the platelet aggregates take much longer to break up; histologic examination shows a fibrin component in these aggregates. Direct proof that fibrin is essential to stabilize the initial platelet mass that forms in response to vessel injury was obtained in the experiments of Hovig et al in which mesenteric vessels were transected in normal dogs and in dogs with hemophilia. In normal dogs, bleeding was usually arrested within three or four minutes by formation of a platelet mass (having the same structure as a thrombus formed from flowing blood) at the end of the cut vessel. In this plug the aggregated platelets were surrounded by a network of fibrin. In the hemophilic dog, the plug formed at the same rate but frequently broke down, evidently as a result of the inability of these animals to form fibrin. Further support for the concept of the importance of fibrin in stabilizing the initial platelet mass comes from the studies of Hirsh and his associates. It was found that after a platelet mass had formed at the end of a cut mesenteric artery in rabbits, activation of plasminogen by adding streptokinase to the surface of the hemostatic plug caused lysis of fibrin around the mass, leading to a break-up of the platelet aggregate and further bleeding. (For a discussion of the fibrinolytic mechanism and its activators, see Chapter 28, "Present Status of Antithrombotic Therapy in Acute Heart Attack," by Sherry.)

Platelets play a key role in blood coagulation. Two steps in the coagulation sequence require phospholipid for maximum activity: the interaction of factors IX and VIII, and the interaction of factors X and V. When platelets are exposed to A D P, the phospholipid on the platelet surface apparently becomes available for the clotting reactions. Furthermore, Walsh has recently demonstrated that A D P-

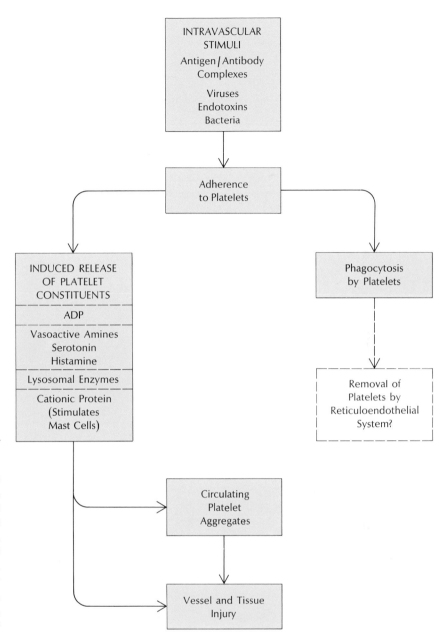

According to recent work, a number of substances involved in inflammatory and immunologic reactions may lead to intravascular platelet aggregation, initiating the events depicted diagramatically above. Release of platelet constituents, as also occurs when platelets adhere to injured vessel wall, causes formation of circulating platelet masses that may themselves induce vessel injury; released constituents may also be damaging.

induced platelet aggregates can activate factor XII and that the interaction of platelets with collagen leads to activation of factor XI. It has been shown that when washed platelets are exposed to activated factor X, traces of thrombin are generated; this observation indicates that the components of the clotting sequence from factor V to factor II, as well as phospholipid, are available on the platelet surface. Platelets also release an antiheparin factor (platelet factor 4), which may

further facilitate the generation of thrombin in and around platelet aggregates.

Another important aspect of the relationship between platelets and coagulation is the interaction of platelets with fibrin. Platelets will not adhere to fully polymerized fibrin, but during the process of polymerization the fibrin adheres firmly to the platelet surface. This is probably the mechanism by which links are formed between fibrin and platelets. Finally, thrombin

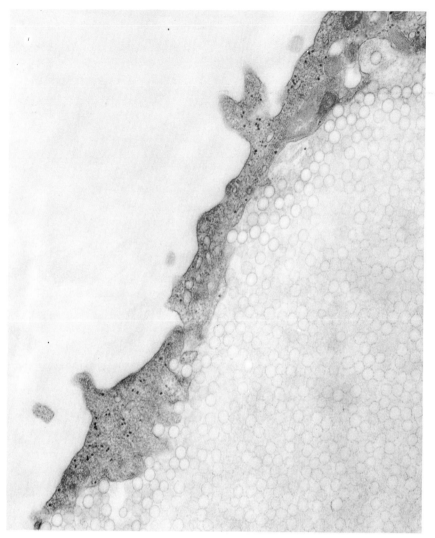

Interaction of platelets with various surfaces has been examined in a number of experimental preparations; for example, platelet shape change on adherence to gamma globulin–coated latex particles is shown above (original x12,500).

and myocardial infarction: the effects of blood flow and the nature and importance of vessel injury. As mentioned earlier, the structure of arterial thrombi is distinctive – they appear as columns of aggregated platelets separated by fibrin and some red blood cells. Arterial thrombi tend to occur around heart valves and in the auricles of the heart, downstream from stenoses, at the origin of luminal expansions, lateral to orifices of perpendicular branches and at the hips of bifurcations. The characteristic structure of thrombi and their localization are profoundly influenced by blood flow.

How hemodynamic forces and blood elements such as platelets interact in thrombosis needs clarification. Interesting observations bearing on this question were made by Goldsmith and coworkers, to the effect that collisions between particles such as platelets occur in areas of disturbed flow, especially if there is vortex formation. Because of very low return velocities in the vortex close to the vessel wall, there is minimal inward radial migration of formed elements, which increases the likelihood that a platelet mass once formed will adhere to the wall. Thus, repeated collisions of platelets with each other and with the vessel wall in regions of disturbed flow and vortex formation could facilitate thrombus formation. The size of the platelet mass that forms at a site of vessel injury will be considerably influenced by the blood flow pattern at the site. Injury to the intima with loss of the endothelium leads to platelet accumulation on the denuded surface. Two types of vessel wall lesion are often suggested as important in the initiation of coronary artery thrombi: hemorrhage into the vessel wall and intimal breaks or rupture of an atherosclerotic plaque. The most recent evidence indicates that bleeding from vessels within the vessel wall is not associated with thrombosis, but hemorrhage into the vessel wall from the lumen, because of rupture of an atherosclerotic plaque, is associated with thrombosis.

Constantinides found that occlusive thrombi in coronary arteries were almost always associated with breaks in atherosclerotic or fibrotic vessel walls. This was shown by complete serial-sectioning (every 10 microns) of

can cause the release of platelet constituents, and it is probably this effect of thrombin that leads to further growth of an initial platelet mass. The relationship between coagulation and platelets is probably responsible for the characteristic layered structure of arterial thrombi – a mass of aggregated platelets surrounded by fibrin, covered by more aggregated platelets and a further layer of fibrin.

A pitfall in any discussion of thrombosis is that it may be incorrectly assumed that thrombus formation usually follows an orderly sequence: from the initial platelet-fibrin mass to a transformed fibrin-rich mass to an organized connective tissue–rich thickening of the intima. In fact, the thrombotic process is both dynamic and variable. Experimentally, if one

injures a blood vessel in the microcirculation and then observes the effects, the mass that forms at the injury site can be readily seen building up and then breaking down. A platelet mass may be so unstable that it fragments before much fibrin can accumulate, or fibrin, once formed, may be degraded through the action of the plasma fibrinolytic system or enzymes from the leukocytes, leading to the fragmentation of the thrombus. Several of these processes may proceed simultaneously; what happens in a given instance depends on whether factors leading to the growth and persistence of a thrombus overcome those causing its disruption.

There are two additional points concerning the relationship among platelets, thrombosis, atherosclerosis,

thrombosed arteries of patients who had died of coronary disease. More than 55,000 sections were examined; in nearly every case, thrombi were associated with breaks of various sizes and shapes in the arterial wall, and almost all hemorrhages could be traced to passage of blood through the same breaks. Fischer and Jørgensen and their associates consider that there are two types of thrombi: those associated with rupture of an atherosclerotic plaque and those associated with small breaks in the intima. In patients with rupture of a plaque it appears that the thrombi take time to develop after the onset of symptoms, whereas with the other type of lesion the thrombus appears to develop coincidentally with onset of symptoms. In this latter type of thrombus, the break in the endothelium may occur after the thrombus has formed. However, these breaks may be artifacts caused by the methods used in preparing the sections (see Chapter 18 by Roberts).

The factors causing damage to the endothelium could be stretching, blood flow, or injury caused by the formed elements of the blood. There is some evidence that the endothelial attachment to the vessel wall is much weaker where there is an atherosclerotic plaque.

There is considerable debate on the question of how important occlusive thrombi are in precipitating clinical complications of atherosclerosis, in particular myocardial infarction. A widespread belief, of course, is that thrombotic occlusion of major arteries is a principal factor. However, it is also recognized that in cases studied postmortem shortly after the acute event, evidence of fresh thrombotic occlusion is often not present. As Roberts points out, patients who die suddenly from what appears clinically to be myocardial ischemia usually do not have major thrombi in the main coronary arteries. Those who develop symptoms and live longer do show evidence of large thrombi. Again, the incidence is not 100%, but something like 60%. Subjects with massive infarcts of the heart do show a high incidence of occlusive thrombi in their major coronary arteries. However, since most patients who develop myocardial ischemia and die do so during the first few hours, it appears that occlusive thrombosis is only a single factor (but admittedly an important one) in causing death from myocardial ischemia and infarction. The lack of evidence that occlusive thrombosis is the major cause of myocardial ischemia and infarction has led to alternative explanations to account for the acute event. Among these are rupture of an atherosclerotic plaque with embolization of sclerotic material and immediate death, hemorrhage into a plaque, abnormal myocardial metabolism, and abnormal blood flow.

Another possible mechanism is obstruction of the microcirculation resulting when a platelet-rich thrombus forming in a coronary artery fragments and showers the distal circulation with platelet emboli. That mural thrombi formed at sites of vessel injury in animal experiments do fragment and embolize in the microcirculation has been observed repeatedly. It is also likely that intravascular stimuli could cause the formation of platelet aggregates that obstruct flow in small vessels. In either case, if a portion of the myocardial microcirculation were affected, significant organ dysfunction and tissue injury might result.

To date, the most convincing clinical evidence that such a mechanism occurs in man has been obtained not in reference to the heart but to the cerebrovascular system. But a similar mechanism might well operate elsewhere, since so far as we know thrombus formation proceeds by essentially the same mechanisms in all parts of the arterial bed. A number of investigators (e.g., Millikan and coworkers and Gunning et al) have linked platelet microemboli to clinical cerebrovascular disease. Some fairly direct observations were made by Fisher and coworkers, who followed passage of microemboli through the retinal arterioles during transient visual loss. Histologic studies by others confirmed that the microemboli were platelet aggregates. In Norway, Jørgensen and colleagues reported interesting findings from an autopsy study of cerebrovascular disease. Checking for the presence of platelet aggregates in the vascular bed of arteries supplying the brain, they found the incidence far higher in patients with carotid artery thrombosis than in those with grossly visible emboli from the heart or other intrathoracic sources. This strongly suggested that most platelet aggregates were microemboli from an upstream thrombus.

There is also evidence now that platelet microembolism may cause significant dysfunction and tissue injury in the kidney. More specifically, microembolism from mural thrombi in the aorta has been linked to renal injury associated with hypertension.

Thrombus (arrow) is seen at point of stenosis caused by atherosclerotic lesion. Thrombi also tend to occur at heart valves, at the origins of luminal expansion, and near orifices of perpendicular branches and bifurcations.

Initially, this possibility suggested itself to Moore after autopsy studies in which he noted the frequent occurrence of superficial cortical scars of the kidney and significant aortic atherosclerosis upstream of the renal arteries in patients with hypertension. Subsequently, in a series of experiments in rabbits, dogs, and monkeys, Moore and his colleagues demonstrated that mural thrombi induced in the aorta above the orifices to the renal arteries caused repeated embolic showerings of the renal arteries and development of lesions closely similar to those seen in the human autopsy study. Using A D P infusion in similar experiments in rabbits, Jørgensen et al found that transient showers of platelet microemboli in the renal microcirculation caused necrosis or renal infarcts as well as focal glomerulonephritis.

What of the possibility that similar circulatory disturbances in the myocardial microcirculation could be produced either by platelet emboli from an upstream thrombus or by intravascular platelet aggregates?

In exploring this question, Jørgensen and associates analyzed autopsy findings in patients who had died within 48 hours of onset of acute myocardial ischemia. Of those with thrombosis in a main coronary artery, platelet aggregates were present in downstream epicardial or intramyocardial arteries in about one third of the cases. Of course, some of the aggregates could have been secondary to anoxic damage, but, as Jørgensen suggests, it seems equally likely that some were microemboli from coronary thrombi.

The Norwegian workers also studied patients who had died suddenly, with what clinically appeared to be myocardial ischemia, for evidence of intravascular platelet aggregates. In most of these subjects, no occlusive thrombi were found in the main coronary vessels. As before, platelet aggregates were found in about one third of cases. Again, some of the aggregates could have been secondary to anoxia, but this seemed unlikely since they were more frequent and extensive than in subjects who had died suddenly from other causes.

To explore whether transient platelet aggregation could have significant myocardial effects, Jørgensen et al used the technique of A D P infusion to induce platelet aggregation in the coronary arteries or left ventricles of swine. In control experiments, animals were infused with A M P, which does not cause platelet aggregation. To insure that only transient platelet thromboemboli were produced, the infusion was maintained for four or five minutes and then stopped. During the infusion all animals showed signs of circulatory collapse and, usually, electrocardiographic evidence of myocardial ischemia; in association with these changes there was a sharp drop in the number of circulating platelets. Many of the animals showed arrhythmia during the infusion of A D P and a significant number went into ventricular fibrillation and died. The mesenteric microcirculation was observed during intraventricular A D P infusion; platelet aggregates appeared immediately and the mesenteric circulation was severely impaired. Within 20 to 60 seconds of the start of the infusion there was red cell sludging, followed by complete stoppage of blood flow in many vessels. During

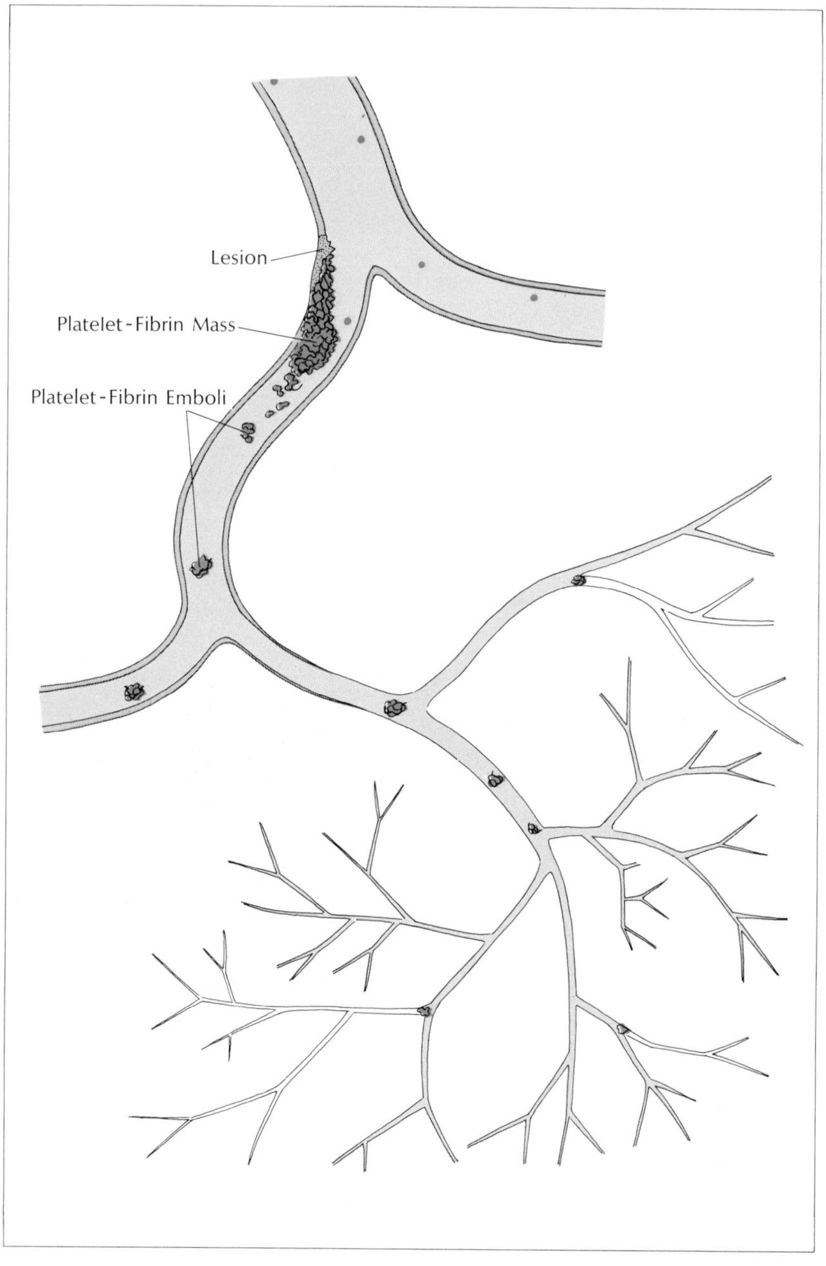

Lesion

Platelet-Fibrin Mass

Platelet-Fibrin Emboli

Fragmentation and embolization of platelet-rich mural thrombi formed at the site of vessel injury could cause damage by obstructing myocardial microcirculation. Conceivably, platelet aggregation induced by intravascular stimuli could have a similar effect.

the remainder of the infusion, flow in veins and capillaries tended to remain arrested, while in arteries it was intermittent and sluggish.

Following the infusion the circulating platelet count and cardiac function returned to normal. However, of the animals that survived the A D P infusion, myocardial infarcts developed within two to three hours in 85% of those given an intracoronary infusion of A D P and in 60% of those infused intraventricularly.

The infarcts appeared to be the result of platelet aggregation, but to be more certain of the relationship Jørgensen et al. examined the effect of A D P infusions into the myocardial circulation of animals made thrombocytopenic by the prior administration of ³²P-orthophosphate. Also, since it was known that platelets are temporarily insensitive to A D P following an initial treatment, another experiment was done in which animals were given a preparatory injection of A D P into another part of the vascular tree before the intracoronary or intraventricular infusion of A D P. None of the animals treated in either way showed changes in cardiac function, died, or developed myocardial infarcts.

In these experiments the duration of ischemia produced by changes in the microcirculation was 10 minutes at most. It is of interest that in experiments in cats, Korb and Schlosser found that up to nine minutes of total ischemia was sufficient to cause histologic evidence of permanent focal myocardial damage. Pearson et al found that 10 minutes of anoxia depressed oxygen uptake of heart muscle slices by 40%. Thus the transient obstruction of the microcirculation such as was produced in swine might produce sufficient ischemia in focal areas of the myocardium to result in fatal arrhythmia or irreversible tissue injury. In the animals given the A D P infusion there was evidence of injury to the walls of vessels in the microcirculation, including swelling of endothelial cells, gap formation, and extravasation of red cells. This would suggest that the initial platelet aggregates caused endothelial cell damage; presumably this could lead to repeated formation of platelet aggregates capable of causing intermittent obstruction of the circulation.

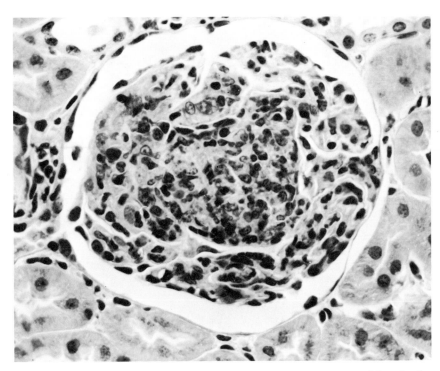

The possibility of significant organ dysfunction and tissue injury caused by platelet embolism to the microcirculation was supported by experiments in which ADP-induced platelet aggregation produced renal infarcts and focal glomerulonephritis in rabbits. In example shown here, profound changes in a glomerulus (note the increase in cellularity and the collapse of capillary loops) are evident at 48 hours after ADP had been infused into the aorta just above the renal arteries.

Obviously it is difficult to establish the clinical importance of temporary or permanent obstruction of the myocardial microcirculation – either by intravascular platelet aggregates or microemboli from upstream thrombi – since myocardial tissue is seldom available for examination at the time of the acute event. It is worth noting too that in the swine experiment platelet aggregates were found in all histologic sections that were taken from animals killed during the infusion or from those killed immediately afterwards. However, in sections taken from animals killed 30 minutes or more after the infusion or from animals that died during the infusion but were not examined until an hour or so after death, platelet aggregates were found in only about 30% of the sections.

In the experiments in swine it was noted that about one third of the animals died either during the A D P infusion or immediately afterward of ventricular arrhythmia. Might something like this happen in humans as well? In a study by Haerem in Norway, more numerous and larger plate-

let aggregates were found in epicardial and intramyocardial arteries in persons who had died suddenly of myocardial ischemia and infarction than in those who had died suddenly from other causes. Perhaps in sudden death due to myocardial dysfunction, a lethal arrhythmia develops as a result of microcirculatory disturbance leading to ischemia and impairment of the conduction system. James has emphasized that disturbances in the small vessels supplying the conduction system of the heart can cause death.

Although platelet thromboembolism of the myocardial microcirculation either from a small upstream mural thrombus or intravascular platelet aggregates can be a cause of myocardial ischemia and sudden death, its importance is at present not known. All this evidence indicates that if attempts are to be made to diminish the incidence of myocardial ischemia and infarction due to thromboembolism, modification of platelet function would be useful. It may be only with this approach that the importance of the role of platelet embolization of the microcirculation will

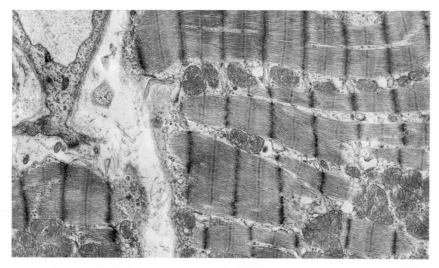

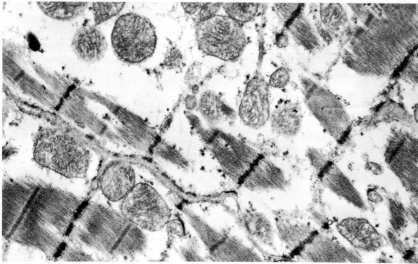

Section of normal pig myocardium (EM at top, original x3,500) is contrasted with section of infarcted myocardium (lower EM, original x9,000) taken a few hours after intracoronary infusion of ADP to induce platelet aggregation. Obvious tissue changes include fragmentation and separation of muscle fibers, disruption of sarcolemma, swelling of mitochondria, and formation of dense intramitochondrial granules.

eventually be determined.

Modification of Platelet Function

The mechanisms in thrombosis could be modified to potentiate the process or inhibit it. There are a number of factors that may enhance the formation and stabilization of thrombi. One is epinephrine, which both causes and enhances platelet aggregation. There is some evidence that cigarette smoking predisposes individuals to an increased risk of coronary artery disease. It has been suggested that cigarette smoking may cause an elevation in blood catecholamine levels and it is possible that one effect of such a process would be to enhance the formation of platelet thrombi at sites of vessel injury. Several studies have demonstrated that platelet survival is shorter and platelet turnover is greater in subjects with a history of thromboembolic disease. Murphy et al found that in patients in metabolic ward conditions who were given a constant diet, platelet survival was shorter and turnover greater when the subjects were permitted to smoke than when smoking was restricted.

Evidence of several kinds has implicated lipids in the development of thrombosis. Epidemiologic data suggest that individuals on a high-fat diet have an increased susceptibility to both arterial and venous thrombosis.

Since atherosclerosis is not a feature of the latter condition, the implications are that diet influences the mechanisms of thrombosis itself. Laboratory studies, particularly those of Connor and his colleagues, have shown that long-chain saturated fatty acids can both enhance blood coagulation and cause platelet aggregation. Renaud and associates have observed that rats maintained on a diet rich in butter are more susceptible to endotoxin-induced thrombosis than control rats on a diet rich in corn oil. In their experiments, the enhancement of thrombosis was associated with an increased sensitivity of the platelets to thrombin. In a study of swine maintained for a year on a high-fat diet rich in egg yolk, more mural thrombus formed in extracorporeal shunts than in shunts connected to animals maintained on a low-fat diet. In man it has been found that subjects given a diet rich in egg yolk and butter fat have a shorter platelet survival and greater platelet turnover than subjects maintained on a low-fat diet or a diet rich in corn oil. Cessation of cigarette smoking and adoption of a low-fat diet might, therefore, reduce the incidence of arterial thrombosis and its complications (see Chapter 20, "The Primary Prevention of Coronary Heart Disease," by Stamler).

It is acknowledged that use of anticoagulant drugs such as dicumarol has had little effect on overall morbidity or mortality from complications of coronary artery disease. Actually this is quite compatible with what we know about arterial thrombus formation and what we know about the relationship among thromboembolism, myocardial ischemia, and infarction. Since coagulation processes are not of primary importance in arterial thrombus formation, anticoagulant therapy should not be expected to provide a complete solution; rather logic suggests that drugs primarily affecting platelet function would be more effective in controlling the thromboembolic component of myocardial ischemia and infarction. This is the approach that is currently being considered by a number of investigators.

Interest in this possibility stems from clinical observations made several years ago in patients being treated with sulfinpyrazone (originally introduced as a uricosuric agent). Tests of platelet function showed a marked decrease in platelet adhesiveness and an increased platelet survival time. This suggested that the drug was affecting platelet function; subsequent in vitro studies showed that two pyrazole compounds – sulfinpyrazone and phenylbutazone – markedly inhibited platelet response to surface stimuli, including collagen, antigen-antibody complexes, or gamma globulin–coated latex. It has since been learned that a variety of compounds can block platelet aggregation and/or inhibit release of platelet constituents. In vitro, prostaglandin E_1 has proven the most potent inhibitor of platelet aggregation; other active inhibitors include some of the pyrimido-pyrimidine compounds such as dipyridamole, the methylxanthines, chloroquine, cyproheptadine, antihistamines, and several adenine compounds including 2-chloroadenosine and 2-methylthio-A M P. In vivo, some of these would be of little practical value since, although they inhibit platelet aggregation, they have side effects such as vasodilation. However, several groups of agents – nonsteroidal anti-inflammatory and related drugs (such as phenylbutazone, acetylsalicylic acid, and sulfinpyrazone), dipyridamole, and chloroquine – can be given orally in doses that alter platelet function in man without causing major side effects.

There are at least four aspects of platelet function that could be modified to inhibit the response of blood to injury. These include 1) the adherence of platelets to constituents of the vessel wall such as collagen, basement membrane, and the microfibrils, 2) the platelet release reaction that is caused by some of these surface stimuli and by other agents such as thrombin or antigen-antibody complexes, 3) the adherence of platelets to each other owing to the effects of A D P, and 4) the accelerating effect of platelets on the reactions of the blood coagulation sequence and the stabilization by fibrin of the initial mass of aggregated platelets.

Dipyridamole has been shown to inhibit A D P-induced platelet aggregation and the platelet release reaction. Its precise mode of action is not fully understood, but it does inhibit glucose metabolism by platelets and also inhibits the platelet phosphodiesterase, leading to an increase in platelet cyclic A M P levels. Chloroquine is known to inhibit A D P-induced platelet aggregation and the platelet release reaction, but it has not yet been studied in terms of its effect on platelet metabolism, cyclic A M P, or other aspects of platelet function. The nonsteroidal anti-inflammatory drugs do not inhibit primary A D P-induced platelet aggregation, but they do inhibit the release reaction caused by surface stimuli.

However, these drugs are poor inhibitors of the thrombin-induced release reaction. They inhibit the adherence of platelets to surfaces and this may be a partial explanation of the mechanism through which they inhibit the release reaction induced by surface stimuli. It is of interest, in respect to collagen, that aspirin has been shown to inhibit the glucosyl transferase on the surface of the platelet, which may be involved in the interaction of platelets with collagen. Although in very high doses drugs such as aspirin inhibit glucose utilization by platelets, the lower doses, which inhibit the platelet release reaction induced by collagen, do not inhibit glucose uptake. There is no evidence that these drugs achieve their effect by increasing platelet cyclic A M P levels. If they did produce their effect by inhibiting glucose utilization or increasing platelet cyclic A M P levels, one would expect them to inhibit A D P-induced platelet aggregation, but they do not, in fact, do so.

Although there is no conclusive evidence that any of these drugs are useful in the management of arterial thrombosis, there is suggestive evidence that they may influence some aspects of the thrombotic process in man. Dipyridamole has received fairly extensive study, but the results are conflicting. One study showed that dipyridamole had no effect on the subsequent fate of patients who had had a myocardial infarct; a second study showed that it did not affect the incidence of clinically detectable deep-vein thrombosis; and in a third study dipyridamole was not found to influence venous thromboembolism in patients subjected to hip surgery. However, when administered in combination with an oral anticoagulant, this drug has been reported to reduce the incidence of thromboembolic complications. Kincaid-Smith reported that dipyridamole with an anticoagulant prevents not only thrombosis in vessels in acute rejection but also the progressive narrowing of vessels that is characteristic of chronic rejection in cadaveric renal allografts. Harken observed, using Cr^{51}-labeled platelets, that platelet survival is shorter and platelet turnover increased in patients with prosthetic heart valves. Administration of dipyridamole to these patients (some of whom were also receiving anticoagulants) restored platelet survival and turnover values towards normal, although there was no detectable effect on A D P- or collagen-induced platelet aggregation. It has been observed that administration of dipyridamole, in combination with an oral anticoagulant, to patients with prosthetic heart valves reduced the

Duration of Feeding	Mean Values				
	Cholesterol	Clotting Time	Amount of Liver Infarcted	Incidence of Thrombosis	Thrombin-Induced Platelet Aggregation
Weeks	mg/100 ml	In Seconds	gm/100 ml	% of Animals Affected	Units
5	589	163	0	0	0.6
7	461	143	1.4	23	1.6
10	423	134	10.0	78	8.3

Possible link between saturated fats and thrombosis was suggested by experiments of Renaud and coworkers in which rats fed a butter-rich diet became susceptible to endotoxin-induced platelet thrombosis (but not when unsaturated fats were substituted). Effect was attributed to an increased sensitivity of platelets to thrombin.

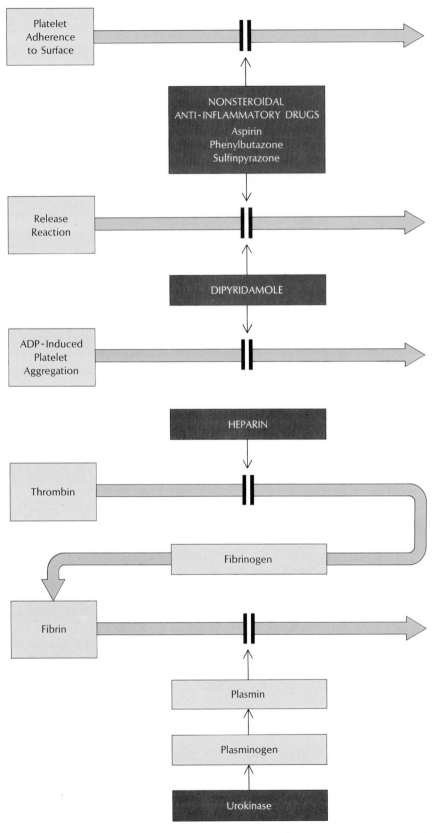

incidence of thromboembolic complications but did not have any effect on mortality.

Chloroquine has been found to reduce significantly the incidence of venous thrombosis and pulmonary embolism in patients undergoing major surgery.

Sulfinpyrazone, an analog of phenylbutazone, has been found by Weily and Genton to prolong platelet survival and decrease platelet turnover in patients with prosthetic heart valves. Evans has found that sulfinpyrazone causes a significant reduction in the frequency of episodes in patients suffering from intermittent attacks of cerebral ischemia. Aspirin inhibits the reaction of platelets with collagen and prolongs the bleeding time in man. Studies of the effect of aspirin on venous thrombosis are in conflict. For example, O'Brien found no effect of aspirin on the accumulation of I^{125}-fibrinogen in leg veins in postoperative patients. On the other hand, Salzman observed that 600 mg of aspirin given twice daily was as effective as warfarin in preventing venous thromboembolism in patients who had undergone hip surgery. Recently it has been reported that aspirin causes a marked reduction in the frequency of intermittent transient attacks of retinal ischemia; in this study, dipyridamole had no effect. Although the nonsteroidal anti-inflammatory drugs are potentially attractive as agents to modify at least one aspect of platelet function that contributes to the formation and growth of thrombi (that is, the release reaction induced by surfaces), their value in the management of thromboembolism is at present uncertain.

Anticoagulant drugs such as dicumarol and heparin have been used fairly extensively in attempts to prevent the occurrence of coronary artery thrombosis in individuals at risk of developing myocardial infarction or in those who have had a myocardial infarct. Theoretically, one would expect that these drugs would modify the process of thrombosis to some extent. In particular, heparin, because of its effect on thrombin, should influence the formation of a platelet mass. There is no conclusive evidence, however, that these drugs significantly influence the course of coronary artery disease. However, dicumarol was

Evidence for a primary role of platelets in arterial thrombus formation has focused interest on agents capable of modifying platelet function, e.g., by decreasing platelet aggregation and inhibiting release of constituents (upper section of diagram). In contrast, since clotting processes appear only secondarily involved, control of the thromboembolic component of myocardial ischemia and infarction probably cannot be expected solely with use of agents interfering with thrombin or fibrin formation (lower section).

found to reduce the extent of arterial thrombosis, which may be further evidence that occlusive thrombosis is not of major importance in myocardial ischemia and infarction.

It is also possible that a drug that inhibited platelet function so as to prevent thrombosis would so alter the response of the blood to injury that hemorrhagic complications would occur. If this were the case, then the prevention of thromboembolism in the arterial side of the circulation may require modification of the response of the endothelium to injury.

Platelets, Thrombosis, and Atherosclerosis

There is one concrete piece of evidence in relation to myocardial ischemia and infarction that seems to have stood the test of time. That is, extensive atherosclerosis of the coronary arteries or stenotic lesions are found in almost all patients who die as a result of myocardial infarction.

There seems little doubt that mural thrombi forming on the surface of arteries can become organized and produce intimal thickening. The type of intimal thickening can range from a fibrous plaque to one that contains foam cells, connective tissue, and deposits of cholesterol. In 1947, Duguid showed that in advanced atherosclerosis the organization of mural thrombi is a significant factor contributing to the development of atherosclerotic plaques and stenotic lesions. An area of vessel disease and stenosis is an excellent site for the formation of thrombi and lesions, as these sites gradually increase in size by repeated episodes of mural thrombosis. Eventually an occlusive thrombus may develop. Alternatively, mural thrombi may fragment and shower the microcirculation with platelet-fibrin emboli. Such an event could produce sudden cardiac death because of the development of ventricular fibrillation.

From what we know about the mechanism of thrombus formation in arteries, it is clear that the platelet must play a key role in the development of such thrombi. Recognition of the fact that the initial platelet-rich thrombus rapidly undergoes transformation to a fibrin mass, has made it possible to understand why one does not characteristically find platelets in

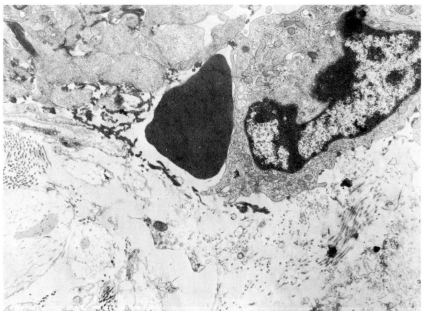

Electron micrographs show contrast between normal vessel wall (EM at top, original x2,600) and vessel wall at site of early atherosclerosis (lower EM, x5,600). At the lesion, platelets, fibrin, a white blood cell, and a red blood cell have accumulated. The wall is edematous, indicating increased permeability to plasma.

atherosclerotic lesions. Wolfe and Carstairs have demonstrated that many advanced atherosclerotic lesions contain material that has antigenic properties similar to those of platelets, and these investigators suggested that there may be residual platelet material in some of these lesions. This is further support for the hypothesis that mural thrombi that become organized contribute to the development of the atherosclerotic lesions.

The relationship between platelets

and thrombosis and the development of early atherosclerosis is less clearly defined. A characteristic of early vessel wall changes in atherosclerosis is the focal nature of lipid accumulation and intimal thickening. Sites of early vessel change show increased permeability to plasma proteins, and in these regions the intima is usually loosened and appears edematous. Examination of these sites has shown that there is injury and, in some cases, loss of the endothelium. Formed elements, chief-

Accumulation of blood elements at site of early atherosclerotic lesions can be demonstrated on the endothelial surface. En face *preparation was obtained from aorta of a pig.*

ly platelets and the white blood cells, are found at these injury sites. A critical question is whether the injury is caused by mechanical factors or by the effects of the formed elements.

Experiments with models of different vessel configurations have shown that the sites of maximum interaction of the formed elements of blood with the wall are in regions of disturbed flow that correspond to some extent to sites of the early lesions of atherosclerosis. Since both the platelet and the leukocyte, when stimulated, release factors that can cause increased vessel permeability, it is possible that the formed elements reacting with each other and with the vessel wall in areas of disturbed flow might contribute to the vessel injury. Studies have shown a correlation between the degree of injury to the vessel wall, as measured by intimal edema, and the

accumulation of platelets and leukocytes. There is a considerable amount of experimental evidence that platelets can cause vessel injury. In the studies that were carried out with ADP infusions it was not uncommon to find the endothelium altered or lost at the site where the thrombus was close to the vessel wall. Sometimes the internal elastic lamina was lost. Often there was intensive polymorphonuclear leukocyte accumulation at the vessel wall site in contact with the platelet aggregate. In one study in rabbits, a vascular reaction of this type occurred in 28% of the animals given the ADP infusion compared with 3% of the animals in which the ADP did not cause aggregation. More recently, Moore and his colleagues demonstrated that the platelet emboli arising from mural thrombi in the aorta and passing into the renal circulation cause injury to the renal arteries. This injury includes alteration or loss of the endothelium, damage to the internal elastic lamina, and changes in the smooth muscle cells. One of the interesting degenerative changes in the smooth muscle cells was the development of lipid droplets within them. All of this occurred in situations in which the animals were not on lipid-rich diets and did not have increased serum-lipid levels.

A number of other theories suggest that the localization of lesions at these sites is related to blood flow and is not dependent upon the formed elements of the blood. Fry has suggested that high rates of shear cause loss of the endothelium, giving rise to increased permeability. Clearly, increased permeability of the vessel wall will lead to increased plasma protein accumulation and, if the serum lipids are elevated, increased lipoprotein in the wall. Caro has proposed that the accumulation of lipoprotein in the wall is due to the effect of disturbed blood flow on the ingress and egress of lipids. It is clear that the diffusion of material must be important, but whether it is a primary factor in causing the lesions, or secondary and related to other mechanisms causing injury, is at present unknown.

All this evidence suggests that the platelets and thrombosis do play some part in the development of coronary atherosclerosis as well as the complications of atherosclerosis.

Material Infused	Number of Pigs		
	With Vascular Lesions	Without Vascular Lesions	Total
ADP	7 (37%)	12	19
AMP	1 (6%)	15	16
Double ADP	0	4	4

Animal experiments indicate that the presence of transient platelet aggregates in flowing blood may be an important factor in initiating vessel wall damage and mural thrombus formation; for example, vascular lesions were produced in a significant proportion of pigs following intracoronary ADP infusion to induce platelet aggregation. In contrast, infusion of AMP (which does not cause platelet aggregation) or double ADP (ADP infusion remote from coronary circulation to make platelets refractory to ADP, followed by infusion of ADP into the coronaries) caused little or no vascular injury.

18

Coronary Artery Pathology in Fatal Ischemic Heart Disease

WILLIAM C. ROBERTS

National Heart and Lung Institute

Nearly 60 years ago James Herrick recorded several observations in reference to heart disease that were to influence medical thinking for many years to follow. One was that acute obstruction of a major coronary artery, or even of a main trunk, was not necessarily lethal. It has since been amply documented that while "acute coronary occlusion" is often fatal it is not invariably so, as Herrick correctly observed. He drew a further inference from his work that also gained general acceptance: that the usual cause of coronary arterial occlusion is thrombus.

Indeed, after Herrick, the terms "coronary thrombosis" and "coronary occlusion" came into wide usage as synonyms to describe events leading to myocardial necrosis. Among many clinicians and pathologists alike the belief persists to this day that without thrombotic occlusion of a major coronary artery, acute myocardial infarction is unlikely to occur. Moreover, coronary arterial thrombosis is considered a prerequisite for myocardial necrosis.

It is not difficult to see why this assumption has taken so firm a hold. Clinically, acute myocardial infarction is often a dramatic event. A patient apparently well to that point is suddenly in cardiovascular collapse; death may come within minutes and often does. Even with a history of cardiac disease there is likely to be an abrupt change in the patient's status at onset of the fatal attack. The pathologist, pressed for an explanation, looks for some new finding in the coronary arteries to account for the acute clinical event. Given the long association of thrombotic occlusion and infarction, both he and the clinician expect to find a fresh arterial thrombus; if none is there, the implication may be that it was somehow missed. A thrombus is found often enough to perpetuate the view that acute myocardial infarction usually results from thrombotic occlusion of a coronary artery.

Careful examination of the facts, however, leads one to question seriously whether there is a causal relationship; rather, the evidence would suggest that arterial thrombi may occur as consequences of acute myocardial infarction and not the other way around.

Reports over the years have indicated a wide range of frequency of coronary arterial thrombi in patients dying of acute myocardial infarction – from as low as 21% in some studies to as high as 100% in others. This discrepancy in itself might argue against a causal role, although other factors, such as differences in techniques of examining coronary arteries, could explain some of it.

Strict definition of terms is a requirement for collecting meaningful frequency data. It must also be taken into account that gross inspection of coronary arteries is not sufficient for assessing their status. Several distinguishing features of thrombi must be confirmed histologically: A true thrombus is adherent at some point along its length (more often distally than proximally) to the luminal surface of the artery; it is composed of platelets or fibrin or both, and usually also of erythrocytes and leukocytes. Actually the composition of a thrombus may differ substantially along its length (usually about 1 cm): Distally it is more likely to consist chiefly of platelets or fibrin or both (white thrombus), whereas proximally it is more often composed chiefly of erythrocytes, with lesser quantities of fibrin, platelets, and leukocytes (red thrombus). Early in their formation, however, thrombi are likely to be composed almost entirely of platelets.

Too often when coronary arteries are sectioned at necropsy, an arterial thrombus is all that is looked for; if something red is spotted, it is usually assumed to be a thrombus. But hemorrhage into an old atherosclerotic plaque may closely resemble a thrombus grossly, as may postmortem clot, although close inspection would show

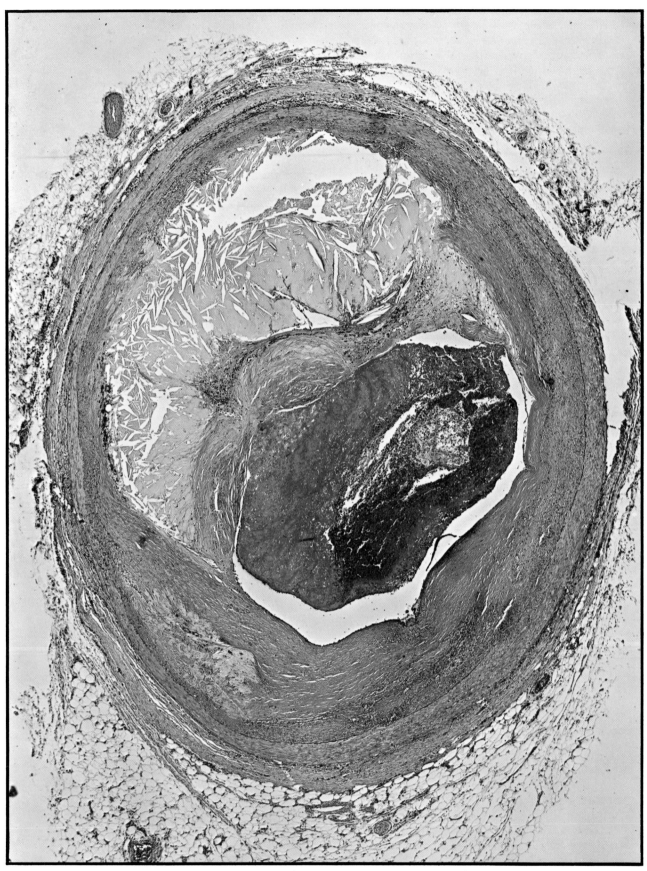

An occlusive thrombus is superimposed on old plaque in the left circumflex artery of a 55-year-old woman who died five days after the onset of acute myocardial infarction. She had had severe congestive cardiac failure. The white space between the thrombus and the plaque represents a shrinkage artifact (Movat stain, original magnification x22, photographic enlargement 100%).

that the latter is nonadherent and composed chiefly of erythrocytes. Histologic examination must be done, therefore, to distinguish a true thrombus from a postmortem clot or from hemorrhage into an old plaque.

A coronary arterial thrombus may not necessarily totally occlude the vessel containing it; this must be kept in mind in considering whether thrombus formation is likely to be causally related to acute myocardial necrosis. When the terms "occlusion" and "thrombosis" are used interchangeably, as they often are, it is overlooked that the occlusion may be only partial rather than complete and that a coronary artery may be occluded by material other than that which forms a thrombus. In the 74 patients with fatal transmural infarction studied personally, about 80% of the thrombi found were totally occlusive; the re-

mainder were either partially occlusive or mural thrombi. Young thrombi composed purely of platelets are usually small and nonocclusive.

Nonocclusive thrombi probably have little functional significance. Indeed, as will become evident, even occlusive thrombi under some circumstances may be of little functional significance. Thus, it is not enough to know whether or not a coronary artery contains a thrombus; knowledge of whether it is totally or only partially occlusive and the degree of luminal narrowing already present as the result of old atherosclerotic plaques is required before the significance of the thrombus can be judged.

In clarifying the relationship of thrombosis to myocardial necrosis, it is important to consider the type of infarction present. Reported variations in frequency of arterial thrombi

in fatal acute myocardial infarction may largely reflect the patient group studied: Frequency of death differs sharply in transmural infarction involving virtually the entire thickness of the myocardial wall, as compared with frequency in subendocardial infarction, with necrosis limited to the inner half of the myocardial wall. There is a third possibility to take into account as well: sudden death, i.e., death within six hours – usually only minutes – after onset of symptoms of myocardial ischemia, occurs before subendocardial or transmural necrosis has had a chance to evolve.

It has been recognized for some time that coronary arterial thrombi are rarely present at necropsy in sudden death cases, whether or not there was a prior history of heart disease; coronary thrombosis is also uncommon in patients with subendocardial infarction. Thrombosis has, however, been closely associated with acute transmural infarction; observations implicating thrombosis in the etiology of acute myocardial infarction have been based chiefly on cases of the latter.

In examining major coronary arteries of patients who died of acute myocardial infarction, we were unable to find either gross or histologic evidence of arterial thrombosis in many patients in whom thrombus might have been expected. Therefore, coronary arteries were examined systematically in consecutive patients with fatal acute myocardial infarction. In each, at least three sections of left ventricular wall were obtained for histologic study. Before the ventricles were opened, the major extramural coronary arteries (left main, left anterior descending, left circumflex, and right) were excised intact. Each major vessel was extended to full length and sectioned transversely in 5 mm segments. A key step in the procedure was decalcification of the vessels – both before and after sectioning – to avoid crushing and distortion of the vessel by cutting. This was essential for accurate measurement of the degree of luminal narrowing by old atherosclerotic plaques.

Another important step in the procedure was to imbed the arteries in paraffin at precise right angles so that they could be cut directly across in segments of uniform size. For identification of arterial thrombi two histo-

Frequency of Coronary Thrombosis in Acute Myocardial Infarction

	Author	Year	Number of Patients	Number (%) with Coronary Thrombosis
1a	Herrick	1912	1	1 (100)
1b	Herrick	1919	3	3 (100)
2	Nathanson	1925	113	24 (21)
3	Davenport	1928	50	30 (60)
4	Parkinson and Bedford	1928	51	33 (64)
5	Levine	1929	46	23 (50)
6	Lisa and Ring	1932	32	13 (41)
7	Saphir et al	1935	34	18 (53)
8	Friedberg and Horn	1939	153	119 (78)
9	Mallory et al.	1939	100	70 (70)
10	Blumgart et al	1940	16	14 (88)
11	Foord	1948	315	274 (87)
12	Yater et al.	1948	68	34 (50)
13	Miller et al	1951	143	92 (64)
14	Branwood and Montgomery	1956	61	13 (21)
15	Spain and Bradess	1960	200	109 (55)
16	Ehrlich and Shinohara	1964	130	57 (44)
17	Mitchell and Schwartz	1965	26	21 (81)
18	Baroldi	1965	449	211 (47)
19	Meadows	1965	100	30 (30)
20	Kurland et al	1965	127	70 (55)
21	Harland and Holburn	1966	53	48 (91)
22	Chapman	1968	292	278 (95)
23	Kagan et al	1968	176	87 (49)
24	Spain and Bradess	1970	391	115 (29)
25	Walston et al	1970	37	19 (51)
26	Bouch and Montgomery	1970	100	66 (66)
27	Page et al	1971	36	30 (83)
28	Roberts and Buja	1972	107	42 (39)
	Totals		3410	1944 (57)

(Documentation of above items is presented on page 395.)

logic sections were prepared from each 5 mm segment (one stained by hematoxylin and eosin, and the second by Movat's method). By examining the many sections in each patient, it seemed unlikely that arterial thrombi might be present but remain undetected. Each section was examined by light microscopy and the maximal degree of luminal narrowing was recorded, often by planimetry.

If a thrombus was found, its composition was noted (an unstained section of thrombus was treated with phosphotungstic-acid hematoxylin to aid in quantifying the several components). The condition of the coronary artery at the site of thrombus formation was carefully observed, to determine in particular whether the lumen there or close by was already narrowed, and to what degree, by old atherosclerotic plaques. The presence of hemorrhage into plaques was recorded as well, since this too has been implicated in precipitating acute infarction.

Of 107 patients investigated in this manner, 74 had acute transmural infarcts, nine had acute infarcts limited to the subendocardium, and 24 patients died suddenly before myocardial necrosis was detectable by histologic examination. (In these studies sudden death was defined as death occurring within six hours following onset of acute symptoms.) It is assumed that necrosis would have developed in these patients also if they

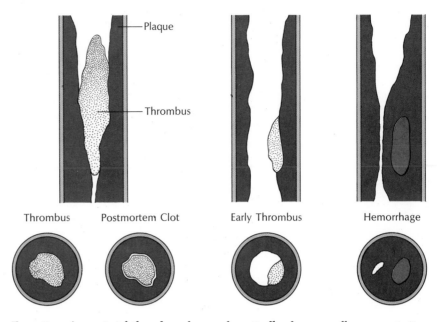

Formation of an arterial thrombus, shown schematically above, usually occurs at sites of luminal narrowing by atherosclerotic plaques; platelets, and later platelets and fibrin, are chief thrombus components, whereas a hemorrhage into an old plaque or postmortem clot is composed chiefly of erythrocytes. Thrombus and postmortem clot also differ in the adherence of the former to luminal surface.

had lived longer; perhaps early signs of necrosis before death would be more evident with improved techniques for recognizing them.

An association between thrombosis and transmural infarction, although by no means a consistent one, was clearly confirmed, as was the relative absence of arterial thrombi in the other two groups. Specifically, only two of the 24 sudden death cases had coronary thrombi, and none of the

nine cases of subendocardial infarction had coronary thrombi. In contrast, thrombi were present in more than half (40 of 74) of the cases of fatal transmural infarction. (As indicated earlier, the thrombi were totally occlusive in most but not all of these cases).

Hemorrhage into atherosclerotic plaques proved fairly common, occurring in 24% of the 107 cases studied. These seemed to be of little functional

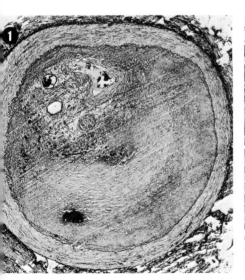
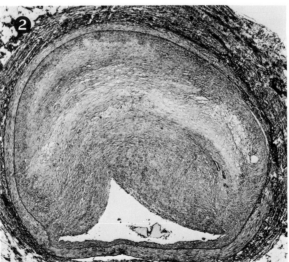

Atherosclerotic plaques accounted for virtually all narrowing of extramural vessels in a 26-year-old female victim of coronary disease; sections of the right (1), the left circumflex (2), and the left anterior descending (3) coronary arteries are shown at the sites of their maximal narrowing. Each of the photomicrographs was taken at the same magnification.

 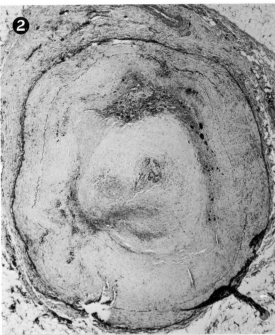 

Sectioning of right coronary artery of 52-year-old woman revealed a partially occluding thrombus (1) and a totally occluding atherosclerotic plaque (2) just distal to it. As suggested schematically (right) and shown histologically (3) presence of an arterial thrombus may have little functional significance in acute myocardial infarction if diffuse atherosclerotic plaquing has already narrowed

significance in terms of initiating infarction. In only one of the 26 patients with hemorrhage into an atherosclerotic plaque was the arterial lumen compromised by the extravasated blood. Such hemorrhages appear to form from either breaks in the fibrous capsule covering a plaque or from rupture of a small vascular channel within a plaque, although either of these mechanisms is difficult to prove in the individual patient. In some patients, hemorrhages into old plaques apparently keep occurring over lengthy periods. In any case, hemorrhage probably has little to do with the onset of acute myocardial infarction.

Our systematic examination of major coronary arteries made clear that "nothing new" appears in these vessels at the time of acute myocardial infarction in most patients stricken. The low frequency of arterial thrombosis in patients dying suddenly of coronary disease, and its presence in only about half of those with transmural myocardial necrosis, increased our belief that a causal relation to myocardial infarction was unlikely. Even in patients in whom fresh thrombi were present, it would be difficult to say whether they developed before or after the infarction.

It has been suggested that fresh coronary thrombi present before death may be undetected at necropsy because of postmortem lysis of thrombi due to excessive fibrinolysin production. Several observations tend to discount this hypothesis. If lysis of thrombi did occur, there should be evidence of the fact in the form of blood or blood products in the affected coronary arteries. This is rarely the case. Indeed, necropsies performed within 15 minutes of death from acute myocardial infarction have disclosed no evidence of lysed or partially lysed thrombi. It is also unlikely that postmortem lysis of thrombi would occur so selectively as to liquefy thrombi in patients with subendocardial but not in those with transmural myocardial necrosis. When the same investigators have checked for the appearance of thrombi in two widely separated studies, they have tended to find a similar incidence of thrombus formation on both occasions. This would be unlikely if lysis is a factor, since it would occur by chance.

Looked at another way, the absence of arterial thrombi in many patients with acute myocardial infarction may in part explain the lack of clear-cut benefit from anticoagulant therapy. The initial rationale given for use of anticoagulants in patients with coronary artery disease was a presumed causal relationship between thrombosis and infarction and the presumed ability of these drugs to reduce arterial thrombus formation or extension. Yet it is now known that the frequency of coronary arterial thrombosis in fatal acute myocardial infarction is similar in patients receiving and those not receiving anticoagulant therapy.

On several grounds, then, it is time to consider the alternative hypothesis in reference to coronary arterial thrombosis. Rather than being causally related to acute myocardial infarction, does coronary arterial thrombosis occur as a consequence of advancing myocardial necrosis?

When we analyzed our transmural infarction cases, a provocative finding emerged. Arterial thrombi appeared to develop only in certain patients dying of myocardial necrosis — those who experienced cardiogenic shock and/or congestive heart failure for a time before death. In the patient with uncomplicated acute transmural infarction — whose death was due not to pump failure but to a lethal arrhythmia — arterial thrombi were rarely present at necropsy.

Interestingly, similar findings were obtained in a study by Walston and coworkers on patients who died of

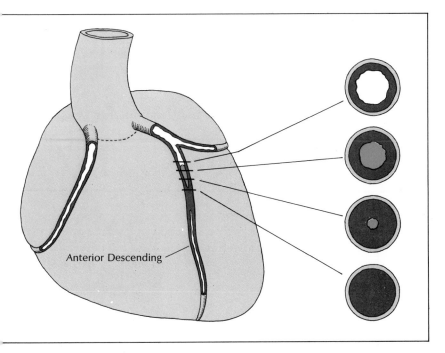

Anterior Descending

extramural arteries severely. The small thrombus present in the anterior descending artery (3) could have caused only minimal luminal narrowing. Patient was a 59-year-old woman who died six weeks following onset of myocardial infarction.

have since become increasingly convinced that this is the case). Other observations began to shed more light on conditions favoring the appearance of arterial thrombi in association with acute myocardial infarction. For example, thrombi were most often located at sites of luminal narrowing; frequently the degree of narrowing was greater than 75% at the distal attachment. It seemed possible, if still speculative, that thrombus formation at this location might be related to introduction of high-velocity gradients as luminal narrowing increases, since this tends to favor platelet aggregation.

One certainty was that examination of the entire coronary tree yielded an unexpected discovery about the condition of the coronary arteries in patients who died of myocardial infarction. Many believe the process of atherosclerosis underlying coronary heart disease is usually localized, with atherosclerotic plaquing often confined to one major vessel. Our studies showed unequivocally that the entire extramural coronary tree is likely to be affected. The degree of luminal narrowing differed in each particular coronary artery and in each patient studied, but there was some atherosclerotic plaquing on the intimal surface of nearly every millimeter of artery examined, not only within the major extramural arteries themselves but in the smaller extramural branches

acute myocardial infarction. The presence of antemortem arterial thrombi could be linked to the occurrence of the "power failure syndrome" – in essence an inability of the myocardium to maintain a level of cardiac output necessary for adequate organ perfusion. In the 37 cases studied, Walston et al found arterial thrombi at necropsy in 71% of patients who before

death had manifested the power failure syndrome and in only 15% of those who had not.

These findings, and ours along the same line, suggested that a markedly diminished cardiac output and the consequent slowdown in coronary blood flow might be required for arterial thrombus formation in association with acute myocardial infarction (we

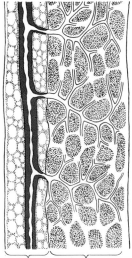

Epicardium   Myocardium

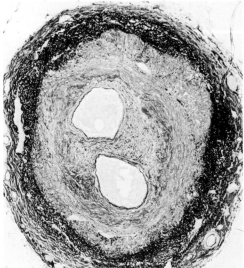

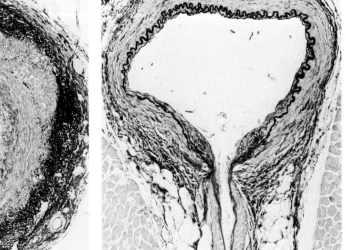

Extensive atherosclerosis usually seen in main extramural arteries and epicardial branches almost never extends into intramural coronary arteries (diagram). For example, in autopsy study of sud- *den death victim with known severe hypertension, severe luminal narrowing was found in left circumflex and other extramural arteries (center) but intramural arteries were essentially normal (right).*

197

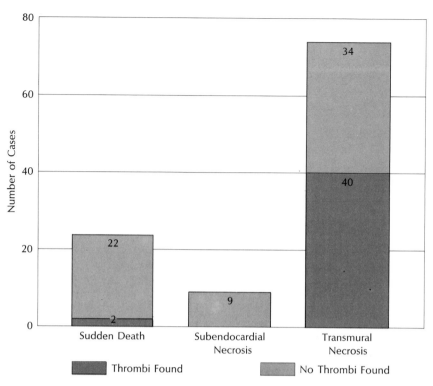

Confirmation of an association between thrombosis and transmural infarction was obtained in the study of 107 patients dying of acute myocardial infarction. Its relative absence in cases of subendocardial infarction or sudden death was also demonstrated.

as well. In all, several thousand histologic sections were examined and only four sections were free of old atherosclerotic plaques, excluding three patients with coronary arterial emboli.

We were aware that despite considerable atherosclerosis a coronary artery may still carry sufficient blood to the myocardium; in general, coronary flow is unlikely to be seriously reduced, with the patient in the basal state, until the original lumen is decreased by 75% or more. Thus our interest was in the degree of luminal narrowing produced by atherosclerotic plaquing.

Sites of maximal narrowing showed wide variation, but with examination of our 107 cases definable patterns emerged. For example, the lumen of the left main coronary artery was rarely stenosed by atherosclerotic plaques. On the other hand, the left anterior descending, left circumflex, and right coronary arteries were often narrowed 75% and more. The average number of these latter three vessels narrowed by more than 75% was 2.4 per patient in the group with transmural infarction, 2.3 in patients with subendocardial necrosis, and 2.4 in the sudden death patients. Vessel nar-

rowing by 90% or more was frequent.

It is significant that, from the point of entry to the myocardial wall of the heart, as well as distally, the artery is likely to appear entirely normal. It seems generally true that conditions involving the extramural coronary arteries do not involve the intramural coronary arteries; likewise, diseases affecting the intramural coronary arteries infrequently affect the extramural coronary arteries. Admittedly, there are dissenting opinions on this point; in our experience, however, this intramural-extramural difference does appear to hold. In the 107 patients studied, none had significant abnormalities of the intramural coronary arteries.

It would appear that the intramural coronary arteries are somehow protected from intimal proliferation and luminal narrowing by the contracting adjacent myocardium. Even in the presence of systemic hypertension, the intramural coronary arteries remain normal or virtually normal; perhaps this is because they are not exposed to systemic systolic pressures, since they are perfused mainly in ventricular diastole. The contracting myocardium may further lower intraluminal

pressure in these small vessels. It may seem puzzling that the intramural arteries remain free of significant coronary atherosclerosis, but there is no doubt that they do. A typical finding: Epicardial branches of major extramural arteries showing almost total luminal narrowing by atherosclerotic plaques were seen to be suddenly wide open as they penetrated the myocardium.

It cannot be assumed that any part of the extramural coronary arterial tree is entirely normal, but some sites are more predisposed to severe narrowing than are others. Typically, in our patients, maximal narrowing of the left anterior descending and left circumflex arteries was found to occur within 2 cm of the bifurcation of the left main coronary artery; in the right coronary artery, the distal third tended to show more luminal narrowing by old plaques than the proximal portion, but this was not always the case. It is worth noting that the main function of the right coronary artery is to supply the posterior wall of the left ventricle via its posterior descending branches; it begins perfusing the left ventricle only after traversing the right atrioventricular sulcus for about 12 cm. Thus, significant narrowing of the right coronary artery 11 cm from its aortic ostium may be as important functionally as similar narrowing much closer to its aortic ostium. In contrast, since the left coronary arterial tree begins supplying the left ventricle about 2 cm from its aortic origin, marked narrowing of the left anterior descending artery far downstream may be of little myocardial consequence if significant proximal narrowing is not present. Since arterial thrombi tended to develop at or proximal to a site of severe luminal narrowing, thrombi in the left anterior descending or left circumflex arteries were usually within 2 cm of the bifurcation of the left main. In the right coronary artery, they occurred more frequently in the distal and middle thirds than in the proximal third.

Almost always, if a thrombus was present in fatal acute myocardial infarction, it was located in the coronary artery that supplied the infarcted area. Thus, in infarction involving the anterior wall of the left ventricle, the

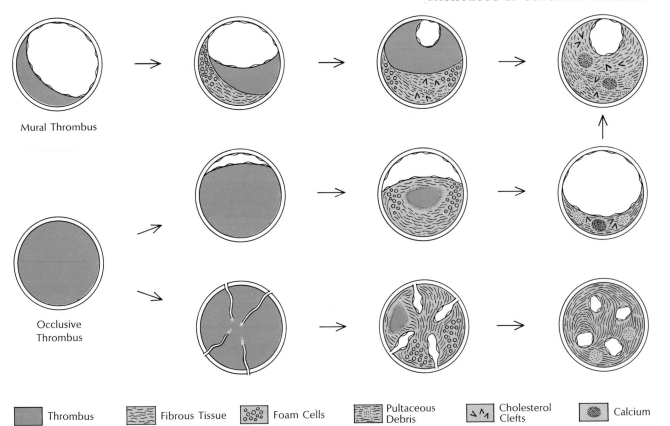

▮ Thrombus	▨ Fibrous Tissue	⊙ Foam Cells	▨ Pultaceous Debris	⌄⌃ Cholesterol Clefts	◉ Calcium

Thesis that both mural and occlusive thrombi may be incorporated into arterial intima as plaques is posed in diagram of postulated sequence of events in formation of both thrombus types. Organization of mural thrombi, beginning with ingrowth of over-

lying endothelial cells and connective tissue, leads to formation of atherosclerotic-type lesions. An occlusive thrombus may organize similarly; alternatively, capillaries growing into its base may dilate as thrombus retracts, resulting in plaque with recanalized channels.

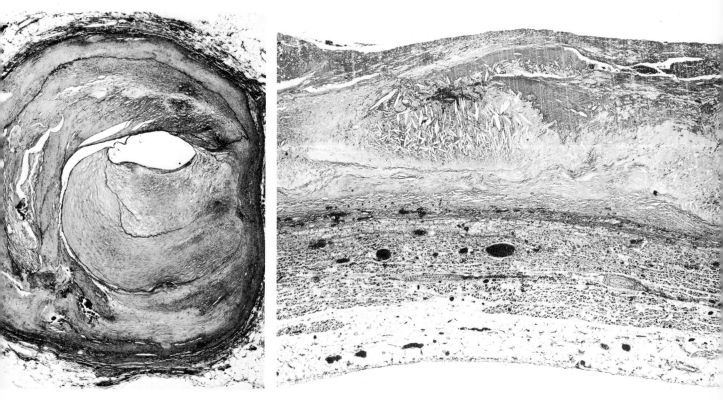

Section of right coronary artery of 65-year-old man (left) shows extensive atherosclerotic plaquing and almost total luminal narrowing. Demarcation lines suggest plaques are of varying ages.

Right: Cholesterol clefts, pultaceous debris, and calcific deposits – key components of arterial atherosclerotic plaques – were all present in left atrial thrombus in patient with mitral stenosis.

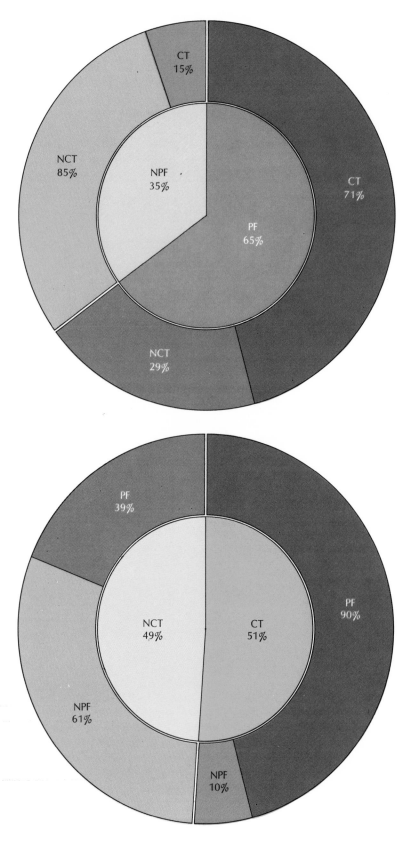

PF = Power Failure   CT = Coronary Thrombus
NPF = No Power Failure   NCT = No Coronary Thrombus

In an analysis by Walston and coworkers, coronary thrombus formation proved clearly related to the occurrence of power failure, as shown in upper diagram; among cases with thrombosis, fully 90% were associated with power failure (lower diagram). Relationship suggests a severely diminished cardiac output may be needed for thrombus formation.

anterior descending coronary artery was the site of thrombus formation, while posterior wall infarction was associated with thrombosis of the right or left circumflex coronary artery.

It is noteworthy that in previous studies relating coronary arterial thrombosis to acute myocardial infarction, the condition of the artery distal to the thrombus has not been considered. The focus of attention has been on the coronary arterial segment containing the thrombus; a number of investigators have carefully examined this portion of the vessel by serial sectioning **techniques**. Usually the inquiry has stopped there, implying that finding a fresh arterial thrombus more or less establishes its functional significance.

But if a coronary artery is already severely narrowed distally – and in nearly all the patients we studied in whom thrombi were found the degree of luminal narrowing by old atherosclerotic plaques *at* or *distal* to the thrombus was greater than 75% – the significance of a proximal thrombus must be questioned. That distal narrowing was found in so many of the **patients we studied was an important** influence moving us to consider thrombus formation more likely the result than the cause of acute infarction. The same inference has been drawn by others from comparisons of the histologic ages of coronary thrombi and of acute myocardial infarcts. Since it is difficult to judge the age of a coronary thrombus histologically, this approach is not reliable.

Nonetheless, several observations, some already alluded to, strongly suggest that fresh coronary thrombi present at death develop only after the myocardial necrotic process is already under way. For example, there is the fact that coronary thrombi do not occur in all patients with acute myocardial infarction. The clinical events in fatal cases may hold the explanation. When Spain and Bradess examined the clinical courses in some 400 fatal cases, they found that in general the longer the interval between onset of symptoms and death, the greater the likelihood of coronary arterial thrombus formation. Thus the incidence of thrombi increased from 17% among patients surviving less than an hour to 36% in patients surviving one to eight hours, and 54% in patients who survived 24 hours or more before death. This finding would indicate that a certain but variable period of survival must elapse after onset of myocardial necrosis in order for an arterial thrombus to form, although it does not identify the factors that influence thrombus formation.

Whether severely decreased coronary flow leads directly to formation of arterial thrombi remains to be established; from the evidence it does seem a possibility worth exploring further. If valid, the slow-flow hypothesis would have to account for occurrence of arterial thrombi at sites of, and proximal to, severe stenoses caused by old atherosclerotic plaques. Sometimes thrombi can be seen covering cracks in plaques and it has been suggested by some that rupture of the innermost layer of plaque may precipitate arterial thrombosis. The evidence given is that rupture occurs particularly in fibrous tissue covering deposits of pultaceous debris; this leads to discharge of necrotic material into the arterial lumen or to bleeding into plaques. The abrupt change in volume of the plaque caused by discharge of plaque material into the lumen or by hemorrhage into the plaque via the rupture causes abnormalities in flow patterns favoring platelet thrombosis, it is further suggested.

However, the postulated relationship between rupture of necrotic plaques and formation of coronary arterial thrombi has yet to be confirmed. Observing cracks in plaques requires serial sectioning techniques, and even when these are done interpretation may be difficult. In our studies, most thrombi formed over plaques with intact surfaces. It should be borne in mind too that rupture of a plaque may sometimes result from cutting an artery and fixing it without prior support of its wall. For example, when Fulton injected coronary arteries with a solid supporting medium before sectioning, no plaque ulceration or cracking was observed in the 25 cases of coronary heart disease (14 of acute myocardial infarction) that were studied.

Even with our limited understanding of conditions favoring formation of arterial thrombi, it is now clear that we must look elsewhere for the events that precipitate myocardial necrosis. But if thrombus formation is not the

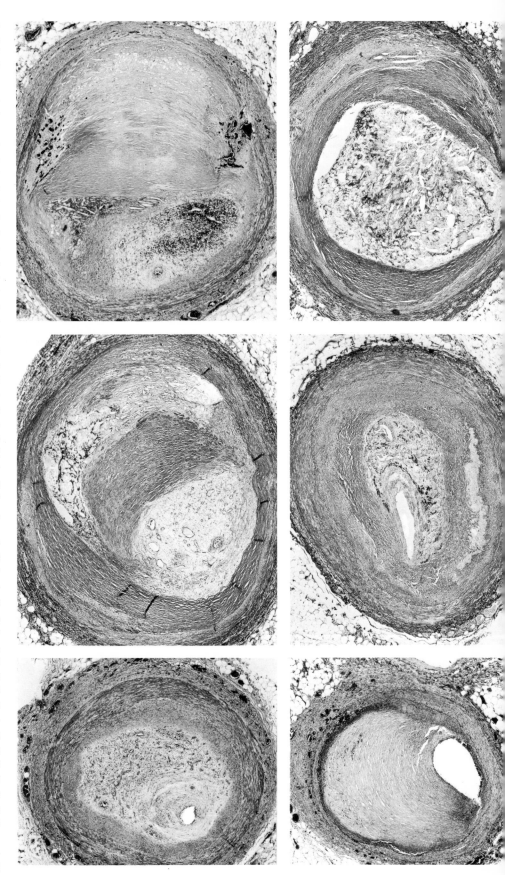

These six sections were taken from a 2 cm segment of the posterior descending artery of a 49-year-old man who died suddenly. A year earlier, this patient had suffered an acute posterior wall infarction. Atherosclerotic plaques apparent in all sections vary greatly in composition. Hemorrhage has occurred into several plaques.

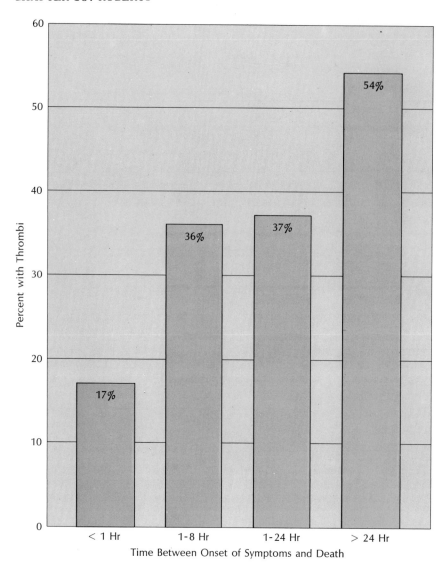

Thrombus formation proved closely related to survival time in close to 400 fatal infarc-tion cases studied by Spain and Bradess, thus frequency of thrombi increased from 17% in patients who survived less than an hour to 54% in those who lived 24 hours or more.

critical factor, what is? We know that fatal acute myocardial infarction is as-sociated with diffuse coronary artery disease that presumably has been pro-gressing for some time prior to the acute episode. Against this setting, is it possible that even minor disturb-ances in coronary artery perfusion could shift the balance from adequate to inadequate flow, producing ischemia and necrosis in myocardium? Perhaps one additional pin on the elephant's back, so to speak, is all that is re-quired to tip the scales.

Another question: Is it possible that, although thrombosis appears not to be a precipitating cause of acute infarc-tion, it figures in the development of coronary atherosclerosis? This possibility would return coronary

thrombosis very much to the center of the stage, though in a very different role than that of curtain ringer. De-spite the apparent paradox, the most logical explanation of atherosclerotic plaquing does seem to be the laying down and organization of mural thrombi.

As is known, atherosclerotic lesions may be primarily *fatty* (yellow), *fib-rous*, or *complicated*. The last are com-posed of cholesterol clefts, pultaceous debris, calcific deposits, and few, if any, foam cells. The atherosclerotic plaques in coronary arteries in fatal acute myocardial infarction are chiefly of the complicated type. Atheroscler-otic plaques are never seen in the intramural coronary arteries. The pos-sibility that formation and organi-

zation of mural thrombi contribute significantly to development of these complicated atherosclerotic plaques is supported, for one, by the presence of fibrin and platelets, both thrombus constituents, in the plaques. This has been demonstrated by immunofluores-cent techniques; fibrin has also been shown both histologically and by elec-tron microscopy. To strengthen the re-lationship, there is the finding of atherosclerotic-type lesions (contain-ing cholesterol clefts, foam cells, pul-taceous debris, and calcific deposits) in organized thrombi, such as those found in the left atrium in mitral stenosis.

The possibility that atherosclerotic plaques may be thrombus derived has been discounted in part because histo-logic evidence is often obscured. As a thrombus becomes covered by a new endothelium, the underlying endothel-ium is replaced by connective tissue from the intima and the original line of demarcation disappears.

Recent findings suggest that organi-zation of thrombi occurs by ingrowth of overlying endothelial cells and con-nective tissue; modified smooth muscle cells capable of synthesizing collagen, elastin, and probably mucopolysac-charides – all present in connective tissue of arterial intima – then invade the bases of attached thrombi. Al-though small mural thrombi usually organize by an avascular process, larger mural thrombi become vascu-larized; capillaries from the new over-lying endothelium provide a direct blood supply from the lumen and from vasa vasorum penetrating thrombi at their bases. With an increased blood supply, enhanced fibrinolysis may con-tribute to the resolution of the throm-bus as it becomes organized. The capillaries may later atrophy or be-come a source of hemorrhage into plaques.

It appears that both occlusive and nonocclusive (mural) thrombi may be incorporated into the arterial intima as atherosclerotic plaques. However, oc-clusive thrombi that retract before en-dothelialization is complete may ap-pear later as mural or nonocclusive plaques.

The source of lipids in atheroscler-otic plaques is of course a matter of great interest. Among other findings, the fact that fatty degeneration can occur in any thrombus suggests that thrombus components, such as platelets and erythrocytes, may contribute to lipid accumulation. The erythrocyte component of thrombi contains less lipid than does the platelet component; nonetheless, repeated hemorrhages might lead to accumulation of considerable amounts of lipid, especially cholesterol. Lipoproteins present in both fresh and organizing thrombi also contribute to lipid accumulation in atherosclerotic plaques.

Experimental findings lend support to the view that thrombosis may be important in development of atherosclerosis: When whole blood clots are injected into systemic veins of rabbits, fibrous intimal plaques containing little lipid form in pulmonary arteries; thromboemboli, at first occlusive, organize by retracting into eccentric plaques. Injection of platelet-rich thrombi rather than whole blood clots results in typical atherosclerotic plaque formation, with plaques containing foam cells and calcific deposits.

As our histologic studies have made clear, atherosclerotic plaques are much like fingerprints—no two are completely alike. Indeed, our examination of the coronary arterial tree revealed tremendous variation in the composition of adjacent plaques. Whereas some contained lipid and large quantities of pultaceous debris, others were composed primarily of fibrous tissue. Differences in composition of atherosclerotic plaques may be explained in part on the basis of differences in composition of underlying thrombi.

It is known, for example, that mixed white and red thrombi tend to form plaques that contain some foam cells but fewer than do plaques derived chiefly from platelet-rich or white thrombi. Occlusive platelet thrombi undergoing transformation to fibrofatty plaques usually do not accumulate fibrin, whereas mural platelet thrombi are usually partially or totally replaced by fibrin before undergoing organization; consequently the plaques that form are chiefly fibromuscular.

Enough may have been said concerning a possible relationship of thrombosis to atherogenesis to suggest that it warrants much more investigation. This leaves still unanswered, however, the question of what

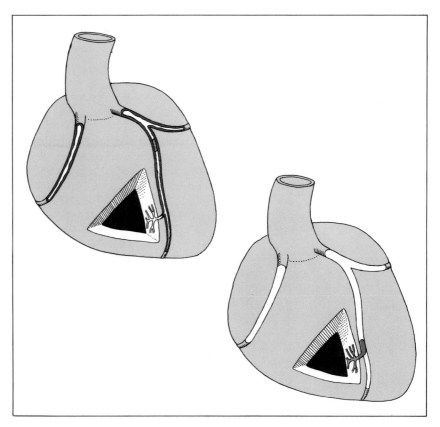

Key differences between coronary arterial thrombosis (left) and embolism (right), as diagrammed above, include the distal occurrence of the latter and its extension into intramural arteries. In addition, the coronary tree is usually devoid of atherosclerotic plaquing.

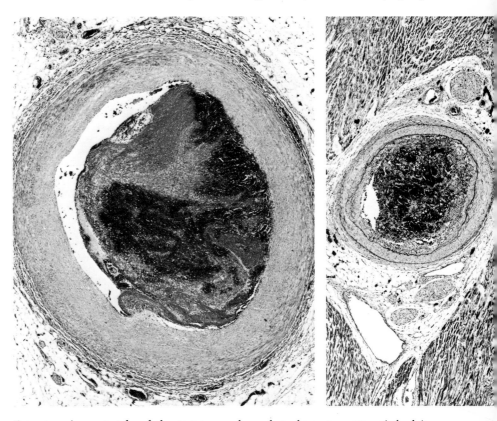

Extension of an arterial embolus to intramural vessels is shown in section of the left anterior descending artery (left) and its intramural branches (right) in man who died of anteroseptal wall infarction. No significant old atherosclerotic plaque is present.

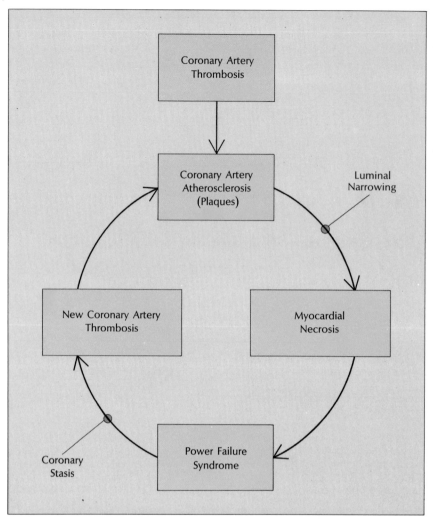

Postulated relationship of coronary artery thrombosis to acute myocardial infarction includes the possibility of a primary role in development of atherosclerosis; in addition, thrombus formation at the time of infarction appears linked to the occurrence of power failure, suggesting that coronary stasis may be required for thrombosis.

precipitates acute myocardial infarction. If not arterial thrombosis, then what? The answer is uncertain, but acute myocardial infarction, except in the case of embolism, occurs when there is already extensive diffuse arterial luminal narrowing by old atherosclerotic plaques. The factor that causes barely adequate oxygenation to become inadequate may not be readily detectable.

To be sure, coronary arterial emboli occur far less frequently than arterial thrombi in acute myocardial infarction. (Only three emboli vs 39 arterial thrombi were found in our 107 patients.) Nonetheless, coronary arterial embolism may occur more often than is generally recognized. The presence of a clot in the distal portion of a major extramural coronary artery

should suggest embolism and not thrombosis; the latter is more often located proximally in the arterial tree. The two can be more accurately distinguished if the following and other differences are kept in mind: In coronary arterial embolism the clot usually extends into the small epicardial branches of major extramural arteries and into intramural coronary vessels as well. As indicated earlier, in thrombosis the intramural coronary arteries are uninvolved and the small epicardial branches of extramural arteries are less often affected than the major vessels themselves. A key distinction is that in the presence of arterial embolism the extramural coronary tree is relatively free of old atherosclerotic plaques while, as we have seen, quite the opposite is true in cases of arterial

thrombosis. Also, patients with arterial emboli are usually relatively young in comparison with those with thrombosis. Predisposing factors such as the presence of arrhythmias, infective endocarditis, and intracardiac mural thrombosis should also suggest that an arterial clot is embolic in origin.

Actually, in studies to date concerning acute myocardial infarction the thrust has been essentially descriptive, aimed at recording significant clinical events and anatomic findings associated with acute myocardial ischemia and necrosis. More quantitative anatomic information is needed. It would be useful, for example, to have more accurate data on the composition of arterial thrombi, in hope of explaining why they often differ distally and proximally; why some consist almost entirely of fibrin, others of red cells and a few fibrin strands; why some contain few platelets and others many. Also, quantitative data on the size of myocardial infarcts would be useful. The area of myocardial necrosis weighs how many grams compared with the weight of the non-necrotic or fibrotic left ventricular myocardium? What percent of left ventricular myocardium needs to remain intact for survival? What percent of necrotic or fibrotic myocardium is fatal?

Another question is why cardiogenic shock and congestive failure develop in some cases of acute myocardial infarction and not in others. The answer may relate primarily to the amount of myocardium infarcted: the larger the infarct the greater the likelihood of reduced cardiac output, reduced blood flow, and pump failure. Recently, Page and associates showed that in patients with fatal acute myocardial infarction associated with shock, more than 40% of the left ventricular myocardium was either necrotic or fibrotic, and in patients without shock, less than 35% of the left ventricular wall was destroyed. The likelihood of thrombus formation is known to be increased with increasing infarct size; perhaps the occurrence of arterial thrombosis in patients with acute transmural infarction complicated by shock or congestive heart failure can be explained on this basis.

The major question centers on the relative roles of thrombosis and lipids in development and progression of coronary atherosclerosis.

Genetic Aspects of Hyperlipidemia in Coronary Heart Disease

JOSEPH L. GOLDSTEIN

University of Texas, Southwestern

"The best known instance is that of the Arnold family. William Arnold, collector of customs of Cowes, died suddenly of spasm of the heart in 1801. His son, the celebrated Thomas Arnold . . . died in his first attack. Matthew Arnold, his distinguished son, was a victim of the disease for several years, and died suddenly in an attack on Sunday, April 15, 1888 . . . ."—Osler, William. Lectures on Angina Pectoris and Allied States, 1897.

Thus it was already appreciated in Osler's time that at least some cases of coronary heart disease reflect a strong genetic influence, or, as he commented in citing the example above, "Since the members of certain families show a special tendency to arterial degeneration, it is not surprising to find cases in father and son, or in brothers, or even in representatives of three generations."

Within recent years the presence of an hereditary component in acute myocardial infarction and other clinical expressions of coronary heart disease has been supported by several lines of evidence – for example, the observed concordance in identical twins and the differences in prevalence among different ethnic groups living under similar environmental conditions. Familial aggregation studies also show close relatives of victims of premature coronary disease to be at an increased risk; for example, in the analysis by Slack and coworkers in England, the coronary death rate among first-degree relatives of men suffering a fatal myocardial infarction prior to age 55 was twice that of age-matched controls in the general population.

Of course, establishing familial aggregation in reference to a given disorder is not proof in itself of a genetic basis, since families usually share common environmental determinants. On the other hand, a number of conditions predisposing to coronary heart disease, such as hypertension, diabetes mellitus, and hyperlipidemia, are known to involve hereditary factors. Of all the risk factors associated with atherosclerosis, elevation in blood cholesterol and/or triglyceride levels is considered by many to be the most significant. For this reason a study of the genetics of the hyperlipidemias as they relate to coronary heart disease becomes of prime importance.

Until recently the role that genetic factors play in the development of most hyperlipidemias has not been well defined. International epidemiologic surveys showing a parallel increase in serum lipid levels and coronary disease incidence were presumed to reflect cultural differences primarily, especially in the amount and type of fat ingested. Similar inferences were drawn from prospective studies (as in Framingham, Mass., and Tecumseh, Mich.) documenting that the risk of coronary heart disease increased in step with the antecedent serum cholesterol level (see Chapter 20, "The Primary Prevention of Coronary Heart Disease," by Stamler). Subsequently, data from other studies indicated that serum triglyceride levels also tend to be increased among patients with coronary heart disease. None of these epidemiologic studies, however, were designed to assess the importance of *genetic* factors in hyperlipidemia.

Historical Aspects

The first convincing evidence that genetic factors may be important in the pathogenesis of the hyperlipidemias came as a result of the pioneering studies in the 1940's and 1950's of several investigators, including Müller, Thannhauser, Wilkinson, and Adlersberg. These investigators, and others, delineated the syndrome of familial hypercholesterolemia, established that it was an inherited disorder, and showed that affected individuals were at high risk for the development of premature atherosclerosis. Although these original observations on hyperlipidemia were confined largely to the most severely affected individuals, questions inevitably arose as to the extent to which genetic factors might contribute to the mild-to-moderate hyperlipidemia typically associated with premature coronary heart disease among the general population.

It was also known from the above studies as well as from those of Holt and coworkers (who described for the first time the syndrome of familial hyperchylomicronemia) and of Ahrens and associates (who separated hypertriglyceridemia into carbohydrate-induced and fat-induced varieties) that hyperlipidemia does not represent a single entity but a heterogeneous group of disorders expressed clinically as an elevation in the plasma cholesterol, the plasma triglyceride, or both.

It was not, however, until the introduction of lipoprotein typing in the mid-1960's by Fredrickson and coworkers at the National Institutes of Health that it became possible to delineate further the heterogeneity and, hence, the genetics of the hyperlipidemias. As is known, the focus of the NIH group has been on classifying hyperlipidemias in terms of lipoprotein patterns. With recognition that the major plasma lipids – cholesterol and triglyceride – are transported as constituents of several different families of lipoproteins, it appeared that blood lipid abnormalities could be adequately classified – whether for diagnostic purposes or for purposes of categorizing patients for therapy – by taking into account the protein components as well as the lipid levels. For the purposes of understanding the lipoprotein typing system, it is important to remember that the major transport protein for cholesterol in blood is the low-density (LD) lipoprotein and that the major transport protein for triglyceride is the very-low-density (VLD) lipoprotein.

Accordingly, in the system devised by Fredrickson et al, lipoprotein patterns were classified either on the basis of flotation rates of protein fractions subjected to ultracentrifugation or of their relative migration on electrophoresis. The World Health Organization, in adopting the system for international use in 1970, subdivided the original type II pattern as IIa and IIb, the former signifying an abnormal increase in cholesterol and its principal transport protein, LD lipoprotein, and the latter signifying an increase both in cholesterol and in triglyceride and *its* carrier, VLD lipoprotein. Otherwise, the original classification of abnormal lipoprotein patterns remained unchanged – type I reflecting a plasma excess of chylomicrons; type III indicating an increase in VLD lipoprotein having a high cholesterol content – the so-called floating-beta or beta-migrating VLD lipoprotein; and types IV and V, both marked by an increase in VLD lipoprotein, but the latter also by the presence of chylomicrons.

From the clinical viewpoint the NIH studies confirmed the data of earlier workers indicating that coronary heart disease is associated with hyperlipidemia. Specifically, their studies, as well as those of Slack in England, left no doubt of the association of enhanced risk of coronary atherosclerosis with at least one of the abnormal lipoprotein patterns – familial type II according to the Fredrickson classification, IIa in the WHO system. Among the other abnormal lipoprotein patterns, the rare type III and the more common type IV were also linked to premature coronary disease.

As the familial component of many hyperlipidemias became better recognized, available evidence was originally interpreted to suggest that each of the abnormal patterns might reflect a specific inherited defect, each defect affecting some discrete phase of lipoprotein metabolism. In particular, the type II pattern among members of a given family was thought to result from a single-gene mutation, transmitted by simple mendelian inheritance as an autosomal dominant trait. Individuals manifesting this disorder in its most florid form – for example, those developing widespread xanthomatosis and major cardiovascular complications in early childhood – presumably were homozygous for the abnormal gene; a heterozygote might also manifest xanthomatosis and premature atheromatosis but his life-span might be close to normal. Since the predominant lipid abnormality expressed in the type II pattern was an excessive elevation in plasma LD lipoprotein cholesterol, the terms familial type II hyperlipoproteinemia and familial hypercholesterolemia came to be used interchangeably to describe essentially the same disorder, a familial form of hypercholesterolemia with several distinct clinical features for which the mode of inheritance seemed well understood.

Genetic Approaches to Hyperlipidemia

In looking back, one can see that the assumptions made in reference to a single-gene mechanism underlying certain familial hyperlipidemias were correct in part, although, as is now evident, while familial hypercholesterolemia is usually associated with a type II lipoprotein pattern, the two cannot be equated. (More will be said of this later.) Moreover, defining the mode of inheritance underlying a familial disorder is difficult without detailed genetic analysis of a sufficient number of individuals – patients and their relatives – to discern meaningful trends. In addition, there must also be observation on a sizable control group. Particularly with disorders as common as hyperlipidemia, large amounts of data must be amassed on unselected families in order to establish when a given form of hyperlipidemia is genetic and then to delineate what the

The Major Abnormal Lipoprotein Patterns

Type	Chylo-microns	LDL	VLDL	Floating β-lipoproteins
I	+			
IIa		+		
IIb		+	+	
III				+
IV			+	
V	+		+	

Classification of the hyperlipidemias in terms of the specific plasma lipoprotein abnormality present in an individual patient was originally described by Fredrickson et al in the mid 1960's. This system of lipoprotein typing has recently been modified (as shown above) by the World Health Organization.

patterns of inheritance may be.

With any of the available methods for determining the presence of hyperlipidemia – such as measuring plasma levels of total cholesterol, L D lipoprotein cholesterol, or plasma triglyceride – one would not expect the results to reflect the primary action of genes as directly as do measurements of specific enzymes in other genetic conditions, such as disorders of amino acid metabolism. Instead, these tests reflect a combination of genetic and environmental influences. Consequently, an elevated lipid plasma value in a patient may simply reflect the uppermost values of the normal continuous distribution, which are usually thought to be determined by many genes *(polygenic)* or the elevated value may be due to the effect of a single mutant gene *(monogenic)*.

The monogenic and polygenic forms of hyperlipidemia require different approaches to genetic counseling, and each may differ in the potential risks for the development of atherosclerosis and in the response to diet and drug therapy. It is therefore important to elucidate the genetic mechanisms of these disorders. In the absence of specific genetic markers, genetic analysis of the family of a hyperlipidemic individual provides a first approach for discerning the mode of inheritance most likely to be involved. The proportion of relatives with the same disorder is of great importance in this context. If a monogenic mechanism involving transmission of a single dominant gene is operative, an affected individual should have at least one affected parent. Among first-degree relatives of an index case (first-degree relatives include the parents, brothers and sisters, and children), approximately 50% would manifest the same abnormal trait. That is, the frequency distribution of lipid values of family members, when plotted on a graph, would show a bimodal pattern reflecting an approximately equal proportion of relatives with and without the familial lipid defect. With dominant inheritance a vertical pedigree pattern would be seen in both near and distant relatives.

In contrast, if polygenic inheritance were responsible, the disorder would be more in evidence among near relatives – siblings, parents, children – of an affected individual, whereas the

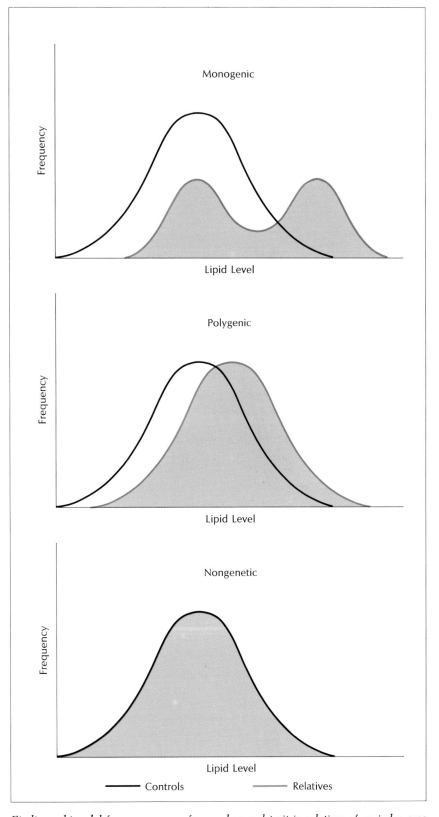

Finding a bimodal frequency curve for an abnormal trait in relatives of an index case suggests that transmission involves a single abnormal gene (top); in the case of autosomal dominant inheritance, about half the first-degree relatives would have the trait, the other half would not. With more than one gene (middle), a unimodal distribution can be expected since the distinction between affected and nonaffected relatives is not all or nothing but one of degree; mean values of the relatives, however, would be higher than those of the controls. In a nongenetic situation, the lipid values of relatives would be the same as those of the controls (bottom).

risk to more distant relatives would be reduced. Lipid values of relatives, when plotted on a graph, would form a single or unimodal distribution, as would be the case in a control population, although mean values would be higher. On the other hand, if the hyperlipidemia occurring in a given individual were nonfamilial and hence nongenetic, blood lipid values of relatives of all degrees would essentially be indistinguishable from those of control subjects.

Although one can best approach these questions by pooling genetic data on a number of individual patients and their relatives (as in our family studies to be described shortly), much can also be learned when a single large kindred can be examined in reference to a given familial disorder. Fortunately, the opportunity for detailed analysis of such a family – including four generations – presented itself to our group at the University of Washington when we were studying genetic aspects of hyperlipidemia in relation to coronary heart disease. My colleagues in this project and others to be described were William R. Hazzard, Helmut C. Schrott, Edwin L. Bierman, and Arno G. Motulsky.

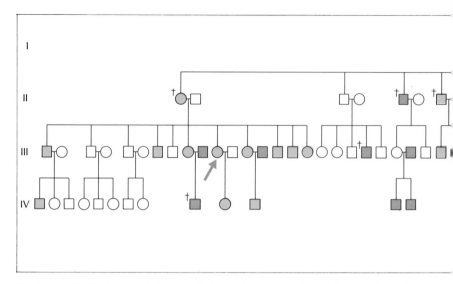

Alaskan kindred with familial hypercholesterolemia was identified through third-generation member who, at age 22, had plasma cholesterol and LD lipoprotein values of

The family came to our attention through a 22-year-old Alaskan woman with severe hypercholesterolemia; total plasma cholesterol when we tested her was 595 mg/100 ml; the L D lipoprotein cholesterol was 497/100 ml. Classical clinical signs of familial hypercholesterolemia – extensive tendinous xanthomas and arcus corneae – were present but she had no cardiovascular symptoms.

As our family study disclosed, this young woman was one of more than 90 descendants of a couple (he of German extraction, she of mixed Aleutian-Russian ancestry) who had settled some 60 years earlier in a small village in the Aleutian Islands. They had 18 children. At the time of the study the kindred also comprised 60 grandchildren (of whom the young woman was one) and 14 great-grandchildren. Virtually all living family members had remained in the village and were available for study; the youngest was under one year old, the eldest, the husband in the first-generation couple, was 87.

Immediate differences were apparent when plasma cholesterol values for kindred members and control subjects were compared. In the latter, values followed the expected continuous distribution and unimodal curve; in contrast, when values for the kindred were plotted it was apparent that there were two distinct populations approximately equal in size, one with hypercholesterolemia, the other presumably unaffected. According to the distribution of cholesterol levels, a value in the 275 to 295 range appeared to be an appropriate cutoff for separating normal from affected family members past the age of 20; most adults with values above 295 manifested typical clinical evidence of severe hypercholesterolemia (for example, 70% of those with a value of 295 or above had tendinous xanthomas).

In the family members designated

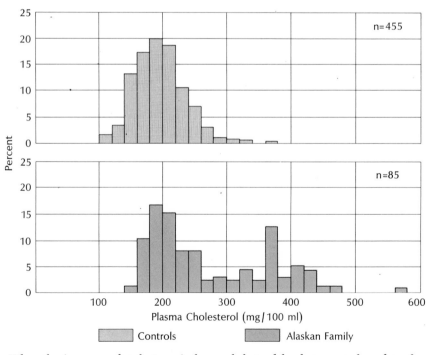

When the frequency distribution of plasma cholesterol levels in controls and in the Alaskan family was compared, the latter clearly had two populations: one normal and resembling the controls, with a mean value of 207 mg/100 ml (control mean 216); the other affected and distinct from the controls, with a mean of 411 mg/100 ml.

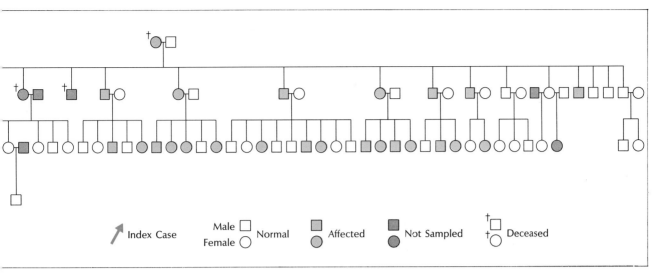

Index Case | Male □ / Female ○ Normal | Affected | Not Sampled | † Deceased

595 and 497 mg/100 ml. When blood lipid levels of kindred were determined, distinct bimodal frequency pattern was found, indi- *cating trait was transmitted by a single dominant gene. It did not appear in offspring of any matings of normal individuals.*

as normal the mean cholesterol level was 207, significantly different from the mean of 411 for those with hypercholesterolemia. There was less of a spread in lipid values among younger family members between normal and affected groups: mean cholesterol levels of 201 vs 350.

A chief aim, of course, was to determine whether the genetic mechanism responsible for the familial hypercholesterolemia entailed a single major gene (monogenic) or multiple genes at several loci (polygenic). The bimodal distribution of cholesterol values in the kindred strongly suggested a single-gene mutation transmitted as an autosomal dominant trait. To reinforce this interpretation, segregation analyses were done on 83 offspring of 18 marriages of family members. In no case did two normal parents have a child with hypercholesterolemia, whereas among progeny of normal X hypercholesterolemia matings the ratio of normal to hypercholesterolemic children was about 1:1, as expected in monogenic dominant inheritance.

In affected relatives hypercholesterolemia was not accompanied by a demonstrable abnormality in triglyceride levels. Rather, plasma triglyceride values tended to increase with age in both normal and hypercholesterolemic individuals, bearing no apparent relationship to the presence or degree of hypercholesterolemia. On the other hand, when values for total plasma cholesterol and L D lipoprotein

cholesterol were compared it was evident that the former closely reflected the latter. Thus, the basic defect underlying the familial hyperlipidemia evidently altered metabolism of cholesterol and its predominant transport protein, L D lipoprotein. Indeed the high correlation between the total plasma cholesterol and the L D lipoprotein cholesterol suggested that total plasma cholesterol was a suitable marker for identifying familial hypercholesterolemia of the type exemplified in this kindred, a point I will return to.

According to family pedigree analysis, the gene mutation causing hypercholesterolemia in this kindred was fully penetrant, with no skipped generations; moreover, the lipid defect was expressed in affected family members in early childhood. During the first decade hypercholesterolemia was the only detectable abnormality, regardless of the degree of blood lipid elevation. Unmistakable clinical manifestations of familial hypercholesterolemia began to appear early in the second decade. By age 20, one third of affected family members had developed arcus corneae or xanthomas or both. In the 20 to 30 age group, 80% had tendinous xanthomas.

Of most pertinence to our discussion was the observation that 50% of the hypercholesterolemic adults had documented evidence of coronary heart disease. There had been three coronary deaths, two at an early age (a man and woman, both at age 38).

The third victim, the first generation wife, had died at age 62. In addition, two younger family members (a man of 31 and a woman of 37) had symptomatic coronary disease in the form of severe anginal attacks.

None of the unaffected family members, or their spouses, had symptomatic heart disease, and there had been no coronary deaths among them. It also should be noted that coronary atherosclerosis and heart disease are relatively uncommon among Aleuts.

The genetic findings in this kindred do not of course establish that a similar single-gene mutation underlies other familial forms of hypercholesterolemia. Nor can any assumptions be made in reference to the type of hypercholesterolemia typically associated with coronary heart disease in the population at large.

Segregation Analysis in Alaskan Family

Parental Matings (Number)	Phenotype of Children	
	Affected	Normal
Normal X normal (5)	0	13
Affected X normal (7)	14	14
Deceased, at risk for hyperlipidemia, X normal	19	17

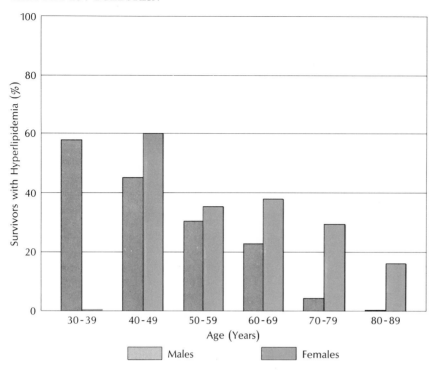

In the Seattle study, analysis of fasting blood cholesterol and triglyceride levels of 500 survivors three months after they had suffered a myocardial infarction showed that 31% of the total were hyperlipidemic; the finding was particularly frequent in the younger male survivors and in women of all age groups.

Hyperlipidemia in Survivors of Myocardial Infarction

In order to determine the frequency of the different forms of hyperlipidemia in "garden-variety" patients with coronary heart disease, my colleagues and I carried out, in Seattle, an extensive genetic analysis, in which index cases for family studies consisted of a large number of unselected patients with both hyperlipidemia and coronary heart disease. A chief goal was to delineate more precisely the various forms of both familial and nonfamilial hyperlipidemias as they relate to coronary heart disease in the general population, and to characterize better the mode of inheritance of the familial varieties.

We began by screening for plasma lipid abnormalities among 1,166 patients who had been hospitalized at any one of 13 Seattle hospitals over an 11-month period for acute myocardial infarction. Since the 13 hospitals treat 95% of Seattle patients suffering an acute coronary episode, a representative sampling of the general population was assured. Criteria for diagnosis of acute infarction included at least two of the following: a compat-

ible clinical history, characteristic electrocardiographic changes in serial recordings, and characteristic serum enzyme changes in serially drawn blood samples.

Of the 1,166 patients hospitalized with acute myocardial infarction, 885 were still alive at three months after hospital admission and 500 of these survivors were selected for study. These 500 index patients comprised virtually all (95%) patients under the age of 60 who survived at least three months following the acute episode plus a random sampling (25%) of three-month survivors 60 and older. Control subjects in this and later phases of the study (a total of 950) included the non-blood relatives of the survivors and the spouses of other family members. For purposes of genetic studies of lipid levels, non-blood relatives such as spouses provide the best control for environmental or nongenetic factors that may aggregate in families and simulate genetic factors. To allow comparison of cholesterol and triglyceride levels of survivors and control subjects of different age and sex, each lipid value was converted by standard methods to its equivalent value in a 45-year-old

man or woman. (According to regression equations, mean cholesterol and triglyceride levels in both sexes were the same at that age).

All survivors with fasting cholesterol and/or triglyceride values exceeding the 95th percentile for the control group were classified as hyperlipidemic. Epidemiologic data from Framingham and elsewhere had made clear that there is no critical level of plasma cholesterol in relationship to development of coronary heart disease. Thus our use of the 95th percentile value as the cutoff point to separate normal and hyperlipidemic survivors was purely arbitrary. Moreover, we recognized that since the index cases were three-month survivors of acute myocardial infarction, our findings would not necessarily be applicable to all infarction cases, given the frequency of sudden and early coronary deaths.

These limitations aside, analysis of the fasting plasma lipid values yielded several findings of interest: Of the 500 survivors some 31% were classified as hyperlipidemic on the basis of elevated plasma levels of cholesterol and/or triglycerides. There was a clear-cut relationship to age and sex: Among male survivors under age 40 hyperlipidemia was identified in 60%, but its frequency decreased with age, and among men of 70 and older scarcely any manifested a lipid defect. Among women, hyperlipidemia was identified in 60% of the below-50 age group but its frequency remained relatively high in the older age groups and about 30% of women in the 70 to 79 decade had elevated blood lipid levels.

Our lipid data on the Seattle survivors confirmed the previously reported association between an elevation in triglyceride levels and concomitant metabolic alterations associated with coronary heart disease. Thus, diabetes mellitus, obesity, and hypertension were all more common in survivors manifesting an abnormal increase in triglyceride alone or in both triglyceride and cholesterol than in those manifesting only hypercholesterolemia alone or having normal blood lipid levels. Among survivors with lipid abnormalities, hypertriglyceridemia in fact proved more common than hypercholesterolemia; hypertriglyceridemia, with or without associated hypercholesterolemia, occurred in survivors at nearly three times the frequency of hypercholesterolemia alone.

Conceivably, the finding of more survivors with a triglyceride increase than a cholesterol increase could have been related to dietary limitations imposed following hospital discharge, since a restricted intake of total dietary fat and cholesterol sometimes causes a relative increase in triglyceride levels at the expense of a reduction in cholesterol levels. This seemed unlikely, however, in the light of observations made in the second phase of our study, in which the pattern of hyperlipidemia among presumably healthy family members was used to classify the form of hyperlipidemia in each index survivor. This type of family approach to genetic analysis is necessary when there is a possibility that the inherited disorder under study varies in its expression.

A parallel can be drawn with regard to the dominantly inherited connective tissue disorder, the Marfan syndrome. In one individual the abnormal gene may be expressed early and fully in the form of congenital dislocation of the lens, tall stature, elongated fingers, dissecting aneurysm of the aorta, and so on. The parent from whom he inherited the disorder may have dislocation of the lens but no heart disease and a normal physical appearance; another affected relative may manifest the Marfan gene only in his stature and other physical signs and be free of heart disease or lens dislocation. The same gene is present in each of these individuals but differently expressed; in some, direct examination may leave no doubt as to the nature of the disorder, whereas for others only a family analysis including many relatives can provide the necessary clues.

Thus in the second phase of our genetic study a total of 2,520 family members were tested for lipid abnormalities. Included were 95% of all living first-degree relatives of the survivors with hyperlipidemia as well as a sizable number of their more distant relatives. Among *all* adult first-degree relatives the fasting values for both plasma cholesterol and triglyceride were significantly elevated over control values: a mean of 235 mg/100 ml vs 218 for cholesterol and a mean

of 126 mg/100 ml vs 93 for triglyceride. Moreover, these differences were accentuated when hyperlipidemic survivors were grouped according to the predominant lipid elevation. Among *all* adult first-degree relatives of survivors with hypercholesterolemia the mean value for cholesterol was 247; among *all* adult first-degree relatives of survivors with hypertriglyceridemia, mean triglyceride value was 140.

Clearly, familial factors were implicated in these hyperlipidemic survivors with coronary heart disease. The familial factors became even more evident when we determined the causes of death among deceased first-degree adult relatives. Death certificates on 95% of such relatives were obtainable, and they disclosed a coronary death rate about twice as high among families with hyperlipidemia than among those without it. Whereas the proportion of coronary deaths among the deceased relatives of the nonhyperlipidemic survivors came to 18.9%, the proportion among relatives of survivors shown to have a familial lipid disorder was between 35% and 40%. Not only were there more coronary deaths among the relatives of hyperlipidemic survivors but also these relatives appeared to die at

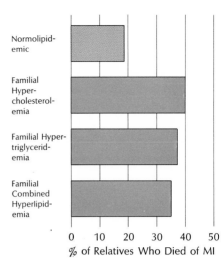

When causes of death among adult first-degree relatives of hyperlipidemic MI survivors were analyzed, their coronary death rate was twice as high as that found among relatives of normolipidemic survivors.

a younger age (10 to 15 years earlier) than deceased relatives of survivors without hyperlipidemia.

When genetic analysis was applied in order to classify each of the index survivors, five forms of hyperlipidemia were identified. In one form, designated *sporadic hypertriglyceridemia*, an elevation in triglyceride

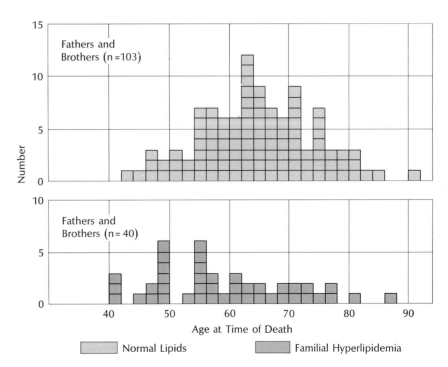

Not only were relatives of hyperlipidemic MI survivors more likely to die of coronary heart disease but, as graph shows, death was likely to occur at an earlier age. (The familial hyperlipidemia group includes data from all families with familial hypercholesterolemia, familial hypertriglyceridemia, and familial combined hyperlipidemia.)

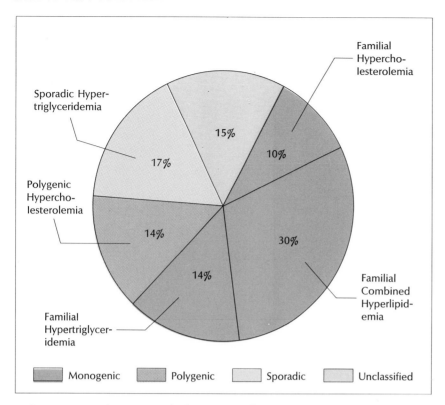

When genetic analysis was applied through study of relatives, more than half of 164 hyperlipidemic MI survivors could be classified as having one of the three types conforming to single-gene transmission. Polygenic hypercholesterolemia reflected complex genetic-environmental influences in which single-gene transmission was not demonstrated; sporadic hypertriglyceridemia was identified as nongenetic; those unclassified represent survivors with fewer than four relatives available for study.

levels presumably reflected exogenous factors (a genetic basis was ruled out when triglyceride curves among relatives were almost identical with those of control subjects). Another, manifested primarily as hypercholesterolemia and designated *polygenic hypercholesterolemia*, presumably reflected complex genetic-environmental influences. However, more than half the cases were classified as having a monogenic or simply inherited form of hyperlipidemia. The monogenic hyperlipidemias occurred in one of three forms, involving either an elevation in cholesterol (*familial hypercholesterolemia*), triglyceride (*familial hypertriglyceridemia*), or a combined increase in both lipids (*familial combined hyperlipidemia*).

As in the Alaskan kindred, a hallmark of familial hypercholesterolemia in the survivors was its complete expression in affected children. In adults with familial hypercholesterolemia, triglyceride levels were sometimes elevated as well, but the plasma ratio of cholesterol/triglyceride was

almost always greater than 2. The degree of elevation in cholesterol levels showed marked variation; while the mean value was close to 350 mg/100 ml, among the affected relatives cholesterol levels ranged from 270 to above 450. This can be explained in terms of the normal polygenic variation in blood lipid levels occurring in all of us whether hyperlipidemic or not; given this normal variability, a major gene effect on lipid levels will be expressed in higher values in some individuals than in others.

In almost half of the families affected by familial hypercholesterolemia clinical manifestations of the lipid defect, chiefly tendinous xanthomas and arcus corneae, were noted in one or more hyperlipidemic members. On several counts, then, this form of familial hyperlipidemia differed from the other two familial disorders (discussed below), both of which are expressed in childhood only in a minority of cases and are rarely if ever accompanied by xanthomas or other clinical signs.

However, one point must be stressed in reference to the clinical manifestations of familial hypercholesterolemia. While xanthomas were present in a high proportion of affected family members and presumably age-dependent in onset, they were absent in other relatives in the same family with a comparable genetic lipid abnormality. As shown in the Alaskan kindred analysis, the same may be true with respect to coronary atherosclerosis. The 50% frequency of overt heart disease among the hypercholesterolemic Alaskans was surely very high, yet why didn't the other 50% of family members of comparable age and with significant hypercholesterolemia show signs of cardiovascular involvement? They might, of course, if restudied later in life, but the genetic data in both family studies suggested strongly that the familial hyperlipidemias under discussion vary markedly in their clinical expression. Thus it would be expected that not all affected individuals would be equally vulnerable to premature myocardial infarction or be affected at the same stage in life.

It was of interest that our analysis of lipid data on the Seattle families showed a higher frequency of familial hypertriglyceridemia than of familial hypercholesterolemia (23 vs 16 of 131 families studied). In families with hypertriglyceridemia, only about 12% of relatives at risk manifested the lipid defect in childhood (prior to age 20).

Familial Combined Hyperlipidemia

No doubt the most intriguing findings uncovered in our genetic study were in reference to the familial disorder in which elevations in both plasma lipids were characteristically observed. This disorder, affecting 47 families, proved more common than the other two together. Familial combined hyperlipidemia, as we termed it, was distinguishable from each of the other disorders on several grounds. First, plasma lipid levels, while significantly increased, tended to show a lesser degree of elevation than in familial hypercholesterolemia or familial hypertriglyceridemia. Moreover, affected individuals rarely manifested an elevation in cholesterol lev-

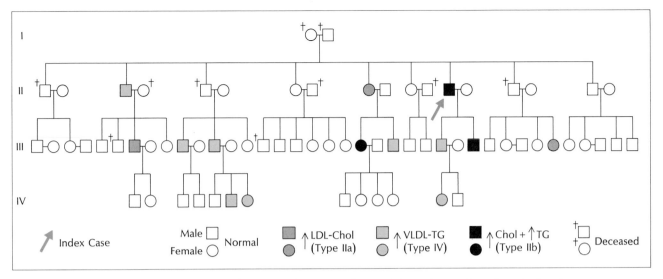

In Seattle study, familial combined hyperlipidemia was the inherited disorder most frequently encountered on genetic analysis of MI survivors; one such analysis is shown above. Note that although the defect may be expressed as an elevation of either plasma cholesterol or triglyceride or both, inheritance pattern is consistent with autosomal dominant transmission. The unique and characteristic feature of this disorder is presence of multiple lipoprotein types among hyperlipidemic family members.

els in childhood, as was almost always the case in familial hypercholesterolemia. What impressed us most were the differing lipid abnormalities in families with presumably the same disorder. Affected members of the same family characteristically showed both hypercholesterolemia and hypertriglyceridemia but often an affected relative manifested either hypercholesterolemia alone or hypertriglyceridemia alone. The variability was striking and proved to be a unique feature of this disorder.

Anticipating that multiple interacting genes might be involved, we looked for evidence of this in the family data. However, the findings simply did not fit any model of polygenic inheritance; rather all data pointed to a monogenic mechanism in familial combined hyperlipidemia just as it did in familial hypercholesterolemia and familial hypertriglyceridemia.

In familial hypercholesterolemia, the frequency distribution of cholesterol values appeared bimodal, whereas that of triglyceride values appeared unimodal, suggesting a familial disorder determined by a single dominant gene affecting blood cholesterol without significant effect on triglyceride — just as we observed in the analysis of the Alaskan family. According to pedigree inspection, the defect was expressed in about half of the off-

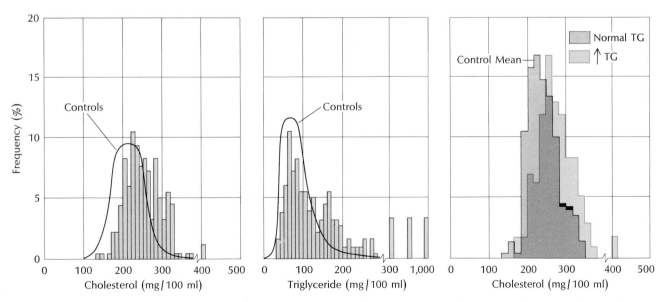

In familial combined hyperlipidemia, cholesterol levels of 234 adult first-degree relatives of 47 index survivors appeared to show a unimodal distribution with a rightward shift (graph at left), while the curve of triglyceride values appeared bimodal and hence suggested monogenic transmission (center). Additional analysis (right) indicated, however, that the cholesterol shift to right was confined mainly to relatives with elevated triglycerides. It was concluded that the cholesterol elevations were secondary to the triglyceride elevations, suggesting that the major gene effect in this disorder is on triglyceride metabolism.

spring of affected individuals, again characteristic of monogenic dominant inheritance. Segregation analysis showed a 50% frequency of familial hypercholesterolemia among siblings of index patients classified as hypercholesterolemic, providing further documentation. A similar pattern prevailed in reference to familial hypertriglyceridemia.

Naturally, curiosity was greatest in reference to the combined disorder, not only because it was more common than the others but, to the best of our knowledge, it represented a newly identified genetic lipid disorder. In affected families, the frequency distribution of triglyceride values was indicative of bimodality, whereas in the same families distribution of cholesterol values appeared unimodal (although shifted to the right of control values). However, when the data were analyzed more closely, the apparently unimodal cholesterol curve proved to be composed of two overlapping distributions—a normal cholesterol distribution in relatives with normal triglyceride values, a shifted cholesterol distribution in relatives with elevated triglyceride values.

This type of analysis suggested the operation of a single gene with its primary action affecting triglyceride metabolism with secondary effects on cholesterol metabolism. According to current thinking, in the normal physiologic sequence, V L D lipoprotein synthesized in the liver is catabolized in the circulation to L D lipoprotein. Thus it is tempting to speculate that the basic defect here is one of overproduction of V L D lipoprotein, which could

theoretically be reflected in the individual patient in a variety of ways — as either hypertriglyceridemia due to elevated V L D lipoprotein, hypercholesterolemia due to elevated L D lipoprotein, or both hypertriglyceridemia and hypercholesterolemia when both V L D and L D lipoproteins are elevated. The striking variability observed among affected individuals in the same family might be due to nongenetic factors such as diet and drugs that secondarily affect the peripheral conversion of V L D lipoprotein to L D lipoprotein.

Results of segregation analysis on families with combined hyperlipidemia essentially excluded the possibility of two independent but interacting genes, such as one elevating cholesterol levels and the other elevating triglyceride. With segregation of two genes in these families, hyperlipidemia would be expected not in about 50% of siblings of patients with the lipid defect, as observed, but in about 75% (25% hypercholesterolemic, 25% hypertriglyceridemic, 25% with both abnormalities, 25% normal). Variability in expression of a single abnormal gene was further supported by the observation that some offspring born of hypercholesterolemic X normal matings manifested significant hypertriglyceridemia, whereas others, born of hypertriglyceridemic X normal matings, showed hypercholesterolemia.

In considering the hyperlipidemias from a genetic viewpoint, familial combined hyperlipidemia warrants further comment. Although it appeared to be a newly recognized genetic disorder, a literature search revealed several examples of large

families that, in retrospect, probably had the same familial defect (for example, a 1968 report by Matthews of a kindred with hypercholesterolemia and hypertriglyceridemia, occurring presumably as different phenotypic expressions of the same mutant gene, and a 1969 report by Schreibman et al on "familial hypertriglyceridemia," in which affected relatives in the same family manifested either hypertriglyceridemia alone, hypercholesterolemia alone, or both).

Recently, Rose and coworkers in New York independently identified in several families combined hyperlipidemia as a distinct genetic entity different from either familial hypercholesterolemia or familial hypertriglyceridemia. In more extensive family studies, Nikkila and Antti in Finland tested first-degree relatives of survivors of acute myocardial infarction (412 relatives of 101 consecutively admitted cases). As in our study, index patients were classified according to the serum cholesterol and triglyceride levels of their relatives. Hyperlipidemia was identified in about 30% of the patients surviving acute myocardial infarction, the "most important" and most common type being a familial disorder in which the basic lipid abnormality was expressed differently in members of the same family. Among family members with this disorder three lipoprotein patterns — types IIa, IIb, and IV—were about equally represented. In light of our earlier discussion, it was of interest that in their affected families about 50% of relatives manifested hyperlipidemia. These findings in Finland were remarkably similar to the observations on familial combined hyperlipidemia we had made in our Seattle study.

Lipoprotein Patterns and Genetic Disorders

To be sure, none of our described observations *prove* a monogenic basis for any of the three familial lipid disorders, although they strongly support the possibility. With this in mind, let us consider the three familial disorders from another vantage point, relating the genetic lipid abnormalities to lipoprotein patterns. As noted earlier, since the advent of lipoprotein typing to classify hyperlipidemias, the terms familial hypercholesterolemia and fa-

Segregation Analysis of Informative Matings from Families with Familial Combined Hyperlipidemia

Mating Type (Number)	Distribution of Phenotypes in Offspring (Number)			
	Normal	↑Cholesterol	↑Triglyceride	↑Both
↑ Cholesterol × normal (6)	4	1	3	2
↑ Triglyceride × normal (9)	10	1	6	5
↑ Both × normal (7)	10	0	8	3

Monogenic transmission of familial combined hyperlipidemia is supported by data such as those given above; if two genes were involved, the proportion of affected offspring would be closer to 75% than the approximately 50% actually found.

milial type II (more recently IIa) hyperlipoproteinemia have been used interchangeably, the assumption being that the two were not only clinically similar but reflected the same genetic defect. Similarly, familial hypertriglyceridemia and familial type IV hyperlipoproteinemia were thought to be genetic equivalents. In truth, however, the type of genetic analysis necessary to establish this thesis as fact had never been done. Accordingly, as part of our family studies we determined lipoprotein patterns among the survivors of myocardial infarction, comparing findings with the genetic diagnosis obtained independently by analysis of plasma lipid levels among their relatives.

Characteristically, the lipoprotein pattern in survivors classified as having familial hypercholesterolemia was type IIa, although some few had type IIb; characteristically, in familial hypertriglyceridemia the pattern was type IV. However, when the comparison was carried further it could be seen that *there was no consistent relationship between lipoprotein pattern and genetic disorder.* None of the patterns proved specific for any of the three familial defects; none of the familial defects was specified by a single lipoprotein pattern. No fewer than four patterns – IIa, IIb, IV, and V – were identified in families with combined familial hyperlipidemia. Moreover, the presumably monogenic hyperlipidemias were indistinguishable on the basis of lipoprotein patterns from those that appeared to be nongenetic and polygenic in origin.

When tested for lipoprotein patterns, several of the patients were on drug therapy to reduce elevated lipid levels. This in itself could have explained some of the discrepant findings; it is known that lipoprotein patterns are alterable by pharmacologic intervention and by varying physiologic conditions (e.g., conversion to a type IV from type V pattern with caloric deprivation). In this context, it is also worth noting that abnormal lipoprotein patterns occurring as secondary effects of various disease states that alter lipid metabolism, or on a hormonal basis, cannot be distinguished from those associated with genetically determined lipid disorders.

A true marker in a genetic sense for a given inherited disorder is of course

Summary of Clinical, Genetic, and Biochemical Characteristics of Hyperlipidemic Survivors of Myocardial Infarction

| Disorder | Typical Lipid Level | | Lipoprotein Types | Mode of Inheritance | Expression in Children |
	Cholesterol (mg/100 ml)	Triglyceride (mg/100 ml)			
Monogenic Familial hypercholesterolemia	353	126	IIa, IIb	Autosomal dominant	Yes
Familial hypertriglyceridemia	241	267	IV, V	Autosomal dominant	Rarely
Combined hyperlipidemia	300	241	IIa, IIb, IV, V	Autosomal dominant	Rarely
Polygenic hypercholesterolemia	308	287	IIa, IIb	Polygenic	Not applicable
Sporadic hypertriglyceridemia	233	243	IV, V	Nongenetic	Not applicable

unique to that defect, does not vary, and remains the same despite changing conditions. In sickle cell anemia, to cite one example, S hemoglobin is always present in blood samples on electrophoresis, whether the hemoglobin level rises or falls. Such discrete genetic markers do not yet exist for the familial hyperlipidemias associated with coronary disease. Thus far, the only lipoprotein pattern that can be considered a genetic marker is the rare type I pattern, which appears to reflect familial hyperchylomicronemia due to lipoprotein lipase deficiency.

The very absence of genetic markers for these lipid disorders probably accounts for the failure to delineate familial combined hyperlipidemia until now. Since affected members of

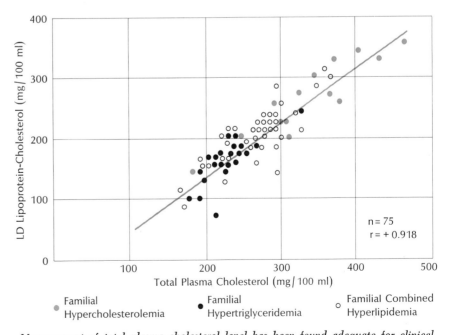

Familial Hypercholesterolemia Familial Hypertriglyceridemia Familial Combined Hyperlipidemia

Measurement of total plasma cholesterol level has been found adequate for clinical purposes in identifying individuals affected with any of the three monogenic hyperlipidemias, as suggested by the excellent correlation of the LD lipoprotein-cholesterol level and the total plasma cholesterol level shown in graph; lipoprotein typing is seldom necessary for routine clinical diagnosis.

Frequency of Hyperlipidemia

| Disorder | Myocardial Infarction Survivors | | | General Population % |
	< Age 60 (a) %	≧ Age 60 (b) %	Ratio a/b	
I Monogenic hyperlipidemia Familial hypercholesterolemia	4.1	0.7	5.9	~0.1-0.2
Familial hypertriglyceridemia	5.2	2.7	1.9	~0.2-0.3
Combined hyperlipidema	11.3	4.1	2.8	~0.3-0.5
Total	20.6	7.5	—	~0.6-1.0
II Polygenic hypercholesterolemia	5.5	5.5	1.0	—
III Sporadic hypertriglyceridemia	5.8	6.9	0.8	—

these families characteristically manifest different lipoprotein patterns, the use of lipoprotein typing for genetic classification of hyperlipidemia would make recognition of a disorder like combined hyperlipidemia difficult, if not impossible.

It goes without saying that discovery of an identifiable biochemical basis for each of the familial hyperlipidemias would provide the necessary means of accurately and rapidly classifying patients with these disorders. For the present, however, measurement of plasma lipid levels in relatives and quantitative analysis of the pattern of variation in families appears to provide a meaningful approach to genetic classification of familial lipid disorders.

When originally introduced at the clinical level, lipoprotein typing was thought potentially more informative to the clinician than the routine measurement of plasma lipid levels. In particular the concern was that the latter might be misleading if a high concentration of the L D lipoprotein cholesterol were obscured by the variable contribution to the total plasma cholesterol level of V L D lipoprotein and H D (high density) lipoprotein; in such a case the presence of types IIa or IIb might be missed. As part of our family studies we tested these relationships directly among survivors of myocardial infarction, plotting levels of whole plasma cholesterol against L D lipoprotein cholesterol measured in the same blood samples. In each of the genetically defined hyperlipidemias the correlation between plasma cholesterol and L D lipoprotein cholesterol was excellent; the correlation also held in blood samples from survivors with normal lipid levels. It would appear, therefore, that for *most* clinical purposes lipoprotein typing – a practice that has now become almost routine in medicine – probably does not provide the clinician with any more significant information than that obtained from the much simpler and less expensive measurement of blood cholesterol and triglyceride levels.

Frequency of Familial Hyperlipidemia

At this point, it seems desirable to focus on another implication of the observations discussed, for example the observed frequency of familial hyperlipidemia among *unselected* patients with coronary heart disease who presumably are representative of the population at large. Since the Seattle

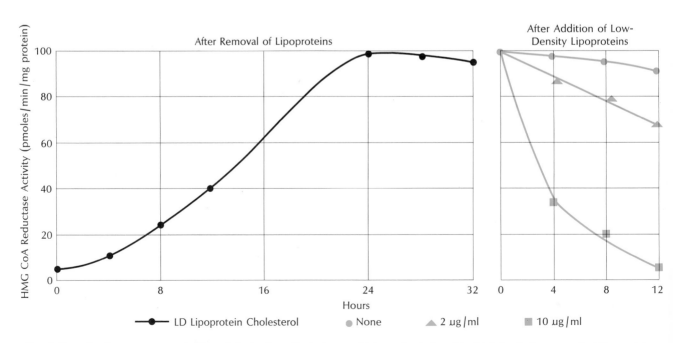

Regulation of a key enzyme controlling cholesterol synthesis in human cells can be studied in cultured skin fibroblasts as in experiments like that graphed above. Note that enzyme activity, *which can be induced to high levels by removal of lipoproteins, was rapidly and proportionately reduced when different amounts of LD lipoprotein cholesterol were added to the medium.*

family studies included virtually all survivors under the age of 60 served by hospitals in a large metropolitan area, the findings may well be applicable elsewhere among patients with premature coronary disease. In Seattle, in the under-60 age group more than one fifth (20.6%) of heart attack victims were classified as having one of three forms of familial hyperlipidemia, each presumably having a monogenic basis. Eleven percent of these survivors had familial combined hyperlipidemia, 5% had familial hypertriglyceridemia, and 4% had familial hypercholesterolemia. Among survivors past the age of 60, the familial hyperlipidemias affected only about 7.5%. The nongenetic and polygenic forms of hyperlipidemia occurred at a similar frequency (5% for each) in the under-60 and over-60 age groups. The rarest form of hyperlipidemia in our survivors was the type III disorder, which was present in only two of the 500 consecutively studied coronary patients.

From our studies, we estimate that probably one in 150 individuals in the general population may be a carrier of a gene predisposing to one of the three familial lipid disorders. Of course, it remains to be proved biochemically that each of the three familial hyperlipidemias is indeed determined by a separate major gene; if so, their combined frequency may make them among the most common disease-producing genes in our population. Assume, however, that our estimates are correct and no more than 1% of the general population carries a gene for one of the monogenic forms of hyper-

lipidemia. It is then predictable that four out of every five individuals in the *general population* who manifest either an elevation in cholesterol or triglyceride (as arbitrarily defined by upper five percentile cutoff values) will turn out to have a polygenic or sporadic (nongenetic) form of hyperlipidemia. Thus, among hyperlipidemic individuals *without* coronary heart disease, the polygenic and sporadic forms of hyperlipidemia are probably more common than the monogenic disorders.

It is obvious, of course, that coronary heart disease is in most cases a multifactorial disorder involving both genetic and environmental causation. In some instances familial hyperlipidemia may be a necessary factor for myocardial infarction, though not sufficient in itself. One can speculate, however, that perhaps one reason for the increased occurrence of premature coronary disease in recent times may be the introduction of noxious environmental influences that interact with one of the genes predisposing to hyperlipidemia. These genes probably have not increased in frequency in the population but their expression may have been "facilitated."

Search for the Basic Defect

The suggestion that each of the three familial lipid disorders occurring in survivors of myocardial infarction may be determined by a single gene mechanism implies that a discrete and different biochemical lesion may underlie each of these disorders.

To identify the basic defects underlying these disorders is the goal of

studies I am now pursuing in collaboration with Michael S. Brown at the University of Texas in Dallas. Specifically, we have begun by examining the regulation of cholesterol biosynthesis in cultured human fibroblasts. Finding that the activity of the rate-controlling enzyme in the pathway known to regulate cholesterol synthesis in the liver is detectable in these cultured skin cells as well, we have been able to relate cellular enzyme activity to the level of specific extracellular lipoproteins. When fibroblasts were cultured in serum containing no lipoproteins, the specific activity of this key enzyme (3-hydroxy-3-methylglutaryl-coenzyme A reductase) increased more than 40-fold as compared with its activity when lipoproteins were present in the medium. The inhibitory factor responsible for the normal suppression of enzyme activity could be localized to the L D lipoprotein fraction of serum. Thus, we have developed an in vitro system using normal human cells for examining the regulation by lipoproteins of the enzymatic synthesis of cholesterol.

In an attempt to detect defects in this regulatory system, we have recently begun a series of studies utilizing cells from patients with different genetic forms of familial hyperlipidemia. Whether any derangements in the normal processes regulating cholesterol metabolism are related to the development of any of the inherited hyperlipidemic states, it is too soon to say. But an experimental system of this type does provide an approach to search for the basic defects in these hyperlipidemic states that appear to be genetically determined.

The Primary Prevention of Coronary Heart Disease

JEREMIAH STAMLER

Northwestern University Medical School

Life expectancy of adults in this country has increased only slightly since the turn of the century; for white men aged 40 and older the increase has been negligible. These are highly discouraging "vital statistics." The 20th century epidemic of premature heart attacks is the single most important factor at the root of this phenomenon. At present, well over a million heart attacks occur annually in the U.S., and about 700,000 coronary heart disease (CHD) deaths per year — 400,000 of them sudden deaths — are being recorded. Of the total CHD deaths, about 175,000 are in persons under age 65. CHD is the most important cause not only of death in this country but also of disability in the prime of life, at great cost to the nation. The NHLI Task Force on Arteriosclerosis estimated the direct costs of this epidemic of heart disease at $2.1 billion in 1967, the indirect costs at $13.5 billion, total costs $15.6 billion – undoubtedly up to about $25 or $30 billion at present, and a major factor in our high costs of medical care.

Major progress in controlling coronary heart disease requires better appreciation of the kind of enemy confronting us. Only with enhanced understanding of the nature of the problem will effective measures be taken to combat it and will they have a chance to succeed.

Presently, a North American male has a 20% probability of having a major coronary episode – myocardial infarction (MI) or coronary death – before age 65. In a high proportion of cases this first event is likely to be the last: about 20% of victims die within three hours of onset of symptoms (see Chapter 24, "Myocardial Infarction and Sudden Death," by Paul). At least another 10% of all cases die within the first weeks of the acute attack. Moreover, for the fortunate ones who recover, the outlook is far from bright: even when recovery is good enough to permit return to full-time work, they are, on the average, about five times as likely to die within the ensuing five years as men without a history of CHD. Death in most cases is due to a recurrent coronary episode.

These grim findings emerge from our group's study of the labor force of the Peoples Gas Company in Chicago and from similar studies throughout the country, combined in the national cooperative Pooling Project (a project for pooling prospective epidemiologic data from the Framingham (Mass.) community, employees of the Chicago Peoples Gas Company and the Chicago Western Electric Company, groups of Albany (N.Y.) civil servants, Los Angeles civil servants, Midwest railroad workers, Minneapolis-St. Paul businessmen, and Tecumseh (Mich.) middle-aged white males).

This effort combines the years-long experience of major U.S. prospective population studies of thousands of middle-aged white men initially free of coronary heart disease. Data from the long-term Peoples Gas Company study, involving 1,329 men aged 40 to 59 and free of CHD on initial examination in 1958, testify further to the catastrophic nature of coronary heart disease as it strikes a prime target, the middle-aged man in his most productive years. In the first 10 years of follow-up, 46 men died of CHD. More than half of the deaths were sudden, occurring within an hour of the acute attack. Almost two-thirds of men dying suddenly had had no prior clinical heart disease. Of these sudden deaths, all but one – 17 of 18 – occurred so rapidly that the victim could not be gotten to the hospital. Usually, time was too short to bring a physician to the scene. The same situation prevailed for sudden deaths from recurrent episodes. In fact, an absolute majority (67.4%) of all deaths, sudden and nonsudden, took place outside the hospital. This is why development of hospital coronary care units, employing advanced techniques and equipment, has done little to

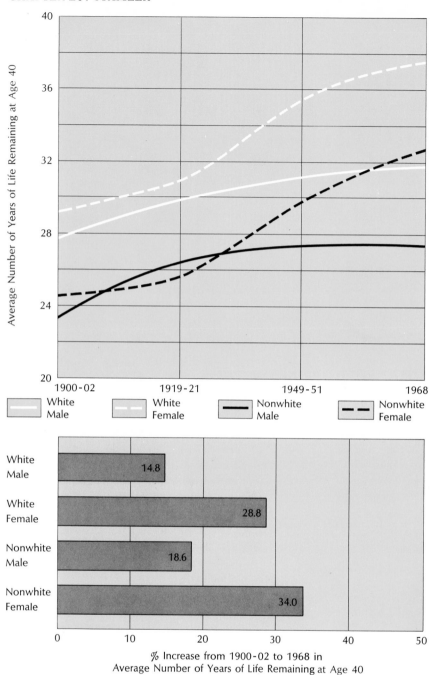

When gains in life expectancy since 1900 are evaluated in terms of years of life remaining at age 40, it can be seen that those for males, both white and nonwhite, have been small; percentage gains of white males have been less than those of nonwhite. Higher susceptibility to coronary disease is single most important factor in the male failure to keep pace with striking gains in life expectancy by both white and nonwhite women.

worldwide. As the World Health Organization Executive Board soberly notes:

"Coronary heart disease has reached enormous proportions, striking more and more at younger subjects. It will result in coming years in the greatest epidemic mankind has faced unless we are able to reverse the trend by concentrated research into its cause and prevention.

"The Board expressed a wish that countries most affected by cardiovascular diseases increase their efforts both to set up efficient services for control and to carry out more extensive research programs."

In most cases of acute myocardial infarction, sudden death, or other clinical expressions of CHD (angina pectoris, congestive failure, arrhythmia, conduction defect, etc.), the underlying disease process is severe atherosclerosis of the coronary arteries. Of course atherosclerosis can be found to some degree in most adults, male and female; but disability and death are almost always the consequence of atherosclerosis sufficient to result in marked narrowing or occlusion of the arterial lumen (see Chapter 15, "Development of Atherosclerotic Plaque," by Wissler). Hence, primary prevention must seek first of all to halt progression of atherosclerosis to severe form.

The Major Risk Factors – Keys to Etiology and Prevention

A fundamental conclusion, solidly based on decades of research data (clinical, pathologic, animal-experimental, epidemiologic), is that severe atherosclerosis is a metabolic disease of multiple causes in which altered lipid metabolism plays a crucial role. More specifically, mass occurrence of severe atherosclerosis and clinical atherosclerotic disease in young and middle-aged adults has as its essential metabolic prerequisite the mass occurrence of *elevated serum cholesterol* levels in the population. Lipid accumulation, most prominently esterified cholesterol, primarily in the intima of major arteries, has been recognized as the hallmark of atherosclerosis for well over a century. Circulating lipoproteins—particularly cholesterol-rich, low-density (beta) lipoproteins – are the primary sources for the accumu-

reduce overall mortality in our population from heart attacks. Even when a patient reaches a unit alive, often little can be done to overcome pump failure (see Chapter 24 by Paul).

The Need – A Strategy of Primary Prevention

For such a disease, hope for mastering its epidemic onslaught is un-

realistic as long as the sole or major reliance is on measures taken after overt illness occurs. Rather, an effective strategy for control requires that major attention be given to treatment before the first acute attack – in other words, to primary prevention. Unless *risk* of its occurrence is reduced, there is little hope of reducing the tragic toll, not only in this country but

lated cholesterol in atherosclerotic arteries (see Chapter 15 by Wissler and Chapter 19, "The Hyperlipidemia Syndromes and Coronary Artery Disease," by Goldstein)

A further conclusion is that the elevation of serum lipids leading to increased susceptibility to premature severe atherosclerosis usually results from *habitual excessive dietary intake of cholesterol and saturated fats.* Strong support for both conclusions has been obtained through several different investigative approaches, including critical laboratory experiments in which atherosclerosis was first successfully produced in animals.

These experiments were performed in the early years of the century (1908 to 1910) by Russian workers whose intent was in quite another direction. Anitschkow and colleagues were initially interested in the renal effects of a high-protein diet. To explore this question, they fed animal tissues to normally herbivorous rabbits. Unmistakable evidence of gross atherosclerosis developed in the hyperlipidemic animals, but which component of animal tissue was responsible? Hypercholesterolemia and atherosclerosis were again seen when cholesterol and fat in pure form were fed, but not when pure protein or carbohydrate were added to usual rabbit foods.

Since that time, atherosclerosis has been produced experimentally in every species used in the animal research laboratory: rabbits, dogs, chickens, rats, guinea pigs, hamsters, pigs, and primates. Almost without exception the means used have been an increased intake of cholesterol and fat, producing sustained hypercholesterolemic hyperlipidemia. Nor did the hyperlipidemia have to be extreme for atherosclerotic lesions to be induced.

Hypertension accelerates development of atherosclerosis in animals fed an atherogenic diet, although it does not produce the disease in those on a low-cholesterol, low-fat diet. Conversely, estrogens are markedly protective in some species on an atherogenic diet. Given such a diet, a complex interplay between endogenous and exogenous factors evidently can either aggravate or impede the disease process. It has also been demonstrated that atherosclerotic lesions in primates and other animals can be re-

Life Expectancy in Years for U.S. White Males, 1900 to 1970

Age	1900	1920	1940	1960	1970
0	52.8	60.3	65.4	67.4	67.7
5	59.9	62.4	64.3	64.4	64.4
20	47.9	49.1	50.1	50.1	50.1
30	39.6	40.8	40.9	40.9	40.9
40	31.2	31.7	31.7	31.7	31.7
50	23.1	23.2	23.2	23.2	23.2

Prepared by E. A. Lew, and E. Seltzer, from basic data presented by P. A. Jacobson, Cohort Survival for Generations Since 1840, Milbank Memorial Fund Quarterly, July, 1964, and publications of the National Center for Health Statistics, Department of Health, Education, and Welfare.

versed by cessation of the cholesterol-fat-supplemented diet, a fact of great importance in its preventive implications for man.

The possibility that atherosclerosis in man might be diet-related was first clearly broached around the time of the early animal experiments. European physicians serving in Africa and Asia consistently found much less atherosclerotic disease than in their own countries and suggested a relation to nutritional patterns. Severe atherosclerosis and coronary heart disease were invariably common among people whose circumstances permitted a diet rich in meat, dairy products, and eggs, and therefore high in cholesterol and saturated fats. Conversely, occurrence rates were generally low

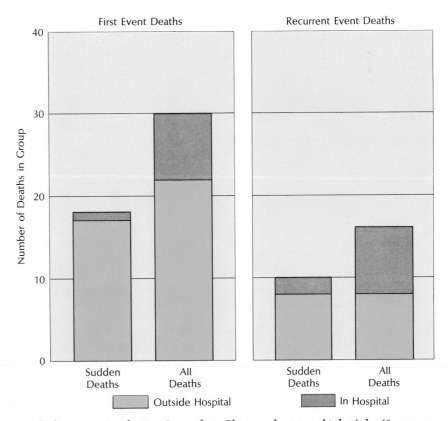

In the long-term Peoples Gas Co. study in Chicago, about two thirds of the 46 coronary deaths in the first 10 years of follow-up occurred outside the hospital, emphasizing the necessity of preventive measures if the coronary disease toll is to be cut. Eighteen of the 30 first-event deaths were sudden, as were 10 of the 16 recurrent-event deaths.

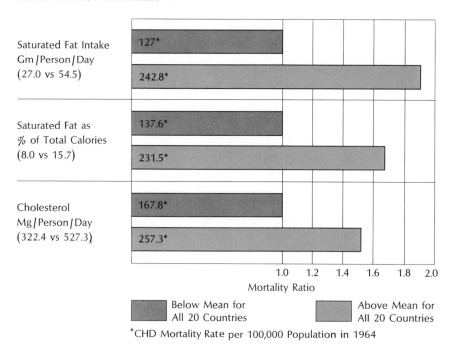

Saturated Fat Intake
Gm/Person/Day
(27.0 vs 54.5)

127*

242.8*

Saturated Fat as
% of Total Calories
(8.0 vs 15.7)

137.6*

231.5*

Cholesterol
Mg/Person/Day
(322.4 vs 527.3)

167.8*

257.3*

1.0 1.2 1.4 1.6 1.8 2.0
Mortality Ratio

Below Mean for
All 20 Countries

Above Mean for
All 20 Countries

*CHD Mortality Rate per 100,000 Population in 1964

Relationship between national diet patterns and death rates from coronary heart disease was clarified by post-World War II epidemiologic studies. Graph compares 20 countries in terms of intake of three nutrient categories. When mortality for men age 45-54 from countries below the mean for the specified nutrient for all 20 is set at 1.0, mortality for men from countries above the mean for the specified nutrient for all 20 countries is consistently and significantly higher.

in populations on less expensive vegetarian diets consisting chiefly of high-starch grains and tubers. The complement to these findings was the observation in the 1920's and 1930's by the first generation of clinical cardiologists – Paul D. White, Samuel Levine, and others – that in their mounting series of cases of M I, individuals with hypercholesterolemia (also hypertension and diabetes) were inordinately represented among the patients.

The expanding epidemiologic research following World War II provided the first mass human data on interrelationships among nutrition, serum lipid levels, and severe atherosclerotic disease and its clinical sequelae. Without significant exception, every large body of data yielded the same conclusion. For example, international statistics gathered by W H O and the Food and Agriculture Organization repeatedly confirmed a close relationship between national diet patterns and death rates from coronary disease among middle-aged men. The greater the habitual intake of cholesterol, saturated fats, and calories, the higher the toll from premature coronary heart disease. Differences were especially marked between popula-

tions of highly developed and underdeveloped countries, but were apparent even from analyses limited to economically advanced countries. In these countries, too, sizable differences in coronary heart disease mortality for middle-aged men could be related to national per capita consumption of cholesterol, saturated fats, and total calories, as well as cigarettes. Habitual lack of exercise, and other nondietary aspects of life in affluent countries, may also play a role in the multifactorial etiology of the heart disease epidemic. Data indicating an association between the number of automobiles per 100 persons and C H D mortality rates are consistent with this possibility. (The problem of the possible role of dietary sucrose is discussed below.)

Autopsy studies of the International Atherosclerosis Project on more than 31,000 persons who died in 15 cities throughout the world documented marked differences in the occurrence of severe atherosclerosis among different populations, and confirmed the relationship between severity of atherosclerotic lesions and intake of fats – as well as with serum

cholesterol levels. Incidentally, in these studies the degree of atherosclerosis was greatest in the U.S. decedents autopsied.

Data on prevalence and incidence of C H D, obtained in an international study of 18 living populations of middle-aged men in seven countries, were entirely consistent with those of both autopsy findings and mortality statistics. Again, differences in occurrence and severity of coronary heart disease were closely related to saturated fat intake and to serum cholesterol levels.

These studies also found that diet-induced hyperlipidemia is not the sole cause of atherosclerosis. Thus, one or more of the international studies implicated hypertension, diabetes, and cigarette smoking; i.e., their findings confirmed the multiple origins of the disease. But the epidemiologic data yielded overwhelming evidence that certain habitual dietary patterns are essential for development of a high rate of clinical coronary disease in a middle-aged population. (The suggestion that excessive ingestion of simple sugars is a key factor in atherogenesis is untenable on several grounds: the clinical basis for this claim has not been reproducible in several studies. Similarly, the epidemiologic basis for this claim is faulted by the data from developing countries, e.g., Colombia and Cuba, with high sugar intake per capita, but low saturated fat and cholesterol intake – and no epidemic of premature C H D. Finally, animal-experimental work gives no indication that high sugar intake as such can induce atherosclerotic changes – in conspicuous contrast to high cholesterol-fat intake.)

Primary prevention of any disease in a population is greatly aided when a "handle" is available for predicting its occurrence. The abundance of epidemiologic research both here and abroad in recent years provided that handle for coronary heart disease – by identifying and quantitating important risk factors. By definition these are traits or habits associated with a significantly increased risk of developing the disease in subsequent years. In terms of primary prevention the key risk factors are necessarily those amenable to influence. This excludes advancing age, which, of course, increases risk of coronary heart disease, and the well-established sex disadvantage for men, which prevails until fairly late in life. (Each year three times as many men as women under age 65 succumb to coronary heart disease in the U.S.)

Of the risk factors that *can* be altered, four are of cardinal importance – habitual diet high in cholesterol and saturated fat, hypercholesterolemia, hypertension, and cigarette smoking. These four are at present properly designated *major risk factors* for premature atherosclerotic disease, especially coronary heart disease. This

designation is appropriate, first because of the impact of these factors on risk, second because of the extent and consistency of the findings now available from multiple studies, third because of the independent and additive contribution of these factors to risk (at least under the conditions of life in economically developed countries), fourth because of the frequency of occurrence of these factors in affluent populations, and fifth because all are potentially amenable to mass public-health preventive efforts.

Almost all Americans are at risk

of CHD from childhood on because of their habitual diet, which is more or less high in saturated fat and cholesterol. This diet produces varying serum lipid-lipoprotein responses, depending on genetically influenced metabolic mechanisms as yet not totally defined (see Chapter 19 by Goldstein). A few metabolically fortunate people maintain optimal low-normal serum cholesterol-lipid-lipoprotein levels into middle age despite their "rich" U.S. diets, but the rest respond with hypercholesterolemic hyperlipidemia hyperlipoproteinemia of varying severity.

Correlation Coefficients: 1964 CHD Mortality Rates and Selected Variables for 22 Developed Countries

	Variable	Mean and Standard Deviation	Correlation between Variable and 1964 CHD Mortality Rate			
			Men 45-54	Men 55-64	Women 45-54	Women 55-64
	Income/person/year—U.S. $	1,373 ± 503	.444*	.515*	.259	.365
	Cigarettes/year	2,198 ± 935	.648**	.643**	.782**	.793**
	Cars/100 persons	18.2 ± 11.5	.516*	.583**	.439*	.490*
	Calories/day	2,959 ± 350	.570**	.634**	.209	.353
gm/day	Total Protein	90.7 ± 14.6	.675**	.722**	.434*	.525*
	Animal Protein	52.1 ± 17.9	.650**	.726**	.351	.491*
	Total Fat	112.9 ± 33.4	.463*	.558**	.065	.244
	Saturated Fat	46.3 ± 16.2	.580**	.654**	.175	.331
	Oleic Acid	43.7 ± 13.7	.518*	.628**	.137	.337
	Poly Fat	18.8 ± 6.9	−.213	−.161	−.382	−.299
	Cholesterol (mg/day)	431.9 ± 153.5	.617**	.685**	.399	.495*
	Total Carbohydrate	394.2 ± 32.7	.191	.124	.209	.150
	Sucrose	98.1 ± 25.8	.579**	.677**	.273	.491*
Calories %	Total Protein	12.3 ± 1.1	.527*	.514*	.648**	.597**
	Animal Protein	6.7 ± 1.7	.604**	.690**	.334	.474*
	Total Fat	33.6 ± 8.3	.391	.489*	.009	.193
	Saturated Fat	13.7 ± 4.1	.546*	.620**	.137	.308
	Oleic Acid	12.9 ± 3.6	.470*	.575**	.102	.298
	Poly Fat	5.6 ± 2.0	−.340	−.334	−.426	−.404
	Total Carbohydrate	54.1 ± 7.7	−.429	−.531*	−.057	−.241
	Sucrose	13.1 ± 2.8	.372	.460*	.183	.400

*p ≤ .05   **p ≤ .01

CHD mortality rates, 1964, 22 countries, means and standard deviations:

men   45-54: 212.3 ± 103.4   women 45-54: 47.3 ± 21.5
men   55-64: 591.6 ± 254.4   women 55-64: 196.0 ± 81.5

Data for CHD mortality rates in table above are from 22 developed countries; data for national income are from 19 of these countries; data on cigarette smoking are from 17; and data on motor vehicles and nutrients are from 20 countries.

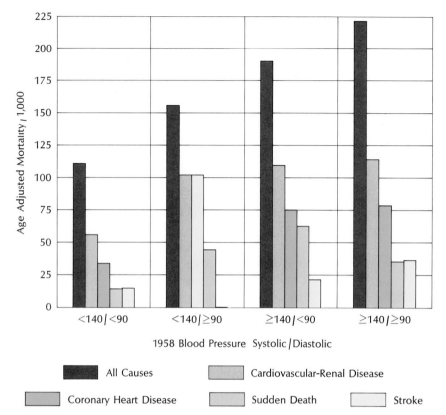

1958 Blood Pressure Systolic / Diastolic

- All Causes
- Cardiovascular-Renal Disease
- Coronary Heart Disease
- Sudden Death
- Stroke

In graph above, 1958 blood pressure and 12-year mortality rates are plotted for 1,329 men, originally aged 40 to 59, who participated in the Peoples Gas Co. Study. The men were free of definite CHD in 1958 and followed long-term without systemic intervention.

Among the several serum lipids, cholesterol has been the most frequently measured for detection of individuals predisposed to coronary heart disease. It has been amply documented that hypercholesterolemia is associated with grossly increased risk. Detailed analyses of the available data indicate that, for U.S. white males age 40 to 44, 45 to 49, 50 to 54, 55 to 59, and 60 to 64, *relative risk* – the ratio of risk for a man in a higher quintile (20%) of serum cholesterol level compared to one in the lowest—remains substantial even for the oldest age group, though it tends to decrease with age. *Absolute excess risk* – the absolute excess in probability of experiencing a heart attack in any given year for a man in a higher quintile compared to one in the lowest quintile, or risk of the former minus risk of the latter – remains the same or even increases with age. For the individual patient and his physician, *absolute risk* and *absolute excess risk* are the decisive matters. From the data of the National Cooperative Pooling Project (see page 226), *relative risk* of a

first coronary event for men with serum cholesterol in the range of 250 to 274 mg per dl was 2.5 times as high as risk for men with values less than 175 (112/45). The *absolute risk* over 10 years for these men in the 250 to 274 range was 112 per 1,000, and the *absolute excess* in risk was 67 per 1,000 (112 minus 45). Clearly, these data indicate the preventive potential of identifying and correcting hypercholesterolemia by safe means as early in life as possible.

Recent data from the Coronary Drug Project indicate that serum cholesterol level remains predictive of risk of dying in men who have recovered from one or more myocardial infarctions in middle age. This new finding indicates also a substantial rationale for secondary prevention – treatment of hypercholesterolemia in patients with frank coronary heart disease. In this regard, the Coronary Drug Project data are consistent with the results of at least one European study.

Finally, data from the Framingham

study indicate that for male decedents at autopsy, serum cholesterol measurements made five and nine years prior to death were significantly correlated with severity of coronary atherosclerosis, as measured by both percentage of intimal involvement and percentage of luminal insufficiency.

Clearly, the evidence on the association between serum cholesterol level and atherosclerosis is extensive and unequivocal.

The amassed data further demonstrate incontrovertibly that there is a steady increment in premature atherosclerotic disease as level of serum cholesterol rises. As cholesterol concentration increases, risk increases, and the relationship is continuous. This is true at all ages, or at least from young adulthood through middle age. There is no evidence of a critical level that divides "normal" subgroups "immune" to premature coronary disease from "abnormal" subgroups prone to coronary heart disease. Nor is there any justification for using the Gaussian distribution to define "normal" levels. It is unfortunate that this distribution was named the "normal curve" by statisticians, since they did not intend to imply anything about biologic or medical normalcy. Yet even now this distribution, particularly the level two standard deviations above the mean in our population, is being used to define upper limit of normal for specific age-sex groups. This is an unjustifiable definition of normal based on what exists – what is prevalent – in our population, without regard to the continuous relationship between serum cholesterol and risk, and without regard to the lessons from comparative studies of other human populations and other species.

For the physician responsible for patients, the basic facts about the continuous relationship between serum cholesterol level and risk are of the utmost practical importance in prescribing measures for prevention. The greater the probability, the greater the need for prophylaxis – but there is no single "screening level" separating those in need of prophylaxis from those who are not.

This basic set of conclusions does not negate, but rather places in proper context, the clinical use of practical cutting points, e.g., serum cholesterol of less than 200 mg per dl as normal,

200 to 249 as borderline, 250 or greater as abnormal for adults age 30 and over. As American Heart Association statements on risk factors have emphasized, this 250 mg per dl level for defining hypercholesterolemia is approximately the 2 to 1 cutting point, or persons positive for this risk factor are approximately twice as susceptible to premature coronary heart disease as those with lower levels, everything else being equal. The impact of these factors is no small 10%, but rather 100% – a doubling of risk. But as useful as this practical approach of cutting points is, it remains a distortion of reality. After all, a person with a serum cholesterol of 240 is at greater risk than one at 210, and this person, in turn, is at greater risk than one at 160. Moreover, a serum cholesterol level of 240 has an entirely different meaning in risk for a pack-a-day cigarette smoker with a diastolic blood pressure of 96 mm Hg, than for a nonsmoker with a pressure of 74. At present, modern biomathematical techniques for multivariate risk function analysis are becoming available to physicians, permitting them to evaluate risk factors simultaneously, as continuous quantitative variables. This will mean further improvement over present, already useful, approaches to assessing the significance of serum cholesterol level and quantitating susceptibility to premature atherosclerotic disease (see below).

As to other serum lipid and lipoprotein measurements and their relationship to risk of atherosclerotic disease, until recently only three sets of definitive data, from long-term prospective studies, were available for a scientific assessment. A fourth has just been published, with data from Sweden on serum cholesterol and fasting triglycerides as predictors. These data show that serum cholesterol and low-density lipoprotein (LDL beta lipoprotein, S_f 0 to 12 and 12 to 20 lipoprotein) are highly correlated – inevitably, since LDL is the main bearer of serum cholesterol. Correspondingly, serum cholesterol and LDL are about equal as predictors of risk of premature coronary heart disease. Further, the first three of these studies indicate that once determination of serum cholesterol has been made, little or nothing is apparently added to predictive power by measurement of very

low-density lipoprotein (VLDL, pre-beta lipoprotein, S_f 20 to 400) and therefore of serum triglycerides (VLDL being the main carrier of serum triglycerides). On the other hand, the report from Sweden concludes that fasting serum triglycerides are independently and additively predictive, although, in my judgment, the published data do not necessarily warrant this inference.

It is very possible that hyperpre-beta lipoproteinemia has significance for atherogenesis chiefly (perhaps solely) because of the associated hypercholesterolemia. No evidence is available indicating that, in the absence of hypercholesterolemia, hypertriglyceridemia (whether from endogenously synthesized VLDL molecules or from absorbed chylomicrons) is associated with intensified atherogenesis. Evidence *is* available indicating that both LDL and VLDL molecules are atherogenic, and LDL is more so. This is not surprising, in view of recent data confirming that the smaller LDL molecules infiltrate across the arterial intima more readily than

the larger VLDL particles, are subject to entrapment in the subintimal tissue (owing in part, at least, to their electrical charge), and bring into this tissue a much greater amount of cholesterol (and cholesterol ester) than VLDL per molecule. And it is this plasma cholesterol, especially cholesterol ester, that accumulates in excess (10-fold, 40-fold above normal levels) as an integral part of atherogenesis, first in smooth muscle cells, then, as these disintegrate due to lipid overloading, in extracellular pools, acting as tissue irritants to stimulate scarification – the sclerotic component of the pathology process (see Chapter 15 by Wissler).

On the basis of currently available data, therefore, serum cholesterol is the best single measurement for assessing risk of premature coronary heart disease. This is particularly true for mass screening in communities or at places of work, since serum cholesterol can be accurately measured without fasting, is subject to less laboratory error than other procedures, and is less expensive. Fasting serum trigly-

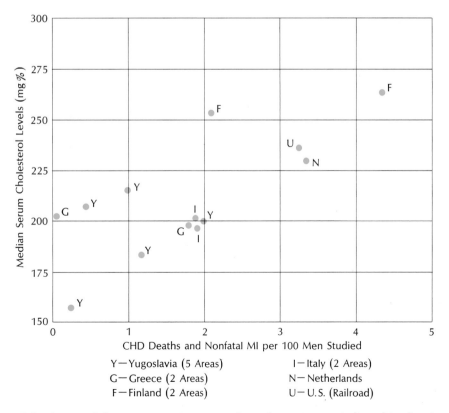

Y—Yugoslavia (5 Areas)   I—Italy (2 Areas)
G—Greece (2 Areas)   N—Netherlands
F—Finland (2 Areas)   U—U.S. (Railroad)

Role of national dietary patterns in coronary heart disease is again indicated in plot of age-standardized, five-year incidence rates of fatal CHD, nonfatal myocardial infarction, and diet-dependent median serum cholesterol levels (International Cooperative Study on Epidemiology of Cardiovascular Disease). Men age 40-59 were free of CHD at the time they entered the studies indicated.

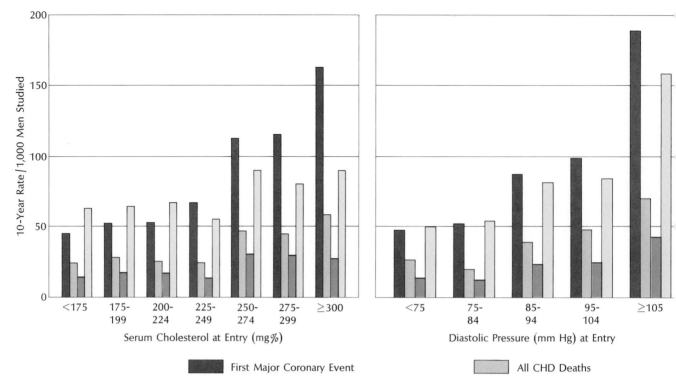

First Major Coronary Event   All CHD Deaths

Data from the national cooperative Pooling Project demonstrate the effects of three cardinal risk factors on incidence of coronary heart disease and the intensification of risk when factors are combined. The three risk factors are defined as follows: hypercholesterolemia, a serum cholesterol level of 250 mg% or greater at entry; hypertension, diastolic blood pressure of 90 mm Hg

cerides or lipoproteins determined by electrophoresis are not superior predictors of risk. Earlier claims that they were, based on preliminary or unsatisfactory data, have not withstood the test of time.

In the management of hypercholesterolemic patients, however, fasting serum triglyceride determination is a useful adjunct to cholesterol measurement. The rare chylomicronemias (hyperlipoproteinemia types I and V) can usually be detected from the serum test sample if the patient fasted for 15 hours after a meal moderate in fat and free of, or low in, alcohol. The technique is to refrigerate a lactescent serum for 24 hours and then to examine it for a supranatant chylomicron layer. It is unclear at present whether serum lipoprotein typing by electrophoresis is also worthwhile – claims to the contrary notwithstanding.

In the general population, the common phenomenon is "moderate" hypercholesterolemia – either without hypertriglyceridemia, or with hypertriglyceridemia slight, moderate, or marked, but without chylomicronemia. Once conditions known to induce hyperlipidemia (e.g., uncontrolled diabetes, hypothyroidism, nephrosis, bili-

ary obstruction, pancreatic disease, alcoholism, myeloma, contraceptive steroids) have been ruled out, it may be concluded that the abnormality is fundamentally diet-induced, i.e., acquired.

This is not to say that genetic factors do not operate in "common" hypercholesterolemia with or without accompanying hypertriglyceridemia. Since a small minority of Americans maintain very low levels of all serum lipids on usual U.S. diets, there must be an element of host response in all acquired cases of hyperlipidemia, and almost certainly this reflects genetic differences in metabolism. Correspondingly, since almost all persons with familial severe hyperlipidemia respond at least in part to diet, their condition is to a degree environmental in origin and related to the usual U.S. diet. Therefore, the distinction between acquired and familial primary hyperlipidemia is relative, not absolute. This conclusion in no way contradicts the fact that among persons with severe hyperlipidemias in particular, disease usually is due predominantly to genetic metabolic abnormalities. Of practical importance, for both diagnosis and treatment, is evaluation

of the entire immediate family.

Another key finding in both international and U.S. studies is that *hypertension* generally increases risk. In industrialized countries, where economic circumstances commonly produce the nutritional-metabolic patterns that lead to severe atherosclerosis, the significance of this phenomenon for morbidity and mortality is apparent. Even "moderate" elevations of blood pressure impose a penalty. This was shown in our Chicago prospective study (Peoples Gas Company) among 1,329 middle-aged men initially free of coronary heart disease. The 12-year death rate from all causes was almost twice as high for men with initial diastolic pressure in the range of 90 to 99 mm Hg as compared with those whose initial reading was below 80. Corresponding data for systolic pressure show a similar relationship to risk. Each measure of blood pressure considered separately is highly predictive. When elevated blood pressures were associated with definite or even suspect evidence of heart disease (e.g., minor E C G abnormalities), risk of dying was even greater.

When both systolic and diastolic

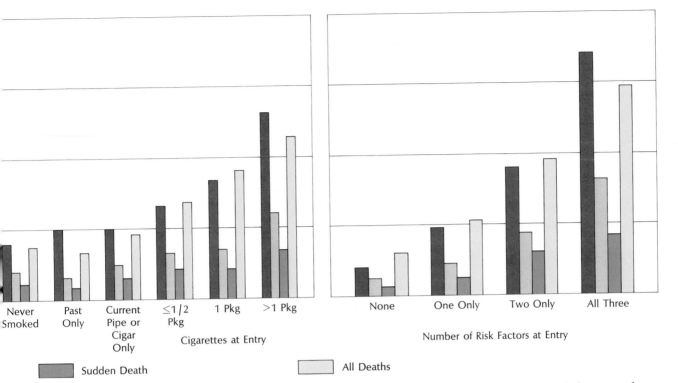

Never Smoked | Past Only | Current Pipe or Cigar Only | ≤1/2 Pkg | 1 Pkg | >1 Pkg

Cigarettes at Entry

None | One Only | Two Only | All Three

Number of Risk Factors at Entry

■ Sudden Death   ■ All Deaths

or higher at entry; cigarette smoking, any current use of cigarettes at entry. "Major coronary event" is defined as including nonfatal and fatal myocardial infarction and sudden death due to coronary heart disease. Populations pooled comprised over 7,000 U. S. white males age 30-59 at entry (all rates age adjusted by 10-year age groups to 1960 U. S. white male population).

blood pressure are considered together, men with true hypertension — an elevation of diastolic, with or without a concomitant elevation of systolic, pressure — are at greater risk than normotensive men. Of course, most hypertensives manifested elevation of both systolic and diastolic pressure.

In the Peoples Gas Company study, about 15% of the middle-aged male cohort free of coronary heart disease at entry exhibited systolic blood pressure elevation without concomitant diastolic elevation — so-called systolic hypertension. This is not truly hypertensive disease, its mechanism being quite different: in most cases, rigidity of major arteries, due to severe atherosclerosis. As expected, since this is a diagnostic sign of atherosclerotic disease in major arteries, this group also was at greater risk.

The data of the prospective studies demonstrate that, at least for affluent populations, hypertension is related to risk of premature C H D independent of and additive to the impact of other major risk factors.

It should be emphasized that casual diastolic pressures in the 90 to 99 mm Hg range are quite common in the U.S. adult population: prev-

alence rates for whites age 30 and over are about 10%, and for blacks about 20%. Unfortunately, many physicians dismiss such readings as clinically insignificant.

Preliminary data from the Pooling Project confirm the hazard associated with any increase in blood pressure above a normal level. When the populations, again initially free of coronary heart disease, were stratified into groups based on initial blood pressure, risk of a major coronary event over the next 10 years was doubled for the group with a diastolic reading of 95 to 104 mm Hg and quadrupled for the group in the 105+ range, as compared with the low-normal group.

The autopsy data of the International Atherosclerosis Project are consistent with these findings. They reveal a significant relationship between hypertension and severity of atherosclerosis in the aorta and coronary arteries. Similarly, findings of the International Cooperative Study on the Epidemiology of Cardiovascular Disease (the Seven Countries Study) indicate that differences among populations in five-year incidence rates for C H D can be attributed, in part, to differences in prevalence of hypertension

among the 18 "chunk" samples of middle-aged men.

Recent national and international epidemiologic findings also confirm the role of *cigarette smoking* as a risk factor for premature C H D. International data demonstrate a high-order correlation between average per capita consumption of cigarettes and coronary heart disease mortality rates for both middle-aged male and female populations of the developed countries. These data are particularly intriguing in that the correlation coefficients between cigarette smoking and coronary heart disease mortality are higher for the female than for the male populations.

In regard to individual differences in cigarette smoking habit and their relationship to risk of atherosclerotic disease, extensive data from several prospective studies in the U.S. and Great Britain demonstrate a clear-cut relationship. The data of the national cooperative Pooling Project are typical. For men smoking cigarettes at initial examination, the risk of experiencing a first major coronary event, sudden death, coronary heart disease death of any type, and death from all causes, was consistently higher in comparison with men who had never smoked or who had quit smoking. Risk generally increased stepwise with the number of cigarettes used daily. For users of pipe or cigar tobacco, 10-year rates were only slightly, and insignificantly, higher than those for men who had never smoked.

The largest prospective study of cigarette smoking, involving one million men and women age 40 to 84 at entry, has furnished follow-up data showing that for each sex and age group, coronary heart disease mortality increased with intensity of cigarette smoking – the younger the age group, the higher the relative risk associated with cigarette smoking. The youngest men smoking two or more packs of cigarettes a day were at highest relative risk. Absolute excess risk remained high for cigarette smokers throughout middle age. Moreover, autopsy studies indicate that atherosclerosis of the aorta and coronary arteries is more severe in persons who were habitual smokers than among those who never smoked.

The massive data from U.S. prospective studies (as well as the data of the International Cooperative Study on the Epidemiology of Cardiovascular Disease) also show that cigarette smoking, like hypertension, operates as a risk factor independent of and additive to hypercholesterolemia. The international and animal-experimental findings further indicate that the effects of both hypertension and cigarette smoking on this disease process are of little or no consequence unless the dietary pattern provides the nutritional-metabolic prerequisite for atherogenesis – hypercholesterolemia. It is evidently a matter of adding insult to injury. This is suggested by the animal experiments showing that hypertension alone never leads to atherosclerosis in any animal species, but when the diet is supplemented with cholesterol and fat, hypertension accelerates and aggravates atherosclerosis.

In relation to cigarette smoking, pertinent experiments involved exposing one of two groups of animals to carbon monoxide in amounts akin to those inhaled by habitual smokers. Both groups were also fed an atherogenic diet. Lesions of far greater extent and severity appeared in animals both exposed to the toxic gas and fed the harmful diet.

Questions of mechanism – how either hypertension or cigarette smoking aggravates atherosclerosis – remain to be resolved. Hypertension could lead to more infiltration of atherogenic lipoproteins into the coronary arteries through increased lateral pressure and by damaging the arterial wall. In reference to cigarette smoking, it is of interest that years ago Anitschkow showed that whereas injection of epinephrine into rabbits produced arterial scarring, atherosclerosis did not appear until animals were fed an excess of fats and cholesterol. Then atherogenesis was of increased severity, compared with rabbits not injected with epinephrine. The fact that nicotine increases circulating catecholamine levels may have a bearing here. Whatever the mechanisms involved, it is clear from the epidemiologic studies that where a population has a high incidence of hypertension and cigarette smoking but its dietary pattern makes hyperlipidemia infrequent (as in Japan) morbidity and mortality from myocardial infarction and other forms of coronary disease remain generally low.

In parts of the world where combinations of these risk factors are likely to be present, as in the U.S., coronary morbidity and mortality differ markedly when persons are classified by these factors. *The risk factors in combination have an additive impact.* This has been demonstrated both by the U.S. prospective studies and for European populations by the International Cooperative Study on the Epidemiology of Cardiovascular Disease. For example, data now available from the Pooling Project show coronary disease mortality to be more than three times higher among men in whom two of the three risk factors were initially present than among men with none of the three risk factors. CHD death rate among men manifesting all three risk factors was six times higher; mortality from all causes, five times higher.

A few details will underscore the significance of this analysis. At first examination 10 years before, men aged 30 to 59, free of CHD, were classified "high" or "not high" for each of the factors. The cut-off points were 250 mg% for serum cholesterol, diastolic pressure of 90 mm Hg, and any use of cigarettes. The analysis is a simple and crude one, in that a single measurement at entry is used to characterize each man, and his status with respect to the risk factors was based on division of the data according to the specified cutting points. Obviously, a serum cholesterol level of 240 mg per dl is not an optimal level in terms of risk, nor is a diastolic blood pressure of 88 mm Hg. Nevertheless, for purposes of this analysis, such values were designated not high. Despite these rather high cut points, only 1,249 of the 7,342 white men age 30 to 59 at entry (only 17%) exhibited none of the three risk factors. The remainder exhibited one or more: 3,320 (45.2%) one abnormality; 2,178 (29.7%) two; 595 (8.1%) all three; and 2,773 (37.8%) two or all three.

Presence of only one risk factor – as compared with none – was associated with an increase in risk over the next decade of almost 100% for the fatal end points, including total mortality. When any two or all three risk factors were present, susceptibility to overt coronary heart disease and fatal disease was substantially higher, reaching levels four or five times greater than for the group with none of the three risk factors. This high-risk group accounted for 62% of sudden deaths, 57% of coronary deaths, and 55% of all deaths in the study population. Detailed age-specific analyses demonstrate that these high levels of both relative and absolute excess risk are present for men with these combinations of factors at all ages through 60 to 64.

Clearly with combinations of these three cardinal risk factors so prevalent, and so lethal, special attention should be given to identifying such very high-risk young and middle-aged adults, and children as well (see Chapter 16, "Prevention of Atherosclerosis: A Pediatric Problem," by Blumenthal and Jesse). A halving of the CHD mortality in such men through early effective control of these risk factors would lower their total death rate by almost 13%. This would be a huge and unprecedented achievement. It is a realistic target to aim at over the next years.

A recently published handbook, which reflects the modern techniques of multifactorial risk analysis, should serve as an invaluable aid to physicians in identifying persons at very high risk of CHD. Titled *Handbook of Coronary Risk Probability*, it makes possible calculation of six-year CHD risk for any middle-aged patient. The book is based on the Framingham studies; the patient's sex, age, serum cholesterol, blood pressure, cigarette smoking habit, glucose tolerance, and ECG are used in risk analysis. This American Heart Association publication deserves wide circulation and use.

Other Risk Factors

Less definitively implicated as a risk factor, but sufficiently to warrant concern in preventive programs, is habitual *physical inactivity*, or a sedentary habit of life. Initial data on this point came from Great Britain: in homogeneous populations of middle-aged men, coronary disease death rates over the long term were higher in groups whose work involved relatively little physical activity (bus drivers and telephone operators) than among others more active (bus conductors and postmen). Similar findings were reported among inhabitants of Israeli farm communes. On the other hand, the five-year follow-up study of European populations is nonconfirmatory. Conspicuous are the findings on the East Finns, who consume a diet very high in saturated fat and cholesterol, and are generally very active and nonobese. The strenuous character of their work apparently gave little or no protection against either hypercholesterolemia or coronary incidence, since they were higher on both these parameters than the U.S. railroad workers.

Some of the prospective studies have shown a positive correlation between activity level and premature development of coronary heart disease; however, the data are inconsistent. Even in regard to the original British investigation there is a suggestion of confounding by preselection of employee groups, i.e., the bus drivers tended to be more obese than the conductors when they first went to work as young adults. Recently, however, the British research group has published significant positive results from their large-scale prospective study.

The most impressive positive data

from U.S. studies come from Framingham. When five indices of activity and fitness were simultaneously evaluated, in a questionnaire-based scale of total daily activity of work and leisure, vital capacity, heart rate, relative weight, and handgrip strength, persons assessed as more fit had fewer fatal heart attacks than the less fit. This association was independent of serum cholesterol, blood pressure, and cigarette smoking. Therefore, light to moderate exercise, of the type enhancing cardiopulmonary fitness (vigorous walking, jogging, bicycling, swim-

ming) may be protective if approached properly to avoid hazards, especially when combined with reasonable alterations in diet and smoking habits.

The role of *obesity* as a coronary risk factor has also not been fully documented. On the basis of the epidemiologic studies, it is incriminated to a lesser extent than the major risk factors. Obese persons are more likely to be hyperlipidemic, hyperglycemic, hypertensive, and hyperuricemic, but if none of these is present in an overweight individual, is he still at increased risk? The findings to date are

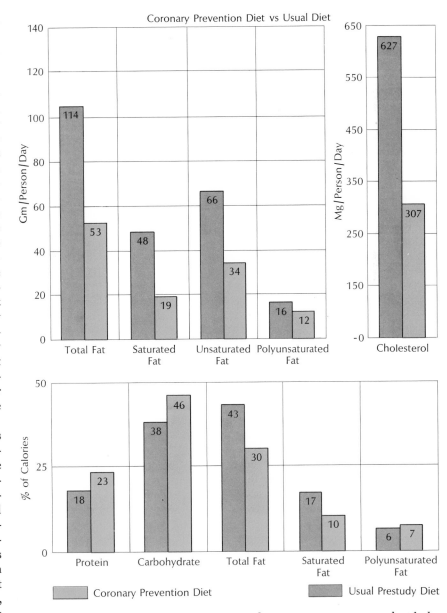

Diet used in Chicago's Coronary Prevention Evaluation Program is compared with the usual American diet (as eaten by participants at entry into study) in terms of composition and percentage of calories from major nutrient classes. The modified diet is low in saturated fats and cholesterol; moderate in calories, total fats, unsaturated and polyunsaturated fats; high in all essential nutrients.

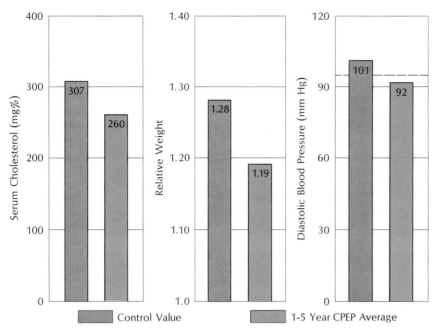

Effects of Chicago's Coronary Prevention Evaluation Program (CPEP) on various risk factors are summarized in terms of findings in men participating for at least five years. Control values are those for these men at entry into study. Relative weight is defined as the ratio of observed weight to desirable weight for height (from life insurance actuarial tables). Dashed line in graph at right is criterion for diagnosis of hypertension (diastolic blood pressure, ≧95 mm Hg at entry).

equivocal. It appears that in the absence of other risk factors moderate obesity adds little to risk, but this is still open. Very marked obesity is another matter. In any case, obesity associated with other risk factors is common, and its correction with a diet of optimal composition remains an important aspect of controlling the obesity-related risk factors.

For years, *clinical diabetes mellitus* has been recognized as a serious risk factor for atherosclerotic disease, although the mechanism is not well understood. The association between diabetes and coronary, cerebrovascular, and peripheral vascular disease has been extensively documented in retrospective studies, clinical and pathologic. Other data confirm that persons with atherosclerotic disease more often manifest abnormal glucose tolerance than do control subjects.

Population studies have presented only limited data in this area to date. Internationally, reports are available in the older literature – from China and Ceylon, for example – indicating that diabetes there was not associated with increased occurrence of severe atherosclerotic disease. Presumably, in the absence of an habitual diet high in saturated fat and cholesterol, dia-

betes per se was not atherogenic.

In the U.S., the study of Du Pont employees identified 370 men with clinical diabetes, and evaluated their mortality rates, compared with matched controls, over 10 years. The death rates were 25.4% and 9.7% respectively, i.e., 2.6 times as great among diabetics as among controls; CHD death rates were 13.2% and 4.6%, 2.9 times as great among diabetics as among controls; and death rates for all cardiovascular causes were 19.1% and 7.0%, 2.7 times as great. Mortality rates were consistently higher for diabetics than controls, whether normotensive or hypertensive, indicating that the diabetic state adds to risk independent of blood pressure. Whether diabetes adds to risk independent of serum cholesterol and cigarette smoking habit cannot be assessed, since no data are given. The more severe the diabetes, the greater the risk – diabetics on 40+ units of insulin per day show a mortality ratio of 5.7:1 compared with controls, and diabetics taking no insulin show a ratio of 2.2:1 compared with controls. Unfortunately, no information is available for diabetics using oral agents in treatment of hyperglycemia. These data do not demonstrate that clin-

ical diabetes, particularly the mild maturity-onset, nonketotic, non-insulin-dependent form, is an independent and additive risk factor for CHD and severe atherosclerotic disease of other sites.

With respect to *asymptomatic hyperglycemia (chemical diabetes as distinct from clinical diabetes)*, the Tecumseh study, based on response at one hour to a 100 gm oral glucose load given in its first round of examinations, reported an association between hyperglycemia and CHD prevalence for both men and women. The finding was independent of, and additive to, the effect of serum cholesterol and blood pressure. This set of prevalence data, indicating that chemical diabetes adds independently to risk, cannot be regarded as definitive pending incidence data and repetition in another study. (The problem in interpreting CHD prevalence data is a well-known bugbear of cardiovascular epidemiology.) Similar prevalence data from the Chicago Heart Association Detection Project in Industry, involving 35,000 young and middle-aged men and women, are not consistent in regard to the key question of whether asymptomatic hyperglycemia contributes to risk independent of, and additive to, the major risk factors. Again, long-term follow-up data are of critical importance.

The Tecumseh study has also reported that its long-term follow-up observations confirm the significant association between hyperglycemia and incidence of CHD. However, no data are available as yet to clarify whether this relationship is independent of other risk factors. Recently, the Framingham study presented multifactor analysis data suggesting that glucose intolerance is an independent and additive predictor of risk. (There the measurement was random blood glucose and glycosuria, not glucose after load.)

The only other set of U.S. prospective data is from our group's study of middle-aged men employed by the Peoples Gas Company in Chicago. While that investigation was begun in 1958, measurement of blood glucose one hour after a 50 gm oral load was done for the first time only in 1965. Several relevant items emerged from the initial set of data: plasma glucose and blood pressure (both systolic and diastolic) were significantly correlated, and this relationship held up after control for age, relative weight, and thiazide therapy. The higher the level of plasma glucose after load, the higher the blood pressure. Men with frank hyperglycemia (plasma glucose equal to or greater than 205 mg%) had a prevalence rate of hypertension of 32%, compared with 18% for men with glucose levels less than 205 mg%. Hyperglycemic men also exhibited higher rates of hypercholesterolemia and hyperuricemia.

For the period 1965 to 1970, age-adjusted C H D death rate was 42.1/ 1,000 for the hyperglycemic men, 15.6/1,000 for the normoglycemic men. Most of the excess mortality among hyperglycemic men was of men who were also hypertensive. (Hypercholesterolemia and cigarette smoking were also implicated.) Numbers of C H D deaths are small so far in these groups, and further follow-up is needed to assess the long-term trends. Nevertheless, the data pose important questions: what are the mechanisms — over and above chronic caloric imbalance — of the associations between hyperglycemia and hypertension, hyperglycemia and hyperlipidemia, hyperglycemia and hyperuricemia? Is a good deal, even all, of the excess atherosclerosis risk of mild maturity-onset, nonketotic, non-insulin-dependent diabetics in our population a result of the concomitant hypertension and/or hyperlipidemia, and not independently related to the hyperglycemia per se?

The posing of these questions is no esoteric exercise in epidemiologic dialectics. Very practical issues are involved. Maturity-onset diabetics number about 10,000,000 in the U.S., and their prime problem far-and-away is risk of atherosclerotic "complications." It is now more than ever clear from the results of the University Group Diabetes Program study that treatment of hyperglycemia with drugs — oral or parenteral (insulin) — is ineffective in averting morbidity or mortality from cardiovascular complications in such patients. Their atherosclerosis is no different in kind, only in degree, from that of nondiabetics. Therefore a total reconsideration and redefinition of control is needed for such diabetics. Even if hyperglycemia does turn out to be an independent

C H D risk factor for the diabetic, his risk of premature atherosclerotic disease is also potently related to his blood pressure, serum lipids, cigarette smoking, i.e., to the major coronary risk factors. Therefore control cannot remain focused exclusively on blood and urine glucose but must become comprehensive. It must include effective control of obesity, to correct hyperglycemia and hypertension; attention to diet composition, to correct hyperlipidemia; and attention to sedentary habit, to correct poor cardiopulmonary fitness and aid in control of obesity. Cigarette smoking must also be eliminated. Hope for the prevention of atherosclerotic disease in diabetics lies only in such a comprehensive approach to control.

What about *hyperuricemia?* When present, it is usually associated with other risk factors such as obesity, hypertension, and hyperglycemia. Evidence is available from the Peoples Gas Company study and others that hyperuricemia may operate as an independent risk factor, but again further clarification is needed.

Certain *personality-behavior patterns, social incongruities and instabilities, and psychosocial tensions* related to personal life situations and/

or those inherent in cultural circumstances have long been suspect as factors related to premature C H D (see Chapter 21, "The Central Nervous System and Coronary Heart Disease," by Rosenman and Friedman). The Report on the Primary Prevention of the Atherosclerotic Diseases of the Inter-Society Commission for Heart Disease Resources noted that this view has received support from several studies. Similary, data have been obtained indicating a detrimental effect of social.and geographic mobility and urbanization. These various psychosocial influences may be conditioning and/or aggravating factors in our society, particularly in the presence of other traits enhancing proneness to premature C H D.

Most of the positive findings indicating associations between various psychosocial factors and premature C H D have been recorded in single investigations and they require confirmation. Obviously this is understandable in view of the complexity of measurement in this area.

Coronary heart disease has long been viewed as related to *family history.* Evidence exists indicating increased risk of C H D in close relatives of persons who experience a heart

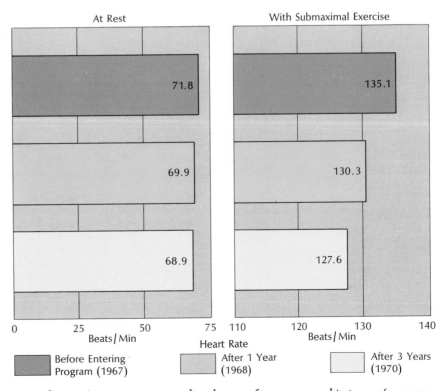

Some degree of improvement in cardiopulmonary fitness, measured in terms of response to submaximal exercise, has been observed in men participating in Chicago's CPEP.

231

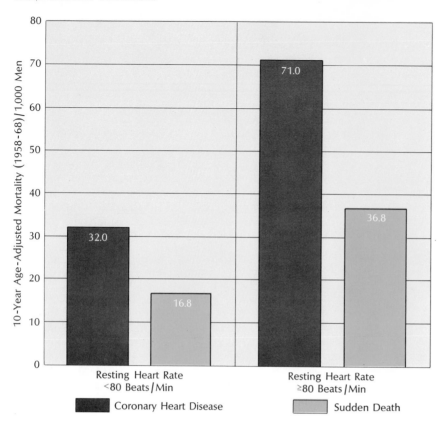

A high resting heart rate ≥80 beats/min) apparently was a coronary disease risk factor in Chicago study among gas company workers, as shown in graph above. If other risk factors were present, the effects were generally additive. As shown in graph below, if heart rate, blood pressure, and cigarette smoking were all judged high (diastolic blood pressure, ≥90 mm Hg; smoking ≥10 cigarettes a day) at entry into the study, the 10-year coronary death rate was about eight times higher than in age-matched men not manifesting any of these three risk factors.

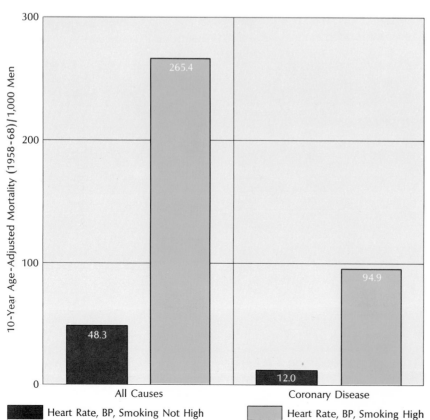

attack early in life, e.g., prior to age 50. There are numerous examples of multiple premature attacks within families. In contrast, there is little evidence for familial aggregation when the disease first occurs late in life. It is likely that much of this predisposition is mediated by familial resemblances in key risk factors, e.g., hypercholesterolemia, hypertension, cigarette smoking, diabetes, etc. Obviously, most of these predisposing influences are under both environmental and genetic control. Families share not only genes but also living habits. In any case, identification of a high-risk person, or an index case of premature CHD, should lead to a survey of the immediate family for risk factor status.

Two other types of risk factor, both involving cardiac findings, need to be mentioned. One is the abnormal electrocardiographic pattern, found with fairly high frequency in presumably healthy middle-aged men. For example, in our Peoples Gas Company study, 10% of apparently healthy men in the 40 to 59 age group had *abnormal resting electrocardiograms.* Electrocardiographic patterns indicative of bundle-branch block or other conduction defects, arrhythmias, and left ventricular hypertrophy have been found highly predictive. Nonspecific T wave changes—low voltage, diphasic, or flat T waves — may also be associated with increased risk. As indicated in the discussion of hypertension, these ECG findings are independent of, and additive to, the effects of the major risk factors.

The *ECG response to exercise* as well as the resting ECG can give important information relative to coronary risk. A significant number of middle-aged adults with normal resting ECG patterns exhibit an abnormal ischemic response (depression of the S-T segment) to moderate exercise. Long-term studies clearly show such persons to be at increased risk of subsequent clinical coronary disease including myocardial infarction. This may also be true for individuals with arrhythmias on the exercise and/ or postexercise ECG, or on the ECG monitoring usual daily activity.

A second cardiac finding that apparently is an important risk factor is a *high resting heart rate.* This was mentioned earlier, in the discussion of sedentary living habits and poor cardiopulmonary fitness. The Peoples Gas Company men showed an association between rapid heart rate (80 or more beats per minute) and risk of coronary death in middle age. The association apparently could not be attributed to the coexistence of other risk factors. If others were present, the effects generally were additive. For example, during a 10-year follow-up period, the combination of rapid resting heart rate, hypertension, and cigarette smoking was associated with a coronary death rate nine times higher than in age-matched men manifesting none of these factors.

Either of the two cardiac risk factors could of course be readily detected if screening for coronary disease risk were linked to routine medical practice. The overwhelming weight of evidence implicating the several risk factors, especially the four major risk factors, makes it mandatory for physicians in practice as well as those in public health to incorporate detection in regular examinations of adults, including the asymptomatic. There seems little justification not to do so, especially since early identification of very high-risk persons – common in our population, including teenagers – is feasible with use of a few simple, familiar, inexpensive procedures.

Hospitals have a unique opportunity to act as centers for detection of coronary-prone persons. All that is needed is a revamping and modernization of the test procedures done routinely on every person seen by a hospital, either as an out- or inpatient. For all too long, most institutions have been doing just a chest x-ray, blood count, urinalysis, and a serologic test for syphilis. Particularly with the availability of automated chemistry, measurement of such risk factors as serum cholesterol, plasma glucose after load, and serum uric acid should become routine. Of course, cigarette smoking habit and blood pressure determination should be a standard part of the evaluation of all patients seen by the hospital. At the very least, an electrocardiogram at rest also should become routine. Its yield nowadays is much greater than that of the chest x-ray. Furthermore, steps need to be taken throughout the hospital system to assure the retrieval of this set of

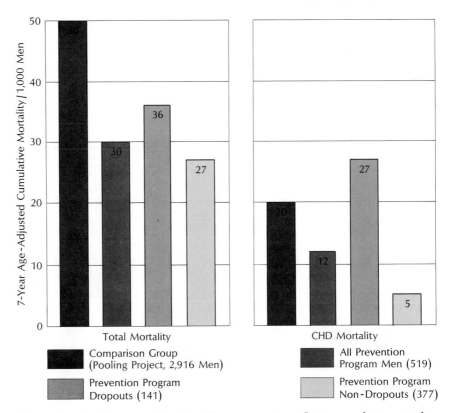

The end point of assessment in the Chicago prevention effort is cumulative mortality as compared with that for matched men from the national cooperative Pooling Project. As graph above shows, efforts to control risk factors appear to pay off. Record of men staying with the program is apparently much better (evaluated in terms of seven-year mortality rates) than that of the dropouts as well as that of the comparison group.

measurements in a special form, so that their meaning for risk assessment is specifically evaluated – and forwarded for essential prophylactic action. Here it is appropriate to call attention once again to the American Heart Association's *Handbook of Coronary Risk Probability*. Recent data from studies by the Coronary Drug Project, the Mayo Clinic, and the Health Insurance Plan of Greater New York show that the methods of risk analysis outlined in the *Handbook* can also be used to evaluate the prognosis of patients who have suffered one or more myocardial infarctions. These methods of analysis are not esoteric exercises in risk "pigeonholing" – they provide the physician with practical "handles" for long-term care aimed at improving prognosis.

Preventive Approaches

The inference is that with such identification of persons at risk appropriate measures can be taken against controllable risk factors. If *reversal* of atherosclerotic lesions is

achievable in primates and other animals by nutritional means (and a similar approach has reportedly caused regression of atherosclerosis in man), surely a prophylactic effort is indicated, with control of the four major risk factors its cornerstone. For the great mass of the population who have not yet experienced a clinical coronary event, the bold goal of reversal of lesions need not be set; the more modest ones of stopping or at least markedly slowing atherogenesis will suffice.

A body of direct experience has demonstrated both the possibility and practicality of a preventive approach. One can cite the long-term studies in Los Angeles, Helsinki, and New York. Each has involved several hundred men and used dietary modification to prevent or control hyperlipidemia as a fundamental approach to primary prevention. The nine-year Los Angeles study, completed in 1967, was conducted in a Veterans Administration VA facility. The second, which recently reported 12-year follow-up data, has involved patients in two mental hospitals. The third, the New York Anti-Coronary Club study initiated in 1957 and also still under way, is comparing volunteers on a modified diet with a similar group in the community on their usual diet. Reports from all three indicate a sizable decrease in the incidence of new coronary events.

In Chicago, we have had a broader preventive program under way since 1958, aimed at controlling multiple risk factors. It was deliberately decided to intervene against several of them – hypercholesterolemia, obesity, hypertension, cigarette smoking, and physical inactivity – to explore the hypothesis that primary prevention hinges on correction of damaging living habits acting synergistically to intensify risk. Modification of eating patterns has been the major focus not only for control of hyperlipidemia but other diet-related risk factors. Any indicated drug therapy for either hyperlipidemia or hypertension has been left to the judgment of the participant's personal physician.

The study cohort of the Coronary Prevention Evaluation Program includes 519 coronary-prone volunteers, at entry aged 40 to 59 and free of clinical coronary disease or other life-limiting illness but manifesting some combination of hypercholesterolemia, hypertension, cigarette smoking, overweight, and fixed minor T wave abnormalities in the baseline resting E C G. A few men with severe hypercholesterolemia, in the range of 325 or greater, have been included on the basis of this risk factor alone.

The diets used are moderate in calories, moderate (not low) in total fat and carbohydrate, low in saturated fat, cholesterol, and simple sugars, moderate (not high) in polyunsaturates and salt. The notion persists in some quarters that high polyunsaturate intake is the key to controlling hyperlipidemia. This is a distortion. In most cases, the decisive elements are significant reductions of saturated fat and cholesterol intake, with a calorie-controlled diet for correction of obesity. A given amount of polyunsaturated fatty acid lowers cholesterol only about one half as much as a comparable amount of saturated fat raises it. What is essential is to reduce saturated fat intake to no more than 9% of calories and to lower cholesterol

intake to less than 300 mg per day. With this approach, polyunsaturates at a level up to 10% of calories are ample. This is a diet composition like that eaten for generations by Mediterranean and Far Eastern populations known to have lower death rates from C H D – and from all causes – for middle-aged men than for our own. No population in the world has ever consumed more than 9% to 10% of calories from polyunsaturates. Therefore no data are available on the long-term safety of high polyunsaturated-fat diets, e.g., 15% to 25% of calories from polyunsaturates. Another mistaken notion is that controlling hypertriglyceridemia requires sharp carbohydrate restrictions, e.g., to less than 30% of calories. Only in very rare, severe familial cases may this apply. Correction of both the caloric imbalance and the high saturated-fat, high-cholesterol composition – with a moderate carbohydrate intake – is all that is needed to accomplish the desired goal for most patients. For some, curtailment or cessation of ethanol consumption is a decisive factor.

As a result of our dietary program, serum lipid levels and weight have been substantially reduced. Moreover, these changes have generally been maintained for years by active participants. Thus, among hypercholesterolemic men in the program for at least five years, serum cholesterol levels declined by an average of 15% (from a baseline average of 307). Serum triglycerides of hypertriglyceridemic men declined approximately 30% (from a baseline of 213 mg%). Weight reduction averaged about 7% and this weight reduction was associated with a significant and sustained decrease in diastolic blood pressure of obese hypertensive men, from a baseline mean level of 101 mm Hg to an average of 92 mm Hg over a five-year period. Undoubtedly, blood pressure of these men could be normalized (diastolics under 90) by judicious addition of antihypertensive drugs. Interview data indicate that most active participants have made a transition from essentially sedentary living to light activity. Serial submaximal exercise tests indicate that a modest enhancement of cardiopulmonary fitness has occurred. About half the long-term active participants who were cigarette smokers at entry have

quit, i.e., have smoked no cigarettes for a year or longer.

What of the results in terms of coronary heart disease? The end points being assessed are cumulative mortality as compared with that for matched men in the national cooperative Pooling Project. From the latest life-table analysis, through seven years of follow-up, the coronary death rate for all men in the program, including dropouts, was 40% lower than for the comparison group. For men remaining active in the program (nondropouts) the rate was 75% lower. For the high-risk men identified in the Pooling Project cohort, coronary disease mortality at seven years accounted for 40% of total mortality. For the high-risk men remaining active in the prevention program, coronary disease mortality represented 19% of total mortality.

Like other "first generation" trials described above, this program has been limited by relatively small sample size and lack of a randomly assigned control population (except in the Los Angeles V A study). Nonetheless, its results to date are certainly encouraging, generally consistent with those of the three other trials, and in agreement with what is to be anticipated from the experimental, clinical, and epidemiologic studies. (Although none of these trials has established specific benefits with cessation of cigarette smoking, this has been demonstrated elsewhere, including the impressive evidence from Great Britain of a substantial decrease in mortality among physicians who have given up the cigarette habit. Similarly, the positive results of the Veterans Administration trials indicate the efficacy of good long-term control of both "mild" and "moderate" hypertension.)

Taken together, the combined experience falls short of providing final proof of the possibility of preventing premature coronary heart disease by control of coronary risk factors. Large-scale, long-term "second generation" trials are needed to evaluate the effects of various interventions, particularly diet modification and multifactor interventions, on rates of premature atherosclerotic disease. This was the urgent recommendation of the Inter-Society Commission for Heart Disease Resources and the N H L I Task Force on Arteriosclerosis.

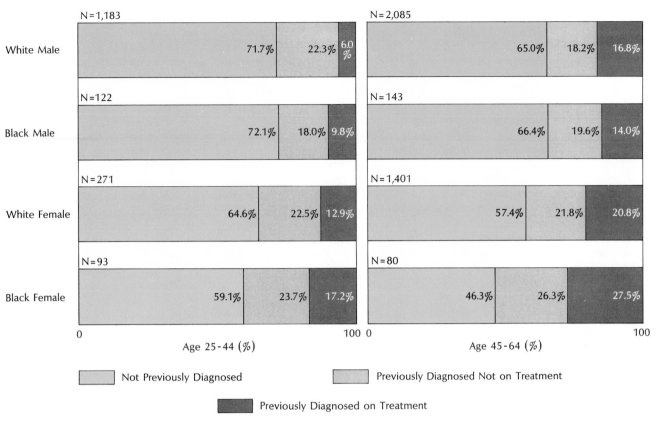

N=1,183

White Male   71.7%   22.3%   6.0%

N=2,085

White Male   65.0%   18.2%   16.8%

N=122

Black Male   72.1%   18.0%   9.8%

N=143

Black Male   66.4%   19.6%   14.0%

N=271

White Female   64.6%   22.5%   12.9%

N=1,401

White Female   57.4%   21.8%   20.8%

N=93

Black Female   59.1%   23.7%   17.2%

N=80

Black Female   46.3%   26.3%   27.5%

0   100   0   100

Age 25-44 (%)   Age 45-64 (%)

☐ Not Previously Diagnosed   ☐ Previously Diagnosed Not on Treatment

■ Previously Diagnosed on Treatment

In the Chicago Heart Association's Detection Project in Industry, a majority of the persons who had hypertension at entry were unaware they had the disease, and most of those whose hypertension had been detected were receiving no treatment. This was true regardless of age, sex, or race. Data cover the period from November, 1967, to May, 1972.

Such trials, e.g., the Hypertension Detection and Follow-up Program and the Multiple Risk Factor Intervention Trial, are just now getting under way, under sponsorship of the National Heart and Lung Institute. It is anticipated that such trials will take up to a decade to complete.

What should we do while we wait for these further answers? All have agreed for years on the need to find the high-risk people (who with their families number in the tens of millions) and bring them under effective long-term care, including diet therapy. But precious little has been done so far to implement this accepted policy. As far as the U.S. population as a whole is concerned, some argue that in the absence of "final" proof from mass field trials, general nutritional-hygienic recommendations to the public as a preventive measure would lack authenticity.

However, is it not wiser (as the Inter-Society Commission Report proposed) to use best judgment based on the huge amount of evidence already available and implement safe meas-

ures that can probably stem the epidemic – rather than suspend judgment? Since contemporary living habits render our entire population more or less at risk with respect to this disease, it seems entirely fitting to urge the public to modify living habits in the direction of removing or reducing the risk factors associated with premature coronary disease. Indeed, the Inter-Society Commission, in the report calling for long-term evaluative trials, emphasized the present need and propriety of primary preventive measures for the general public. In recommendations aimed both at individual physicians and the health professions, the commission called for a three-pronged program: dietary changes to prevent or control hyperlipidemia, obesity, hypertension, and diabetes; elimination of cigarette smoking; and pharmacologic control of elevated blood pressure. Specific advice in reference to diet includes adjustment of caloric intake to achieve and maintain optimal weight, a substantial reduction of dietary cholesterol intake to less than 300 mg per

day (the current average is above 600 mg), limitation of total fat intake to less than 35% of calories and of saturated fats to less than 10%. (For reasons already indicated, substitution of large amounts of polyunsaturates is not considered necessary for control of serum lipid levels.) To achieve these nutritional goals, the commission urged: "*Americans should be encouraged to modify habits with regard to all five major sources of fat in the U.S. diet – meats, dairy products, baked goods, eggs, table and cooking fats.*"

As the report noted, the feasibility of commercial preparation of foods designed to control hyperlipidemia is now well established (specifically by the National Diet-Heart Study). Community and government health officials, along with the medical profession, are asked to "encourage" the food industry to make generally available leaner meats and low-fat processed meat products, dairy products and baked goods reduced in saturated fats-cholesterol and calories, as well as fats and oils for cooking or table use of low saturated fat and cholesterol content. The new food labeling regulations set down by the FDA, if strictly followed by the food industry, should foster widespread marketing of superior fat-modified products that are easily identified by consumers.

In regard to hospital practice, one corollary flowing from these conclusions about nutrition is the need to modernize hospital dietetics. To cite one gross and persistent problem, hospitals throughout the country continue to serve even their coronary patients breakfasts of eggs, buttered toast, cereal with cream, whole milk — and foods similarly high in saturated fat and cholesterol at lunch and dinner — in response to physicians' prescription of a "bland diet." It is long since time to correct this anachronism by using pleasant and varied recipes and menus for truly bland diets low in saturated fat and cholesterol. This is an entirely feasible undertaking, as a series of articles in *Hospitals* (46:1, 1972, through 46:4, 1972) clearly shows.

A "major national effort" was also urged — by both the Inter-Society Commission and the Task Force on Arteriosclerosis — for improved control of hypertension, which, as indicated, is frequently undetected or, if detected, frequently untreated or inadequately treated. (As an example, in the Chicago Heart Association Detection Project among almost 30,000 industrial workers age 25 to 64, we found that 18.4% had findings indicative of hypertension; of these, a majority were unaware of having the disease. Among persons reporting themselves as hypertensive by history, a majority were receiving no treatment. This was true for younger and older, men and women, white and black, more and less educated.)

The commission and the task force also urged that high priority be given to elimination of cigarette smoking as a national habit. It called for multiple measures to achieve this goal.

In line with what has been learned about the hazards associated with multiple risk factors, the commission also urged development and expansion of community programs (using allied health personnel as well as physicians) to detect and treat persons of all ages highly susceptible to premature atherosclerotic disease. On the basis of recent experience such programs could have a large yield, since fully 20% to 30% of middle-aged adults — as well as a sizable proportion of teenagers and young adults — appear to be at very high risk.

Important as this is, emphasis on the high-risk individual should not deflect concern from prophylactic measures aimed at protecting the entire population against the large-scale occurrence of premature atherosclerotic disease. Any decision to withhold general recommendations to the public on the ground that "final" proof of their benefit is not yet at hand must also mean continued acceptance of high incidence and mortality for coronary heart disease among our young adult and middle-aged populations over the next decades. This toleration of the coronary epidemic is unnecessary and indefensible.

The Central Nervous System and Coronary Heart Disease

RAY H. ROSENMAN *and* MEYER FRIEDMAN

Mount Zion Hospital and Medical Center, San Francisco

Q. Do you often have the feeling that time passes much too fast for you to accomplish what needs doing each day?
A. I have felt that way constantly for the past several years.

Q. Are you impatient when someone does a job slowly that you could do faster, enough to step in and try to do it yourself?
A. Always.

These two questions are among a total of about 20 or so comprising a structured interview we have been using to explore the role of certain emotions, as expressed in overt behavior, in the genesis of coronary heart disease. More from the manner of response to interview questions than from their actual content it has been possible to identify a rather specific behavioral complex that appears to enhance risk of development of premature coronary disease and that acts independently of some of the other, traditional, risk factors. (From the replies cited plus various other reactions, the respondent above could be classified as coronary-prone.)

A relationship between emotions and transient cardiovascular changes is one readily perceived by most physicians; admittedly, many find it more difficult to accept the concept that lasting changes in both structure and function may also have a similar basis. Yet the evidence strongly suggests that emotional and behavioral factors operating through the central nervous system may play a major pathogenetic role in coronary heart disease. Although still under exploration, the evidence to date already indicates that this possibility must be taken into account as part of ongoing programs to control coronary risk factors. Otherwise, morbidity and mortality associated with premature coronary disease may well continue at their current high level despite measures to alter diet and lower serum lipids.

If coronary heart disease was a comparative clinical rarity until the 20th century, the probability is that the accelerated coronary atherosclerosis underlying its development was also a rarity. Epidemiologic studies have clearly shown that the increased occurrence both of severe coronary atherosclerosis and of coronary heart disease has essentially been restricted to populations both industrially and socially advanced.

The impact of traditional coronary risk factors – hyperlipidemia, hypertension, heavy cigarette smoking, and the like – is beyond dispute, and the intent here is not to minimize their importance (see Chapter 19, "Genetic Aspects of Hyperlipidemia in Coronary Heart Disease," by Goldstein and Chapter 20, "The Primary Prevention of Coronary Heart Disease," by Stamler). Their significance has been demonstrated in all prospective epidemiologic studies including ours, initiated a decade ago in California with more than three thousand middle-aged men (39 to 59 years old) as participants. Myocardial infarction or angina pectoris has indeed occurred with significantly increased frequency among men who at intake had elevated blood pressure, elevated serum lipid and lipoprotein levels, diabetes, and a parental history of coronary disease, and who were heavy cigarette smokers. The combination of two or more of these findings further enhanced the risk.

However, despite their acknowledged role, the traditional risk factors must not be oversold. In our prospective study population – no exception in this regard – factors such as hyperlipidemia and hypertension have been present in only a minority of subjects at intake, and also in only a minority of those who have since developed coronary heart disease. Indeed, most subjects considered at higher risk on the basis of such classic factors still remain free

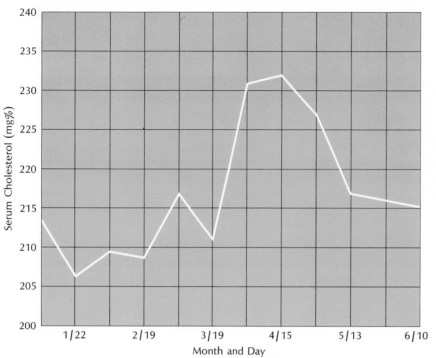

Impact of socioeconomic and psychological stress factors on serum cholesterol levels is evident in sharply increasing values recorded in a group of tax accountants as April 15 deadline neared for filing tax returns. Values promptly declined as pressure eased.

of clinical disease after a decade, and a considerable incidence of clinical disease has occurred in subjects not exhibiting the traditional factors at intake. In actuality, while prospective studies have permitted identification of traits that increase susceptibility to coronary disease, the findings unfortunately are predictive only for *groups* of people and lack individual specificity. Indeed, Keys and associates, after elegant statistical analyses of many population groups, recently concluded that relative risk in middle-aged men is well predicted by the classic risk factors, but that only about half of the total coronary incidence in middle-aged American males can be accounted for by such risk factors. Their findings clearly implicated another major risk factor, and it seems clear that some other factor or factors must often be present for classic risk factors to be pathogenetic.

Our own interest in these questions dates back at least 15 years, to our then growing conviction that dietary patterns and serum lipids did not provide sufficient explanation by themselves for the observable rise in coronary morbidity and mortality during recent decades. For one thing, studies up to that point (and many since) had

omitted consideration of other findings that might also be operative, for example, social and economic forces affecting people's lives. Actually their importance had been forecast more than 70 years ago by Osler in his comment that "in the worry and strain of modern life, arterial degeneration is not only very common but develops at a relatively early age. For this I believe that the high pressure at which men live and the habit of working the machine to its maximum capacity are responsible rather than excesses in eating and drinking." Since other explanations did not fully account for the increased occurrence of coronary disease, perhaps the interplay of external stresses and individual response to their challenge might prove to be a controlling factor.

To begin investigation of the role of social and environmental conditions, we measured serum cholesterol levels biweekly for six months in a group of accountants when they were beset by tax deadlines, as well as before and after when they were under far less pressure. Cholesterol levels were much higher during the period of deadline pressure, independent of changes in diet or physical activity. Serum lipid levels were later also

found by others to go up in other temporarily stressful situations, for example, in medical students facing major examinations. It seemed of importance, next, to study a larger group of men not seasonally but chronically stressed, especially since clinical experience had alerted us to certain personal and behavioral traits that might increase vulnerability to external pressures. These traits were by then seen so often in middle-aged and younger coronary patients that we felt they could be considered quite typical.

The emotional interplay, subsequently termed Behavior Pattern Type A, comprises a rather specific combination of personality traits including ambition and competitive drive, aggressiveness, impatience, and a strong sense of time urgency. To be sure, these are traits present to varying degrees in most men in today's world; the type A man has them to an enhanced, often excessive, degree. Our concept, then as now, was that pattern A arises in a subject more or less perpetually involved in a struggle in which he is determined to persevere. Sometimes the struggle is with other individuals he feels are out to best him; more often he is "at war" against time, racing to attain his perhaps unattainable goals before his chance runs out. The busy clinician can understand this ongoing time pressure and sense of time urgency. The type A individual is not coronary-prone by personality alone. His problems arise because the environment presents a challenge he feels impelled to overcome. In other words, it is the interaction of the susceptible type A personality and the modern environment that evokes the specific pattern of overt behavior associated with increased risk of coronary heart disease. The type A individual's "coat of arms" might well feature a clenched fist wearing a stopwatch.

We sought to evaluate the pathogenetic effect of behavior type A in a group of men exhibiting it in extreme form. For comparison we set up a converse group, designated type B, of men who manifested extreme passivity and lack of drive, and also a group beset by chronic anxiety and fear because of a severe physical handicap, blindness, since these emotions are not characteristic of type A men. The first two groups were recruited at their place of employment by lay selectors asked to choose subjects most closely fitting the two contrasting patterns; 96% of the men chosen agreed to cooperate.

As a group, the type A men had much higher serum cholesterol levels, shorter blood clotting times, and increased prevalence of arcus senilis. More significant was the far greater frequency of coronary heart disease in the type A men as compared with the other two groups. Twenty-three of 83 type A men were found to have definite symptoms or ECG evidence of clinical coronary disease, as against 3 of 83 type B men and 2 of 46 in the chronically anxious group of blind men. Comparisons of dietary intake of calories and fat, smoking habits, and exercise patterns revealed little variation in any of the three groups. Moreover, whatever was responsible for the type A behavior pattern, it obviously was not confined to any single socioeconomic group since men at both

high and low job levels were included among those showing typical A behavior.

As these studies proceeded, the presence of type A behavior proved to be related to the prevalence of coronary heart disease in other groups investigated, including women as well as men, and also with other biochemical correlates of coronary heart disease, including elevated triglyceride and beta and pre-beta lipoprotein levels as well as cholesterol. Type A subjects tested during their working day also consistently showed increased catecholamine excretion.

If type A behavior and its concomitants played a significant role in the advent of coronary heart disease, then their presence in individuals free of disease should have useful predictive value. Pursuing that important question would require systematically following a large enough group of subjects classified prospectively as coronary-prone on the basis of be-

havior pattern. Such a study was initiated by our research group in 1960-61 with some 3,500 men aged 39 to 59 at intake, employed in 10 California companies. Collaborating investigators in Los Angeles classified the men prospectively on the basis of serum lipoproteins (beta/alpha lipoprotein ratio); data on blood coagulation were obtained by other collaborators then in San Antonio.

Our earlier work had convinced us that an oral interview administered by trained personnel would be the best approach to behavioral typing. This would allow assessment of both the intensity and emotional overtone of responses, usually more revealing in distinguishing A from B than the actual words used in answering the structured questions. The subject's motor behavior — gestures, grimaces, and other "body language" — is also readily evident. Emphatic, often explosive, replies are typical of the type A person; his voice, for example, is

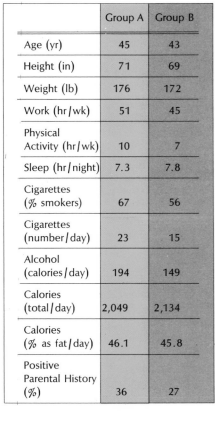

	Group A	Group B
Age (yr)	45	43
Height (in)	71	69
Weight (lb)	176	172
Work (hr/wk)	51	45
Physical Activity (hr/wk)	10	7
Sleep (hr/night)	7.3	7.8
Cigarettes (% smokers)	67	56
Cigarettes (number/day)	23	15
Alcohol (calories/day)	194	149
Calories (total/day)	2,049	2,134
Calories (% as fat/day)	46.1	45.8
Positive Parental History (%)	36	27

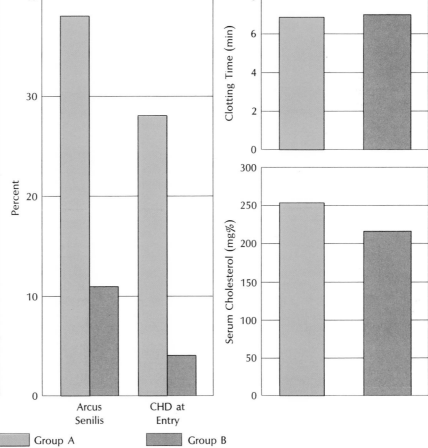

Group A   Group B

In 1959 prevalence study of 83 group A and 83 group B subjects, men in each group were essentially comparable in age, weight, and dietary habits (table at left); however, the incidence of pre-existing clinical coronary disease and of arcus senilis was significantly higher in group A (graph at center). On the average, serum cholesterol levels for group A men were also noticeably higher.

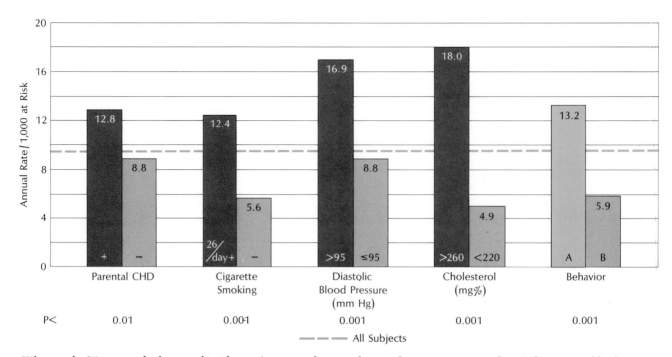

When, at the 8½ year mark, the annual incidence of coronary disease among the study population of approximately 3,500 men was classified according to presence of risk factors at entry, the contribution of group A behavior pattern does not appear at first glance to be quite as great as that of elevations in blood pressure or serum cholesterol. However, analysis of incidence by behavior pattern in addition to traditional risk factors yielded the findings shown in the graphs on page 241.

loud and at times even hostile in tone. In his impatience he anticipates what others will say, including the interviewer, and frequently interrupts to answer questions before they are fully asked.

Interview questions were designed in part to elicit angry and aggressive feelings, both past and present, as well as the degree of drive and ambition throughout a subject's working life, and above all his sense of time urgency, since this factor more than any other appears to intensify and sustain the type A pattern. As his responses indicate, the type A person is invariably punctual and greatly annoyed if kept waiting; he rarely finds time to indulge in hobbies, and when he does, he makes them as competitive as his vocation. He dislikes helping at home in routine jobs because he feels that his time can be spent more profitably. He walks rapidly, eats rapidly, and rarely remains long at the dinner table. He often tries to do several things at once and carries a second line of thought if he can possibly manage it. Admittedly, some type B subjects may reply similarly to certain interview questions, but differences in tone and mood usually are unmistakable.

In the procedure followed in the prospective study, all intake interviews were tape-recorded and the recordings, plus descriptive information provided by the interviewers, were used by us for behavioral typing. To insure against bias neither of us met any of the study subjects ourselves or had access to other information about them; behavioral typing was based on interview data alone. The intent was not to single out extreme forms of the two behavior patterns, as in the earlier prevalence studies, but rather to identify type A and type B behavior more broadly as each might occur in the general population. Hence, subjects strongly exhibiting type A behavior were classified as A-1, the remainder in the A group as A-2; similarly, subjects exhibiting type B behavior in clearest form were classified as B-4, the others as B-3. As learned then, and since confirmed, some 10% of urban, employed subjects are likely to be type A-1, another 10% type B-4. The majority exhibit either type A or type B behavior to a lesser degree, but nevertheless enough for classification.

The behavioral type arrived at for each man in the prospective study, along with information on serum lipoproteins and blood coagulability obtained by the collaborating groups, was funneled directly to an independent data repository committee; other material obtained at intake, including medical and family history, diet, exercise, and smoking habits, anthropometric data, and cardiovascular findings, was also entered in the data bank.

From the outset, type A behavior proved strongly associated with clinical coronary disease. Preexisting coronary disease was found at intake in 113 of the 3,524 subjects. A type A classification had been given to 70.9% of these men (and to 52.0% of the total group). By the end of 1963 (after a mean interval of 2½ years) 70 of 3,182 subjects then at risk had developed coronary heart disease (52 were cases of myocardial infarction, 9 of them fatal; the remainder were angina pectoris). Before developing coronary heart disease these men had shared many similarities with the unaffected group, e.g., dietary and exercise patterns were similar, as were smoking habits. Mean serum cholesterol and triglyceride levels were somewhat higher in coronary cases: 249 mg% vs 224 mg% for cholesterol; 159.6 mg% vs 147.7 mg% for triglycerides. More coronary men (27.1% vs 9.4%) had an elevated diastolic blood pressure. A far greater proportion had been classified as coronary-prone on the basis of behavior pattern

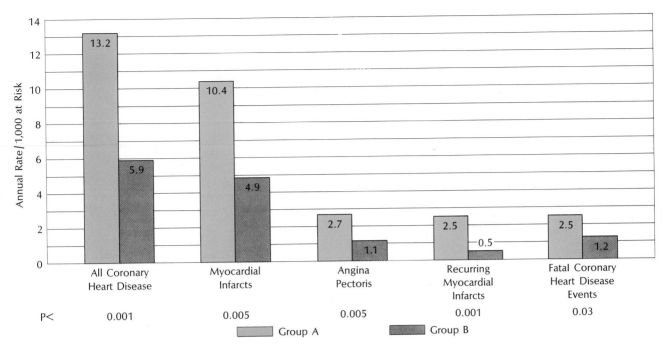

After 8½ years of follow-up the incidence of new coronary disease events in the study population was found to run at least twice as high among group A as among group B subjects; a similar relationship applies when cases are classified as to type of heart disease. Moreover, in the presence of type A behavior, the risk of recurrence of myocardial infarction is markedly increased; in addition, there is a definite trend to type A behavior in cases of myocardial infarction that terminated in death.

(85.2% vs 47.0% of all subjects aged 39 to 49 at intake and 72.1% vs 57.9% of all those aged 50 to 59). Significantly, while the presence of hypercholesterolemia or hyperbetalipoproteinemia or both clearly increased the risk of coronary disease, this effect was much less obvious in subjects who had been classified as type B in behavior. Similarly, though there was a threefold greater incidence of new coronary disease in men with pre-existing hypertension, almost all hypertensives who developed heart disease had exhibited type A behavior before the latter became manifest. It became clear that elevated diastolic blood pressure or serum lipids (or both) carried major prognostic significance only when they occurred in association with type A behavior. These relationships continued to apply as the study continued.

Within a mean follow-up period of 4½ years, 133 of the men developed clinical coronary disease (acute myocardial infarction in 104). Behavior pattern proved significantly related among younger men in particular: In the 39-to-49-year age group 71.5% of the heart patients came from the type A group. In the disease-free group the two behavior types were about equally represented.

A separate analysis was done on cases of clinically unrecognized infarction, either present at intake or occurring in the follow-up period. (There had been 42 such cases detected at intake; at the 4½-year mark, 31 of the 104 new infarction cases were of the "silent" type.)

Comparison with age-paired non-coronary subjects revealed significant differences, again most marked for younger men. In the 39-to-49-year age group, men developing unrecognized infarction significantly more often reported a parental history of coronary disease, had elevated serum triglycerides and elevated systolic blood pressure, and were heavy smokers; 71.4% had been classified as type A in behavior, as compared to 46.4% of age mates without heart disease. It seemed noteworthy that in this younger age group the frequency of unrecognized infarction was not significantly increased among men exhibiting diastolic blood pressure above 94 mm Hg, nor among subjects who had serum cholesterol levels exceeding 259 mg%. Rather, the risk factor that appeared with greatest frequency was the type A behavior pattern; from the evidence, both in reference to clinically evident and silent heart disease, it appeared to operate independently of blood pres-

sure, serum lipid or lipoprotein levels, cigarette smoking, parental history, or any of the other factors under study.

It was felt, however, that further statistical testing was necessary to ensure that the predictive power of type A behavior could not be "explained away" by its association with classic risk factors often also present. With bivariate analysis, it was shown that the impact of type A behavior remained despite statistical control of another risk factor such as elevated serum cholesterol or parental history of coronary heart disease. Subsequently, a multiple regression procedure was used to control a broad series of effective risk predictors simultaneously; the impact of the coronary-prone behavior pattern remained highly significant. In the 39-to-49 age group, the coronary disease risk of type A proved to be twice that of type B men when serum lipids, blood pressure, smoking, obesity, and several other influences were all held constant. In the older (50 to 69) group, type A men were still at increased risk, although the differences were no longer as significant.

By the 6½-year mark, clinical heart disease had developed in 195 of the 3,182 subjects; 139 of the 195 had been classified at intake as exhibiting type A behavior. The increased incidence of coronary disease in type A men continued to prevail when behavior pattern again was stratified by "high" or "low" values for other risk factors. By this study, the coronary disease incidence for type A men with a "low" value for some other risk factor was found to approximate the incidence in type B men with a "high"

value for the same factor. With multiple risk factors in addition to type A behavior the latter could still have an overriding effect.

At latest count, after 8½ years, 257 men in the prospective study have experienced clinical heart disease; the impact of type A behavior as a risk factor continues to be unmistakable. To be sure, the effect was greater in

the early prevalence studies, in which the coronary disease rate was sevenfold higher among type A subjects; in the prospectively followed population, which includes a range of type A and type B behavior instead of only the extreme forms, the incidence of heart disease is two to three times higher among type A subjects, still surely enough of a difference to warrant concern.

If type A behavior were associated not only with occurrence of coronary heart disease but with risk of recurrence it would of course be important to know that too. Hence the prospective study data were analyzed to compare findings in recurring and nonrecurring infarction; the critical question of whether the risk of fatal infarction was increased was also investigated. These analyses were done at the 4½-year point; of the 104 new cases of myocardial infarction to that time, 23 had been fatal; 13 of the 104 men had had a second episode. Comparison of younger men with recurring and nonrecurring infarction showed a higher frequency of serum lipid elevation and type A behavior in the former prior to either the first or second attack; in older subjects only the higher frequency of diastolic hypertension proved statistically significant.

Among men with fatal vs nonfatal infarction, higher serum lipid values proved to be the chief distinguishing feature; there was a trend to more type A behavior in fatal cases but this difference was not statistically significant. Clearly, though, in both fatal and nonfatal cases, type A behavior was far more frequent than among men remaining free of heart disease.

At the 8½-year follow-up in which 257 men had experienced clinical morbidity, 41 had suffered two or more myocardial infarctions and 50 had suffered fatal coronary events. Type A behavior had been classified prospectively in 34 of the 41 subjects with recurring coronary events and in 34 of the 50 subjects suffering fatal coronary events. At this point the much higher incidences of recurring and of fatal coronary events in type A men was highly significant statistically.

From the epidemiologic evidence, then, the presence of type A behavior carries profound prognostic import, particularly for younger men, in terms

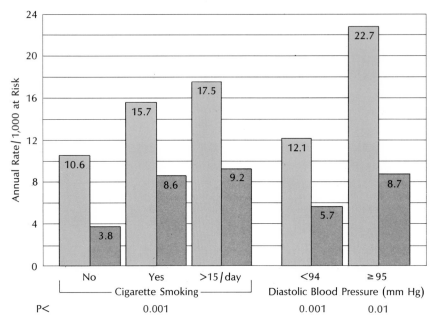

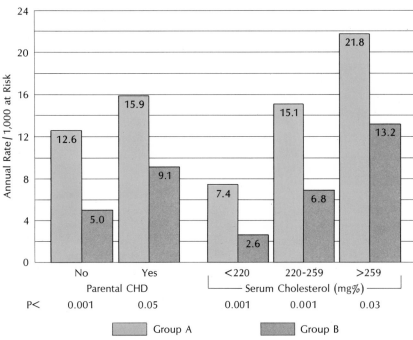

The apparent overriding effect of type A behavior is reflected in coronary disease incidence rates after 8½ years of follow-up of subjects who had been rated "high" or "low" at entry in reference to traditional coronary risk factors. As can be seen, incidence rates among type A men free of one or another risk factor may approximate or even exceed those among type B men rated "high" for the same risk factor.

of occurrence of coronary disease as well as its outcome. From what we now know it seems safe to say that serious coronary disease will occur infrequently before the age of 60 or thereabouts in the absence of type A behavior, except in subjects with diabetes, hypertension, or more marked hyperlipidemias. The behavioral assessment increases the predictive value of other risk factors; if it is not included, then no matter how large the population sample or how carefully other entities are studied, the probability exists of serious error in evaluating risk.

It must be made quite clear, however, that from a practical viewpoint the findings do not permit use of behavior typing to predict occurrence of coronary heart disease in a given patient. Type A behavior, like any of the other risk factors identified thus far, has been detected in many more subjects remaining free of heart disease than in those affected by it. Nevertheless, a considerable incidence of clinical disease still occurs in type A individuals not exhibiting any of the other classic risk factors. A physician observing these factors, behavior included, can only advise a patient that he has a higher risk of coronary disease than the average individual his age. He cannot yet be more definite.

On the other hand, one can with more certainty predict relative immunity to premature coronary heart disease in a subject with fully developed type B behavior. An analysis done after 4½ years of our prospective study convinced us that a B-4 type middle-aged man manifesting normotension and low values for two or more of the lipid entities (serum cholesterol below 226 mg% and either triglycerides below 126 mg% or a beta/alpha lipoprotein ratio below 2.01) could be given rather definite assurance that he would not incur coronary heart disease at least within the ensuing 4½ years. Subsequent follow-up studies indicate that such prediction for the type B-4 man can safely be extended for a longer period. In contrast, no combination of low lipid or blood pressure values permits similar assurance for men exhibiting type A behavior.

Our method of behavioral typing utilizing the taped personal interview has yielded a high degree of agree-

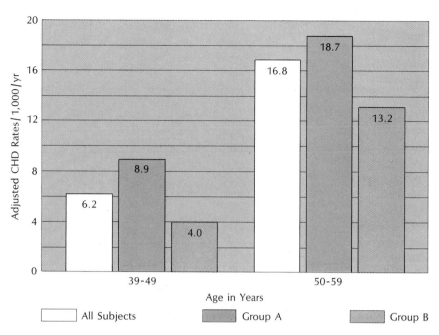

With statistical control of a broad series of other coronary risk factors by means of a multiple regression procedure, the predictive power of type A behavior persisted, especially among younger men in the study group. Among men in the 39-49-year age group at entry, the coronary disease risk was at least twice that among type B men of the same age. Older men manifesting type A behavior were also at increased risk although the difference here was less significant. The 12 risk factors held constant in this analysis (made after 4½ years of follow-up) included (among others) hypercholesterolemia, hypertension, excessive cigarette smoking, obesity, and parental history of coronary disease.

ment among evaluators (in the range of 85% to 90%); moreover, results are reproducible over an extended period. Nonetheless, we have also been searching for other, more objective, methods in which the subjective role of the rater becomes less critical. One such approach is a "voice analysis" test wherein a graphic record is obtained of the rhythm, tone, and timing of the subject's speech. Most type A and type B subjects can be differentiated by use of this test and it is now considered a useful adjunct.

Until recently our work on the role of behavior and emotional factors in coronary disease had received little confirmation elsewhere; independent assessment of our approach by several other investigators has now begun to provide corroboration. For example, using our interview procedure, Quinlan, Barrow, et al found the prevalence of myocardial infarction in Benedictine and Trappist monks to be four times higher in men classified as type A than in comparable type B men. Angina pectoris was twice as prevalent. Earlier, employing their own psychological technique, Brozek, Keys, and Blackburn could readily distin-

guish the potential heart disease victim among men prospectively followed during a 14-year period. The former exhibited a higher activity drive, was more likely to be "on the go" and to "speak, walk, write, drive, and eat fast even when he does not have to do so," a quite accurate description of our type A individual. In a pertinent Swedish study, Liljefors and Rahe obtained psychosocial histories on identical twins discordant for coronary disease. They found significant intrapair differences for the category of "life dissatisfactions" as well as total psychosocial score; in contrast, correlations run on subjects' medical history, smoking habits, cholesterol levels, and the like proved inconsistent and generally insignificant.

To be sure, none of the epidemiologic correlations permit conclusions as to whether the relationship between behavior and heart disease is causal or merely associative. As our prospective investigation proceeded, we attempted to answer an important basic question related to a possible causal relationship: Does type A behavior accelerate the atherosclerotic process in the coronary arteries? An autopsy study per-

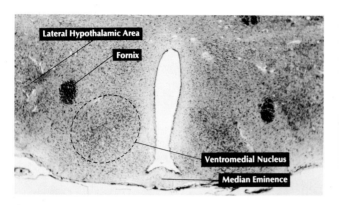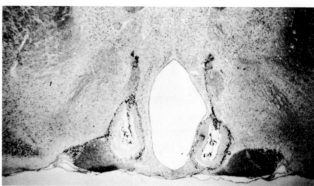

Hypothalamus may be CNS region involved in hypercholesterolemia seen in group A individuals. Experiments in rats suggest that the specific areas involved are fornix, medial portion of lateral hypothalamic areas, and ventromedial nucleus. Above, left, is intact midhypothalamus of a normal rat; right, lesions that produced chronic hypercholesterolemia and aggressive behavior.

formed after 5½ years yielded relevant information on this point. By then there had been 82 deaths — 40 from heart disease and 42 from other causes; coronary arteries of 51 of the victims were available for study of the relationship between the nature and severity of atherosclerosis present at death and the type of behavior manifested during life. Eighty-five percent of the men dying of heart disease were found to be type A in behavior; moreover, regardless of cause of death or age group, type A victims were found to have a greater degree of underlying coronary atherosclerosis. This was demonstrated by grading severity of coronary atherosclerosis on a 6-point scale; in younger men the average grade of atherosclerosis in the right and left coronary arteries was 2.5 and 3.1 respectively in type A and 1.8 and 2.0 in type B subjects. In the older men, the averages were 3.5 and 3.8 in type A and 1.8 and 1.9 in type B.

Concerning the possible mechanisms whereby behavior pattern might accelerate atherosclerosis, our earlier findings linking fully developed type A behavior and various biochemical correlates of coronary heart disease could of course have a bearing. In further work, we have also seen that type A subjects as compared with type B manifest a significantly increased insulin response to glucose. As before, this cannot be ascribed to differences in age, weight, habits of physical activity, or dietary intake. Although the role of these abnormal lipid and insulin responses in pathogenesis is not known, other laboratory observations may have a bearing.

Earlier experiments in rabbits suggested that the hypothalamus may be the crucial area of the central nervous system through which the damaging behavior pattern is expressed; our more recent observations have strengthened our belief that this may be so. The experiments showed that electrical stimulation of the diencephalon prompted significant elevation in plasma cholesterol levels. Efforts were then made to determine the precise region of the hypothalamus responsible for the serum lipid increase by creating discrete electrolytic lesions. In rats, it was found that destruction of nuclei in the anterior portion of the hypothalamus did not alter concentration of cholesterol in plasma; neither did isolated destruction of the ventromedial, dorsomedial, or arcuate nuclei. However, chronic hypercholesterolemia almost invariably resulted from lesions involving the fornix, the medial portion of the lateral hypothalamus, and either the ventromedial or dorsomedial nucleus. Interestingly, these animals' behavior has been markedly altered, specifically showing greater activity and aggressiveness.

Precisely how the hypothalamic lesions induce hypercholesterolemia remains to be determined; notably, while a diet rich in cholesterol intensified the effect, it was also seen in animals on a diet low in cholesterol.

Whether the hypothalamic lesions raise the serum cholesterol by somehow interfering with normal turnover of dietary cholesterol, or whether hormonal changes occur as the result of the effect of the hypothalamic lesions on the pituitary or other endocrine glands are questions now being explored. Whatever the basis for this type of hypercholesterolemia, clearly the experiments point up the importance of the central nervous system and in particular the hypothalamus in regulating serum cholesterol levels.

At this juncture we would conclude that the hypothalamus surely provides part of the mechanism whereby behavior alters lipid levels; however, we are not convinced that the lipid abnormalities and their atherosclerotic effects will provide the sole explanation for the cardiovascular findings observed. Conceivably the increased catecholamine discharge in type A individuals could also intensify the atherosclerotic process. Conceivably, too, the increased discharge could cause arterial damage associated with increased deposition of thrombogenic elements. The known influence of catecholamines on clotting mechanisms suggests this as a possibility.

That emotional and behavioral factors such as we have been describing lead in some way to organic changes in the coronary vasculature now seems to us well demonstrated, even if all the mechanisms involved have yet to be fully clarified. Surely from the evidence already in hand, the suggestion that such factors are of little influence in development or acceleration of coronary heart disease is no longer tenable. On the part of researchers and clinicians both, a behavioral assessment should be included in efforts to prevent coronary heart disease by controlling risk factors. As of now, more **investigators are at least considering** that the way a man lives may be as important as what he eats in increasing his vulnerability to heart disease. This is an encouraging sign.

Section Six

Consequences of Myocardial Ischemia

Biochemical and Morphologic Changes in Infarcting Myocardium

BURTON E. SOBEL

Washington University, St. Louis

Knowledge of the specific metabolic changes that occur in the myocardium in response to ischemia is basic not only to improved understanding of pathogenesis of the disease process but also to more effective treatment. The availability of surgical procedures for myocardial revascularization and of other aggressive measures has made it imperative to define how much damage heart tissue can tolerate while still maintaining viability. Valid indices of irreversible injury would be extremely helpful. In addition, recent evidence indicating that increased size of an infarct underlies increased likelihood of fatal complications heightens the need for accurate means of quantifying the effects of ischemic injury (see Chapter 33, "Myocardial Revascularization During Postinfarction Shock," by Mundth, Buckley, and Austen and Chapter 29, "Protection of the Ischemic Myocardium," by Braunwald and Maroko).

As will become evident later in our discussion, tangible gains have been made in the development of methods of assessing the extent of infarction and predicting its ultimate extent during early evolution. Much has been learned, too, about the sequence of metabolic changes beginning with the onset of ischemia and culminating in cell necrosis. Here, however, some critical events are still incompletely understood.

Myocardium dies when the flow of arterial blood is reduced below that required to maintain vital cell processes. The prime insult, of course, is oxygen deprivation. But it need not follow that this is the only important factor in cell death; indeed, it has been shown that tissue hypoxia or anoxia alone may not be immediately lethal. The contribution of other changes resulting from the reduced blood supply — deficiency of exogenous substrates ordinarily supplied by arterial blood and/or impaired diffusion of end products of metabolism from poorly perfused ischemic tissue — must also be taken into account.

Until relatively recently, little was known of the sequence of early changes in ischemic injury since, with conventional laboratory techniques, virtually all ischemic cells were already dead for some hours before proof of damage appeared. Now a combination of new procedures applied in animal studies of acute myocardial infarction has made possible delineation of very early biochemical and structural changes. Within seconds following onset of ischemia the injured area may be characterized with use of redox-sensitive indicators; electron microscopy may provide evidence of structural changes in some cells within 20 minutes; and selected histochemical changes may be manifest promptly.

Available evidence suggests that the sequence initiated by onset of ischemia begins with potentially reversible changes and unless interrupted usually ends in irreversible changes and cell death. Recent work by several investigators has aimed at defining both reversible and irreversible changes; one of the most significant observations has been that drastic histologic or histochemical alterations may be induced in cell constituents without signifying permanent damage. If blood flow to ischemic tissue is restored before too much time has elapsed, affected cells recover rapidly and may redevelop full functional competence.

Onset of myocardial ischemia is followed by striking intracellular changes: Within 8 to 10 seconds the affected myocardium becomes cyanotic and noticeably cooler; there is also significant hydrogen ion accumulation. Simultaneously, electrocardiographic changes appear, and within 30 to 60 seconds after onset of ischemia, contraction ceases in the injured area. These changes relate directly to local anoxia resulting from cessation of blood flow. Within minutes thereafter intracellular glycogen stores are significantly reduced, reflecting activation of glycolysis as anaerobic metabolism subserves energy production, and there is rapid accumulation of lactic acid, the principle end product of anaerobic glycogen degradation. Marked elec-

MORPHOLOGIC	Normal Mitochondrion	 Swollen Mitochondrion		Aggregation of Nuclear Chromatin	Enlargement of Mitochondrion Formation of Granule Loss of Matrix Densit

0	5 sec	30 sec	1 min	5 min	20 min

BIOCHEMICAL AND FUNCTIONAL	Cyanosis Hydrogen Ion Accumulation Lactic Acid Accumulation	Reduced Glycogen Potassium Loss		Nonspecific Electrocardiographic Changes	Severe ATP Depletio ($<2.5\ \mu moles/gm$) Cessation of Glycolytic Flux Lysosomal Degradation

Studies aimed at defining the sequence of events following onset of myocardial ischemia have indicated that even profound biochemical and functional changes can be reversed if blood flow to the ischemic area is restored prior to a critical time limit (about 20 minutes in experiments to date). As myocardial cells lose viability, signs of irreversible structural damage – particularly in the mitochondria – can be seen immediately by electron microscopy, or some hours later by light microscopy. Myocardial cell

trolyte disturbances, in particular intracellular potassium loss, are evident also within the first few minutes; this change is reflected in an acute increase in potassium in coronary sinus blood derived from areas of acute ischemia.

Studies by Jennings and colleagues at Northwestern University have been particularly helpful in characterizing the early changes in dying myocardial cells and in establishing the minimum period after which damage becomes irrevocable. In their work, myocardial injury was induced in dogs by occlusion of the circumflex branch of the left coronary artery. The posterior papillary muscle provided a readily sampled area of ischemic tissue; since the anterior superior portion of the left ventricle was not involved, it could be used as nonischemic control tissue.

In experiments in which blood flow was restored to the ischemic area after varying intervals, it was shown that none of the early changes cited above were indicative of irreversible injury. Although cells were metabolically altered and nonfunctional, they maintained viability provided blood flow was reestablished within about 20 minutes. In that case there was a prompt return in aerobic metabolism and contractile function.

As Jennings and coworkers observed: "Within a few seconds, or certainly minutes, after restoration of flow, the affected tissue becomes indistinguishable by biochemical, morphologic, or functional techniques from control myocardium."

Once occlusion is maintained beyond the 20-minute point, restoration of flow no longer consistently reverses cell injury. As might be expected, the metabolic changes seen during the reversible phase grow more profound as cells lose viability. Although cells still appear histologically normal by light microscopy, histochemical techniques reveal major changes reflecting increased utilization or destruction of tissue components; there is also a marked decrease in stainable glycogen. Moreover, ultrastructural damage detectable by electron microscopy is identifiable shortly after cells enter the phase of irreversible damage. Obvious changes appear after 20 minutes of

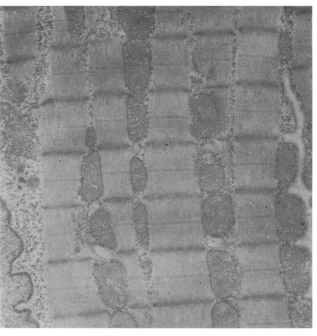 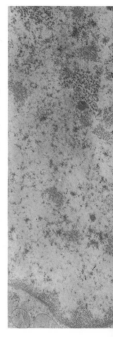

Electron micrographs by Dr. Robert B. Jennings and colleagues at Northwestern demonstrate the sequence of mitochondrial and other ultrastructural changes observed in myocardial cells of experimental animals (dogs) with progressive ischemia. In control view at left, mitochondria have a dense and orderly appearance prior to ischemia

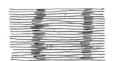

Disintegration of
Myofibrillar
Pattern

| 1 hr | 8-12 hr |

Myocardial
CPK Depletion

death is believed to occur when intracellular ATP drops below 2.0 μmoles/gm, forcing cessation of anaerobic metabolism on which the ischemic heart depends.

occlusion; they are prominent after 60 minutes. Chief among these are peripheral aggregation of nuclear chromatin, disruption of the regular myofibrillar pattern, and development of marked relaxation bands. The most profound changes are in the mitochondria – in particular, loss of matrix density, enlargement, and the appearance of intramitochondrial granules.

Following several lines of evidence, these workers pursued the hypothesis that mitochondrial damage was the critical event leading to irreversible injury. The normal heart is almost wholly dependent on mitochondrial energy production and the structural changes seen in mitochondria of cells that are irreversibly damaged are indeed striking. Moreover, Jennings' group also showed that mitochondria isolated from irreversibly injured cells are defective in their capacity to metabolize representative substrates such as α-ketoglutarate or pyruvate, and that they manifested impaired respiratory control. In electron microscopy studies, it was found that mitochondria isolated from irreversibly injured cells showed evidence of increased fragility; however, the deficient metabolism of pyruvate persisted even when their morphology was preserved with use of special isolation techniques.

Although these observations strongly support the view that mitochondrial damage is associated with irreversible injury, they do not of course identify the critical defect within the mitochondria. As Jennings et al note, the possibilities include inactivation of mitochondrial enzymes, loss of essen-

tial cofactors, or maldistribution of essential anions or cations within the mitochondria. The Northwestern group has been investigating the role of alterations in mitochondrial electrolyte distribution, since the dense granules uniformly present in the mitochondria of dying cells appear to contain an excess of calcium and phosphate.

Ischemic myocardial cells may die when the energy level is reduced sufficiently to render them incapable of integrated function. In addition to mitochondrial damage, other biochemical changes seen in reversibly injured cells may impair viability. For example, supplies of glycogen for anaerobic metabolism may become exhausted, or accumulation of lactic acid and hydrogen ions in the ischemic area may cause a lethal decrease in intracellular pH.

Morphologic studies indicate no sharp dividing line between reversible and irreversible ischemic damage. Also, although metabolic and functional changes may become irrevocable in some cells after about 20 minutes, not all damaged cells die at once. In the Jennings study, for example, after 45 minutes of ischemia more than 60% of affected cells re-

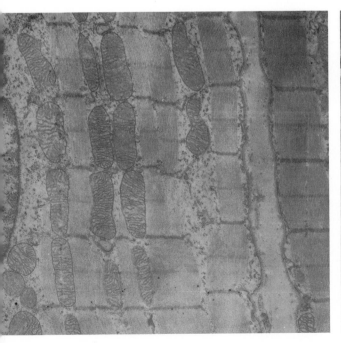

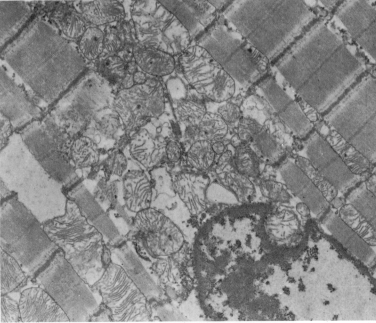

(original x13,600). In view at center, made after 15 minutes of ischemia (original x12,000), nucleus shows some margination of chromatin material but the mitochondria are relatively unchanged; injury may still be reversible. In EM at right, made after

60 minutes of ischemia – when irreversible damage has occurred – margination of nuclear chromatin is prominent and profound mitochondrial changes are apparent, including loss of matrix density, presence of intramitochondrial granules (original x14,000).

mained viable, but after 60 minutes there were virtually no viable cells within the severely affected area.

Significantly, the extent of cell damage observed morphologically following prolonged ischemia depends in part on the site from which the sample is taken. Irreversibly injured cells near the center of an infarct die without marked microscopic change, whereas those closest to normally perfused areas, at the periphery of the infarct, develop marked morphologic abnormalities.

Brachfeld and others have called attention to curious differences between cells irreversibly damaged by permanent coronary occlusion and those subjected to transient occlusion followed by restoration of circulation to the ischemic area. In a pertinent study, Sommers and Jennings observed histologic and histochemical changes in myocardium subjected to 40 minutes of ischemia followed by up to four hours of recirculation of arterial blood through the previously ischemic area. They compared these changes with those resulting from occlusion of the same vessel, also for a 40-minute period, not followed by reperfusion. In both cases cells were irreversibly injured and cell death occurred. However, electron microscopy revealed striking cellular changes following return of blood supply to areas of transient ischemia, changes more severe than any seen following permanent arterial occlusion. After 20 minutes of recirculation there was extensive disruption of intracellular structure. Disorganization of myofibrils was the most prominent finding, accompanied by the appearance of dense contraction bands. Intracellular edema, inflammatory cell infiltration, calcium deposition, and total loss of stainable glycogen were seen as well. In addition there were marked alterations in intracellular potassium, phosphorus, sodium, and chloride. In areas to which circulation was not restored these changes occurred either much later or in milder form.

Sommers and coworkers suggested that the severity of structural and metabolic changes was related to restoration of arterial flow. With return of the blood supply, inflammatory cells, calcium, sodium, intermediary products of metabolism, and other substances gain ready access to the area of injury; at the same time lactic acid, cofactors, enzymes, potassium, and nucleotides diffuse away. Some of the changes seen could well be accounted for on this basis. These workers note: "It is probable that resumption of active myocardial contraction in the adjacent, formerly contracting portion of the heart is a significant factor in production of the most prominent microscopic changes in the heart, i.e., the stretched, separated fibers with a disrupted myofibrillar pattern and the formation of contraction bands."

Unfortunately, although morphologic techniques have provided important information on early changes following ischemic injury, they have been of limited value is defining the critical events in onset of cell necrosis. Structural changes appearing in some dying cells and not in others are unlikely to hold the key to irreversible injury. The frequent dissociation of structural changes and viability of specific myocardial cells and the heterogeneity of structural damage make it difficult to apply anatomic criteria to quantify

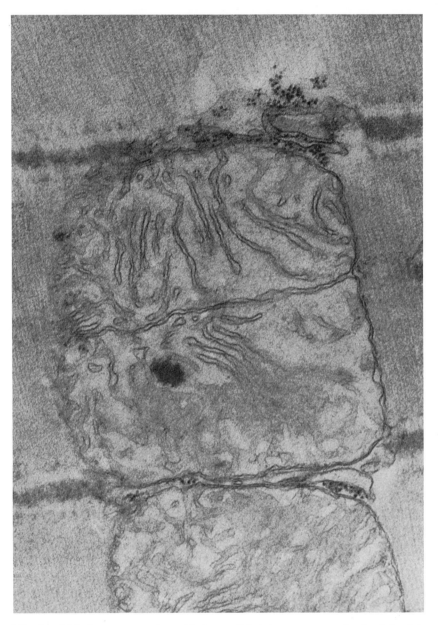

Mitochondrial changes occurring with irreversible injury are more clearly defined in this higher power view (original x45,000) of a single mitochondrion from tissue subjected to 60 minutes of ischemia (also Jennings et al). Matrix is relatively clear, with loosely packed cristae; prominent dense body is of type that appears in all dying cells.

the extent of severity of ischemic injury.

For these reasons a number of investigators have been focusing attention on the biochemistry of myocardial ischemia and infarction, both in pursuit of valid methods of quantifying damage and in seeking to identify the critical factor or factors precipitating cell death.

In an informative study, Braasch et al recorded changes in energy metabolism of ischemic cardiac muscle in dogs with experimental myocardial infarction: Initial biochemical measurements were made within hours of ischemic injury; animals were sacrificed after varying intervals for analysis of myocardial adenosine triphosphate (ATP), creatine phosphate (CP), and lactate content. In addition, tissue taken from the same areas – the center and periphery of the infarcts as well as noninfarcted portions of the left ventricle – were analyzed for enzymatic activity of the glycolytic and oxidative pathways and the hexose-monophosphate shunt.

In determinations made 24 hours after artery ligation, enzyme activity of both the glycolytic and oxidative pathways was significantly reduced in ischemic myocardium; lowest values for activity of both pathways were recorded 10 days postocclusion (between 11% and 15% of normal activity in the center of the infarct for the oxidative pathway; between 5% and 30% of normal activity in the center of the infarct for the glycolytic pathway).

In sharp contrast, there was a striking increase in activity of enzymes of the hexose-monophosphate shunt (see Chapter 3, "Biochemical Processes in Cardiac Function," by Davies). These enzymes are of minor importance in the myocardium under normal conditions; their activation following ischemic injury may reflect their role in processes of repair and their activity in nonmyocardial elements. Pronounced changes were seen both in the center and periphery of infarcts. Thus by the end of the 10th day, glucose-6-phosphate dehydrogenase (G-6-PD) activity at the center was 30 times greater than in control samples; in the periphery it was increased 20-fold. Interestingly, there was a smaller but still substantial – two- to threefold – increase observed in non-

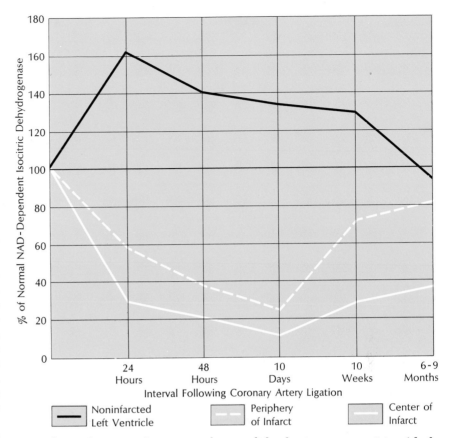

At 24 hours after onset of experimental myocardial ischemia, enzyme activity of both oxidative and glycolytic pathways was significantly reduced both in center of the infarct and at its periphery. As study in dogs by Braasch and coworkers also showed, enzyme activity in center of infarct remained low as long as nine months after onset of infarction. In the noninfarcted portion of the left ventricle, an initial increase was followed by a gradual decline to normal levels. Values shown here for isocitric dehydrogenase were comparable to those found for several other enzymes measured.

infarcted left ventricle from the same heart. Activity of shunt enzymes decreased somewhat in the months following infarction, but up to nine months later it was still significantly higher in scar tissue of the healed infarct than in normal cardiac muscle.

For further insight into biochemical aspects of myocardial ischemia, other workers have attempted to record very early changes in activity of mitochondrial enzymes, developing sensitive histochemical techniques for the purpose. For example Schnitka and Nachlas, using a substrate medium containing nitrobluetetrazolium (NBT) as electron acceptor, identified changes in succinic dehydrogenase activity at six hours. Initially, the loss was confined to the mitochondria and activity was increased in myofibrils; this was true also of cytochrome oxidase. Between one and five days there was a progressive reduction of activity in ischemic muscle, cytochrome oxidase disappear-

ing at a slightly slower rate than succinic dehydrogenase. Significantly, Purkinje fibers located beneath the endocardium remained viable and retained normal stores of both mitochondrial enzymes and glycogen.

Despite the information provided, observations such as these made it unlikely that enzymic changes of the type described could serve as indicators of irreversible cell injury. For one thing, the heterogeneity referred to earlier in reference to morphologic damage was also true of enzyme denaturation and degradation; in addition, the decrease or increase in enzyme activity seen in some myocardial cells did not necessarily hold true for all. Most important, the source of increased activity of a given enzyme need not be solely within the ischemic myocardium; for example, white cell infiltration is known to contribute significantly to increased activity of en-

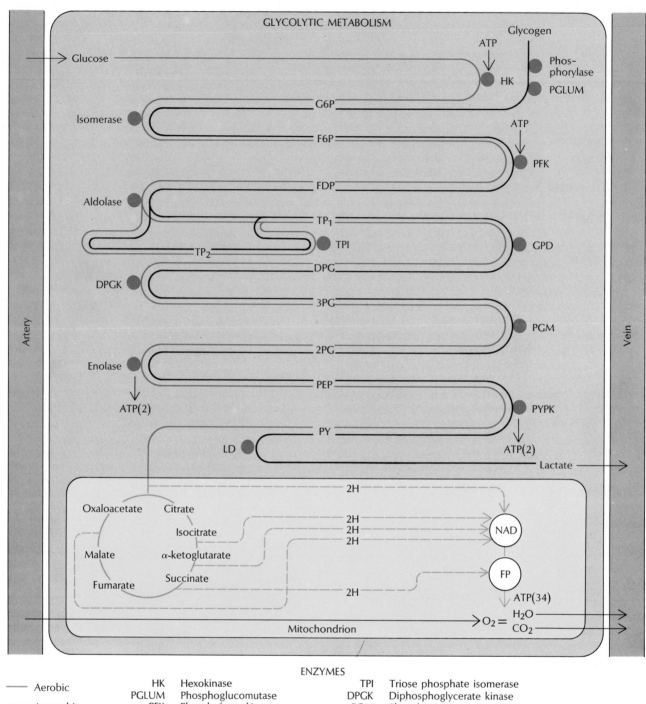

GLYCOLYTIC METABOLISM

Legend:
— Aerobic
— Anaerobic

ENZYMES

HK	Hexokinase		TPI	Triose phosphate isomerase
PGLUM	Phosphoglucomutase		DPGK	Diphosphoglycerate kinase
PFK	Phosphofructokinase		PGM	Phosphoglyceromutase
GPD	Glyceraldehyde phosphate dehydrogenase		PYPK	Pyruvate phosphokinase
			LD	Lactic dehydrogenase

INTERMEDIATES

G6P	Glucose-6-phosphate		DPG	1, 3-diphosphoglycerate
F6P	Fructose-6-phosphate		3PG	3-phosphoglycerate
FDP	Fructose 1, 6-diphosphate		2PG	2-phosphoglycerate
TP$_1$	3-phosphoglyceraldehyde		PEP	Phosphoenolpyruvate
TP$_2$	Dihydroxyacetone phosphate		PY	Pyruvate

ELECTRON DONORS

NAD	Nicotinamide adenine dinucleotide	FP	Flavoprotein

Primary biochemical changes in ischemic heart muscle relate to the shift from aerobic to anaerobic metabolism for the production of ATP so that at least marginal energy production can be maintained for a brief period. Sequential steps in anaerobic glycolysis, as schematized above, result in breakdown of glucose to lactic acid, whereas in the presence of sufficient arterial oxygen and hence normal mitochondrial metabolism, glucose would be oxidized further to CO_2 and H_2O. As also shown, the ATP yield from oxidative carbohydrate metabolism is many times higher than that from anaerobic glycolysis.

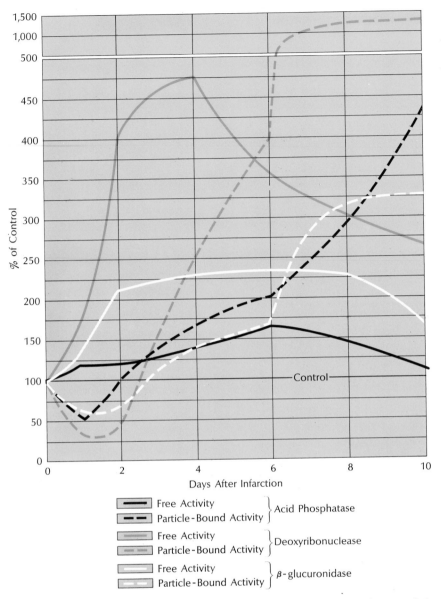

	Free Activity	} Acid Phosphatase
	Particle-Bound Activity	
	Free Activity	} Deoxyribonuclease
	Particle-Bound Activity	
	Free Activity	} β-glucuronidase
	Particle-Bound Activity	

Changes in lysosomal enzyme activity seen following onset of experimental myocardial infarction began with an increase in soluble enzyme activity; as this activity reached its peak following the onset of infarction, the activity of the particle-bound fractions was also increased. Study by Ravens and coworkers included measurement of γ-glutamyl transpeptidase as well as the three lysosomal enzymes graphed above.

zymes involved in the hexose-monophosphate shunt.

Thus, other approaches were required to pinpoint early sequential changes in ischemic injury that might be crucial to maintaining cell viability The primary biochemical changes in ischemic heart muscle, of course, relate to the shift to glycolytic metabolism as the major pathway of energy production. With onset of tissue hypoxia the energy produced through glycolysis is a small fraction of that yielded by oxidative metabolism. Activation of anaerobic metabolism in hy-

poxic myocardium appears to begin with the decrease in concentration of high-energy phosphates normally produced by oxidative phosphorylation and the corresponding increase in inorganic phosphate. Since ischemic myocardial cells were known to survive for a time following onset of anoxia, energy metabolism in ischemic myocardium and in perfused, anoxic myocardium was examined by Kübler and coworkers.

As Kübler noted in the ischemic dog heart, myocardial oxygen reserve is used up very shortly (within about

eight seconds) after cessation of all coronary flow; when arterial oxygen tension falls below a critical level ($<pO_2$ 5 mm Hg) oxygen delivery becomes rate-limiting for oxidative phosphorylation, which is then insufficient to meet energy demands. The breakdown of high-energy phosphates consequent to the energy deficit at first involves mainly C P, shortly thereafter A T P as well.

In Kübler's experiments it was shown that the transition from aerobic to anaerobic energy metabolism entails a 20-fold increase in the rate of glycolytic flux, as judged by lactate output; nonetheless, in the ischemic myocardium glycolysis was found to cover only about 65% to 70% of total energy requirement. (As will be seen, this proved to be substantially less than in myocardium perfused by deoxygenated medium, suggesting that some factor associated with ischemia but not with anoxia must account for at least part of the gap between energy requirement and energy production in the ischemic heart.)

Essentially, the Kübler studies involved analysis of substrates, intermediary metabolites, end products of the multiple enzyme reactions in the glycolytic pathway, and of the role of allosteric regulators in governing enzyme activity. In view of differences already alluded to between ischemic myocardium and anoxic-perfused heart preparations, key findings will be discussed separately.

In the ischemic myocardium, substrate concentration was found not to be rate-limiting for glycolytic flux; for example, lactate production ceased after a period of ischemia despite a high myocardial glycogen content. Hence attention was focused on mechanisms responsible for regulation of glycolytic enzyme activity in governing glycolytic flux.

As Morgan and his coworkers have elegantly shown, the enzymes first activated are hexokinase (H K) and phosphorylase. The shift to glycolytic metabolism depends also on activation of phosphofructokinase (P F K), occurring in part because allosteric inhibition of P F K by A T P is removed as the A T P deficiency increases. Significantly, however, under conditions of ischemia the P F K activation is not persistent, apparently because it is inhibited by the intracellular acidosis.

Thus, despite the sharp increase in glycolytic flux with onset of anaerobic metabolism, myocardial PFK activity is considerably decreased as ischemia persists. Indeed, as Kübler found, the PFK reaction becomes rate-limiting for glycolysis and high-energy phosphate production; it is this that largely accounts for the incapacity of anaerobic energy production to meet more than about two thirds of total energy demands.

As long as the PFK reaction remains rate-limiting, activity of other glycolytic enzymes is also adversely affected. In particular, there is accumulation of glucose-6-phosphate (G-6-P), the substrate for PFK, which in turn inhibits HK activity; thus both glucose and glycogen utilization are impeded. The finding that in the ischemic myocardium, metabolites of the glycolytic pathway show no changes in concentration beyond the PFK reaction suggested that glycolytic flux is controlled by a reaction at the end of the metabolic pathway — involving the enzyme pyruvate kinase (PK) — in addition to the control exerted by the HK, phosphorylase, and PFK reactions.

At a later stage of ischemia, the reactants in the PFK step approach equilibrium concentrations and glycolytic flux is regulated chiefly by the phosphoglucomutase (PGLUM) reaction. This enzyme catalyzes transformation of glucose-1-phosphate to glucose-6-phosphate via G-1,6-diphosphate; since synthesis of the intermediary product is ATP-dependent, limitation of glycolytic flux via the PGLUM reaction appears to result largely from the decreased cell content of ATP.

Kübler and coworkers found that the transition of the rate-limiting step from the PFK to PGLUM reactions occurs when myocardial ATP content falls to about 3.5 μmoles/gm (about 50% of normal). This shift of the rate-limiting step appears to correspond to the clinical limit of tolerable ischemia, since it was shown in the dog heart that when ischemia was maintained only until the ATP level decreased to this level, full recovery could still be achieved postischemia.

At a still later stage of ischemia, glycolytic flux is again governed chiefly by the PFK reaction when its reactant concentrations again deviate from equilibrium. According to Kübler, this occurs when myocardial ATP content decreases to 2 μmoles/gm, or below the tolerable limit. The ATP level is then too low to "prime the pump" as it were, so that production of more ATP via phosphorylation of fructose-6-phosphate to fructose-diphosphate is no longer possible. At this point glycolysis essentially ceases and myocardial viability can no longer be maintained. Since lactate production stops despite high stores of glycogen and glucose and high concentrations of both glucose-6-phosphate and fructose-6-phosphate (G-6-P and F-6-P), clearly breakdown of anaerobic energy production is not due simply to substrate exhaustion.

In the anoxic perfused heart prep-

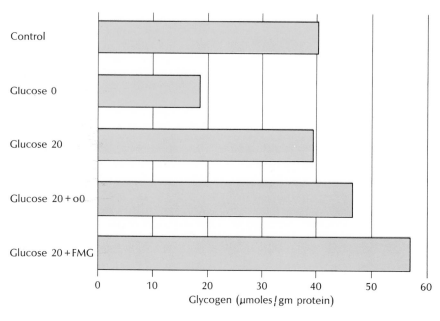

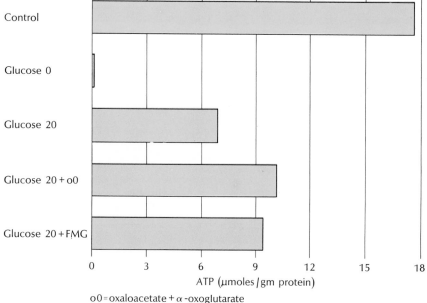

o0 = oxaloacetate + α-oxoglutarate

FMG = fumarate + malate + glutamate

Anaerobic cardiac function might be enhanced by use of tricarboxylic acid metabolites to stimulate ATP synthesis, as suggested by results of experiments of Penney and coworkers in which rat heart preparations were perfused with glucose and oxaloacetate + α-oxoglutarate or fumarate + malate + glutamate. After 40 minutes of anoxia, concentrations of both glycogen and ATP were higher than in preparations perfused only with medium (glucose 0) or glucose (20 millimoles) alone. Control hearts were not perfused.

aration, as under ischemic conditions, glycolysis virtually ceases when intracellular A T P falls below 2 μmoles/ gm. However, before that point is reached, the pattern of glycolytic intermediary metabolism differs sharply from that in the ischemic myocardium, chiefly with respect to the P F K reaction. There is early activation of P F K, reflecting decreased allosteric inhibition by A T P. One reason is simple: Lactate is produced as in the ischemic myocardium but is promptly washed out, preventing the buildup of intracellular acidosis. In the deoxygenated perfused heart preparation, concentrations of G-6-P and F-6-P decrease markedly at onset of anoxia because of activation of P F K; with the decrease in G-6-P there is increased H K activation, hence enhanced utilization of glucose as well as of glycogen.

Thus, total glycolytic flux is considerably higher than in the ischemic heart with comparable myocardial oxygen tension. In the anoxic perfused heart, as Kübler's studies showed, anaerobic energy metabolism can cover between 75% and 80% of total energy need. Moreover, addition of glucose to the perfusion medium brings a further increase in lactate production, and fully 85% to 90% of energy needs can accordingly be met. In contrast, in the ischemic myocardium the P F K rate-limiting effect resulting from intracellular acidosis puts the injured cells in double jeopardy: under ischemic conditions, constituents such as A T P assume a critical regulatory role at several reaction sites, yet A T P is synthesized at a slower rate because of P F K inhibition.

From these and related studies it is clear that the impairment and eventual fate of ischemic cells relate quite directly to development of intracellular acidosis. Whether acidosis itself is the key factor dictating onset of cell necrosis remains to be determined; in any case, the particular susceptibility of the heart to acidosis and accumulation of hydrogen ions must be kept in mind. Function is known to be impaired at a higher pH in the heart than in skeletal muscle. Furthermore, because of the relatively poor buffering capacity of myocardium, the decrease in intracellular pH for a given increase in lactic acid production is greater in the heart.

Several investigators have called at-

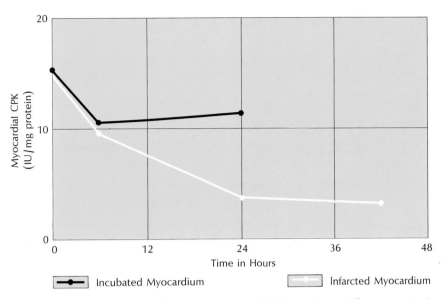

A striking decrease in myocardial CPK activity in the first six hours following onset of experimental infarction is evident in extracts from tissue in the center of the ischemic areas; activity is further reduced by 24 hours but shows only minimal reduction thereafter. A similar early decline in myocardial CPK activity occurs in the noninfarcted isolated heart, which has been incubated at 37°C. The reduction in enzyme activity in the heart in situ in excess of that seen in the incubated tissue reflects the release into the circulation of enzyme from necrotic cells.

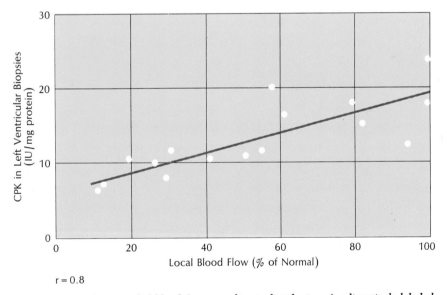

r = 0.8

Measurement of myocardial blood flow according to distribution of radioactively labeled microspheres in biopsies obtained 24 hours after onset of experimental infarction in dogs indicated that blood flow was markedly reduced in center and marginal zones of infarct. Homogenates from biopsies showed a corresponding depression in CPK activity.

tention to the possibility that intracellular acidosis may make myocardial cells more vulnerable to damaging effects of lysosomal enzymes. "The myocardium is undoubtedly more sensitive to the effects of ischemia than any other tissue in the body and therefore presents a favorable environment for hydrolase activity," as Brachfeld points out. "Anaerobic production of excessive amounts of lactic acid may overcome the buffering capacity of the sarcoplasm and decrease cellular pH to a point within the range of enzyme activation. In addition, such a decrease may in itself trigger a cyclic mechanism by inhibiting glycolysis, leading to a further decrease in A T P production and contractility, a fall in blood pressure and consequently in myocardial perfusion, and further decrease in pO_2."

There is some evidence that lysosomal enzyme activity is increased in myocardial tissue following ischemic injury. For example, in studying experimental myocardial infarction in dogs, Ravens and coworkers measured changes in activity of four lysosomal enzymes (acid phosphatase, glucuronidase deoxyribonuclease, and γ-glutamyl-transpeptidase) following coronary artery occlusion; within the first 48 hours there was a moderate increase in soluble, i.e. free, enzyme activity, thought to reflect the autolytic phase of cell and tissue destruction. Between the second and sixth day – coinciding with the major phase of tissue degradation and removal of cell debris – soluble enzyme activity reached its maximum level and activity of particle-bound enzyme fractions was also increased. These findings have been confirmed in several laboratories. However, it must be recognized that myocardium differs markedly from other tissues with respect to its complement of identifiable lysosomes. Observations made with the electron microscope fail to reveal appreciable quantities of lysosomal particles in heart muscle analogous to those seen in organs such as liver or kidney. Furthermore, the amount of acid-activated hydrolytic enzyme activity that can be obtained from disruption of particles from centrifugated myocardium is very small compared with that seen in preparations from other organs. Thus, although activation of lysozymes in cells participating in the exudative reaction to myocardial infarction may contribute to late degradation of myocardium after ischemic injury, it appears unlikely that the ischemic heart muscle cell destroys itself with a suicidal burst of activation of myocardial lysosomal enzymes.

From what is known thus far of the sequence of biochemical changes following onset of ischemia, several prospects suggest themselves. As Braunwald and his associates have shown, increased availability of glucose contributes to maintenance of viability in the ischemic dog heart (see Chapter 6, "The Autonomic Nervous System in Heart Failure," by Braunwald). Other alternatives include finding a means of supporting anaerobic metabolism

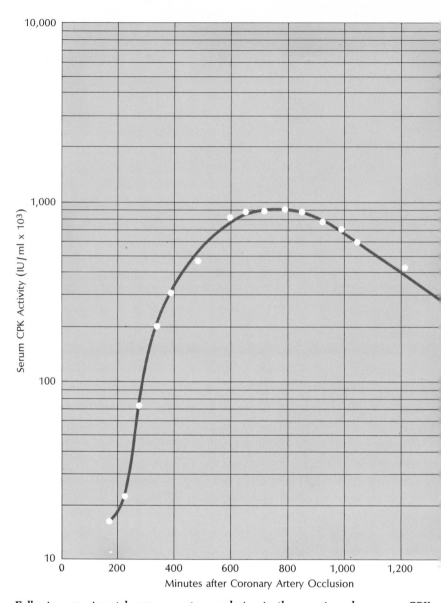

Following experimental coronary artery occlusion in the conscious dog, serum CPK levels change slowly at first but (as shown by serial determinations in a representative animal) increase rapidly in subsequent hours. The delay in serum enzyme elevation apparently corresponds with the delay in myocardial CPK depletion; the marked depletion in myocardial CPK is accompanied by a sharp rise in serum CPK levels.

by stimulating ATP synthesis. In this connection Penney and coworkers observed that under anaerobic conditions the capacity of rat heart preparations to produce ATP could be potentiated by mitochondrial metabolites of the tricarboxylic acid cycle (fumarate + malate + glutamate or oxaloacetate and α-oxoglutarate). Addition of glucose plus metabolites to the perfusate stimulated cardiac function and anaerobic energy production to a greater extent than did glucose alone; tissue concentration of both ATP and glucose were higher than in preparations perfused only with glucose. Other possi-

bilities are suggested by the finding of Whereat and colleagues that mitochondria have the capacity to synthesize fatty acids via two separate pathways: one localized to the inner mitochondrial membrane where fatty acids are synthesized de novo from acetyl groups, the other localized to the outer membrane where fatty acids are produced by a chain elongation mechanism. The two synthetic pathways differ in cofactor requirements, but both utilize nicotinamide adenine dinucleotide in the reduced form (NADH). Since NADH accumulation resulting from excess lactate is a key step in

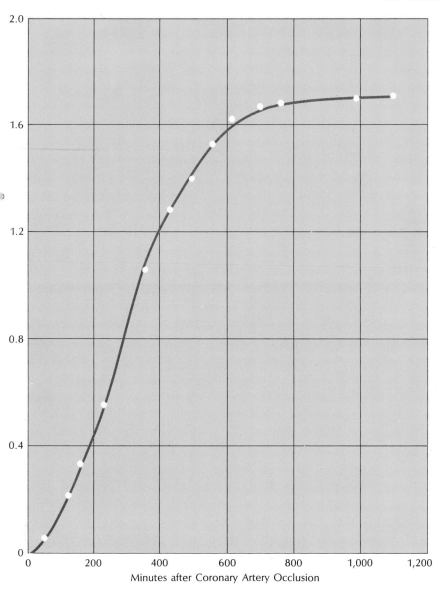

Analysis of the rate of appearance of CPK in serum as a function of time following acute coronary occlusion indicates a relatively rapid initial rise; release of CPK then continues to increase slowly at a progressively diminished rate. Values plotted here were derived from serially measured CPK changes shown in preceding graph. Each value represents cumulative CPK released into 1 ml of serum at the time indicated after artery ligation.

inflammatory response following onset of acute myocardial infarction. However, one enzyme, creatine phosphokinase (C P K), is found mostly in the myocardium and skeletal muscle, where it has an essential role in energy production. For this reason we thought that measurement of myocardial C P K activity might provide a relatively specific index of the extent of myocardial cell damage following acute coronary occlusion.

Accordingly, myocardial C P K activity was measured in heart muscle from rabbits with infarction produced by ligation of the left circumflex artery; a spectrophotometric-kinetic C P K assay was used for measurements of enzyme activity in samples from injured and normal ventricular myocardium. Six hours following occlusion, C P K activity in extracts of tissue in the center of the ischemic area was significantly depressed (from a mean of 15.5 ± 0.9 I U/mg supernatant protein to a mean of 9.2 ± 1.0). After 24 hours, activity was further reduced (to a mean of 3.4 ± 0.3). This represented a decline to about 22% of control values; since the reduction began so shortly after coronary artery occlusion it could be assumed that it occurred before marked inflammatory changes would be apparent. The consistent diminution of C P K activity is in contrast to the variability of changes seen in activity of other enzymes in the heart, such as those involved in oxidative or glycolytic metabolism. The consistency of the fall in C P K activity suggests that overall activity in the heart is not affected by enzyme activity in other cell types involved in the inflammatory response. It should be noted that in presumably nonischemic tissue peripheral to areas of infarction, myocardial C P K activity was not different from that in sham-operated animals.

Since it might be argued that the C P K changes observed could be influenced by an increased workload imposed on normal left ventricular tissue following onset of myocardial infarction, C P K activity was measured in the myocardium of guinea pigs 24 hours after severe aortic constriction. Values were virtually identical with those in whole homogenates from left ventricle of normal or sham-operated animals.

The rabbit experiments also estab-

breakdown of anaerobic metabolism, glycolysis might continue longer if some of the accumulated N A D H could be diverted to intramitochondrial fatty acid synthesis.

One can only speculate about the possible benefits of altering the metabolic milieu of the ischemic heart until more is known of the critical biochemical events precipitating cell necrosis. Although several of the factors thus far discussed are clearly major steps in onset of irreversible injury, no single factor or specific combination can be identified as *the* cause of cell death. However, recognition of the

significance of several is an important step in arriving at more definitive answers.

As noted at the opening of this chapter, substantially more progress has been made toward a second major goal: development of reliable biochemical indices of the extent and severity of tissue damage following onset of myocardial ischemia. Earlier in our discussion it was pointed out that there were difficulties in correlating myocardial enzyme changes with the irreversibility of cell damage, in part because of the appearance of other enzyme-producing cells in the

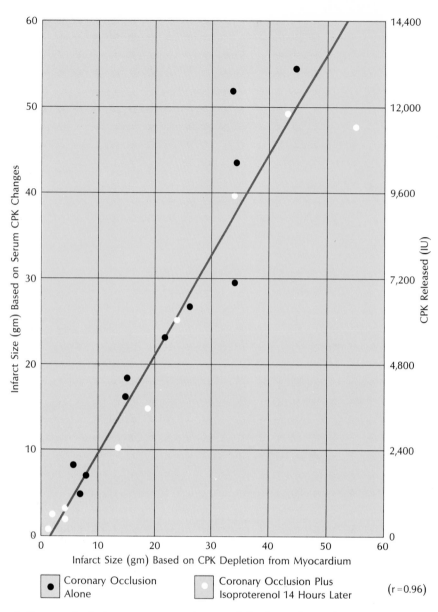

Indirect method of measuring size of myocardial infarcts, by analysis of serum CPK changes, yields values closely comparable to those obtained by direct method entailing analysis of myocardial CPK depletion. The validity of this method is corroborated when infarct size is modified by administration of isoproterenol 14 to 17 hours after occlusion. Again, the direct and indirect measurements of infarct size are in agreement.

lished a direct, linear relationship between the size of the infarct and the extent of CPK depression. Additional evidence linking CPK depression with infarct size was obtained in dogs with experimental infarcts by measuring myocardial blood flow with use of radioactively labeled microspheres. Just prior to sacrifice of the animals at 24 hours, the microspheres were injected through an indwelling catheter into the left atrium; relative blood flow was measured by counting the radioactivity in full-wall biopsy specimens of various portions of the left ventricle,

and CPK activity was measured in homogenates of the same specimens.

In the center of infarcts, labeled microsphere content per gram of tissue was only about 12% of that in nonischemic peripheral tissue. The reduction in blood flow correlated with depression of CPK activity in homogenates prepared from the same biopsy specimens; thus, although coronary occlusion resulted in heterogeneous diminution of perfusion in the area of gross infarction, depression of CPK activity was directly related to the extent of reduction of flow. In other ex-

periments, the extent of derangement in oxidative phosphorylation in mitochondria isolated from ischemic areas was closely correlated with the magnitude of depletion of myocardial CPK activity in the same sample. It was concluded that CPK depression reflected the extent of necrosis, which in turn depended on the severity of ischemia.

Despite the utility of myocardial CPK depletion as a means of assessing ischemic injury, it obviously does not provide a practical method of determining infarct size in man. If changes in serum enzyme activity could be shown to reflect myocardial CPK depletion, a clinically useful index for quantitating infarct size would result. Observation that the fraction of myocardial CPK released into the circulation following onset of experimental infarction was relatively constant and proportional to infarct size encouraged us to explore the possibility.

Earlier studies by other investigators had indicated a relationship between the peak magnitude of elevations of serum enzymes and the extent of infarction; this, however, was insufficiently specific. One reason, already noted, is that serum enzyme activity may reflect release not only from myocardial cells but from other components participating in the inflammatory response; this could be considered a minor problem with respect to CPK. Accordingly, we performed studies in dogs to examine the kinetics of serum CPK disappearance following intravenous injection of purified enzyme, in order to define the effective distribution space of CPK and the fractional disappearance rate of CPK from the circulation. A mathematical model for determining infarct size from serum CPK changes was developed, taking into account the rates of appearance and disappearance of CPK activity in serum. The effect of local denaturation of enzyme was considered also, since it is an important determinant of the fraction of myocardial CPK released into the circulation following ischemic injury. The mathematical model was based on several considerations:

1) A constant fraction (F) of the total myocardial CPK depleted 24 hours after coronary occlusion is released into the circulation, while the remainder is degraded locally in the heart.

2) After coronary occlusion, the CPK released from the heart is distributed in a volume representing a constant fraction of body weight, the CPK distributon space (CPK_{ds}). CPK_{ds} was determined independently in 20 experiments in which CPK purified from myocardium was injected intravenously in conscious dogs.

3) The activity of CPK remaining per gram of myocardium (CPK_I) in the center of infarcts 24 hours after coronary occlusion is relatively constant. Hence, CPK depletion per gram $= CPK_N$ (CPK activity in normal myocardium) $- CPK_I$.

4) Following coronary occlusion, the instantaneous rate of change in serum CPK activity, dE/dt, is a result of two competing phenomena: the rate of appearance of enzyme activity (f(t)) released from heart, and the fractional rate of disappearance of enzyme, k_d. The k_d was determined from the fractional disappearance of purified, intravenously injected enzyme in 11 conscious dogs and averaged $0.005 \pm .0003$/minute. Disappearance was found to be monoexponential. Thus, k_d was constant and the amount of enzyme disappearing during any given interval was equal to the prevailing serum CPK concentration (E) multiplied by k_d. Accordingly, the kinetics of the system can be represented by the equation $dE/dt = f(t) + k_dE$.

By simple rearrangement of terms and integration

$$\int_0^{24 \text{ hrs}} f(t)dt = \int_0^{24 \text{ hrs}} [dE/dt - k_dE]dt$$

Since k_d is known and dE/dt can be obtained from serial serum CPK determinations following coronary occlusion, one can calculate the value of the left-hand term in the above equation. This value multiplied by $K =$ infarct size.

$$K = \frac{[\text{body weight}] \times CPK_{ds}}{F \times (CPK_N - CPK_I)}$$

As noted previously, the total amount of CPK depleted from the heart (CPK_d) is linearly related to infarct size in grams. Hence, infarct size can be determined noninvasively by simply measuring serial serum CPK changes.

This model was utilized in a study of quantification of infarction pro-

duced in conscious dogs by constriction of a snare placed around the left anterior descending coronary artery in an operation the previous week. Animals were sacrificed 24 hours after artery occlusion. Representative results are illustrated on these pages. Serial serum CPK values following coronary occlusion are depicted on page 256. The figure on page 257 illustrates the cumulative CPK appearance, derived from the serial values analyzed according to the model developed. As can be seen, the cumulative CPK appearance reaches a plateau approximately 800 minutes after coronary occlusion, at which time serum CPK is still elevated. Thus, the analysis indicated that virtually all the CPK released from the heart had appeared in the circulation by this time. The correlation between infarct size assessed indirectly, from serial serum CPK changes, and infarct size assessed directly, by analysis of myocardial CPK depletion, is shown in the illustration on page 258. In all 22 dogs, infarct size measured by both methods was found to agree closely.

When the extent of infarction was modified by administration of isoproterenol, estimates of infarct size based

on serial changes in serum CPK activity again conformed quite closely to actual infarct size measured by analysis of myocardial CPK depletion.

Thus, a means is now at hand for quantitating, biochemically, the extent of myocardial damage following production of experimental infarction in the conscious animal. In the clinical setting, analysis of serum CPK activity is proving useful in assessing infarct size in patients suffering acute myocardial infarction, provided that artifacts related to disease affecting skeletal muscle can be excluded. With the use of CPK isoenzyme determinations it is possible to avoid spurious estimates of infarct size when enzyme release from tissues other than heart would distort the picture.

Application of this method to patients with acute myocardial infarction has demonstrated that infarct size is a major determinant of prognosis. Thus, among patients admitted with acute myocardial infarction that was initially uncomplicated or associated with only mild left ventricular failure, mortality within the first 30 days was 12-fold greater in patients with large infarcts compared with those with small infarcts.

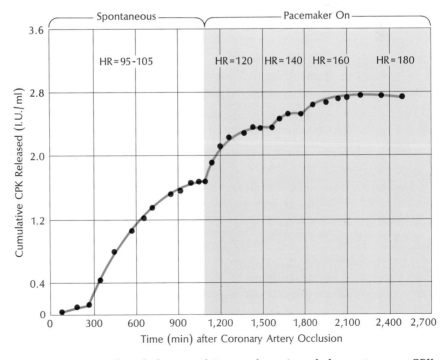

Cumulative CPK released, determined from analysis of serial changes in serum CPK and reflecting the extent of myocardial necrosis, indicates the deleterious effects of an increased heart rate occurring spontaneously or augmented stepwise by means of ventricular pacing. Study was in dog with induced infarction. As shown, as heart rate was increased modestly, cumulative CPK released rose, indicating extension of infarction.

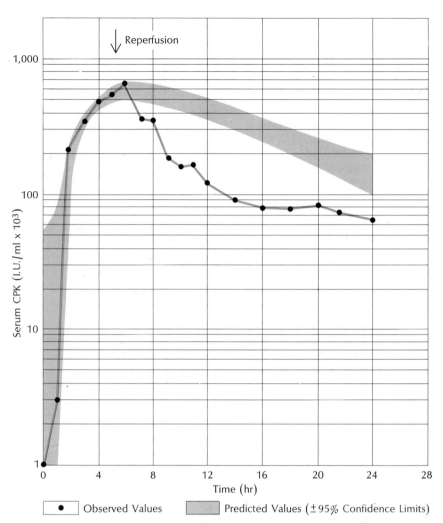

Final infarct size, calculated from all observed serum CPK values in a dog with induced coronary occlusion, was significantly less than that predicted by projection of serum CPK curve calculated on the basis of initial enzyme changes and application of non-linear curve-fitting technique. This difference was attributable to release of the constricting coronary cuff after five hours and reperfusion. Application of the curve-fitting technique to patients has indicated that appreciable salvage of the myocardium can be achieved when therapeutic interventions designed to favorably modify infarct size by reducing myocardial oxygen requirement are undertaken early in an evolving infarction.

More recently we have attempted *prediction of infarct size* on the basis of initial changes in serum enzymes – by means of on-line computer analysis of early data points on the serum C P K curve and projection of the entire curve by nonlinear curve-fitting techniques. These studies, performed with Drs. William E. Shell and James W. Covell, were begun in dogs with experimental coronary occlusion and have since been extended to patients with complicated and uncomplicated infarction. By following the serum C P K changes the first few hours after the initial elevation, one can project the infarct size that can be expected when necrosis is complete.

This technique permits recognition and quantification of the effects of deleterious or therapeutic interventions on experimental and spontaneous evolving acute myocardial infarction. For example, when heart rate is increased by ventricular pacing in a conscious dog with coronary occlusion, the amount of cumulated C P K released increases, indicating extension of infarction (see page 259). With the use of curve-fitting techniques, infarct size can be predicted prior to acceleration of heart rate and projected serum C P K values can be obtained based on initial changes observed prior to the intervention. After acceleration of heart rate, observed serum C P K values significantly exceed those predicted, and the extent of the completed infarct is greater than that predicted from serum C P K changes projected prior to the intervention (see graph at left).

In preliminary studies with patients, we have demonstrated that diminution of ventricular afterload during evolving myocardial infarction results in appreciable salvage of myocardium, recognized by comparison of observed to projected serum C P K values.

The availability of these and other means of quantifying damage in myocardium undergoing infarction should facilitate further studies of the effect of various pharmacologic interventions. With the use of this same approach, some of the suggestions raised earlier for maintaining myocardial viability with metabolic interventions can also be appraised, in the hope that they may be effective in limiting the extent of cell necrosis following onset of ischemic injury. With the advent of intensive explorations of procedures for coronary revascularization and the availability of techniques such as intra-aortic balloon counterpulsation, even small temporal gains achieved with metabolic and pharmacologic protection of ischemic myocardium may be amplified dramatically. Thus, modest maintenance of myocardial viability may be sufficient to set the stage for definitive therapy when it would otherwise be prohibited by rapid evolution of massive infarction.

23

Hemodynamic Changes in Acute Myocardial Infarction

JOHN ROSS JR.

University of California, San Diego

There is no question that prognosis following acute myocardial infarction reflects the degree of functional impairment of the heart. Even with optimal care in a coronary unit, early death rates of 90% or more have been the rule when the infarction is initially large and complicated by power failure and cardiogenic shock, compared with rates in the 5% range when hemodynamic complications are absent and the infarction is small. Fortunately, there are reasons for believing that the outlook may be substantially improved even for patients with severe left ventricular dysfunction. Bolder treatment approaches are now being applied earlier in the course of the infarction process – for example, use of intra-aortic balloon counterpulsation combined with myocardial revascularization surgery in patients with shock – and occasionally are accomplishing reversal of even the gravest complications and making rehabilitation possible (see Chapter 33, "Myocardial Revascularization During Postinfarction Shock," by Mundth, Buckley, and Austen).

Another advance, less dramatic to be sure, but also of critical importance, relates to improved techniques for assessing left ventricular function while the patient's life hangs in the balance. With the increased understanding made possible by application of these newer methods, it has now become clear that virtually all patients with acute myocardial infarction exhibit some evidence of left ventricular dysfunction or failure. The techniques employed to detect this dysfunction are not too traumatic for use during the acute postinfarction phase, yet are sufficiently reliable and reproducible for monitoring purposes. Developments along these lines, to be described in detail, are providing a sounder basis for therapeutic decisions. As more treatment options become available, it is obviously desirable to have more accurate indicators of cardiac functional status before a course of action is decided upon, particularly in a patient with a large myocardial infarc-

tion or other complication, as well as to assess the results of various forms of therapy.

Even without sophisticated measurements, however, it often is evident that left ventricular function is promptly affected with onset of acute myocardial infarction. An atrial or ventricular diastolic gallop usually is audible on physical examination; reduced intensity of the first heart sound and paradoxical splitting of the second are common signs (see Chapter 9, "The Clinical Manifestations of Cardiac Failure in Adults," by Perloff), and when indirect graphic tracings are obtained, a prolonged preejection period and increased ratio of the preejection period to ejection time may be seen. These clinical findings reflect in part acute hemodynamic changes: decreased rate of development of left ventricular pressure (dP/dt), decreased left ventricular ejection rate, and a decreased stroke volume, often despite a compensatory increase in ventricular end-diastolic volume.

Plainly, such findings signify depressed myocardial function and indeed some degree of dysfunction is usually detectable by objective methods, even when overall pump performance is maintained. In effect, there is a spectrum of left ventricular dysfunction following acute myocardial infarction, at one end of which some degree of dysfunction exists even in the absence of clinical evidence of cardiac decompensation, and at the other end of which is the power failure or cardiogenic shock syndrome.

To understand the pathophysiology of this spectrum of left ventricular myocardial failure, it is necessary to consider the factors capable of influencing ventricular performance in the basal state and under conditions of stress. Classically, analysis of cardiac function has been within the Frank-Starling framework, centering on the relationship between ventricular end-diastolic volume or pressure and stroke volume or stroke work. Experiments by numerous investigators, first in isolated heart preparations and later in the intact animal, showed stroke volume to

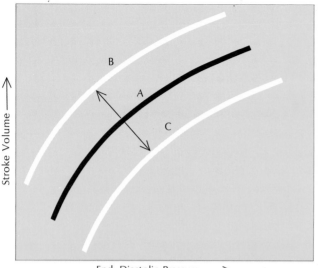

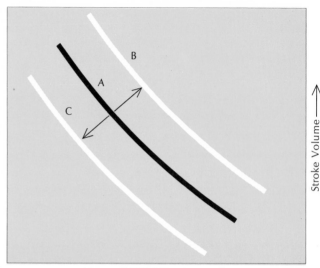

Ventricular performance is influenced by two mechanical factors, preload and afterload, and also by the inotropic state of the myocardium, which affects performance at any level of preload and afterload. The curves in the figure at the left (preload) depict the relationship between stroke volume, i.e., ventricular performance, and the end-diastolic pressure (an index of muscle fiber stretch). An increase in contractility resulting from augmentation of the inotropic state by sympathetic stimulation or, say, exogen-

ous norepinephrine would shift the normal curve (A) to the left (B), while a decrease in inotropism would move it to the right (C). The figure at the right (afterload) shows that with end-diastolic volume constant, stroke volume is inversely related to aortic pressure and, via the LaPlace relation, to intraventricular pressure and ventricular size (wall tension). Note that in this context positive inotropic influences shift the normal curve (A) to the right (B), negative influences move it to the left (C).

be dependent on muscle fiber length at the onset of systole, fiber length in turn being determined by ventricular end-diastolic volume or pressure. The inotropic state, or contractility, could be defined by a ventricular function curve reflecting the relationship between end-diastolic volume or end-

diastolic pressure and stroke work or stroke volume. An increase in the level of contractility would shift the curve upward and to the left, whereas depression of contractility was indicated by downward and rightward displacement. The failing heart, then, delivered a less-than-normal stroke vol-

ume despite a normal or even increased end-diastolic volume.

In a series of studies begun by our group in the early 1960's, myocardial performance in man was examined by acutely altering loading conditions on the heart, such as by partially inflating a balloon catheter

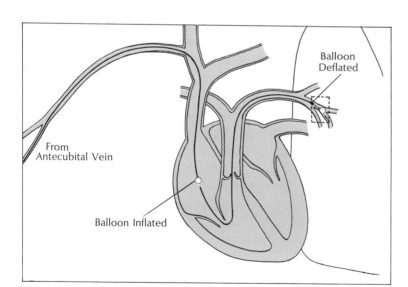

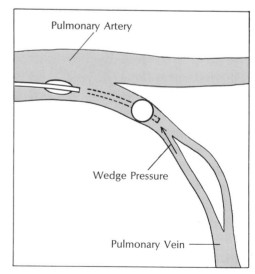

For measurement of pulmonary arterial wedge pressure in the acute postinfarction period, a balloon-tipped, flow-directed catheter is inserted through an antecubital vein under continuous pressure- and ECG-monitoring into the superior vena cava and thence to the right atrium where the balloon tip is inflated. Car-

ried downstream into the pulmonary artery, the catheter balloon is deflated and advanced further until it is in position for pulmonary artery or wedge pressure recordings (as shown in detail at right). When wedge pressure measurement is required, the balloon is reinflated without further catheter manipulation.

within the vena cava to impede venous return or infusing a pressor agent to change aortic pressure. In patients with normal left ventricular function, decreased venous return caused a substantial decrease in stroke volume, and left ventricular end-diastolic pressure was reduced to half the normal value. However, in the presence of chronic left ventricular disease, an elevated end-diastolic pressure was markedly reduced when venous return was impeded, but the initially low stroke volume was unchanged or only slightly further decreased, that is, the function curve was depressed and flattened.

Altering loading conditions by infusion of a pressor agent such as angiotensin or methoxamine elicited the following responses: In patients without disease, no change or an increase in stroke volume was accompanied by a substantial compensatory increase in left ventricular end-diastolic pressure, but in those with chronic left ventricular disease a significant reduction in stroke volume occurred despite augmentation in left ventricular end-diastolic pressure. Thus, although end-diastolic fiber length was increased, the diseased myocardium was evidently unable to meet the load imposed by heightened aortic pressure.

Studies such as these provided insight into ventricular function under both normal and abnormal conditions and, together with other quantitative studies in which cardiac performance was analyzed in terms of the behavior of the muscle during ventricular contraction, allowed identification of four major factors that regulate the manner of shortening of myocardial muscle fibers and hence stroke volume. One, already referred to, is the length of muscle fibers prior to onset of contraction – the *preload* – which profoundly affects the force, speed, and extent of fiber shortening at any level of the inotropic state. The stroke volume also is a function of the tension developed in the myocardium during each contraction; this is the *afterload* imposed on the muscle. Independent of fiber length as well as contractility, afterload is highly dependent both on aortic pressure during ventricular ejection and on ventricular size, according to the LaPlace relation (whereby a large ventricle has a higher afterload to meet than a small one at the same level of aortic pressure). If afterload is increased when preload is experimentally held constant, there is a decrease in stroke volume and velocity of ejection (a reflection of the force-velocity relation).

Both of these mechanical determinants are greatly influenced by the *inotropic state* (contractility) of the myocardium, which can alter performance at any level of preload or afterload. Under physiologic conditions, the chief mechanism regulating the inotropic state is, of course, sympathetic nerve activity and the quantity of norepinephrine released by sympathetic nerve endings both inside and outside the heart (see Chapter 6, "The Autonomic Nervous System in Heart Failure," by Braunwald), but it is also influenced by several biochemical, humoral, and pharmacologic factors. For example, the inotropic state and hence the force, speed, and extent of fiber shortening at any level of preload or afterload can be significantly enhanced by drugs such as digitalis, norepinephrine, and isoproterenol; conversely, acidosis, hypoxia, and many antiarrhythmic agents and anesthetics have a negative inotropic effect.

Finally, the inotropic state is influenced by the *frequency of contraction*. In the experimental animal, when ventricular end-diastolic volume is held constant, peak aortic flow rate, peak rate of left ventricular pressure development, and stroke power all significantly increase with increasing frequency of contraction. Variations

Systemic Hemodynamic Patterns Following Acute MI

Clinical Classification	Systemic Arterial Pressure	Cardiac Output	Peripheral Vascular Resistance	Central Venous Pressure
Uncomplicated	Normal or ↓	Normal	Normal	Normal
Mild congestive heart failure	Usually normal	Usually normal	Usually normal	Usually normal
Severe congestive heart failure	Normal or ↑↓	↓↓	↑↑	Usually ↑ or ↑↑
Shock: Cardiogenic (usual)	↓↓↓	↓↓↓↓	↑↑↑	May be normal ↑↑
Cardiogenic (unusual)	↓↓↓	↓↓	↑	↑
Hypovolemic	↓↓↓	↓↓↓	↑↑↑	↓↓

Although cardiac output may be maintained following onset of myocardial infarction unless severe congestive failure or shock supervenes (table above), some degrees of functional impairment can often be detected by measurement of pulmonary wedge pressure (table below), a reliable indicator of left ventricular dynamics. Note, however, the wide range of PA wedge pressures in the different clinical groups. In a minority of cardiogenic shock patients the degree of hemodynamic abnormality is less marked than usual; it can also be seen that central venous pressure measurements assist in differentiating hypovolemic from cardiogenic shock (table above).

PA Wedge Pressure in Acute Myocardial Infarction

Clinical Classification	Percent of Patients	Mean PA Wedge Pressure (mm Hg)		Percent Having Abnormal PA Wedge Pressure (> 12 mm Hg)
		Average	Range	
Uncomplicated	30	10	2-25	25
Mild LV Failure	45	15	5-25	65
Severe LV Failure	15	17	5-30	70
Cardiogenic Shock	10	24	10-30	90

PA = Pulmonary arterial

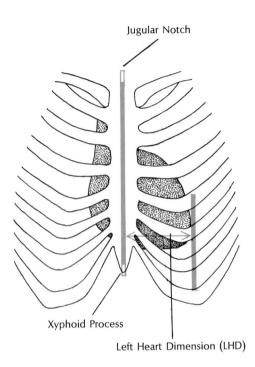

Jugular Notch

Xyphoid Process

Left Heart Dimension (LHD)

To measure left ventricular size externally, vertical lines are drawn on ECG-synchronized x-ray film, one from jugular notch to xyphoid process, another tangential to widest point on left ventricular border; connecting horizon is left heart dimension.

in heart rate also can affect the cardiac minute work: With severe tachycardia, or if heart rate is below 60 per minute (as during sinus bradycardia in acute myocardial infarction), cardiac output may be significantly reduced.

In other experimental studies, comparisons of the force-velocity relation or other measures of the speed of contraction (such as dP/dt) with the standard ventricular function curve (the end-diastolic pressure–stroke work relationship) showed the former to consistently reflect minor alterations in the inotropic state, while the latter often was unchanged. This suggested that measures of velocity might be more sensitive to changing myocardial contractility than the usual hemodynamic data. Subsequent exploration of these relationships in patients with and without left ventricular myocardial disease confirmed that the velocity of shortening of the ventricular wall and the maximum dP/dt during the isovolumic phase of contraction could be reduced in myocardial patients though hemodynamics were normal.

Thus far, studies on left ventricular function in patients with acute myocardial infarction, utilizing standard hemodynamic techniques and some specialized approaches, have substantially added to our understanding of the pathophysiology of this disease. An important initial observation has been that the *clinical* condition following onset of infarction may not reflect the functional state of the myocardium. Evidence of mild left ventricular dysfunction may be missed because overall pumping function of the heart is not visibly affected, and sometimes even relatively severe degrees of hemodynamic impairment may not be reflected clinically.

When Hamosh and coworkers, a few years ago, related hemodynamic features within the first hours after onset of acute symptoms to clinical status, they found by direct retrograde catheterization that the left ventricular end-diastolic pressure was usually elevated in patients with transmural infarction, whether or not there was clinical evidence of cardiac decompensation; they also noted that the left ventricular end-diastolic pressure was markedly elevated in patients with cardiogenic shock. Since that time, other investigators also have noted the frequent occurrence of end-diastolic or pulmonary artery wedge pressure elevations in transmural infarction. Moreover, recent studies by our group using precise cumulative measurements of creatine phosphokinase (CPK) released from the infarcted tissue indicate that the size of an infarction rather than its location primarily determines the hemodynamic pattern and often the outcome (see Chapter 22, "Biochemical and Morphologic Changes in Infarcting Myocardium," by Sobel).

Let us now examine in more detail the way in which development of more accurate techniques for monitoring cardiac function in the early postinfarction period has aided understanding of the hemodynamic patterns associated with acute myocardial infarction and its complications. Central venous pressure is the hemodynamic parameter most commonly measured in clinical practice. The assumption has been that function of the right ventricle, as reflected by this pressure measurement, parallels that of the left ventricle. One need only recall that

since the right ventricle usually is only minimally involved by the infarction process, this is unlikely to be the case. Indeed, central venous pressure may even be distinctly abnormal while left ventricular end-diastolic pressure is normal or nearly so; this pattern, for example, may occur in patients with associated chronic pulmonary disease. More often, left ventricular end-diastolic pressure is substantially elevated, but the central venous pressure is normal. Hence central venous pressure measurement cannot be relied upon for information concerning left ventricular function. On the other hand, the pulmonary arterial wedge pressure is a useful and usually reliable indicator of left ventricular dynamics. This pressure accurately reflects the mean left atrial pressure. The pulmonary artery end-diastolic pressure also usually correlates reasonably well with the mean left atrial pressure.

Until recently, measurement of pulmonary arterial pressures in acutely ill patients presented difficulties that limited the usefulness of this approach. Available techniques required insertion of semirigid catheters through the right ventricle under fluoroscopic guidance. Even if carried out with skill, the procedure carried a considerable risk of cardiac arrhythmias, which is hardly a complication to invite in patients with compromised cardiac function. These difficulties have largely been surmounted with use of a balloon-tipped, flow-directed catheter (developed by Swan, Ganz, and coworkers) that allows for rapid cannulation of the pulmonary artery with minimal risk, even in seriously ill patients.

As the procedure is usually performed, the catheter is advanced under continuous pressure and electrocardiographic monitoring into the right atrium, the balloon tip is inflated, and the catheter is then carried by the bloodstream through the right ventricle and into the pulmonary artery. Once in position the balloon is deflated and subsequently reinflated without further manipulation when pulmonary arterial wedge pressure is to be recorded. By this method, serial monitoring can be performed in the acute postinfarction period with relative simplicity and safety.

In a recent comparison of this technique for obtaining the wedge pressure with central venous pressure monitoring, Forrester et al (of the same group that developed the balloon-tipped catheter) simultaneously performed both measurements in patients with acute myocardial infarction. Whereas the level of pulmonary artery wedge pressure and x-ray evidence of pulmonary congestion were often correlated, central venous pressure did not always reflect the presence of left ventricular failure, as indicated earlier. Indeed, accurate prediction of pulmonary artery wedge pressure from knowledge of central venous pressure was not possible in any of the patients studied, and measurement of central venous pressure was often of little value as a means of observing even directional changes in pulmonary artery wedge pressure following acute volume manipulations. As these investigators commented: "The complications associated with pulmonary artery balloon catheterization have been small, and the greater relevance of the measurements obtained suggests that this procedure be substituted for central ven-

ous pressure monitoring whenever careful evaluation of left-sided pressures is indicated for patient management."

Hemodynamic monitoring of pulmonary artery wedge pressure has added considerably to our understanding of the spectrum of left ventricular dysfunction in patients with acute myocardial infarction. Recently, preliminary analysis of patients studied in our Myocardial Infarction Research Unit indicated clearly that clinical assessment can be misleading. Thus, about three quarters of patients were either clinically uncomplicated (without abnormal physical signs) or exhibited clinical evidence of only minimal left ventricular failure. However, within the completely uncomplicated group, about one quarter of the patients had an elevated pulmonary arterial wedge pressure (over 12 mm Hg), and in some instances this was as high as 25 mm Hg. Among the patients with clinical evidence of mild left ventricular failure, two thirds had an abnormal pulmonary arterial wedge pressure. Of those remaining, about 15% exhibited clinical evidence of se-

vere left ventricular failure; another 10% had cardiogenic shock. Among the patients with clinically severe left ventricular failure, 30% did not exhibit an elevated pulmonary arterial wedge pressure at the time of study, a finding that might not have been anticipated in this group of critically ill patients and that may carry therapeutic implications. On the other hand, over 90% of the patients with cardiogenic shock had a markedly elevated pulmonary arterial wedge pressure (average 24 mm Hg); in the few patients having a normal wedge pressure the indication for a trial of volume expansion was, of course, clear. In general, among all groups, as the clinical category became more severe, the average pulmonary artery wedge pressure for the group increased. Finally, it was of interest that in the great majority of patients who recovered from acute myocardial infarction, initially elevated pulmonary arterial wedge pressures returned toward normal over the first few days after the infarction.

With reference to other measures of left ventricular function, there has

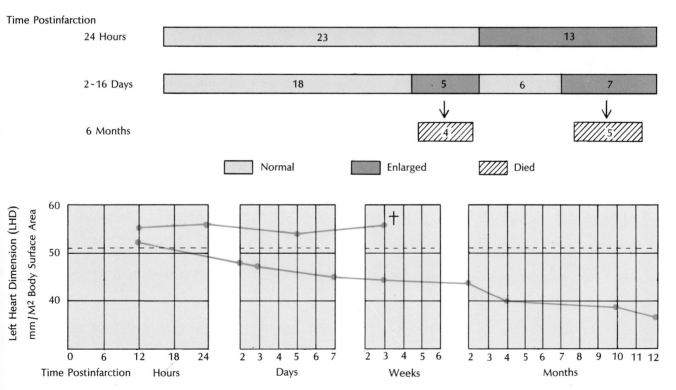

Serial studies have not only established the frequent occurrence of left ventricular enlargement in the acute postinfarction period but confirmed the prognostic value of such calculations. Thus in the initial 36 patients studied (upper graph) few deaths occurred among those whose LHD remained within normal limits; however, when left ventricular size was initially increased or became so in the weeks after infarction, the mortality risk was substantially increased. Actual measurements obtained in two patients (lower graph) again show that whereas a temporary increase in ventricular size may be of little importance, residual enlargement carries with it a less favorable prognosis. The dashed line indicates the upper limit of normal left ventricular size.

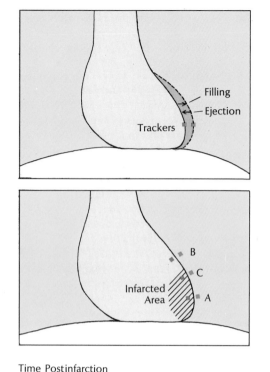

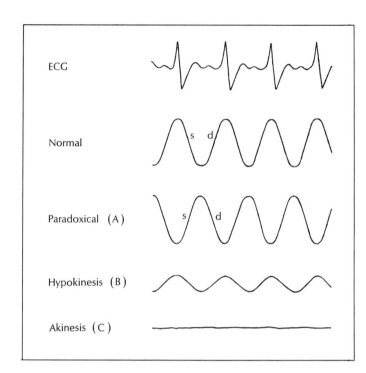

Time Postinfarction

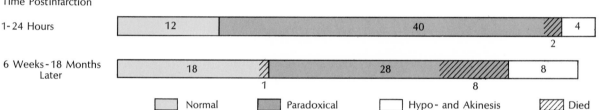

Noninvasive technique of radarkymography for detecting regional loss of contractile function employs video-tracking system to record horizontal heart wall motion during left ventricular ejection and filling (top left). Normal inward motion during systole and outward motion during diastole are recorded as a downward deflection (s wave) followed by an upward deflection (d wave), as shown in panel at right. Paradoxical pulsations marked by complete reversal of the normal wave form reflect dis-

ordered wall motion at the site of acute myocardial injury, a frequent finding in the postinfarction period; recordings from the periphery of the infarcted area may show hypokinetic or akinetic patterns (center left and right). Whereas transient wall motion abnormalities following acute infarction may be of little consequence, persistence of paradoxial pulsations has proved an important prognostic sign, as was observed in a group of 56 postinfarction patients who were followed for up to 18 months (bar graph).

been need for diagnostic techniques suitable for use in seriously ill patients who require serial measurements. For example, a key measurement following the onset of myocardial infarction is the left ventricular size, because of its obvious importance in determining cardiac performance and energy requirements. The procedures usually employed almost always require left heart catheterization, which usually is not desirable and is difficult to repeat. Although its dependability for serial monitoring requires further evaluation, the noninvasive technique of echocardiography holds promise as an alternative. However, a radiographic method with which we have been working proved sufficiently accurate and reproducible to allow serial studies over prolonged periods, and

it appears to offer several advantages over radiographic techniques formerly in use. Plain x-ray methods for calculating cardiac size and volume have been standardized with the patient in the upright position. In this new approach the patient is positioned in a specially modified, radiolucent bed with the head either at a 45° angle or horizontal, usually comfortable positions for the acutely ill. Standardized first on normal subjects, the method has since been applied in patients with acute myocardial infarction and other forms of cardiac disease.

In developing the method, it was postulated that the horizontal distance from the midline to the external margin of the left heart should be relatively free of influence of right heart filling and thus should closely reflect altera-

tions in left ventricular size. This dimension, determined from the frontal plane roentgenogram, was compared with the left ventricular cavity diameter measured directly from cineangiograms in patients undergoing diagnostic left ventriculography. In some patients, resistance to left ventricular ejection was increased or decreased in order to induce alterations in left ventricular size, and the direct and indirect measurements were again compared.

The close correspondence in left heart dimension as determined by the two techniques encouraged us to pursue a further investigation in which the radiographic method was evaluated in healthy subjects to establish a range of normal values and determine the practicability of the method for repeated measurements of left heart dimensions. E C G-synchronized roentgenograms were exposed at end-diastole (by means of a circuit consisting of a Q R S detector and a variable delay electronic network that triggered the exposure); a hand respirometer monitored the degree of inspiration prior to exposure. On the developed x-ray film, a vertical line was drawn from the jugular notch to the xyphoid process (small lead markers were placed on the chest to mark these sites), and a second parallel line was drawn tangential to the widest point on the left ventricular silhouette. The horizontal line joining these two represented the left heart dimension when corrected for x-ray magnification.

Measurements in healthy subjects established an upper limit of normal for left heart dimension at 52 mm/M² body surface area. Variation in the left heart dimension on different days was at most 3 mm, establishing reproducibility. As part of the same study, cardiac dimensions as computed by this method were compared with cardiothoracic ratios in patients with coronary heart disease. In about one fourth of the cases the cardiothoracic ratio was apparently normal in the presence of an abnormal left heart dimension on roentgenography.

Several cautions on use of this approach are in order: For example, subjects must be instructed not to perform a Valsalva maneuver, since this can induce a marked reduction in heart size. Rotation of the thorax in the sagittal plane can cause errors in measurement. Also, in patients with severe pulmonary infiltrates, the left heart border may be difficult to define. An abnormal left heart dimension in patients suspected of having pericardial effusion should not be attributed to left ventricular enlargement unless confirmed by echocardiography or other studies.

However, if these limitations are kept in mind, the technique can be utilized to reveal changes in left ventricular volume associated with both chronic and acute cardiac disease. Serial measurements in 125 patients with acute myocardial infarction in our coronary care unit have confirmed the early occurrence of left ventricular enlargement in over 40% of patients with acute myocardial infarction. Moreover, this measurement proved to

have predictive value: The left heart dimension became normal, or remained persistently normal in 60% of 115 patients without shock, and it became enlarged or remained persistently enlarged in 40%. If the patients with cardiogenic shock are excluded, early death (within 4 weeks) occurred in 3 of 68 patients (4%) with an initially normal left heart dimension, and in 12 of 47 patients (26%) with an initially enlarged left heart dimension. The left heart dimension remained normal or became normal in 62 of 96 patients who survived more than one month. During the follow-up period, 8% of patients with a normal left heart dimension have died and the remainder (with one exception) are in New York Heart Association (N Y H A) class I or II. In 34 patients, the left heart dimension became or remained persistently enlarged. Of these patients, 24% have died, 42% are in N Y H A class III, and only 34% are in classes I and II. Considered together, the findings strongly suggest that residual left ventricular enlargement has important prognostic significance.

Recently, another technique that does not require cardiac catheterization – radioisotope angiography using a gamma scintillation (Anger) camera – has been evaluated in patients with acute myocardial infarction. With injection of the radioisotope into a peripheral vein, it has been found that ventricular volume as well as the ejection fraction can be calculated: In more than 80% of patients with acute myocardial infarction studied by our group, the ejection fraction has been found to be reduced. This technique also offers the possibility of calculating the mean velocity of shortening of the left ventricular wall in acutely ill patients.

Another factor only recently appreciated for its prognostic importance following acute myocardial infarction is disordered motion of the left ventricular wall. Translocation of blood in and out of aneurysmal cavities, as described 25 years ago by Tennant and Wiggers, is one circumstance under which major hemodynamic abnormalities may occur; dyssynergy in the absence of any alteration in the anatomy of the left ventricular wall can have similar effects. It has also been suggested that a re-

gion of abnormal pulsations may act as a "slack" elastic element in series with the contractile portion of the left ventricle, thereby increasing cardiac work and myocardial oxygen consumption. The precise sequence of events is not clear, but evidence does suggest that when the proportion of surface area of the ventricle that becomes dyskinetic or akinetic is sizable, the remainder of the normally contracting myocardium may be unable to sustain normal cardiac output.

Although compensatory changes in left ventricular size may keep stroke volume at near-normal levels for a time, when this mechanism fails, regional loss of contractile function could lead to generalized ventricular failure. Studies by a number of investigators have documented the relatively common occurrence of left ventricular dyssynergy in late postinfarction patients with heart failure.

For these reasons it is important to be able to identify abnormalities of left ventricular pulsation as early as possible in the course of acute myocardial infarction. However, left ventricular cineangiography, the most reliable method of doing so, is imprac-

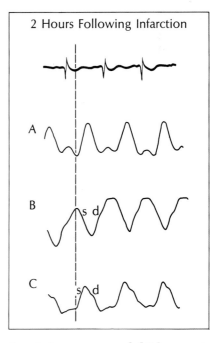

2 Hours Following Infarction

In radarkymogram recorded 2 hours postinfarction, onset of systole (dashed line) is accompanied by paradoxical expansion of lower left ventricular wall (C) at site of injury whereas normal wave pattern prevails (B) in upper ventricular wall. Expansion of the aorta with systole is also recorded (A).

ticable for serial studies in the acutely ill patient. Fluoroscopy relies heavily on subjective impressions of the observer; measurements by techniques such as apexcardiography and kinetocardiography are affected by the structure of the thoracic wall. Recently, however, the combination of image intensification and closed circuit television with fluoroscopy has provided a more precise indirect method for assessing regional wall motion. Using radar to scan the heart image on a television monitor and to track the motion of multiple sites along the heart border, a method has been developed that allows detection and serial follow-up of the course of left ventricular wall motion disorders in patients with both acute and chronic coronary heart disease.

In essence, radarkymography records horizontal movements of the cardiac silhouette as projected on a television screen; wall motion abnormalities are detected by changes in density at the interface of the cardiac border and the lung. Normally the left ventricular border moves medially during ejection and laterally during filling; the dark-to-light transition indicating the cardiac border creates a

voltage peak onto which a tracker is locked. The motion of the tracker as it follows density changes at the heart-lung interface is in turn translated into an analog signal that is displayed on an oscilloscope and recorded as a radarkymogram.

In a normal radarkymogram three wave patterns are recorded during each cardiac cycle: an upward a wave at onset of systole, reflecting outward motion of the left ventricular wall, followed by a downward s wave reflecting rapid inward motion during ejection; and an outward motion of the heart during diastole, recorded as an upward deflection (d wave). The abnormal pattern seen with complete reversal of pulsation (paradoxical pulsation) consists of an upward deflection during ventricular systole and a downward deflection during diastole. With localized diminution of motion (hypokinesis), the distance between the peak of the a wave and the nadir of the s wave is sharply reduced. In the presence of akinesis the radarkymographic waves bear no temporal relation to electrical events in the heart.

With radarkymography, disordered wall motion of one type or another is often found in the first hours

following onset of acute myocardial infarction, before characteristic serum enzyme changes or ECG abnormalities have appeared. Moreover, according to recent evidence, a persistent abnormality in wall motion, like persistent left ventricular enlargement, may be an ominous sign.

In a study with this technique by our group, sequential radarkymograms were recorded in patients with acute myocardial infarction, beginning within the first hour after onset of symptoms and continuing up to 18 months in some cases. Disordered motion of the left ventricular wall was recorded on the initial radarkymogram in about 80% (44 of 56) of patients studied; two of the 44 died on the first day. The persistence of paradoxical movement appeared to carry the greatest risk, since 8 of 28 in whom this pattern persisted died in the ensuing period. In contrast, there was one death among 15 patients who manifested paradoxical motion only temporarily or had no wall motion abnormalities at any time. Patients with acute myocardial infarction involving the lateral wall showed paradoxical pulsations at some time in all 23 such instances; of the 18 who retained paradoxical pulsations, 5 (28%) died in the ensuing period.

Patients with abnormalities confined to the posterior and inferior ventricular wall are more difficult to evaluate by this method. Radarkymography can be used to good effect only where there is a visible interface between the cardiac silhouette and adjacent structure; pulsations of the diaphragmatic wall are usually missed. There are recording problems, too, in the presence of extensive pulmonary edema or fibrosis, pleural effusions, and bony distortions of the chest cage; in dyspneic patients, extraneous motions of the heart produced by respiration can introduce artifacts.

Within these limitations, radarkymography does appear useful as a prognostic indicator in patients with acute myocardial infarction. It should prove useful also in assessing results of active intervention in the postinfarction period: to determine, for example, whether restoration of coronary flow by means of myocardial revascularization also restores ventricular function to the damaged area.

Techniques such as radarkymogra-

Therapeutic Implications of Altered Hemodynamics in Acute MI

Physiologic Variable	Usual Findings	Therapeutic Implications
Preload	Increased	Maintenance of elevated left ventricular end-diastolic volume may be necessary to sustain cardiac output Optimum atrial booster pump function is important
Afterload	Normal or low	Adequate systemic arterial pressure during *diastole* is necessary to maintain coronary perfusion Elevated *systolic* arterial pressure may reduce cardiac output and will increase myocardial oxygen consumption
Inotropic State	Decreased	Acidosis and hypoxia and anti-arrhythmic agents depress the inotropic state of surviving myocardium Positive inotropic agents augment myocardial performance. In excess (particularly with isoproterenol) they may increase myocardial O_2 consumption and adversely affect ischemic areas
Heart Rate	Slightly increased	Mild increase in heart rate may serve to maintain minute output of failing heart; mild bradycardia may result in decreased cardiac output Severe tachycardia increases myocardial oxygen consumption and adversely affects ischemic areas

Pathophysiology of Cardiogenic Shock

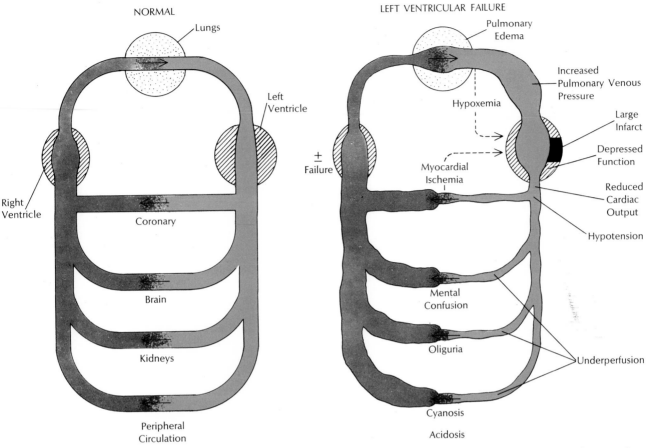

As the diagram suggests, cardiogenic shock represents an extreme form of the left ventricular dysfunction that usually accompanies acute myocardial infarction. With a large infarct the likelihood of severe left ventricular failure and serious hemodynamic abnormalities that result in shock is substantially increased; right heart failure may or may not develop.

phy and external measurement of left ventricular size have proved most useful in cases not complicated by severe heart failure or cardiogenic shock. When these complications occur, assessment of left ventricular function and choice of therapy can be better accomplished with precise knowledge of hemodynamic parameters. In addition, the form of shock associated with hypovolemia often can be detected with certainty only by measurement of the pulmonary arterial wedge pressure or left ventricular end-diastolic pressure, and this form of shock may respond well to volume replacement.

The pathophysiology of cardiogenic shock is shown in the diagram above. The underlying problem of severe left ventricular failure is complicated further by certain relations between aortic pressure and coronary blood flow. It is well known that the normal heart exhibits a remarkable capacity

to regulate coronary flow to meet metabolic needs. When there is an acute change in oxygen needs, as with onset of myocardial infarction, autoregulation of coronary blood flow to surviving tissue is maintained up to a point by reduction of coronary vascular resistance to assure sufficient dilation of the coronary vascular bed.

However, local autoregulation is lost when the aortic pressure falls to a critical (shock) level; coronary vessels are dilated to the limit and flow becomes pressure dependent. In the normal coronary circulation this does not happen until perfusion pressure drops to 65 mm Hg or below. But in patients with acute myocardial infarction, the coronary vasculature is rarely normal and narrowed blood vessels outside of the region of the infarction are likely to be unusually sensitive to alterations in perfusion pressure. Hence, beyond an area of narrowing, perfusion pressure may be far lower

than in the aorta, and distal coronary flow is likely to be highly pressure dependent. Maintaining aortic pressure above the danger point is essential to improve flow both to the region around the infarction and to marginally perfused areas elsewhere.

Since a pressure increase necessarily imposes a higher afterload on an already failing left ventricle, it can create other problems. Thus, when pure peripheral vasoconstrictors such as methoxamine are given to patients in cardiogenic shock, the already low cardiac output is further reduced; moreover, such pressure agents augment myocardial wall tension and heart size, leading to increased oxygen consumption. Thus, instead of increasing aortic pressure alone when it has fallen to hypotensive levels, it makes more sense to increase both aortic pressure and heart contractility by administering a positive inotropic agent such as norepinephrine. The dual aim

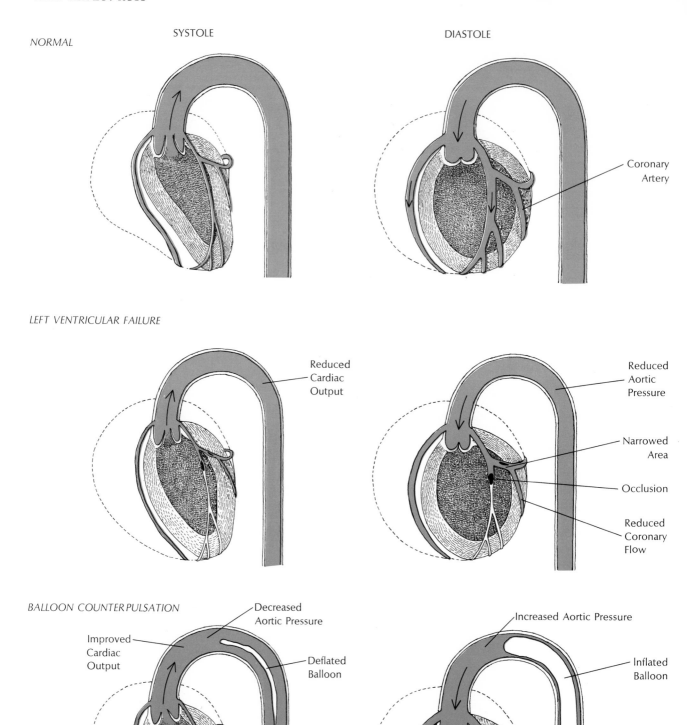

NORMAL

SYSTOLE

DIASTOLE

Coronary Artery

LEFT VENTRICULAR FAILURE

Reduced Cardiac Output

Reduced Aortic Pressure

Narrowed Area

Occlusion

Reduced Coronary Flow

BALLOON COUNTERPULSATION

Decreased Aortic Pressure

Improved Cardiac Output

Deflated Balloon

Increased Aortic Pressure

Inflated Balloon

Increased Coronary Flow

Collateral Flow

A left heart assist system that has improved prognosis in cardiogenic shock entails use of an intra-aortic balloon pump as a counterpulsing device. Balloon deflation at onset of systole reduces systolic aortic pressure and improves cardiac output;

inflation at onset of diastole increases diastolic aortic pressure and coronary perfusion. Thus, time may be gained for development of collateral circulation or for employing a myocardial revascularization procedure if indicated.

in this situation is to produce the least increase in afterload consistent with adequate coronary perfusion, while avoiding an excessive inotropic effect and hence a further increase in myocardial oxygen requirements.

However, despite their potentially beneficial effects, catecholamines carry the threat of inducing local hypoxia (see Chapter 29, "Protection of the Ischemic Myocardium," by Braunwald and Maroko). Experimentally, isoproterenol has extended the area of ischemia in dogs subjected to coronary artery ligation; this results not only from its stimulation of the inotropic state, heart rate, and oxygen consumption but also from its peripheral vasodilating action and adverse effect on diastolic aortic and hence coronary perfusion pressure. The experimental observation that marked tachycardia can increase the size of an infarct also bears noting in this connection. Thus, in shock, doses of norepinephrine sufficient to raise diastolic aortic pressure to 65 mm Hg are preferable.

It should be kept in mind that the factors that affect cardiac performance also are the major determinants of the heart's oxygen consumption (the preload, afterload, heart rate, and inotropic state). But of the several determinants of myocardial performance, preload has the least effect on myocardial oxygen consumption; increasing cardiac output by altering fiber length does not greatly augment myocardial oxygen consumption, particularly if arterial pressure remains fairly stable. Thus, as far as possible, it would also seem logical to make maximum use of the Frank-Starling mechanism for augmenting the force and extent of fiber shortening – for example, by expanding volume with plasma or dextran – taking care that this does not produce or aggravate pulmonary edema.

In management of patients with severe congestive failure and cardiogenic shock, one is often faced with the therapeutic dilemma of trying to improve coronary perfusion pressure and ventricular function, while reducing pulmonary edema and secondary hypoxia, without overly increasing myocardial oxygen consumption or further inhibiting cardiac output. In cardiogenic shock, the reduction in cardiac output and elevation in left ventricular end-diastolic pressure are likely to be extreme. Given the limited options for the therapy of power failure or shock, development of intraaortic balloon counterpulsation and external counterpulsation have been particularly welcome additions to the management of cardiogenic shock (see Chapter 32, "Assisted Circulation: A Progress Report," by Soroff and Birtwell). Counterpulsation offers the highly desirable combination of a reduced systolic aortic pressure (thereby favoring cardiac output and lowered left atrial pressure) while elevating diastolic aortic pressure (and hence coronary perfusion pressure). Experience outlined by Mundth et al in Chapter 33 indicates that mechanical circulatory assistance by this means can provide important hemodynamic support in the shock patient. When balloon counterpulsation is combined with myocardial revascularization surgery, reduction in mortality is seen, from 95% to 70% or 80% – still far too high but surely a significant gain.

Aside from the management of arrhythmias, in the final analysis the therapeutic regimen selected for a given patient with acute myocardial infarction depends on the degree of left ventricular dysfunction that is present. Most clinically uncomplicated cases require little or no intervention from a hemodynamic viewpoint, since the abnormalities seen in the early postinfarction period are likely to correct themselves; watchful waiting thus becomes the treatment of choice. In the presence of mild to moderate congestive failure, treatment must be aimed both at strengthening the contractility of surviving myocardium and alleviating secondary effects of left ventricular failure upon the lungs, as with diuresis and digitalis therapy. In addition, considerable research has now indicated that with appropriate therapy, areas of myocardium destined to die may be salvaged (see Chapter 29 by Braunwald and Maroko). No doubt the outlook for clinically complicated cases could be improved further with more specific criteria for determining in advance whether a given patient is destined for cardiogenic shock, so that a technique such as counterpulsation could eventually be used to prevent rather than reverse this lethal complication. Indeed, one of the chief goals of current hemodynamic studies is to provide reliable indirect means of predicting events in the acute postinfarction period, as a guide to clinical management and for evaluating new forms of therapy. One hopes that these aims can be achieved in the not too distant future.

Myocardial Infarction and Sudden Death

OGLESBY PAUL

Northwestern University

The threat of sudden, unexpected death has haunted humankind throughout history, though we are no longer quite so defenseless against some of its forms. The demonstration barely more than a decade ago that so simple an emergency measure as external manual cardiac compression could reverse imminently fatal circulatory arrest gave proof that sudden death was at least an approachable adversary. Kouwenhoven and coworkers deserve our gratitude not only for devising the resuscitative procedure but for their contribution toward making electrical countershock a practical method for control of ventricular fibrillation.

In a real sense these accomplishments provided the impetus for development of the more sophisticated techniques now available for reversal of cardiac arrest and lethal arrhythmias. For patients requiring – and receiving – such treatment the threat of sudden death has been measurably reduced. But in acknowledging these gains we must not overlook certain sobering truths: In terms of absolute loss of life, sudden, unexpected death today poses our greatest single medical problem. Though the actual incidence of sudden death is unknown, recent estimates suggest an incidence as high as 30% of all natural deaths. It is certain that the most common cause of sudden death in our adult population is due by and large to coronary heart disease. Reportedly, sudden death is the first clinical manifestation of acute myocardial infarction in 20% to 25% of all cases. In addition, of more than 500,000 coronary deaths per year, fully 60% are sudden deaths that often occur without any warning at all; moreover, the fraction of coronary deaths occurring suddenly is higher in younger than in older adults. The tragedy is heightened when an autopsy shows, as it sometimes does, a basically normal myocardium with only moderate disease of coronary arteries and no evidence of thrombotic occlusion.

It should be borne in mind, however, that sudden death may be due also to other cardiovascular diseases. Valvular defects, including aortic stenosis and aortic insufficiency, are familiar causes. Serious rhythmic abnormalities such as AV block with Stokes-Adams attacks carry a particularly high risk. Both myocarditis and myocardiopathy precipitate sudden death more often than realized. Primary pulmonary hypertension and pulmonary embolism are also more frequent causes than was formerly recognized. Cerebral lesions as a group usually do not produce immediate death; however, cerebral hemorrhage is more likely to produce sudden death than are cerebral embolism and thrombosis. Assuming that sudden death is likely to occur only in association with coronary disease can mean excluding other important possibilities. Better understanding of underlying mechanisms in sudden death – and hope for prevention – must begin with appreciating all possible causes.

To pursue meaningful studies of sudden death a standard definition is surely a first requisite. However, even the most cursory review of medical literature on the subject indicates that, unfortunately, a standard definition does not exist. The term has been so variously defined – or sometimes used without definition at all – that comparison of case material becomes difficult and the disparate findings confusing.

To guide clinicians and also to provide a basis for further research, a committee representing both the American Heart Association and the International Society of Cardiology agreed recently on a definition of sudden, unexpected death as death that occurs within an estimated 24 hours of onset of acute symptoms and signs. (An *instantaneous* death is one that occurs within seconds or

Total Deaths (64)

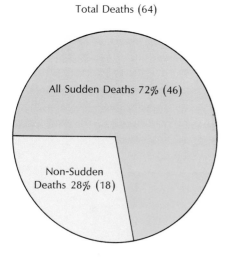

Sudden Deaths (46)

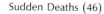

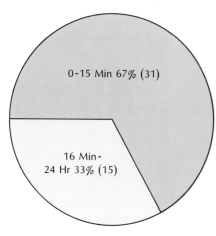

Sudden Deaths (46)

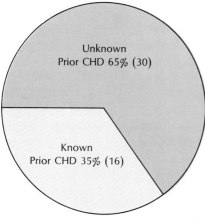

Sudden deaths accounted for nearly three fourths of total coronary deaths at 10-year mark in prospective study of Chicago telephone workers (top diagram). As shown, most sudden deaths occurred in subjects with no prior history of clinical coronary disease (bottom diagram) within minutes of the onset of acute symptoms (center).

minutes.) The 24-hour limit was intentionally set because there is often some ambiguity as to exactly when death has occurred; for various reasons a number of hours may elapse between the event and its discovery. But the liberality of this definition should not divert us from a critical fact about sudden cardiovascular deaths, most particularly those caused by coronary disease—most such deaths occur in the first hours of the 24-hour period, too rapidly for effective medical aid to be obtained. A variety of studies, both retrospective and prospective, have made it clear that the majority of victims die at home or en route to the hospital.

To illustrate the problem I might cite findings in our long-term study of coronary heart disease among some 2,000 middle-aged men (40 to 55 years at entry) employed by the Western Electric Company in Chicago. As in other prospective studies, the men were initially free of heart disease and have now been followed for well over a decade. Within the first 10 years there were 64 coronary deaths, all but 18 of them sudden. However, nearly half (31 of 64) the victims died not only suddenly but instantaneously, within 15 minutes of onset of the acute episode. The Framingham community study, covering a broader age range (29 to 62 at entry) and both sexes, yielded similar findings: There were 120 coronary deaths, half of them sudden, in a 14-year follow-up period. In a retrospective study of sudden death by Kuller and coworkers — covering virtually all such deaths in the city of Baltimore in a one-year period — some 60% of victims of coronary heart disease died at home or in transit to a medical facility.

Feinleib and Davidson reported on a survey conducted of all death certificates filed in 1969 in a Maryland suburban community. During the year, there were 719 deaths in both sexes in the age group 35 to 74, and 257 or 36% of these were due to coronary heart disease. It was observed that at least 155 (60%) of these 257 died before definitive medical care could be provided. Of those reaching a hospital dead or alive, 61% came by rescue squad and 19% by ambulance. These authors also emphasized that patient delay was the chief impediment to more prompt medical attention; the

major delay was not in the transport system.

The gravity of the problem is reflected, too, when we consider the events preceding death. For example, in the Baltimore study approximately half the patients dying suddenly of coronary disease had been free of cardiac symptomatology until the fatal event. In our Western Electric study group, too, only half the victims dying within 24 hours were known to have coronary disease; in the group dying within 15 minutes only one third had known prior disease. It is noteworthy that these patients, as in other prospective studies, were receiving repeated routine cardiovascular examinations as part of the study protocol; thus it is unlikely that symptomatic disease would have been overlooked if present. In Framingham, more than 90% of patients who died (either suddenly or otherwise) were free of clinical coronary disease, or had only mild forms, at the last examination within two years of death.

In the past few years attention has been focused on treatment of patients with acute myocardial infarction surviving long enough to reach a medical facility. Without a doubt inhospital mortality from acute infarction has been significantly reduced since the establishment of well-equipped coronary care units, chiefly because of effective prevention and treatment of life-threatening cardiac arrhythmias by means of defibrillation, drug therapy, and pacemaker insertions. Among patients receiving optimal care in such a unit, death rates can usually be reduced by about 30%; more recently reductions of up to 50% have been reported (see Chapter 22, "Biochemical and Morphologic Changes in Infarcting Myocardium," by Sobel and Chapter 27, "Management of Arrhythmias in Acute Myocardial Infarction," by Killip).

Gratifying as this is, the success of these units must be viewed as only a partial victory. Their use has meant a substantial saving of lives among victims reaching such a unit in time; given the high mortality in acute myocardial infarction within the first few hours, we must now focus more purposefully on the prehospital phase of illness. Two basic directions are being followed, with research aimed at improved understanding of underlying mechanisms triggering sudden death, and at earlier identification and perhaps prediction of the acute episode.

Precise data have been lacking both on the pathophysiology of sudden death and the terminal electrocardiographic events, in part because the prehospital phase of illness is only beginning to receive its fair share of systematic attention. Also, of course, the very nature of sudden death has made it difficult to study.

Most cases are not associated with pathologic evidence of acute infarction, although it may be surmised that infarction would have evolved if the terminal period had been longer. Severe coronary atherosclerosis is usually present and diffusely distributed in the majority of cases examined at postmortem. But coronary arterial lesions of equal severity are also found in patients who died of other causes, while some patients dying suddenly of heart disease have less extensive lesions than others surviving longer.

Pathologists who have studied the incidence of fresh thrombi in sudden death victims have come up with variable findings (see Chapter 17, "Platelets and Thrombosis in Acute Myocardial Infarction," by Mustard and Chapter 18, "Coronary Artery Pathology in Fatal Ischemic Heart Disease," by Roberts). It is generally thought however that they are present in only a minority of cases, probably no more than 30%. Even when thrombi are found we cannot say that they necessarily provide an explanation for death. Other possibilities must also be considered, though again not with any degree of certainty. In the absence of thrombi, a tear or fracture in an atherosclerotic plaque might narrow a vessel sufficiently to produce ischemia followed by an arrhythmia. Arterial spasm might have the same result.

In cases of sudden death in which there is gross atherosclerosis of coronary arteries but not to the extent one would expect to cause death, disease of the microcirculation affecting the conduction system could be the underlying disorder. This intriguing possibility is raised by findings of James and coworkers in cases of sudden death in young adults. At death, evidence was found of obliterative lesions within sinus node arteries, and of significant damage to both sinus and AV

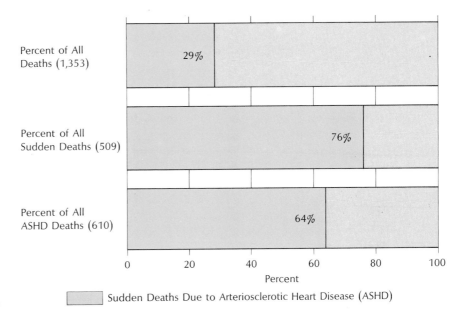

Analysis of virtually all sudden natural deaths occurring in the city of Baltimore over a one-year period points up the overwhelming impact of coronary heart disease. Data (from Kuller et al) graphed above – reflecting the experience of white males aged 40 to 64 at death – are consistent with the findings of other epidemiologic studies.

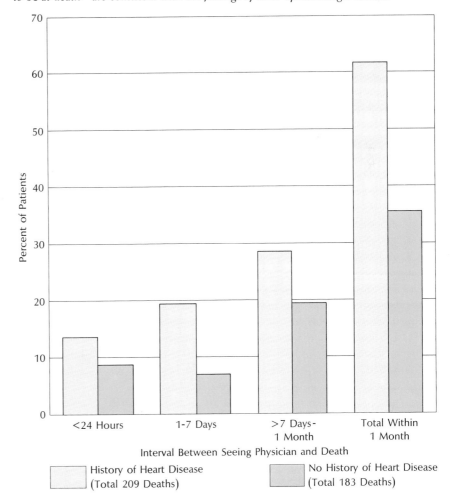

A high proportion of sudden death victims have no prior history of overt heart disease to explain the acute fatal event; however, many are known to have consulted a physician within a week of death, perhaps because of disturbing premonitory signs. Representative data on both points come from Baltimore study (white males aged 40 to 64).

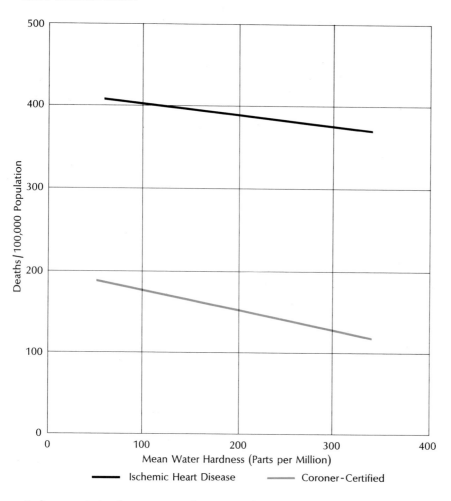

A close association between mineral content of local water supplies and heart disease mortality was documented in Canadian study by Anderson et al, graphed above. Higher mortality in soft-water regions was attributed chiefly to an excess of sudden deaths. This became clear following an analysis of coroner-certified deaths, since many of the latter can be presumed to have occurred before medical aid could be summoned.

nodes. It was concluded that the high incidence of lethal arrhythmias and conduction disturbances preceding sudden death in such cases might well have been due to small vessel disease involving the blood supply to these critical regions of the heart. Whether this will prove to be a major factor in many of the sudden deaths now attributed to coronary artery disease remains to be determined; the findings make it essential that examination of the conduction system and its blood supply become a more routine procedure in cases of sudden cardiac death.

One certainty is that the pathologic findings thus far associated with sudden death in coronary disease need more study and often are incomplete evidence of the nature of the final event.

It is known from experience with inhospital coronary care units that the danger of life-threatening arrhythmias is greatest in the first few hours after onset of an acute episode; reportedly, ventricular fibrillation is 25 times more likely to occur in the first four hours than in the ensuing 24. Most early inhospital deaths are the result of arrhythmias rather than heart muscle damage, and ventricular fibrillation is the type of arrhythmia usually identified. It seems probable that death in the prehospital phase is also most often due to ventricular fibrillation; however, as we have seen, cases treated in a hospital coronary care unit may represent a different phase of acute infarction. There is some evidence that bradycardias may be relatively common in the very early period, with ventricular ectopic rhythms occurring somewhat later in the course of acute infarction. More needs to be known about the immediate electro-

cardiographic events in prehospital sudden death in order to clarify the importance both of ventricular arrhythmias and bradycardias. Moreover, if arrhythmias are the cause of most sudden cardiovascular deaths in or out of the hospital, their genesis needs to be better defined. Plainly, with better understanding, there might be a better chance of preventing lethal arrhythmias.

A number of speculations have been voiced, for example, that occurrence of arrhythmias is somehow related to the mineral content of local water supplies. Studies in several countries have shown higher death rates from ischemic heart disease among residents of soft-water regions. In a recent investigation, Anderson and colleagues in Canada correlated sharp regional differences in death rates from ischemic heart disease in Ontario with local water hardness; the latter was expressed in terms of parts per million of calcium carbonate in the three regions studied. Death rates ranged from 365 per 100,000 population in a hard-water region (200 ppm or higher) to 416 per 100,000 in a soft-water region (below 100 ppm). In an intermediate region the death rate was 390 per 100,000.

Moreover, the higher death rate in soft-water areas could be attributed almost entirely to an excess of sudden coronary deaths. This was indicated by a comparison of deaths certified by private physicians and those certified by coroners, who were more likely to handle deaths that occurred before medical aid could be summoned. The rate of deaths reported to coroners in the region with the softest water was almost double that in the region with hardest water, but noncoroner-certified deaths were virtually the same. This suggested that any effect of the water was more likely on the mechanism causing death than on the process underlying myocardial infarction. Conceivably, a lack of calcium or other ions in soft water could adversely affect myocardial muscle contractility and hence increase susceptibility to fatal cardiac arrhythmias. As of now there is no proof that this occurs, or that other differences between hard- and soft-water regions in addition to their water supplies might not explain the findings.

It is recognized that profound

changes in myocardial cell metabolism accompany acute myocardial infarction; currently, the possibility that some arrhythmias may be explained on a metabolic or biochemical basis is being vigorously pursued. More specifically, interesting research by Kurien and Oliver in Scotland links development of lethal arrhythmias to increases in plasma and intracellular levels of free fatty acids (FFA). A known effect of elevated plasma FFA is to increase oxygen requirements of tissues; their research further suggests that accumulation of intracellular FFA consequent to elevation of plasma levels may have detergent effects on cellular membranes, with cation loss and resultant ectopic pacemaker activity.

This thesis is supported by a number of observations: In clinical studies plasma FFA levels were shown to be markedly increased with onset of acute infarction; subsequently, in several hundred consecutive patients, high plasma FFA levels were significantly correlated with arrhythmic deaths. It was theorized at first that the arrhythmogenic effect might result primarily from increased catecholamine activity during infarction, which is reflected also in increased lipid mobilization from adipose tissue. Later experiments indicated that free fatty acids themselves could have an arrhythmogenic effect. Thus, in dogs with induced myocardial infarction, serious arrhythmias could be consistently produced by elevating plasma FFA levels, which was shown to be accompanied by triglyceride infiltration of the myocardium. Other evidence suggested that with onset of infarction, simple diffusion of unbound extracellular FFA increases their entry into the cell. When hypoxia is severe, locally released norepinephrine further increases intracellular FFA levels by lipolysis of stored triglycerides. As another complicating factor, the impairment in glucose metabolism often associated with myocardial infarction may deplete myocardial glycogen stores. As a result, alpha-glycerophosphate may be inadequate to permit maximal esterification of intracellular FFA. Free fatty acid accumulation increases further as these acids rather than glucose become the principal substrates used for energy production. As tissue binding sites are exceeded, accumulated FFA may exert detergent effects on cellular metabolism, leading to potassium loss and electrical instability.

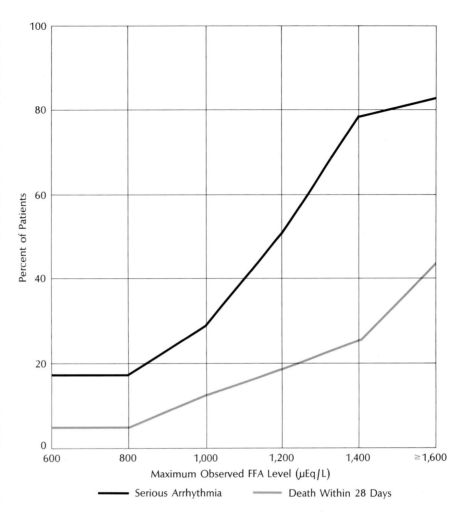

Incidence of serious ventricular arrhythmias and of death within 28 days was significantly increased in the presence of elevated plasma free fatty acids in study by Kurien and Oliver of 200 consecutive patients with acute myocardial infarction. Such findings appear to support thesis that some arrhythmias have a metabolic or biochemical basis.

Of course, further work is needed to prove whether some arrhythmias and sudden deaths are explainable on this basis. Some investigators (e.g., Nelson in Belfast and Opie et al in London) have failed to find an association between free fatty acid levels and arrhythmias. But if an association is confirmed, treatment of acute infarction could properly be directed towards suppressing excess mobilization of FFA from adipose tissue, and trying to ensure that myocardial energy requirements are met as far as possible by oxidation of glucose.

Studies we have undertaken on the circadian rhythm of certain biochemical constituents on a small group of six male patients who had recovered from myocardial infarction have been compared with the findings in six male patients believed to be free of clinical coronary disease. It was of interest to observe certain significant differences, notably a decided drop in the serum potassium levels in the myocardial infarction group around midnight, at a time when the potassium level was actually rising in the control group. More observations need to be made, but it is intriguing to speculate that certain nocturnal sudden deaths may be due to arrhythmias triggered in susceptible individuals by biochemical changes.

One question that appears pretty well resolved involves the role of physical stress in precipitating sudden death. According to several studies, only a small fraction of sudden coronary deaths (reportedly between 2% and 5%) are preceded by strenuous

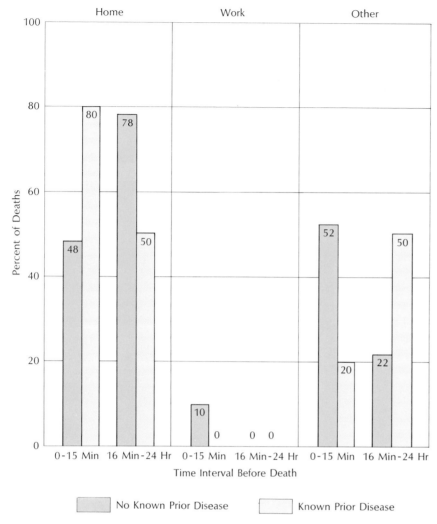

Most sudden death victims are stricken at home – often while resting or sleeping – according to Chicago study among Western Electric workers. Other studies corroborate that relatively few sudden coronary deaths are preceded by strenuous physical activity.

physical activity; somewhat more (8% to 12%) occur at work. In contrast, at least half the victims are stricken at home, most often while in bed. This was borne out among our Western Electric subjects with known prior disease: 80% of those dying within 15 minutes were at home when stricken; so were 50% of those dying in the 16-minute to 24-hour period. Among men without known prior disease, death came at home to 48% of those dying instantly and to 78% of those dying in the remainder of the 24-hour period. Virtually no deaths occurred at work.

Although case reports suggesting otherwise appear in the literature from time to time, there is scant evidence that either unusual mental or emotional stress is likely to trigger most sudden deaths, even in individuals with organic heart disease. The problem

has been studied by Greene, Goldstein, and Moss in an industrial plant in Rochester, N.Y. A review of 26 persons who died suddenly appeared to show both that a majority of these had been depressed for some time and that there had also been a more recent incidence of acute anger or anxiety. Such retrospective studies are decidedly valuable; they do have the limitations imposed by the effects of the recent tragedy on those interviewed. Studies that have attempted to resolve the question have included measurement of E C G responses to stressful automobile driving, as performed by Taggert and coworkers in London. During a test drive in busy city traffic, ischemic E C G patterns were seen in normal subjects and even more so in subjects with coronary disease; half of the latter showed ischemic patterns. Nonetheless, this and other studies

confirm that cardiac arrhythmias originating in traffic stress infrequently cause fatal road accidents.

Considering that most sudden deaths are not as yet convincingly related to either mental or physical stress, and that evidence of recent occlusion is seldom found, we are left with the consideration of other contributing or underlying factors.

In recent years a considerable amount of epidemiologic research has been done on risk factors associated with clinical arteriosclerotic heart disease – most notably hypercholesterolemia, hypertension, hyperglycemia, and excessive cigarette smoking (see Chapter 20, "The Primary Prevention of Coronary Heart Disease," by Stamler). These same factors can heighten the risk of fatal as well as nonfatal infarction. For example, among the Western Electric subjects, two or more of the above risk factors were present in 76% of men without known prior disease who suffered instantaneous death. Among victims of instantaneous death with known prior disease, 90% exhibited two or more of the risk factors.

It would be wrong to assume that factors related to nonfatal myocardial infarction necessarily carry the same weight in reference to sudden death. Indeed, data now available through the national cooperative Pooling Project (combining a 10-year follow-up of several prospectively studied populations, including our Western Electric group) suggest that there may be important differences. In short, the findings indicate that whereas hypercholesterolemia is the factor most strongly correlated with nonfatal infarction (see Chapter 19, "Genetic Aspects of Hyperlipidemia in Coronary Heart Disease," by Goldstein), other risk factors may play a more critical role in cases of sudden death.

One of the factors may be cigarette smoking. A recent pertinent study by Spain and Bradess suggests that cigarette smoking may exert "some if not its major harmful effect on the acute clinical event rather than on the chronic atherogenic process." When they classified subjects dying suddenly of a first clinical episode of coronary heart disease according to whether they survived less than one hour or from one to eight hours, they found that only 5% (2 of 40) of men who smoked more than a pack a day were in the latter group. In contrast, 26.6% (8 of 22) of men who smoked less than a pack a day and 33.3% (6 of 18) of nonsmokers were in the one-to-eight-hour group. Whether the known effect of nicotine in stimulating cate-cholamine production and free fatty acid mobilization has a bearing here is not really known.

Plainly, then, neither all the facts regarding the underlying pathology, the precipitating factors, nor the final event in sudden death have been sufficiently delineated. From what we know now the only sure deterrent to the majority of cases of sudden death would be a means of preventing coronary atherosclerosis. On the other hand, there are reasons to believe that the problem of sudden death may be more approachable than is generally realized.

For example, although a high proportion of victims were without symptomatic heart disease when last examined, this should not be taken to mean that sudden death casts no shadow before it. Actually it is often heralded by premonitory signs that may not be recognized as such. Despite the difficulty of estimating the proportion of patients experiencing significant prodromata, it is undoubtedly greater than has been appreciated.

This is suggested, for example, by the fact that in the Baltimore retrospective study cited above, nearly 25% of patients had seen a physician within a week of the fatal event. Among the Western Electric subjects, half of those who consulted a physician shortly before death did so seeking a "checkup." Although information is not available for either group on *why* a physician was consulted, presumably at least some of the patients did so because of symptoms that might have sounded an alarm to a physician on the lookout for them.

Until recently few hard data were available on the frequency or significance of prodromata in acute infarction. However, careful inquiries such as the one by Killip et al in New York have provided pertinent information, at least in reference to patients surviving long enough to reach a coronary care unit. Detailed questioning of some 100 patients shortly before hospitalization revealed that fully

65% had had a clear-cut warning during the month preceding the acute episode. Chest pain or discomfort was the dominant warning symptom; it was the sole sign in more than 70% of patients with prodromata. Chest pain was associated with other symptoms (including dyspnea, diaphoresis, and "light-headedness") in close to 20%. About 10% had no pain; their pre-infarction symptoms included "burning in the chest," dyspnea, vertigo, weakness, and fatigue. Moreover, more than 85% of patients with prodromata had recurrent episodes that usually increased in frequency, intensity, or duration before the culmination in acute infarction. The longest interval between onset of prodromata and occurrence of the definitive attack was two months, the shortest 14 hours. A key finding was that patients with preexisting angina hospitalized for acute infarction almost always had

had some warning; according to the data there was at least an 80% chance they would develop prodromata. Occurrence of prodromata also proved related to the extent of myocardial damage; their incidence was significantly lower among patients with transmural rather than nontransmural infarction.

The investigators suggest that appearance of prodromata may represent a "dynamic interplay" between the coronary and systemic circulations; these tend to emerge when the myocardial circulation has been sufficiently compromised or the work of the heart exceeds available oxygen supply, or both factors are present. "A significant rise in blood pressure during spontaneous and exertional angina pectoris is now well recognized," Killip and his colleagues point out. ". . . If the patient with gradually progressive coronary artery disease

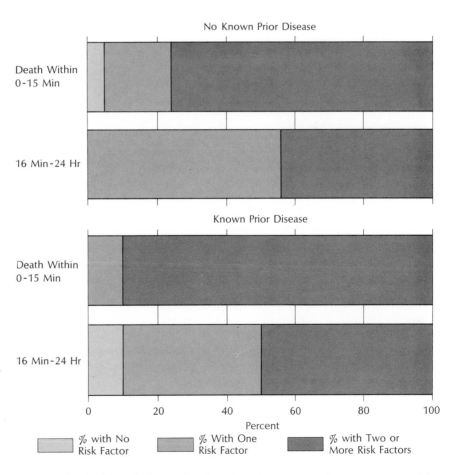

Likelihood of sudden death was heightened in the presence of major coronary risk factors, whether or not victims had a prior history of clinical heart disease; among victims of instantaneous death, at least 75% manifested multiple risk factors. Data are from Chicago epidemiologic study among telephone company workers; risk factors considered included hypercholesterolemia (>255 mg%); hypertension (systolic blood pressure >150 mg Hg, diastolic >90 mg Hg); and a cigarette intake of 10 or more daily.

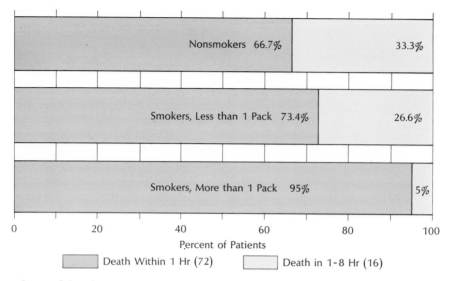

The possibility that excessive cigarette smoking may be a critical factor in precipitating
sudden death is supported in New York study of fatal coronary disease by Spain and
Bradess; as shown in graph above, survival time after onset of acute myocardial infarction was sharply decreased among those who were "heavy" smokers.

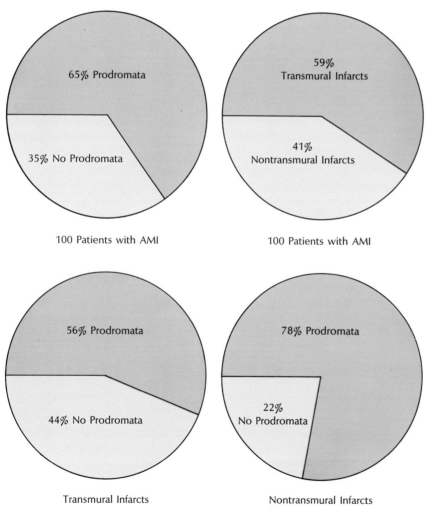

Fully two thirds of sudden death victims had clear-cut warning signs during month
preceding the acute episode in New York study by Killip et al The occurrence of
prodromata also proved inversely related to the extent of myocardial damage; hence it
was significantly lower in patients with transmural rather than nontransmural infarction.

has an exaggerated pressor response
to his ischemic pain, the stage may be
set for a crescendo cycle of ischemia,
pain, pressure rise, more ischemia expressed as prodromata, and finally
acute infarction."

Another commentary on the significance of prodromata is provided by a
community study reported by Fulton
and her collaborators in Edinburgh,
in cooperation with general practitioners in the area. They discovered
only three sudden deaths among 167
patients with "unstable" angina and
concluded that sudden death was not
common among such patients. They
have thus offered more reassurance
regarding this condition than has
generally been recognized by most
clinicians.

In analyzing the Western Electric
data we attempted to see if we could
have anticipated sudden death by reviewing ECG findings. Although no
definite pattern could be discerned in
reference to arrhythmias, other ECG
abnormalities did appear to have some
predictive value. These abnormalities
included nonspecific T waves, S-T
segment depression of the ischemic
type, and signs of left ventricular hypertrophy. They were present on one
or more earlier occasions in 48% of
men without prior symptomatic disease dying within 15 minutes, and in
33% of those dying within the remainder of the 24-hour period. The
abnormalities were present in an even
higher percentage of those with prior
symptomatic disease: in 70% of those
dying in 15 minutes and in 84% of
those dying in the remainder of the
24-hour period.

Although increased interest in identifying probable victims of sudden
death in advance of the fatal event
makes it likely that other premonitory
signs will also be found, something
further is urgently needed if mortality
from this cause is to be substantially
reduced. Since risk of sudden death is
highest in the prehospital phase, the
promptest possible hospitalization is
essential. According to several systematic studies, the median elapsed
time between onset of acute symptoms
and hospital admission is now about
eight hours; only about 15% of patients reach the hospital within four
hours. Availability and accessibility of
medical facilities are rarely the reason
for the delay. All studies substantiate

that it is mostly due to indecision on the part of the patient or his family.

This problem was recently underscored in a report by the Inter-Society Commission for Heart Disease Resources, a panel charged with developing national guidelines for improving facilities for prevention and treatment of cardiovascular disease (see Chapter 20 by Stamler). Among a number of factors that contribute to patient delay, the commission cited "lack of information regarding the significance of symptoms and the urgency of seeking immediate medical care . . . misinterpretation of symptoms as reflecting disorders of other organ systems . . . denial of the importance of chest discomfort because of fear of myocardial infarction and its consequences."

The last mentioned—denial of symptoms — is highly significant. In a study by Hackett and Cassem in Boston on randomly selected patients with acute infarction admitted to one of three hospital coronary care units, it was found that only half knew that their symptoms were related to the cardiovascular system. In the remainder, strong denial was expressed by displacement of symptoms to other organs, in particular the respiratory and/or gastrointestinal systems. Longest delays in seeking help occurred among patients who interpreted their symptoms to exclude the heart; when they consulted a physician it was only after a relative or friend had repeatedly urged them to do so. Unrelated to patient delay were such factors as age, sex, socioeconomic status, or prior history of myocardial infarction.

Significantly, in more than 10% of cases, a physician contributed to delay. Sometimes he showed the same tendency as the patient to shift blame to another organ system, or insisted that symptoms referable to the heart did not constitute a medical emergency.

When denial is not a dominant factor, patient delay may reflect chiefly inability to distinguish the symptoms from usual complaints. As matters now stand, often the patient "is his own physician during the period of greatest risk," as Bondurant pointed out at a symposium on the prehospital phase of acute myocardial infarction, "[since] we have been able to provide him with no systematic, organized, and proved criteria for judging when

Past History	Number of Patients	Decision Time (Min)
MYOCARDIAL INFARCTION		
Present	18	202 ± 69
Absent	46	199 ± 45
ANGINA PECTORIS		
Present	35	176 ± 39
Absent	29	228 ± 68
HYPERTENSION		
Present	21	234 ± 59
Absent	43	182 ± 47
CONGESTIVE HEART FAILURE		
Present	18	263 ± 75
Absent	46	175 ± 43

Patient indecision in seeking emergency medical aid has been found to be a major factor contributing to mortality in prehospital phase of acute myocardial infarction. In study by Moss and coworkers of 64 patients admitted to a CCU over a five-month period, decision time averaged 200 minutes. A prior history of myocardial infarction, angina pectoris, hypertension, or congestive heart failure did not affect decision time significantly.

he should seek assistance."

With the high frequency of coronary heart disease in our adult population, increased patient awareness of the nature and gravity of acute coronary symptoms must be ensured not only by public education but on an individual basis by the patient's physician, especially for high-risk cases. More detailed instruction on this matter could cause some false alarms for physicians; it could also make some patients unduly fearful about the possibility of an acute coronary episode. On the other hand, experience gained through informing women about the value of the Pap smear indicates that the benefits from education of the public should far outweigh any problems created.

Knowing as we do that some patients are at high risk because of such factors as a family history of premature cardiovascular disease — or the presence of hyperlipidemia, hypertension, and addiction to cigarettes — we should take special pains to provide this group with more explicit information and instructions to follow in the event of an attack.

Hospitalization is sometimes un-

necessarily delayed because patients believe the only significant symptom is acute chest pain. In fact, many patients having acute infarction experience only a sensation of dull discomfort; in the absence of pain they do not recognize that an attack is occurring. Unfortunately, too many physicians also focus only on "chest pain," failing to elicit needed information by using other terms. Moreover, prodromal episodes of dyspnea, weakness, and diaphoresis are not always viewed with appropriate concern. A single normal E C G in an individual at high risk is allowed to provide undue reassurance. It has been suggested that individuals at high risk might be instructed on self-administration of antiarrhythmic drugs such as atropine or lidocaine upon onset of acute coronary symptoms; this has been suggested also for patients with angina pectoris, or those who have already had one or more infarctions. However, the benefits of this approach remain to be proved; perhaps new antiarrhythmic drugs or drug combinations may prove more suitable for this purpose than those presently available.

Clearly it would be helpful if patients having acute coronary symptoms were educated to proceed directly to a hospital emergency room rather than try to reach a physician by telephone. Reorganization of emergency rooms may be needed, however, to ensure that the necessary assistance is promptly provided. At present, emergency room personnel are sometimes less concerned than they should be with management of cardiovascular emergencies. Better training, and periodic drilling, may be necessary to make certain the staff can provide cardiopulmonary resuscitation, initiate antiarrhythmic therapy, and do whatever else is necessary to stabilize the patient before transferring him to the coronary care unit.

With recognition of the high mortality from acute myocardial infarction in the earliest phase, increasing effort has been made to bring such aid to patients either at home or en route to the hospital. Use of fully equipped mobile coronary care units can appreciably shorten the interval between onset of symptoms and initiation of intensive inhospital care; arrhythmic deaths at home or during transport can often be prevented. In the experience of Pantridge and coworkers in Belfast — where mobile units have probably been in use longest — median time between onset of symptoms and commencement of hospital therapy was reportedly reduced from eight hours to one hour and 40 minutes. However, most of the reduction was in the time used for admission and administrative procedures; there was little change in the interval between onset of symptoms and the patient's call for medical aid. As long as the major source of delay in securing needed medical help is generated by the patient himself, innovations along these lines will probably have only a limited effect on mortality.

In terms of priorities, major emphasis must be placed on finding ways to reduce patient decision time. With efforts now oriented not only to the need for improved community facilities for the prehospital phase of coronary care but to the critical role of the patient in deciding when to seek emergency medical aid, there is hope that many more lives can be saved.

Section Seven

Treatment of Myocardial Infarction

The Cardiac Care Unit in 1974

BURTON E. SOBEL

Washington University, St. Louis

Innovations in medicine are often introduced at the same time by independent investigators in the forefront of rapidly developing areas. That is what happened more than a decade ago when hospital coronary care units first were initiated by Day in Kansas City, Meltzer in Philadelphia, and Brown in Toronto.

Establishment of these units was abetted by two practical advances: external cardiopulmonary massage to cope with cardiac arrest and electrical countershock to correct lethal ventricular dysrhythmia. Experience with these techniques in hospitalized patients soon established that sudden death following acute myocardial infarction was potentially reversible if manual massage was used to maintain the circulation during the brief time required to initiate countershock and restore cardiac rhythm. However, successful resuscitation depends on prompt availability of individuals with the requisite skills and the necessary equipment. Day, Meltzer, and Brown recognized the value of admitting patients with acute myocardial infarction to a specialized facility appropriately equipped and staffed with experienced personnel trained in resuscitation techniques.

The first generation of coronary care units had the important but restricted aim of responding to cardiac emergencies after their occurrence. With the addition of reliable electrocardiographic monitoring it soon became apparent that lethal ventricular fibrillation was often heralded by ectopic ventricular complexes or bradyarrhythmias. Accordingly, the objectives of coronary care units soon included the immediate recognition and treatment of harbingers of lethal dysrhythmias to prevent cardiac arrest and reduce the need for resuscitation.

The benefits – and often dramatic successes – of this preventive approach are now well recognized. In hospitals with effective coronary care units, early postinfarction mortality rates 50% lower than those previously observed have become the rule. However, realistic evaluation of the impact of coronary care units on the overall problem of acute myocardial infarction must include consideration of several aspects in addition to the substantial gains made in reducing mortality from lethal dysrhythmias in the acute postinfarction period. Thus, one must view the coronary care unit in the context of mortality due to sudden cardiovascular collapse and death in the prehospital period (see Chapter 24, "Myocardial Infarction and Sudden Death," by Paul) and that due to myocardial infarction and cardiogenic shock (ventricular power failure). The latter presently accounts for the great majority of deaths in coronary care unit patients following hospital admission. One of the rapidly growing areas undergoing exploration in coronary care units with investigative capability is accurate prediction of the development of power failure in individual patients and implementation of physiologic and pharmacologic interventions early in the evolution of infarction designed to limit infarct size and avert cardiogenic shock with its associated high mortality. Diagnostic and therapeutic approaches along these lines will be discussed later.

Death Before Admission to the CCU

Most deaths due to acute myocardial infarction occur prior to hospitalization, usually before medical aid can be obtained. Estimates indicate that close to 70% of deaths due to coronary artery disease occur not only suddenly but unexpectedly, often in the absence of prior overt cardiovascular disease. The yearly toll from sudden death exceeds 400,000 in the United States alone, representing a public health problem of enormous magnitude. The need to understand this phenomenon better and to reduce the mortality from sudden death is giving rise to extensive investigation designed to improve identification of patients at very high risk, to develop practical and safe approaches to prophylaxis, and to speed implementation of definitive care after onset of infarction with the use of mobile intensive care units (see Chapter 24 by Paul).

Delay in hospitalization following onset of infarction is

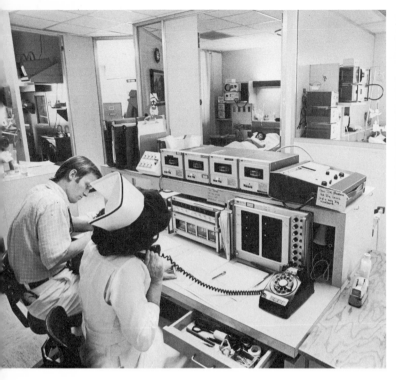
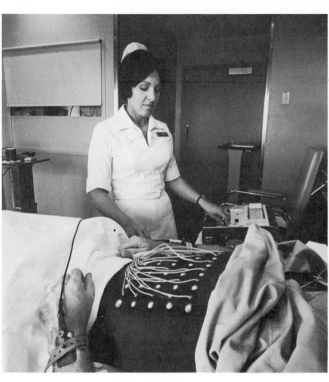

In the Cardiac Care Unit at University Hospital in San Diego, constant patient monitoring from central station is primarily the nurses' responsibility but medical decisions rest with full-time staff physician (left). Use of a 35-lead ECG system like the one shown at right aids in accurate localization of the infarct and facilitates detection of its possible extension.

common, often prolonged, and may contribute significantly to overall mortality from acute myocardial infarction. It often results from indecision on the part of the patient or his relatives about seeking medical assistance. Neither the significance of the symptoms nor the urgency of immediate medical care is recognized, usually because of lack of information, sometimes through denial. Denial by the physician may also contribute to the delay. Although prodromata (usually chest pain) occur in the weeks prior to infarction in most cases (up to 80% in some series), similar symptoms are common in individuals without impending infarction as well, making it difficult to recognize promptly the individual at risk of sudden death. For such reasons the time lag between onset of acute infarction and hospital admission averages at least three to five hours in most communities.

Unquestionably, part of this delay can be reduced by effective emergency transport. For example, analyzing the first 2,000 calls to their mobile unit, Grace and coworkers in New York City found that 50% of patients were being treated and transported within five minutes, 75% within 11 minutes.

In Los Angeles, response time averaged 5.6 minutes from receipt of the alarm, according to Criley and colleagues. But this achievement, and achievement it is, has to be viewed in context. Reducing response time even to within six minutes may not help the victim of sudden circulatory collapse, since irreversible brain damage occurs after as little as two minutes of cardiac arrest, and appears inevitable after four minutes. In the Los Angeles study, attempts at resuscitation of patients with ventricular fibrillation by the rescue crew failed in 35 of 45 cases, presumably because as swiftly as the mobile unit responded the response was not swift enough. Similarly, according to Pantridge and colleagues, who introduced and popularized the concept of mobile coronary care (their facility in Belfast has been operative since January 1966), successful resuscitation following circulatory collapse has been accomplished in only a small percentage of cases.

Even among patients who are transported without mishap the benefits provided by the mobile unit may be negated on arrival at the hospital when patients are consigned first to the hospital emergency area. Too often emergency admissions are handled through a triage clinic largely run by a paramedical staff. Further delay may occur because personnel in the emergency area sometimes fail to recognize the gravity of the situation and the need for immediate transfer to the coronary care unit. As a result a large proportion of inhospital deaths following acute infarction (probably in the range of 15%) occurs within emergency areas prior to the patients' arrival in the coronary care unit.

The Role of the Coronary Care Unit

In evaluating the overall contribution of hospital coronary care units to reducing mortality associated with coronary artery disease, it becomes clear that the factors cited above limit their impact. Nevertheless, intensive coronary care has a great deal to offer the patient who has survived the prehospital phase of infarction.

Of course the outlook is brightest if the infarction process is essentially uncomplicated, that is, unaccompanied either by a serious rhythm disorder or ventricular failure enhancing the risk of disability or death.

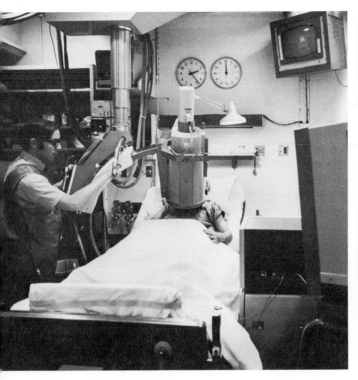 

In assessing ventricular function and extent of akinesis with radioisotope angiocardiography, image intensifier fluoroscope is used with gamma scintillation camera (left) Unit's resources also include computer setup (right) for on-line analysis of patient data obtained during stay in CCU, to guide clinical management as well as assist in ongoing research studies of acute infarction.

Indeed, for such a patient, admission to a coronary care unit is only a precautionary measure, although, of course, it is difficult to know prospectively whether or not complications will develop. Serious complications affecting either cardiac rhythm or ventricular function develop after admission to the coronary care unit in approximately one third of cases; both types of complications occur with similar frequency. Virtually all the gain in mortality statistics resulting from intensive coronary care is attributable to control of disturbances of cardiac rhythm or conduction. But since effective control of electrical disorders extends the potential for salvage to some 50% of patients formerly at risk of death, another 50% are at risk of death from power failure and shock. These patients are the targets of current efforts to improve prognosis after acute infarction, some of which will be discussed later.

Effective management of dysrhythmias depends on adequate staffing of the coronary care unit—that is, round-the-clock coverage by trained medical and nursing personnel. This is most readily obtainable in a unit affiliated with a medical teaching center. Community hospitals may well have facilities comparable to those in university centers but, with some exceptions, they are less able to assure full-time staffing by both medical and nursing personnel. In recent years, as coronary care units have proliferated in community hospitals, both large and small, the major burden has often fallen on the nursing staff because of limited physician coverage. Some units in community hospitals are staffed virtually entirely by nurses, the rationale being that properly trained and motivated nurses can provide the necessary continuous E C G monitoring and can institute promptly the interventions necessary to control acute disturbances in cardiac rhythm.

The essential role of the nursing staff has long been appreciated. As Lown noted (1967) in reviewing the first five years of intensive coronary care: "The coronary unit functions most effectively when staffed with highly trained nurses permitted to assume responsibilities hitherto within the exclusive domain of the physician." Killip and Kimball commented at the same symposium: "The overriding fact is that the nurse is frequently the only medically trained professional at the bedside during important clinical events."

Both statements are no less true after more than a decade of experience with coronary care units. Even with round-the-clock medical coverage, coronary care unit nurses must be skilled in cardiac resuscitation and recognition of dangerous dysrhythmias. The nurses' contribution to diagnosis of dysrhythmia goes beyond merely observing the oscilloscope and detecting an abnormality; their judgment as to the nature of the problem is also essential. Nurses must also be alert to early signs of circulatory failure, and must be able to assess a patient's hemodynamic status by checking for abnormal distension and pulsation of neck veins as well as for restlessness and diaphoresis. However, it is another matter when nurses in the coronary care unit are expected to function in place of a hospital staff because there is none. In these circumstances the nurses must institute resuscitative measures and make critical decisions regarding the nature and treatment of dysrhythmias during prolonged intervals, often on the basis of optional standing orders to be implemented at the nurses' discretion. This approach to coronary care may entail significant danger resulting from de facto abdication of the primary responsibility of the physician for medical decisions.

Several years ago, when open heart techniques suitable for correction of valvular defects came into wide use, it was soon realized that hospital mortality associated with the procedure was inversely proportional to the number of operations performed in the specific institution. In centers equipped and staffed to perform many operations yearly the death rate was comparatively low; in those in which only a few operations were done it proved disturbingly high. The lesson learned was that open heart surgery is best attempted in centers with not only appropriate facilities but also with a caseload sufficient to ensure maintenance and continued improvement of skills of highly specialized personnel. It seems likely that the same concept applies to hospital intensive care. Not every hospital can or should maintain a pediatric unit for intensive care of the sick newborn, or a coronary unit for management of patients with acute myocardial infarction. The decision to establish or maintain such units should

depend on several factors: the availability of trained physicians, nurses, and allied health personnel for staffing; the number of patients likely to require care in the unit; and the extent of other community facilities undertaking the same task.

The contributions of a community physician meeting the needs of a large number of patients and those from a physician who devotes full time to investigative cardiology and intensive coronary care in a university medical center are complementary. The university-based unit within a given community is often the appropriate setting for managing patients with complex problems. With suitable emergency transport, patients requiring this kind of attention can be transferred to such a facility early enough in the course of their illness to derive most benefit; the remainder – that is, the majority of patients – can be managed well within an effective community hospital unit.

Some details concerning operation of our unit at University Hospital in San Diego may clarify its role as a clinical facility and as a setting for investigative work aimed at improv-

ing intensive coronary care.

The six-bed unit (serving a 500-bed hospital) is staffed on a 24-hour basis by a medical intern, medical resident, and cardiology fellow. The intern or resident are physically present in the unit or adjacent to it virtually constantly; the cardiology fellow evaluates all admissions and is available at all times for help with emergency procedures and consultation. All orders are written by the intern and reviewed with the resident. Overall responsibility for patient care rests with the full-time director of the unit and the patient's personal physician. The unit serves patients with a wide variety of acute cardiac problems in addition to acute myocardial infarction, including valvular disease or cardiomyopathy with severe congestive heart failure, or potentially serious dysrhythmias unrelated to coronary heart disease. Accordingly, it has been called a cardiac care unit (C C U) from the outset. Patients with unequivocal acute myocardial infarction (occurring within the preceding 48 hours) have top priority for bed space in the C C U. Infarction is considered unequivocal in the presence of acute E C G changes, serial

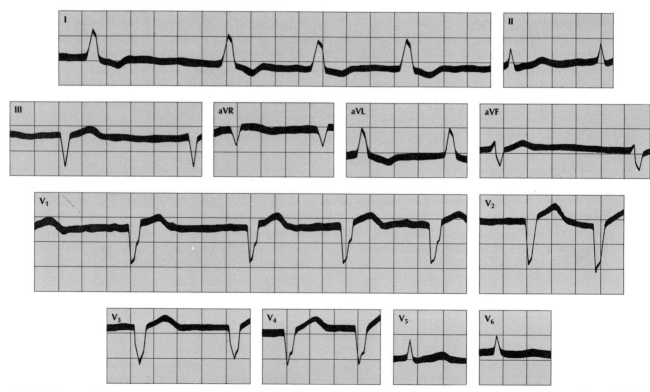

CCU staff must be adept at recognizing subtle ECG changes to avoid injudicious therapy, as in example above (after Lown and Levine), which shows not atrial fibrillation, which might suggest additional digitalis, but paroxysmal atrial tachycardia with block resulting from digitalis toxicity. Some features of toxicity are diminutive P waves, A-V block, associated VPC's.

serum enzyme elevations, and classic clinical signs, including oppressive, persistent chest pain. (Two of the three are considered sufficient to establish the diagnosis.) Patients with suspected acute infarction are also given priority over patients with noncoronary disease. Transfer of patients from the emergency room to the CCU is expedited as promptly as possible (usually within 10 minutes) and ECG monitoring is instituted immediately. Frequently, the suspected diagnosis is not confirmed during subsequent observation, and this is what we expect. If a diagnosis of infarction were confirmed virtually always, it would suggest that, in patients with equivocal symptoms, our index of suspicion was too low.

The role of the CCU nursing staff (usually three nurses per shift) is no less central because there is full coverage by physicians. Nurses are prepared to administer drugs prophylactically or on an emergency basis as defined in the individual patient's orders and to implement electrical countershock or cardiac massage on an emergency basis to avoid ·even a few seconds delay while a physician is summoned. An intensive training course for nurses prior to CCU assignment ensures that they can promptly recognize signs of circulatory collapse (impaired cerebration, syncope or seizure, pallor or cyanosis, absence of heart sounds and peripheral pulses) and distinguish whether it is due to primary asystole or ventricular fibrillation. CCU nurses' training includes formal lectures and demonstrations, participation in attending rounds, written examinations, and practical experience in the animal laboratory or with patients under supervision prior to certification for administration of countershock and performance of other technical procedures.

Clearly, the nurses' role is of critical importance to our unit's effectiveness. With a CCU physician present in the unit or on call down the hall, the nursing staff functions essentially as an extension of his presence in facilitating evaluation and management of CCU patients. To do this effectively a CCU nurse must possess the requisite knowledge and skills plus something more in attitude. The latter may be defined as combining a sufficient measure of self-confidence, decisiveness,

Differentiation of Hypovolemic and Cardiogenic Shock

	Hypovolemic Shock	Cardiogenic Shock
Systemic arterial pressure	↓	↓
Cardiac output	↓	↓ ↓
Peripheral vascular resistance	↑	↑ (usually)
Central venous pressure	↓	↑ (often)
PA wedge pressure (mean)	↓ (usually less than 10 mm Hg)	↑ (usually exceeds 18 mm Hg)

and tact. The nurse has a vital role, too, in easing the CCU patient's course psychologically, by providing needed reassurance and encouragement, and preparing him for diagnostic and therapeutic procedures the medical staff deems necessary.

Physicians and nurses serving in the unit know that in the event of circulatory collapse, restoration of effective endogenous cardiac rhythm must be the immediate goal, since external massage can provide only limited cardiac output ($1 L/M^2$ maximum). If collapse is due to known or suspected ventricular fibrillation unresponsive to a thump on the chest, electrical countershock is applied immediately; another attempt is made within a few minutes if fibrillation persists. In the interim, external cardiac massage is begun and endotracheal intubation and artificial ventilation are promptly instituted; acid-base and electrolyte imbalance are also quickly corrected, since they may be aggravating the dysrhythmia. If effective rhythm is restored by countershock but then rapidly deteriorates, lidocaine is administered in bolus form (100 mg IV) and continued by IV infusion, and countershock is attempted again.

In contrast, circulatory collapse due to unequivocal asystole is managed by immediate heart pacing. As a rule the transthoracic route is employed, since application of the pacemaker requires only a few seconds; our CCU policy does not include insertion of a transvenous pacing catheter on a standby basis, since the catheter may increase ventricular irritability and since pacing is required in only a minority of cases.

In patients without circulatory col-

lapse accurate identification of dysrhythmias is essential to ensure appropriate intervention. For example, minor changes in P-wave morphology may indicate occult digitalis toxicity; in a patient with a catheter-electrode pacemaker, minor changes in QRS morphology may indicate that the catheter has shifted and may require repositioning; a rapid run of anomalous beats may not necessarily be a run of ventricular ectopic beats—rather the mechanism is often ventricular aberration of beats of supraventricular origin. Distinguishing one from the other is crucial, because while ventricular ectopic beats frequently precipitate ventricular fibrillation and demand immediate correction, aberrant ventricular conduction is usually more benign. The latter disturbance develops because a supraventricular impulse enters the specialized conducting system before it has recovered fully from the previous beat. Often, the portion remaining refractory is in the distribution of the right bundle branch; hence many aberrantly conducted ventricular beats exhibit electrocardiographic features of right bundle branch block. Thus, the ECG shows a triphasic pattern of RSR' form in lead V_1, often with the initial deflection identical with that of the adjacent normal sinus beat. In contrast, in most cases of ectopic beats arising from the left ventricle the initial deflection differs from that of normally conducted beats; typically the right precordial leads manifest a monophasic (R) or diphasic (qR) shape.

An ECG lead system such as the one devised by Marriott is useful for distinguishing between these two abnormalities. An advantage is that it

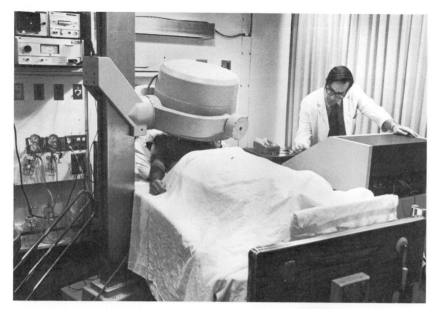

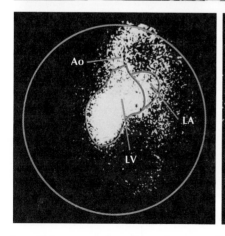
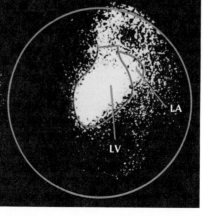

In radioisotope angiocardiography a scintillation camera records the heart image at various times during the cardiac cycle (top); scintillation camera data and the simultaneously recorded ECG are then replayed and displayed (center) and an ECG gating device used to sum up consecutive images so that their area can be determined by planimetry. Akinesis of anterior wall of left ventricle is evident in end-systolic (bottom left) and end-diastolic (bottom right) images obtained in patient with infarction.

records ECG complexes resembling those obtained with a V_1 lead; while the latter provides the most information about disturbances of rhythm and conduction, it is inconvenient for routine cardiac monitoring since four limb electrodes are required. In Marriott's modified CL_1 system, as it is termed, the exploring electrode is placed at the C_1 position (fourth right interspace at the right sternal edge) and the indifferent electrode near the left shoulder; the ground wire is attached to the right shoulder. As Marriott notes, the triphasic (RSR') pattern associated with aberrant conduction is usually readily identified with use of a CL$_1$ lead. Should the diagnosis remain in doubt, a prompt switch to a left precordial lead should settle the question. Aberration of the right bundle branch type usually produces a qRs pattern in a left precordial lead, whereas an rS or QS pattern suggests ventricular ectopic beats.

The CCU staff must not only be adept at recognizing the origin of ventricular dysrhythmias but appreciate their significance. Some types of ventricular premature complexes (VPC's) are considered most hazardous – for example, the occurrence of more than five VPC's per minute, three VPC's consecutively, VPC's with different foci, or any VPC's early in the cycle. Accordingly, these are usually treated with bolus IV lidocaine (1 mg/kg) and a lidocaine drip (15 μg/kg/min); procainamide or some other antiarrhythmic drug is tried if the problem persists. A ventricular rate dropping below 40 may set the stage for ventricular ectopic beats and is often treated with atropine (0.6 to 1 mg IV) or ventricular pacing. If the specific diagnosis of a rhythm or conduction disorder is not clear from conventional electrocardiograms, His bundle recording may be useful. For example, definition of the site of atrioventricular block may be critical, since distal block (often trifascicular block) is more frequently associated with extensive infarction and is more likely to progress to complete heart block. For His bundle recordings a catheter electrode is introduced percutaneously via the femoral vein into the right ventricle and pulled back until the tip of the electrode is adjacent to the tricuspid valve (see Chapter 27, "Management of Arrhythmias in Acute Myocardial

Infarction," by Killip). Recordings from the tip as well as from the other portions of the catheter reflect not only His bundle depolarization but its relation to atrial and ventricular depolarization; this information may be essential in clarifying the nature of electrical disturbances. Although His bundle recordings require an invasive procedure, the benefits in selected patients often outweigh the minimal discomfort and risk.

The same concern must properly be considered regarding all invasive procedures in the C C U. When techniques involving cardiac catheterization were introduced in the C C U on a research basis a few years ago it was feared that they might increase morbidity and mortality. This has not been the case in our unit and the same appears to be true in many similar units elsewhere. If anything, the ability to assess ventricular filling pressure and ventricular function more directly following acute infarction has reduced overall mortality. Determinations of cardiac output and left ventricular filling pressure can be extraordinarily helpful in effective management. Measurement of pulmonary artery wedge pressure with the Swan-Ganz catheter has greatly facilitated reliable estimation of left atrial pressure and hence left ventricular filling pressure (see Chapter 23, "Hemodynamic Changes in Acute Myocardial Infarction," by Ross).

Through the diagnostic facilities of the C C U the important distinction between cardiogenic and hypovolemic shock is readily made. Reduction in cardiac output because of depletion of vascular volume will be indicated by inappropriately low pulmonary artery wedge pressure values, since the latter reflect left ventricular filling pressures. It has been our experience that a significant proportion (nearly 25%) of patients referred from community hospitals, presumably because of cardiogenic shock and power failure, have hypovolemic shock. Since hypovolemic shock usually responds to administration of fluids, its presence must be appreciated promptly.

The concentration of complex equipment for monitoring, diagnosis, and therapy within the C C U demands that the highest safety standards be maintained. Indeed, such a unit should not function without regular access to a well-staffed biomedical engineering group well versed in practical aspects of safety, to avert accidents from current leakage or inadequate grounding of equipment. Even minor leakage – as little as 10 microamperes – can precipitate ventricular fibrillation in patients with intracardiac conductors, for example in a patient who is undergoing catheterization and is also connected to another device providing a return path to ground.

Electrical beds are not used in our unit because of the electrical hazards they impose; only battery-operated artificial pacemakers are used to avoid current leakage from line-operated equipment. All electrical devices are checked weekly to ensure against current leakage and other deficiencies. Equipment used for defibrillation and pacing is also checked regularly to assure adequate electrical output.

It should be stressed that elaborate diagnostic studies are not performed as a matter of course in all patients with myocardial infarction under care in the typical university hospital C C U. An I V line is placed on admission, but intra-arterial pressure measurements and other invasive procedures are utilized generally only if specific problems arise. In our unit, the only procedures employed routinely are E C G monitoring and serial sampling of serum enzymes, the latter because of its value in assessing the extent of infarction (as will be elaborated later). To simplify sampling for serial enzyme analysis, a "heparin lock" is installed on admission so that blood samples can be drawn without the need for repeated venipuncture. As a rule patients with uncomplicated infarction remain in our unit for four days. If infarction is complicated by a major dysrhythmia or severe impairment of left ventricular performance, the stay is extended for at least several days following correction of the problem.

Additional Developments

In developing both diagnostic and therapeutic approaches for application in the CCU, a chief goal of our group and others has been to implement procedures less hazardous than those presently available, yet of comparable value. For example, we have utilized and modified procedures for radioiso- tope angiocardiography to assess ventricular function safely in patients with acute infarction. Evaluation of ventricular performance by standard angiocardiographic methods necessitates not only cardiac catheterization but injection of contrast medium, which depresses myocardial function. Accordingly, this technique is often not suitable for patients acutely ill with complications of infarction, especially if serial studies are indicated. For a substitute we have utilized radioisotope angiocardiography, initially performed by pulmonary arterial injection of the radioisotope – technetium-99m – via a Swan-Ganz catheter and use of an Anger scintillation camera for scanning. In pioneering applications of radioisotope angiocardiography, R. Ross and collaborators at Johns Hopkins demonstrated the accuracy of this technique for determining left ventricular volume and ejection fractions at various times during the cardiac cycle; its diagnostic value in patients with chronic cardiovascular disease has also been documented. Extending radioisotope angiocardiography to patients with complications of myocardial infarction, we found it suitable both for acute and serial studies in the C C U; patients experienced

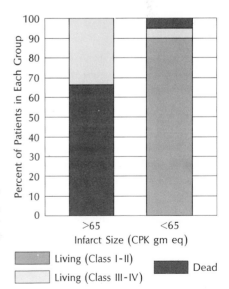

Mortality following acute infarction as well as clinical class of survivors proved clearly related (p <0.001) to infarct size. Here infarct size has been calculated by analysis of serial changes in serum CPK and expressed as CPK gram equivalents. Thirty-six patients were studied in this initial series and followed for an average of 5.3 months after infarction.

no discomfort during the procedure and no hemodynamic perturbations occurred. To reduce the hazard even further we frequently perform these studies with peripheral venous instead of pulmonary arterial injections. Although resolution of cardiac images is somewhat better following pulmonary arterial injection, essentially comparable results can be obtained by peripheral venous injection.

With both approaches, the recorded scintiscans are replayed with the simultaneously recorded ECG and an ECG gating device that sums consecutive cardiac images at end systole or end diastole. Summed images are then photographed, projected on a flat surface, and their areas determined by planimetry for calculation of stroke volume (the difference between end-systolic and end-diastolic volume) and of ejection fraction (the ratio of stroke volume to end-diastolic volume).

The depression in ventricular performance characteristic of acute infarction is reflected in an elevation in end-diastolic volume, reduced ejection fraction, and decreased myocardial fiber shortening, all evident in isotope angiocardiograms. Although this procedure lacks the resolution possible with contrast medium and conventional cineangiographic studies, it is extremely useful for evaluating ventricular function during evolution of infarction and for detection of gross abnormalities such as perforated ventricular septum or severe mitral regurgitation.

Other techniques suitable for serial assessment of ventricular function, such as determination of cardiac output with the thermal dilution catheter developed by Swan, Ganz, and their colleagues, are becoming increasingly useful in the CCU. The ability to perform procedures such as these within the CCU, when circumstances indicate a need for them, facilitates effective patient care. If intracardiac catheterization is required, the equipment is at the patient's bedside; there is no necessity to move him to a catheterization laboratory or operating room for the procedure. The same applies when an artificial pacemaker is indicated. In addition to reducing delays, so important in patients precariously ill, this approach has the advantage of continuity of care by a CCU staff

already familiar with the patient's condition.

The nature of therapeutic procedures becoming available for patients with acute myocardial infarction, some of which are associated with significant risk, has made it obligatory that we be able to assess prognosis in selecting a course of action. Only then can a well-based decision be made that a particular added risk is worth imposing because there is a fair chance of benefit. It is also important to know when a given procedure is unnecessary because recovery is likely without it. In part, choices can be made on the basis of common sense: Given a young patient with stable ventricular function and no evidence of serious dysrhythmia it is not difficult to decide against a major intervention. On the other hand, a somewhat older patient showing evidence of impaired ventricular function and enlargement of the heart, plus electrical instability, is in a different position. In that case recommending a given procedure with inherent risks – for example, circulatory assistance with use of an intra-aortic balloon pump or surgery to revascularize the myocardium – must be balanced against the risks of leaving the patient alone.

Making a judgment requires among other things knowledge of the natural history of acute infarction, and only recently has definitive information begun to accumulate. Recently, investigators in several centers have developed prognostic indices founded on research and clinical findings among patients managed in hospital CCU's. For example, Norris et al in England have defined criteria for estimating outcome on the basis of patient age; presence or absence of hypertension, cardiomegaly, or pulmonary vascular congestion; electrocardiographic localization of the infarction; and past history of overt coronary disease. In a large series of cases, reportedly both early prognosis and the later course of illness could be anticipated quite accurately.

In our unit we've tried to predict the outcome of CCU care in terms of several kinds of information available at the time of admission or soon after: the patient's age and cardiac history, left ventricular function as assessed by diagnostic techniques already re-

ferred to and a roentgenographic method developed by Dr. John Ross Jr., and the extent of myocardial necrosis quantified by analysis of serial changes in serum creatine phosphokinase (CPK) activity. Among some 160 patients studied in our Myocardial Infarction Research Unit, physically a component of the CCU, the overall inhospital mortality proved to be 22%. However, in the group of advanced age (60 or older), with hemodynamic complications without shock (diminished cardiac output and elevated pulmonary wedge pressure) and large myocardial infarcts (exceeding 50 CPK gram equivalents) the mortality was above 85% (see Chapter 22, "Biochemical and Morphologic Changes in Infarcting Myocardium," by Sobel). At the other extreme, mortality was only 3% in patients with small infarcts and adequate ventricular function. Thus far this type of prognostic index has been applied chiefly to define prognosis among groups of CCU patients. If further prospective studies support its validity it would seem applicable in individual cases as well.

Given what we know today, it seems likely that the amount of myocardial tissue damaged as a result of an episode of infarction is a key factor determining mortality and morbidity. Indeed, this concept, first put forth by Braunwald, and the corollary concept that reduction of tissue damage sustained might favorably affect outcome have spurred much current research in reference to acute myocardial infarction. Neither possibility was clearly recognized or articulated when intensive coronary care was focused on preventing or reversing electrical catastrophes. Only later, when power failure and shock emerged as major complications to be faced in the CCU, did the question arise as to why certain patients developed hemodynamic complications resulting in early death while others did not. Braunwald's studies and those of others have indicated that infarct size influences prognosis through its role in development of cardiogenic shock and power failure. Investigators both here and abroad have associated shock with necrosis of substantial portions of myocardium; pathologic evidence of extensive infarction has been confirmed in patients who died of ventricular failure.

In studies by our group, analysis of serum enzyme changes has been utilized to quantify infarct size in CCU patients, in order to define more precisely the relationship between infarct size and prognosis, particularly the development of power failure. A related approach is now being used to predict infarct size during early evolution of infarction, at a time when salvage of myocardium might still be attainable. These clinical studies have been based in part on our earlier experimental work establishing that myocardial depletion of creatine phosphokinase has a linear relationship to the amount of myocardium undergoing cell death, and that infarct size is reflected by the amount of CPK lost from the heart and appearing in the blood. Thus infarct size can be accurately calculated by analyzing serial changes in serum CPK and predicted by obtaining best fit curves from early serum CPK changes (see Chapter 22 by Sobel).

In extending these studies to patients we utilized a new method of CPK isoenzyme detection and analysis (entailing cellulose acetate electrophoresis and fluorescence scanning) in order to determine whether recorded elevations of serum CPK reflected myocardial damage rather than enzyme release from skeletal muscle or other tissue. Infarct size was measured in terms of CPK gram equivalents (CPK gm eq), one unit being the amount of myocardial CPK depletion occurring per gram of myocardial tissue undergoing homogeneous infarction as calculated from changes in serum CPK activity.

Among the findings: In patients who developed power failure and died of refractory congestive heart failure or cardiogenic shock, infarct size measured before development of ventricular decompensation averaged 109 ± 10 CPK gm eq. In those who survived, but only with marked functional impairment, infarct size averaged 91 ± 8; in contrast, in those surviving without functional impairment it averaged 31 ± 4. Viewed from another perspective, in patients with small infarcts (<50 CPK gm eq) the overall inhospital mortality rate was <5%, compared with 38% in those with large infarcts. Among patients who were discharged alive, the subsequent mortality was much higher in those with large infarcts. Clearly, this kind of information can help in selecting patients for procedures with significant risk.

Our initial experience indicates that prediction of infarct size will provide a firmer basis for selecting a specific course of therapy. Clinical research involving prediction of infarct size has already suggested several possibilities for limitation of the ultimate extent of myocardial necrosis, now being pursued (see Chapter 29, "Protection of the Ischemic Myocardium," by Braunwald and Maroko). One possibility makes use of agents or techniques to limit infarct size by reducing ventricular afterload in the presence of hemodynamic complications. Analysis of predicted vs observed CPK curves in a small pilot study has indicated that infarct size may be reduced by diminution of ventricular afterload.

In conducting this type of research in the CCU, as in clinical management of patients admitted for CCU care, the aim is to increase the chance of survival as well as to reduce cardiovascular disability among the survivors. Although the original mission of the CCU – to prevent death following acute infarction – remains paramount, recent developments have broadened its scope. In all probability, the CCU will play an increasingly central role in helping to favorably influence the outlook for patients with acute myocardial infarction.

26

Antiarrhythmic Drugs
in Ischemic Heart Disease

J. THOMAS BIGGER JR.

Columbia University

Therapy with drugs that control cardiac rate and rhythm should be founded on several basic principles, among them that an arrhythmia is present and has been precisely identified and that its nature dictates intervention with an antiarrhythmic drug. Further, there should be reason to believe that the drug selected is likely to modify or, preferably, abolish the arrhythmia without unacceptable toxicity, and that controlling the arrhythmia can make a difference in the course of the patient's illness. Although these are all vital considerations, they are seldom met in full in antiarrhythmic regimens. Limited understanding of the genesis of these arrhythmias, and hence of the best means of approaching them, may be partly responsible. However, therapeutic errors may also be made because of inferences drawn from experience in managing a critically important though limited group of patients: those who develop a rhythm or conduction disorder as a complication of acute infarction.

It is well known that arrhythmias of one form or another occur in almost 90% of patients who survive acute infarction long enough to reach a hospital coronary care unit; control of ventricular arrhythmias has been the chief factor in reducing mortality among patients receiving intensive coronary care. Monitoring of literally tens of thousands of patients in coronary units throughout the country has taught us a great deal about the natural history of arrhythmias in the acute postinfarction period and their response to treatment. The pattern of their appearance is amply documented. Arrhythmias are often present at admission to a coronary unit and may demand aggressive treatment; by 72 hours after onset of infarction the heart's vulnerability has greatly decreased. Our current concepts of management during this period are discussed in Chapter 27, "Management of Arrhythmias in Acute Myocardial Infarction," by Killip.

A common assumption made is that the fundamentals of arrhythmia management established in an intensive care setting apply equally to arrhythmias encountered at other times, for example in the first two hours of acute myocardial infarction. A similar assumption is made in reference to arrhythmias occurring not as a complication of a recent infarction but in ambulatory patients with coronary heart disease. Such extrapolation is, at best, uncertain and may be counterproductive. Experience gained in hospital coronary units is most relevant to arrhythmias developed during the period of intensive care—that is, from about 4 to 72 hours after onset of acute infarction. Since the total experience with arrhythmias occurring in the first two or three hours after onset of symptoms is only a few hundred cases, there are still many unknowns. The same is true of arrhythmias developing in ambulatory patients. From the evidence in hand there seems little doubt that electrocardiographically identical arrhythmias may have a different meaning in terms of morbidity and mortality according to when they occur in the course of ischemic heart disease.

The risk attached to a given arrhythmia, as well as response to treatment, is bound to be influenced not only by the type of arrhythmia but the state of the heart in which it develops and the patient's overall clinical state. Obviously the situation may differ in ambulatory patients with coronary heart disease and those with massive infarction. Crucial differences appear to exist too in the pre- and in-hospital phases of acute infarction, which may explain dissimilar responses to treatment. (For example, sustained ventricular tachycardia or frequent ventricular depolarizations, readily controlled by lidocaine in small doses at four to six hours after onset of infarction, appear much more resistant to the same drug within the first hour or two, as shown by Pantridge and coworkers.)

These limitations should be kept in mind as we discuss the specific effects of five commonly employed drugs—quinidine, procainamide, propranolol, lidocaine, and diphenylhydantoin—in relation to their antiarrhythmic

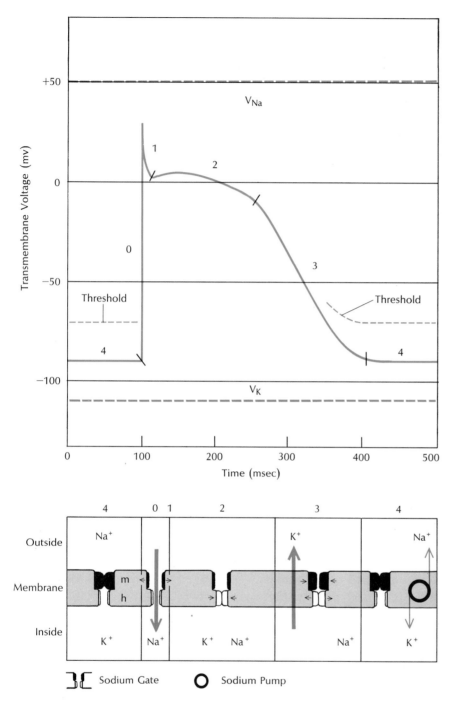

A schematic diagram of a cardiac action potential is shown at top, and the events that determine the time voltage course of the action potential are shown in the lower diagram. When the cell is quiescent (phase 4), its membrane is much more permeable to potassium than any other ion, so that its resting transmembrane voltage is near the potassium equilibrium potential (V_K). At excitation (0), the cell membrane suddenly becomes permeable to sodium; the intense inward sodium current carries sufficient positive charge into the cell to carry the transmembrane voltage to a value near the sodium equilibrium potential (V_{Na}). In the several phases of repolarization (1 through 3), changes in transmembrane action potential initially reflect the decreasing sodium conductance and subsequently the marked increase in potassium conductance, which returns the membrane potential to its resting value. Movement of sodium across the cell membrane from outside to inside is controlled by two component sodium channels, m and h, which appear to work in opposition to each other. With sufficient depolarization, activation of the m site permits rapid influx of sodium. In succeeding phases of the depolarization-repolarization cycle, sodium conductance is decreased by closure of the h site; in phase 4 the sodium-carrying system is again available and awaiting activation.

properties. The orientation here will be largely in terms of arrhythmias developing in the acute postinfarction period; without question, however, proper selection of an appropriate drug at any time in the course of ischemic heart disease depends on awareness of important distinctions among available drugs, all of which may be equally effective clinically against a given arrhythmia. I refer specifically to differences in electrophysiologic properties and pharmacokinetics of individual antiarrhythmic drugs, and to differing effects on mechanical function of the heart.

To put these several aspects of antiarrhythmia therapy in proper perspective, it is reasonable first to consider the electrophysiologic basis for initiation and conduction of the normal cardiac impulse and the ways in which alterations in electrical activity are thought to precipitate arrhythmias and conduction defects. Normally there is a significant voltage difference across the cardiac cell membrane. Maximum transmembrane voltage has been found to vary with cell type; in the resting cell the range varies from −55 to −70 mv inside the cell relative to extracellular fluid in sinoatrial (SA) or atrioventricular (AV) nodes to −85 to −95 mv in Purkinje fibers of the specialized conduction distal to the AV node.

Studies of Purkinje and ventricular fibers in various mammalian systems have made it clear that transmembrane resting potential is determined chiefly by the concentration gradient for potassium across the cell membrane and its permeability to potassium relative to other ions. With the cell at rest, permeability of the membrane to potassium is about 20 times greater than its permeability to sodium; on excitation, permeability to sodium increases more than 100-fold. Although the increased sodium conductance lasts but an instant (about 1 millisecond) the intense inward current carries enough positive charge across the membrane for the voltage inside to quickly approach Na^+ equilibrium voltage (+40 mv). As the inward sodium current subsides there is a period of slow repolarization (the plateau or phase 2 of the action potential); although the ionic basis for this phase is not well delineated, it appears to reflect a decrease in potas-

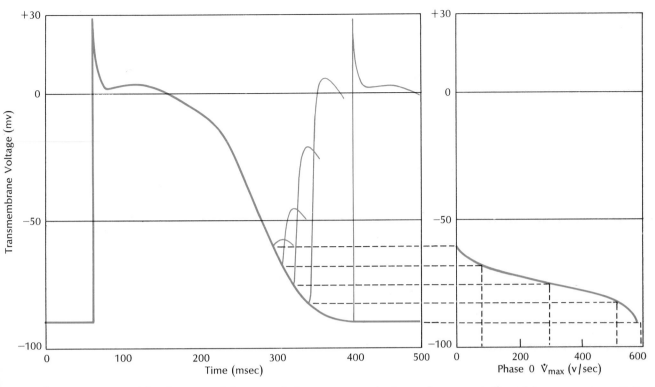

Since the maximum rate of depolarization of the myocardial contractile cell depends on the transmembrane action potential at the moment of excitation, membrane responsiveness is reduced by factors causing depolarization, e.g., excitation before the repolarization phase is complete and the cell returns to its resting *state. As shown diagrammatically at left, response to excitation is minimal at an action potential in the range of −60 mv but increases as the potential moves toward the resting value (−90 mv). Maximum rates of depolarization ($\dot{V}_{max}$) at various transmembrane voltage levels are shown at right.*

sium conductance as well as increased membrane conductance to calcium and some residual increase in sodium conductance. The key ionic shift during rapid repolarization (phase 3) is a marked increase in membrane potassium conductance, which returns transmembrane potential to resting value.

Movement of sodium across the cell membrane appears to be both voltage- and time-dependent. At normal resting potential, most if not all sodium "gates" or channels in the membrane are available but not active. With sufficient depolarization, activation of the sodium channels occurs and the inward movement of sodium causes additional depolarization and further activation of Na^+ channels; as shown by Weidmann and coworkers, in cardiac Purkinje fibers the maximum rate of depolarization (phase 0 of the action potential) provides a useful index of the inward sodium current. After a brief lag, the sodium-carrying system becomes inactivated and remains so until transmembrane voltage reaches −55 mv or so (during phase 3 of repolarization). Cardiac fibers regain their ability to develop a normal re-

sponse only when membrane voltage reaches a maximal value of about −90 mv (end of phase 3) and the sodium system is again available for ion transport.

The maximum rate of phase 0 depolarization (designated $\dot{V}_{max}$) is a function of the level of transmembrane potential (V_m) at the moment of excitation. This relationship is of considerable importance since it determines membrane responsiveness, that is, the nature of the response of a cardiac fiber when acted on by a propagating action potential (or experimentally by an applied electric pulse). The stimulating efficacy of an action potential, its propagation velocity, and the likelihood that it may undergo decrement and blockage all hinge on the slope and magnitude of the response.

When V_m is reduced, membrane responsiveness at a given level of transmembrane voltage is similar regardless of how the reduction comes about, e.g., by steady depolarization induced by injury, ischemia, or hypoxia; by incomplete depolarization during phase 3; or by diastolic depolarization in automatic fibers. It should be noted

that the voltage required for activation of the resting membrane (threshold voltage or V_{th}) depends on a number of factors, including cellular ionic environment, drug exposure, and the level of V_m at the time a propagating action potential or other stimulus arrives, as well as membrane responsiveness. The ability of a given stimulus to bring V_m to threshold level is also affected by passive electrical properties of the membrane.

While the $\dot{V}_{max}$–V_m relationship has been worked out principally in Purkinje fibers, it applies as well in atrial and ventricular myocardium. However, in SA nodal and perinodal cells or AV nodal cells the typical relationship (S-shaped curve) between transmembrane potential and the rate of phase 0 depolarization is not seen. $\dot{V}_{max}$ after activation shows a stronger time dependence in these fibers, and membrane responsiveness may not return to normal until well after repolarization is complete.

Certain cardiac fibers possess the property of automaticity, that is, the ability spontaneously to generate action potentials. In these fibers, transmembrane voltage is not maintained at a steady value after full repolarization, as in other cardiac cells; rather, after membrane potential has been carried to its maximum diastolic value (during phase 3 of repolarization) there is a slow spontaneous decrease in membrane potential (phase 4 depolarization). If this spontaneous decrease reduces membrane potential to the value of the threshold (activating) voltage, the cell will excite itself. Automaticity is a property of cardiac fibers normally controlling heart rhythm but not of "working muscle" in the atria or ventricles. It is readily evident in cells of the SA node, specialized atrial fibers, distal AV nodal fibers (NH), and fibers of the His-Purkinje system. In automatic cells the spontaneous decrease in V_m during diastole appears to be due primarily to a steady decline in potassium conductance. With outward movement of potassium reduced, transmembrane potential moves to more positive values (is depolarized) under the influence of small but steady inward currents carried by sodium and/or calcium. Changes in a number of variables – the maximum diastolic V_m, V_{th}, the rate of phase 4 depolarization – can change the spontaneous firing rate in automatic fibers.

The complex series of changes in the electrophysiologic properties of cardiac cells during acute myocardial infarction and their genesis is not well understood. However, a great deal is known or can be surmised. The changes in individual cells are complex not only by virtue of their time course but also because of the complex geometry of the injured area in which these cells reside. Although many ventricular cells die in the center of the infarct, many gradations of cellular response can be seen in or around a myocardial infarct. Cells in all stages of depolarization can be seen, action potential duration may vary from much shorter to much longer than normal, conduction in and around the infarct may be very slow, and an active impulse may wander for very long times in the labyrinth created by inexcitable barriers. The electrophysiologic properties of the tissues at the margins of an infarct must vacillate markedly under the electrotonic influence of the nearby infarct and a fluctuating blood supply. Also, depending on the thickness of the endocardium, much of the dense subendocardial Purkinje network will be adequately nourished from blood in the ventricular cavity but subject to influence by electrical changes in and chemicals released from the subjacent infarct. With regard to automatic rhythms, it is entirely reasonable to suppose that flow of current from depolarized ischemic sites would augment the normal automatic process in Purkinje fibers in the immediate vicinity. The deeper layers of Purkinje fibers, which lie within the purview of the infarct, may depolarize and oscillate by mechanisms that are quite different from normal automaticity. Less likely, but possible, is that the depolarized tissues in the infarct act as a source of current strong enough to activate adjacent, more normally polarized, tissues.

Now let us consider these aspects of cardiac electrophysiology as they apply to development of cardiac arrhythmias. To put it simply, arrhythmias may be due to alterations in formation of the cardiac impulse related to automaticity, to alterations in impulse propagation affecting conduction, or to a combination of altered automaticity and altered conduction. An arrhythmia related to automaticity is presumed usually to involve a derangement in *normal* automatic mechanisms, that is, in phase 4 depolarization. It has been suggested, however, that *abnormal* automatic mechanisms may play a role – for example, sustained focal depolarization, membrane oscillations, or afterpotentials (marked delays in repolarization at V_m levels near -60 to -70 mv). These phenomena are readily evoked by administration of certain drugs (such as high concentrations of certain beta-adrenergic blocking agents) to cardiac fiber preparations, by reduction of sodium or calcium in the perfusate, or by thermal or mechanical injury. Conceivably, a steady flow of current from a depolarized ischemic site might either excite adjoining repolarizing muscle or augment normal automaticity in automatic fibers in the immediate vicinity. However, the contribution of such automatic mechanisms in the genesis of arrhythmias remains unknown.

Probably, altered conduction of the cardiac impulse rather than altered automaticity accounts for the majority of human arrhythmias. The conduction disturbance may result from propagation of the cardiac impulse in depolarized cardiac muscle. In either case conduction velocity of the propagating action potential is slowed and the likelihood of a block in conduction increased. Certain regions of the heart – the SA node, perinodal fibers, and AV node – are relatively poor conductors at best. But under abnormal conditions any region of the heart may transmit a propagating impulse too slowly or act as the site of conduction block, for example, when depolarization is caused by hypoxia or ischemic injury.

The conduction block that results from injury must be unidirectional to cause reentry; this type of behavior is easy to produce experimentally at the junction of distal Purkinje and ventricular muscle fibers. Normally a cardiac impulse propagating toward ventricular muscle enters the ventricles through the terminal branches of the Purkinje system; under the conditions we are describing, a given impulse may become blocked in a zone depolarized as a result of ischemic injury but spread through a normal terminal branch and reach the ventricle and successfully traverse the depolarized branch in the other direction. In the time occupied by the reentrant conduction, repolarization in normal Purkinje tissue has already reached a voltage at which Purkinje cells, and subsequently ventricular cells, can be reactivated, giving rise to a ventricular premature beat. In the ventricle this type of reentry mechanism may account in large part for the two types of ventricular arrhythmia so commonly seen in ischemic heart disease: premature depolarizations, produced by single reentrant impulses, and tachycardia, resulting from continuous circulation of impulses in a reentrant circuit. In truth, we are not certain as to how these arrhythmias occur, but the fixed coupling of the premature ventricular depolarization suggests a reentrant mechanism. Reentrant impulses may also result from increased automaticity in cells of the His-Purkinje system due to the reduction in V_m phase 4 depolarization. If the automatic activity is focal, it is highly probable that reentrant beating will occur.

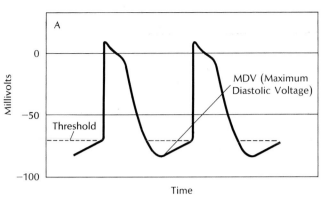

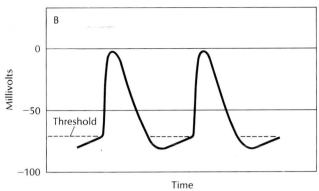

In cells with the property of automaticity, transmembrane voltage does not remain steady during the diastolic interval as it does in other cardiac cells. Instead, membrane potential progressively decreases after it has been carried to maximum diastolic voltage (phase 4 depolarization), as shown schematically in A. In cardiac arrhythmias related to derangement of automatic mechanisms, the maximum diastolic voltage during phase 4 may be reduced,

but excitation occurs when spontaneous depolarization lowers voltage to the threshold value, as in more normal cells (B). Both group I drugs (C) and group II drugs (D) may abolish arrhythmias related to cell automaticity by decreasing or abolishing the slope of phase 4 depolarization and thus increasing the length of the cycle. However, group I drugs also appear to extend cycle length by increasing the threshold voltage for fiber activation.

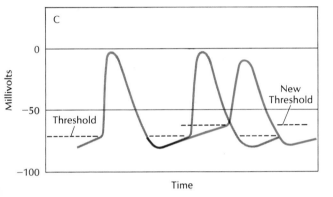

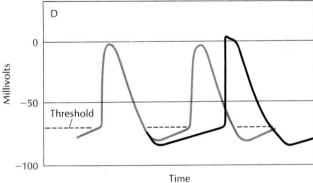

A finding that may bear on development of reentrant arrhythmias is that of Carmeliet and Vereecke who found that Purkinje fibers depolarized to a degree that would ordinarily inactivate the sodium channel can cause impulse propagation at a *very slow* rate on exposure to catecholamines. Considering the extremely long refractory period of cardiac muscle, very slow conduction is required to produce reentrant impulses. Indeed, Wit, Cranefield, and Hoffman have shown that this type of slow response can generate reentrant activity. We do not know that this type of response underlies human arrhythmias associated with reentry mechanisms, but it certainly seems a reasonable possibility. There is a high density of autonomic nerve terminals in distal Purkinje fibers, providing a rich supply of catecholamines from local sources. Any factor causing abnormal depolarization of a Purkinje fiber could depolarize sympathetic nerve terminals in the area, producing loci of slow conduction and block, lead-

ing to impulse reentry. To cite just one possibility, depolarization might result from alterations in intra- and extracellular concentrations of potassium released as a result of myocardial ischemia.

Let us now focus on how antiarrhythmic drugs may act to control cardiac arrhythmias. Although a number of drugs are capable of controlling abnormalities of cardiac rate and rhythm, we will confine ourselves chiefly to the five named earlier since they share a high degree of clinical efficacy against ventricular arrhythmias characteristic of ischemic heart disease. These drugs can be classified as belonging to either of two groups on the basis of their electrophysiologic properties. Thus, in group I are quinidine and procainamide; in group II, diphenylhydantoin and lidocaine. Propranolol has properties common to both but is tentatively classified with group I drugs. This classification is based primarily on laboratory studies of electrophysiologic properties, but

group I and II drugs also differ in their effects on the electrocardiogram in human subjects and, clinically, in the types of arrhythmias that they control. Thus the electrophysiologic properties shared – or not shared – by these agents may provide a clue to their antiarrhythmic action.

It should be stressed that neither electrophysiologic nor E C G differences appear directly related to chemical structure of drugs in the two groups. If anything, structural differences are greater within the two groups than between them, for example, procainamide and lidocaine are far more similar structurally than procainamide and quinidine.

One property common to all five drugs is suppression of the normal automatic mechanism; through this "antiautomatic" action presumably they also can abolish arrhythmias generated by enhanced automaticity in the ventricular specialized conducting system or other ectopic sites. The

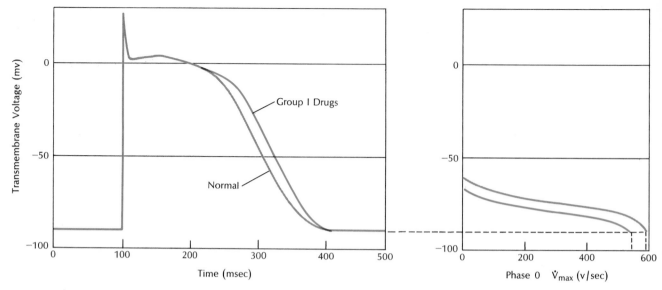

Transmembrane potential from Purkinje fiber shows that group I antiarrhythmic drugs alter membrane responsiveness to excitation so that maximum rate of phase 0 depolarization and conduction velocity are decreased at any given transmembrane voltage.

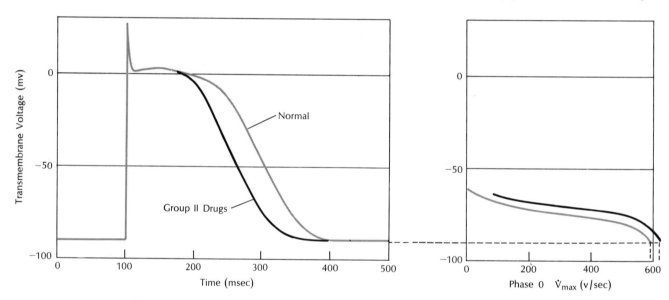

Group II drugs appear to act by abolishing responses to stimuli delivered at low transmembrane voltages and shifting curve on its voltage axis so that maximum depolarization rate is increased at any transmembrane voltage at which a response can be elicited.

ability of these drugs to prevent spontaneous depolarization could also overcome slowed conduction and block that would otherwise produce arrhythmias through impulse reentry. Fortunately, these drugs usually extinguish automaticity in ectopic sites, at concentrations that exert only minimal effects on the automaticity of a normal SA node. Thus, automatic ectopic rhythms can be abolished without inducing asystole. But when function of the SA node or perinodal fibers is altered by disease, SA nodal control of the heart may be impeded by administration of either group I or group II drugs in therapeutic concentrations. Of the two, however, group I drugs are much more likely to induce bradycardia (more will be said of this later).

Group I drugs affect automaticity through a concentration-dependent decrease in the slope of phase 4 depolarization and increase threshold voltage for fiber activation. In toxic concentrations quinidine and procainamide have the opposite effect, causing depolarization of Purkinje fibers and inducing accelerated automatic firing. Group I drugs also have significant indirect effects on automaticity. At least in animals, quinidine and procainamide decrease the vagal influence on cells of the SA node, atrium, and AV node; they also have some alpha-adrenergic blocking activity, which may reflexly augment impulse traffic along cardiac sympathetic nerves. In this way the two differ from propranolol, which impedes the effect of sympathetic influences throughout the heart by its beta-adrenergic blocking action; this leads to sinus slowing, prolonged AV conduction, and anti-automatic effects in Purkinje fibers.

Group II drugs also reduce automaticity in the specialized conducting system by a concentration-dependent decrease in the rate of phase 4 depolarization, probably by increasing potassium conductance, thus increasing outward potassium current and preventing spontaneous depolarization in diastole. Group II drugs do not significantly alter threshold voltage for fiber activation. Moreover, automaticity is not induced in Purkinje fibers with toxic doses as occurs with quinidine and procainamide. Although group II drugs do not interfere to a significant degree with peripheral autonomic influences, sudden injection of large doses in animals or man can cause hypotension and reflex sympathetic augmentation.

Group I drugs in therapeutic concentrations increase the effective refractory period (ERP) as well as action potential duration (APD), the former to a greater extent; group II drugs shorten both the ERP and APD. Drugs in both groups share the ability to prolong ERP relative to APD, both in Purkinje fibers and ventricular muscle. Obviously, group I and group II drugs must affect the ERP-APD relationship through different mechanisms. Group I drugs do so by shifting the membrane responsiveness relationship, so that the maximum rate of phase 0 depolarization and conduction velocity is decreased at any given transmembrane voltage.

In Purkinje fibers exposed to group I drugs in low concentrations there is little change in resting transmembrane voltage, APD, or action potential slope (however, antiautomatic effects are seen). Phase 0 amplitude is not reduced, but the membrane responsiveness curve shifts significantly on the voltage axis. When the drugs are given in toxic doses these changes are intensified, and the marked reduction in responsiveness leads to a substantial QRS widening on the ECG.

In contrast, group II drugs in therapeutic concentrations reduce responsiveness of Purkinje fibers to stimuli delivered at low transmembrane voltages and shift the curve on its voltage axis in a direction opposite to that seen with group I drugs. Thus responses cannot be elicited at very low values of V_m. Lidocaine – like diphenylhydantoin – abbreviates both APD and ERP in the two fiber types, the effect in Purkinje fibers being greatest where APD is the longest, i.e., these drugs tend to minimize the

	GROUP I		GROUP II
	Quinidine Procainamide	Propranolol	Lidocaine Diphenylhydantoin
Automaticity	Decrease	Decrease	Decrease
Excitability	Decrease	Decrease	No Change
ERP[1] and APD[2]	Increase	Decrease	Decrease
ERP Relative to APD	Increase	Increase	Increase
Conduction Velocity	Decrease	Decrease	No Change/Decrease
Atrioventricular Conduction Time	No Change/Increase	No Change/Increase	No Change/Increase
Efficacy Against Digitalis Arrhythmia	+	+ +	+ + +

[1] Effective Refractory Period   [2] Action Potential Duration

◐ Increase   ● Decrease   ○ No Change

Whereas some electrophysiologic properties are shared by both group I and group II antiarrhythmic drugs – for example, the capacity to suppress automaticity in pacemaker fibers – differences may be critical in choosing the proper drug for therapy.

			GROUP I		GROUP II	
			Quinidine Procainamide	Propranolol	Diphenyl-hydantoin	Lidocaine
ECG *Duration*		PR	No Change/Increase	No Change/Increase	No Change/Increase	No Change/Increase
		QRS	Increase	No Change	No Change	No Change
		QT	Increase	Increase	Increase	No Change/Increase
Blood Pressure			Decrease	No Change/Decrease	No Change/Decrease	No Change/Decrease
Cardiac Output			Decrease	Decrease	No Change/Decrease	No Change/Decrease
Left Ventricular End-Diastolic Pressure			Increase	Increase	No Change/Increase	No Change/Increase

● Increase   ● Decrease   ○ No Change

In addition to differences in electrophysiologic properties, group I and group II drugs also have dissimilar electrocardiographic and hemodynamic effects. These too must be considered in drug selection, particularly when patients are critically ill.

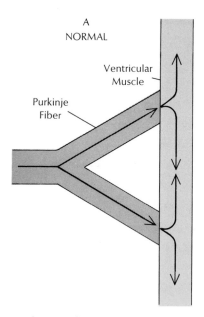
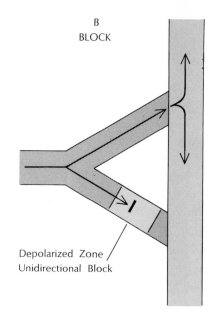
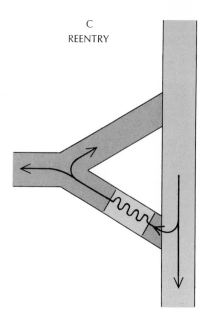

A
NORMAL

Ventricular
Muscle

Purkinje
Fiber

B
BLOCK

Depolarized Zone
Unidirectional Block

C
REENTRY

Schematic diagram of experimental model of cardiac arrhythmia due to reentry mechanism shows how normal impulse conduction from terminal branches of Purkinje fibers to ventricular muscle (A) may be impaired because of unidirectional block in zone depolarized as a result of ischemic injury (B). However, the same impulse spreading through a normal terminal branch may reach the ventricle to traverse the depolarized zone in the other direction, permitting premature reexcitation of ventricular muscle (C).

differences in A P D that normally exist throughout the system. Suppression of automaticity in Purkinje fibers without depression of the amplitude or rate of rise of phase 0 depolarization has also been demonstrated. This strongly suggests that part of lidocaine's antiarrhythmic action could be accomplished by improving conduction in ventricular tissue.

It is worth citing a few details of relevant studies on the effects of lidocaine on conduction in the Purkinje fibers and in the region where the specialized conducting system adjoins ventricular muscle. Lidocaine at a concentration of 2.3 μg/ml (equivalent to a therapeutic concentration in vivo) can substantially accelerate the propagation of premature impulses at the normal Purkinje fiber–ventricular muscle junction.

Lidocaine can also restore conduction in some instances of experimental block at this junction. Also, Bassett et al have shown that diphenylhydantoin delays the decline both in resting and action potential amplitude and in the maximum rate of rise of phase 0 of the action potential caused by hypoxia. Obviously, some of the experimental findings cited above could bear on control of clinical arrhythmias since lidocaine or diphenylhydantoin reduces the possibility that the specialized conducting system can

participate in rhythm disturbances due to block and reentry. Ability of group II drugs to control ventricular premature depolarizations (V P D's) and ventricular tachycardias associated with myocardial ischemia presumably can be explained on the basis of improved conduction, although studies in humans are not conclusive.

Clearly, another mechanism must underlie control of reentrant arrhythmias by group I drugs, given their different – in many instances opposite – effects on the cardiac membrane. Quinidine and procaine not only prolong E R P duration at the junction of Purkinje fiber and ventricular muscle but also significantly slow conduction time. Because of the shift in membrane responsiveness on its voltage axis, the $\dot{V}_{max}$ of the response evoked at a low V_m is so diminished that successful propagation of the impulse is impossible in either direction; in effect the area of conduction delay is pharmacologically extirpated. Reentrant arrhythmias dependent on unidirectional block could thus be promptly terminated. Recent experiments done by Giardina et al have shown that procainamide probably works in this way in man to extinguish premature ventricular depolarizations with fixed coupling. As drug plasma concentration increases, the coupling interval grows longer and longer as conduc-

tion is increasingly slowed, until finally the arrhythmia disappears, suggesting total block in the reentrant pathway.

Interestingly, bretylium tosylate, in concentrations considered comparable to therapeutic, produces no alteration in peak $\dot{V}_{max}$ or membrane responsiveness. In fact bretylium lacks most of the electrophysiologic properties associated with antiarrhythmic drugs. It does not suppress phase 4 depolarization or spontaneous firing in Purkinje fibers; indeed, it can induce firing in quiescent fibers. It does not alter E R P relative to A P D as the other drugs do; furthermore, it has no significant effect on conduction velocity. Thus the actions of bretylium cannot be explained in terms of electrophysiologic properties of the cell membrane, yet it does appear to have an antiarrhythmic action against some forms of ventricular arrhythmia. Although we do not know how bretylium tosylate works, its effects on the autonomic nervous system may be important in its antiarrhythmia action. Bretylium is preferentially taken up by adrenergic nerve terminals where it prevents release of norepinephrine, and recent work by several investigators has linked the autonomic nervous system to genesis of some arrhythmias, on the theory that neural factors could alter conductivity, automaticity,

D
GROUP I DRUGS

E
GROUP II DRUGS

F

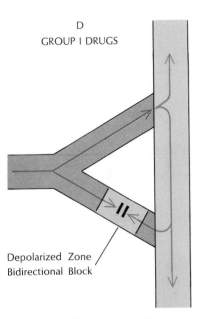

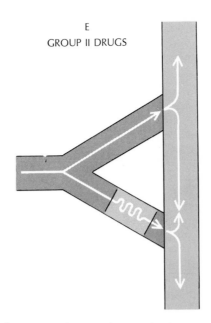

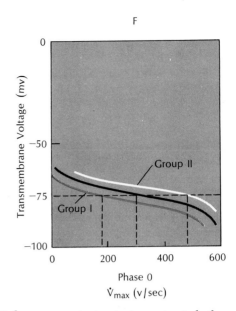

Depolarized Zone
Bidirectional Block

Since the effect of group I drugs is to reduce responsiveness of the cardiac cell membrane to stimulation and hence decrease conduction velocity, presumably these drugs abolish reentry by converting the unidirectional block to bidirectional block (D). In contrast, group II drugs appear to terminate reentrant rhythm by increasing membrane responsiveness and thus eliminating unidirectional block (E). Differing effects on maximum rate of depolarization of cardiac fibers are shown at right (F).

and excitability of cardiac fibers.

At present, electrophysiologic properties of group I and II drugs defined in the animal laboratory can be related to their antiarrhythmic actions in man in only a limited way, but significant differences between the drug groups in ECG effects have direct clinical applicability. Awareness of ECG effects helps both in planning and monitoring therapy. Group I drugs tend to prolong the QRS duration, evidence that they are slowing ventricular conduction, and the rate-corrected QT interval (QT_c). In man, changes in the QRS or QT_c duration induced by quinidine correlate very closely with plasma concentrations of the drug; changes in QRS duration can be detected at plasma quinidine concentrations as low as 2 μg/ml; ECG changes increase linearly as plasma concentration increases. A similar relationship exists for procainamide. In monitoring therapy, an increase in QRS duration in the range of 25% should alert the physician to observe the patient closely for toxicity. When the increase approaches 50%, the dose should be promptly reduced or the drug discontinued. Plasma drug concentration should be determined at this point and a search made for factors that might be altering responsiveness to the drug or slowing drug elimination. In the doses employed

therapeutically, neither the group II drugs nor propranolol tend to increase the QRS duration; they may cause a slight decrease in QT_c interval.

For the clinician, knowing the differing effects of group I and II drugs on AV conduction can be important in selecting the proper drug in crucial circumstances. Group I drugs and propranolol may prolong the PR interval, particularly if the heart rate remains constant. These drugs also significantly increase refractoriness in the AV conducting system; the effect of quinidine and procainamide is more pronounced on the ventricular portion of the system, while propranolol primarily affects the AV node. Thus when either intraventricular or AV conduction is impaired, a group II drug may be preferable; these drugs usually do not affect PR interval and their ability to decrease refractoriness of the AV conduction system can provide advantages.

In atrial arrhythmias – tachycardia, flutter, or fibrillation – quinidine and procainamide may slow the atrial rate to a marked degree. In the presence of fibrillation (occasionally in flutter) this atrial slowing reduces concealed conduction in the AV conducting system; thus the ventricular rate may be increased despite the direct depressant effect of the drugs on AV conduction. Propranolol signifi-

cantly decreases the ventricular rate in the atrial arrhythmias. In contrast, the group II drugs have less pronounced and consistent effects on atrial rate; depending on the initial atrial rate and the intrinsic state of the AV conducting system, the positive dromotropic effect of lidocaine and diphenylhydantoin may act either to decrease or increase ventricular rate. Clinically, quinidine and procainamide are most effective in converting atrial arrhythmias to sinus rhythm, whereas group II drugs are relatively ineffective except in atrial tachycardia. Of all the drugs, diphenylhydantoin and lidocaine are most useful against digitalis-induced atrial tachycardia.

Knowledge of hemodynamic effects of antiarrhythmic drugs is also basic to a sound therapeutic program. It should be kept in mind that all five drugs are capable of inducing severe hypotension after rapid IV injection. Indeed, any intravenous use of quinidine in acute situations is probably ill-advised because of the risk of hypotension. Significant hypotension need not occur after injection with any of the other drugs. If it does, it is usually because the drug is administered too rapidly and in excessive doses. IV injections of procainamide or diphenylhydantoin are given in 100-mg doses over one to two minutes; the dose is repeated as needed at five-minute intervals and blood pressure and ECG are monitored. After about six doses of either drug, there is usually a mild but moderate reduction in blood pressure; subsequent doses produce a further graded decline. In our hands, administration of these drugs in this way has never produced shock or heart failure. Lidocaine probably offers the widest margin of safety for intravenous injection, since even sudden injections usually produce little decrease in arterial blood pressure. Despite its effectiveness against many ventricular arrhythmias, propranolol should be used with great caution in the acute situation because of its ability to block the effect of the sympathetic nervous system, which is often playing a major role in supporting the circulation. Giving a beta-blocker in these circumstances can cause significant decreases in heart rate, myocardial contractility, cardiac output, and arterial blood pressure. A point to remember is that an injection of any antiarrhythmic drug that would cause minimal hemodynamic changes in a patient in functional class I or II (New York Heart Association classification) may cause severe circulatory impairment in a class III or IV patient.

Only propranolol is likely to cause hemodynamic problems after oral administration. Lidocaine is not useful orally since a large fraction of an oral dose is inactivated by the liver and also side effects – nausea and abdominal distress – are common.

It is generally advisable to use only one antiarrhythmic drug at a time. In clinical practice it is becoming common for patients to be treated with two or more simultaneously; I believe this is unwise as initial therapy. In the management of acute situations, optimal use of a single antiarrhythmic agent combined, if necessary, with intracardiac pacing is likely to achieve a good result. When more than one drug is used it is difficult to distinguish the actual effect of either one; more important, it is more difficult to distinguish adverse drug reactions from changes in the underlying condition.

Since antiarrhythmic drugs have a relatively narrow therapeutic ratio, the possibility of toxic reactions must always be kept in mind. The nature of the toxicity differs considerably

between group I and II drugs. Group I drugs are more likely to have direct cardiac effects, expressed as alterations in the mechanical or electrical behavior of the heart. Even with therapeutic concentrations they may significantly reduce myocardial contractility. After toxic doses, a drop in cardiac output and blood pressure may be seen. Electrically, they can cause marked suppression of automaticity, including the SA node, resulting in asystole or, on the other hand, induced automaticity. Impairment of AV conduction and severe slowing of intraventricular conduction may also be anticipated. This combination of effects can usually be overcome with molar sodium lactate and catecholamines. For drug-induced asystole or heart block, pacemaker application or other electrical measures may be required.

In contrast, group II drugs, even in toxic doses, usually do not produce severe cardiac effects. Toxicity is usually manifested by central nervous system effects. It is usual for diphenylhydantoin to produce CNS signs and symptoms at plasma concentrations above 20 μg/ml – well above the effective level for control of responsive arrhythmias. At concentrations above 20 μg/ml, nystagmus, lethargy, and ataxia begin to be seen. Symptoms commonly produced by lidocaine toxicity include drowsiness, disorientation, apprehension, paresthesia, difficulty in hearing, and muscle fasciculation – at plasma concentrations of about 5.5 μg/ml or greater (effective concentration is 1 to 5 μg/ml). These symptoms may be considered the patient's emotional reaction to his illness and drug toxicity may be overlooked. Severe toxic effects – generalized convulsions and respiratory arrest – can occur at plasma concentrations as low as 7 μg/ml. (Lidocaine convulsions can be interrupted almost instantly by injection of short-acting barbiturates, but discontinuing the infusion immediately is usually sufficient.)

Admittedly, when antiarrhythmic drugs are used in critically ill patients, it may be difficult to maintain effective plasma levels without toxicity. The physician must be aware that a patient's changing condition may modify drug absorption, the volume and sites of drug distribution, the mode or rate of drug elimination, or the effect of a

given plasma concentration.

A consideration of the pharmacokinetics of these drugs assumes particular importance because effective plasma concentrations and antiarrhythmic action are so closely related. This relation generally holds in patients with many forms of heart disease and in a variety of clinical situations. Nonetheless, special circumstances may significantly modify the response to a given plasma concentration of drug. For example, patients with hypokalemia are often unresponsive or resistant to antiarrhythmic agents (particularly group I drugs), while hyperkalemia augments the effect of a given plasma concentration of any antiarrhythmic drug. It is important to remember that a prime determinant of plasma concentration is the apparent volume of distribution. Following an IV injection, the initial rapid decline in plasma drug concentrations is almost entirely due to movement of the drug into the total volume in which it is ultimately distributed. Drug elimination accounts for the slower terminal phase of decline in plasma concentration. In the presence of heart failure the volume of distribution of many antiarrhythmic drugs is likely to be reduced, which will cause a given drug dose to produce unexpectedly high plasma concentrations.

When an antiarrhythmic drug is introduced into the circulation by constant-rate IV infusion (e.g., lidocaine and procainamide), it takes several hours for the final steady-state plasma concentrations to be reached (90% of steady-state concentration is reached at 3.3 times the elimination half-life); however, this method of administration produces the least fluctuation of plasma concentrations once a steady-state value is reached. The delay in attaining steady-state plasma concentrations deserves emphasis. A physician impatient with lack of results in the first hour or two might increase the infusion rate rather than wait longer; this will produce an earlier antiarrhythmic effect but greatly increases the risk of late toxicity if the high infusion rate is maintained.

Changes in the function of the organs that metabolize a given drug are also important. All five of the antiarrhythmic drugs under discussion are metabolized to some extent by the liver; in patients with hypotension or congestive failure – in whom hepatic blood flow is reduced – the rate of metabolism is reduced, and the plasma drug concentration may be excessively high for the dose and infusion rate. This is particularly important for group II drugs and propranolol, which are extensively metabolized by the liver and should be used with caution in the presence of hepatic or circulatory insufficiency. On the other hand, a significant proportion of both quinidine and procainamide is excreted unaltered by the kidneys; thus high plasma concentrations occur when ordinary doses are given to patients with renal insufficiency. Lidocaine or diphenylhydantoin do not present this problem in patients with renal insufficiency, since the proportion eliminated by the kidneys is small.

Factors affecting drug metabolism and excretion must also be kept in mind when antiarrhythmic drugs are given orally, which is usually the case except in the immediate postinfarction period. After a single oral dose of a drug, the time required to reach peak plasma concentration and the concentration reached depends not only on the size of the dose but on delay in absorption, the fraction of the dose absorbed, and the absorption rate. Drugs such as quinidine or procainamide may be poorly absorbed from the stomach, diphenylhydantoin is absorbed slowly, and propranolol erratically. As mentioned above, lidocaine is not used orally. Nonetheless, absorption of each antiarrhythmic drug is rapid relative to the rate of excretion; hence effective plasma concentrations are reached almost as soon after an oral dose as after an IV or IM injection. After an oral dose of quinidine or procainamide, plasma concentration usually peaks between 60 and 90 minutes; for diphenylhydantoin peak concentrations are not reached for several hours. Should absorption be delayed or slowed, a given dose of a drug produces lower peak plasma concentrations, the peak is later, and the decline in plasma drug concentration may also be slower because of continued absorption.

On a regimen of repeated oral doses of constant size and frequency the rate of reaching steady-state concentrations varies directly with elimination half-

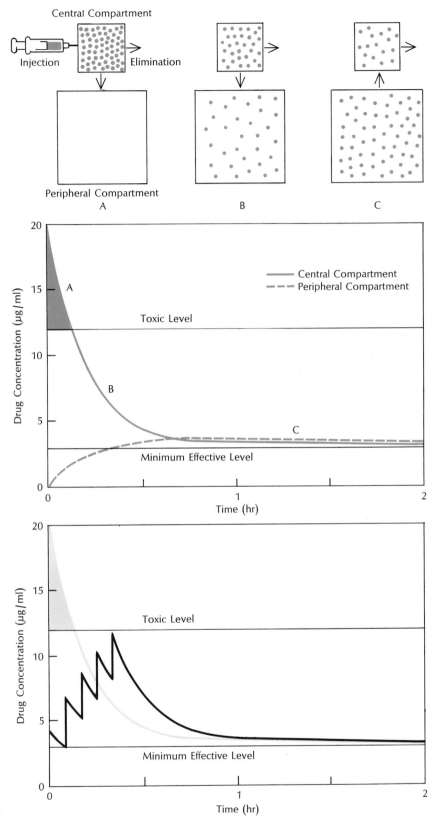

The events following a single IV injection of an antiarrhythmic drug, in this case 500 mg procainamide, are shown at top. Before distribution of the drug from the well-perfused organs (central compartment) to peripheral tissues, plasma concentration remains above the toxic level (center); drug concentration does not fall below toxic level until distribution to peripheral compartment takes place. In contrast, when same drug is given by multiple injection (five 100 mg doses five minutes apart), minimum effective level is also exceeded but toxicity is avoided (bottom).

time: the more rapidly elimination takes place, the sooner a steady state is reached. Procainamide (t½ elim = 3.5 hours) steady-state concentration is reached within 24 hours; with diphenylhydantoin (t½ elim = 36 hours) it takes more than a week.

The duration of antiarrhythmia therapy may range from a few days or weeks to months and years. Regardless of the duration, the goal must always be to maintain the plasma concentration above the minimum effective level without producing toxicity.

One important question is how long treatment should be continued after acute myocardial infarction. In our coronary unit, once an acute arrhythmia is brought under control we attempt to stop treatment after three or four days, arguing that the tendency to arrhythmia has abated. Others consider this unwise, on the ground that continuing therapy may prevent recurrence of arrhythmias. Which view is correct? Nobody knows; only controlled studies will bring the answer.

In recent years, several university centers have evaluated prophylactic use of antiarrhythmic drugs (quinidine, procainamide, lidocaine) in the immediate postinfarction period; patients with arrhythmias requiring immediate treatment or with hemodynamic complications were not admitted to these studies. Such studies fail to show any difference in mortality between treated and untreated groups. Investigations using effective doses of antiarrhythmic drugs do show a significant reduction in arrhythmias in the drug-treated group. On the basis of these investigations our view of prophylaxis is that, even if effective, in a university setting it is probably unnecessary; the availability of highly trained, hospital-based staff and excellent coronary care facilities assures

that the patient needing treatment receives it without delay.

However, in a community hospital the situation may be quite different. Because staff and facilities are likely to be more limited – and the office of the patient's personal physician may be at some distance – routine prophylaxis may well prevent serious problems that might otherwise ensue because premonitory arrhythmias were overlooked. On the other hand, prophylaxis as a universal practice might be ill-advised. Patients who develop cardiac failure or shock on the one hand or severe conduction defects or bradyarrhythmias on the other might be exposed to added risk by routine drug treatment. Thus even in community hospitals the case for routine prophylaxis is not yet clear and its usefulness remains to be demonstrated.

The situation in reference to arrhythmia prophylaxis among ambulatory patients is even less well-defined. For one thing, ventricular arrhythmias (chiefly in the form of premature depolarizations) are very common in asymptomatic coronary patients. A finding of v p d's – more than 10/1,000 beats – has been linked by Hinkle et al to added risk of subsequent sudden death in middle-aged men (see Chapter 24, "Myocardial Infarction and Sudden Death," by Paul). Whether the incidence of these arrhythmias can be reduced with long-term use of available drugs without other intolerable problems is not known. Neither do we know whether the incidence of sudden death would be reduced even if the frequency of v p d's was very significantly reduced.

Another suggestion is that some arrhythmias causing very early death after such myocardial infarction might be prevented by antiarrhythmic self-medication. Since such deaths are

likely to be due to ventricular fibrillation or severe bradyarrhythmias, it is argued that patients known to be at risk should be taught to administer a drug such as lidocaine or atropine by intramuscular injection on appearance of symptoms of myocardial ischemia, and then report to the hospital. Such a practice is fraught with hazard: the presence of chest pain does not necessarily mean that the patient has or will have an arrhythmia, and if one is present it is certainly preferable to determine the type before treatment is begun. Beyond this, we are not sure these medications will be successful or without significant harmful effects. Inhospital studies or outpatient studies conducted without electrocardiographic recordings will not answer this question. Again, in this area controlled and careful studies are badly needed. Until self-administered antiarrhythmic drugs are proven of benefit, measures to get patients into immediate contact, e.g., by telephone, with the health care system at onset of acute symptoms would seem a sensible course. In the future some form of self-medication may prove practical, following further development of miniaturized cardiac monitors that permit the patient's e c g to be transmitted to the hospital and specific advice given (indeed, this is already being done to a small extent on an experimental basis).

We badly need new, improved antiarrhythmic drugs and the answers to many questions about currently used drugs. Despite this, rational and effective therapy is possible with available antiarrhythmic drugs by utilizing to advantage their critical differences in electrophysiologic properties, toxic effects, and pharmacodynamic qualities. This approach provides the maximum probability for successful therapy of cardiac rhythm disturbances.

Management of Arrhythmias in Acute Myocardial Infarction

THOMAS KILLIP

Cornell University

Late in 1965, when the coronary care unit at New York Hospital had been open for about 10 months, the clinical course of the first 100 patients admitted to the unit with acute myocardial infarction was compared with that of 100 consecutive cases on regular care during the same period. The functional severity of myocardial infarction was the same in both groups according to standard clinical measures of cardiac compensation; age and sex distribution were also comparable.

To our dismay, the patients receiving intensive care in the new unit fared better only while remaining there; with transfer to regular care, any advantage was lost. Thus the overall incidence of cardiac arrest was almost identical in the two groups, and no more of the patients treated in the coronary unit left the hospital alive.

Our review disclosed that the patients who died following transfer from the coronary care unit had had serious arrhythmia or had shown severe cardiac decompensation, or both, while in the unit. Moreover, nearly all deaths occurred within five days of transfer to regular care. We concluded that more aggressive medical tactics were necessary: early treatment of potentially serious complications and delegation to the nurse of responsibility for both recognition and treatment of many arrhythmias.

The key change came in the management of cardiac arrhythmias. Emphasis was shifted from prompt resuscitation of patients *after* cardiac arrest had occurred (as was the rule when such units first opened in the 1960's) to early recognition and treatment of arrhythmias likely to precipitate cardiac arrest. Patients with rhythm disorders or other complications were kept in the unit for at least five days after control of the last serious episode; moreover, antiarrhythmic therapy was continued as indicated following transfer to regular care.

Since that time, mortality of patients admitted to hospital coronary units because of acute myocardial infarction has been markedly reduced (up to 50% at many centers), mostly by immediate and vigorous therapy for potentially lethal arrhythmias. It is assumed, although proof is lack-

ing, that sudden death occurring prior to hospitalization is largely due to catastrophic arrhythmias that occur too rapidly for prevention or treatment. Both Pantridge and Grace have reported a high incidence of bradycardia and drug-resistant ventricular arrhythmia soon after acute infarction. Continuous E C G monitoring of patients who reach a hospital unit alive has left no doubt that arrythmias of varying severity are the most common complication in the acute postinfarction period, occurring in about 90% of cases in most units.

The pathogenesis of arrhythmia in ischemic heart disease is not sufficiently understood. Knowing more precisely how and why arrhythmias develop might help us in designing improved therapy; thus far we can only speculate as to specific precipitating events. (It would be more accurate, of course, to refer to these disorders as dysrhythmias, since rhythm is usually disturbed rather than absent, but the term arrhythmia will be used here since it is more familiar.) As discussed by Bigger (see Chapter 26, "Antiarrhythmic Drugs in Ischemic Heart Disease"), premature depolarizations may reflect abnormality of either automaticity or conduction. Altered conduction or reentry probably accounts for the majority of arrhythmias observed in patients with acute myocardial infarction. However, studies in man to confirm this supposition are lacking.

Several factors have been identified that appear to enhance the risk of cardiac arrhythmias. One is cardiac size; an enlarged heart is more vulnerable to arrhythmia than a small one, and arrhythmia is more likely to have an adverse effect. Any preexisting impairment in the conduction system also increases the hazard of arrhythmia. A third factor is myocardial ischemia, which is known to increase vulnerability to fibrillation. Thus the patient with acute myocardial infarction may be at increased risk on at least two counts: He has myocardial ischemia, and, depending on his past history, he may have an enlarged heart. A conduction defect may also be present, either a local impairment in the infarcted area, or less commonly, a type of bundle branch block.

As discussed by Sobel (see Chapter 22, "Biochemical and Morphologic Changes in Infarcting Myocardium"), myocardial ischemia is capable of inducing profound metabolic alterations in the myocardium. Vital metabolites leak into surrounding tissue, and the accumulation of end products may culminate in acidosis. Local extracellular potassium concentration increases markedly. Thus, the unstable metabolic situation that prevails, as well as the ischemic process itself, could well set the scene for development of cardiac arrhythmia. The pacemaker function of the sinoatrial (s a) node may be preempted by cardiac tissue bordering on the ischemic area, favoring the development of ectopic foci. Alternatively, as the excitory impulse encounters partially refractory tissue affected by the infarction process, the normal sequence of depolarization and repolarization is disrupted. An impulse approaching an affected area is diverted and slowed, permitting reentry and coupled extrasystoles or sustained tachycardia. Either reentry or a sustained ectopic

focus with varying degrees of exit block could account for the increased risk of arrhythmia associated with acute myocardial infarction. However, while it is agreed that local metabolic changes secondary to ischemia could account for ectopic rhythms occurring in either way, the precise cellular events remain unknown.

Monitoring of patients in coronary care units has clearly shown that arrhythmias most often appear within the first hours following admission. The risk of fatal arrhythmia is also known to be highest shortly after onset of infarction and then decreases exponentially. These findings would suggest that there is a finite period during which the ischemic process heightens vulnerability to arrhythmia. The individual who dies suddenly from acute infarction may be the unfortunate victim of ischemia, arrhythmia, and altered intraventricular conduction occurring all at once. Hence the disordered cardiac rhythm precipitates fatal cardiac arrest within minutes of the acute event. We can only presume that the latter is true, of course, since virtually all current

knowledge of cardiac arrhythmias following acute infarction is based on observations in patients monitored in hospital coronary units. The patient hospitalized for an acute myocardial infarction has survived moments of high risk and reached the coronary unit alive. His arrhythmia may be different in important ways from that of a patient who dies before medical aid·can be provided. Nonetheless, experience gained by observations within coronary care units has provided valuable insights into the incidence and management of complications of acute myocardial infarction. This may be exemplified by the experience in the New York Hospital unit over the past seven years, which the remainder of this chapter will discuss.

It should be emphasized, however, that the lessons from the c c u are not always applicable to other clinical situations. Arrhythmia occurring in one context, in this case the patient with acute myocardial infarction, does not necessarily have the same import in another. For example: v p c's are common in many clinical situations. Their occurrence in the individual without other evidence of heart disease would warrant a quite different and probably more leisurely therapeutic approach than when encountered in the patient with a fresh infarct.

Obviously, not all arrhythmias are of equal clinical urgency; a distinction must be made between arrhythmias that are relatively benign and those that are potentially life-threatening or of such immediate urgency that mere recognition should impel immediate action. Generally, supraventricular arrhythmia poses little danger; however, one form of supraventricular arrhythmia — significant slowing of the primary pacemakers — is often far from trivial. Many ventricular arrhythmias are potentially lethal since either of the two major types — ventricular tachycardia or ventricular premature contractions — may be harbingers of ventricular fibrillation and cardiac arrest. Ventricular fibrillation may however occur in a primary form without any premature contractions or tachycardia.

From a clinical viewpoint it is essential to distinguish arrhythmias that can be managed on an elective basis from those demanding attention as medical emergencies. The chief arrhythmias in the first group are atrial

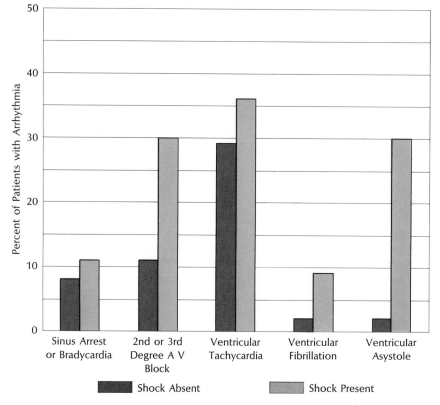

When analysis of the New York Hospital series was confined to potential lethal arrhythmias, ventricular tachycardia was found to be the most common arrhythmia whether shock was present (as in 203 patients) or absent (as in 47). As shown by the bars at far right, however, there was a much higher rate of asystole when shock was present.

fibrillation and flutter; arrhythmias in the second group include sinus bradycardia, heart block in its several forms, ventricular tachycardia or multiple ventricular extrasystoles, and ventricular fibrillation. Although it cannot be predicted with certainty whether a given type of arrhythmia is likely to occur in any individual case, patterns observed in groups of patients have made several generalizations possible.

For example, in a study in our coronary unit, it proved useful to relate the occurrence of arrhythmia to the functional severity of infarction. For this analysis some 250 consecutively admitted patients were classified according to the presence of clinical signs of heart failure, pulmonary edema, and cardiogenic shock, it being assumed that these findings represented increasing degrees of left ventricular dysfunction. Approximately one third of the patients had no clinical signs of cardiac decompensation (class I). Another third had mild-to-moderate heart failure (class II), diagnosed by the presence of rales, S_3 gallop rhythm, or venous hypertension. The remainder had severe heart failure with frank pulmonary edema (class III), or cardiogenic shock (class IV), manifested by a systolic blood pressure of 90 mm Hg or below, signs of peripheral vasoconstriction (including oliguria, cyanosis, and diaphoresis), and usually also heart failure with pulmonary edema.

Although arrhythmias were observed in the great majority of patients in all groups, there were definite variations in incidence according to the clinical severity of infarction. All patients with pulmonary edema or cardiogenic shock developed some sort of arrhythmia, whereas among those showing no signs of cardiac decompensation, arrhythmias occurred in 83%; in the group with mild-to-moderate pump failure the incidence was 90%. More important, when only potentially lethal arrhythmias were considered, there was a marked predilection among patients also manifesting signs of cardiogenic shock. Thus, life-threatening arrhythmias were detected in 94% of patients developing cardiogenic shock and in 45% of those without shock. Ventricular tachycardia proved to be the most common type of arrhythmia in patients with or without shock, occur-

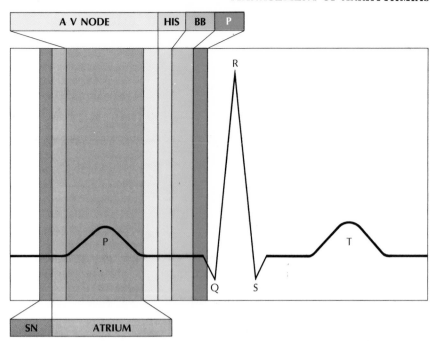

As is suggested by schematic above, the standard ECG does not record transmission of the impulse through the specialized conducting fibers; the tracing between P and QRS is essentially flat. In contrast, the His bundle electrogram, or HBE (drawing below), provides specific information on activation of the different parts of the system. To obtain the HBE, an electrode catheter is introduced into a femoral vein, advanced into the right ventricle, then slowly withdrawn across the tricuspid valve until the sharp biphasic spike representing His electrical activity appears. In general, delay of conduction at the AV node is less hazardous than delay distal to the His bundle.

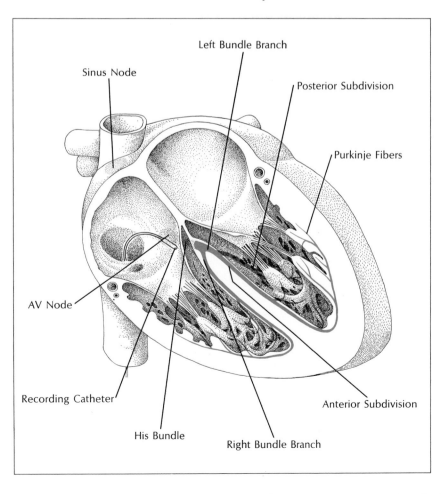

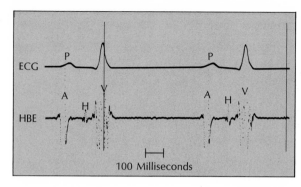

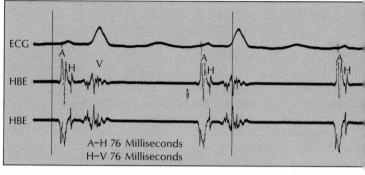

In the normal HBE at left, His deflection (H) appears between the atrial (A) and ventricular (V) activity. Note that A precedes P wave of ECG. Prolongation of the A-H interval (normal 80-120 milliseconds) with constant H-V interval would suggest block at AV node; prolongation of H-V (normal 45 milliseconds), would suggest block distal to His bundle. In HBE at center, obtained from patient with episodes of syncope, prolongation of H-V interval indicates intraventricular delay. Clinical designation was

ring in about one third of both groups. In contrast, atrioventricular (AV) heart block was three times as common in the group with shock; ventricular fibrillation was more than twice as common.

Not surprisingly, the mortality rate also increased with the degree of functional impairment: While the hospital death rate was 6% in class I patients, in class IV patients it was above 80%; thus prompt treatment of serious arrhythmia, despite its importance, could not turn the tide once the shock state was sufficiently advanced.

We continue to classify our patients according to functional status since further experience has confirmed that both morbidity and mortality predictably increase with the clinical severity of the disease. However, it has also become apparent that serious disorders of cardiac rhythm may suddenly appear in presumably uncomplicated cases, that is, in patients manifesting no evidence of cardiac decompensation. Indeed, there really is no uncomplicated case. No patient with proved acute myocardial infarction is a "good risk" since in all a catastrophic arrhythmia such as ventricular fibrillation may develop.

One of the lessons learned from coronary care has been the importance of primary ventricular fibrillation. It can and does occur in well-compensated patients who have not previously had significant arrhythmia. In effect, any arrhythmia may occur in any patient with acute myocardial infarction, although the more ventricular function is compromised the more likely is the chance of life-threatening arrhythmia developing.

With this in mind, let us discuss each of the major types of arrhythmia in turn, considering first the less serious disorders and then focusing our attention on the potentially or actually lethal.

As already noted, most supraventricular arrhythmias are benign in the patient with acute myocardial infarction. Usually they are self-limited and will terminate spontaneously, but this does not mean they should be ignored. As in more serious types of arrhythmia, proper management depends chiefly on the patient's clinical response to the abnormal heart rate. For a patient who appears able to tolerate supraventricular tachycardia, prompt digitalization is considered the treatment of choice; a similar course would be followed in a patient with atrial flutter or fibrillation not showing adverse hemodynamic effects. However, if the sudden rapid heart rate is associated with inadequate cardiac output and hypotension or failure, synchronized precordial shock may be indicated. The problem here is that atrial arrhythmias, particularly flutter and fibrillation, tend to recur despite treatment; for this reason we reserve precordial shock for the patient with an extremely rapid ventricular rate or persistent flutter or fibrillation who seems to be showing signs of advancing pump failure.

While digitalis remains the preferred drug for treatment of supraventricular arrhythmias, propranolol in small doses has also been found useful in controlling atrial flutter and fibrillation. Because the toxicity of digitalis may be significantly enhanced in the acute postinfarction period, standard doses may prove excessive. Our policy is to use no more than 70% of the calculated digitalizing dose for the first 48 hours or so while this effect is at its peak.

Among the possibly serious rhythm disorders – to turn our discussion to them – one that has aroused considerable interest of late is sinus bradycardia. The frequency of sinus bradycardia as a complication of acute MI has only recently been appreciated. Its occurrence in up to 15% of patients in our unit has been the rule elsewhere as well. It should be recognized that when marked sinus slowing occurs in the absence of an adequate nodal or junctional escape rhythm two pacemaker sites are malfunctioning: the sinus node and the AV node, or junctional region.

Sinus bradycardia is not necessarily life-threatening; the danger may be of inducing a progressive ventricular arrhythmia. The excessively slow heart rate significantly prolongs diastole, producing an electrical instability that increases the likelihood of ventricular ectopic beats or various escape rhythms, which may lead to sustained ventricular tachycardia or fibrillation. However, sinus bradycardia per se is not necessarily innocuous and should be recognized as a potentially serious threat in its own right. Most of those patients with an acquired heart disease who develop sinus bradycardia have a fixed cardiac output and a relatively fixed stroke volume; they are unable to adjust the ejection fraction as the heart rate changes. Once the heart rate drops to about 55 or thereabouts, a steady decline in cardiac output can be anticipated, particularly in an elderly individual. Unless the ventricular rate is raised, progressive hemodynamic

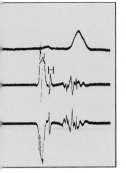
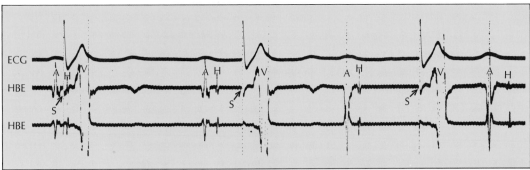

type II second degree AV block; QRS pattern is that associated with left bundle branch block. HBE at right shows third degree (complete) heart block. Patient has an implanted, continuous ventricular pacemaker; S indicates stimulus. Each nonconducted P wave in the ECG is followed by a His deflection in the HBE but V activity is absent (except following stimulus). Block was thus distal to the common bundle (adapted from Damato and Lau, Prog Cardiovasc Dis, 13:2:119).

problems may ensue.

Recently Epstein and coworkers have suggested that sinus bradycardia in patients with acute infarction is a benign condition that seldom leads to further difficulty. The incidence of bradycardia is highest in the first few hours after the attack and it has been suggested by Hinkle that bradycardia carries an increased risk of sudden death. It is clear that the clinical significance of sinus bradycardia is far from settled.

Treatment of sinus node dysfunction must be twofold, to increase cardiac output and prevent the development or progression of ventricular arrhythmias. As with other arrhythmias, the need to maintain an adequate ventricular rate determines the choice of therapy. Atropine (in a dose of 0.6 to 0.8 mg IV) is useful in the management of sinus bradycardia. If necessary the injection is repeated once or at most twice. Atropine is a relatively safe drug, but its use is best limited. Some degree of urinary retention is virtually inevitable, nor can the possibility of central nervous system effects and glaucoma be dismissed.

Infusion of isoproterenol is also useful in management of bradycardia. The infusion rate must be precisely controlled, however, since the drug may cause sinus tachycardia or atrial or ventricular arrhythmias. Furthermore, isoproterenol sharply increases myocardial oxygen demand, a potentially adverse effect in the patient with coronary artery disease, and may extend the size of infarct (see Chapter 29, "Protection of the Ischemic Myocardium," by Braunwald and Maroko). Some other groups favor a longer trial

of drug therapy, but we have come to feel that, in experienced hands, pacing entails less risk. We turn to it promptly if one or two injections of atropine do not have the desired effect, or use it as primary therapy if sinus node dysfunction is associated with progressive cardiac decompensation.

Indications for insertion of intracardiac pacing electrodes on a standby basis have narrowed within the past few years. For example, about three years ago pacing electrodes were inserted in some 35% of our cases and actually used in fewer than half of those. Presently they are inserted in under 20% – and are used in almost all.

Sinus bradycardia that persists despite atropine therapy continues to be our most frequent indication for temporary pacing, and, as will be discussed shortly, pacing is also often used in some (though not all) forms of AV block. In addition, some patients with recurrent ventricular tachycardia that does not yield to drugs will respond to pacemaker overdriving, that is, pacing the ventricle faster than the ventricular tachycardia rate and then gradually slowing the heart rate until a rate is achieved at which the tachycardia does not occur.

Our current practice is to insert the pacing electrode into the right atrium or right ventricle percutaneously, using the subclavian approach, since this does not require a cutdown incision and there is little likelihood of dislocation of the catheter from motion of the arm or shoulder. We favor a semifloating type of electrode catheter because of the ease of blind insertion with ECG guidance. When necessary – in less than 5% of cases – a portable

fluoroscope is used to visualize passage of the electrode. A major advantage of our approach is that the patient need not be moved to the operating room or catheterization laboratory for pacemaker insertion.

Any consideration of intracardiac pacing in reference to heart block – the second major indication for pacemaker use – must take into account changing concepts of AV conduction disturbances. For years the assumption was that these disturbances were limited primarily to the area within or surrounding the AV node and that the degree of block related to the extent of nodal abnormality. Thus, in first-degree block, conduction is delayed at the AV node, hence the prolongation of the PR interval. In second-degree block, a greater degree of nodal abnormality prevents some impulses from reaching the ventricle. In third-degree block, all transmission to the ventricle is blocked. It was speculated that significant AV conduction disturbances might occur subnodally, in the common bundle of His or its major branches, but this concept was difficult to prove since lower conduction pathways manifest no specific electrical activity on a standard surface ECG.

A few years ago, Damato and coworkers developed a relatively simple method of recording His bundle activity by using an intracardiac lead. This technique has made it possible to localize the site of conduction disturbances more precisely than ever before. Conduction defects were shown to originate at many levels in the conduction system. AV blocks due to abnormality in the bundle branches are likely to be more serious in their effects on cardiac function than blocks originating at the level of the A V node. Recognition that blocks within the A V node or above the His bundle seldom progress to complete heart block or asystole has been a factor in the decline in pacemaker insertion.

A fresh view of both the location of various types of heart block and their prognostic significance has emerged through His bundle recordings and other recently developed techniques. In first-degree block the delay in conduction is usually within the node; the conduction defect is also localized within the node in one of the two varieties of second-degree block—so-called Mobitz type I with the Wenckebach phenomenon, in which intermittent dropped beats result from a progressive delay in A V conduction and increase in the P R interval. In the other form of second-degree block, namely, intermittent or 2:1 A V block, the block may be either at the A V node or below. If the Q R S complex is narrow, the block is usually at the A V node and is a form of Mobitz I. If the Q R S is wide, the block is usually an expression of intermittent bilateral bundle branch block or Mobitz type II.

In Mobitz II or intermittent complete heart block the condition usually arises from lesions not within the node but in the His-Purkinje systems. According to current evidence, most instances of established complete heart block are instances of bilateral bundle branch disease rather than disease of the A V node.

One point to remember in management is that Mobitz type I blocks (prolonged P R interval and Wenckebach phenomenon) appear to result from reversible ischemic damage of nodal tissue; neither is likely to progress to complete heart block. Both are especially common in the first few hours after an inferior diaphragmatic infarction. A V dissociation may develop as a result of the Wenckebach phenomenon. However, the escape rhythm usually originates high in the bundle so that an adequate ventricular rate is preserved. (In discussing the varieties of heart block and their management, the importance of accurate E C G diagnosis cannot be overstressed; unfortunately, episodes of A V dissociation are sometimes interpreted incorrectly as heart block. The hallmark of heart block is the

failure of P waves to capture the ventricles when they should; in contrast, A V dissociation most often occurs when a lower pacemaker is faster than the normal pacemaker.)

As a rule, no therapy is required for first-degree heart block, although intravenous atropine may be administered in some cases. Mobitz type I block (Wenckebach) is usually treated with atropine with favorable results. The decision to insert a pacing electrode, as in the bradyarrhythmias, depends chiefly on the patient's clinical status. The possibility that Mobitz type I block may occasionally progress to a higher degree of block must also be kept in mind.

Mobitz type II block, on the other hand, presents quite a different situation. The problem is to recognize those situations in which type II may occur. Unlike the lesser degrees of heart block discussed above, this variety appears to be associated with severe structural damage at some level of the conduction pathway. Aggressive therapy is essential to prevent progression to complete heart block and cardiac arrest. In most instances of type II the Q R S complex is prolonged and anterior infarction is present. Since temporary intracardiac pacing is often indicated, a pacing electrode is usually inserted and connected promptly to a demand pacemaker.

If complete heart block is going to develop, it usually does so within the first three days of onset of infarction and is due to bilateral complete heart block. The immediate aim in complete heart block must be to increase the ventricular rate (nodal or idioventricular escape rhythm at a rate of 45 or so is not uncommon) both to sustain the circulation and to prevent ventricular fibrillation or asystole. If an intracardiac pacemaker is not already in place, electrode insertion must be accomplished without delay, yet the slow heart rate must not be allowed to persist even for a brief period while this maneuver is completed. Thus drugs are used initially to maintain the ventricular rate; once intracardiac pacing is established, medication may be discontinued. Intravenous atropine in a dose of 0.6 to 1.0 mg may be administered, although there is seldom a satisfactory response in this situation. Isoproterenol by slow infusion is the drug of choice to maintain an adequate ventricular rate prior to

pacing. One milligram of the drug may be diluted in 500 ml of 5% dextrose and the infusion rate adjusted to achieve the desired rate. The potential for sudden complete heart block appears fairly high in the presence of severe heart failure or cardiogenic shock, especially if response to medical treatment has been poor. With this possibility in mind, it is often our practice to insert a pacing electrode in the severely decompensated patient whether or not heart block seems imminent.

A few words must be said too about preexisting bundle branch block, in view of evidence that it may frequently underlie development of Mobitz type II or complete heart block in the acute postinfarction period. Recent studies have documented that mortality in acute M I is substantially increased — often approaching 50% — in the presence of bundle branch block. Insertion of an intracardiac pacing electrode as a routine has been strongly urged to prevent progression to a lethal arrhythmia. Unfortunately, it is difficult to prove that this approach improves mortality. At least in a study by our group, even with a policy of prophylactic pacemaker insertion, few of those developing complete heart block were salvaged. Perhaps this is because when complete heart block does occur in such a patient there is already massive myocardial injury, and the heart block is only incidental to the overall cardiac damage. Julian has made similar observations. Also, the incidence of ventricular tachycardia or ventricular fibrillation is disconcertingly high in patients with bundle branch block, particularly if the left bundle branch is involved.

Complete heart block continues to be associated with a high mortality in myocardial infarction, regardless of whether the patient is also in shock or not and despite generally successful treatment of slow heart rates. It is worth emphasizing, however, that if an adequate ventricular rate can be maintained by temporary pacing or other means and the patient survives, the block usually resolves. Acute heart block due to myocardial infarction seldom progresses to chronic block requiring permanent pacing. Thus, if therapy can insure an adequate ventricular rate for a few days, the block will almost always disappear.

Experience has shown that v p c's – the most common of all rhythm disturbances following acute myocardial infarction – are often the forerunner of ventricular fibrillation and cardiac arrest. A frequent mechanism in this progression is the occurrence of a ventricular extrasystole closely coupled to the previous conducted beat (R on T wave). Antiarrhythmic therapy of v p c's must be initiated without delay. Although the urgency is greatest when the v p c's appear in salvos during the vulnerable period, the occurrence of more than four to five extrasystoles per minute warrants immediate action.

In management of v p c's or any potentially lethal ventricular arrhythmia, one must decide which antiarrhythmic agent to employ and how long to continue therapy after the acute episode has passed. The question of instituting prophylactic therapy in the hope of preventing a serious ventricular arrhythmia must also be considered.

In the coronary unit setting there is no question that lidocaine is the drug of choice for overcoming ectopic ventricular arrhythmias. Lidocaine is classified as a type II antiarrhythmic (see Chapter 26 by Bigger). While it suppresses automaticity, it significantly shortens the effective refractory period and action potential duration. It is most likely effective in abolishing v p c's by speeding conduction and abolishing reentry. It is almost universally effective and it is safe. Experience has shown that it can be given rapidly in large doses, with very little immediate toxicity. Significant change in blood pressure or cardiac function is uncommon and prolongation of the P R or Q R S intervals is not a problem. As is true with any of the antiarrhythmic agents developed to date, the possibility of toxicity exists, but in this respect lidocaine is greatly to be

Management of Arrhythmias in Acute Myocardial Infarction

Arrhythmia	First Choice	Second Choice	Comments
Atrial premature complexes (APC's)	Digitalis	Quinidine	APC's are frequently forerunners of atrial fibrillation or flutter. Caution: Avoid excessive dosage of digitalis because of increased susceptibility to arrhythmia in acute myocardial infarction.
Paroxysmal atrial tachycardia	Digitalis	Precordial DC shock	An uncommon complication of acute infarction. Avoid excessive digitalis.
Atrial fibrillation	Digitalis	Precordial DC shock	Arrhythmia tends to recur, hence first aim of treatment is control of ventricular rate. If patient tolerates arrhythmia poorly, needs "atrial kick," or if stroke volume is low, immediate DC conversion may be necessary. Eventual spontaneous reversion is the rule.
Atrial flutter	Digitalis	Precordial DC shock	Comments above on atrial fibrillation are applicable to flutter. Some authorities recommend immediate DC shock in all instances of atrial flutter or fibrillation.
Paroxysmal nodal tachycardia	Digitalis	Precordial DC shock	See atrial tachycardia. If rate is only moderately increased and associated with A V dissociation, consider digitalis toxicity as causative.
Ventricular premature complexes (VPC's)	Lidocaine	Quinidine Procainamide Diphenylhydantoin Overdriving with pacemaker	Decision to treat depends on setting. More than 5 VPC's per minute, occurrence in salvos, or R on T phenomena (closely coupled) demand immediate and adequate treatment. Once VPC's are initially suppressed with lidocaine, a plan for long-term therapy with longer-acting agent should be considered.
Ventricular tachycardia	Precordial DC shock	Lidocaine Quinidine Procainamide Diphenylhydantoin Overdriving with pacemaker	Forerunner of ventricular fibrillation. Best combination is immediate precordial shock followed by long-term administration of suppressive drugs.
Ventricular fibrillation	Precordial DC shock	Closed-chest cardiac massage Intubation and ventilatory support	When cardiac arrest occurs in the CCU, precordial shock should be administered immediately. If unsuccessful, it may be necessary to resort to cardiopulmonary resuscitation. The longer fibrillation persists, the less likely is survival.

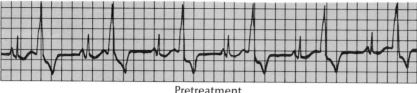

Pretreatment

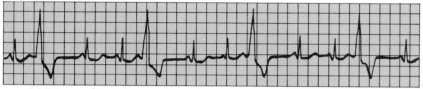

2 Minutes After Lidocaine 75 mg IV (First Dose) Blood Level 0.4 μg/ml

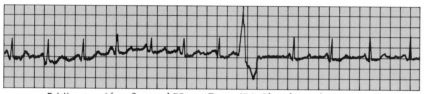

5 Minutes After Second 75 mg Dose (IV) Blood Level 1.5 μg/ml

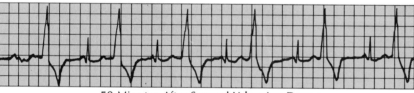

50 Minutes After Second Lidocaine Dose

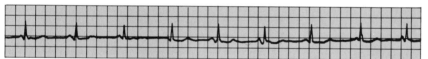

30 Minutes on 2 mg/min IV Lidocaine Drip Blood Level 1.0 μg/ml

Lidocaine is drug of choice for overcoming ectopic ventricular premature complexes in acute myocardial infarction; its value is demonstrated by ECG above. Note that two minutes after the first dose (1.0 mg/kg), the frequency of ectopic beats is reduced; second dose, with blood level higher, is more effective. Continuous suppression requires continuous IV drip and maintenance of adequate blood levels.

preferred over other compounds of comparable effectiveness, such as procainamide or quinidine.

Current practice in our unit, as in others, is to administer the drug via continuous intravenous drip after first building up the blood level with a single dose in bolus form. Without an adequate loading dose, lidocaine administered by infusion is unlikely to reach an effective level for at least 6 hours, 12 in some cases. Measurement of blood levels has taught us that dosages cannot be standardized. The usual loading dose is between 1 and 2 mg/kg body weight followed by an infusion at the rate of between 2 and 3 mg/min. In some cases it is necessary to supplement the loading dose 30 minutes later with an additional 50 to 70 mg of lidocaine to ensure an adequate blood level. The infusion rate should be adjusted, preceded by boluses as needed to achieve the desired effect, abolition of the V P C's. If V P C's remain suppressed, as fortunately they often do, the lidocaine administration is continued for 24 to 48 hours and the dosage is gradually reduced until the patient is weaned from the drug.

A similar approach is taken toward ventricular tachycardia, although the urgency of this arrhythmia depends greatly on the heart rate involved in the particular case. Little if any treatment is probably required for the "slow" tachycardias, that is, when the idioventricular rate is only slightly higher than the basic sinus rate so that there is oscillation between the two. On the other hand, a "fast" ventricular tachycardia demands immediate treatment; what is done depends on how the patient is tolerating the arrhythmia. If there are adverse hemodynamic effects, precordial shock is applied immediately, followed by continuous infusion of lidocaine. A patient tolerating the arrhythmia fairly well may be put directly on drug therapy, according to the regimen followed in treatment of V P C's.

In our coronary unit, as in others, early and aggressive treatment of ventricular extrasystoles has greatly reduced the incidence of cardiac arrest due to either sustained ventricular tachycardia or ventricular fibrillation. Indeed, the greatest contribution of specialized coronary care since its introduction has been to demonstrate that most life-threatening arrhythmias can be effectively controlled. This is largely because the necessary combination of well-trained medical and nursing personnel for adequate staffing at all times, plus the equipment required for monitoring and therapy, has been clustered within the coronary unit setting (see Chapter 25, "The Cardiac Care Unit: 1974," by Sobel). The same principles can be applied with equal success in other settings, such as emergency rooms, receiving rooms, and I C U's.

The cost effectiveness of the C C U has recently been challenged. There is an increasing trend to treat a wide variety of patients with cardiac problems in the C C U, not just those with infarction. Such treatment is not cheap: both manpower and equipment are expensive. It is apparent, however, that C C U concepts and practices have greatly improved the standard of care of cardiac disorders throughout the hospital. A control situation no longer exists and prospective evaluation of the C C U is probably not now possible.

Speed no less than teamwork has been responsible for the effectiveness of coronary care units. A defibrillator at each bedside permits precordial shock to be initiated within 30 to 60 seconds in cardiac arrest caused by ventricular tachycardia or fibrillation. Experience has shown that this is none too soon. The notion that the brain can escape irreversible damage if arrest persists for as long as four minutes is an unfortunate exaggeration. For the typical victim of acute myocardial infarction — middle-aged or elderly with at least some degree of vascular disease – circulatory arrest for more than one minute may be intolerable. There are not even seconds to waste in attempting to ventilate the patient or performing cardiac massage. On the other hand, if ventricular fibrillation is reverted to sinus rhythm within 60 seconds, other resuscitative measures are rarely required.

Regrettably, in some patients vulnerability to fibrillation is so great that within a few beats after defibrillation the heart begins fibrillating again. In such cases sufficient cardiopulmonary support must be provided,

if possible, to keep the patient alive until an effective drug program can be worked out. In this situation a variety of agents may be tried, including lidocaine, quinidine, and procainamide. There have been promising reports on the experimental use of bretylium tosylate in control of recurrent fibrillation, but this drug is not generally available. In any case, if defibrillation alone is not effective within the 60-second limit, the usual alternatives, such as closed-chest cardiac massage and intubation, should be carried out, although the chances of survival decline sharply as the moments pass.

The high mortality still associated with ventricular fibrillation points up the need for more effective means of preventing its occurrence; knowledge that a less serious ventricular arrhythmia does not always give forewarning of fibrillation makes this all the more urgent. But what should be done in the way of prophylaxis remains an open question. Current practice in most coronary units is to begin anti-arrhythmic therapy – usually a lidocaine infusion – on the appearance of repetitive premature ventricular contractions, particularly if these are of the R on T type. However, some workers have urged that antiarrhyth-

Cardiac Drugs of Use in the Coronary Care Unit in Management of Arrhythmias

Drug	Dosage	Indications	Comments
Atropine	0.5 to 1.0 mg IV	Bradycardia due to sinus slowing AV dissociation	May be repeated 2 or 3 times. Urinary retention common. May rarely cause atropine psychosis or acute glaucoma. Excess dosage may cause sinus tachycardia.
Lidocaine	60 to 100 mg IV	Ventricular premature complexes	Effective in 3-5 minutes. May be repeated 3 times. Duration of action variable, usually 20-40 minutes. Bolus should be followed by steady infusion at 2-4 mg/min to maintain desired effect.
*Quinidine	0.2 to 0.4 gm every 6 hr *po*	Long-term suppression of ventricular arrhythmia	Aim is to achieve adequate blood level (3-6 mg/l) for effective suppression. May depress ventricular function, lower blood pressure, or widen QRS.
*Procainamide	2.0 to 4.0 gm daily in divided doses every 3 to 6 hr	Long-term suppression of ventricular arrhythmia	Aim is to achieve adequate blood level (5-8 mg/l) for effective suppression. May depress ventricular function, lower blood pressure, or widen QRS.
Isoproterenol	1.0 mg in 500 ml 5% dextrose as a continuously regulated infusion	Bradycardia Sinus slowing AV block Asystole	Provides short-term support until pacemaker or other definitive therapy is instituted. May induce ventricular arrhythmia. Markedly increases myocardial oxygen demand. Probably contraindicated in cardiogenic shock.
Propranolol	0.5 mg IV every 2 minutes; total dosage no more than 5 mg	Recurrent atrial fibrillation or flutter with rapid ventricular rate	Use with great caution. May induce profound AV block or asystole. Reserve for special situations only.
Digoxin	0.5 mg IV, followed by 0.25 mg in 6 hours, then 0.125 at 12 and 18 hours Maintenance dose 0.125 to 0.375 mg daily, *po* or IV	Congestive failure Supraventricular arrhythmias	Use cautiously in acute myocardial infarction because of apparent reduced toxic threshold. Excreted by kidneys, thus reduce dose when blood urea nitrogen is elevated. Avoid hypokalemia.

*In general, quinidine and procainamide are reserved for long-term suppression of ventricular arrhythmia after initial treatment with lidocaine. Problem is to give adequate dosage without incurring toxicity. Although "usual" dosage is often too little to achieve therapeutic blood levels, a higher dosage may suppress myocardial function.

Idiosyncrasy to quinidine is well known. Procainamide may cause fever, leukopenia, or lupus erythematosus. Quinidine and procainamide are classified as type I antiarrhythmics and lidocaine and diphenylhydantoin as type II; electrophysiologic and toxic effects differ. Propranolol is an antisympathetic and antiarrhythmic drug.

mia prophylaxis be initiated in all patients in the acute postinfarction phase whether a disturbance in cardiac rhythm is present or not. In fact, it has been established in several carefully controlled trials in coronary units that the frequency of all types of ventricular arrhythmia following acute myocardial infarction is significantly reduced by prophylactic administration of antiarrhythmic agents — either procainamide, quinidine, or lidocaine. The frequency of R on T premature ventricular contractions has reportedly been decreased up to 70% in this way.

Certain problems in reference to these studies require comment. For one thing, only patients with relatively uncomplicated acute myocardial infarction were included in the trials since it would have been difficult to institute such a restrictive protocol in others. Thus, the findings cannot be applied to patients with left ventricular failure or shock or those with major conduction disturbances prior to admission to the coronary unit. Moreover, none of the studies demonstrated a significant reduction in mortality from cardiac arrhythmias despite the reduced incidence of VPC's, doubtless in part because sicker patients were excluded from the drug trials. In addition, the results may have been somewhat clouded by the practice of continuing to administer antiarrhythmic therapy on detection of potentially serious arrhythmias in both treatment and control groups. Life-threatening rhythm disorders in any of the patients were promptly and vigorously treated. Finally, in each study there have been deaths or complications ascribed to toxicity.

As Koch-Weser commented editorially in the *New England Journal of Medicine*: "Since ventricular premature beats, including those accepted as forewarnings of serious arrhythmias, are the rule after acute myocardial infarction, most patients in coronary care units where all dysrhythmic activity is detected receive prophylactic therapy at some time during their stay. In such a setting, universal antiarrhythmic therapy merely assures that prophylactic therapy will never be excessively delayed [and] that those patients in whom serious arrhythmias would develop without any warning would also be protected.

. . . When these advantages are balanced against adverse effects of the drugs in occasional patients who would ordinarily not be treated, no strong case remains for routine administration of antiarrhythmic agents in optimal coronary care units."

In our judgment, too, routine antiarrhythmia prophylaxis scarcely seems justified in a coronary unit that is already equipped to detect rhythm disturbances as soon as they appear and to provide instant corrective treatment if they progress to more serious form. Although the possibility of primary fibrillation or sudden complete heart block may seem reason enough for preventive therapy, these arrhythmias are relatively uncommon compared with those in which there is a gradual progression that can be recognized and treated. On the other hand, there might well be justification for routine prophylaxis, at least in some patients, when coronary care facilities are limited. This would be true at many community hospitals where most patients with acute myocardial infarction are more likely to be treated in intensive rather than coronary care units and where staff coverage may be a problem.

The problem, as Koch-Weser suggests, is that since none of the available antiarrhythmic agents is free of toxicity, their administration to patients on a routine basis raises the prospect that some who may not need the drug may suffer harm. This dilemma is faced also in deciding whether to continue antiarrhythmic therapy in a patient who has survived a serious ventricular arrhythmia while in the coronary unit and is ready to go home. Although there are few objective data, clinical observations suggest that some instability of cardiac rhythm may persist for a considerable period after the acute event and that such patients are at risk of sudden death. This would suggest that prophylactic antiarrhythmia therapy should be maintained at least for a time. Or is it preferable to allow some degree of arrhythmia to persist rather than use an antiarrhythmic agent that might prove toxic to the heart or other organs? The physician's final decision must be based on a careful consideration of the patient's clinical condition and the therapeutic choices available.

Of the available compounds, lidocaine has the advantage of lowest toxicity but its administration is difficult outside the hospital. Procainamide and quinidine are easier to use outside the hospital but their greater toxicity may be limiting, and additional problems are raised by the multiple daily doses required. Recent observations by Lown and coworkers of patients on maintenance therapy with procainamide following acute myocardial infarction are disturbing. They found that fully two thirds of their patients stopped taking the drug despite physicians' instructions, either because of unpleasant reactions or annoyance with the treatment regimen. Because of the variable absorption characteristic of all the antiarrhythmic drugs, dosage is best regulated by repeated blood level determinations. Yet these determinations are not generally feasible outside a hospital setting, which may present difficulties if the drugs are to be used on a long-term basis.

What is needed, of course, is an effective and relatively nontoxic antiarrhythmic agent, simple to administer and having a prolonged action, which could be expected to maintain a blood level in a reasonable range. The kind of compound we are looking for would offer the advantages currently provided by digitalis for the supraventricular arrhythmias: relatively nontoxic (except in the immediate postinfarction period), long-acting, convenient to take for many years, if necessary. Indeed, digitalis has been used for upwards of 20 years or more by many patients with no side effects or toxicity. Of how many drugs can this be said?

Without question, the risk factors that increase vulnerability to recurrent cardiac arrhythmia following acute myocardial infarction need to be better defined. Then one might decide with greater confidence whether a given patient needed to be kept on antiarrhythmic therapy following discharge from the hospital despite the risk of some drug toxicity. Conversely, one might be better able to predict that therapy could be safely discontinued since a recurrence of the arrhythmia was unlikely. It is to be hoped that current work directed toward this end will bring cardiac arrhythmias under better control not only in the acute phase following onset of myocardial infarction but thereafter as well.

Present Status of Antithrombotic Therapy in Acute Heart Attack

SOL SHERRY

Temple University

"In summary, the total world evidence suggests that in the absence of compelling contraindication, and with the availability of satisfactory laboratory and clinical facilities, patients suffering with acute myocardial infarction should receive adequate ....therapy during the first month, and that the risk of reinfarction and death is reduced if this is continued for one or two years after the first month" (*Circulation*, September 1964).

"It is disconcerting to realize that after such prolonged and extensive clinical trial the scientific justification for the use of .... is not available in many clinical situations in which they are used; it is even more disconcerting to recognize that in some of these areas, because of the difficulty in assessing the clinical data, a final conclusion may never be available" (*American Heart Journal*, January 1969).

The form of therapy evoking such sharply opposing comments was of course the same in both instances: use of anticoagulants in management of acute myocardial infarction. Few medical questions have fired as much controversy over so lengthy a period, and if the issue is less hotly debated at this writing that is not because it is resolved. More accurately, one has to speak of the multiple issues involved, for the controversy has included use of anticoagulants in the several phases of acute myocardial infarction – not only in management of the acute stage following onset of ischemia but in the preinfarction phase, if such can be identified, and, after the fact, to prevent reinfarction. At the clinical level, probably most practitioners continue to employ anticoagulants, at least during the acute illness and often for a considerable period thereafter, on the ground that both immediate and later hazards may be reduced. In the final analysis, however, the benefits achievable with any form of therapy are likely to be limited by the nature of the disease being treated. When the nature of acute myocardial infarction is considered, it becomes evident that other forms of therapy – to be discussed as we proceed – may be more applicable both in treating the acute stage of illness and on a prophylactic basis.

Introduction of anticoagulant therapy for myocardial infarction in the mid-1940's was based on two suppositions about this disease: One was that coronary artery thrombosis probably played a role in development of the obstructive arterial lesions underlying onset of myocardial ischemia and necrosis; the other was that thromboembolic complications of the infarction process contributed significantly to morbidity and mortality during the acute phase of illness. Anticoagulant therapy following onset of infarction aimed at preventing or controlling such complications; anticoagulant therapy after recovery aimed at minimizing the thrombotic process that might precipitate a recurrence.

Without a doubt the early studies favoring use of anticoagulants in treatment of acute myocardial infarction demonstrated a reduced frequency of thromboembolic complications affecting the venous system, including pulmonary embolism and systemic arterial embolism from endocardial mural thrombi. This effect of anticoagulants probably produced most of the benefits recorded. However, when these studies were in progress (the landmark trial under the aegis of the American Heart Association was completed in the early 1950's), thromboembolic complications of this type accounted for considerably more of the morbidity and mortality associated with acute myocardial infarction than they do at present. Possible reasons for the present-day reduced frequency of thromboembolic complications (earlier ambulation of patients with acute myocardial infarction, more vigorous treatment of heart failure) are readily cited. In any case, the effectiveness of anticoagulants was more convincing when such complications accounted for a higher proportion of all deaths in patients with acute myocardial infarction — perhaps 10% to 15% as against 2% to 3% today. This low mortality from thromboembolic complications makes it unlikely that anticoagulants can play more than a minor role in the saving of lives; however, anticoagulation is still a valuable adjunct in management by virtue of its ability to reduce morbidity and disability from certain thromboembolic complications, e.g., cerebral, peripheral, pulmonary, and other emboli.

The other supposition in reference to acute myocardial infarction — that arterial thrombosis may play a causal role — is still being debated (see Chapter 17, "Platelets and Thrombosis in Acute Myocardial Infarction," by Mustard and Chapter 18, "Coronary Artery Pathology in Fatal Ischemic Heart Disease," by Roberts). While it is well known that occlusive disease of coronary arteries is often associated with a combination of atherosclerosis and thrombosis, the relative importance of the two in development of acute myocardial infarction continues unresolved. As is known, pathologists' testimony to the infrequent occurrence of fresh thrombi in patients dying shortly after onset of acute symptoms has been a chief reason why thrombogenic factors tend to be discounted. The argument is extended by the suggestion that when arterial thrombi are detected in patients with acute myocardial infarction they are more likely to represent an effect of the infarction process than its cause; this would fit with the observation that the incidence of arterial thrombosis tends to increase with the duration of survival following onset of myocardial ischemia.

However, other observations cast these relationships in a somewhat different light: For example, the incidence of coronary arterial thrombosis has usually been calculated as if sudden cardiac death (within an hour or so following onset of acute symptoms) may be assumed to be due to the same event which leads to a classical acute transmural myocardial infarction. In actuality no one can be certain that if the victim survived he would have developed a typical infarction. Recent observations suggest that most sudden, unexpected deaths are due to a catastrophic arrhythmia, not heart muscle injury, but in reality the patho-

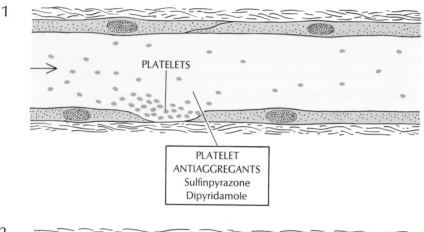

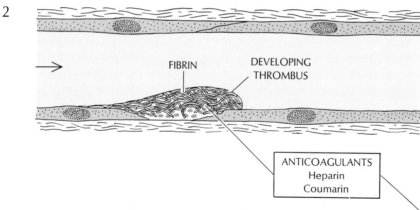

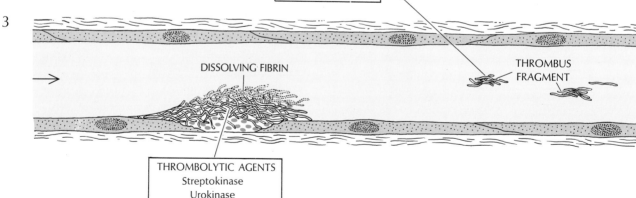

Given evidence that the initiating factor in arterial thrombus formation is platelet aggregation at the site of vessel injury, interest has focused on effective prevention through use of platelet antiaggregating agents (1). At this stage anticoagulant therapy appears of little value since it does not significantly influence platelet aggregation. Anticoagulants do have a limiting effect on thrombus growth through deposition of fibrin in and around the original platelet mass (2); they are useful too in preventing embolization of thrombus fragments (3). Once an arterial thrombus is fully formed, its resolution is facilitated by use of thrombolytic agents, such as streptokinase and urokinase, which have proved capable of dissolving fibrin.

genesis of such deaths is really not well understood. Plainly, though, the relative absence of coronary arterial thrombosis among sudden death victims tells little about its relevance to proved infarction. Indeed, in several recent studies limited to cases of proved transmural infarction, the incidence of coronary thrombosis has been 50% to 90% (see Chapter 18 by Roberts).

To be sure, formation of fresh thrombi could result from factors that come into play after rather than before onset of myocardial ischemia. This view, however, is difficult to reconcile with observations of several investigators that thrombi typically are superimposed on cracks or fissures in the intima of atheromatous or fibrosed arterial wall. Such vascular damage precedes onset of infarction.

If coronary artery thrombosis does play a causal role, as we believe, in most cases of acute transmural myocardial infarction, either before or after the onset of ischemia, then thrombus prevention is of prime importance in reducing risk of occurrence or recurrence. Elimination of underlying atherosclerosis, if feasible, would be one approach to thrombus prevention; for practical purposes, however, anticoagulant therapy — either in the presence of symptoms of impending infarction or on a long-term basis to prevent reinfarction — is the principal measure taken to interfere with the thrombotic process. Implicit in this practice is the assumption that anticoagulants can strikingly affect arterial thrombus formation, when in fact this is not the case.

As work by other investigators has shown (see Chapter 17 by Mustard), an arterial thrombus begins as an accumulation of platelets at the site of vascular injury. As a secondary event, release of platelet factors results in deposition of fibrin sufficient to initiate formation of a fibrin–red coagulum superimposed on the original platelet mass. From all evidence, anticoagulant therapy has no demonstrable effect on platelet aggregation except in the isolated circumstance where thrombin is the primary stimulus for aggregation.

Growth of an already formed arterial thrombus through fibrin deposition is another matter, for there anticoagulants can be expected to have a

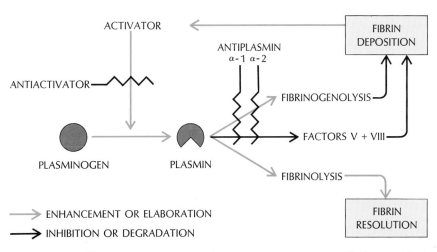

Deposition of fibrin in response to vascular or tissue injury is normally kept in check since its occurrence triggers the body's fibrinolytic enzyme system, in turn dependent on the presence of specific activators for conversion of the proenzyme plasminogen to plasmin. The latter is capable of hydrolyzing not only fibrin but fibrinogen and at least two clotting factors as well; however, excessive plasma proteolysis is averted because fibrinogen and clotting factor degradation is checked by potent antiplasmin factors as well as by natural antiactivators. Thus, conversion of plasminogen to plasmin is limited as is the duration of plasmin action in the circulating plasma. Fibrinolysis, however, proceeds by other mechanisms.

limiting effect; their use can also prevent embolization from an arterial thrombus, since by the time embolization is likely to occur, fibrin is the major thrombus constituent. On the other hand, there is little gained by using anticoagulant therapy in hope of influencing either formation of an arterial thrombus or subsequent resolution; it is unlikely to do either.

If the goal is to prevent thrombus formation, a more direct — and more logical — approach is to utilize an agent capable of interfering with the platelet aggregation initiating the thrombotic process. Indeed, several of the pharmacologically active antiaggregating agents identified to date (aspirin, sulfinpyrazone, and dipyridamole) are considered potentially useful in antithrombotic therapy (see Chapter 17 by Mustard). Now a major question is whether or not the promising experimental findings can be applied to coronary arterial thrombosis in man. Some relevant clinical data showing encouraging results have been obtained through study of two disorders associated with arterial platelet aggregation: embolization from cardiac vascular prostheses and transient cerebrovascular ischemic attacks. With development of less thrombogenic types of heart valves and increasing use of surgical approaches for transient cerebrovas-

cular ischemic attacks, the availability of suitable patients for such studies has diminished.

Given the mounting evidence that implicates platelet aggregation in coronary arterial thrombosis, pressures are increasing for an adequate large-scale trial of platelet antiaggregants as prophylactics against thrombus formation. However, there are still other questions to be answered as to the agent or agents that might best be employed and the preferable dosage regimen. Whether or not the platelet antiaggregants now under investigation will prove clinically useful remains to be seen. In this respect, it is interesting to note that aspirin is now under evaluation in the National Heart and Lung Institute's Coronary Drug Study.

But if anticoagulants are of little value in averting coronary artery thrombus formation, what of their place in therapy of patients undergoing acute infarction? As noted earlier, use of heparin and coumarin compounds over the years has taught that these agents are primarily effective in controlling venous thrombosis and pulmonary and systemic embolization. These benefits, however, as previously noted, have had little impact on the *survival* of patients following acute myocardial infarction; survival depends far more on the extent of myo-

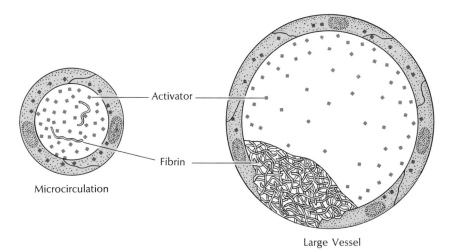

Activator

Fibrin

Microcirculation

Large Vessel

Endothelial cells lining blood vessels appear to be the principal source of specific kinases required for conversion of plasminogen to plasmin and activation of the fibrinolytic enzyme system. Because the concentration of such cells is relatively greater within smaller vessels, the body's natural fibrinolytic system is oriented primarily toward the microcirculation, where it functions to maintain fluidity of the capillary bed. Because of the greater volume of circulating blood in larger vessels, there is proportionately less activator present to initiate fibrinolysis; hence, in the presence of a sizable thrombotic mass, the levels of activator in the immediate vicinity of the clot may be inadequate. Thus, pharmacologic enhancement of fibrinolysis is indicated.

cardial necrosis as it affects cardiac function. With the availability of coronary care units to control arrhythmias, pump failure and the accompanying manifestations of cardiogenic shock are the most urgent considerations during the acute phase of illness; the most appropriate therapy for pump failure is that which can effectively restore blood flow to the damaged myocardium before necrosis develops or before it is extensive enough to cause incapacitating or fatal heart failure (see Chapter 23, "Hemodynamic Changes in Acute Myocardial Infarction," by Ross and Chapter 33, "Myocardial Revascularization During Postinfarction Shock," by Mundth, Buckley, and Austen).

Since coronary arterial thrombi are most often present, as is a plugging of the microcirculation with fibrin and platelets, and these contribute to obstruction of flow, it now seems only logical to suggest that their removal would provide a most effective means of reperfusion. Accordingly, a series of investigations in recent years by ourselves and others have sought to develop effective thrombolytic agents, in the hope that these could have a major impact on morbidity and mortality resulting from acute myocardial infarction. The remainder of this chapter will be a report on this work.

Whether thrombosis occurs in the arterial or venous systems, a chief component of a fully formed thrombus is the insoluble fibrin matrix giving it structural integrity. Thus an effective thrombolytic agent must be capable of dissolving fibrin; in fact, finding ways to mimic and accelerate natural mechanisms for fibrinolysis has been the key to development of effective thrombolytic agents for in vivo use.

As is known, fibrin deposition is a natural response to a multiplicity of vascular and tissue injuries; normally its occurrence activates the plasma proteolytic enzyme system responsible for clearing such deposits, so that the patency of vascular and other channels is maintained. Like other enzyme systems, this one comprises an inactive proenzyme – plasminogen – and an active component – plasmin – capable of rapidly solubilizing fibrin (by splitting off peptides responsible for maintaining the insolubility of the parent molecule). Conversion of plasminogen to plasmin – in other words, activation of the fibrinolytic system – is dependent on the presence of kinases specific for plasminogen. These are apparently present in the circulation and in most tissues and body fluids.

The proteolytic activity of plasmin is not limited to fibrin dissolution, a fact highly pertinent to our discussion.

The enzyme hydrolyzes fibrinogen at a similar rate; it acts also on at least two clotting factors (V and VIII) and on other plasma proteins. Fortunately, potent plasmin inhibitors present in plasma serve to keep the enzyme system in check. Thus far two antiplasmins have been identified in the alpha globulin plasma fraction (chiefly as a result of the work of Norman et al). One is an immediate inhibitor, alpha-2 antiplasmin or alpha-2 macroglobulin, which produces a reversible reaction (the presence of fibrin, fibrinogen, or other protein substrate can disrupt the plasmin inhibitor complex). The other is a slowly reacting inhibitor (alpha-1 antiplasmin or alpha-1 antitrypsin), which has greater capacity and produces irreversible inhibition. (Some work suggests that the alpha-1 globulin component may exhibit both slow and immediate antiplasmin activity.) Reportedly, the antiplasmin capacity of plasma is many times greater than its plasmin potential; thus the presence of plasmin cannot readily be demonstrated in normal blood unless it is treated to remove natural inhibitors of fibrinolysis.

As the functioning of the fibrinolytic system· in vivo became better understood, it became evident that regulation of its activity was related to the concentration of plasminogen activator. Direct observations confirmed that the level of fibrinolytic activity of blood was a function of its plasminogen activator content. With the knowledge that plasmin is a proteolytic enzyme of undifferentiated specificity, the puzzle was how it could achieve selective lysis of fibrin without also lysing other susceptible plasma proteins. However, under some circumstances, hyperplasminemia and excessive plasma proteolysis did occur; this too required explanation.

Matters were clarified when it was learned that plasminogen is deposited with fibrin whenever the latter is formed, and that plasminogen activation near a fibrin deposition (as in the interstices of a clot) is the most sensitive mechanism for fibrinolysis. Observations by our group led to formulation of a hypothesis to account for the findings: Plasminogen in vivo appears to exist in a two-phase system – in soluble form in plasma and other body fluids and in gel form in thrombi and fibrinous deposits. Activation of gel phase or clot plasminogen results in plasmin formation expressed chiefly by fibrinolysis. Activation of soluble phase or plasma plasminogen results in circulating plasmin formation, with the activity expressed chiefly by fibrinogenolysis. In recent years, an additional link to our understanding of this system has come from the observation that insoluble fibrin has the ability to bind plasminogen activators selectively.

Under conditions predisposing to overactivity of the plasma enzyme system, activation of the soluble phase results in hyperplasminemia and excessive proteolysis of plasma factors; however, under physiologic conditions, the presence of plasminogen activator in the circulation does not have these effects because activation of plasminogen to plasmin is effectively impeded by plasma inhibitors. In contrast, incorporation of plasminogen activator into a clot normally produces rapid fibrinolysis. Here the proteolytic enzyme is activated in close spatial relation to fibrin, usually the only substrate available.

Both in natural fibrinolysis and in pharmacologically induced fibrinolysis, the mechanism appears to involve diffusion and binding of activator into the thrombus with conversion of plasminogen therein to the active enzyme form. Another hypothesis (proposed by Ambrus and Marcus) holds that plasminogen activation occurs predominantly in the circulation. According to this theory, plasmin formed in the circulation immediately complexes with inhibitor, and when the plasmin-antiplasmin complex encounters a thrombus, plasmin is selectively released for local fibrinolysis. However, several findings make diffusion and binding of activator into the clot a more likely possibility; for example, observations on the localization of activators on a thrombus, significant concentrations of plasminogen known to occur in clots and the continued fibrinolysis when circulating plasminogen levels are grossly depleted.

Endothelial cells of the microcirculation are probably the principal source of plasminogen activator—both the small amounts normally present in the circulation and the increased levels found in abnormal fibrinolytic states. Since plasminogen activator is rapidly cleared from the systemic circulation by the liver and circulating inhibitors, the basal level of activator continuously present presupposes an almost continuous cellular release.

Significant arteriovenous differences have been shown by direct measurements of plasminogen activator concentrations across pulmonary, renal, mesenteric, and gastric circulations. This and related observations would suggest that the body's natural fibrinolytic system is oriented primarily toward the microcirculation, where it functions to maintain fluidity of the capillary bed. Fibrinolytic activity is high and continuous in this part of the circulation and fibrin deposition is promptly followed by fibrinolysis.

On the other hand, fibrin formation in the systemic circulation is not dealt with nearly as well. Since clot formation occurs there in the presence of relatively low plasminogen activator levels, resolution necessarily proceeds at a much slower pace. In the presence of a sizable thrombotic mass the high levels of activator required in the immediate vicinity of the clot may not be obtainable through normal physiologic mechanisms; thus, for rapid thrombus dissolution to occur, some means of enhancing natural fibrinolytic activity is required. Actually, two pharmacologic approaches have been pursued: One, which rather quickly proved unsatisfactory, involved stimulation of endogenous fibrinolytic activity, the other, infusion of exogenous plasminogen activators. Fortunately, this more direct approach has proved relatively effective. (Needless to say, an agent suitable for thrombolytic therapy should dissolve fibrin without excessive digestion of fibrinogen and other plasma clotting factors.)

Two biologic compounds have been the focus of most studies: streptokinase, a secretory protein of hemolytic streptococci, and urokinase, a product of human urine, produced by the kidneys presumably to keep the tubules and urinary tract free of fibrinous deposits. Both have proved ability to induce in vivo a predictable, controllable thrombolytic state that results in effective thrombus dissolution. Both have been actively investigated clinically in recent years in a variety of thromboembolic disorders; they offer the prospect that by controlling its thrombotic aspect, morbidity and mortality associated with acute myocardial infarction may be reduced.

The clinical potential of intravascular use of streptokinase for thrombolysis was first explored by our group and others more than a decade ago; this followed laboratory observations indicating that streptokinase could liquify clotted hemothorax and lyse experimental venous thrombi in rabbits. (W. S. Tillett, who initiated this research, had been the first to identify the fibrinolytic capacity of products of hemolytic streptococci as early as 1933.) In further experiments, streptokinase effectively dissolved induced

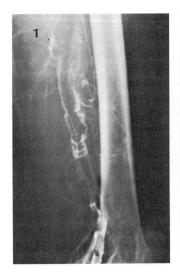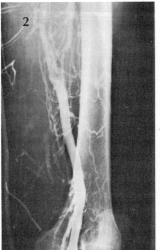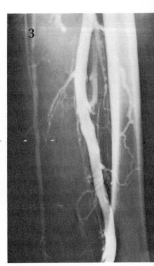

Thrombosis of femoral-popliteal vein (1) is effectively resolved by regimen combining 72-hour streptokinase infusion, then heparin for 7 days and warfarin thereafter. In venograms 4 and 12 days after start of therapy (2, 3) vessel patency is demonstrated.

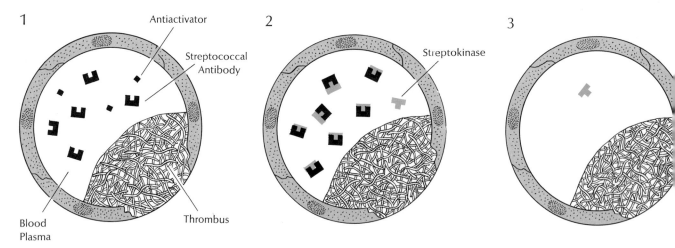

For effective thrombolytic therapy with use of streptokinase (SK) as a plasminogen activator it is necessary first to overcome problems of antigenicity, since the drug will interact immunologically with antibodies produced by previous streptococcal infections (1).

Thus, the loading dose of SK must be sufficiently large to neutralize antibodies (2) and overcome the effect of natural antiactivators. Antigen-antibody complexes are rapidly cleared from the bloodstream through activity of the reticuloendothelial sys-

arterial thrombi in dogs, paving the way for preliminary human studies in which streptokinase showed an impressive capacity to dissolve both venous and arterial thrombi. In one of these early studies in a small series of patients we assessed the effect of administering streptokinase in the acute stage following onset of myocardial infarction. Inhospital mortality was lower in the treated group than in controls. In terms of later work with plasminogen activators, a more tangible result was that the enhanced thrombolytic activity of the circulating blood was apparently well tolerated by the infarcting myocardium.

Admittedly, early clinical work with streptokinase raised serious practical problems. Some preparations had a tendency to elicit pyrogenic reactions that proved difficult to eliminate; the suspicion was raised that these batches might contain toxic contaminants. A major problem proved to be the immediate inactivation of streptokinase by circulating streptococcal antibodies (antistreptokinase) present in most patients as a result of earlier streptococcal infections. To ensure adequate antibody neutralization, a preliminary titration of the patient's plasma was necessary to determine the antibody level; individualized dosage schedules were required, as was careful monitoring throughout therapy. The antigenicity of streptokinase further complicated matters, since rapid immunization made retreatment difficult if not impossible.

For these and related reasons, further clinical testing of streptokinase as a thrombolytic agent was suspended indefinitely in the U. S. in 1960 (and only recently resumed on an investigational basis). However, workers abroad took a different route and intensified efforts to produce preparations that would be readily tolerated by patients. Succeeding in this, they were also able to overcome the problem of resistance to streptokinase, showing that despite variations among patients in this regard, the dosage of streptokinase need not be individualized for effective antibody neutralization. A standardized dosage schedule was developed, combining a loading dose sufficient to convert plasma plasminogen to plasmin and initiate thrombolysis with a maintenance dose given by infusion to sustain the activity. The maintenance dose was low enough to avoid excess plasma proteolysis yet high enough to ensure conversion of plasminogen in the thrombus to the active enzyme.

In view of evidence that the most sensitive mechanism for thrombolysis involves adsorption and diffusion of plasminogen activator into the thrombus, the question was whether local perfusion of an occluded vessel with streptokinase would be preferable to systemic intravenous administration of the agent. While the question is still not fully resolved, most investigators consider systemic administration probably equally effective; hence unless a catheter already in place will permit local perfusion, there is no need to insert one.

Studies abroad (in both Europe and Australia) provided convincing evidence that streptokinase could accelerate dissolution of a variety of intravascular clots. Since it has been available for clinical use, streptokinase has been extensively employed, chiefly for thromboembolic disease of the peripheral vessels and pulmonary embolism. Clinicians abroad (and investigators here, now involved in re-examining the potential of streptokinase with European preparations) generally employ a loading dose of 250,000 units followed by a sustaining infusion of 100,000 units/hr. This regimen appears to contain sufficient streptokinase to overcome the resistance of 85% to 90% of patients; it also provides free circulating levels of the agent sufficient to sustain an active yet safe thrombolytic state.

As a rule, therapy can be monitored with a single laboratory test — speed of clotting on addition of an excess of thrombin to plasma. Thrombin clotting time (or, alternatively, the prothrombin time), which closely reflects the appearance and accumulation of fibrinogen breakdown products, serves as a useful though indirect measure of fibrinolytic activity. If the test induces no change in thrombin time, a higher dose of the thrombolytic agent may be needed to overcome streptokinase resistance. A marked increase in thrombin time suggests excessive plasma proteolysis; the dosage may

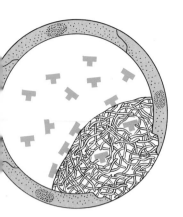

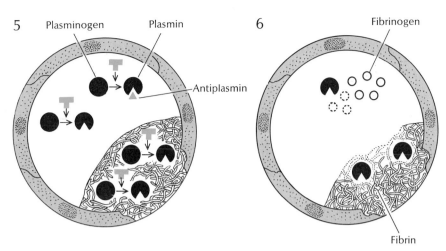

5 Plasminogen   Plasmin

Antiplasmin

6 Fibrinogen

Fibrin

tem and little drug remains (3). Any plasmin formed in the plasma during this phase of treatment is rapidly inactivated by antiplasmins; hence, there is a minimum of plasma proteolysis. Streptokinase subsequently administered in a sustaining infusion

adsorbs to and penetrates in and around the thrombus (4), activates plasminogen therein, and yields sufficient plasmin for fibrin dissolution and thrombus lysis (5). The absence of circulating antiplasmins in the thrombus enhances the SK effect (6).

have to be reduced to avoid digestion of essential clotting factors or increased so as to pass through this potentially dangerous phase more quickly. European workers acknowledge that the antigenicity of streptokinase imposes restrictions on its use, particularly if retreatment seems indicated. In practice, however, this has not proven a serious deterrent.

Favorable experience abroad with use of streptokinase in thromboembolism of peripheral arteries naturally turned attention to its potential for accelerating dissolution of coronary arterial thrombi. The key issue became whether immediate thrombolytic therapy might be useful in restoring patency of occluded or partially occluded coronary vessels including the microcirculation and thus reduce the extent of infarction.

Animal experiments supported this possibility (for example, those by Ruegsegger and coworkers in which fibrinolytic treatment significantly reduced the size of myocardial infarcts induced by thrombotic occlusion of a coronary artery). Since both animal and human studies were indicating that the likelihood of heart failure or cardiogenic shock was largely determined by the extent of necrosis (see Chapter 29, "Protection of the Ischemic Myocardium," by Braunwald and Maroko), it made sense to limit the necrosis by removing any thrombotic obstruction of blood flow in the myocardium. It would also be essential to initiate thrombolytic therapy as early

as possible after onset of acute symptoms, since irreversible necrosis begins within 30 minutes or less of complete occlusion of a coronary artery. Although this process is delayed if occlusion is partial, it is also known that thrombolysis in vivo is a relatively slow process (incipient lysis is first demonstrable angiographically at two hours in most cases, complete lysis not for 10 hours or more).

Although interest in thrombolytic therapy for acute myocardial infarction has always been strongest among

investigators who believe a preformed thrombus usually precipitates the event, in point of fact, whatever the causative role of thrombosis, i.e., whether it initiates the necrosis or contributes to it as a secondary event, its presence immediately post-infarction can only add to a patient's difficulties.

Restoration of blood flow by lysis of arterial thrombi in a main coronary artery or of fibrin-platelet masses in the microcirculation might therefore salvage not yet irreversibly dam-

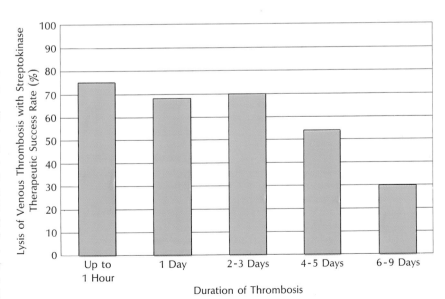

Thrombolysis is most readily achieved in freshly formed thrombi, according to clinical experience in treating both arterial and venous thrombosis. The importance of duration of thrombosis is exemplified here in data from an Australian study of streptokinase therapy of venous thrombosis by J. C. Biggs and coworkers. These investigators reported that no successes were achieved after nine days.

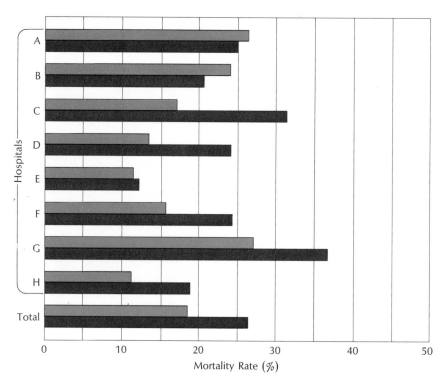

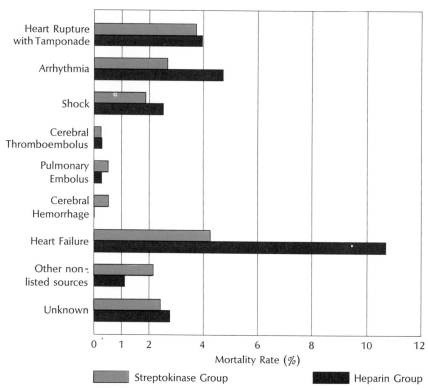

In a large-scale controlled trial to compare thrombolytic and anticoagulant therapy of acute myocardial infarction – involving eight European hospitals – total inhospital mortality (top) was significantly lower among patients treated with streptokinase than in those given conventional heparin therapy. The 730 patients admitted to the trial had a clinical diagnosis of recent acute infarction. Treatment with either drug was administered as a 24-hour infusion. Clinical findings among patients who died (bottom) revealed key differences in cause of death. More than twice as many patients on heparin therapy died of heart failure; a greater number also died of arrhythmia. This pattern lends support to the thesis that thrombolytic therapy may help by restoring blood flow to the infarcting myocardium before extensive damage to the muscle precipitates circulatory and/or electrical failure.

aged muscle tissue, perhaps preventing extension of the infarction. Improved flow might also lessen the risk of electrical instability in marginally ischemic regions, known to increase the possibility of disabling or fatal arrhythmias. Additionally, lysis of incipient thrombi formed on damaged myocardium and in peripheral veins at sites of stasis might reduce embolic complications.

A valid end point in assessing any form of therapy in reference to coronary heart disease is mortality rate: If it could be shown that thrombolytic therapy made a measurable difference in outcome, its usefulness would be confirmed whether or not the pathogenic mechanisms remained unsettled.

Actually, several investigating teams abroad have undertaken controlled trials of such therapy in acute myocardial infarction, comparing results in terms of early and late mortality in patients treated with streptokinase (a 24-hour infusion followed by anticoagulant therapy) or with conventional anticoagulant therapy. For example, two German trials (by Schmutzler, Poliwada, et al.) have involved some 800 patients in six hospitals. In the first (involving 558 patients), both early and late mortality were significantly lower in the streptokinase-treated group. Mortality between the second and 40th day after infarction was reduced from 22% to 14%. Serial changes in the electrocardiogram also indicated beneficial effects of streptokinase therapy. A higher incidence of rudimentary infarction in the streptokinase group suggested that thrombolytic therapy had decreased the extent of cardiac muscle necrosis; however, full-thickness infarcts did not appear to differ in size in the two groups.

A second German trial began when it was seen that strict randomization was not assured in the first. According to an analysis   these results, the benefits observed earlier still prevail, with mortality again apparently reduced by about 30% from that observed in the group that did not receive streptokinase. A multicenter European trial – among hospitals in Germany, Holland, Austria, and Belgium – also yielded similar encouraging results. More specifically, the mortality rate for the first 30 days was 18.5% in the streptokinase group (373 patients) as compared with a rate of 26.3% for the anticoagulant group (357 patients), treated with heparin for the first 24 hours and later with a coumarin derivative. Again there was a notable difference in cause of death: In more than twice as many patients on anticoagulant therapy, heart failure was the cause of death.

Taken together, results of these earlier trials in general hospital beds suggest that thrombolytic therapy may have a useful place in the treatment of acute myocardial infarction (the sole exception was a Finnish investigation but it differed in design, dosage regimen, and time of accession into the study). Nevertheless, with the advent of coronary care units, it is no longer feasible to equate mortality as influenced by a particular therapy in general hospital beds with that observed in these highly specialized facilities; thus the 25% to 30% reduction in mortality previously achieved may already have been accomplished by the care and procedures utilized in units which have reduced the death rate by approximately 60%. Accordingly, several recent trials, as described below, have been undertaken in coronary care units but the results have been contradictory.

No effects were noted in an Italian streptokinase trial (unfortunately therapy was given for only 12 hours as compared to the 24-hour period used in all trials reporting a significant reduction in mortality) or in a European urokinase study. In the Australian streptokinase trial, in progress since 1968, the mortality among the first 253 patients treated with anticoagulants alone was 12.6%, while among the group receiving the thrombolytic agent (264 patients), the mortality was 9.8%. While this difference is not statistically significant for the number of patients studied, the trend in favor of streptokinase was present from the very beginning of the study; this implies that significance might be established when a sufficient number of patients (i.e., 2,000 to 2,500) is studied. However, since analysis of the data has suggested that streptokinase therapy is more likely to benefit those over 60 years of age, those with a history of past infarction, and those with a poor prognostic index, the study is being continued until significance is achieved for this higher risk group

alone. (It is projected that this will be accomplished when 1,000 patients have been entered into the trial.)

Another study with encouraging observations is a United Kingdom trial still in progress at this writing; at last report, 370 patients had been entered (190 streptokinase treated, 180 controls). The mortality for the streptokinase group has been 14.1% and for the controls, 19.9%. Somewhat bothersome is the high mortality among patients treated in coronary care units. One assumes that this is due to earlier admission or selection of patients into these particular units; if not, then the comparability of this study to others may be in question.

An appropriate controlled trial in the U. S. would be of great help in settling this important issue. Until recently, this seemed a remote possibil-

ity, in part because of the discouraging early experience with streptokinase, but a major trial (sponsored by the National Heart and Lung Institute with participation of eight medical centers) is currently in a pilot phase. Unlike the earlier trials abroad, it would be desirable to include in this one a thorough comparison of the relative effectiveness of streptokinase and of urokinase, which came under active investigation in this country after work with streptokinase was aborted. The nonantigenicity of urokinase, of course, gave it an immediate advantage over streptokinase. Early in vitro studies indicated that its use would not require individualization of dosage or as strict laboratory control. Moreover, addition of urokinase to plasma resulted in a higher fibrinolytic/fibrinogenolytic ratio than with streptokinase,

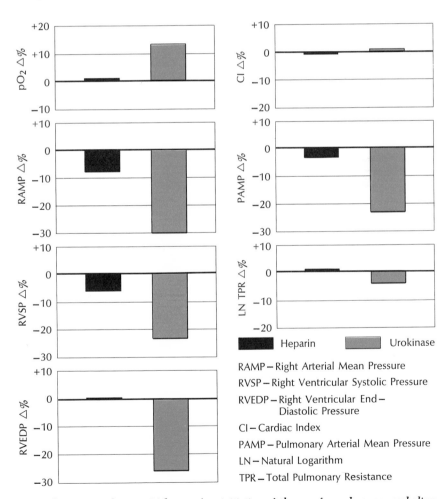

Heparin   Urokinase

RAMP — Right Arterial Mean Pressure

RVSP — Right Ventricular Systolic Pressure

RVEDP — Right Ventricular End-Diastolic Pressure

CI — Cardiac Index

PAMP — Pulmonary Arterial Mean Pressure

LN — Natural Logarithm

TPR — Total Pulmonary Resistance

Hemodynamic evaluation 24 hours after initiation of therapy for pulmonary embolism showed an advantage for thrombolytic over anticoagulant therapy. Right ventricular systolic and right ventricular end-diastolic pressures were reduced by 25% to 30% in the urokinase-treated patients as against less than 10% in the heparin-treated group; a 30% decrease in pulmonary arterial mean pressure obtained with urokinase contrasts with a 4% decrease with heparin. The change in total pulmonary resistance, plotted as the natural logarithm, also favored urokinase.

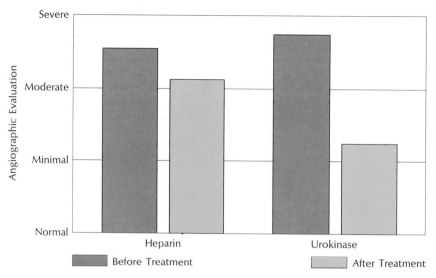

A comparison of results of urokinase and of heparin therapy in patients with massive pulmonary embolism (without shock) showed significant advantage for the former. Pulmonary angiograms were made before and 24 hours after the start of therapy.

suggesting that a more reliable thrombolytic state could be induced with milder aberrations of the hemostatic mechanism.

On the other hand, there were logistic problems in obtaining a trace enzyme from urine in sufficient quantity for subsequent human studies (to provide enough urokinase to treat one thromboembolic episode required processing of 200 to 300 gallons of urine). Elimination of contaminating urinary thromboplastin or adventitious viruses from urokinase preparations had to be assured before they would be suitable for human use. Accordingly, the NHLI supervised development of reproducible assay methods and established a standard urokinase unit for dosage purposes. (Currently it is encouraging the development of tissue culture methods for the production of urokinase.)

In the dosage currently being used in patients, the partially purified preparations developed have been shown to increase thrombolytic activity of plasma some 300 times. This level can be maintained at will by a sustained infusion, and on termination of the infusion the activity promptly disappears. Preliminary clinical observations by ourselves and others showed that urokinase could effectively lyse both arterial and venous thrombi, and a large-scale controlled trial was planned. (From the outset, investigation of urokinase has been limited by both restricted supplies and NHLI

stipulations concerning its use under controlled conditions for specified disorders; hence total clinical experience to date has been far less extensive than that abroad with streptokinase.)

For a national cooperative trial the disorder first focused on was acute pulmonary embolism, purposely selected since results could be better quantified than in other conditions in which the direct effect of the drug could not be as readily measured. Evaluation was based on angiographic, lung scan, and hemodynamic data prior to treatment and 24 hours after its initiation. (The 160 patients studied received either urokinase or heparin by a sustained infusion over a 12-hour period; all were then on heparin therapy for a minimum of five days.)

Dissolution of pulmonary thromboemboli was found to be significantly accelerated by urokinase therapy; patients with massive emboli and in shock appeared to benefit the most. Admittedly, lysis of the entire pulmonary lesion rarely occurred within the period of observation, nor were hemodynamic abnormalities fully corrected. It appeared that the goal of complete medical thrombectomy might require a longer treatment period. A second phase of the trial (launched in the fall of 1970) therefore compared results obtained with a 12-hour urokinase infusion, as before, with those following a 24-hour infusion of either urokinase or streptokinase.

In effect, the pulmonary embolism

trial is providing the first clinical comparison between the two thrombolytic agents in terms of relative activity and also of disadvantages associated with their use. Final results, which should be available fairly soon, will of course be taken into account in finalizing plans for the projected NHLI trial that should establish the effectiveness — and the limitations — of thrombolytic therapy in patients with acute myocardial infarction.

Neither clinical nor investigational experience to date suggests that these agents are likely to be universally effective in managing any thrombotic disorder; success in completely dissolving either arterial or venous thrombi has approximated 50%. Why only partial or no dissolution can be achieved in the remainder is not certain, although it is clear that a newly formed thrombus is far more vulnerable to thrombolysis than one several days old. The observation that plasminogen activator must be in immediate proximity to the thrombus for maximal effect also may have a bearing. That clot lysis may not occur for several hours (and then be incomplete) following administration of a thrombolytic agent may also be a limiting factor determining its clinical efficacy. But even partial dissolution that restored some of the circulation to the damaged area might make a major difference.

Needless to say, any discussion of thrombolytic therapy cannot overlook the hazard of excessive bleeding. Some impairment in hemostasis appears to be inevitable during therapy and often for a few days thereafter as the result of the rapid dissolution of fibrin and the accumulation of fibrin and fibrinogen degradation products in the blood. (Other factors, such as increased fibrinolytic activity itself and altered platelet function, also are important but the extent of their contribution needs further clarification.) However, in the streptokinase and urokinase trials to date, bleeding has most often occurred at the site of invasive procedures — venous cutdowns, arterial punctures, and the like — required to obtain needed information. (Hemorrhagic complications at other sites occurred with the same frequency seen in patients on anticoagulant therapy.) Bleeding with use of streptokinase or urokinase can usually be controlled by a local pressure bandage; on occasion there may be more serious bleeding into areas of trauma or operative wounds. In severe cases, transfusions or perhaps administration of an antifibrinolytic agent such as epsilon aminocaproic acid may be necessary.

In centers where either of these agents is under study, thrombolytic therapy is usually not begun within 10 days of surgery because of the increased risk of bleeding, but there seems to be no reason why surgery cannot be performed immediately on completion of thrombolytic therapy. Although anticoagulants apparently may be safely given following use of a thrombolytic agent, as in the strep-tokinase and urokinase trials, it is agreed that at current dosage schedules (streptokinase, 100,000 units/hr, or urokinase, 2,000 cta units/lb body wt/hr) they probably should not be given together since this may magnify the bleeding hazard. (Lower dosage schedules in combination with anticoagulants are now under study for the treatment of venous thrombotic disease.)

Despite encouraging experience abroad it is still far from certain whether the benefits of thrombolytic therapy in acute myocardial infarction are likely to outweigh the risks. That critical question will be answerable only on completion of the national cooperative trial.

The question of the role of coronary thrombosis in acute myocardial infarction also may be finally resolved when the effects of thrombolytic therapy are evaluated under controlled conditions in a sufficient number of patients. It is estimated that the trial will probably require 2,000 patients for each group, i.e., 2,000 controls and 2,000 for each treatment category. If the natural course of acute myocardial infarction is significantly altered, there no longer will be any doubt of the importance of thrombosis in the infarction process. If the outcome is not only affected but improved, thrombolytic therapy will have provided us with an effective new weapon for treatment.

Protection of the
Ischemic Myocardium

EUGENE BRAUNWALD *and* PETER R. MAROKO

Harvard University

It has long been assumed that the myocardium perfused by a coronary vessel that has become occluded rapidly becomes ischemic and that once the infarction process begins, only a brief interval elapses before the damage is irreversible. Since it became apparent that clinical prognosis following infarction depends directly on the quantity of residual viable, normally functioning myocardium, these widely held assumptions have taken on fresh significance. Cardiogenic shock due to pump failure has now emerged as the chief cause of death in patients hospitalized for acute myocardial infarction (see Chapter 23, "Hemodynamic Changes in Acute Myocardial Infarction," by Ross); this complication has indeed been shown to be closely linked to loss of some portion of contractile myocardium (see Chapter 33, "Myocardial Revascularization During Postinfarction Shock," by Mundth, Buckley, and Austen). Despite heroic measures, many such patients are doomed because too little viable myocardium remains. If only one could effectively limit tissue damage following coronary occlusion, pump failure and its consequences might be averted.

To what extent can prognosis be improved by measures aimed at aborting the necrotic process? Our focus in this chapter will be on gains now being made toward the development of such measures. In animals with experimentally induced infarcts it has been conclusively demonstrated that substantial amounts of myocardium can be salvaged by any of several forms of intervention. We would emphasize at the outset that immediate applicability of these research findings to the human situation is not yet at hand. But the experimental observations, combined with limited data in humans, are pointing toward a new approach to management of acute infarction that could have major impact – not only in reducing mortality risk following a given occlusion but in ensuring survivors

a greater reserve of functioning myocardium should another occlusion occur.

Basic to our discussion is the progression of myocardial ischemic injury, as presently understood, following coronary artery occlusion. It is agreed that myocardial cells reach the point of irreversible injury when the biochemical processes of energy production can no longer maintain cellular integrity. Studies by Jennings and others have demonstrated marked functional and structural changes in cell mitochondria after approximately 20 minutes of ischemia; as ischemia is prolonged, the proportion of surviving cells rapidly decreases (see Chapter 22, "Biochemical and Morphologic Changes in Infarcting Myocardium," by Sobel). On the basis of these findings, it would appear that, at the tissue level, death following ischemic injury also occurs within a matter of minutes. If this were the case, examination of myocardial tissue supplied by an occluded vessel should show an essential homogeneous area of necrosis. Yet, in studies of experimentally induced infarcts in animals, this has not been the usual finding. Rather, these studies have documented that following occlusion the affected myocardium is likely to manifest a region of central necrosis surrounded in patchy fashion by a substantial amount of abnormal but still viable tissue. Moreover, this ischemic "twilight zone," as it has been termed, may increase in size for some time, while the necrotic zone remains relatively small. Indeed, according to Cox and coworkers, the ischemic zone may continue to enlarge for up to 18 hours after occlusion; thereafter the region of central necrosis expands rapidly at the expense of ischemic tissue.

The absence of a clear demarcation between normal and necrotic tissue on histologic examination in patients with myocardial infarction coming to autopsy has been well illustrated by Mundth et al in Chapter 33. Although it appears likely, one cannot confirm with certainty that the progression from ischemic damage to necrosis follows a time course in man similar to that in dogs. What does seem evident is that for an indeterminate period following interruption of blood flow in a coronary artery – surely more than a few minutes and very likely more than a few hours – a significant portion of myocardial tissue served by the occluded vessel remains capable of essentially full recovery *or* of further damage leading to necrosis. In other words, obstruction of a major coronary artery appears to set off a dynamic process variable in outcome, *not* an unalterable sequence beginning with myocardial ischemia and ending with necrosis.

Since integrity of the myocardium depends primarily on its oxygen supply, it seemed logical to us that a critical factor in determining how much myocardium would remain viable following coronary artery occlusion might be the precise balance between local need for and local supply of oxygen. On that premise, factors that tend to augment myocardial consumption of oxygen – or further decrease oxygen availability – should act to enlarge the area of ischemic injury and of ultimate necrosis. Therefore, ischemic myocardium might be protected against progressive damage and death by interventions capable of improving myocardial oxygenation, if such could be found. This has been the major aim of a number of related

investigations conducted over the past several years with our colleagues. Results to date, which have been encouraging, will be detailed as our discussion proceeds. As will also become evident, direct improvement of myocardial oxygenation is but one way of favorably influencing energy balance. The goal may also be approached in terms of increasing the diffusion of oxygen and/or energy substrates to the involved cells or enhancing anaerobic metabolism.

The concept of a critical relationship between myocardial oxygenation and ischemic injury derives in part from a series of studies in cardiovascular physiology which we began prior to 1958 at the National Institutes of Health. Each of these studies

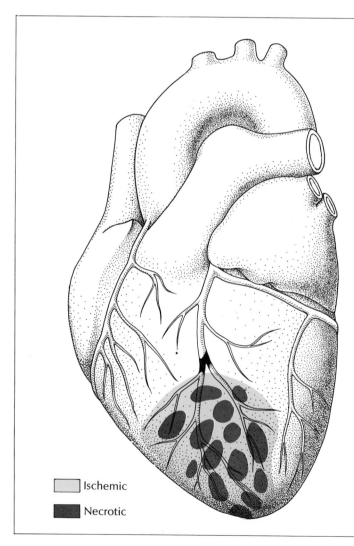

Interventions that reduce myocardial injury

A. *By decreasing myocardial oxygen demands*
1. Propranolol
2. Practolol
3. Ouabain in the failing heart
4. Intra-aortic balloon counterpulsation

B. *By increasing myocardial oxygen supply*
1. Directly
a. Coronary artery reperfusion
2. Through collaterals
a. Elevation of coronary perfusion pressure
b. Intra-aortic balloon counterpulsation

C. *By enhancing anaerobic metabolism*
1. Glucose-insulin-potassium
2. Hypertonic glucose (also acts by increased osmolarity)

D. *By enhancing transport to the ischemic zone of substrates utilized in energy production (presumed)*
1. Hyaluronidase

E. *By protecting against autolytic and heterolytic processes (presumed)*
1. Hydrocortisone

Interventions that increase myocardial injury

A. *By increasing myocardial oxygen requirements*
1. Isoproterenol
2. Glucagon
3. Ouabain
4. Bretylium tosylate
5. Tachycardia

B. *By decreasing myocardial oxygen supply*
1. Reduction of coronary perfusion pressure

Ischemic

Necrotic

For some time following myocardial ischemic injury, as drawing suggests, affected heart tissue served by occluded coronary arteries consists of a relatively small, patchy necrotic zone surrounded by a zone of abnormal yet still viable tissue at high risk of further irreversible damage or possibly amenable to salvage through medical or surgical interventions. The goal of limiting infarct size in man and thus influencing both the immediate and long-term prognosis in acute infarction is now being actively pursued. It has already been learned (see table) that certain interventions have a positive, others a negative, effect on prognosis.

was concerned, in part, with the mechanism of action of those drugs commonly prescribed for patients with coronary artery disease. Among the first examined was nitroglycerin, which was shown to act in angina pectoris not merely by dilating coronary vessels but by decreasing the heart's oxygen consumption. Given this lead, we examined the effect of carotid sinus nerve stimulation in controlling anginal pain, on the theory that it might overcome a transient oxygen deficiency by reducing sympathetic efferent traffic and thus oxygen need.

These observations alerted us to the possibility that in the more serious clinical situation following occlusion of a major coronary artery, the extent of myocardial ischemic injury and necrosis might be affected by underlying hemodynamic factors affecting the balance between local oxygen supply and demand. Also, administration of suitable pharmacologic agents might alter the relationship between the oxygen available to the affected segment of myocardium and its energy requirements.

Our observations on the effects of diverse hemodynamic and pharmacologic stimuli on the course of myocardial injury are worth reviewing in some detail, within the context of what was learned through studies in cardiovascular physiology about control of myocardial energy balance. Actually it has been known for many years that total metabolism of a quiescent heart (arrested with excess potassium) is only a minor fraction of that of a beating heart. In the quiescent heart, oxygen consumption is about 1.3 ml/min/100 gm of left ventricle as compared with a range of 3 to 15 ml/min in the beating heart. In one of the NIH studies, oxygen requirements for electrical activation of the heart were defined in an isolated canine heart preparation, the coronary bed of which was perfused at a constant rate. The oxygen cost of depolarization proved to be trivial, amounting to only 0.5% of the total oxygen consumed by a normally contracting heart.

This turned our interest to delineating those aspects of contraction that do require substantial quantities of oxygen. Many years earlier, studies by Rohde (reported in 1912) had

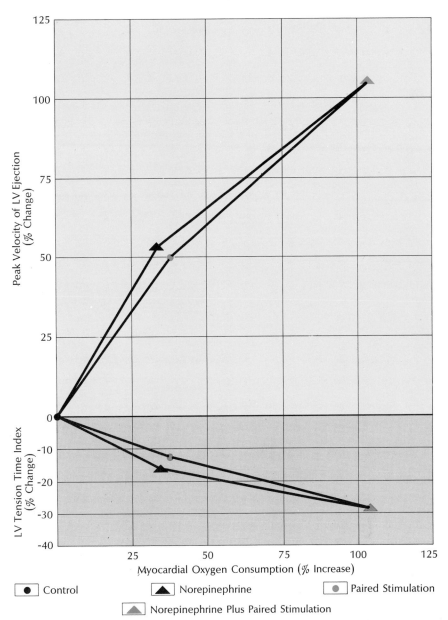

Myocardial O₂ consumption and velocity of contraction were increased in parallel in canine heart preparation by interventions enhancing myocardial contractility. Tension-time index was reduced, since measures shortened duration of left ventricular ejection.

shown that myocardial oxygen consumption varies directly as a function of the product of developed pressure and heart rate. Not long afterwards Evans and Matsuoka cited the important relation "between the tension set up on contraction and the metabolism of contractile tissue." With development (in the 1950's) of improved techniques for externally regulating heart performance, the NIH group, working first in Sarnoff's laboratory, undertook a systematic investigation of the relative effects in the normal heart of aortic pressure, stroke volume, and heart rate on myocardial

oxygen consumption.

When aortic pressure was progressively increased and heart rate held constant, myocardial oxygen consumption proved closely related to the tension-time index per minute (calculated from the area beneath the left ventricular pressure pulse curve) at all levels of cardiac output. Similarly, the tension-time index and myocardial oxygen consumption changed in parallel when cardiac output was progressively increased while arterial pressure and heart rate were kept constant, or when heart rate was varied while arterial pressure and cardiac output were kept constant. Subsequently, it was recognized that a more definitive factor in myocardial energy utilization than pressure developed by the ventricle is myocardial wall **tension** during systole. This is a direct function of intraventricular pressure and ventricular radius and is inversely related to ventricular wall thickness.

But when studies along these lines began to be performed in intact animals rather than in isolated heart preparations it became apparent that something besides wall tension must be at work in determining the heart's metabolic requirements. In pertinent canine experiments, Gregg found that myocardial oxygen consumption correlated poorly with the tension-time index during exercise or sympathetic nerve stimulation; in man, Krasnow, Gorlin, et al noted a discrepancy in the relation between the tension-time index and myocardial oxygen consumption when isoproterenol was given.

Accordingly, the N I H group explored the possibility that in addition to developed ventricular tension, the peak velocity of contraction – reflecting the heart's contractile or inotropic state – might be a second major determinant of myocardial oxygen consumption. This hypothesis was tested with use of a canine right heart bypass preparation, in which blood was pumped at a constant rate into the pulmonary artery so that a constant left ventricular output could be maintained; aortic pressure and heart rate were also held constant.

Against this background, various interventions known to enhance myocardial contractility were introduced: first, repetitive paired electrical stimulation (sustained postextrasystolic potentiation) and, subsequently, administration of catecholamines and digitalis. It was consistently found that myocardial oxygen consumption increased in parallel with increased velocity of contraction (obtained from the peak left ventricular ejection rate). Moreover, in all instances, while myocardial oxygen consumption increased, the tension-time index declined, reflecting a shortened duration of ejection. The importance of myocardial contractility as a determinant of oxygen consumption was corroborated in other experiments in which peak vel-

ocity of contraction was reduced by cardiac depressant drugs such as propranolol, procainamide, or pronethalol. With these interventions, myocardial oxygen consumption was significantly reduced.

Later it was shown that developed tension and contractility had a comparable quantitative influence; this was in experiments in an isovolumetric left ventricular preparation in which wall tension but not contractility was altered nor peak velocity increased at any given tension level. Heart rate was held constant throughout to eliminate its effect, since by then it was apparent that heart rate in itself raises myocardial oxygen consumption 1) by increasing frequency of tension development per unit of time, and 2) by increasing contractility through the force-frequency relationship.

Let us now consider these experimental observations as they might apply to the clinical situation following acute coronary occlusion. If in this period influences were at work to augment myocardial tension and/or contractility, and hence local oxygen consumption, presumably they could cause an extension of ischemic injury and necrosis. To compound the problem, the unfavorable energy balance could depress ventricular function at the margins of already infarcted tissue and result in adverse hemodynamic changes, including elevated ventricular pressure and volume and elevated wall tension. This might then cause further functional impairment in tissue, which until then had maintained marginal viability, and lead to a vicious cycle.

Having postulated this sequence of events it behooved us to elucidate the kinds of factors that might operate to augment tension or contractility, and thus oxygen consumption, and to document their effects, if possible. For although pathologic and other evidence strongly suggested that the extent of irreversible tissue damage following occlusion depended on local energy balance, there was no direct proof. Certainly, at that point, we could not have predicted that ischemic injury was still in a reversible stage several hours after coronary occlusion and that one could limit the size of an infarct by applying measures to improve oxygenation at this time.

The indicated experiments required a reliable means of confirming the occurrence and progression of ischemic **injury** following coronary artery ligation, and preferably in the same animal(s), to avert errors introduced by variations in coronary arterial distribution when several animals are compared. With the technique that we employed, together with J. Ross Jr. – open-chest epicardial electrocardiography – measurements could be readily made before and after coronary artery occlusion, including successive occlusions and various interventions, and each dog could serve as its own control. Moreover, animals could be subjected to relatively brief periods of occlusion and the effects immediately seen, since the E C G changes appear within a relatively few minutes after coronary artery ligation and disappear when the ligature is released.

With this technique, tracings can be obtained from 10 to 14 epicardial leads on the anterior surface of the left ventricle; by intent the sites selected include some within the area supplied by the occluded vessel, some in areas immediately adjacent, and some in remote portions of the left ventricle that presumably are adequately perfused. S-T segment elevation of more than 2 mv 15 minutes after artery ligation indicates the presence of ischemic injury; the number of sites with this degree of elevation defines the area of injury.

Initially, reproducibility of the method was established by demonstrating E C G changes at identical sites after repeated occlusions and little variation in the magnitude of S-T segment elevation. From there we went on to test the effect of various interventions, both pharmacologic and hemodynamic, which, in view of their effect on myocardial oxygen balance, might be expected to intensify – or limit – ischemic injury.

One intervention was the infusion of isoproterenol, which was shown in the nonfailing heart to increase both the extent and severity of ischemia as reflected by S-T segment elevation. To identify the specific contribution of drug-induced tachycardia, heart rate was increased by electrical stimulation. Such pacing-induced tachycardia also augmented the S-T segment elevation produced by occlusion, but did so to a lesser extent than when a similar heart rate was attained with isoproterenol, indicating that the effects of the latter were due in part to the positive chronotropic effect and in part to the positive inotropic effect of the beta-adrenergic stimulant. Administration of digitalis, which ordinarily depresses the S-T segment, did so at sites remote from the occluded vessel; however, like isoproterenol and bretylium tosylate, digitalis in the nonfailing heart increased both the number of sites showing S-T segment elevation and the peak elevation attained. In contrast, propranolol and practolol reduced myocardial oxygen demands and ischemic injury by producing beta-adrenergic blockade. S-T segment elevation following occlusion was greatly decreased, as was the number of sites showing these changes.

Before any inference is drawn from these findings it is fair to ask whether epicardial S-T segment elevation might not represent merely an electrocardiographic change of little significance in reference to ischemia. How-

ever, there is convincing evidence that S-T segment elevation does directly reflect myocardial ischemic injury early in its course. For example, in experiments by Wegria et al, epicardial S-T segment elevation varied with the degree of coronary artery constriction. Others have associated elevation of the S-T segment with the magnitude of ischemia-induced alterations in myocardial cellular membrane potentials. Scheuer and Brachfeld found that with reduction of coronary blood flow, there is a close correlation between the development of S-T segment elevation and anaerobic metabolism.

Having granted that S-T segment elevation is a valid indicator of early cellular changes associated with myocardial ischemia, we wished to use this measurement predictively, to anticipate the extent of necrosis that might ensue after ischemic injury. We found that in fact it could be so used. A close correlation was observed between the early ECG tracings following coronary artery ligation and later findings in reference to myocardial enzyme activity — specifically, to

depletion in myocardial creatine phosphokinase (C P K), a quantitative indicator of the extent of cell death after coronary artery occlusion (see Chapter 22 by Sobel). In dogs with induced occlusion, epicardial ECG maps were recorded, as usual, 15 minutes after onset of occlusion, and myocardial C P K activity was determined in multiple corresponding tissue specimens obtained on sacrifice of the animals at 24 hours. Invariably, S-T segment elevation greater than 2 mv was associated with a decrease in myocardial C P K activity; on this basis the early S-T segment changes clearly presaged later cell and tissue damage. (We have since developed a noninvasive technique of precordial ECG mapping that can provide comparable information in closed-chest animals and in man. More will be said of this later.)

Since S-T segment mapping proved so informative in regard to ischemic injury, it was of special interest that the same electrocardiographic changes were seen whether isoproterenol was administered shortly before onset of occlusion (as was done intially)

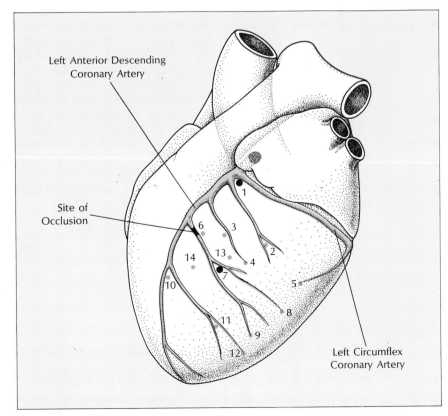
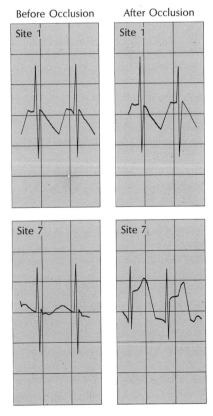

Ischemic injury is revealed in epicardial ECG's obtained shortly after induced occlusion from sites on anterior surface of dog heart, as shown schematically at the left. Whereas ECG from a *site in the area distal to the occluded vessel (lower right) shows marked S-T segment changes, none are seen in tracing from a site that is remote from the injured zone (upper right).*

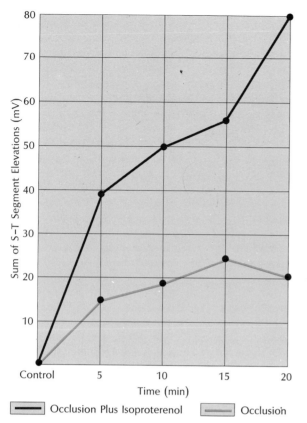

Isoproterenol infusion augmented both severity and extent of myocardial injury, as reflected in sum of S-T segment elevations recorded after coronary occlusion (left). As shown schematically *(right), area of injury after occlusion alone (A) was greatly extended by pretreatment with drug (B); region of heart remote from occlusion site did not show S-T segment changes (C).*

or after occlusion had been maintained for some time. Infusion of isoproterenol begun after three hours significantly increased both the extent and severity of ischemic injury. Propranolol had a protective effect, manifested both by a reduction in s-t segment elevation and less enzyme depletion, as compared with control animals (operated on to induce occlusion but untreated). Clearly, the assumption that only a relatively brief time elapses between ischemic injury and irreversibility of damage could not be true if intervention three hours after onset of occlusion (or even later as will be seen) could have so significant an effect.

To return to the initial round of experiments, the effects on the epicardial ECG map of altering blood pressure were also examined. Arterial pressure was elevated above baseline levels by methoxamine infusion and maintained during occlusion, or it was lowered by acute arterial hemorrhage. Paradoxically, the pressure elevation decreased the extent and severity of ischemic injury; one would have an-

ticipated that the increase would tend to augment myocardial oxygen consumption. In contrast, arterial hypotension, which decreases myocardial oxygen consumption, was associated with increased ischemic injury. Superficially, this might imply that myocardial oxygen balance bears less of a relationship to ischemic injury than other work had indicated. However, the most probable explanation is that (at least under the conditions of these experiments) an increase in coronary perfusion pressure brought about by the rise in arterial pressure caused an increase in collateral blood flow and thus increased oxygen supply to the ischemic myocardium. Thus, in this case the increase in oxygen supply appears to override the effect of an increase in oxygen needs, tilting favorably the oxygen balance to spare myocardial cells. The greater ischemia seen following arterial hypotension might be explainable on the basis of decreased coronary flow.

If these measures designed to reduce myocardial oxygen demand and/or improve coronary perfusion re-

duced the extent of ischemic injury in our animals, how applicable were the observations to patients with acute coronary artery disease? Apart from the usual cautions concerning extrapolation of findings in animals to man, the experimental situation imposed major artificial differences. Except for one occluded vessel, the dogs had normal coronary vasculature. In many patients with coronary artery disease, much of the arterial tree is likely to be diseased long before luminal narrowing is sufficient to precipitate occlusion. But if direct extrapolation of the findings is not warranted neither should their potential clinical relevance be discounted.

Perhaps the complication of hypotension does contribute to extension of ischemic injury in some patients; even in uncomplicated infarction, the presence of severe pain or anxiety, by increasing sympathetic stimulation of the myocardium, could augment heart rate, contractility, and local oxygen consumption. The metabolic cost of positive inotropic agents, such as isoproterenol and digitalis, must be considered as well, since under some conditions there might be deleterious effects resulting in increased ischemia. The same applies to bretylium tosylate, which has been suggested for use in acute infarction on the basis of its antiarrhythmic action as well as its positive inotropic properties.

This is not to suggest that these drugs have no place in treatment of acute infarction, but an understanding of their actions in relation to myocardial ischemia and necrosis can guide us in using them wisely. It must be stressed, however, that the research described thus far was in animals that not only had normal coronary arterial vasculature except for the occluded vessel but were without signs of ventricular dysfunction. Yet some degree of left ventricular failure is almost invariably present in patients with acute myocardial infarction, and conceivably the same drugs might act differently when administered to a patient with an enlarged, failing heart. For example, the presence of ventricular dilatation associated with pump failure — by increasing ventricular radius and thus wall tension — might well modify the effects of positive inotropic agents, which in themselves influence myocardial energy balance.

Certain findings regarding digitalis first prompted the thought that the interrelationship of myocardial energy balance, level of contractility, and ischemic injury probably could not be considered without regard to the heart's underlying hemodynamic status. Prior to the N I H studies referred to earlier, work by others had shown little or no effect of digitalis on myocardial oxygen consumption despite substantial increments in velocity of contraction. Yet, consistently, the two had changed in parallel in our experiments. This seemed puzzling until it was recalled that most previous work had been on enlarged hearts in failure, whereas our group had studied normal hearts. Would this account for the discrepancy? With J. Covell and others, we compared the effects of digitalis in a relatively normal heart and one in acute failure, using the right heart bypass preparation. In both, administration of acetylstrophanthidin increased peak velocity of contraction; however, the directional change in myocardial oxygen consumption depended on whether the heart was normal

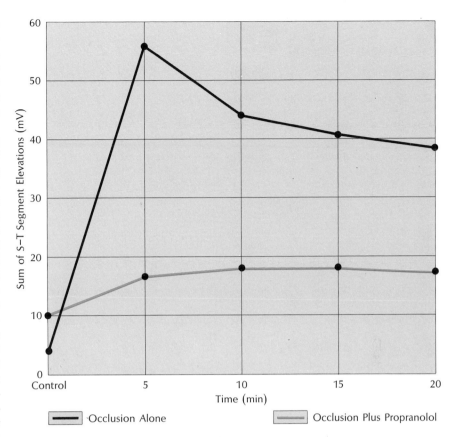

By reducing myocardial oxygen demand, propranolol reduced the extent and severity of ischemic injury in dogs subjected to coronary artery occlusion, as shown in the sum of S-T segment elevations from all recording sites 15 minutes after vessel ligation.

or failing at the time of drug administration. Whereas in the normal heart myocardial oxygen consumption was increased, in the failing heart it was unchanged, or sometimes even reduced. Thus in either a normal or failing heart, the change in myocardial energy balance following an inotropic stimulus appeared to depend on the degree to which one determinant of oxygen consumption — tension developed by the ventricle — is altered in relation to the other determinant — velocity of contraction. In the failing, dilated left ventricle, along with the improvement in contractility effected by a positive inotropic agent, there is a substantial decrease in end-diastolic pressure and volume and therefore in intramyocardial wall tension. The net effect may be little or no change in energy balance, since the influence of increased contractility is offset by the decrease in tension.

These relationships were explored further in dogs with use of epicardial E C G mapping, under experimental conditions paralleling acute infarction complicated by heart failure. Dog

hearts were acutely depressed (with sodium pentothal or propranolol) and the effects of pretreatment with digitalis or isoproterenol compared with those in the absence of heart failure. Whereas in the nonfailing heart, administration of digitalis prior to occlusion had been associated with a twofold increase in S-T segment elevation, in the failing heart S-T segment elevation was reduced by 70%, evidently because the decrease in ventricular wall tension overcame the effect of increased contractility. Infusion of isoproterenol caused at most a modest increase in E C G response in the failing heart, whereas in the normal heart S-T segment elevation was increased by 400%.

It was of interest, too, that while in the normal dog heart an increase in aortic pressure was associated with decreased myocardial injury, in the depressed heart there were small but directionally opposite effects. Evidently in this situation the elevation in aortic pressure caused a marked further increase in left ventricular volume and tension, and these effects predominated over any increase in diastolic coronary pressure and flow that may have taken place.

In more recent related work in our laboratory it was shown that in the presence of decreased coronary blood flow, propranolol improves heart contractility, whereas in the presence of normal flow it has a depressive effect. Conversely, isoproterenol improves contractility in the latter situation but not in the former.

The observations have been discussed at some length to point up the necessity in the clinical situation of tailoring therapy to the functional state of the myocardium. It is as important to know when a given course of action may possibly compound a patient's problems by intensifying myocardial ischemia and necrosis as it is to do what we can to modify the extent of ischemic injury.

These animal experiments have given us much food for thought. For example, in recent studies Epstein and his collaborator at NIH found that in conscious dogs with bradycardia, any increase in the heart rate attained by atropine administration – even from a very low level to within the normal range – was associated with increased S-T segment elevation. On this basis, the usual practice of treating bradycardia associated with acute infarction with atropine may be ill-advised (unless hypotension makes it necessary), except that again these were animal experiments and we do not know what would be the ideal heart rate, or blood pressure, to limit myocardial injury in man.

According to our findings in regard to propranolol, this drug might well be of value clinically in limiting the extent of ischemic injury, although its use would probably not be indicated in the presence of heart failure. A first step in finding out would be a small clinical trial, with suitably selected patients and adequate controls; since in animals pretreatment with propranolol also had a favorable effect, such a study might also include patients with unequivocal symptoms of impending infarction. However, at this stage we are also concerned with devising additional approaches to modifying myocardial injury, both to validate further the concept and to find the means most applicable for use in man.

In this context we have been exploring other modalities that might favorably affect energy balance of the heart, for example mechanical counterpulsation. As is known, counterpulsation has emerged as an important form of therapy for cardiogenic shock complicating acute myocardial infarction (see Chapter 32, "Assisted Circulation: A Progress Report," by Soroff and Birtwell, and Chapter 33 by Mundth et al). The possibility of counterpulsation influencing the infarction process early in its evolution – before the amount of myocardium destroyed is sufficient to precipitate shock – was suggested by a consideration of its physiologic effects in relation to myocardial energy balance. In theory, counterpulsation might bring about improvement in two ways: Withdrawal of blood from the aorta during ventricular systole reduces aortic systolic pressure and impedance to left ventricular emptying; it thus reduces ventricular wall tension. Return of blood during diastole, and the resultant elevation of aortic diastolic pressure, increases coronary perfusion pressure and flow, thus improving myocardial blood supply.

To define the changes in ischemic injury under controlled conditions we again utilized the ECG mapping tech-

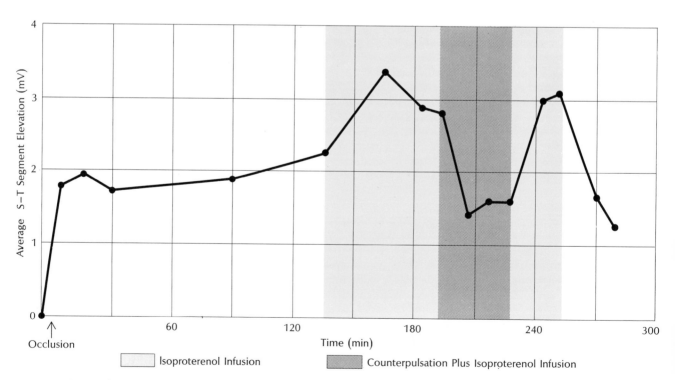

Counterpulsation begun after three hours of maintained occlusion consistently reduced area of injury, as shown by decrease in average S-T segment elevation; moreover, extension of injury produced by isoproterenol could be offset by counterpulsation.

The response of one treated dog (above) suggests a possible clinical combination in suitable infarction cases: isoproterenol to elevate cardiac output plus counterpulsation to counteract the increase in myocardial oxygen consumption isoproterenol induces.

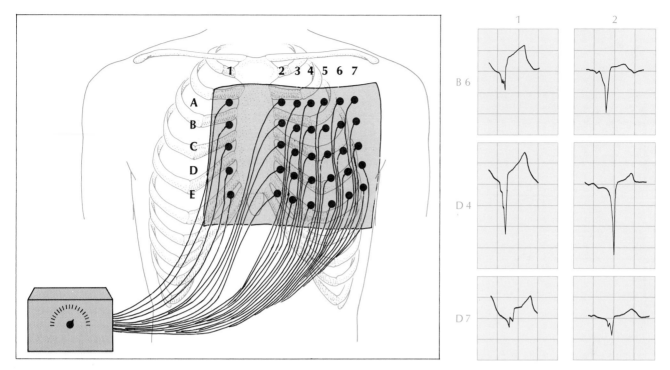

Precordial ECG mapping technique employing a 35-lead electrode blanket such as the one schematized at left is proving useful in following the course of patients hospitalized after onset of infarction. Tracings at right are of three selected leads from the 35-lead ECG recorded from the precordium of a 50-year-old male patient with acute myocardial infarction. The elevation of S-T segments (column 1) was decreased abruptly following propranolol administration (column 2).

nique. Counterpulsation was begun either shortly before an occlusive episode or after occlusion had been maintained for up to three hours. The area of injury was consistently reduced in both circumstances, as shown by reduction in S-T segment elevation. It is worth noting that these experiments were in normotensive dogs, implying that this technique has potential applicability for altering the early course of uncomplicated infarction as well as in controlling cardiogenic shock. As with propranolol, there is also the possibility of employing counterpulsation as an approach to impending infarction, since dogs pretreated by this means showed reduced ischemic injury.

In one series of counterpulsation experiments, isoproterenol was administered two hours after onset of occlusion to intensify ischemic injury, and pumping was begun an hour later. It was intriguing to note that the increase in injury associated with isoproterenol administration could be offset by concurrent counterpulsation. Thus, this therapeutic combination could have a place in management of certain patients; as isoproterenol ele-

vated cardiac output, the disadvantage accruing from increased myocardial oxygen consumption might be overcome with counterpulsation. True, in the experiments described, counterpulsation was accomplished by intra-aortic balloon pumping, necessitating an invasive procedure that makes it inappropriate in managing uncomplicated infarction. But external counterpulsation is also available (see Chapter 32 by Soroff and Birtwell) and we are now considering its potential usefulness in this context.

For human use, a noninvasive technique to monitor myocardial damage is obviously needed. Consequently, a precordial E C G mapping technique has been developed and tested in closed-chest dogs to assess infarct size. Results proved comparable to those observed when open E C G epicardial mapping was employed.

Precordial E C G mapping was used to study the natural course of E C G changes in patients hospitalized following onset of infarction. E C G maps were obtained within 24 hours of admission and again the following day. In uncomplicated cases, average S-T segment elevation declined within

this interval by 29%; in some patients, S-T elevation increased, presumably as a consequence of arterial hypotension or after recurrence of ischemic chest pain.

On the other hand, in a small number of patients being treated for cardiogenic shock with intra-aortic counterpulsation, recordings obtained with a 35-lead precordial "electrode blanket" showed decreased S-T segment elevation, a prompt increase when pumping was interrupted for a brief period, and another decline as soon as pumping was resumed. Also, both propranolol and hyaluronidase (see below) strikingly decreased myocardial injury. A systematic examination of the effects of both hemodynamic changes and drug administration in both complicated and uncomplicated cases is currently in progress. When the possibility of intervening to modify the extent of myocardial injury becomes more of a reality it would seem relatively simple to assess the effect of a given intervention by this means; a limitation is that only infarcts affecting the anteroseptal, anterior, and lateral walls can be accurately assessed in this way.

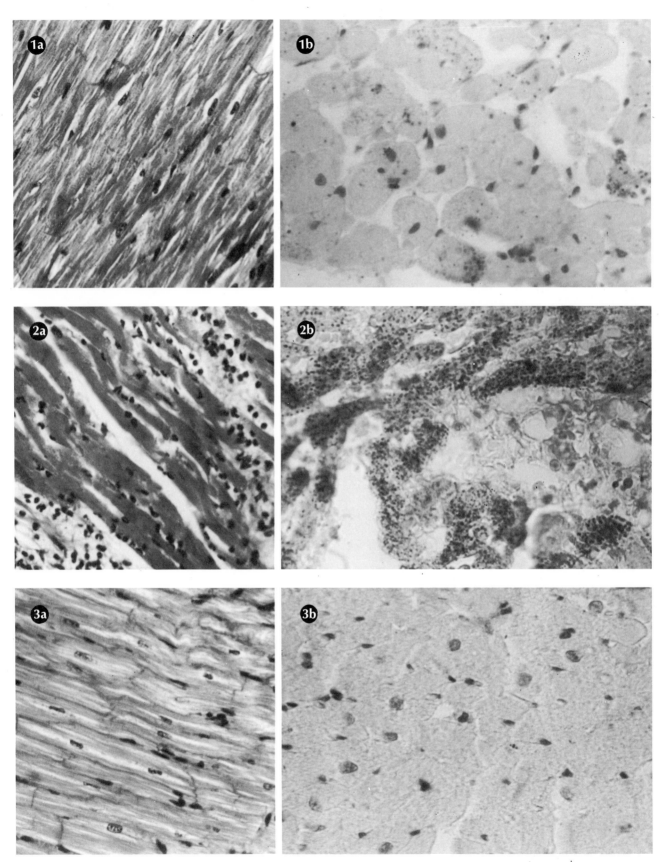

Histologic effects of GIK solution on myocardial ischemic injury are demonstrated in experimental animals. In light micrographs on this page, at 24 hours after artery ligation, tissue remote from occlusion site is essentially normal on H & E or oil red O staining (1a, 1b); fragmentation of myocardial fibers and other signs of necrosis expected on the basis of early ECG changes are evident in tissue served by occluded vessel (2a) and fat granules can be seen (2b). In contrast, in other animals necrotic changes are averted by treatment with GIK solution 30 minutes after onset of occlusion (3a, 3b). Parallel EM's are shown opposite.

Thus far we have considered possible means of modifying ischemic injury in relation to myocardial oxygen balance. But when myocardial oxygen supply is impaired by ischemic injury, might extension of ischemia and necrosis be retarded by facilitating anaerobic metabolism? Under normal conditions, of course, the heart derives essentially all of its energy from oxidation of various substrates in the Krebs cycle, but it is well known that in the absence of sufficient oxygen it can shift for short periods to the anaerobic, or glycolytic, metabolic pathway. If infarct size depends on the local balance between energy production and supply, perhaps cellular integrity could be preserved by supplying additional glucose to myocardial cells to enhance anaerobic glycolysis.

Observations by a number of investigators provided a rationale for believing that this might be an effective approach. For example, in studying muscle glucose uptake (in the isolated perfused rat heart), Morgan and coworkers found that under aerobic conditions it was negligible if the perfusate contained glucose in physiologic concentration. However, when the medium was glucose-enriched, uptake increased in parallel with increasing glucose concentration of the perfusate. With addition of insulin, glucose uptake at low perfusate concentrations also increased, an effect attributed to accelerated transport by the hormone. Under anoxic conditions the effect of insulin was magnified and glucose uptake became maximal over the entire range of perfusate concentrations used.

In other studies, Weissler et al examined electrical and mechanical heart performance in an anoxic rat-heart preparation after addition of glucose to the perfusion medium; there was significant improvement in both parameters. And whereas cell ultrastructure as revealed by electron microscopy had been markedly disrupted in the anoxic heart, when the medium was glucose-enriched the abnormalities disappeared. Moreover, Scheuer et al have shown that the glycogen content of the myocardial cell closely parallels its capacity to withstand anoxia.

Since the normally oxygenated heart derives a substantial fraction of its energy from oxidation of free fatty

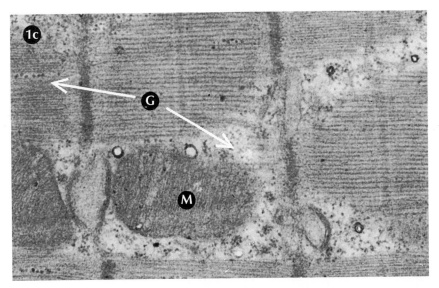

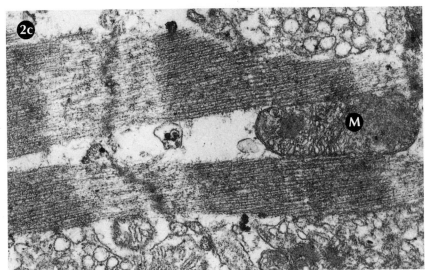

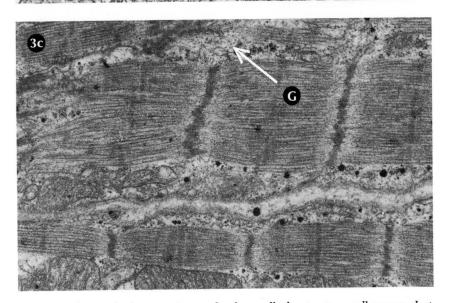

In untreated animal, electron micrographs show cell ultrastructure well preserved at uninjured site (1c), while characteristic ultrastructural signs of necrosis appear in site that showed S-T segment elevation (2c), such as loss of glycogen granules (G) and swelling of mitochondria (M). In animal treated with GIK solution (3c), site that showed S-T segment elevation is relatively free of necrotic changes 24 hours later.

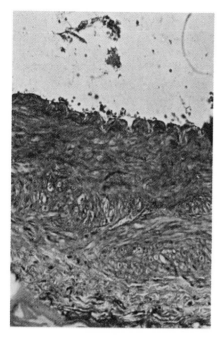 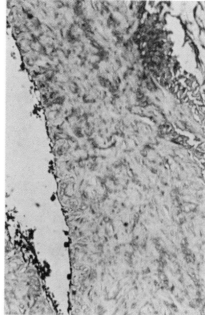

Positively stained material specific for hyaluronic acid is abundant in specimen from untreated animal (left) but much less in specimen from animal treated with hyaluronidase (right), indicating that enzyme penetrates infarct center. Finding is consistent with the view that by depolymerizing hyaluronic acid, hyaluronidase improves transport of energy-producing nutrients to myocardial cells.

acids, it is interesting to compare myocardial uptake of both substrates – free fatty acids and glucose – following experimentally produced infarction. When Owen and coworkers did so, they found that uptake of glucose by the ischemic zone (defined by epicardial E C G mapping) increased three- to fourfold as compared with that of free fatty acids; the investigators attributed this to a shift to anaerobic glycolysis in the ischemic zone.

We accordingly undertook a study in which a glucose-insulin-potassium (G I K) infusion (potassium added to avoid hypokalemia associated with accelerated glucose transport) was given to dogs 30 minutes following acute coronary artery occlusion. As before, epicardial E C G's were recorded 15 minutes after coronary artery ligation and periodically thereafter, and 24 hours later transmural tissue specimens were obtained from the same sites for determining myocardial C P K levels. However, something new was added this time: histologic analysis of tissue sections to demonstrate the extent of cell damage and staining for glycogen depletion, since the latter is one of the earliest histologic signs of myocardial necrosis. In addition, ultra-

structural changes at 24 hours were recorded by electron microscopy.

By all criteria, the degree of myocardial damage was strikingly reduced by the G I K infusion. Many sites that, on the basis of early S-T segment changes, would have been expected to show marked enzyme depletion, instead maintained normal enzyme levels. In the same specimens, expected histologic changes were absent and glycogen depletion was similarly reduced. The appearance of fat granules in myocardial fibers, a later sign of cellular injury, was also less evident in treated animals.

The histologic findings have special relevance, since, classically, the diagnosis of acute infarction is based on histologic rather than biochemical changes. In treated vs untreated animals, electron microscopy documented a decreased frequency of such severe ultrastructural changes as swelling of the mitochondria, myofibrillar stretching, and rupture of the sarcolemma, although prior to treatment both groups had shown comparable epicardial E C G changes. In other experiments, a G I K infusion and propanolol were given starting three hours after onset of occlusion. A protective effect was demonstrated both by enzymatic

and by histologic analysis of involved tissue, though it was less than when treatment was begun sooner.

The hyperosmolar effect of G I K infusion has been proposed to account at least in part for its action. While the protective effect of hyperosmolar solutions in ischemic tissues has been well demonstrated by Powell, Leaf, and their associates, to us it seems likely that some of the additional glucose provided to myocardial tissue does enter into glycolysis, or is stored as glycogen for future use. Of course regardless of *how* G I K infusion may act, *whether* it can act will depend on glucose reaching ischemic tissue in adequate amounts. It was of interest that in the animal experiments, areas of myocardium protected by the infusion (i.e., exhibiting little or no histologic damage) were generally at the periphery of zones of tissue showing ischemic injury. Although oxygenation was reduced enough to threaten viability, presumably these cells were perfused sufficiently by patent collateral vessels to allow exposure to the G I K solution.

As is probably known, clinical use of G I K therapy in acute infarction was introduced some years ago both on this continent and abroad, and while some benefit was reported, in most cases the outcome was inconclusive. Little should be inferred from that experience, however, since there was often no record of how soon treatment was begun following onset of symptoms, and varying concentrations of glucose, insulin, and potassium were employed. Moreover, results were evaluated primarily on the basis of mortality, which is really only one parameter to be considered in evaluating the effect of any intervention on clinical prognosis in acute myocardial infarction.

No one would question that improving the chance of survival is crucially important, but the potential gain from intervention early in the course of infarction may be even greater than that. Taking a longer view, since prognosis is so closely tied to the total amount of viable myocardium remaining, preservation of as much myocardial tissue as possible is of utmost importance. Should another occlusive episode occur some time later, as often happens, any further reduction in myocardial tissue will be better tolerated, and again sufficient viable myocardium may remain to permit survival.

Thus far we have not tried G I K infusion clinically, though observations in animals suggest that it may be well worth trying (perhaps in combination with beta-adrenergic blockade) in patients without concomitant heart failure.

In theory, the goal of modifying myocardial necrosis could be approached in still another way – by facilitating delivery of energy substrates to ischemic cells. In this connection, we decided to examine the effects of hyaluronidase, since this agent is known to increase diffusion of a variety of substances through interstitial spaces. Perhaps with the shift from aerobic to anaerobic metabolism as myocardial ischemia advances, cellular glucose uptake and anaerobic glycolysis could thus be enhanced. To evaluate the effects of hyaluronidase in dogs with coronary artery occlusion, we utilized the epicardial E C G mapping technique and analysis of tissue from the same sites for enzymatic and histologic changes. Among animals given hyaluronidase 30 minutes after coronary artery ligation, there was a protective effect comparable to that seen following G I K infusion – a one third reduction in the extent and severity of ischemic damage (see photos opposite).

Administration of hyaluronidase may, in fact, offer several potential advantages over other approaches: It requires no special equipment (as does counterpulsation); it does not depress cardiac contractility (as does propranolol); in itself it does not alter the s-t segment (as does G I K). In addition, wide clinical usage of hyaluronidase has established its lack of toxicity.

On this basis, hyaluronidase was recently employed in a pilot clinical study at our hospital, involving 22 unselected patients with acute myocardial infarction (12 treated, 10 controls). A single dose (500 mg/kg) was given on admission; results were assessed by comparing the initial precordial E C G map with one obtained eight hours later. During this period the s-t segment elevation decreased significantly more rapidly in treated patients. These results are encourag-

ing, and further clinical study is planned.

Naturally we should like to know more about how hyaluronidase exerts its effect. In hearts with coronary occlusion, tissue sections were examined by Alcian green staining, which detects the presence of hyaluronic acid. Considerable Alcian-positive material was seen in specimens obtained from untreated animals and relatively little in hyaluronidase-treated animals.

Thus we know that hyaluronidase does penetrate into the center of an infarct. But while it seems likely that hyaluronidase acts by improving transport of energy-producing nutrients from the bloodstream to myocardial cells, there is no proof that this is the case.

There are even fewer clues as to the mode of action of yet another agent also being tested experimentally. In recent animal studies in our

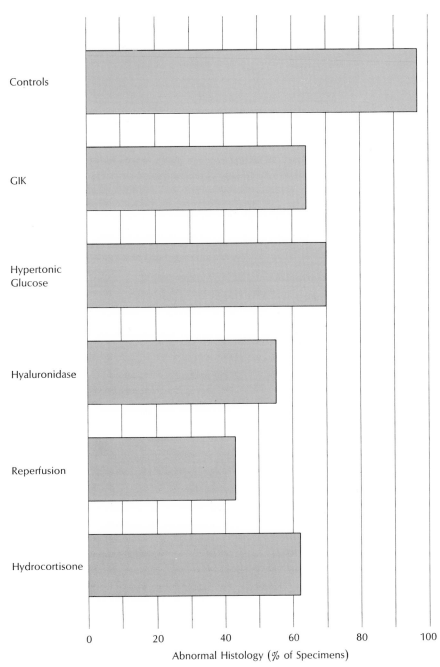

Graph shows percentage of myocardial specimens having S-T segment elevation 15 minutes following occlusion that showed necrosis 24 hours later. In the control group most specimens (97%) were necrotic. In animals treated by a variety of interventions a substantial percentage of the myocardium was spared.

laboratory, hydrocortisone (50 mg/kg) effectively modified infarct size to a degree comparable to that seen with use of hyaluronidase or G I K infusion. Earlier experimental and clinical work by others had yielded conflicting reports concerning the potential usefulness of hydrocortisone in treating acute infarction, but the availability of the E C G mapping technique made it feasible to reopen the question. Like the other interventions described, hydrocortisone evidently could protect substantial portions of ischemic myocardium from undergoing necrosis. In our study no attempt was made to elucidate the mechanism of action of hydrocortisone, but it is not difficult to suggest explanations. For one, it is known that lysosomes within myocardial cells are likely to be disrupted by acidotic conditions produced by hypoxia, and recent work suggests that release of acid hydrolases may hasten irreversible cell damage. Thus steroids might protect the myocardium by their stabilizing effect on lysosomal membranes, decreasing cellular autolysis.

It must be noted that in these experiments very large doses of hydrocortisone were employed, and there is also no information on how administration of hydrocortisone early in the course of infarction might affect the healing process. However, an important observation confirmed in this study is that some portion of myocardium can be spared from necrosis by intervention as late as six hours after onset of coronary artery occlusion— or within the time period that many patients are admitted to a hospital coronary care unit and their condition diagnosed.

It stands to reason that no form of medical intervention is likely to be as effective in preserving myocardial cells as the restoration of blood flow to the obstructed vessel. This is the rationale, of course, behind the use of surgery in management of acute infarction. In order to study this question experimentally, coronary artery occlusion was induced in dogs and epicardial electrocardiographic maps were obtained at fifteen minutes and again on reperfusion (the ligature was released after three hours). Without doubt, reperfusion had a greater impact than any of the medical interventions discussed. More than half (57%) of sites initially showing s-t segment elevation were normal histo-logically 24 hours later; myocardial C P K values followed a similar pattern, and there was objective evidence of improved left ventricular function. When the extent of myocardial damage was assessed following sacrifice of the animals a week later, little depletion of myocardial C P K or tissue necrosis was observed in the treated (reperfused) animals, but in the controls myocardial C P K values were profoundly decreased and extensive cell destruction was documented histologically.

While these findings provide experimental documentation of the value of restoring the myocardial blood supply, medical rather than surgical intervention to salvage myocardium might well be preferable in many cases. Should the concept of such medical intervention be further validated, as we hope it will be, the requisite clinical trials would necessarily involve a number of institutions in a broadly based cooperative trial. The major effort and costs involved would surely be worthwhile if they offered the prospect of significantly improving both the immediate and long-term prognosis for patients with acute myocardial infarction.

Revascularizing the Myocardium: The Saphenous Vein Bypass

DONALD B. EFFLER *and* WILLIAM C. SHELDON
Cleveland Clinic

The Case

A 62-year-old retired executive had been suffering from chest pain on exertion and also at rest. His pain, which was not associated with shortness of breath, was relieved promptly by nitroglycerine. He was admitted for evaluation at the Cleveland Clinic in September 1970.

History

The patient had first experienced substantial precordial pain in 1964 when climbing two flights of stairs to his office. The pain, which did not radiate, was relieved by rest and did not recur until early in 1969 when he began having attacks of pain while walking short distances, sometimes on waking or at rest. In the spring of 1970, when the chest pain was occurring several times each night, he retired from his job. Despite a comprehensive medical regimen the attacks continued to become more frequent and severe.

The patient had been diabetic for 20 years; the disease was controlled and he reported no sequelae. He also gave a history of alcoholism, for which he had been treated, and he had not drunk since November 1969. In 1968, a lesion on his tongue had been diagnosed as malignant and treated by surgery and radiation.

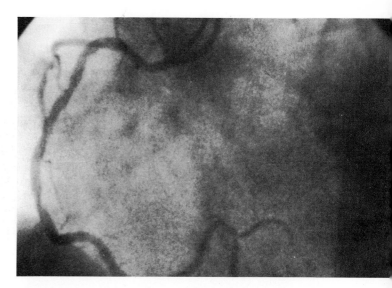

Patient's right coronary artery is demonstrated in left anterior oblique view (above), showing diffuse involvement with mild lumen irregularities. Left coronary artery is also shown (below). Arrows indicate locations of segmental constrictions in proximal anterior descending and circumflex branches.

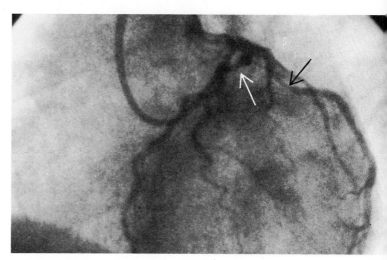

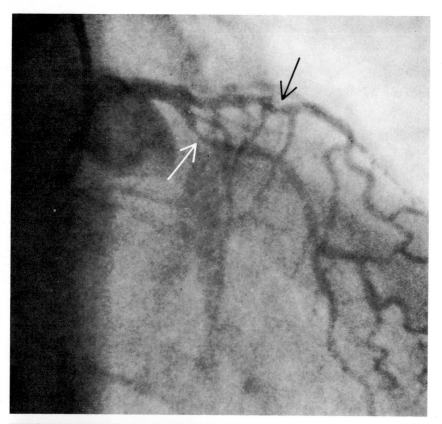

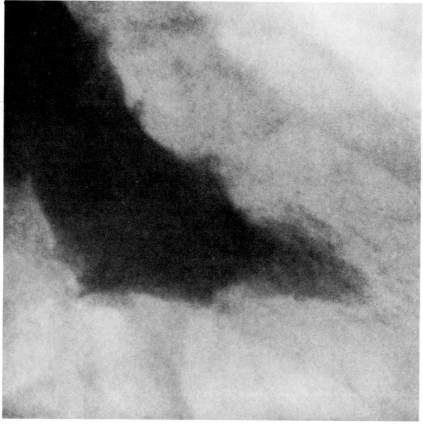

Left coronary artery is shown in right anterior oblique view (top). Segmental stenoses are seen in proximal circumflex and anterior descending branches (arrows). Frame from left ventriculogram (bottom), exposed during systole, shows normal end-systolic volume. Motion study demonstrated full and symmetrical excursions of left ventricular contraction, excluding significant damage to left ventricular myocardium.

Physical Examination

The patient was a well-formed man, somewhat ruddy in complexion and in no distress. He was 68½ inches in height and weighed 151 pounds. The blood pressure was 170/80 mm Hg and the pulse regular at 78 beats per minute. Auscultation disclosed no cardiac murmurs or arrhythmias; bruits were heard over the left carotid and right femoral arteries. A healed scar was seen in the middle of the tongue on the dorsal surface. There was no palpable adenopathy.

Investigations

An SMA-12 survey was normal. A chest x-ray was within normal limits; electrocardiographic studies were unremarkable. His serum cholesterol level was 160 mg%. The triglyceride level was 130 mg%. A serum lipoprotein electrophoresis showed a slight increase in the beta lipoprotein fraction (see Chapter 19, "Genetic Aspects of Hyperlipidemia in Coronary Heart Disease," by Goldstein). Other routine hematologic studies were normal.

Left heart catheterization was performed via the right brachial artery, and a series of coronary arteriograms were made in the left and right anterior oblique projections. These showed the proximal left circumflex coronary artery to be narrowed 75% to 80%. Mild occlusive changes compromised the proximal and middle segments of the large posterolateral circumflex branch. The anterior descending left coronary artery was narrowed 65% to 75% near the junction of the proximal and middle thirds. The dominant right coronary artery showed mild, diffuse lumen irregularities in the proximal and middle segments. No intercoronary collateral channels were seen. A left ventriculogram revealed normal contractility of the left ventricle; there were no valve defects or ventricular aneurysms. The pressure in the left ventricle was 165/18 mm Hg, and in the aorta, 165/85 mm Hg. These procedures were well tolerated by the patient.

Surgery to improve the myocardial blood supply was recommended and carried out as shown on the following pages.

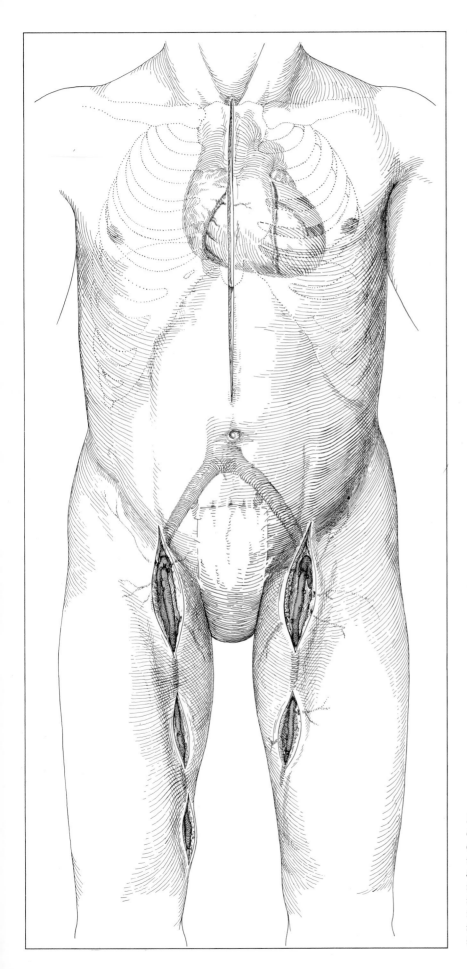

Exposure of the heart will be made through a sternal splitting incision, as shown in drawing. This step is accompanied by the mobilization of the saphenous veins so that segment (tied between ligatures) may be taken for the grafts. First, however, tributaries must be located and tied. Interruption of these superficial veins does not lead to complications, since adequate drainage is provided by the deep saphenous vessels.

345

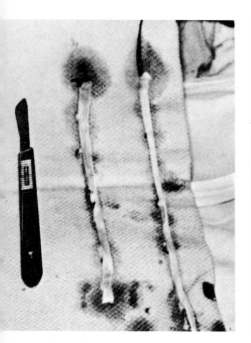
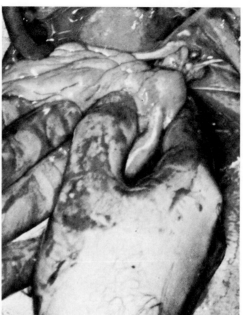
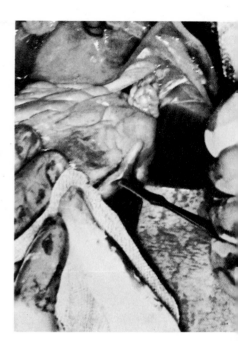

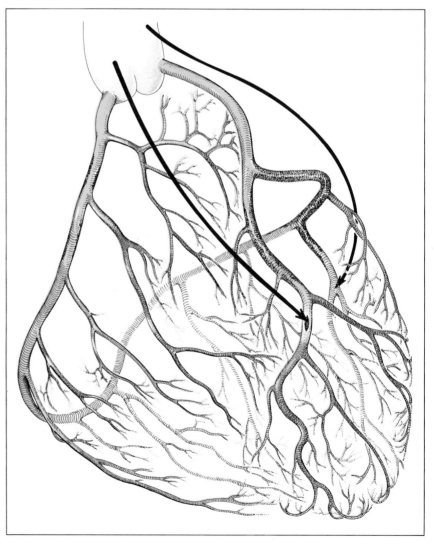

With the patient under general anesthesia and in the supine position, the saphenous veins have been taken from both groins and their tributaries "stick tied" (as shown in the photograph at left above).

After the heart has been exposed, opening of the pericardium, which is normal in appearance, discloses no adhesions nor any scars suggesting previous myocardial infarction. The ventricles appear to be normal in size. After the patient is heparinized, routine cannulations are made, the arterial line being placed high in the ascending aorta. The heart is then put on total bypass and a still field obtained by electrically induced ventricular fibrillation. As the revascularization procedure gets under way, the heart is elevated manually (center photo above), and inspection and palpation reveal an excellent descending branch of the circumflex artery, which is unusually large in this patient. It is incised and the arteriotomy extended for 1.5 cm (photo at upper right), revealing a good proximal lumen that admits a #8 dilator; distal end admits large lacrymal probe.

The drawing at right shows the locations of the severe stenoses in the circumflex and anterior descending branches of the left coronary artery; there is also moderate atherosclerosis of the right coronary artery. The arrows indicate the routes to be taken in creating the two vein graft bypasses that are required for revascularization of the left ventricle.

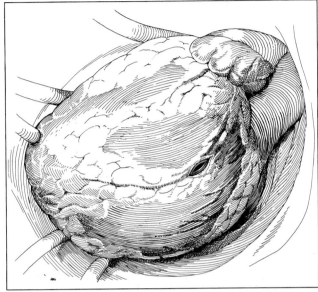

A spurt of blood (photo at left) indicates backflow is adequate in the distal segment of the arteriotomized circumflex vessel. A vein graft will therefore provide both antegrade and retrograde flow when the bypass has been constructed. As seen in the drawing below, the heart is elevated manually and kept rotated slightly to the right throughout the procedure on the circumflex branch to expose the distal portion of the vessel. The vent in the apex of the left ventricle was placed prior to inducing fibrillation.

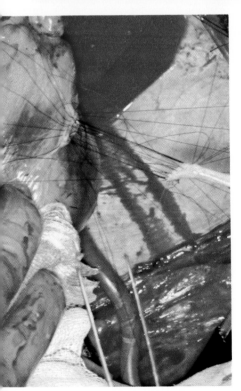

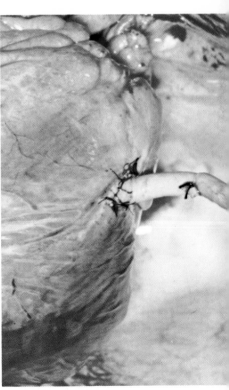

Lubricated 6-0 interrupted silk arterial sutures are placed at margins of the arteriotomy in preparation for anastomosis (left). A reversed length of vein, cut on the oblique, is now sutured in place (center), and the anastomosis completed (right). For this, total anoxic arrest is obtained by clamping the aorta. When clamp is removed, heartbeat spontaneously returns; on occasion, ventricular fibrillation ensues and DC defibrillation is required. The vein graft shows good retrograde filling.

*To complete the first bypass the heart is put back in normal posi-
tion and a partial occluding clamp placed on the ascending aorta,
in which an arteriotomy is made to receive the proximal end of
the vein graft (photo at right). As shown in the drawing of the
cannulated heart (below), this incision is made about 2.5 cm below the cannula and extends for about 1 cm to permit the oblique
section of saphenous vein to be approximated to the aortotomy.*

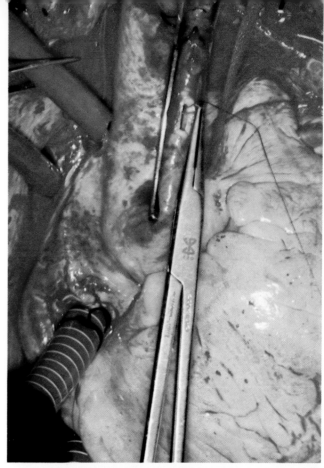

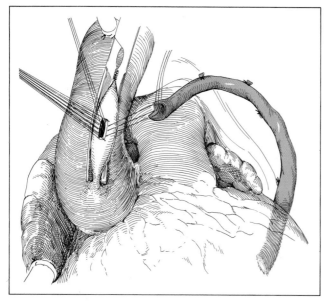

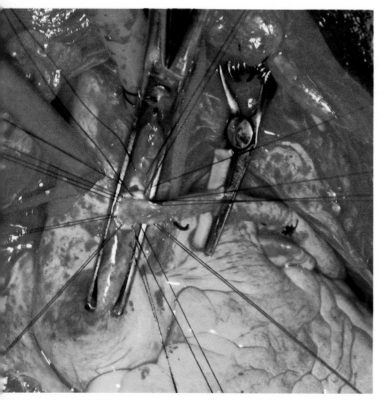

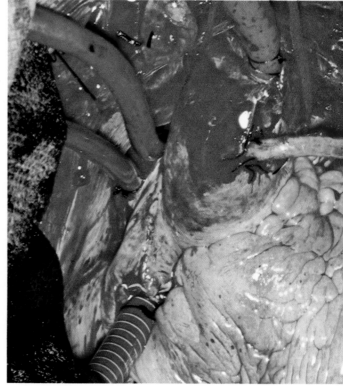

*Sutures have been placed in the aortotomy and are now being
pulled in to secure the proximal anastomosis (left). If cardiac output is adequate, extracorporeal circulation may be discontinued*
*at this stage; the partially occluding aortic clamp does not impair
normal cardiac function. At the completion of the procedure the
vein graft looks very promising (right).*

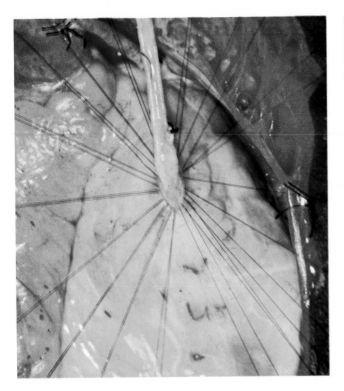

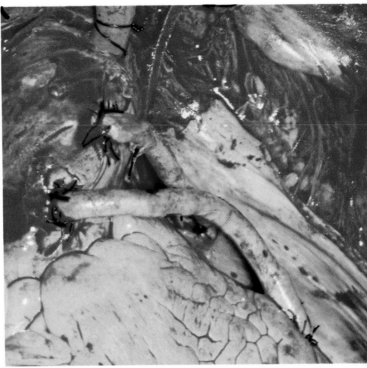

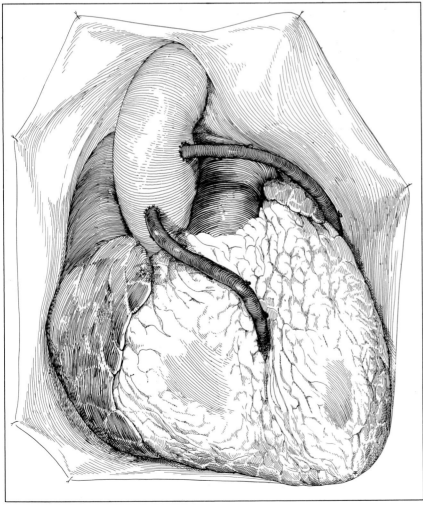

Extracorporeal circulation and ventricular fibrillation have been reestablished for the second procedure, the aorta-to-anterior-descending-artery vein graft. The artery was opened at the level of the first diagonal branch, where luminal caliber was found to be adequate (approximately 4 mm in diameter). A vein graft, cut on the oblique, is being anastomosed oblique-to-side (photo at left above); it filled well when the aortic clamp was removed. The heartbeat returned spontaneously as soon as the period of anoxic arrest was terminated.

A partial occluding clamp was placed on the ascending aorta below the first anastomosis and the proximal anastomosis completed. As shown at right above, the clamp has been removed and the vein graft fills very well. The completed revascularization procedure is shown in the drawing. Now, extracorporeal circulation can be withdrawn and the cannulas removed. The patient was given protamine to neutralize the heparin effect and the incisions closed in routine fashion. His vital signs were very stable at end of operation and he was transferred to the Intensive Care Unit.

349

The Case in Context

This case history illustrates the value of selective coronary arteriography both in diagnosis and selection of the patient for revascularization surgery. Although the patient's symptoms were severe, he was far from being incapacitated by his disease and had not sustained previous myocardial damage.

Coronary arteriography had clearly established the degree and extent of atherosclerotic involvement in this particular patient and, in our judgment, his needs would be best served by bypass vein grafts to the anterior descending and circumflex branches of the left coronary artery. The dangers of a serious myocardial perfusion deficit would be overcome by the double vein graft procedure. The gradual acceleration of angina pectoris during the preceding six years in spite of an adequate medical regimen suggested that little would be gained by

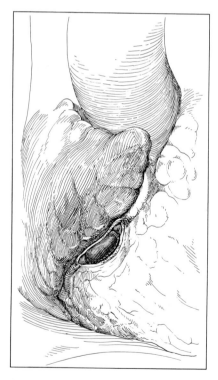

Expanding the lumen of an obstructed coronary vessel by "roofing" it with a patch of pericardial tissue was one method of myocardial revascularization that preceded the saphenous vein graft bypass. Lasting benefit was limited to the relatively few patients with "ideal" lesions.

alteration in his medical program. The relatively low risk of surgical treatment and the likelihood that one or both grafts would remain patent and augment his deficient coronary circulation were considered strong arguments for operative intervention.

Had this patient come under our care a few years earlier, he would have been considered for indirect revascularization surgery using the internal mammary arteries for single or double implant procedures. At that time, direct revascularization with the left coronary artery carried a prohibitive mortality rate and was only recommended for left main trunk lesions. Whereas mammary implantation might have been beneficial, the fact remains that he would have received no immediate benefit from surgery since months would be required before the implanted artery could develop collaterals and augment the deficient coronary circulation. Yet our experience with the bypass vein graft procedure, which spanned five years, clearly showed that the deficit in myocardial perfusion could be relieved by this technique. Had his saphenous veins been unsuited for graft purposes because of varicosities or previous surgery, the same might be achieved by utilizing direct internal mammary artery-coronary artery anastomosis.

The presence of carotid and femoral bruits did not disqualify the patient for surgical consideration as these were unassociated with symptoms. Generally speaking, the presence of a peripheral vascular lesion has little bearing on the selection of treatment for myocardial ischemia unless it is associated with impaired renal function, transient episodes of cerebral ischemia, or other conditions that might affect the outcome of surgery.

Neither did his mild diabetes disqualify the patient for surgery. The well-known association between diabetes and atherosclerosis may be clinically significant, particularly in younger patients, but a controlled diabetic state can be well tolerated by the surgical patient who suffers from myocardial ischemia.

In theory, any procedure that removes or circumvents a coronary ob-

struction should improve a deficient myocardial circulation. Our first efforts along this line were in 1962 with coronary endarterectomy. Unfortunately, the mortality rate was prohibitive and the procedure was soon abandoned in favor of "patch graft" reconstruction of a segmental occlusion, usually in a dominant right coronary artery. Patch graft reconstruction of a coronary artery carried less immediate hazard than endarterectomy, but this method was also found to have severe limitations. The poor results of these earlier direct coronary procedures can be explained, to a large degree, by the disease process itself. The atherosclerotic plaque, whether partially removed or left in place, creates undue turbulence and frequently accelerates thrombosis; this is most likely to occur in patients with an inflammatory type of coronary atherosclerosis. It is immediately apparent that the patch graft procedure is suited to short and incomplete segmental occlusions. Its clinical application is restricted, therefore, since coronary atherosclerosis is usually diffuse and tends to produce obstructions that may be both lengthy and multiple. Nevertheless, many patients did benefit from these surgically primitive procedures.

The first major breakthrough in direct revascularization surgery came in May 1967. A routine patch graft to the right coronary artery had been scheduled by our associate, Dr. René Favaloro, but at operation the diseased coronary artery was unsuited for that procedure. Therefore, Favaloro removed the diseased segment and replaced it with a segment of the patient's saphenous vein, reestablishing continuity with two end-to-end anastomoses. This procedure had been used in treating popliteal artery obstructions and proved to be quite simple. We hadn't used the interposed vein graft before largely because we feared an arterialized vein graft would be doomed to thrombosis, calcification, aneurysm formation, or intimal proliferation when it was exposed to an arterial flow.

Favaloro's introduction of the interposed saphenous vein graft for segmental occlusions of the dominant right coronary artery offered a new dimension to revascularization surgery. The operation was comparatively easily performed and provided "instant revascularization." However, the approach had one serious drawback: it was limited to comparatively short segments of obstruction well below the coronary ostia and proximal to the final arterial run-off. Since coronary occlusions are frequently found in high proximal locations, the interposed vein graft was, ironically, least useful where it was most needed. Direct surgery upon ostial lesions is notoriously hazardous and the long-term results most disappointing.

The obvious solution was soon provided by the saphenous vein bypass technique, which provides a conduit from the ascending aorta to the more distal element of the involved major coronary artery. Like the interposed vein graft, a bypass graft also produces "instant revascularization," but the range of application is obviously much greater. Most importantly, it was applicable to the anterior descending and to the circumflex branches of the left coronary artery. The bypass vein grafts were adopted as procedures of choice in October 1967.

By February 1969, the Cleveland Clinic team had performed vein graft procedures in 224 patients; the results were most encouraging when compared to the earlier endarterectomy and patch graft procedures. As would be expected, the majority of these were performed for right coronary artery disease. The first 207 operations were attended by 8 hospital deaths. By current standards, this would be high mortality; in 1969 it represented considerable improvement in direct revascularization surgery.

At this writing, the vein graft techniques have been employed for almost six years by the Cleveland Clinic team. Approximately 4,000 patients have undergone this form of direct revascularization surgery. On the basis of our experience between 1971 and 1973 it is apparent that the expected hospital mortality for all patients undergoing vein graft techniques will be between 1% and 2%. Follow-up studies in over 1,000 patients indicate that patency in primary vein grafts is 85% or greater. More important, there seems to be little evidence to suggest that patent vein grafts tend to deteriorate with the passage of time; on the contrary, vein graft thrombosis, when it does occur, seems to take place within a few weeks or months

after operation. The most important data has to do with the prognosis of the patient who undergoes successful vein graft bypass surgery. Evaluation of these 1,000 patients indicates that the prognosis for patients with critical two and three vessel disease is appreciably better with bypass vein grafts than when they are treated medically.

It seems appropriate to mention here a newer form of revascularization surgery using anastamosis of the internal mammary artery to the coronary artery. Green and his associates, who popularized this technique in the U.S., reported an impressive surgical record from the standpoint of hospital mortality and postoperative patency of the mammary-coronary anastomoses. In the past two years, Loop and Cheanvechai have operated on over 500 patients in the Cleveland Clinic Hospital using various modifications of the mammary-coronary anastomotic procedures. The initial hospital mortality rates compare favorably with the single and double vein graft procedures and the measurable flow rates are very impressive, but most exciting

is the patency rate of more than 95%.

Criteria for Patient Selection

The "ideal" candidate for saphenous vein graft operations will have severe obstruction (more than 75%) of one, two, or more coronary vessels and a myocardium that is either undamaged or within the range of salvage.

This ideal candidate is of course not identified until he has been studied by coronary cinearteriography. Therefore, the primary question is: Who should by studied by this technique? Opinion on this question has been divided between those who would perform coronary arteriography on a majority of patients, if not all, with suspected coronary atherosclerosis and those who would restrict the investigation to atypical cases or patients with "end stage" disease refractory to medical treatment. An argument for mass coronary arteriography can be made on the theoretical grounds that the natural history of coronary occlusive disease, while notoriously unpredictable, usually includes a period

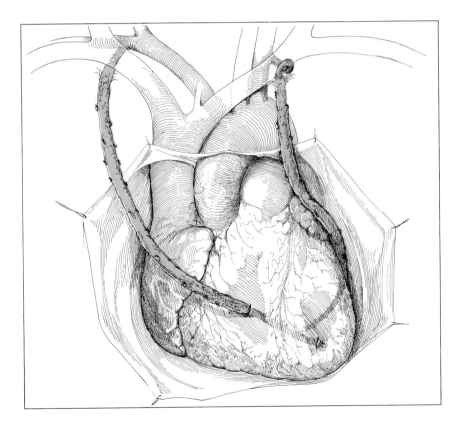

The internal mammary artery implant (Vineberg procedure) is an older method of myocardial revascularization that is still well suited to patients in whom multiple distal obstructions rule out the use of a bypass graft. Two implants, as shown here, may be used; or in some cases an implant may be combined with a bypass procedure.

during which surgery might help.

There are, however, only about 200 medical centers in the U.S. that have the facilities for performing coronary arteriography. The number of centers falls far short of the need. In practice, therefore, selection of patients will tend to be made on a fairly narrow basis, no matter how liberally the method may be advocated in theory. We recommend angiographic study of all patients with suspected or known coronary heart disease.

It follows that for more efficient utilization of coronary arteriography, every effort should be made to establish a diagnosis by other means. We stress this admittedly pedestrian observation because large-scale arteriographic studies have shown that many practitioners fall considerably short of the 95% accuracy that is widely claimed for the diagnosis of ischemic heart disease. Our experience with more than 30,000 patients referred for cineangiography at the Cleveland Clinic has revealed a diagnostic error rate of more than 30%.

Many patients, incorrectly diagnosed as having coronary artery disease, had pursued a needlessly restricted existence in anticipation of a "heart attack," while others had endured lengthy treatments with vasodilators, sedatives, and anticoagulant drugs. In some cases, the internal mammary artery had been needlessly ligated; in others, myxedema had been induced by the administration of radioactive iodine.

In practice we find that the largest group of patients in whom studies are warranted are those in whom the diagnosis of coronary artery disease is suspected but either poorly defined or in doubt because of atypical clinical features. The most common error is in the patient who has chest pain of neuromuscular origin. Typically, such patients tend to experience pain *after* a period of exertion has ended, as opposed to the pain of angina pectoris, which characteristically arises during the exertion itself. True angina is also reproducible in most cases, and the exercise tolerance electrocardiogram is sometimes helpful.

When a patient has pain brought on by effort, relieved promptly by rest or by vasodilators (within two to three minutes), and that is reproducible with effort, there is a 95% chance that

the diagnosis of coronary atherosclerosis is correct – and, in our experience, a 60% chance that one of the coronary arteries is already obstructed. In general, symptoms are of little value in predicting the location or extent of the disease.

Whether to study the asymptomatic patient who presents himself only because of high "risk factors" in his own or his family history is a frequently raised question to which there can be no clear-cut answer. We are inclined to study the patient who is concerned because of a strong family history of early death from coronary artery disease. In some cases, a patient with no ascertainable risk factors may be psychologically incapacitated by minor symptoms until he has been completely evaluated.

Contraindications to coronary arteriography include severe associated disease, such as leukemia, cancer, or psychosis. Congestive failure should be regarded as a relative contraindication until it has been brought under control. Another relative contraindication is acute myocardial infarction, although we are becoming more flexible in our approach to emergency surgery on the coronary arteries. We have performed preoperative arteriography on more than two dozen patients with acute or impending myocardial infarction, and the surgical results were, fortunately, satisfactory. But we do not really know the degree to which emergency surgical intervention will improve the morbidity or the mortality in these acute cases. Certainly, the situation is not yet sufficiently well explored to advocate routine arteriography and coronary artery surgery for all such patients (see Chapter 31, Evaluation and Surgery for Impending "Myocardial Infarction," by Harrison and Shumway and Chapter 33, "Myocardial Revascularization During Postinfarction Shock," by Mundth, Buckley, and Austen). Healed myocardial infarction is not a contraindication, but rather constitutes a very compelling reason to evaluate the full extent of the disease process.

We can now return to our criteria for selecting patients for surgery by appropriate procedures. The arteriograms for each of the three main coronary systems — the right, left main, and anterior descending arteries – are evaluated in turn and independ-

ently, since no one operation will serve for every patient. A vein graft, for example, requires that the distal segments of the diseased artery are sufficiently large and free of major obstructions. From the standpoint of the surgeon making anastomoses, the lower limit of artery size is about 1 to 2 mm.

With good technique, coronary vessels with a lumen of 100 to 200 mμ can be visualized; narrowing that obstructs the lumen by more than 20% can be detected in vessels larger than 1 mm. In particular, we look for collateral channels arising above obstructed segments or from adjacent branches and perfusing distal branches of the obstructed vessel.

In addition, the state of the myocardium itself influences the choice of surgical procedure. Extensive infarction, for example, may require the removal of scarred tissue before constructing a vein graft. In some instances, the myocardium is so scarred nothing can be gained from a vein graft. On the other hand, we sometimes discover angiographically that a coronary artery has multiple obstructions in its distal branches, yet the muscle has remained intact. Here, we usually recommend an internal mammary implant.

Very frequently, the selective study of each of the major coronary vessels indicates the need for a combination operation. Thus, one patient might have a vein graft to the right coronary artery and excision of an aneurysm due to obstructional anterior descending artery. Or a vein graft to the right coronary may be combined with an internal mammary artery implant beneath a circumflex artery too small to accept a graft. With modern coronary artery surgery there is practically no limit to the number of feasible reconstructive arrangements.

In fact, the criteria for surgery in coronary artery disease have been broadened to the extent that virtually all patients can (in theory) at least be considered for operation. Our own patients have ranged in age from 19 to 72 and presented with every degree of coronary involvement, from the clearly localized single obstruction with mild anginal syndrome to the acute emergency with multiple lesions requiring a complex variety of reconstruction procedures.

Evaluation and Surgery for Impending Myocardial Infarction

DONALD C. HARRISON *and* NORMAN SHUMWAY

Stanford University

In the development of myocardial infarction there appears to be a transitional phase preceding actual necrosis of cardiac muscle when, for a brief time, a precarious balance is maintained between myocardial oxygen supply and metabolic demand (see Chapter 29, "Protection of the Ischemic Myocardium," by Braunwald and Maroko). If at this point in time the means were available to us to restore adequate blood flow to the compromised myocardium, acute infarction and its unfortunate sequelae might be successfully averted. Until recently the likelihood of achieving this goal through either medical or surgical intervention seemed remote; now, however, prevention of threatened infarction is becoming a realistic prospect, made possible by development and refinement of techniques for revascularization of the myocardium by direct surgery to bypass obstructive lesions in the major coronary arteries.

A variety of surgical approaches to ischemic heart disease have been introduced in the past, often with considerable enthusiasm, only to meet with frustrating and frequently tragic results; to some it seems improbable that attempts at myocardial revascularization at any stage of ischemic heart disease are likely to provide sufficient clinical benefit to outweigh the risks involved. Skeptics readily recall the disappointments following attempts to restore blood flow by implanting systemic vessels into the left ventricular myocardium, or to expand with patch grafts the lumen of damaged coronary vessels. However, there is little doubt that coronary bypass surgery that employs a segment of saphenous vein to link the aorta and the affected artery (see Chapter 30, "Revascularizing the Myocardium: The Saphenous Vein Bypass," by Effler and Sheldon) can accomplish what the other approaches could not: immediate perfusion of the region of the myocardium at risk of infarction by establishing flow from a source above the obstruction to a relatively healthy portion of the artery beyond it. To cardiologists dismayed by earlier surgical failures, this is the first approach that seems sound physiologically, since it can provide blood to the specific myocardial tissue likely to need it urgently.

Following the introduction in 1966 of saphenous vein bypass surgery for the management of chronic ischemia, experiences at a number of centers have documented that coronary blood flow can be effectively restored – and symptoms relieved – in at least 80% of patients, provided cases are appropriately selected. Such saphenous vein bypass surgery has usually been undertaken on an elective basis in patients with stable angina pectoris. Our focus in this chapter is on use of essentially the same procedure on an emergency basis in the presence of unstable angina associated with acute ischemia, in the hope of averting imminent infarction.

Needless to say, those who continue to doubt the advisability of attempting coronary artery surgery in patients in relatively stable condition are all the more wary when the procedure is extended to patients already gravely ill. Potential hazards of the operation in such cases are considered too great to justify its use, especially in view of the added hazard represented by the coronary arteriography needed to locate obstructive lesions prior to surgery. But potential and actual dangers in any situation are not always the same. In this situation, diagnostic and surgical interventions do entail some risk and it would be pointless to deny it. But it is a risk that to us seems to fall within acceptable limits, considering not only the possible benefits but the alternatives. Once acute infarction occurs, even with rapid admission to a modern coronary care unit, the outlook may be bleak: Among patients receiving intensive coronary care, the 30-day mortality stands at close to 20%; of those fortunate enough to attain long-term survival, some 15% remain significantly disabled.

Fundamental to our approach is the premise that there

is a recognizable stage in ischemic heart disease when premonitory signs forewarn that infarction may be impending. Prompt intervention of the right kind at this moment may turn the tide. It is well recognized that acute infarction, like sudden cardiac death, may occur unexpectedly as the first clinical expression of coronary heart disease. On the other hand, retrospective studies have indicated that in at least 50% of infarction cases there are prodromal symptoms, chiefly chest pain, in the weeks or months preceding the acute event. (According to the New York Hospital study of Solomon et al, 65% of patients reported prodromata during the preceding two months.) In a patient already manifesting symptoms of myocardial ischemia there may be a noticeable clinical change in the period immediately prior to onset of infarction. Whereas anginal pain formerly was brought on by physical effort, it now occurs at rest as well; also, the pain is clearly different in intensity, frequency, and duration from that of classic angina pectoris. It resembles more the pain of acute infarction, but electrocardiographic changes diagnostic of infarction are absent and serum enzymes remain within normal range.

A variety of terms had been used to describe this symptom complex: intermediate coronary syndrome, unstable angina, persistent angina, and status anginosus. More recently the term preinfarction angina has come into usage, although it is considered misleading by some since it presupposes knowledge of a future event not certain to occur. In truth, however, a clinical state foreshadowing imminent infarction can be defined with a high degree of certainty on the basis of standardized criteria. The syndrome will accordingly be referred to in this chapter as preinfarction angina, or impending infarction, to point up its seriousness, although it is acknowledged that infarction will not necessarily ensue in all patients fitting the description.

By inference a patient's history must be known to establish the presence of preinfarction angina, since, as suggested, its appearance marks a major clinical change. The change may take the form of an altered symptomatic pattern in previously recognized disease, or the sudden appearance of disabling symptoms as the first clinical evidence of overt heart disease. Typically, an individual previously asymptomatic experiences severe and prolonged anginal pain in the absence of known precipitating factors; as a rule, several such episodes occur within a brief period. Or a patient accustomed to anginal pain on exercise suddenly begins having pain of greater intensity with far less exertion; in another with a history of angina on effort, episodes of severe pain occur at rest or nocturnally. In both of the latter, prior to these developments the patient's condition may have remained fairly stable for months or even years. The same may be true of another sub-group: patients with angina at rest who become completely unresponsive to medical therapy, whereas formerly symptoms were well controlled with the standard drugs used – nitroglycerine and long-acting nitrites. In all the above, a key change is in the duration of anginal pain: while previously pain usually subsided within a few minutes, attacks of 20 to 30 minutes duration become more the rule; in some cases pain persists for an hour or longer, even with the patient in the hospital and under direct care.

It should be noted that pain associated with impending infarction may be quite atypical in location. To be sure, most patients experience oppressive chest pain of the classic variety. In some there is left arm (less commonly right arm) pain with or without concomitant chest pain; in others, the pain is felt in the neck or the jaw, usually on the left side, or in the epigastrium.

It is not known why preinfarction angina develops when it does. However, close study of such episodes discloses that often they are preceded by sinus tachycardia and paroxysmal hypertension. Why these occur is not known, but the result is surely an increased myocardial oxygen demand, a demand that may remain unmet if coronary arterial narrowing has reached the critical point and blood flow is diminished. Ischemic pain is one result; another appears to be a significant increase in left ventricular filling pressure. Hemodynamic mea-

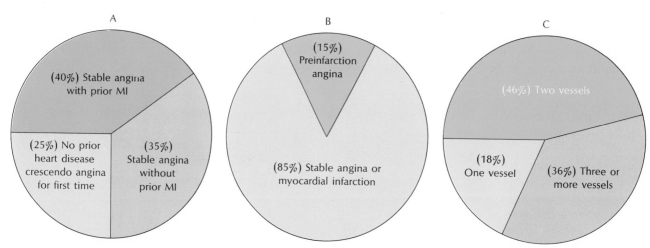

Although in most instances preinfarction angina develops following a period of stable angina or in patients with an earlier healed infarct, symptoms have appeared de novo in some 25% of patients studied by Stanford group (A). Among patients with coronary disease of any type (B) preinfarction angina is the first clinical sign in about 15%. Luminal narrowing of 70% or greater in at least two major coronary vessels has been demonstrated in more than 80% of preinfarction cases to date (C).

surements at this point document the pressure increase (measured as pulmonary arterial wedge pressure or left ventricular end-diastolic pressure) and reduced cardiac output.

Clinically, it may be difficult to identify impending or actual infarction on the basis of a patient's symptoms; in any event identification should not be attempted without reference to the electrocardiogram. If appropriate E C G leads reveal characteristic new Q wave patterns, the tissue is already infarcted; preinfarction angina is thereby ruled out. In preinfarction angina, E C G changes are limited to those of myocardial ischemia – chiefly flattened depression of the s-t segment and, on occasion, T wave inversion. (In an occasional patient the E C G pattern reflects an anginal variant or so-called Prinzmetal's angina; instead of classic ischemic s-t depression there is s-t segment elevation.)

However, since Q wave changes are typical only of transmural infarction, their absence is no proof that infarction has not occurred. Infarction localized to subendocardial layers of the myocardium (which occurs in about 25% of cases) cannot be distinguished from preinfarction angina on the basis of E C G patterns; serum enzyme changes may then become the crucial factor in differentiating between the two. Any change above normal in serum glutamic oxaloacetic transaminase (s G O T) or lactic dehydrogenase (L D H) levels may be assumed to indicate infarction. However, a small increase in creatine phosphokinase (C P K) – up to twice the normal value – may occur in the absence of cell necrosis; preinfarction rather than infarction is suggested if this is the only enzyme change. Care must be taken to assure that intramuscular injections have not been given, since they produce muscle necrosis and three- or fourfold increases in C P K and rises in L D H.

When all three criteria are met – the presence of anginal pain at rest in a crescendo pattern and the absence of both E C G and serum enzyme changes indicating gross myocardial damage – the affected patient may be considered to be in a preinfarction state. It cannot be predicted whether infarction will occur in a given individual if not somehow prevented; what

Differential Diagnosis of Preinfarction Angina

	Stable Angina	Impending Infarction	Acute Infarction
Pain Pattern	Brief pain episodes, usually of substernal origin and lasting 3 to 5 minutes. Onset related to physical effort, emotion, eating, or other stress. Prompt response to rest or nitrates.	Severe pain, usually of substernal origin and lasting 15 to 30 minutes. Onset unrelated to effort or other known precipitating factors. Responsive to nitrates, but narcotics may be required for relief.	Crushing pain, usually of substernal origin and lasting 15 minutes or more. Onset usually unrelated to effort or other known precipitating factors. Narcotics required for relief.
Physical Signs	A 3rd or 4th heart sound may appear, related to pain episode.	Arterial blood pressure usually normal or initially decreased, followed by moderate decline.	May develop shock or heart failure. Cold extremities, sweating, peripheral cyanosis present.
Serum Enzymes	Within normal range.	SGOT and LDH levels within normal range. CPK levels normal or slightly elevated to no more than twice maximal normal level.	SGOT, LDH, and CPK levels elevated and show evolutionary pattern.
ECG Changes	S-T-segment displacement or T-wave inversion in some cases.	Flattened depression of S-T segment. Deep symmetrical T-wave inversion. Elevation of S-T segment in anginal variant syndromes (occasional) Transient changes.	Appearance of Q waves. Elevation of S-T segment. T-wave inversion. Evolutionary changes over days.

can be said is that a substantial proportion of such patients do develop infarction within the ensuing days or weeks, although as yet there are insufficient data on which to base firm estimates of risk. Until recently, relatively few investigators have directly addressed this question, in part because after identifying such patients there was little one could do to protect them. In addition, the studies that have been conducted have differed in their clinical definitions and terminology, producing differing conclusions that have clouded the issue.

In a retrospective survey of some 250 patients with preinfarction angina, Vakil and coworkers (in Bombay) observed development of infarction within three months in 50%, with an associated mortality of 30%. On the other hand, Fulton et al (in an Edinburgh community survey) found that acute infarction developed within three months in only 16% of patients reporting symptoms indicative of unstable angina. (Unstable angina was defined as chest pain suggestive of myocardial ischemia occurring de novo or recurring after a pain-free

period within the preceding month, or abruptly and inexplicably increasing in frequency and severity during the same period.) However, these investigators also collected data on cases of proved infarction occurring within the same population and found that unstable angina had occurred prior to the acute event in 60% of cases. Significantly, only a minority of the patients – 17% – had complained of their symptoms to a physician.

In studying events preceding onset of acute infarction, De Sanctis and coworkers analyzed records of all patients admitted to the Massachusetts General Hospital coronary care unit over a 27-month period; of those with symptoms of ischemic heart disease 19% were classified as having acute coronary insufficiency (episodes of anginal pain lasting at least 30 minutes, occurring within 24 hours of admission and unrelated to obvious precipitating factors, with ECG and serum enzyme levels in the normal range). Despite these prodromal signs comparatively few (6 of 100) patients developed infarction while in the hospital; all six survived. A year later

Control

Impending Infarction

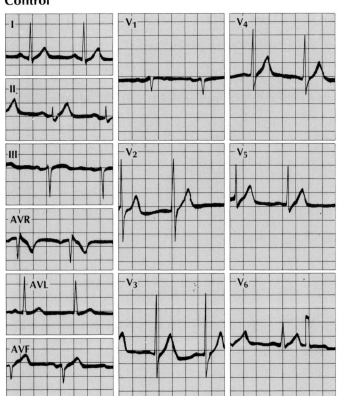

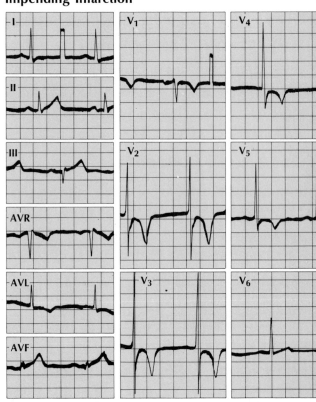

ECG tracings above at left were recorded in 52-year-old man prior to onset of preinfarction angina; changes indicative of

myocardial ischemia appeared when infarction was imminent (right). Angiography demonstrated critical narrowing of anterior

Control

Acute Infarction

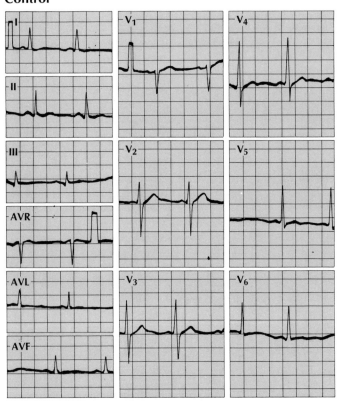

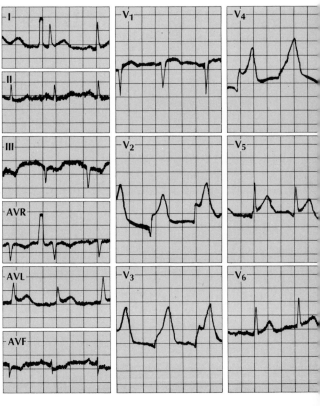

Before onset of acute anterior septal myocardial infarction, ECG tracings of 62-year-old man showed typical preinfarction pattern

(left); appearance of Q waves and other specific changes marked development of acute infarction a few hours later (right). Evolu-

operative

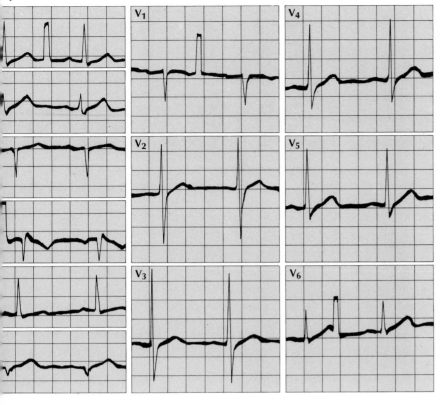

descending coronary artery; bypass surgery was performed. Tracings obtained one month after the revascularization procedure (above) show essentially normal ECG pattern.

ays Postinfarction

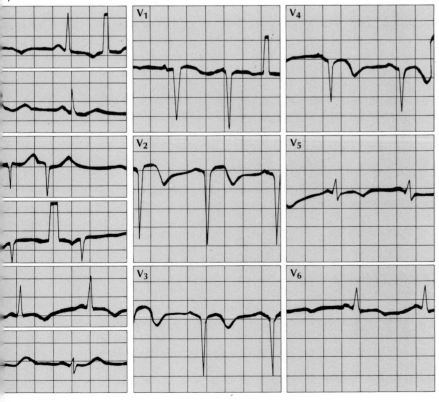

tion of infarction process is indicated in repeat ECG tracings recorded four days after the acute event. This pattern was accompanied by diagnostic serum enzyme changes.

85% were still alive. Remarking on the "benign" hospital course in most cases, the investigators cautioned against aggressive (i.e., surgical) intervention in patients with prolonged ischemic pain. "For the most part patients with acute coronary insufficiency should be treated conservatively," they advised, "and after recovery, studied electively." But it is worth noting that at a later point in the follow-up period (20 months), some 40% of the original group had died, most of acute infarction. On this basis perhaps the approach we are suggesting would have been the more conservative.

As of now it is uncertain what proportion of cases of preinfarction angina or its equivalent will progress to actual infarction; weighing the evidence to date, however, a fair estimate would probably be that in the natural course of events, some 30% to 40% of such patients would develop infarction within the year. A fair estimate of the yearly mortality would be in the range of 20%. Contrast this with a 4% mortality per year for patients with stable angina.

This is not to suggest that all or even most patients with preinfarction angina should be considered for surgery. Clinical evidence of impending infarction is only one factor to be considered. The anatomic condition of the coronary vessels is a major consideration in determining whether a given patient is a suitable surgical candidate. Selective coronary arteriography is essential to establish the presence of substantial narrowing in a major vessel — in the main left coronary artery or in the proximal 1 cm of its anterior descending branch, the proximal right coronary artery, the circumflex artery, or a branch of a dominant circumflex vessel. In our view an obstructive lesion in a nondominant vessel supplying only a small portion of heart muscle does not warrant surgery even if severe anginal pain is present. To justify surgery, narrowing of a major vessel must be equivalent to 70% or more of the lumen. Admittedly, assessing the degree of stenosis can be difficult — especially in the 50% to 70% range; to increase accuracy it is important and necessary to visualize each vessel in two views (usually the right anterior oblique and left anterior oblique). Considerable

357

experience by the team in interpreting arteriograms is necessary, too, of course.

Recent reports warning of excessive mortality (up to 2%) resulting from extension of coronary arteriography to include sicker patients have generally not been substantiated in hospitals where large numbers of studies are performed; there is also no question that morbidity and mortality associated with arteriography vary inversely with the technical skill of the team performing the procedure. Certainly we would exercise greater caution in treating the patients under discussion here than in those whose condition is more stable, and the procedure is completed as rapidly as possible. Injection during an ischemic episode is avoided by monitoring the ECG; arterial blood pressure is also monitored throughout to avoid a precipitous drop in blood pressure. Care is taken in premedicating the patient (usually with barbiturates) and ensuring that premedication is having the desired effect. Among our last 500 patients undergoing coronary arteriography—including the group with impending infarction—mortality associated with the procedure has been 0.2%.

If surgery is indicated (and accepted by the patient) it is performed without delay. With infarction threatening, there is no time to send him home until his condition stabilizes and then schedule surgery electively. This is an emergency situation and any postponement may give cause for regret. In the 125 or so preinfarction cases operated on by our group in the past three years, surgery has often been under way within two or three hours after completion of arteriography; the longest interval has been five days.

The operation is basically the standard saphenous vein–coronary artery bypass (introduced by Favaloro and colleagues at the Cleveland Clinic along with Dudley Johnson of Milwaukee) whereby a reversed segment of the patient's saphenous vein is anastomosed to the aorta and to the distal end of the diseased artery beyond the obstructive lesion; the proximal portion of the artery is left intact (see Chapter 30 by Effler and Sheldon). At our hospital, as elsewhere, the procedure has been employed electively in the past several years in a sizable number of patients with disabling exertional angina (to date our series of elective and emergency revascularizations includes over 1,300 cases). The heart is put on total cardiopulmonary bypass and a still field obtained by electrically induced ventricular fibrillation; moderate hypothermia is used. In cases of impending infarction, great effort is made to limit cross-clamping of the aorta to the absolute minimum of time necessary. Ordinarily, traction on Silastic tapes encircling the affected artery provides adequate and atraumatic hemostasis; when this does not suffice, cross-clamping is employed but limited to 20 minutes at most.

The number of grafts placed at operation depends, within limits, on the number of major coronary vessels affected. Almost always there are two, frequently three; however, in our total series of 1,300, all but 50 to 60 have been limited to three grafts or fewer. Attempting more seems unwarranted, since the vessels involved are usually less essential in maintaining adequate coronary flow; technical difficulties are more likely to occur because of the small lumen size.

Although in its essentials the procedure is the same as in an elective situation there is some added risk of complications. It is only prudent to keep this risk in mind – but it should be placed in its proper perspective. A chief argument voiced against surgical treatment of impending infarction is the possibility of inducing acute infarction either intraoperatively or in the immediate postoperative period. Clearly, this risk is related to the time required for operation. As techniques have been refined it has become possible to complete the several stages of the procedure more quickly; as a result the incidence of serious operative complications has been reduced.

It is worth citing a few details from an analysis of our first 103 emergency revascularizations. The patients met the stated criteria defining impending infarction, including angiographic confirmation of a critical reduction in coronary blood flow. All 103 were in functional class IV (New York Heart Association classification) in regard to anginal pain. The average age was 54 with 11 of the patients past 60 (thus far age 70 has been our upper limit in preinfarction cases). About a third had had heart disease for less than a year; in most of these individuals, the appearance of preinfarction angina was the first clinical sign of heart disease. On the other hand, more than half of the total group had previously had one or more infarctions. Whether or not there was a history of overt heart disease, at least two of the recognized atherosclerosis risk factors (hypercholesterolemia, hypertension, diabetes, obesity, a family history of premature coronary disease, and excessive cigarette smoking) were present in nearly all of the patients (92 of 103). In 22 of the 103, there was evidence preoperatively of congestive heart failure, usually moderate in degree (left ventricular end-diastolic pressure >12 mm Hg but$<$ 20 mm Hg), but in two, severe failure (LVEDP >30 mm Hg) was present.

Operative mortality proved unrelated to a number of factors that deserve mention: age, years of heart disease, severity of ECG changes, number of vessels shown on angiography to be diseased, or number of grafts. Nor did a history of previous infarctions or the time elapsed since the most recent attack increase surgical risk; (in few, however, had these been massive infarctions that destroyed large areas of heart muscle). Certain of the above factors in combination did make a difference: patients with single-vessel disease and no prior infarction had significantly lower operative morbidity and mortality than those with two- or three-vessel disease and one or more prior infarctions.

Surgical risk also proved related to the degree of congestive failure. Indeed, more than any other single factor, ventricular function at the time of surgery affected not only the operative course but events thereafter. Along with others, we have come to feel that revascularization is relatively fruitless in patients in severe congestive failure who have insufficient myocardial reserve. At present such patients are generally not considered for surgery, not only because operative morbidity and mortality are increased but because revascularization is rarely successful in those who survive the procedure. Patients with significant akinesis or dyskinesis are also likely to be turned down, for similar reasons.

To cite a few statistics: In the 103

cases referred to, operative mortality for the group as a whole was 8% among patients with uncomplicated preinfarction angina (without heart failure or shock) it was 6.5%. With greater selectivity as to appropriate candidates, operative mortality currently is about 3%—still higher than the mortality at our hospital for elective bypass (1.5%) but improving steadily.

Critics continue to refer to the high morbidity and mortality associated with revascularization by means of saphenous vein—coronary artery bypass and, frankly, our reason for dwelling on the point is to indicate that a high surgical risk is not inevitable. The high mortality (20% or greater) being reported from some centers mostly reflects the fact that controversy still surrounds the procedure, whether it is employed on an elective or an emergency basis. That is, a cardiologist who is dubious about the merits of surgery and concerned about

possible hazards is likely to refer a patient only after every other resource has been exhausted; at this stage in the patient's disease, there is little chance of a favorable outcome no matter what the surgeon does. Disappointed with the result, the next time the cardiologist may wait even longer to make the referral — and again be disappointed.

Thus a vicious cycle is created and perpetuated, since, under these circumstances, the surgical team cannot gain the necessary experience to perform the procedure with minimal risk and maximal chance of benefit to the patient. To put it another way, in the centers where surgical treatment of myocardial ischemia and impending infarction is associated with the lowest operative morbidity and mortality, no doubt a major factor is the more accepting attitude of referring cardiologists. Aware that any medical treatment yet devised has been of limited value, they are more open to

the possibility of surgery as an alternative.

As noted, rapid completion of the procedure as well as proper patient selection contribute to a successful result. Improvements in suturing — more specifically the use of continuous arterial sutures of a new synthetic filament rather than the interrupted silk sutures originally used — have helped appreciably to shorten operating time. Anastomoses now usually require no more than 15 minutes apiece.

When it comes to discussing results of emergency revascularization, at least two factors must be considered: 1) whether the procedure can alleviate the patient's disabling symptoms, and 2) whether it can protect against infarction in the period following surgery. There is no question that emergency revascularization provides immediate symptomatic relief in the majority of cases. After recovery from the operation 70% of

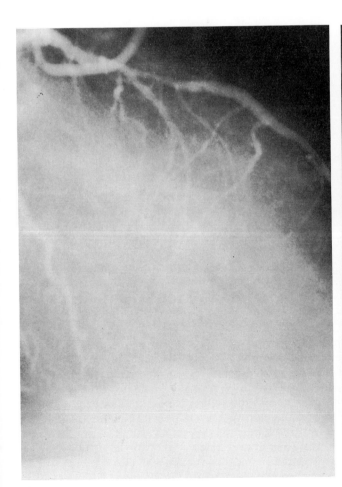

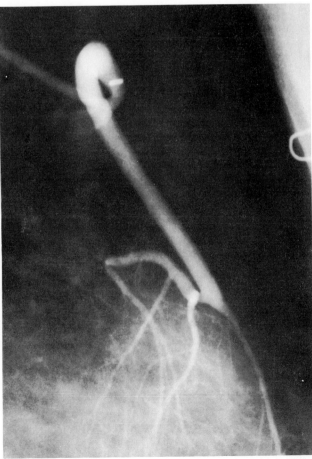

Selective coronary angiography prior to surgery in patient with impending acute infarction showed critical narrowing of anterior descending artery (left); in postoperative angiogram (right) vein graft is shown bypassing obstructive lesion. Criteria for surgery include clinical and ECG evidence of imminent infarction and 70% narrowing or greater of one or more major coronary vessels.

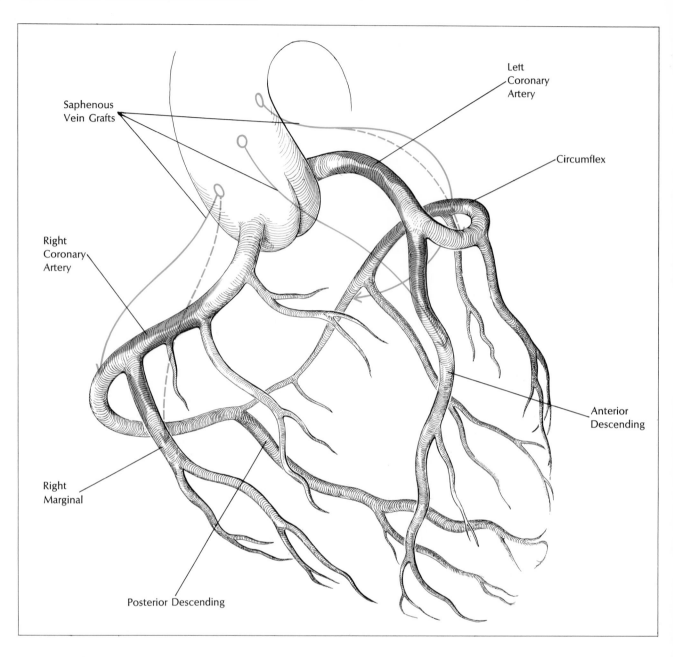

Saphenous
Vein Grafts

Left
Coronary
Artery

Circumflex

Right
Coronary
Artery

Anterior
Descending

Right
Marginal

Posterior Descending

In coronary bypass surgery for impending acute infarction, revascularization of the left ventricle is attempted with use of (usually) up to three saphenous vein grafts to link the aorta with stenosed vessels beyond the point of obstruction. Selective coronary angiography is required first to document substantial narrowing of a major vessel significantly affecting coronary flow. Arrows indicate the routes taken in placing vein grafts in the left coronary, left anterior descending, and right coronary arteries in a typical case. When the obstruction is in a vessel supplying only a small part of the muscle, bypass grafting is not undertaken.

our patients treated to date have had complete and lasting relief from anginal pain (at follow-up 12 months postsurgery). In this group any signs of congestive heart failure have usually been resolved, also as shown by standard hemodynamic measurements. Patients relieved of anginal pain also show increased exercise tolerance when tested on a treadmill or bicycle ergometer. Many have returned to full-time employment.

On the negative side, within the 12-month follow-up period some 8% have developed infarction, usually uncomplicated by heart failure or shock and fatal in only one case thus far. Since our series includes a limited number of such cases, only tentative conclusions are warranted. But it does seem fair to suggest that emergency revascularization does more than relieve symptoms of acute ischemia; it will be recalled, from the experience of others cited earlier, that without intervention considerably more than

8% of patients with preinfarction angina or its equivalent are likely to develop infarction in the period following onset of acute symptoms.

As indicated, a history of one or several previous infarctions need not increase the risk of operating on patients with preinfarction angina; neither does it preclude a gratifying result. To be sure, if the extent of prior damage is too great, the patient will probably not profit much even if the graft remains patent. The chances of success are clearly best in patients with single-vessel lesions, without a history of previous infarctions, and without evidence of circulatory failure in the current episode. Our results thus far indicate that probably 90% of such patients can benefit, both symptomatically and in terms of protection against infarction. In patients with multiple-vessel disease and several past infarctions, only palliative effects can be anticipated, but their impact should not be discounted. A number have been enabled to resume productive lives and thus far are faring well.

Where atherosclerosis risk factors are present preoperatively, an attempt is made to correct them in the period following by appropriate drug therapy or dietary means. Most of these patients can be readily persuaded to modify their eating habits or stop cigarette smoking, having been made aware of the gravity of the situation; even so, preventive efforts are not always successful.

The elective use of coronary bypass surgery has taught us that the fate of a saphenous vein graft often depends on the location of the obstruction as determined preoperatively by arteriography; as a rule the larger the affected vessel, and the more proximal the lesion, the greater the likelihood that a graft will maintain patency. The degree of obstruction also has an important bearing: a graft in a vessel 90% obstructed prior to surgery is more likely to remain open than one in a vessel 50% to 70% obstructed. These observations have proved valid for emergency revascularization as well. In the 67 cases discussed above, the late patency rate was in the range of 75% (patients were restudied angiographically an average of 8.8 months after operation); today the late patency rate is probably closer to 85%. Generally, there has been a good correlation between graft patency and clinical result.

By measuring flow rates through the graft at the time of operation, it can be predicted, within limits, whether a given graft is likely to maintain patency. If these measurements show good distal runoff, chances are the graft will stay open; conversely, there is a relationship between low flow rates at surgery and later loss of patency. An important advantage

of the bypass procedure is that its effect on coronary blood flow is so quickly apparent, as is the effect on cardiac function. This can be seen by standard measurements of cardiac mechanics and contractility, for example recording left ventricular end-diastolic pressure and the acceleration factor of the left ventricle as soon as the operation is completed and comparing readings when the graft is occluded with a clamp. Differences in E C G patterns under the two conditions also attest that the affected area of myocardium served is no longer ischemic.

As will be recalled, a major limitation of older procedures like internal mammary artery implantation was that several months had to elapse before improvement in blood flow could be expected; additionally, there was often little relation between graft patency and clinical result. This appears not to be the case with saphenous vein bypass. More recently, use of the internal mammary artery rather than the saphenous vein has been advocated for bypass grafting, partly on the basis of greater structural similarity to the coronary artery; according to one report (by Green and coworkers) patency rates were improved as a result.

In our view there is little reason to seek a substitute for the saphenous vein unless for some reason the vein, or a sufficient portion, is unavailable; in that case the internal mammary artery is a good second choice. A point to remember is that the saphenous vein in man differs from other veins because of our upright posture. To accommodate the weight of the blood the vein is thick-walled; thus structurally it resembles an artery far more than a vein. When employed for bypass grafting, the saphenous vein can as readily bear arterial blood flow as a graft fashioned from an artery. In using it, we have not confronted problems such as dilatation or aneurysm. The expendability of the saphenous vein as compared with other blood vessels also should not be overlooked. Given the double system in the limbs, it is almost as if the vein were put there just for our purposes!

Something should be said about the combined use of saphenous vein bypass grafting and coronary endarterectomy, that is, preparing the vessel for grafting by endarterectomy to

remove atherosclerotic plaques – or often a fresh thrombus – that may be present in addition to the target lesion. Although critical narrowing of the arterial lumen is usually localized to a limited area (in about 80% of cases), bypassing the obstructive lesion may be of little avail if the vessel is diseased throughout. In probably half of our cases some "cleaning out" of the affected artery has been indicated to achieve the best clinical result from bypass grafting.

Unfortunately, combining endarterectomy with bypass surgery has tended to increase operative risk significantly. To be more specific, in our first 67 cases endarterectomy was performed in four of the six patients who died of intraoperative or immediately postoperative infarction. In two of the four, death was considered due to technical factors related to endarterectomy. However, it must be emphasized that in these cases gas (CO_2) was utilized for dissection; since then, the inherent dangers in gas dissection of the adventitia have been recognized and the technique generally abandoned. At present, endarterectomy is usually performed by dissection with lacrimal probes. Intraoperative infarction is a rare occurrence.

Technically, endarterectomy is simplest in the right coronary artery because of its single bifurcation; the left coronary artery with its several perforating and septal branches presents greater difficulty. Nonetheless, endarterectomy is performed when needed. Although it would be difficult to say how many inoperable cases of impend-

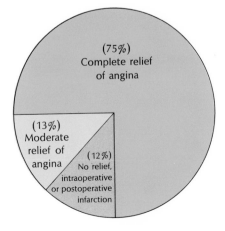

Bypass surgery brings prompt and lasting symptomatic relief in most cases; protection against infarction may also occur.

361

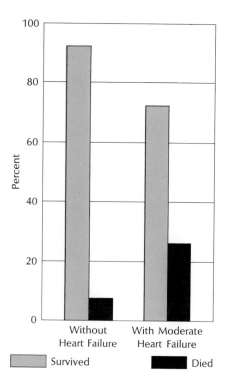

Operative risk appears to be reduced in the absence of congestive failure; in severe failure, surgery is usually contraindicated because of increased risk and poor result.

ing infarction have become suitable for bypass grafting because of endarterectomy, unquestionably this has been true in a considerable number.

Whether performed in conjunction with endarterectomy or not, the saphenous vein bypass seems to us not only warranted but strongly indicated in management of certain patients with impending infarction. These are the patients with a major obstruction in the left main coronary artery or proximally (within the first centimeter) in the anterior descending coronary artery, provided there is no compelling reason to avoid surgery. Judging by results to date – and considering

the options – we no longer feel justified in withholding bypass surgery in such cases. Naturally, a patient is free to decline if he prefers. We usually consider the situation less urgent if the obstructive lesion is in the right coronary or circumflex arteries. Depending on the circumstances, surgery may be advised or it may not. At other centers where bypass surgery is performed for impending infarction, coronary surgeons generally consider it virtually imperative in the presence of a major obstruction of the left main coronary artery. Some are less insistent than we if the lesion is in the left anterior descending artery.

Clearly, the question now to be answered in reference to the saphenous vein bypass, performed either electively or in an emergency, is no longer *whether* the operation can be of clinical benefit. Sufficient experience has accumulated for the appropriate question now to be *how great* is the benefit. As noted, our patients have been formally restudied after an average of about a year. What can be said of how long the gains observed are likely to be maintained? We do not yet have the data for a satisfactory answer. For one, we cannot yet say whether atherosclerotic changes similar to those in the diseased artery are likely to develop in the vein graft.

But even without the answer to this question, our conclusion from the evidence in hand is that the operation is the treatment of choice under specific conditions. What then of the view held by many cardiologists that in patients already acutely ill, vigorous medical therapy could accomplish as much?

These issues are too critical to be put aside. To resolve them, however, it is necessary to do more than compare patients treated medically at one institution with patients treated sur-

gically at another. They can be resolved only by suitably controlled therapy trials to compare medical and surgical treatment in patients identified as in a preinfarction state on the basis of uniform clinical and arteriographic criteria. Only in this way can the pitfalls of earlier studies be avoided, since both the definition of impending infarction and the evaluation methods will be the same for all. Currently, such a study, involving nine cooperating centers coordinated by the National Heart and Lung Institute, is being undertaken.

Considering medical vs surgical therapy of impending infarction brings to mind a point raised earlier: although it is uncertain what proportion of patients with unstable angina would develop infarction unless it were somehow prevented, it is known that infarction can and does develop without being preceded by unstable angina or indeed any overt symptoms of heart disease. The same is true of sudden cardiac death (see Chapter 24, "Myocardial Infarction and Sudden Death," by Paul). At present there are no sound means of predicting that either event is in the offing in an asymptomatic patient with coronary atherosclerosis; nor do we know why these events occur when they do. As studies of coronary arterial function become increasingly safe, it would seem reasonable to try to obtain answers by employing arteriography more broadly in the susceptible age groups with a large number of significant coronary risk factors, for example to include it on a more routine basis in periodic medical examinations in these susceptible groups. Obstructive lesions in the coronary arterial circulation might thus be identified – and appropriately dealt with – before they cause trouble.

Assisted Circulation:
A Progress Report

HARRY S. SOROFF *and* WILLIAM C. BIRTWELL
State University of New York at Stony Brook

In 1966, prospects seemed good that one or more circulatory assistance devices would, within a year or two, move into general clinical use as much needed additions to the physician's sparse armamentarium for dealing with severe cardiac disorders.

It should be said at the outset that this prognosis seems to have been oversanguine; progress in circulatory assistance has been considerably less rapid than might reasonably have been expected then. There have been any number of causes for this lag, some of which will be discussed later. A major one, however, has been money; like most kinds of research, medical research has been feeling the cold wind of appropriations cutbacks.

In saying this, however, we do not mean to imply that circulatory assistance has spent the last decade marking time. Though no line of investigation has been crowned with success, in the sense of winning wide clinical application, we have nonetheless learned much about which lines seem most profitable to pursue and the different clinical situations under which each seems most likely to succeed.

In particular, we have learned that circulatory assistance, for the present at least, will find its main relevance in the treatment and perhaps prevention of acute cardiac failure or cardiogenic shock. Chronic failure secondary to long-standing degenerative heart disease (e.g., cardiomyopathy, myocardial fibrosis) is a far more intractable problem and one to which no current approach to circulatory assistance promises a quick solution. For some years, several research groups have been working on various devices that, it was hoped, could be permanently implanted to supplement the efforts of a severely damaged heart, but all

of them have run into a triple roadblock: hemolysis (chiefly a problem of materials), power supply, and difficulty of implantation. Overcoming these barriers would seem to require several "breakthroughs"; meantime, a solution could very well evolve out of the experiments in heart transplantation – though here, too, the clinical results to date have been rather unimpressive

In today's context, then, assisted circulation refers primarily to temporary assistance in situations where relatively acute developments – e.g., surgical trauma, myocardial infarction – have reduced, or might reduce, the heart's pumping capacity to a degree that endangers life. Here then is every reason to believe that artificial assistance to the circulation, promptly applied, can at the very least sustain life in many patients long enough for the heart's natural recuperative processes to restore a semblance of normal functioning. There is likewise good reason to think that some devices can actively speed these processes in certain circumstances, thereby minimizing the amount of permanent damage to the organ. Finally, there is persuasive, though by no means conclusive, evidence that in some individuals suffering from coronary insufficiency, assisted circulation could serve as a partial prophylaxis against death from coronary occlusion.

Basically, there are two contrasting approaches to assisted circulation: the "shunt" or bypass pump and the "in-series" or counterpulsation pump. The first of these is also the older, since it operates on the principle of the heart-lung machine. Part of the blood flow is removed from the venous circulation via a cannula, bypassed around the heart through the external pump (with or

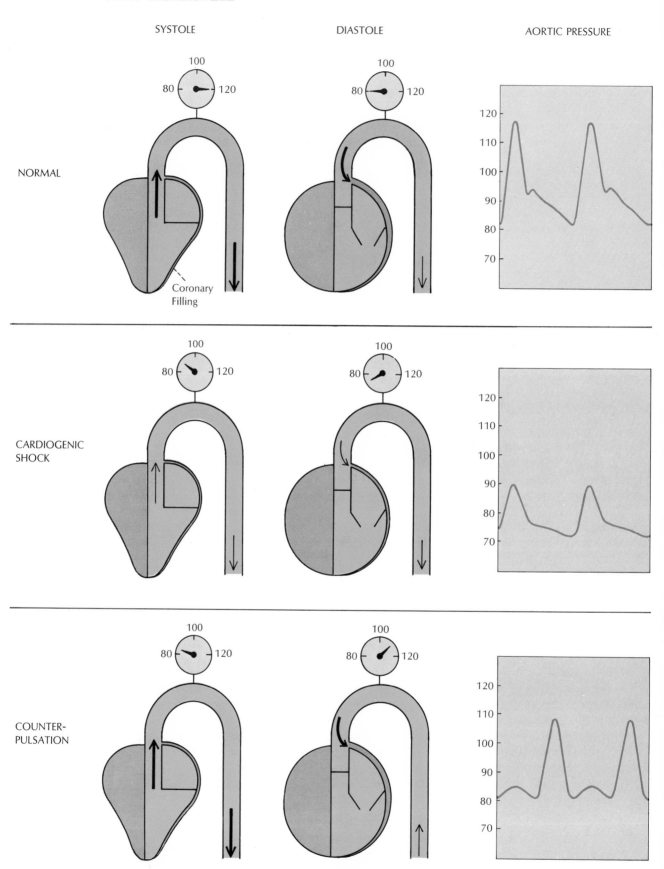

SYSTOLE   DIASTOLE   AORTIC PRESSURE

NORMAL

Coronary
Filling

CARDIOGENIC
SHOCK

COUNTER-
PULSATION

The basic concept of counterpulsation is shown by comparing flow and pressure patterns under various conditions. Normally (top), pressure peaks sharply during systole, but the diastolic level is adequate for full coronary filling during that part of the heart cycle. In cardiogenic shock, both systolic and diastolic pressure drop, reducing both peripheral flow and coronary filling. With counterpulsation, pressure is lowered still further during systole, allowing the weakened heart to pump more blood, while the sharply raised pressure during diastole restores the coronary blood flow and improves systemic perfusion.

without the addition of an oxygenating device), and returned to the circulation via an arterial cannula. Its effect is to reduce the volume of blood pumped by the heart. But, at the same time, the pressure exerted by the pump increases the aortic pressure against which the organ works. This by itself can produce deleterious effects on an already damaged heart — specifically, dilatation of the left ventricle because of its inability to discharge its contents against the elevated aortic pressure.

For this and other reasons, some of them to be given later, we feel that the shunt approach, though it may well prove valuable in certain restricted clinical contexts, will probably be of very limited utility in the much larger area of coronary occlusion or insufficiency. The reader should be aware, however, that our own work has been almost entirely concerned with counterpulsation, and that researchers who have been pursuing the shunt approach may well take a somewhat different view of its potential.

In counterpulsation, there is no bypass around the heart; the pumping action is not exerted "in parallel" but "in series" with the organ. Thus the flow of blood through the heart is not reduced, and may — as we shall see — be increased. In addition, counterpulsation, as its name indicates, is synchronized with the heart's own action but in the opposite (counter) sense: the pump pressure peaks during diastole and bottoms out during systole, so that diastolic pressure is increased while systolic pressure, depending on the underlying circulatory situation, tends either to fall or to remain constant but in any case does not increase.

The physiologic rationale for counterpulsation has two aspects. First, a number of classic studies have shown that both the amount of work done by the left ventricle and the myocardial oxygen consumption are more closely related to the systolic pressure, against which the ventricle works, than to the volume of blood pumped (i.e., the stroke volume). Thus to the extent that counterpulsation reduces systolic pressure, which it invariably does under normal conditions, it will reduce the work of the heart. Animal experiments have demonstrated that counterpulsation can decrease the so-called tension-time index by as much as 28% and myocardial oxygen consumption by 21%. (Experiments with the shunt approach, by contrast, have shown that myocardial oxygen consumption does not drop significantly until virtually the entire blood flow is routed through the bypass.) Under pathologic conditions, the circulatory response to counterpulsation is somewhat more complicated; briefly, the heart tends not to do less work but to do the same quantity of work more efficiently, in the sense that the same amount of effort produces greater blood flow.

The second important aspect of counterpulsation has to do with the rise in diastolic pressure. As is well known, most (about 70%) of the perfusion of the myocardium with arterial blood occurs during diastole, since during systole the pressure exerted by the heart's contraction markedly decreases the volume of its own vasculature. Counterpulsation, by increasing diastolic pressure, markedly increases coronary perfusion — by as much as 48% in the animal experiments mentioned above.

Let us consider now the situation of an individual in cardiogenic shock resulting from a developing myocardial infarct due to coronary occlusion. The impairment of the heart's pumping capacity will tend to lower the aortic pressure, both systolic and diastolic. For a while, this drop may be compensated for by the body's protective mechanisms, whereby blood is shunted away from the peripheral circulation to maintain the perfusion of the vital organs, C N S, and the heart itself. Beyond a certain point, however, these compensatory mechanisms become inadequate; systolic pressure falls, leading to a further diminution in corporeal perfusion, and so does diastolic pressure, leading to reduced coronary flow and a consequent further reduction in the heart's pumping capacity. The result is a vicious circle that can rather quickly lead to death — and in fact does so more than 80% of the time.

Counterpulsation here should have two results (see Chapter 29, "Protection of the Ischemic Myocardium," by Braunwald and Maroko and Chapter 33, "Myocardial Revascularization During Postinfarction Shock," by Mundth, Buckley, and Austen). By raising diastolic pressure it increases myocardial perfusion, reversing the trend toward lower pumping capacity. By itself, this may increase blood flow somewhat, but further improvement will come about through the counterpulsation pressure drop during systole. This, by "taking the pressure off" the impaired ventricle, will enable it to increase its stroke volume (which in these cases may well be something like 15% of normal). The actual drop in systolic pressure will probably be very small — just large enough, in fact, to allow for the increased stroke volume, which in this situation is a pressure-limited phenomenon. Peripheral perfusion will also be enhanced by the rise in mean perfusion pressure (systolic almost constant, diastolic up).

This generalized picture of counterpulsation in the healthy and in the shocked individual is based partly on theoretical considerations and partly on animal experiments. A number of investigators, for example, have simulated myocardial infarction in dogs by various methods, such as injecting into the coronary arteries plastic microspheres that lodge in and block some of the myocardial arterioles, or serially ligating some of the coronary arteries. In one series, approximately 70% of the untreated animals died, while counterpulsation reduced the death rate to 30%.

We now turn to methods of counterpulsation in man. The first technique employed cannulas and an external pump, much like those used in the shunt approach but with both cannulas on the same side of the heart, i.e., in the femoral arteries. The pump was controlled by a timing device, which, in turn, was controlled (usually) by the E C G, so that the apparatus "knew" at what point during the heart's cycle it should exert pressure. Early results were encouraging: if counterpulsation was applied promptly in younger patients, the expected death rate directly ascribable to cardiogenic shock could be cut on the order of one half (e.g., from 80% to 40%). However, this technique also produced a number of problems. Not the least of them was hemolysis, which has dogged so many attempts at cardiac assistance. There was also the fact that the volume of blood that could be pumped quickly (i.e., in the space of a single systole) was sharply

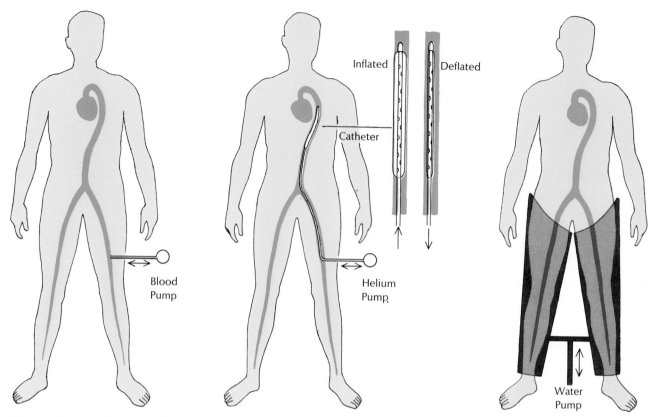

Three techniques of counterpulsation show the progression to less and less interference with the vasculature. Originally blood was led outside the body to an external pump (left). With the balloon technique (center), blood is not exteriorized but pumping balloon must be passed into the aorta by a catheter. With the external pressure system, the vessels remain completely intact.

limited, chiefly by the inelasticity of the vessels (which would help explain, of course, why the results were best in younger subjects). A too-vigorous extraction of blood, moreover, could induce collapse and fluttering of the vessels, which aggravated hemolysis and also slowed blood flow through the diseased femoral vessels.

An improved counterpulsation technique has been tested by Adrian Kantrowitz (now at Mount Sinai Hospital, Detroit) and associates at Maimonides Hospital in Brooklyn. Here the "pump" is a slender balloon supported by a catheter that is inserted into the patient's aorta via the femoral artery. By alternately inflating and deflating the balloon (during diastole and systole respectively), aortic volume is alternately decreased and increased, precisely as it occurs in the pumping chamber of any reciprocating pump. The intra-aortic balloon technique has been employed clinically by several groups (see Chapter 33 by Mundth, et al), again with some encouraging results. Its wider adoption, however, has lagged. For one thing, it is not

without hazards. Insertion of catheter and balloon is a surgical procedure, albeit a minor one – if one can say any surgery is minor in one who has just suffered a myocardial infarction – and it must be performed under local anesthesia, with a sterile field. More remote but still real dangers are the possibility of damage to the vascular intima and of a "blowout" in the balloon, which is inflated with gas (usually helium). At the relatively low pressures used, the latter hazard is highly improbable – but its consequences would be catastrophic.

These dangers probably help to explain why cardiologists and internists have been reluctant to allow their patients to undergo the procedure; a further complication is hospital logistics, whereby the patient must be transferred from the medical to the surgical service.

Our own approach to counterpulsation is both more complex and simpler than either of the foregoing. More complex because somewhat more complicated apparatus is required; simpler because the vascular system remains intact, so that the procedure is

completely nonsurgical and can be performed at the bedside. We have worked on the principle that if minimal alteration of the vasculature is good (the aortic balloon vs the external pump), no alteration is better. We manage this by, in effect, using the patient's legs as pumping chambers.

Our apparatus consists of two tapered, rigid cylinders that enclose the legs from ankle to thigh, with the feet sticking out of the narrow ends. Between leg and cylinder is a water-filled bag that completely fills the intervening space, making the device adaptable for a wide variety of anatomic configurations. Through a connecting tube, water is pumped into and out of the bag, exerting a uniform pressure over the entire surface of the legs and on the veins and arteries within. The pump is, as usual, controlled by the electrocardiogram and is provided with delay and duration electronic circuits that permit proper phasing of the pump with cardiac action. This is necessary because effective counterpulsation under these circumstances requires that the pump produce the pressure variation slightly before the desired response of the heart, since there is a delay of a fraction of a second in the transmission of the pressure wave along the aorta. The control system is completed by apparatus for sensing and visualizing the aortic pressure curve, so that the delay can be adjusted for maximal flattening during systole and for maximal elevation during diastole. Originally we used a catheter inserted into the aorta as the pressure sensor, but we are now employing external sensors, which obviate even this minimal invasion of the vessels.

The actual pressures used are quite modest: a maximum of 200 mm Hg, which is roughly equivalent to that produced by diving to the bottom of a six-foot-deep pool. Our most recent model can, by means of airtight seals at both ends of the cylinders, also induce up to 100 mm Hg of negative pressure during systole.

There are several other aspects of our device that are worth pointing out, apart from those already mentioned. Now incorporated into a console, it can easily be wheeled to the bedside (and could also be used in an ambulance). It, as distinct from the intra-aortic balloon, can exert negative as well as positive pressure – a capability we were not able to incorporate into our clinical equipment until 1970. Because external counterpulsation affects both the veins and the arteries of the legs, it not only increases arterial flow but actively steps up venous return – thereby, so to speak, assisting the heart from both directions.

Though the basic principle of our device is quite simple, the translation of it into actual hardware – including the "debugging" that seems an inevitable aspect of any new invention – was not. Nor, for that matter, was it a cheap device to build. For these and other reasons, it was not until 1968 – after several years of animal experiments, using a scaled-down version, and trials with healthy volunteers – that we undertook our first clinical application. The patient was a 48-year-old woman, who had undergone open-heart surgery for replacement of the aortic and mitral valves. She developed severe hypotension five hours postoperatively and was referred to us after a further lapse of 12 hours, at which point she was unconscious, cyanotic, and in profound shock that had failed to respond to inotropic and vasoconstrictor drugs. During circulatory assistance extending intermittently over six hours, her diastolic pressure increased slightly but her condition was otherwise unchanged; she died 14 hours later.

These results were naturally discouraging but, given the extremely unpropitious circumstances, hardly surprising. A major barrier was the patient's drug-induced vasoconstriction, which drastically limited the amount of blood that could be pumped. Subsequent patients received vasodilator drugs to increase the capacity of the vascular bed. In addition, both our own experience with animals and previous clinical experience with other modalities of counterpulsation had made clear that, as with so many other forms of therapy, delayed treatment is often equivalent to no treatment. In dogs, for example, a short period of coronary occlusion – 30 minutes or less – does not gen-

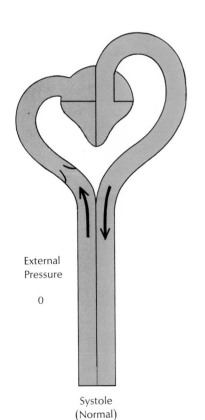 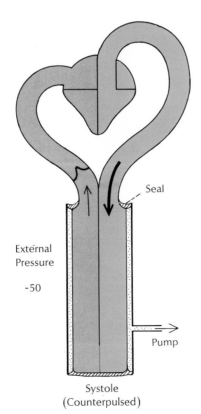 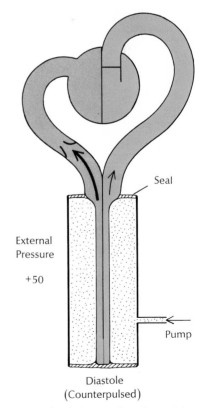

External Pressure	External Pressure	External Pressure
0	-50	+50
Systole (Normal)	Systole (Counterpulsed)	Diastole (Counterpulsed)

Airtight seals coupled with external pumping allow both positive and negative pressure during heart cycle. In systole, negative pressure in effect "sucks" blood out of heart (reverse flow in veins is prevented by natural venous valves). During diastole, positive pressure forces venous blood back toward right heart; arterial backflow increases systemic perfusion, enhances coronary filling.

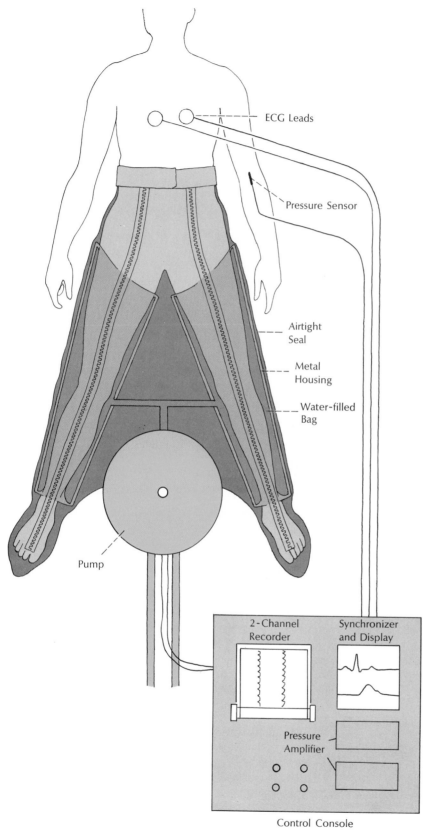

ECG Leads

Pressure Sensor

Airtight
Seal

Metal
Housing

Water-filled
Bag

Pump

2-Channel
Recorder

Synchronizer
and Display

Pressure
Amplifier

Control Console

External pressure device operates by means of water-filled bags enclosed in rigid metal cylinders, with a plastic "bag" over all to form an airtight seal. Control console synchronizes pump action with heartbeat, sensed through ECG leads; pressure pattern is sensed via catheter in the brachial artery (as shown) or externally, and visualized on the display tube with the ECG. Controls actuate variable "delay" and "duration" circuits that allow pump cycle to be adjusted for maximally beneficial pressure pattern.

erally cause permanent damage to the myocardium in untreated animals, but beyond 45 minutes something like 85% of the affected tissue suffers irreversible injury. Counterpulsation during the 45-minute period can limit tissue damage to about 15%, but has little effect if instituted later, even if the ligature was removed.

Subsequent clinical experience was distinctly more encouraging, even if something less than an unalloyed success. Of six patients treated, all in terminal cardiogenic shock, every one was significantly aided: color improved, urine production increased markedly, and arterial lactate concentrations dropped. In two cases the improvement was sufficient for them to be discharged from the coronary care unit, though both died several weeks later of pneumonia. The other four, despite their evident circulatory improvement, died fairly rapidly of their underlying disease. At autopsy, all proved to have structural changes in the heart so severe that no form of assist could have been expected to provide more than transient benefit; all of them, moreover, had been in prolonged shock (an average of seven hours) before counterpulsation was instituted.

As we have already mentioned, our newest equipment for external counterpulsation allows application of negative pressure during cardiac systole as well as positive pressure during diastole. With the new portable system we treated 20 patients at ten hospitals in the Boston area over a period of a year. The average age of the patients was 63. The time between myocardial infarction and the onset of shock ranged from about an hour in one case to over 100 hours in two instances. The average interval between the onset of shock and the application of counterpulsation was just under ten hours. (It might be worth pointing out that in most cases our assist team was able to assemble at the patient's bedside within an hour of the attending physician's call.)

All the patients had failed to respond adequately to vasopressors. The average peak systolic pressure was 80 mm Hg, the urine output at the time of diagnosis of shock ranged from zero in nine patients to 40 cc per hour in one, and the arterial lactate levels were extremely elevated. Coun-

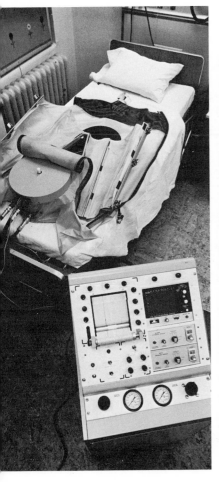
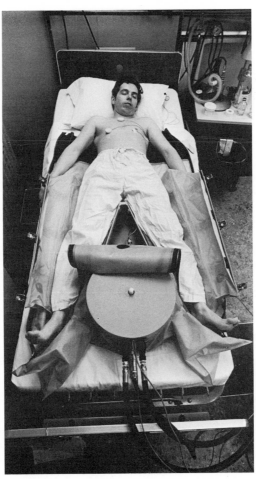
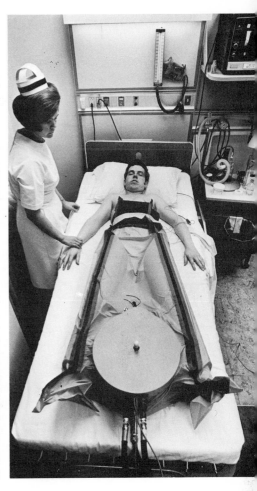

Photos show external assist device kept in the Coronary Care Unit at Boston City Hospital; others are available at a number of other CCU's in the area. Device can be applied to a patient in minutes, without sterile procedures or anesthesia. Center: positioning within apparatus is demonstrated. Right: machine is operating and vacuum stage of pulsation is visible.

terpulsation was applied for an average of 3.7 hours. In three cases, treatment was prolonged to no avail; it seems that if a patient does not respond to counterpulsation within six or eight hours at the most, further application of this treatment will be of little or no value.

Six of the patients died during counterpulsation. Five showed temporary improvement in hemodynamic status but died within hours after treatment. There were nine survivors, counting one patient who recovered from shock completely but died three days later of pneumonia and peritonitis, and another who succumbed to pulmonary edema and pneumonia after three weeks in a coma. Seven patients were able to be discharged from the hospital; one died of myocardial infarction eight months later, but the others remained well. Although the 45% survival rate was a significant (and heartening) improve-

ment over the usual 15%, we feel that the death rate could be lowered even further by earlier application of external counterpulsation – ideally, within two hours of the onset of shock.

It is worth emphasizing that no patient, even the first completely unsuccessful one, has shown any signs of deterioration while under treatment, nor any deterioration after treatment that was not perfectly consistent with the expected course of their disease. (The same is true, of course, of our normal volunteer subjects.) Indeed, we find it almost impossible to imagine any way in which the machine, unless egregiously misused, *could* harm a patient. Thus, whatever the ultimate clinical value of external counterpulsation, it appears completely to meet at least one venerable requirement of any new therapy: *primum non nocere.*

One point should be specially noted because of its wider implications: even

in our first clinical series, of the two patients in whom counterpulsation was most successful, neither one was treated for more than a few hours – yet the circulatory improvement persisted for many days afterward. It seems clear that counterpulsation, in some situations at least, does not merely sustain life for the duration of its employment but in some manner helps the heart to move back toward normal functioning. At a minimum, it buys time in which the heart's natural healing processes can move to ameliorate the circulatory deficiency; at a maximum, it may actually accelerate those processes. Our own belief, based on considerable experimental, though as yet limited clinical, evidence is that the latter is what actually occurs.

Several studies of animals in which experimental coronary occlusions have been induced show very clearly that counterpulsation does not merely increase survival – and to a marked de-

369

gree – but also reduces the size of the resulting infarct (see Chapter 29 by Braunwald and Maroko). It does so by accelerating the opening or development of collateral circulation. (As is well known, collaterals develop to some degree in any patient with coronary occlusion, provided the patient survives long enough.) Postmortem studies have consistently shown clear evidence of more and larger collaterals in counterpulsated animals. By themselves, indeed, these might be dismissed as artifacts produced in some manner by the counterpulsation process, but taken together with the marked increase in survival rates, it seems evident that the "new" channels are not only real but represent at least part of the explanation for the improved survival.

It is worth noting that the possibility of collateral development in the myocardium following coronary occlusion was widely disbelieved as recently as the mid-1950's. Even more recently, the efficacy of the Vineberg procedure for implanting the internal mammary artery in the myocardium was questioned because there was no objective evidence that collaterals did in fact develop from it. However, the development of coronary arteriography by F. Mason Sones and others has provided abundant evidence that collaterals do develop, opening the way to a much wider use of the Vineberg operation in its many variants.

There is an important difference, one with interesting physiologic implications, between what one might call post-Vineberg and post-counterpulsation collaterals. The former develop very slowly, over a period of weeks or months after the operation; the latter, certainly within days and probably almost immediately. We have not yet obtained positive proof of this, but there seems no very plausible alternative explanation of how a few hours, or less, of counterpulsation can produce such long-lasting effects.

One tends to think of the slowly developing post-Vineberg collaterals as new vessels growing in response to the stimulus provided by myocardial ischemia (there is a good deal of evidence that in the absence of ischemia they will not develop). This concept, however, seems hardly consistent with the very rapid development of collaterals, or of improved cardiac func-

tioning presumably reflecting their development, after counterpulsation. An alternative – or additional – process, postulated earlier on other grounds, is that the "instant" collaterals represent existing but nonpatent vessels that are opened by the increased diastolic pressure. Once open, presumably they remain so. A number of vessels in the circulatory system are known to open only in response to a critical internal pressure that is considerably greater than that required to keep them open. And anyone who has ever tried to blow up a long, narrow balloon will probably recall that the problem is in getting it started; if the blower can summon enough breath to do this, the rest of the inflation process goes much more easily.

If relatively brief periods of counterpulsation can call to "active duty" an existing reserve of myocardial vasculature – a belief that is now beginning to be supported by clinical evidence – this would raise exciting prospects for counterpulsation not "merely" as a potentially lifesaving procedure in cases of coronary occlusion but also as a way of relieving coronary insufficiency and, by no means incidentally, lessening the impact of any future occlusion in such patients. This is the more significant in view of the fact that some 50% of coronary occlusion patients die within a few hours – many of them even before they get to a hospital. A serious attack on the coronary death rate must obviously be concerned with prevention as well as therapy after the occlusion has occurred.

A preliminary clinical study of this question by Dr. Thomas Ryan at St. Elizabeth's Hospital in Boston produced encouraging results in that the patients showed evidence of improved cardiac functioning. And quite recently, Dr. John Banas, Jr., of the New England Medical Center, reported that 17 of 21 patients with severe chronic angina pectoris were relieved – in some cases dramatically – by treatment with external counterpulsation. The patients underwent treatment an hour a day for five days. Prior to that they had been taking an average of 54 nitroglycerin tablets (0.4 mg each) a week; a few weeks later they were averaging two tablets a week. Propranolol, which 17 of the patients had also been taking, was

discontinued altogether. In 14 cases coronary angiograms were taken before and after treatment. Four showed no change, but five appeared possibly improved, while the other five showed distinct improvement of the coronary vasculature. In cases where angina redevelops – typically six to eight months after the course of treatment – a second course of treatment again provided relief.

From everything we have said thus far, it will be obvious that we regard the counterpulsation approach to circulatory assistance as the one likely to yield maximum dividends in terms of numbers of patients helped. What about the shunt approach?

The most likely area of application of shunt pumping, we believe, is likely to be in cases of impaired pulmonary function – pulmonary hypertension, right heart failure, and the like. Here the shunt pump in combination with an oxygenator may well prove to be lifesaving. In addition, the shunt pump might find application in patients who are in such profound shock that counterpulsation would be useless, its effects being sharply reduced by the very limited amount of blood already in the arterial tree. Here a shunt pump, again including an oxygenator, might prove to be a way of "cranking up" the circulation, after which the patient could be shifted over to counterpulsation for longer periods. In such cases, however, one might well wonder whether patients so deteriorated could ever be restored to anything like normal. Circulatory assistance is, we believe, a potentially powerful tool – but not so powerful as to work miracles.

Despite our own research commitment to counterpulsation, we feel it would be a mistake to suggest that any approach to circulatory assistance would be applicable in all cases. And, for that matter, it would be equally incorrect to suggest that, in the development of what is still a very new field of medicine, any given device is the "final" answer. There is still a lot to be discovered about how the circulatory system works, and how, in various pathologic situations, it can be most effectively assisted and restored as nearly as possible to normal functioning.

Myocardial Revascularization During Postinfarction Shock

ELDRED D. MUNDTH, MORTIMER J. BUCKLEY, *and* W. GERALD AUSTEN

Harvard University

In employing either a medical or surgical procedure carrying substantial risk, one must weigh the potential benefits against the probable prognosis if the action is not taken. In the case of cardiogenic shock occurring as a complication of acute myocardial infarction it is acknowledged that prognosis has improved little despite intensive therapy in modern coronary care centers (see Chapter 23, "Hemodynamic Changes in Acute Myocardial Infarction," by Ross). Ventricular power failure associated with shock remains the chief cause of hospital death in patients with acute infarction. Among patients with cardiogenic shock who may initially respond to standard treatment, including administration of vasopressor and inotropic agents, mortality in the range of 80% is still the general rule; among those who fail to respond to such therapy, chances of survival are virtually nil.

Cardiogenic shock, unfortunately, is a fairly common occurrence, complicating some 15% of cases in most centers where acute infarction has been studied. Given the grave consequences of cardiogenic shock as well as its frequency, bold measures to improve upon present therapy surely seem warranted.

Only a short while ago direct coronary artery revascularization would have been deemed too traumatic in patients far less critically ill. Recently this mode of therapy has been employed on an investigational basis in management of refractory cardiogenic shock, in the hope that improving blood flow to the compromised myocardium may help to overcome left ventricular failure and thus reverse the shock state. The surgical technique usually employed is the aortocoronary bypass graft, using a segment of saphenous vein to circumvent obstructive lesions in the coronary circulation. It is essentially the same procedure that has been widely used within the past few years in management of chronic myocardial ischemia (see Chapter 30,

"Revascularizing the Myocardium: The Saphenous Vein Bypass," by Effler and Sheldon) and more recently on an emergency basis in patients developing unstable angina or other warning signs of imminent infarction (see Chapter 31, "Evaluation and Surgery for Impending Myocardial Infarction," by Harrison and Shumway).

When coronary revascularization surgery was cautiously extended to patients with preinfarction angina, the possibility of extending its use to the period following onset of acute infarction still seemed beyond consideration to most observers. It was thought unlikely that patients could tolerate revascularization surgery in the face of acute infarction; in the presence of acute infarction and cardiogenic shock, one would expect tolerance to be even more reduced. Yet there is little question that in appropriate cases surgery can be performed with a reasonable possibility of reversing cardiogenic shock that otherwise would undoubtedly be fatal.

Evaluating any therapeutic approach to cardiogenic shock requires first that the criteria used in defining shock be clearly stated. In the past, mortality with shock complicating acute infarction, although invariably high, has varied because of the wide diversity of cases included. With the development of transmural infarction, the initial physiologic insult in most instances causes some decrease in left ventricular function, manifested by a decline in cardiac output and/or arterial perfusion pressure and an elevation of left ventricular filling pressure. In some patients these hemodynamic consequences are negligible; in others they are sufficient to induce a transient shock state that responds readily to conventional medical therapy. A study that includes the latter type of patients will surely come up with a significantly lower mortality than one including only those patients in whom shock persists despite intensive conventional treatment. Obviously a standard

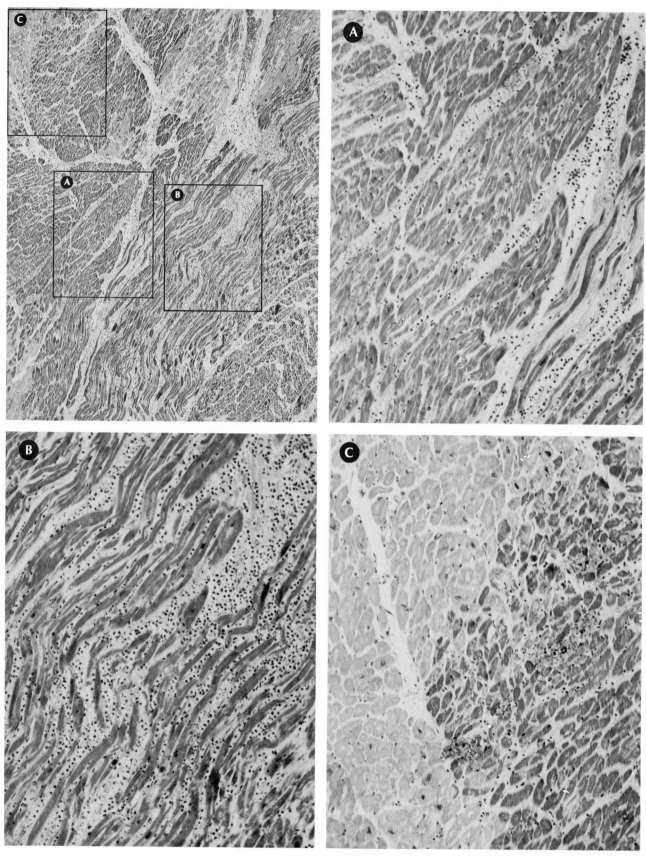

Marginal extension of myocardial necrosis is evidenced by zone of densely staining myocytes centrifugal to neutrophils in border of a four-day-old infarct (top left, x52), as seen in microscopic studies by Caulfield et al of myocardial changes in shock. Central necrotic zone of infarct and its original border of neutrophils are identified in the insets and shown at higher power (x160) in A and B. Region of infarct extension is seen in C (x160); myocytes show smudging of band pattern and some nuclear loss. In cases uncomplicated by ventricular failure and shock, the infarct border retains a homogeneous appearance.

definition of cardiogenic shock is mandatory for evaluation of therapy and comparison of data from different institutions.

To this end, consistent clinical criteria have been agreed on by our group and others currently studying shock and other complications of acute infarction in myocardial infarction research units across the country (sponsored by the National Heart and Lung Institute). The accepted criteria provide that a shock state exists when systolic arterial pressure is below 80 mm Hg, the cardiac index is less than 2.1 l/min/m², urine output is less than 20 ml/hour, and perfusion to the brain and periphery is diminished sufficiently to produce signs of mental confusion or obtundation and peripheral vasoconstriction. In the ensuing discussion, it is assumed that the patients in question have had a trial of conventional medical therapy directed at correcting the classic manifestations of the shock state (such as acidosis, hypoxia, and hypovolemia), control of arrhythmia, and use of vasopressor or inotropic agents to elevate blood pressure, and that the shock state has persisted despite these measures. It is in this group of patients that mortality with conventional therapy approaches 100%.

Recent work clarifying the pathophysiology of cardiogenic shock helps to explain why conventional therapy, even if promptly and vigorously applied, has had such limited success. Refractory cardiogenic shock has been closely linked to the extent of left ventricular necrosis; chances of improving myocardial contractility and ventricular function sufficiently to alleviate or reverse shock are slight if there is loss of ventricular myocardium beyond a critical mass necessary to support essential circulation (see Chapter 29, "Protection of the Ischemic Myocardium," by Braunwald and Maroko).

Consistently in cases ending fatally it is found that more than 40% of the ventricular myocardium has been destroyed (see page 375). Studies in this connection, conducted by Page, Caulfield, and coworkers at our hospital, compared autopsy findings in some 40 patients who had died of acute myocardial infarction, half of whom had been in shock for several hours prior to death despite vigorous

treatment in a coronary unit. The remainder had manifested no clinical shock in their hospital course. In both groups transverse sections of the ventricles at several levels were obtained for microscopic analysis; both the fresh infarct and earlier healed infarcts were taken into account to provide an estimate of total myocardial damage. Among patients with shock, at least 40% — and as much as 70% — of the left ventricular myocardium had been lost in virtually all cases. Among patients without shock, the loss was almost always limited to 30% or less.

Pathologic examination of myocardial tissue following acute infarction also has revealed that whether or not shock is involved, the necrotic area of the myocardium is initially surrounded by an identifiable zone manifesting signs of ischemic injury. For example, Cox and coworkers, observing the evolution of tissue damage following coronary artery ligation in dogs, identified three distinct morphologic zones in the region served by the obstructed artery. There was a central area showing obvious disruption of normal myocardial architecture and

depletion of cellular enzyme (succinic dehydrogenase) activity. Surrounding this was an intermediate zone showing inflammatory changes indicative of myocardial ischemia. In the zone beyond, tissue was normal both morphologically and enzymatically. With the passage of time following interruption of blood flow, the zone of complete necrosis continued to extend at a faster rate than did the ischemic zone. This appeared to be due to progressive destruction of myocardial tissue that began early in the course of infarction and continued until virtually all the damaged area was necrotic rather than merely ischemic.

There seems little doubt that a similar progression may occur in human infarction, particularly if complicated by ventricular failure and shock. In their postmortem studies Page, Caulfield, et al found striking differences in patients with or without cardiogenic shock. In those without shock, the infarct border was relatively homogeneous in appearance; demarcations between zones of necrosis, inflammation, and undamaged muscle were readily discerned. Significantly,

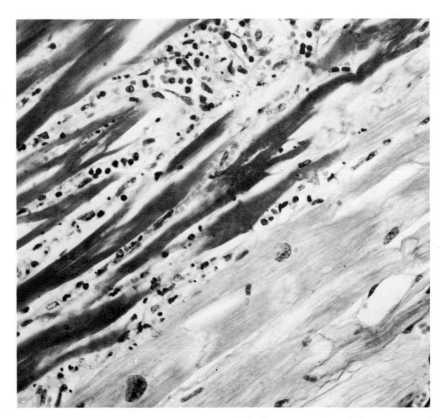

In early myocardial infarct, region of irreversible damage is indicated by presence of densely staining cells in upper portion of tissue section; in lower portion, swollen vacuolated cells characteristic of ischemic zone are still viable (original x320, H & E).

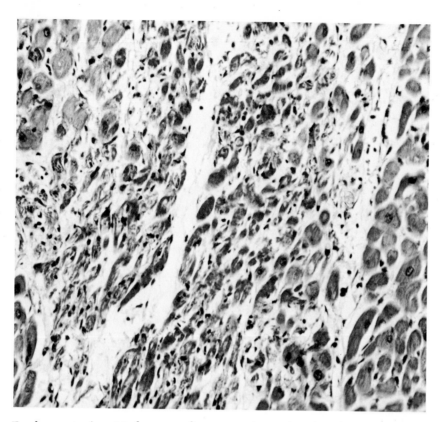

Focal necrosis of ventricular myocardium remote from infarct (x180) is apparently related to reduced coronary perfusion pressure and is consistent finding after death from cardiogenic shock. Similar changes are associated with persistent shock of any cause.

changes in the intermediate zone appeared to occur over a 48-to-72-hour period after onset of infarction and then subsided, suggesting a reversible lesion. In contrast, in the shock cases the border of the infarct was usually irregular in appearance; a mixture of both dead and damaged cells in an irregular concentric ring surrounded most or all of the infarct, suggesting marginal extension of the infarct into the border zone. The depth of tissue involved varied, but unmistakably the proportion of necrotic vs injured cells in this region could be related to the duration of shock prior to death. The areas of myocardial necrosis were found to be histologically of varying ages, suggesting a progression of the infarction process subsequent to the initial infarction. The longer shock had persisted prior to death, the greater the proportion of necrotic cells. As a rule, extension of necrosis to the border zone was most prominent in the region of the infarct served by the coronary artery showing greatest luminal narrowing.

In all the shock cases, the investigators also identified scattered focal areas of necrosis throughout both the right and left ventricles; in number and extent these lesions also appeared to have been increased with the duration of shock prior to death. No such changes appeared in any of the nonshock cases. Interestingly, similar changes were seen in a third group of patients without clinical or anatomic evidence of acute infarction who had died in shock of another cause. Decreased coronary perfusion, occurring because of its dependence on systemic blood pressure, which was already reduced as part of the shock state, was held responsible for the progression of cellular injury in the region of the infarct. The areas of focal necrosis appeared explainable on the same basis.

Cardiogenic shock may thus be viewed as a self-perpetuating state that results in progressive loss of myocardial contractility and ventricular performance and extension of necrosis. As the area of myocardial ischemia becomes enlarged, the possibility of further irreversible damage is increased and an even greater reduction in cardiac function occurs. And so the vicious cycle continues, until death occurs in most cases (see Chapter 22, "Biochemical and Morphologic Changes in Infarcting Myocardium," by Sobel).

Patient survival following a major infarction clearly depends chiefly on the balance between the myocardial need for oxygen for metabolic and functional activity and the capacity of the coronary circulation to deliver the oxygen needed. Obviously, if the initial insult to the myocardium is massive enough, there may be insufficient viable myocardium left to make survival possible.

However, in a good many cases the extent of myocardial necrosis, while enough to induce clinical manifestations of shock, might be compatible with survival were it not for the enlargement of the initial infarct associated with advancing left ventricular failure. It is in this context that the balance between myocardial oxygen need and the available supply can make a critical difference. If the need remains greater than the supply, the ischemic changes are likely to affect an increasing proportion of the myocardium and progress to irreparable damage. But effective means either of reducing oxygen need in the ischemic zone or of increasing the supply might reverse this process (see Chapter 29 by Braunwald and Maroko).

In employing aortocoronary bypass surgery in management of refractory shock, the emphasis is on the second of these two possibilities, that is, increasing the oxygen supply to preserve or restore function to the compromised myocardium and prevent further necrosis and its sequelae. However, before our group considered surgical intervention, another mode of therapy, aimed at reducing myocardial oxygen need as well as increasing supply, was already in use at our hospital and achieving a degree of success. We refer to counterpulsation as a means of mechanical circulatory assistance (see Chapter 32, "Assisted Circulation: A Progress Report," by Soroff and Birtwell). This approach is applied in the management of refractory shock in virtually all cases, either alone or in combination with coronary artery revascularization. Our experience with counterpulsation bears describing in some detail since it led quite directly to the possibility of surgical intervention. As will be seen, neither the revascularization procedure nor the diagnostic studies that precede it could be performed with their present degree of safety or possibility of benefit were it not for the circulatory support provided by counterpulsation.

It may be recalled that the first circulatory support device employing the principle of counterpulsation was developed more than a decade ago (by Clauss and coworkers). It entailed arterioarterial pumping through a cannula in the femoral artery. Several clinically effective approaches have since been devised, alike in that they can provide partial and temporary support to the failing circulation. These include more modern versions of the arterioarterial pump, the intra-aortic balloon pump, and systems for external regional pressure variation (see Chapter 32 by Soroff and Birtwell).

Our preference has been for the intra-aortic balloon pump. The minor surgery required for insertion (placement of a catheter balloon retrograde through a femoral artery into the descending thoracic aorta) requires only local anesthesia. Regardless of technique, the physiologic basis of counterpulsation is the same: peak arterial pressure during systole is lowered, allowing for a reduction in left ventricular afterload as a result of decreased aortic impedance to ventricular emptying and decreased tension in the myocardial wall. Thus, myocardial contractility is enhanced while ventricular ejection occurs at a lower left ventricular end-diastolic pressure and with less stroke work. As studies by Braunwald et al have shown, a major effect of these hemodynamic changes is to reduce myocardial oxygen consumption, thus improving the balance between demand and available supply. Research has confirmed that the effects of counterpulsation are enhanced when it is employed in the presence of reduced coronary flow such as occurs in shock. Helium is the gas used as driving agent because its low viscosity permits inflation and deflation of the balloon with the needed rapidity.

When intra-aortic balloon pumping was introduced experimentally in our unit some four years ago, it was soon apparent that counterpulsation could successfully overcome ventricular failure and shock and permit survival in

some cases. Whatever the outcome, there was likely to be an initial favorable response to counterpulsation, as shown by hemodynamic measurements of cardiac index, systemic arterial pressure, and pulmonary artery wedge pressure as an indicator of left ventricular end-diastolic volume. Later experience confirmed that the shock syndrome could be reversed by counterpulsation in 80% of cases. However, experience also taught that only a minority of patients – in the range of 20% – were likely to benefit sufficiently from counterpulsation to survive when pumping was discontinued.

Initially, the practice was to continue counterpulsation for a week or more in the hope that a satisfactory cardiac output and blood pressure could be maintained. The safety of intra-aortic balloon pumping in critically ill patients was amply demonstrated; pumping for as long as 14 days without interruption did no significant damage to the aorta nor did it induce other complications such as hemolysis or blood clotting. However, among patients failing to respond initially there proved to be little point in hoping that continuing counterpulsation would turn the tide. If there was a hemodynamic response, its peak was reached within about 24 to 48 hours.

By that point, patients could be grouped in three distinct categories. Some had shown minimal clinical or hemodynamic benefit despite balloon pumping and catecholamine infusion;

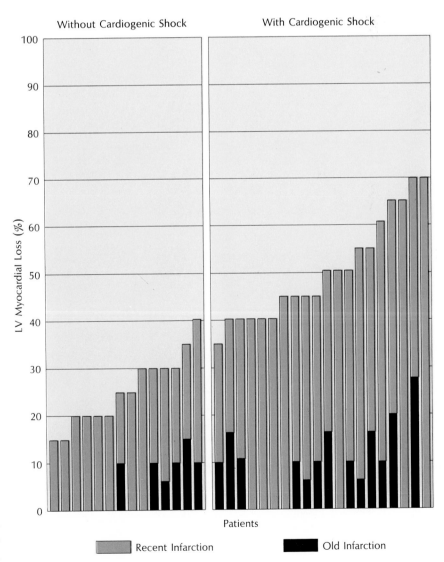

Among patients dying of cardiogenic shock following acute infarction, necrosis affecting 40% or more of left ventricular myocardium was a consistent finding in study by Page, Caulfield, et al; in fatal cases without shock, loss was usually limited to 30% or less.

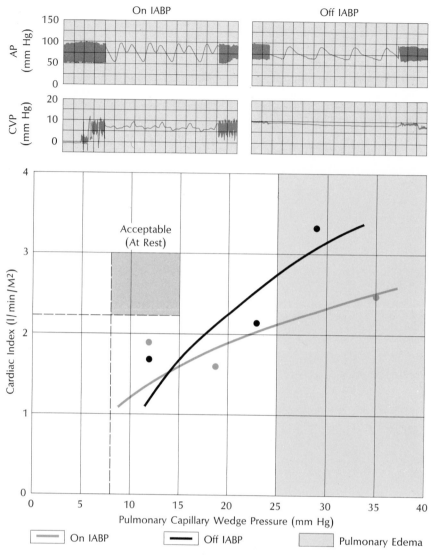

Despite intra-aortic balloon counterpulsation (IABP), a patient in shock complicating acute infarction showed inadequate hemodynamic improvement, as indicated by tracings of arterial and central venous pressures. With or without counterpulsation, left ventricular function (graph) failed to reach the acceptable physiologic range; an excessive increase in left-sided filling pressures was required to elevate cardiac index to levels above 2 l/min/m² and pulmonary edema was the result.

relation between cardiogenic shock and loss of functioning myocardium, presumably the different responses could have reflected differences in the extent of myocardial necrosis. Whether patients saved by counterpulsation alone had infarcts of moderate size could not be determined; however, it seemed safe to assume that they probably had. Postmortem examination of patients unresponsive to counterpulsation almost invariably demonstrated infarction affecting more than 40% of the left ventricle.

In those patients responding initially but remaining balloon-dependent, evidently the benefits of counterpulsation in terms of improving myocardial oxygen balance were inadequate to meet the need when partial circulatory support was stopped. Coronary angiography showed that some patients in this group had areas of necrosis extensive enough to explain counterpulsation failure. In others, dependence on the balloon pump appeared to result from a combination of infarction and ischemia. It was in this setting that direct coronary revascularization in combination with mechanical circulatory assistance emerged as a new therapeutic approach. The concept was that with use of counterpulsation to reduce left ventricular work and myocardial oxygen requirement, the progressive ischemic changes leading to irreversible loss of myocardium might be brought to a temporary halt or at least slowed. Coronary artery revascularization might then effectively increase oxygen delivery to the ischemic "peri-infarction" zone and prevent further loss of myocardium.

The first patient so managed by our group (in June 1970) was a 50-year-old man who had two acute infarcts complicated by cardiogenic shock within a four-week period. During the first episode, intra-aortic balloon pumping was begun some 30 hours following admission, after progressive clinical deterioration and failure to respond to vasopressor and inotropic agents. Circulatory assistance was continued for four days while his condition improved and stabilized. However, anginal pain recurred and left ventricular failure increased in the days that followed. After the second infarct, counterpulsation was again begun in an attempt to overcome refractory shock. There was initial

further counterpulsation was unlikely to be of benefit. Others had improved so substantially that it was anticipated that counterpulsation could eventually be discontinued. Tests in this group after acute cessation or a reduction in circulatory assistance showed that the cardiac index and other hemodynamic measures remained in the normal range. When counterpulsation was completely stopped the improvement was usually maintained. Most of these patients survived at least for a time following discharge from the hospital. The third group – the majority – although responding well at first, obviously could not be saved by counter-

pulsation alone. Although shock was improved the patients were still dependent on the balloon hemodynamically; attempts to wean them from the pump brought immediate clinical and hemodynamic deterioration. In retrospect, it was not possible to forecast, on the basis of clinical signs or hemodynamic status prior to mechanical circulatory assistance, which course a patient would follow. Peak hemodynamic response to counterpulsation was not prognostically indicative, since in some cases marked hemodynamic impairment soon ensued despite continued balloon pumping.

Taking into account the observed

hemodynamic improvement as before, only this time his condition rapidly deteriorated despite balloon pumping and an increasing catecholamine dosage to maintain blood pressure. Since death seemed imminent, more definitive therapy seemed justifiable.

Selective cinecoronary angiography and left ventricular cineangiography were performed with continuous balloon pump support. The former showed 95% stenosis of the mid-right coronary artery with a patent distal vessel and total occlusion of the proximal left anterior descending coronary artery with a patent distal vessel filling via collaterals from the right coronary artery. On the left ventricular angiogram there was akinesis of the apex and a large portion of the inferior and anterolateral wall; it was estimated that more than 50% of the ventricle was contracting poorly or not at all.

Counterpulsation was continued during induction of anesthesia and the initial stage of surgery to maintain arterial blood pressure; it was discontinued during the period of cardiopulmonary bypass and graft placement in the distal right coronary and the distal left anterior descending artery (endarterectomy was first required in the latter). Postoperative recovery was uneventful. The patient eventually returned to full-time work and remains essentially symptom-free.

A similar combination of intra-aortic balloon counterpulsation, diagnostic angiography, and direct coronary artery revascularization — with important modification — has since been employed by our group in some 40 patients. If standard medical therapy of shock does not appear to be effective, it is now terminated much sooner and mechanical circulatory assistance begun. Whereas earlier the practice was to delay counterpulsation for 48 hours or more, currently we are likely to intervene if a patient does not respond to medical treatment within four hours. It is clear that if counterpulsation is to be effective against cardiogenic shock, either alone or in conjunction with surgery, it must be used early, before myocardial damage is extended and further clinical and hemodynamic deterioration occurs.

In the presence of profound hypotension, the medical treatment employed prior to counterpulsation may

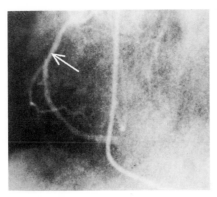
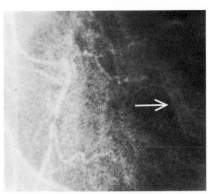

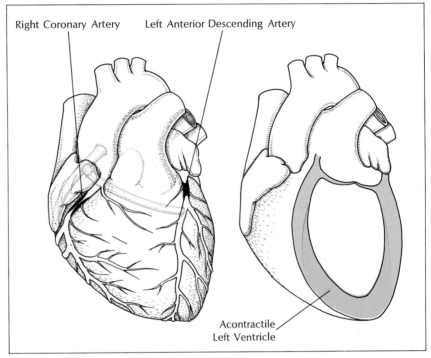

Right Coronary Artery   Left Anterior Descending Artery

Acontractile Left Ventricle

With counterpulsation failure (opposite page) patient underwent angiographic evaluation, which revealed a 95% occlusion of distal right coronary artery (top left, arrow) and occlusion of proximal left anterior descending artery, only faintly visualized at top right (arrow). Saphenous vein bypass grafting was carried out with excellent results (diagram at left); schematic (right) shows preoperative area of ventricular akinesis. An atheromatous core was also removed by endarterectomy from left anterior descending artery.

include levarterenol in addition to epinephrine and isoproterenol to increase blood pressure. All are used cautiously because of their effect of increasing myocardial work and hence oxygen requirement. Once balloon pumping is begun it is assumed that peak hemodynamic response will be attained within one to two days. A patient treatable by counterpulsation alone will show continuing hemodynamic improvement during this period and may be weaned from the pump within three or four days thereafter. On the other hand, lack of steady improvement in this period, or a sudden deterioration in the cardiac

index or pulmonary artery wedge pressure, should warn that the patient probably cannot recover with mechanical circulatory assistance alone. Continuing counterpulsation, by prolonging the period of marginal cardiac output and blood flow, may only lead to extension of infarction and increasing cardiac failure.

If counterpulsation fails to yield the desired result within 48 to 72 hours, selective coronary angiography and left ventricular angiography are performed to establish whether there is a condition remediable by coronary artery revascularization and enough viable myocardium to warrant it.

Cardiogenic Shock

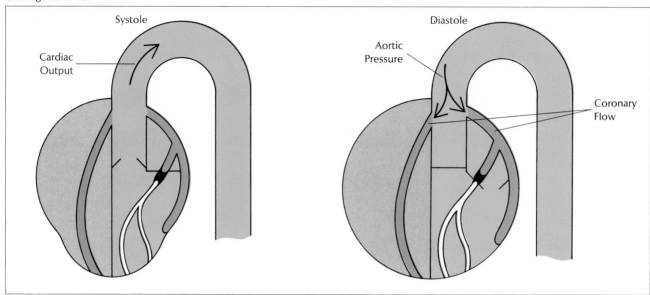

Balloon Counterpulsation (IABP)

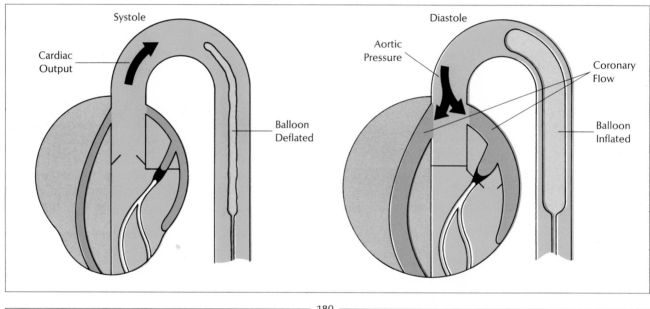

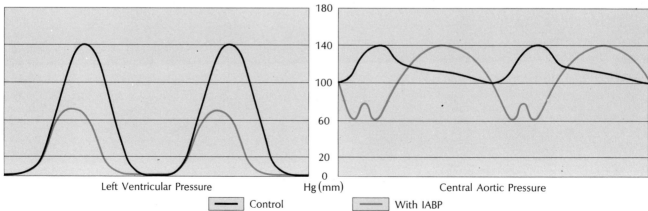

Mechanical circulatory support provided by intra-aortic balloon counterpulsation effects at least temporary hemodynamic improvement in patients with cardiogenic shock complicating acute infarction and permits survival in some cases. Balloon deflation at onset of systole causes a decrease in systolic aortic pressure and reduces impedance to ventricular emptying, thereby enhancing cardiac output; balloon inflation at onset of diastole causes an increase in aortic pressure, thus increasing coronary perfusion pressure when coronary flow is normally at its peak. Typical pressure changes are shown in the tracings at bottom.

Cardiac catheterization is also part of the diagnostic work-up, to determine left ventricular end-diastolic pressure and other hemodynamic values.

That there are hazards in angiography and other diagnostic intervention in this group of patients is undeniable. Ventricular irritability can be increased, hardly to be desired in patients so critically ill. These hazards are tangibly reduced when diagnostic procedures are performed with continuing mechanical circulatory support, which in our institution is done in all cases of this type.

Where surgery is indicated, there is nothing to be gained by delay; indeed, any hope of benefit hinges on early intervention before the extent of myocardial damage is too great. Allowing time for a trial of medical therapy and counterpulsation and the necessary diagnostic studies, it still may be only three or four days between onset of infarction and the revascularization procedure. At the time of operation, these patients are desperately sick and sometimes virtually moribund. Balloon pumping is used to facilitate induction of anesthesia and to increase the margin of safety in the early intraoperative stages; it is resumed immediately after the patient comes off cardiopulmonary bypass and continued after the operation, usually for several days, since the patients are often still acutely ill.

The special hazards encountered in this group are not in our view a reason to deny operation when it may be lifesaving; on the other hand, they are a reason to exercise precautions that might be unnecessary in other circumstances. In addition to circulatory support before and after operation, every effort is made to protect the myocardium by ensuring the least interruption of blood flow. In aortocoronary bypass grafting for chronic angina, a frequent practice is to clamp off the aorta and stop circulation to the heart for long enough to insert two or more grafts if needed. We think this is unwise in the presence of ventricular failure and shock and the aorta is usually not cross-clamped. Use of the pump oxygenator is also limited as much as it can be because of possible damaging effects. Selective hypothermia is employed for its protective effect on myocardial metabolism (the patient is cooled to 28° C; iced saline is then used to lower the heart temperature to approximately 15° C). The dual aim is to reduce the risks of surgery and to prevent, if possible, the progressive myocardial necrosis accompanying the shock state.

Performed with these cautions exercised, coronary artery revascularization apparently can improve perfusion of the ischemic myocardium sufficiently to restore left ventricular function and reverse the shock state in some cases. The effect on left ventricular function is often apparent immediately after the procedure is completed. Left ventricular contractility may be visibly enhanced and left ventricular hemodynamics improved.

To be sure, the benefits are maintained long enough to affect survival only in a minority of cases. Thus far approximately 40% of the patients treated surgically have lived two months or more (up to two and a half years). Needless to say, without surgery virtually all would have died. A 40% survival rate is therefore not unimpressive; moreover, this gain is in addition to that achieved by counterpulsation alone.

At this time, surgical treatment of cardiogenic shock must be viewed as still an experimental procedure; in this regard it differs from intra-aortic balloon counterpulsation which, on the basis of both efficacy and safety, we now consider established therapy for cardiogenic shock not promptly responsive to medical management. Thus far, criteria for selecting patients for coronary artery surgery have not been completely delineated. If a patient has a discrete lesion and substantial ventricular function despite refractory shock, the decision for surgery is clear enough. If an infarct is very extensive, neither surgery nor any other therapy can offset the lack of adequate viable myocardium; this is clear as well. It is the cases in between that can pose a dilemma.

Among patients succumbing despite surgery, pathologic examination at autopsy usually reveals left ventricular wall loss of greater than 60%. As a rule, preoperative left ventricular angiography has shown severe akinesia or hypokinesia, also involving more than 60% of the left ventricle. Given such a finding on angiography, surgery probably would be of little benefit. Plainly it would help to know better how much viable myocardium is required, minimally, to permit survival after acute infarction. Empirically, we have felt that about 50% of functioning myocardium must remain for surgery to have a reasonable chance of success. However, other factors, such as the patient's age, also enter into the decision.

In attempting to define criteria for surgical intervention, Sanders et al have done segmental analysis of left ventricular angiograms of patients undergoing coronary artery surgery. Angiograms were divided into six segments based on right and left anterior oblique views; the presence or absence of contraction in any segment was related to coronary perfusion in the area. In general, contraction and perfusion proved directly related. Among patients who survived, most segments manifested some degree of contraction and perfusion; nonsurvivors showed contraction in no more than half the segments. Although a technique such as this can provide a rough idea of whether surgical intervention is likely to prove beneficial, more definitive criteria are needed.

Of course, the status of the coronary vessels must also be considered in deciding for or against surgery; the situation differs to some extent, however, from that in patients with chronic myocardial ischemia who undergo coronary revascularization as an elective procedure. In the latter, surgery may be considered inadvisable if there is diffuse disease involving distal as well as proximal portions of the affected artery. In patients under discussion here, it may be necessary to proceed in less than ideal circumstances or forfeit all chance of sustaining life. On this basis, distal endarterectomy is performed in a significant number (about 20%) of cases to facilitate vein bypass grafting, even though we appreciate that the risk of early or late thrombosis is increased by endarterectomy.

As already noted, the decision to intervene surgically in the face of cardiogenic shock may be based in part on the presence of a mechanical defect associated with infarction that also needs correction. While death from myocardial infarction most often results from shock, mechanical complications – although relatively rare – also carry a high mortality. Until recently any attempt at surgical correction of such complications – chiefly related to rupture of the interventricular septum or papillary muscle – was usually delayed until a month or more from the time of infarction, since the mortality was prohibitively high when correction was attempted sooner. Surgery after a suitable interval could be performed with fairly good results and without unacceptable risk. The difficulty, of course, is that many patients who die of complications of acute infarction do so within days of its onset or, at most, within one or two weeks.

Our approach to either the hemodynamic or mechanical complications of acute infarction has been to attempt to utilize the potential benefits of surgery during the period when effective therapy can mean the difference between life and death. Bypass surgery to revascularize the myocardium is performed in suitable cases to reverse shock if possible, and if there are also surgically repairable mechanical defects complicating infarction, steps are taken to repair them.

Without doubt a procedure such as closure of a ventricular septal defect presents greater complexity in the presence of acute infarction; for ex-

ample, in tissue involved in the necrotic process it may be difficult to place sutures where they will hold. Nonetheless successful closure has been accomplished in several cases and substantial hemodynamic improvement has resulted. The operative approach taken is usually through a left ventriculotomy in the infarcted areas; if indicated, the infarct is then excised. From earlier experience of others attempting closure of a septal defect in the acute postinfarction period, it was evident that operating through a right ventriculotomy could impose an overwhelming burden on an already severely compromised right ventricle. Since most septal ruptures following acute infarction occur low in the septum in association with a low anteroseptal or posteroseptal infarct, surgical closure through a left ventriculotomy seems preferable.

Papillary muscle rupture, which allows prolapse of a mitral valve cusp during ventricular systole, usually results in severe mitral regurgitation, which, when imposed on a ventricle already functionally compromised, is likely to make intractable left ventricular failure and shock inevitable. In any event, acute infarction complicated by papillary muscle rupture carries an exorbitant risk. Reportedly some 70% of patients die within 24 hours of the appearance of the murmur; within two weeks 90% have succumbed.

Although papillary muscle rupture is usually evidenced by characteristic clinical signs (abrupt development of a loud systolic murmur and rapid hemodynamic deterioration usually occurring within 2 to 10 days after infarction), differentiating it from rupture of the ventricular septum may be difficult without cardiac catheterization. In any case, mitral valve replacement should not be considered until catheterization studies have established a definitive diagnosis.

As with surgery to repair rupture of the ventricular septum, the chances of surviving valve surgery are increased when at least several weeks have elapsed from time of infarction. The first reported successful repair of this mechanical defect complicating acute infarction was performed at our hospital in 1965. In a recent evaluation, 15 of 18 patients who underwent mitral valve replacement three to

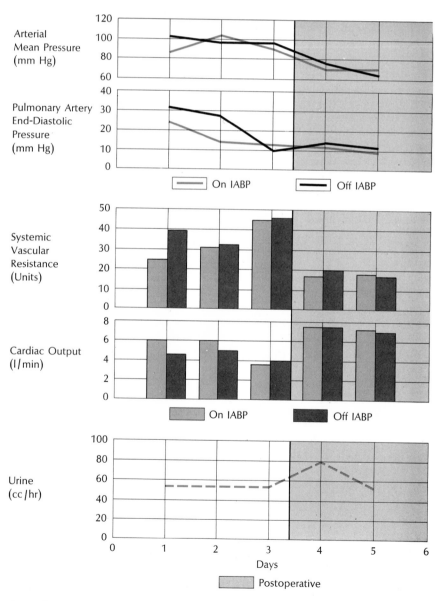

Hemodynamic improvement temporarily achieved by intra-aortic balloon pumping was enhanced and sustained by myocardial revascularization procedure in patient operated on for cardiogenic shock complicating acute infarction. As shown, following surgery hemodynamic values are comparable with or without counterpulsation.

seven months following infarction were alive and clinically well. In contrast, in a small group operated on within 2 to 10 days following infarction about 50% survived. Considering the prospects without such intervention, this is an acceptable result.

The feasibility or necessity of infarctectomy at the time of coronary artery revascularization or other surgery must be carefully weighed; the decision is often a difficult one to make. Theoretically, excision of the infarct might be expected to have a beneficial effect in view of evidence relating left ventricular function to the amount of left ventricular damage. According to an analysis by Klein and coworkers, once a region of akinesis approaches 20% to 25% of left ventricular surface area, the Starling mechanism of functional compensation probably no longer operates. Thus infarctectomy might help by reducing the area of damage relative to ventricular size and allowing improved function in remaining healthy myocardium.

However, clinically, the contribution of infarctectomy in management of complicated acute infarction has still to be clarified. We tend to favor its use only under some circumstances; for example, if there is a large paradoxically bulging infarct or acute aneurysm tending to impede left ventricular function, or if a localized infarct is associated with significant ventricular irritability and recurrent arrhythmia. Infarctectomy is also likely to be performed in the presence of a thinned-out necrotic infarct that appears in danger of rupture.

In considering both possible bene-

Steps in the Treatment of Cardiogenic Shock	
1. Supportive	Oxygen, morphine, blood volume adjustment, correction of acidosis
2. Electrical pacing techniques	Atrial or sequential atrioventricular pacing
3. Pharmacologic	Antiarrhythmic drugs, catecholamines, digitalis
4. Circulatory assistance	Intra-aortic balloon pump
5. Surgery	Revascularization by saphenous vein aortocoronary bypass grafting

fits and risks of surgery in the acute postinfarction period, the possibility of even earlier intervention of course comes to mind. The suggestion that coronary revascularization surgery might better be performed after onset of infarction but before refractory ventricular failure and shock ensue seems to us premature at this time. However, our experience has indicated that surgical therapy should be considered as early as possible when a complication of infarction appears to be evolving. In our view the course we have followed seems sensible as long as surgical treatment of acute infarction remains on an investigational basis. Our present feeling is that immediate use of intra-aortic balloon pumping to prevent refractory shock also is not warranted. Prophylactic counterpulsation has been suggested by others. Despite the relative safety and effectiveness of intra-aortic balloon pumping, some hazard is involved; hence our preference for waiting until standard therapy fails to bring the desired result.

It goes without saying that to employ surgery and counterpulsation in the management of refractory cardiogenic shock, an appropriate setting is required. Considering the precarious state of the patients and the nature of the procedures, it is essential that such treatment be confined to centers where surgeons have appropriate training and experience in coronary artery surgery, and where sufficient professional staff and technical facilities are available. Both preoperatively and postoperatively, these patients require round-the-clock medical and nursing coverage. Resources must be at hand to manage complex respiratory problems, lethal arrhythmias, or hepatic or renal failure, all of which may occur.

If these requirements are met, direct coronary artery revascularization performed with the support of mechanical counterpulsation appears to offer a chance of survival and clinical recovery to a significant proportion of selected patients otherwise doomed by advancing ventricular failure and shock.

34

Rehabilitation of
The Postinfarction Patient

HERMAN K. HELLERSTEIN
Case Western Reserve University

That more liberal attitudes toward the management of myocardial infarction prevail today than a generation ago is obvious. Confinement to bed is as brief as possible; patients are permitted to resume at least mild activity early in the course of illness unless a significant complication supervenes. For uncomplicated cases the total hospital stay is often as brief as two weeks, rarely more than three. From all evidence, patients managed on such a regimen come to no harm provided they are properly selected. However, the combination of early mobilization and resumption of activity as an important first stage in active rehabilitation of the uncomplicated postinfarction patient is considered less often than it should be. My thesis here will be that a planned program featuring exercise training among other measures will predictably enhance physical and emotional function in the majority of patients, and may tangibly reduce the risk of reinfarction and greater myocardial damage. A detailed approach to total cardiac rehabilitation must recognize and cope with the impact of coronary disease on the social, vocational, psychological, and physiological balance of the individual.

By definition, the goal of rehabilitation is restoration of an individual to his optimal status in physiologic, psychologic, and vocational terms; a further goal is to prevent progression of the underlying disease process. Traditionally, the principles of rehabilitation have been applied chiefly to disorders of the musculoskeletal and nervous systems. But they also have a valid and necessary place in the management of the patient with acute infarction or other coronary disease.

Physical conditioning in reference to heart disease is actually far from new. Fully 200 years ago Heberden observed the beneficial effects in a patient he advised to saw wood for 30 minutes daily over a six-month period. Although that was long before the first mention of acute myocardial infarction in the medical literature, no doubt some of Heberden's patients had sustained an infarct as

the condition is understood today. Needless to say, his counsel was all but forgotten following Herrick's original clinical description of acute myocardial infarction in 1912: the worry lest physical exertion heighten the risk of ventricular aneurysm or rupture, or aggravate arterial hypoxemia, kept patients virtually immobilized in bed for six or eight weeks. On discharge, anything as strenuous as stair-climbing was forbidden for at least a year. A few patients returned to work many months after hospital discharge; for most, all chance of a normal life was past.

Credit is due Samuel Levine for being probably the first to question the wisdom of enforced bedrest and inactivity for a prolonged period following onset of infarction; his "armchair" method, recommended largely on an empiric basis to avoid thromboembolic or respiratory complications, has since been well supported and extended both on a clinical and research basis. Without doubt, extenuating circumstances at the time (manpower needs during World War II) spurred efforts to shorten the period of hospitalization and invalidism of postinfarction patients; they also helped to change attitudes among physicians as well as patients as to the feasibility of returning at least some heart attack victims to work after the healing process was complete. Even so, when Leonard Goldwater and colleagues assessed their experience at the country's first cardiac work classification clinic in the 1940's, it came as a surprise to many that fully 60% to 70% of patients could return to work, although not necessarily at the same job as before.

Our experience at the Cleveland Area Work Classification Clinic, the second to be established (in 1950), indicated that an even higher proportion of heart attack victims – 80% to 85% – could resume working. Moreover, it became clear that patients with coronary disease could work safely and productively in a great variety of jobs, many requiring relatively high energy levels. This was established in a series of studies with techniques borrowed from physiologists to measure the energy cost of on-the-job activities. In essence, the energy cost of most jobs proved relatively small; for sedentary workers, often the maximal effort required by their jobs proved to be less than that imposed by walking. In any case, patients with coronary disease could perform most tasks with no more "strain" than healthy coworkers.

These were somewhat unexpected findings in our initial studies among workers in light manufacturing (a metal-fabrication plant); subsequent observations in heavy industry – a steel mill – proved that even there the energy requirements of most jobs were far lower than anticipated. Indeed, in every area of the mill except the open hearth and blast furnaces, there were jobs requiring no greater energy expenditure than in the light manufacturing plant. (Average energy cost per work shift was less than 2.5 Calories per minute.)

Measuring energy cost of any activity in terms of Calories is but one way of determining the physiologic work involved. Since the energy derives from oxidation of food, it can be measured also as oxygen cost – 5 Calories and 1 liter of oxygen being approximate equivalents. A Met (for metabolic unit), the standard frequently employed today as it is the most convenient, refers to the energy expenditure per kilogram body weight per minute of an average subject sitting quietly in a chair or at supine rest (see table, page 384).

As might be expected, the capacity for energy expenditure above the basal level varies both with health status and previous physical conditioning. Among champion athletes the capacity is likely to be in the range of 20 Mets/min, whereas in healthy but untrained young men it is likely to be closer to 12 Mets/min. On the average, a middle-aged man recovered from uncomplicated infarction has a capacity in the range of 8 or 9 Mets/min; if less than ordinary activity produces symptoms, his capacity is probably closer to about 4 Mets/min.

Recent determinations made early in the postinfarction period indicate a greater capacity for energy expenditure than many have assumed. On the average, in the uncomplicated case, capacity increases from a level of 1 to 2 Mets in the first week or so to

3 Mets during the remainder of the hospital stay. While the patient convalesces at home his capacity is likely to be in the range of 4 to 5 Mets; within the ensuing weeks it increases to the 8-to-9-Met level. Relating the physiologic capacity of postinfarction patients to the energy costs of typical activities makes it all the more evident that the capacity of most, even before healing is complete, is well above their needs. Walking on a level at the rate of 3 miles/hr requires only 2.1 Mets/min; walking uphill (5% grade) at the same rate requires 3.0.

Admittedly, other factors – emotional tension, for one – can modify response to a given activity and hence increase its cost. For example, several years ago we studied activity levels among surgeons. As expected, during an operation their average energy expenditure was low (1.5 Mets/min). However, this was a measurement of total body energy consumption. Consumption of energy by the heart itself was another matter. When this was estimated, we learned that myocardial oxygen consumption was probably at least equal to that among

workers in a steel mill or of the surgeons themselves when exercising on a treadmill. (As was established by Sarnoff and Katz, myocardial oxygen consumption can be estimated indirectly by measurements of peak systolic blood pressure and heart rate, the product of the two being proportional to myocardial oxygen consumption.) Thus, allowance must be made for the additional physiologic cost imposed by psychological and other factors. Even so, the postinfarction patient is likely to have a far greater capacity for energy expenditure than he needs.

Recognition of this fact has been partly responsible for a major shift in thinking about cardiac rehabilitation within the last few years. Whereas earlier the emphasis was on restoring the level of functioning in daily activities to what it had been before the patient was stricken, the concept now is that functional capacity – at home or at work – can be enhanced by active physical conditioning, and should be, since this may be protective.

To understand the role of physical activity in risk of coronary disease and in its course after infarction,

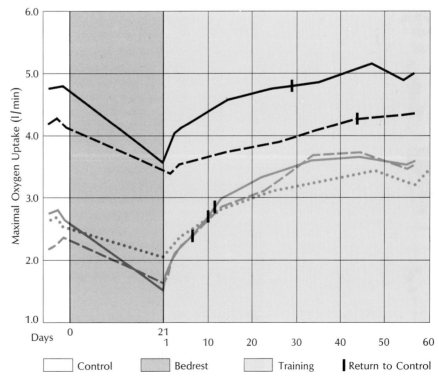

Control   Bedrest   Training   ▌Return to Control

Maximal oxygen uptake – an index of cardiovascular function – decreased markedly during prolonged inactivity in five healthy young men studied by Mitchell and Blomqvist. During the physical training period that followed, oxygen uptake in response to a maximal work load returned to pre-bedrest levels after varying intervals. It took longer to do so in the two habitually active (black lines) than in the three sedentary subjects.

Mean Energy Cost in Metabolic Units (Mets) of Various Activities

Activity	Mets
Sleep	0.8
Awake, lying at ease	0.9
Wash, shave, dress	2.1
Sit at ease	1.0
Stand at ease	1.2
Walk on level at 3 mph	2.1
uphill (5% grade) at 3 mph	3.0
upstairs	6.0
Ski cross-country	6.6-11.0
Bicycle at 5.5 mph	3.2
9.5 mph	5.0
13.1 mph	7.9
Swim breaststroke at 20 yd/min	3.6
30 yd/min	5.4
40 yd/min	7.2
Dance foxtrot	3.7
waltz	4.1
rhumba	5.0

it helps to begin by considering the cardiovascular effects of exercise in normal and particularly in sedentary individuals, and how these might be altered by a conditioning program to improve exercise capacity. Since the major limiting factor determining the level of physical activity any individual can perform is the capacity to provide oxygen to body tissues, a critical measure of physical fitness is maximal oxygen uptake; in turn this depends on maximal cardiac output, as determined by heart rate, stroke volume, and the arteriovenous oxygen difference of the body, reflecting the amount of oxygen extracted by the tissues as blood passes through the capillary bed. Thus, measurement of maximal oxygen uptake provides an index to maximal cardiac function.

In normal subjects, oxygen uptake increases in near linear fashion with increasing work loads imposed through use of standard testing equipment such as a bicycle ergometer or motor-driven treadmill. However, there is a point at which oxygen uptake reaches its upper limit for a given individual; he may continue to exercise at or above maximal work load but

there is no further increase in either oxygen uptake or cardiac output. As one would expect, hemodynamic parameters affecting oxygen uptake all show significant changes as oxygen uptake reaches its peak level. In a normal man going from standing rest to maximal exercise, oxygen consumption has been found to increase by a factor of 12 (in studies by Mitchell and coworkers), reflecting a fourfold increase in cardiac output and a threefold increase in A V oxygen difference. However, the increase in cardiac output is achieved chiefly by an increase in heart rate, since stroke volume appears to reach its maximum while oxygen uptake is still well below maximal. Thus, when oxygen uptake is at about 40% of peak value, stroke volume is already at about 85% of the maximum.

An individual's habitual level of physical activity must also be kept in mind as a major determinant of oxygen transport capacity; when, for one reason or another, the level of activity is reduced, maximal oxygen uptake decreases as well. This was evident when Mitchell and Blomqvist recently evaluated the effects of prolonged inactivity (21 days of bedrest) in five healthy young men. All five subjects showed a decrease in maximum oxygen uptake – from 20% to 46% less – after the extended rest. The decrease correlated closely with a drop in maximal cardiac output and stroke volume. The young men then undertook vigorous physical training for a 55-day period. In habitually sedentary subjects (three of the five), oxygen uptake in response to a maximal work load was twice as great as immediately following bedrest. Interestingly, it took 8 to 13 days for maximal oxygen uptake to return to pre–bedrest levels in the sedentary group; in the two habitually active subjects 20 and 43 days were required.

As the investigators observed: "A long history of a high level of activity associated with high maximal oxygen uptake offers little or no protection against loss of performance capacity following a drastic reduction in physical activity. Correspondingly, a long history of restricted physical activity and extremely low maximal oxygen uptake does not preclude rapid improvement following . . . training."

The latter also proved true in mid-

dle-aged men (studied by Siegel, Mitchell, and Blomqvist) who were sedentary by necessity, having been blind for 10 years or more. Maximal oxygen uptake prior to training was uniformly low; after 15 weeks of a moderate exercise program involving only 30 minutes of training per week, uptake increased by an average of almost 20%. This suggests a greater effect of exercise training than many anticipated.

When our physical reconditioning program was initiated in Cleveland over a decade ago, we arrived empirically at a schedule of 60 minutes three times weekly for full participants. There was no experience to assure that this would achieve the best result; neither were we certain that the principles of conditioning applied in sedentary individuals would prove beneficial in patients with coronary disease. Observations by Turell and myself in the Cleveland Area Work Classification Clinic had convinced us that patients who returned to work improved more in terms of overall functioning than those with the same original degree of disability who did not resume work. On that basis, a planned program of exercise training for coronary patients was cautiously begun. Experiments in dogs (by Eckstein) had suggested that, in animals at least, exercise could induce development of collateral vessels when a main coronary artery was occluded. The hope was that this might happen in humans as well. From clinical experience to date, there has been little proof that such collaterals develop.

The underlying principles of conditioning apply equally to the normal or abnormal situation: The conditioning program must provide for a progressive yet gradual increase in exercise level. Some overload on the muscle – heart as well as skeletal – is required; unless functional capacity is taxed, conditioning is not likely to succeed. Overload is defined as being greater than customary activity and does not imply exceeding the individual's maximal capacity. Paradoxical though it may seem, this does not preclude active reconditioning in cardiac patients. Moreover, there have been few problems with use of pre-training exercise testing in planning a suitable conditioning program. Despite concerns to the contrary, even with exercise testing at maximal levels, the occurrence of infarction or reinfarction in patients with known heart disease has been extremely rare. (Based on the accumulated experience of a number of investigators the likelihood of acute infarction or sudden death is in the range of 1:10,000 tests.) Risks are minimal provided exercise testing and a training program based on test results are limited to patients with uncomplicated infarction. From the beginning, the presence of a serious arrhythmia or heart failure has been considered a contraindication to physical conditioning.

If there were a way to predict exercise tolerance in a given individual on the basis of measurements made *at rest*, testing could of course be dispensed with; there being none, testing must be used as a guide in formulating an exercise prescription. Multilevel testing — as with use of a bicycle ergometer or motor-driven treadmill — is necessary to arrive at a prescription, which will be based on an individual's existing functional capacity but aimed at enhancing it.

In evaluating patients with coronary disease we have purposely kept exercise testing at a submaximal level; the electrocardiogram as well as heart rate and blood pressure are monitored before, during, and after testing. Exercise testing at a maximal work load is recommended by some, and, as already noted, it has been done without significant complications. In our view, testing the limits of exercise capacity is not only inadvisable but unnecessary, since it is feasible to calculate maximal capacity indirectly from other data with reasonable accuracy.

Our long-term study extending over an eight-year period included more than 650 men. Two hundred and fifty-four had recovered from acute infarction and/or were subject to anginal attacks; 402 were considered coronary prone on the basis of acknowledged risk factors (hyperlipidemia, hypertension, obesity, physical inactivity). The two groups were set up by design — in an effort to determine whether a program of exercise training could affect either the progression of known coronary disease and its sequelae or its early development, i.e., whether it would be helpful in either secondary or primary prevention, or both. From the outset,

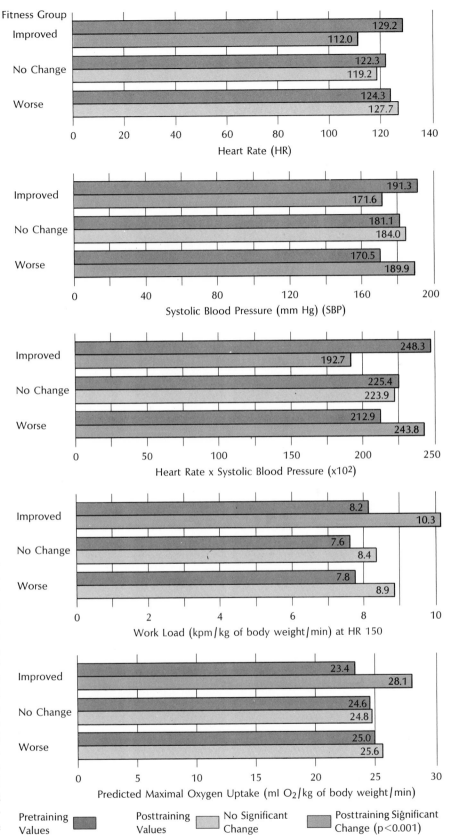

Among 100 men (of 650) with coronary disease participating in Cleveland training programs, improved physical fitness was associated with significant improvement in cardiovascular response to exercise. A greater work load could be performed at a lower heart rate and at lower total oxygen cost. Moreover, myocardial oxygen consumption was apparently reduced, as reflected by the HR x SBP product. In contrast, responses were unchanged or impaired in subjects whose fitness did not improve or became worse.

exercise training was only one part of a multifaceted regimen attacking the other risk factors as well (see Chapter 20, "The Primary Prevention of Coronary Heart Disease," by Stamler).

Men who had sustained infarcts were enrolled in the program after at least three months had elapsed following the acute event. Now that both the benefits and relative safety of exercise training are better established, entry into a conditioning program at two months, or earlier in some cases, is permitted and in fact encouraged.

A bicycle ergometer was used for the prior testing; after a warm-up period, subjects were expected to pedal for six minutes, beginning at a level of 300 kilopond meters/min; the load was increased by increments of 150 kilopond meters with rest periods of four minutes until a heart rate of 150 beats/min — or as close to it as possible in the individual case — was reached. (As defined by work physiologists, a kilopond is the force exerted when a mass of one kilogram is subjected to the normal force of gravity; a kilopond meter of work is performed when this force acts through the distance of one meter.) In each case, maximal oxygen uptake was calculated from the known submaximal work load using a nomogram as suggested by Astrand, or by extrapolation if the highest attained heart rate approximated 90% to 95% of the age-predicted maximal heart rate.

Parenthetically, a heart rate of 150 was chosen because it was assumed to be attainable with submaximal effort and would represent about 85% of the maximal rate for the age group being studied. A number of the men, including some who were coronary prone, were not able to reach that level, however. As we learned, in exercise testing or training the age-determined decline in maximal heart rate must be taken into account. Whereas at age 35 maximal heart rate is in the range of 188 beats, by age 55 it is in the range of 165. In patients of the same age with coronary disease it is often closer to 140 to 145.

Physical fitness on entry into the program (and later to evaluate training effects) also could be characterized in terms of the highest attainable myocardial oxygen uptake by calculating the product of the heart rate times the systolic blood pressure (H R x S B P) and by the associated electrocardiographic changes during exercise testing. A target level for training was worked out for each subject, based on multilevel testing that taxed him to within 70% to 85% of estimated maximal aerobic capacity. Testing was cut off sooner if warning signs appeared; for example, ventricular arrhythmias or conduction defects, disproportionate blood pressure or heart rate responses for the work load, severe chest pain, confusion, or dyspnea. Marked s T-T changes on the electrocardiogram indicating myocardial ischemia also signified excessive strain (displacement of 0.3 or more millivolts in bypolar precordial leads in C5 and C6 positions in the absence of other symptoms, less if associated with severe angina or its equivalent).

In subjects who could complete the exercise testing without adverse signs or symptoms, the exercise prescription was set below work load limit of the ergometer test for continued training — at about 60% to 75% of maximal aerobic capacity. This could usually be achieved with an average target heart rate during exercise sessions of 70% of the attained or predicted maximum for the subject's age and condition; for brief periods during each session it was allowed to reach 85%. Recent investigations by myself and Richard Ader have demonstrated that a constant relationship exists between oxygen uptake, expressed as a percent of the maximal oxygen uptake (Max vO_2), and heart rate, expressed as a percent of maximal heart rate (M H R), regardless of age, fitness, or coronary disease. This relationship can be represented by the regression line $Y = 1.41X - 42.1$ for normal males, and $Y = 1.32X - 35.2$ for A S H D subjects, where $Y = \%$ Max vO_2 and $X = \%$ M H R. The heart rate expressed as % M H R bears a significant relationship to coronary blood flow, myocardial oxygen uptake, body oxygen consumption as percent of maximal oxygen consumption, respiratory exchange ratio, lactate and fibrinolysin production, and catecholamine excretion. At the levels of 70% and 85% M H R, which correspond to 57% and 78% Max vO_2 respectively, significant beneficial adaptive changes transpire and are reflected in these parameters. When testing had to be

stopped because of untoward effects, the target heart rate for training sessions was set at 70% of the peak rate reached, and again at 85% for brief periods. In both situations the work load during training was initially low and increased stepwise until the target level was reached.

Several points must be made in reference to the type of exercise training used. Speaking generally, the aim of physical conditioning can be to increase muscle strength or endurance, or both. Muscle strength can be improved by brief isometric contractions against heavy resistance. Exercise of this type does not involve the body's oxygen transport system; hence it cannot be expected to improve cardiovascular function. If anything, it is likely to be extremely dangerous for an individual with cardiac impairment because of the marked rise in blood pressure and reflex cardiac slowing. Exercise involving short bursts of intense activity may require more energy than is immediately available from oxygen transport; hence it chiefly involves anaerobic not aerobic capacity.

It is a third type of exercise that is of most importance in training patients with coronary disease, since

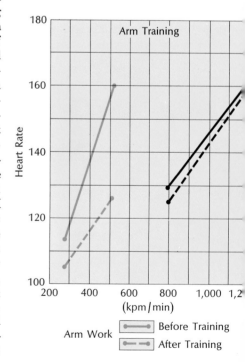

Importance of peripheral response in adaptation to physical training is shown in differential effects of bicycle ergometer testing using either upper or lower limbs. In subjects studied by Clausen and Trap-

only this type offers the prospect of improving their condition. It consists chiefly of repeated actions requiring maximal or submaximal effort, preferably using large antigravity muscle masses so that the greatest demand for oxygen is made. To meet these requirements our exercise program has featured calisthenics and sequences of running and walking; calisthenics for 30 minutes, run-walk sequences for 15 minutes, recreational activity – swimming, volleyball, etc.– for another 15 minutes. (The facilities used are at the Jewish Community Center of Cleveland.) On entering the program most subjects have to be able to manage about half the full sequence of calisthenics, running, and walking; over time, the work load is progressively increased. In the course of our long-term study, it became increasingly apparent that more than exercise capacity is improved through training. Average heart rate and blood pressure responses to exercise are substantially reduced. Calculations of the HR x SBP product indicate reduced myocardial oxygen consumption for a given work load and a greater capacity to attain a higher HR x SBP product before ischemic ST changes

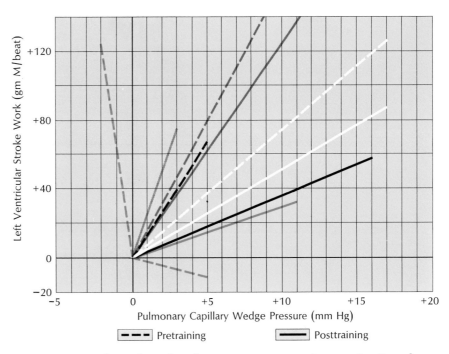

In patients entered in a physical conditioning program two to four months after a documented myocardial infarction, left ventricular function curves during exercise tolerance testing were improved in most subjects after training (Frick and Katila).

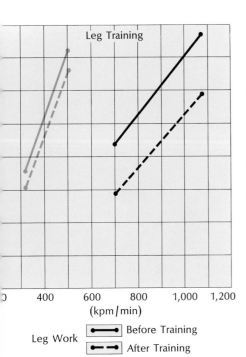

Jensen, heart rate response following arm training was reduced only during arm work; training of leg muscles was associated with lower heart rate response only when leg exercises were performed.

appear. A given work load is apparently attainable at a lower oxygen cost, suggesting improved ventricular performance.

Detailed studies on a subgroup of 100 men with coronary disease (66 with an infarct) after an average of 33 months in training demonstrated sustained improvement in physical fitness in 65%; in contrast, 10% to 12% of control subjects improved spontaneously. Improvement in one parameter was usually accompanied by improvement in another; for example, among subjects with initially abnormal or "borderline" ECG findings during activity, the exercise ECG improved in 84% of those who also improved in physical fitness (see graph on page 385). Not unexpectedly, improvement proved dependent on adherence to the program. Thus, among men who participated fully (three sessions weekly) physical fitness improved in 86%; among those who participated less regularly improvement ranged from 35% to 69%. Changes in the exercise ECG followed a similar pattern: Among subjects with initially abnormal or borderline ECG findings there was improvement in 65% of men who attended the program regularly, as against 14% of men with inconsistent attendance.

Since the inception of our conditioning program, more than 1,200 men have participated, about 450 of whom have clinical coronary disease. Those not participating much at first due to chest pain or other symptoms are soon able to perform the entire sequence of exercises with minimal discomfort (use of nitroglycerin is encouraged if needed). Improvement is documented electrocardiographically by elimination or reduction of ST-T segment changes; physiologically, improved heart rate and blood pressure responses are a consistent finding in more than 75% of subjects. In addition, biochemical tests show decreased lactate production for the same work load and a reduction in serum lipid levels – the latter attributable chiefly to diet modification. Evaluation has also included psychologic testing before and after training; this has confirmed that a feeling of depression is virtually universal in the period following onset of infarction. The basis for this depression is the fear of invalidism and of loss of life, autonomy, and economic independence. "The depression that occurs in the wake of myocardial infarction is reactive and exogenous in type. Like the grief following the loss of a loved one, it occurs in response to an incident . . .

that is appropriate for its development" [Hackett]. The enforced passivity and inactivity following an acute infarction are antithetic to the usual self-sufficient, aggressive, dynamic, and driven personality of many young males (see Chapter 21, "The Central Nervous System and Coronary Heart Disease," by Rosenman and Friedman). Restrictions of activity, either physical or mental, impose an enormous tax on their emotional economy. Planned physical conditioning counteracts the threat of invalidism, enhances the sense of independence, and serves as a potent antidote against and prophylaxis for depression. An indirect benefit of exercise training has been the significant improvement in outlook, self-esteem, mood, and the documented scores of the hypochondriasis, hysteria, and depression scales of the Minnesota Multiphasic Inventory, and, unexpectedly, in the frequency and quality of sexual activity.

As already noted, the program is considered well within the capacity of subjects recovered from uncomplicated infarction. (The average energy cost of the calisthenics is 4.4 Mets/min; the average cost of running exercises, 5.2.) Nonetheless, at entry, cardiovascular status is carefully evaluated in addition to exercise toler-

More or less vigorous calisthenics may be prescribed for Cleveland program participants, as can be observed in photo above.

ance, and appropriate consent forms are completed. The exercise prescription arrived at for each patient is made as specific as possible concerning the magnitude, frequency, and duration of effort. This task must be approached with the same care as the prescription of a potent drug.

Once training is under way, adequate supervision is mandatory. In our facility a physician is always immediately available; physical therapists and other paramedical personnel are trained in cardiopulmonary resuscitation and defibrillation equipment is always on hand.

With experience has also come better appreciation that there are limitations as well as benefits to exercise training Many of our subjects have remained in the program for extended periods and close to 70% have been able to maintain improvement in exercise tolerance and cardiovascular responses for longer than five years; in another 15% the limit of improvement has been closer to two years. In analyzing our results we found that the remainder, about 15% of subjects, have never shown improvement, sometimes despite faithful attendance. Coronary arteriography revealed severe vascular disease among these patients; frequently at least two coronary arteries were stenosed 90% or more. Hence, exercise could not have been expected to be of much value; in such patients, earlier consideration is now given to surgery (see Chapter 30, "Revascularizing the Myocardium: The Saphenous Vein Bypass," by Effler and Sheldon). At present, coronary arteriography is performed on a fairly routine basis to exclude patients unlikely to profit from the program.

Until fairly recently few attempts had been made to evaluate directly the hemodynamic consequences of exercise training, using catheterization and other appropriate techniques. However, within the past few years several groups here and abroad have conducted relevant studies along these lines, both in normal subjects — young and middle-aged — and in coronary patients. Significant changes resulting from exercise training at submaximal levels are found in all groups studied. As we had observed, heart rate response to a given work load is consistently lower after training. Blood pressure is not altered much in young

subjects but is significantly reduced in older subjects and more so in those with coronary disease. Stroke volume during exercise increases in some patients with coronary disease, though less consistently than in normal subjects, young or old. In all groups, oxygen uptake after training remains about the same at similar work loads.

The findings among patients with coronary heart disease are worth noting in some detail. For example, Frick and Katila in Finland entered a group of men in an exercise program two to four months after a documented infarction. The exercise included 30 minutes on a bicycle ergometer, plus 15 minutes on a rowing device, and 5 minutes each of jogging, walking, and step-testing. The intensity of exercise was progressively increased on the basis of intervening fitness tests, but always kept just below the pain threshold. All subjects developed increased exercise tolerance; those with angina remained pain-free at higher exertion levels. Hemodynamically, some, though not all, of the patients manifested increased stroke volume with training, as shown by standard left ventricular function curves; there was also evidence of decreased heart volume in patients with heart enlargement prior to entry. Measurement of the AV oxygen difference showed no change, suggesting to these workers that the improvement in exercise tolerance was not due to greater extraction of oxygen by skeletal muscles.

On the other hand, Varnauskas and coworkers in Sweden, exercising patients with coronary disease on a bicycle ergometer, found that AV oxygen difference increased with training and considered that this probably resulted from adjustment in peripheral circulation. Detry and associates, studying patients at the University of Washington and the University of Louvain in Belgium, also found the AV oxygen difference increased. The arterial oxygen content was also higher after training, suggesting that the wider AV oxygen difference might be due to improved oxygenation rather than peripheral circulatory changes. In these and other studies some patients with coronary heart disease have responded to training with an improved capacity to perform exercise and a lowered cardiac output while others have not.

The differing findings leave unanswered a key question about the effects of exercise training: whether the improvement in exercise tolerance and the cardiovascular effects involve principally peripheral or central mechanisms. Some investigators maintain that the chief effect of training is on the muscles used for training; thus the heart and central circulation would be affected only indirectly. Others believe it likely that there may be direct cardiac effects. If ventricular function or contractility were affected, this might have important implications in terms of the course of coronary disease. Thus far the issue is unresolved.

Without question, peripheral response is important in adaptation to exercise. This has been shown in a number of ways, for example by Danish workers Clausen and Trap-Jensen in training two groups of men – one group exercised using their arms, the other using their legs. In tests after training, both groups alternated between arm and leg exercises, using the same exercise protocol. The result? Training of arm muscles affected heart rate response only during arm exercises, and vice versa. The lack of cross adaptation is a cogent reason for including arm and torso exercises, as in calisthenics, and not restricting training to jogging alone.

According to Clausen and Trap-Jensen, one important effect of training is a redistribution of cardiac output; this was found in studies in which cardiac output and blood flow in regional vascular beds were measured in patients with coronary heart disease before and after physical training (two levels of submaximal exercise were used during 4 to 10 weeks). After training at a "moderate" work load, cardiac output was reduced, largely because of a decreased heart rate. Increasing to a higher work load produced a small increment in cardiac output, reflecting a small increase in stroke volume. Significantly, hepatic blood flow, normally reduced by exercise in the untrained subject, was less reduced after training than before, suggesting that a greater fraction of left ventricular output was being directed to tissues not directly involved in exercise. Indeed, when changes in quadriceps muscle blood flow were estimated after submaximal exercise

training (from the clearance rate of locally injected ^{133}Xe), blood flow was shown to be lower after training than before. Thus skeletal muscles seemed able to perform the same submaximal work load with lesser perfusion; presumably some factor had increased oxygen extraction by muscle.

The possibility now under study is that various changes in skeletal muscle associated with adaptation – among them lower lactate levels and slower glycogen depletion in response to exercise – may be mediated by biochemical changes within the muscles themselves. There have been intriguing findings, by Holloszy and coworkers at Washington University, in rats trained to run on a treadmill to increase endurance. On visual examination, the animals' leg muscles, and homogenates thereof, manifested a deep red color accounted for by increased myoglobin concentration. In fact, the myoglobin level in the muscles increased by 80%; all of the increase was confined to exercised muscles. Recently, at a postgraduate course on exercise testing and training of patients with coronary disease given by Case Western Reserve and George Washington schools of medicine, Holloszy suggested that whatever accounted for the increased myoglobin, its presence might facilitate oxygen utilization in tissues by enhancing its transport.

In response to training, animals' leg muscles also showed a twofold increase in activity levels of the mitochondrial respiratory chain enzymes vital to oxidative metabolism; activity of mitochondrial citric acid cycle enzymes increased significantly as well. Other adaptive responses to exercise included an increased activity of enzymes involved in the transport and catabolism of long-chain fatty acids; an increased capacity of homogenates and mitochondrial fractions to oxidize palmitate, oleate, and linoleate; and a rise in the capacity to regenerate A T P via oxidative phosphorylation.

Holloszy and coworkers suggest that the increases in enzymatic activity and oxidative capacity may both be due to an increase in enzyme protein; evidence for this is a 60% increase in the protein content of the mitochondrial fraction and a doubling in the concentration of cytochrome C. These changes occurred, however, only in

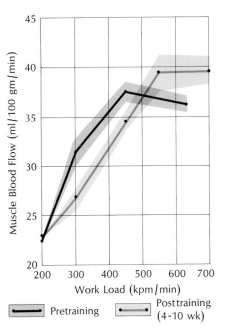

Redistribution of cardiac output following submaximal exercise training is suggested by findings in patients with coronary disease studied by Clausen and coworkers. After training, quadriceps muscle blood flow, as measured by clearance rate of locally injected ^{133}Xe, was lower at a submaximal work load than before training and higher at a maximal load. This suggested that skeletal muscle could handle a submaximal load with less perfusion, perhaps because of increased O_2 extraction.

skeletal, not cardiac, muscle, suggesting that the reduction in heart rate and other cardiovascular effects of exercise training are probably secondary to alterations in skeletal muscle.

If intracardiac factors are involved, how do they relate to the apparent changes in myocardial oxygen consumption seen with exercise training? Within the past few years factors determining oxygen consumption by the heart have been better defined. Earlier, the major determinant was thought to be the tension generated in the wall of the heart as indicated by changes in intraventricular pressure; indeed this is the basis of the systolic tension-time index reflected by the H R x S B P product. However, work by Braunwald, Sonnenblick, et al showed that when heart contractility was augmented in dogs under controlled conditions, myocardial oxygen consumption rose while the tension-time index fell; augmentation was demonstrable regardless of the means used to increase contractility. Thus, although oxygen consumption per beat appears to relate directly to ventricular wall tension, oxygen consumption for any given beat is also markedly affected by the state of contractility of the myocardium.

It is well known that cardiovascular response to exercise involves sympathetic stimulation; some have suggested that exercise bradycardia associated with conditioning may be largely due to a decrease in general sympathetic tone. Experiments by Stephen Salzman of our group in mice adapted to muscular exercise provide some support. Adapted animals showed decreased myocardial uptake of tracer quantities of tritiated epinephrine. However, these findings are not readily reconciled with others suggesting contractility is increased by physical conditioning; for example those by Hanson showing an increase in the mean rate of systolic ejection and an increase in the rate of development of left ventricular pressure (dP/dt).

Thus we do not yet have an adequate explanation for the cardiovascular effects of physical conditioning. The uncertainties do not, however, alter the fact that both subjective and objective improvement can be attained through exercise training, provided patients are properly selected and contraindications observed.

Moreover, in those in whom exercise training is indicated, it makes sense to begin it as early as possible. In patients with acute myocardial infarction, as noted, training of the type we have described should await completion of the healing process. However, preparatory measures can and should be taken in the immediate postinfarction period. Early in the first week the patient with uncomplicated infarction can handle feeding himself, shaving, other selfcare; he can sit in a bedside chair and use a commode (or bathroom with assistance). By the end of the first week he can probably walk around his room; by the second week he may be able to venture down the hall and back, or perhaps try a couple of steps. As a rule these activities are well within his capacity; carried out under supervision and at a gradually increasing level, they should prepare him for greater activity when he reaches home, including stairclimbing if necessary. Walking around the neighborhood, progressively increasing both distance and speed, enhances exercise capacity during the convalescent period.

By the sixth to eighth week after the acute event, most patients are more than ready for activity at higher levels and should be encouraged to try it. Our recommendation is for their enrollment in an exercise training program such as has been described. Admittedly, this may not be easy to arrange since there are few such programs in existence. As of 1970 there were throughout the U.S. about 90 conditioning programs of all types for patients with coronary disease, of which 30 at most did appropriate stress testing to evaluate participants before entry. In the subsequent three years, many additional facilities have been established in the U. S. for evaluation and supervised physical conditioning of the post–myocardial infarction patient, with partial financial coverage by some insurance carriers.

Frankly, chances of improvement will depend on whether more physicians and others involved in caring for patients with acute myocardial infarction come to see physical conditioning as an integral aspect of management. Not long ago an American Heart Association committee concerned with rehabilitation surveyed physicians throughout the country on management of acute myocardial infarction. Respondents (a total of 2,491 out of 3,600 queried) had managed some 70,000 patients with myocardial infarction during the preceding 12 months. Among patients surviving to enter the hospital, nearly 45% were classified by respondents as having uncomplicated infarction.

In other words, these were patients who would be candidates for an active conditioning program following recovery. Few of the responding physicians had considered the possibility, however, although nearly all gave general advice about progressively increasing activity after discharge. Few thought it necessary to employ exercise testing in evaluating a patient's status, some because they considered that clinical judgment would be equally helpful, when, in fact, it cannot substitute for objective evaluation. Others were concerned for their patients' safety during exercise testing, assuming that even a submaximal work load is beyond the capacity of most postinfarction patients, although the contrary has been demonstrated.

To some extent the excessive concern and caution in reference to acute myocardial infarction of an earlier day still seem to persist despite all the changes that have taken place. This is reflected in some of the survey responses: Most physicians were allowing patients with uncomplicated infarction to sit in a chair by day 8, to walk in the room by day 14, and down the hospital corridor by day 17. Typically, stair-climbing was not permitted before day 30. All these activities can probably be managed sooner by most patients with uncomplicated infarction. Significantly, 13% of these patients had not returned to work within the year.

From other findings it is evident that resumption of sexual activity is often unduly delayed, again because it is assumed it will be too taxing physiologically. Actually, when the heart rate was measured in a group of our patients (by means of a Holter type portable ECG recorder worn throughout a 24-to-48-hour period) it proved surprisingly modest. Maximal heart rate during intercourse averaged 117 beats per minute (range 90 to 144), usually lasting no more than 10 to 15 seconds. The energy expenditure was equivalent to that of climbing a flight of stairs. What is also sometimes forgotten is that most of the patients are in the middle years or beyond; like heart rate, the frequency of sexual relations tends to decrease with age. For both reasons sexual activity seems permissible by the sixth week or so.

Given the evidence of enhanced cardiovascular functioning through exercise training, there remains the question of whether conditioning can modify the course of coronary disease, reducing the risk of reinfarction or influencing survival. To date no controlled study has been undertaken to determine if this is the case; it would certainly be desirable to evaluate exercise training along with control of coronary risk factors in secondary prevention. Meanwhile, there is little doubt that active participation in a reconditioning program can go a long way toward improving the quality of life for a patient who has survived an acute infarction. To us this has seemed dividend enough.

Selected References

Index

Illustration and Data Source Credits

Selected References

CHAPTER 1

Braunwald E, Ross J Jr, Sonnenblick EH: Mechanism of Contraction of the Normal and Failing Heart. Little, Brown and Company, Boston, 1968

Huxley HE: The mechanism of muscular contraction. Sci Am 213:18, 1965

Leyton RA, Sonnenblick EH: The ultrastructure of the failing heart. Am J Med Sci 258:304, 1969

Ross J Jr, Sonnenblick EH, Taylor RR, Covell JW: Diastolic geometry and sarcomere lengths in the chronically dilated left ventricle. Circ Res 28:49, 1971

Sonnenblick EH: Correlation of myocardial ultrastructure and function. Circulation 38:29, 1968

CHAPTER 2

Bárány M: ATPase activity of myosin correlated with speed of muscle shortening. J Gen Physiol 50:Suppl 197, 1967

Hill AV: The heat of shortening and the dynamic constants of muscle. Proc R Soc Lond [Biol] B:126, 1938

Katz AM: Contractile proteins of the heart. Physiol Rev 50:63, 1970

Katz AM, Brady AJ: Mechanical and biochemical correlates of cardiac contractions. I. Mod Concepts Cardiovasc Dis 40:39, 1971

Weeds AG, Frank G: Structural studies on the light chains of myosin. Cold Spring Harbor Symp Quant Biol 37:9, 1973

Wilkinson JM, Perry SV, Cole HA, Trayer IP: The regulatory proteins of the myofibril. Separation and biological activity of the components of inhibitory-factor preparations. Biochem J 127-215, 1972

CHAPTER 3

Bing RJ, Fenton JC: Cardiac metabolism. Annu Rev Med 16:1, 1965

Braunwald E: 13th Bowditch Lecture. The determinants of myocardial oxygen consumption. Physiologist 12:65, 1969

Braunwald E, Ross J Jr, Sonnenblick EH: Mechanism of Contraction of the Normal and Failing Heart. Little, Brown and Company, Boston, 1968

Davies RE: Essays in Biochemistry, Vol. I. Campbell PN, Greville GD, Eds. Academic Press, Inc., New York, 1965, 29 ff.

Davies RE: A molecular theory of muscle contraction: calcium-dependent contractions with hydrogen bond formation plus ATP-dependent extensions of part of the myosin-actin cross bridges. Nature (Lond) 199:4898, 1963

Huxley HE: Muscle cells. The Cell, Vol 4. Brachet J, Mirsky AE, Eds. Academic Press, New York, 1960, 365 ff.

Huxley HE: The mechanism of muscular contraction. Sci Am 213:18, 1965

Jobsis F: Basic processes in cellular respiration. Handbook of Physiology. Respiration I. Fenn WO, Rahn H, Eds. American Physiological Society, Bethesda, 1964, pp 63-124

Katz AM: Contractile proteins of the heart. Physiol Rev 50:63, 1970

Olson RE: Physiology of cardiac muscle. Handbook of Physiology. Circulation I. Hamilton WF, Dow P, Eds. American Physiological Society, Bethesda, 1962, pp 199-233

CHAPTER 4

Alpert NR, Gordon MG: Myofibrillar adenosine triphosphatase activity in congestive heart failure. Am J Physiol 202:940, 1962

Ebashi S, Endo M: Calcium ion and muscle contraction. Progress in Biophysics and Molecular Biology. Butler JA, Noble D, Eds. Pergamon Press, Inc., New York, 1968, p 123

Harigaya S, Schwartz A: Rate of calcium binding and uptake in normal animal and failing human cardiac muscle. Membrane vesicles (relaxing system) and mitochondria. Circ Res 25:781, 1969

Ito Y, Chidsey CA: Intracellular calcium and myocardial contractility. IV. Distribution of calcium in the failing rabbit heart. J Mol Cell Cardiol 4:507, 1972

Sandow A: Excitation-contraction coupling in skeletal muscle. Pharmacol Rev 17:265, 1965

Suko J, Vogel JHK, Chidsey CA: Intracellular calcium and myocardial contractility. III. Reduced calcium uptake and ATPase of the sarcoplasmic reticular fraction prepared from chronically failing calf hearts. Circ Res 17:235, 1970

CHAPTER 5

Meerson F: The myocardium in hyperfunction, hypertrophy and heart failure. Circ Res 25: Suppl 2:1, 1969

Meerson F, Pomoinitsky VD: The role of high-energy phosphate compounds in the development of cardiac hypertrophy. J Mol Cell Cardiol 4:571, 1972

Opie LH: Metabolism of the heart in health and disease. I, II, III. Am Heart J 76:685, 1968; 77:100, 1969; 77:383, 1969

Pool PE: Congestive heart failure: biochemical and physiologic observations. Am J Med Sci 258:328, 1969

Pool PE, Braunwald E: Fundamental mechanisms in congestive heart failure. Am J Cardiol 22:7, 1968

Pool PE, Chandler BM, Spann JF Jr, Sonnenblick EH, Braunwald E: Mechanochemistry of cardiac muscle. IV. Utilization of high-energy phosphates in experimental heart failure in cats. Circ Res 24:313, 1969

Rabinowitz M, Zak R: Biochemical and cellular changes in cardiac hypertrophy. Annu Rev Med 23:245, 1972

CHAPTER 6

Burn JH: Adrenergic transmission. Pharmacol Rev 18:459, 1966

Chidsey CA, Braunwald E, Morrow AG: Catecholamine excretion and cardiac stores of norepinephrine in congestive heart failure. Am J Med 39:442, 1965

Cooper T: Terminal innervation of the heart. Nervous Control of the Heart. Randall W, Ed. The Williams & Wilkins Company, Baltimore, 1965, pp 130-153

Covell JW, Chidsey CA, Braunwald E: Reduction of the cardiac response to postganglionic sympathetic nerve stimulation in experimental heart failure. Circ Res 19:51, 1966

Eckberg DL, Drabinsky M, Braunwald E: Defective cardiac parasympathetic control in patients with heart disease. N Engl J Med 285:877, 1971

Epstein SE, Robinson BF, Kahler RL, Braunwald E: Effects of beta-adrenergic blockade on the cardiac response to maximal and submaximal exercise in man. J Clin Invest 44:1745, 1965

Higgins CB, Vatner SF, Braunwald E: Parasympathetic control of the heart. Pharmacol Rev 25:119, 1973

Higgins CB, Vatner SF, Eckberg DL, Braunwald E: Alterations in the baroreceptor reflex in conscious dogs with heart failure. J Clin Invest 51:715, 1972

Levy MN: Sympathetic-parasympathetic interactions in the heart. Circ Res 29:437, 1971

Pool PE, Covell JW, Levitt M, Gibb J, Braunwald E: Reduction of cardiac tyrosine hydroxylase activity in experimental congestive heart failure. Its role in the depletion of cardiac norepinephrine stores. Circ Res 20:349, 1967

CHAPTER 7

Bunnell IL, Grant C, Greene DG: Left ventricular function derived from the pressure-volume diagram. Am J Med 39:881, 1965

Dodge HT: Determination of left ventricular volume and mass. Radiol Clin North Am 9:459, 1971

Dodge HT, Baxley WA: Hemodynamic aspects of heart failure. Am J Cardiol 22:24, 1968

Dodge HT, Baxley WA: Left ventricular volume and mass and their significance in heart disease. Am J Cardiol 23:528, 1969

Dodge HT, Sandler H, Ballew DW, Lord JD Jr: The use of biplane angiocardiography for the measurement of left ventricular volume in man. Am Heart J 60:762, 1960

Dodge HT, Sandler H, Baxley WA, Hawley RR: Usefulness and limitations of radiographic methods for determining left ventricular volume. Am J Cardiol 18:10, 1966

Grant C, Greene DG, Bunnell IL: Left ventricular enlargement and hypertrophy. A clinical and angiographic study. Am J Med 39:895, 1965

Hood WP, Rackley CE, Rolett EL: Wall stress in the normal and hypertrophied human left ventricle. Am J Cardiol 22:550, 1968

Hugenholtz PG, Ellison RC, Urschel CW, Mirsky I, Sonnenblick EH: Myocardial force-velocity relationships in clinical heart disease. Circulation 41:191, 1970

Kennedy JW, Baxley WA, Figley MM, Dodge HT, Blackman JR: Quantitative angiocardiography. I. The normal left ventricle in man. Circulation 34:272, 1966

Kennedy JW, Trenholme SE, Kasser IS: Left ventricular volume and mass from single-plane cineangiocardiogram. A comparison of anteroposterior and right anterior oblique methods. Am Heart J 80:343, 1970

Russell RO Jr, Porter CMcG, Frimer M, Dodge HT: Left ventricular power in man. Am Heart J 81:799, 1971

Sandler H, Dodge HT: Left ventricular tension and stress in man. Circ Res 13:91, 1963

Sandler H, Dodge HT, Hay RE, Rackley CE: Quantitation of valvular insufficiency in man by angiocardiography. Am Heart J 65:501, 1963

Sarnoff SJ: Myocardial contractility as described by ventricular function curves; observations on Starling's law of the heart. Physiol Rev 35:107, 1955

CHAPTER 8

Auld RB, Alexander EA, Levinsky NG: Proximal tubular function in dogs with thoracic caval constriction. J Clin Invest 50:2150, 1971

Davis JO: The physiology of congestive heart failure. Handbook of Physiology. Circulation III. Hamilton WF, Dow P, Eds. The Williams & Wilkins Company, Baltimore, 1965, p 2071

Davis JO: The role of the adrenal cortex and the kidney in the pathogenesis of cardiac edema. Yale J Biol Med 35:402, 1963

Ham AW: Histology, 2nd ed. J. B. Lippincott Company, Philadelphia, 1953

Huxley AF, Simmons RM: Proposed mechanism of force generation in striated muscle. Nature (Lond) 233:533, 1971

Johnson JA, Davis JO: Effects of an angiotensin II analog on blood pressure and adrenal steroid secretion in dogs with thoracic caval constriction. Physiologist 15:3:184, 1972

Johnston CI, Davis JO, Howards SS, Wright FS: Cross-circulation experiments on the mechanism of the natriuresis during saline loading in the dog. Circ Res 20:1, 1967

Schneider EG, Dresser TP, Lynch RE, Knox FG: Sodium reabsorption by proximal tubule of dogs with experimental heart failure. Am J Physiol 220:952, 1971

Urquhart J, Davis JO, Higgins JT Jr: Simulation of spontaneous secondary hyperaldosteronism by intravenous infusion of angiotensin II in dogs with an arteriovenous fistula. J Clin Invest 43:1355, 1964

CHAPTER 9

Adams CW: Symposium on exercise and the heart. Am J Cardiol 30:713, 1972

Barden RP: Pulmonary edema: correlation of roentgenologic appearance and abnormal physiology. Am J Roentgen 92:495, 1964

Braunwald E: The control of ventricular function in man. Br Heart J 27:1, 1965

Guntheroth WG, Morgan BC, Lintermans JP, McGough GA, Figley MM: Pulsus alternans. Supernormal character of the strong beat in pulsus alternans. Circulation Suppl 31, 32:II-104, 1965

Linzbach AJ: Heart failure from the point of view of quantitative anatomy. Am J Cardiol 5:370, 1960

Logue RB, Rogers JB Jr, Gay BB Jr: Subtle roentgenologic signs of left heart failure. Am Heart J 65:464, 1963

Losowsky MS, Ikram H, Snow HM, Hargeave FE, Nixon PGF: Liver function in advanced heart disease. Br Heart J 27:578, 1965

Perloff JK, Roberts WC: The mitral apparatus. Functional anatomy of mitral regurgitation. Circulation 46:227, 1972

Chapter 10

Harris LC, Nghiem QX: Cardiomyopathies in infants and children. Prog Cardiovasc Dis 15:255, 1972

Heymann MA, Rudolph AM: Effects of congenital heart disease on the fetal and neonatal circulation. Prog Cardiovasc Dis 15:115, 1972

Rudolph AM: The changes in the circulation after birth. Their importance in congenital heart disease. Circulation 41:343, 1970

Talner NS: Congestive heart failure in the infant. A functional approach. Pediatr Clin North Am 18:1011, 1971

Talner NS, Campell AG: Recognition and management of cardiologic problems in the newborn infant. Prog Cardiovasc Dis 15:159, 1972

Chapter 11

Abelmann WH: Experimental infection with *Trypanosoma cruzi* (Chagas' disease): a model of acute and chronic myocardiopathy. Ann NY Acad Sci 156:137, 1969

Cardiomyopathy. Burch GE, Ed. Cardiovasc Clin 4:1-395, 1972

Goodwin JF: Congestive and hypertrophic cardiomyopathies. A decade of study. Lancet 1:732, 1970

Hudson REB: Cardiovascular Pathology, Vol. I, Chapters 17-19; Vol. II, Chapter 27; Vol. III, Chapters S17-S19 and S27. The Williams & Wilkins Company, Baltimore, 1965-1970

Hypertrophic Obstructive Cardiomyopathy. Wolstenholme GEW, O'Connor M, Eds. CIBA Found Study Group No. 37, J and A Churchill, London, 1971, p 4

Idiopathic Hypertrophic Subaortic Stenosis. Braunwald E, Lambrew CT, Rockoff SD, Ross J Jr, Morrow AC, Eds. American Heart Association Monograph 10, 1964, pp 1-213

Mattingly TW: Diseases of the myocardium (cardiomyopathies): the viewpoint of a clinical cardiologist. Am J Cardiol 25:79, 1970

Primary myocardial diseases and the myocardiopathies. Friedberg CK, Ed. Prog Cardiovasc Dis 7:1, 1964

Shah PM, Gramiak R, Adelman AG, Wigle ED: Role of echocardiography in diagnostic and hemodynamic assessment of hypertrophic subaortic stenosis. Circulation 44:891, 1971

Chapter 12

Bates DV: Chronic bronchitis and emphysema. N Engl J Med 278:546 and 600, 1968

Fishman AP, Goldring RM, Turino GM: General alveolar hypoventilation: a syndrome of respiratory and cardiac failure in patients with normal lungs. Q J Med 35:261, 1966

Kirby BJ, McNicol MW, Tattersfield AE: Arrhythmias, digitalis and respiratory failure. Br J Dis Chest 64:212, 1970

Laurenzi GA, Turino GM, Fishman AP: Bullous disease of the lung. Am J Med 32:361, 1962

Macklem PT: Obstruction in small airways—a challenge to medicine. Am J Med 52:721, 1972

Mellins RB, Levine OR, Ingram RH Jr, Fishman AP: Obstructive disease of the airways in cystic fibrosis. Pediatrics 41:560, 1968

Thomas AJ: Chronic pulmonary heart disease. Br Heart J 34:653, 1972

Thurlbeck WM, Henderson JA, Fraser RG, Bates DV: Chronic obstructive lung disease. Medicine 49:81, 1970

Chapter 13

Baker PF, Blaustein MP, Hodgkin AL, Steinhardt RA: The influence of calcium on sodium efflux in squid axons. J Physiol (Lond) 200:431, 1969

Digitalis. Fisch C, Surawicz B, Eds. Grune and Stratton, Inc., New York, 1969

Fawcett DW, McNutt NS: The ultrastructure of the cat myocardium. I. Ventricular papillary muscle. J Cell Biol 42:1, 1969

Glynn IM: The action of cardiac glycosides on ion movements. Pharmacol Rev 16:381, 1964

Langer GA: The intrinsic control of myocardial contraction—ionic factors. N Engl J Med 285:1065, 1971

Langer GA, Serena SD: Effects of strophanthidin upon contraction and ionic exchange in rabbit ventricular myocardium: relation to control of active state. J Mol Cell Cardiol 1:65, 1970

Lee KS, Klaus W: The subcellular basis for the mechanism of inotropic action of cardiac glycosides. Pharmacol Rev 23:193, 1971

Schwartz A, Allen JC, Harigaya S: Possible involvement of cardiac $Na^+ - K^+$ – adenosine triphosphate in the mechanism of action of cardiac glycosides. J Pharmacol Exp Ther 168:31, 1969

Skou JC: Enzymatic basis for active transport of Na^+ and K^+ across cell membrane. Physiol Rev 45:596, 1965

Chapter 14

Cannon PJ, Heinemann HO, Stason WB, Laragh JH: Ethacrynic acid. Effectiveness and mode of diuretic action in man. Circulation 31:5, 1965

Heinemann HO, Demartini FE, Laragh JH: The effect of chlorothiazide on renal excretion of electrolytes and free water. Am J Med 26:853, 1959

Laragh JH: Hormones and the pathogenesis of congestive heart failure: vasopressin, aldosterone, and angiotensin II. Further evidence for renal-adrenal interaction from studies in hypertension and in cirrhosis. Circulation 25:1015, 1962

Laragh JH: The proper use of newer diuretics: diagnosis and treatment. Ann Intern Med 67:607, 1967

Laragh JH, Heinemann HO, Demartini FE: Effect of chlorothiazide on electrolyte transport in man. Its use in the treatment of edema of congestive heart failure, nephrosis, and cirrhosis. JAMA 166:145, 1958

Laragh JH, Sealey JE, Brunner HR: The control of aldosterone secretion in normal and hypertensive man: abnormal renin-aldosterone patterns in low renin hypertension. Am J Med 53:649, 1972

Stason WB, Cannon PJ, Heinemann HO, Laragh JH: Furosemide. A clinical evaluation of its diuretic action. Circulation 34:910, 1966

Chapter 15

Fisher-Dzoga K, Jones RM, Vesselinovitch D, Wissler RW: Ultrastructural and immunohistochemical studies of primary cultures of aortic medial cells. Exp Mol Pathol 18:162, 1973

Getz GS, Vesselinovitch D, Wissler RW: A dynamic pathology of atherosclerosis. Am J Med 46:657, 1969

Haust MD, Geer JC: Smooth muscle cells in atherosclerosis. Monographs in Atherosclerosis, Vol. II. Pollak OJ, Simms HS, Kirk JE, Karger B, Eds. Phiebig, Basel, 1972, p 72

Kritchevsky D, Tepper SA, Vesselinovitch D, Wissler RW: Cholesterol vehicle in experimental atherosclerosis. II. Peanut oil. Atherosclerosis 14:53, 1971

The Pathogenesis of Atherosclerosis. Wissler RW, Geer JC, Eds. The Williams & Wilkins Company, Baltimore, 1972

Wissler RW: The arterial medial cell, smooth muscle or multi-functional mesenchyme? J Atheroscl Res 8:201, 1968

Wissler RW, Vesselinovitch D: Comparative pathogenic patterns in atherosclerosis. Adv Lipid Res 6:181, 1968

Wissler RW, Vesselinovitch D: Experimental models of human atherosclerosis. Ann NY Acad Sci 149:907, 1968

Wissler RW, Vesselinovitch D, Hughes RH, Turner D, Frazier LE: Atherosclerosis and blood lipids in rhesus monkeys fed human table-prepared diets. Circulation Suppl II: 43-44, 57, 1971

References for Chart (Chapter 18, Page 194)

"Frequency of Coronary Thrombosis in Acute Myocardial Infarction"

1a. Herrick JB: Clinical features of sudden obstruction of the coronary arteries. JAMA 59:2015,1912

1b. Herrick JB: Thrombosis of the coronary arteries. JAMA 72:387,1919

2. Nathanson MH: Disease of the coronary arteries. Clinical and pathologic features. Am J Med Sci 170:240-255, 1925. (Type of infarct, i.e., transmural or subendocardial, or whether there was sudden death without myocardial necrosis, was not specifically stated.)

3. Davenport AB: Spontaneous heart rupture –a statistical summary. Am J Med Sci 17662-65, 1928. (Rupture of the left ventricle occurred in at least 80%. Thus, most had transmural infarcts.)

4. Parkinson J, Bedford DE: Cardiac infarction and coronary thrombosis. Lancet 214: 4-11, 1928. (Type of infarct, i.e., transmural or subendocardial, or whether there was sudden death without myocardial necrosis, was not specifically stated.)

5. Levine SA: Coronary thrombosis: its various clinical features. Medicine 8:245-418, 1929. (Only 26 of the 46 cases died within 30 days of the onset of symptoms of acute myocardial infarction.)

6. Lisa JR, Ring A: Myocardial infarction or gross fibrosis: analysis of one hundred necropsies. Arch Intern Med 50: 131-141, 1932. (Type of infarct, i.e., transmural or subendocardial, or whether there was sudden death without myocardial necrosis, was not specifically stated.)

7. Saphir O, Priest WS, Hamburger WW, Katz LN: Coronary arteriosclerosis, coronary thrombosis and the resulting myocardial changes. An evaluation of their respective clinical pictures including the electrocardiographic records, based on the anatomical findings. Am Heart J 10:567-595, 762-792, 1935. (Type of infarct, i.e., transmural or subendocardial, or whether there was sudden death without myocardial necrosis, was not specifically stated.)

8. Friedberg CK, Horn H: Acute myocardial infarction not due to coronary artery occlusion. JAMA 112:1675-1679, 1939.

9. Mallory GK, White PD, Salcedo-Salgar J: The speed of healing of myocardial infarction. A study of the pathologic anatomy in seventy-two cases. Am Heart J 18:647, 1939 (Type of infarct, i.e., transmural or subendocardial, or whether there was sudden death without myocardial necrosis, was not specifically stated.)

10. Blumgart HL, Schlesinger MJ, David D: Studies on the relation of the clinical manifestations of angina pectoris, coronary thrombosis, and myocardial infarction to the pathologic findings with particular reference to the significance of the collateral circulation. Am Heart J 19:1-91, 1940. (Type of infarct, i.e., transmural or subendocardial, or whether there was sudden death without myocardial necrosis, was not specifically stated.)

11. Foord AG: Embolism and thrombosis in coronary heart disease. JAMA 138:1009-1012, 1948. (Type of infarct, i.e., transmural or subendocardial, or whether there was sudden death without myocardial necrosis, was not specifically stated.)

12. Yater WM, Traum AH, Brown WG, Fitzgerald RP, Geisler MA, Wilcox BB: Coronary artery disease in men eighteen to thirty-nine years of age. Report of eight-hundred-sixty-six cases, four-hundred-fifty with necropsy examination. Am Heart J 36: 334-372; 481-526; 683-722, 1948. (All patients were aged 18 to 39 years. Cases not divided according to location of infarction.)

13. Miller RD, Burchell HB, Edwards JE: Myocardial infarction with and without acute coronary occlusion. A pathologic study. Arch Intern Med 88: 597-604, 1951

14. Branwood AW, Montgomery GL: Observations on the morbid anatomy of coronary artery disease. Scott Med J 1:367-375, 1956. (26 patients died suddenly before myocardial necrosis and 5-20%-of them had coronary thrombi. The 26 are included among the 61 total.)

15. Spain DM, Bradess VA: The relationship of coronary thrombosis to coronary atherosclerosis and ischemic heart disease. A necropsy study covering a period of 25 years. Am J Med Sci 240:701-710, 1960

16. Ehrlich JC, Shinohara Y: Low incidence of coronary thrombosis in myocardial infarction. A restudy by serial block technique. Arch Pathol 78:432-445, 1964. (17–94%– of 18 with "unicentric" infarcts, presumably transmural involving left ventricle only, had coronary thrombi.)

17. Mitchell JRA, Schwartz CJ: Arterial Disease. FA Davis, Philadelphia, 1965

18. Baroldi G: Acute coronary occlusion as a cause of myocardial infarct and sudden coronary heart death. Am J Cardiol 16:859-880, 1965. (241 of the 449 died suddenly and the frequency of coronary thrombosis in them was identical to that in the 208 patients who did not die suddenly. Many patients with small (< 1 cm) infarcts were included.)

19. Meadows R: Coronary thrombosis and myocardial infarction. Med J Aust 2:409-411, 1965

20. Kurland GS, Weingarten C, Pitt B: The relation between the location of coronary occlusions and the occurence of shock in acute myocardial infarction. Circulation 31:646-650, 1965. (Type of infarct, i.e., transmural or subendocardial, or whether there was sudden death without myocardial necrosis, was not specifically stated.)

21. Harland WA, Holburn AM: Coronary thrombosis and myocardial infarction. Lancet 2: 1158, 1966

22. Chapman I: Relationships of recent coronary artery occlusion and acute myocardial infarction. J Mt Sinai Hosp 35: 149-154, 1968. (Type of infarct, i.e., transmural or subendocardial, or whether there was sudden death without myocardial necrosis, was not specifically stated.)

23. Kagan A, Livsic AM, Sternby N, Vihert AM: Coronary-artery thrombosis and the acute attack of coronary heart disease. Lancet 2:1199-1202, 1968. (84 of the 176 patients died suddenly (< 6 hours after onset of symptoms) and 55 (65%) of them had coronary thrombosis.)

24. Spain DM, Bradess VA: Sudden death from coronary heart disease. Survival time, frequency of thrombi, and cigarette smoking. Chest 58:107-110, 1970. (100 of the 391 had transmural infarcts and 57% of them had coronary thrombi. The remaining 291 patients died suddenly and 20% of them had coronary thrombi.)

25. Walston A, Hackel DB, Estes EH: Acute coronary occlusion and the "power failure" syndrome. Am Heart J 79:613-619, 1970. (Of 29 with transmural infarcts 17 had thrombi, none of the 5 with subendocardial infarcts had thrombi, and 2 of 3 who died suddenly had coronary thrombi.)

26. Bouch DC, Montgomery GL: Cardiac lesions in fatal cases of recent myocardial ischemia from a coronary care unit. Br Heart J 32:795-803, 1970

27. Page DL, Caulfield JB, Kastor JA, deSanctis RW, Sanders CA: Myocardial changes associated with cardiogenic shock. N Engl J Med 285:133-137, 1971

28. Roberts WC, Buja LM: The frequency and significance of coronary arterial thrombi and other observations in fatal acute myocardial infarction. A study of 107 necropsy patients. Am J Med 52:425-443, 1972. (Of 74 with transmural infarcts, 54% had thrombi; of 9 with subendocardial infarcts, none had thrombi; and of 24 who died suddenly (< 6 hours) 2 had thrombi.)

CHAPTER 16

Clarkson TB, Lofland HB Jr, Bullock BC, Goodman HO: Genetic control of plasma cholesterol. Studies on squirrel monkeys. Arch Pathol 92:37, 1971

Fredrickson DS, Levy RI, Lees RS: Fat transport in lipoproteins – an integrated approach to mechanisms and disorders (In 5 sections). N Engl J Med 276:34, 94, 148, 215, 273; 1967

Kannel WB, Dawber TR: Atherosclerosis as a pediatric problem. J Pediatr 80:544, 1972

McGill HC Jr, Eggen DA, Strong JP: Atherosclerotic lesions in the aorta and coronary arteries of man. Compartive Atherosclerosis. Roberts JC Jr, Straus R, Eds. Hoeber Medical Division, Harper & Row, New York, 1965, pp 311-326

Strong JP, McGill HC Jr: The pediatric aspects of atherosclerosis, J Atheroscler Res 9:251, 1969

Zinner SH, Levy PS, Kass EH: Familial aggregation of blood pressure in childhood. N Engl J Med 284:401, 1971

Arteriosclerosis: Report by NHLI Task Force on Arteriosclerosis. (NIH) 72-137, 1971; 72-219, 1972, Washington, D.C.

CHAPTER 17

Marcus AJ: Platelet function. N Engl J Med 280:1213, 1278, 1330, 1969

Mustard JF, Kinlough-Rathbone RL, Jenkins CSP, Packham MA: Modification of platelet function. Platelets and their Role in Hemostasis. Weiss HJ, Ed. Ann NY Acad Sci 201: 343, 1972

Mustard JF, Packham MA: Factors influencing platelet function: adhesion, release, and aggregation. Pharmacol Rev 22: 97, 1970

Mustard JF, Packham MA: The reaction of blood to injury. Inflammation, Immunity and Hypersensitivity. Movat HZ, Ed. Harper & Row, Publishers, New York, 1971

CHAPTER 18

Chandler AB: Thrombosis and the Development of Atherosclerotic Lesions. Atherosclerosis, Proceedings of the Second International Symposium. Jones RJ, Ed. Springer-Verlag, New York, 1970, p 88

Constantinides P: Plaque fissures in human coronary thrombosis. J Atheroscler Res 6:1, 1966

Fulton WFM: The Coronary Arteries. Arteriography, Microanatomy, and Pathogenesis of Obliterative Coronary Artery Disease. Charles C Thomas, Publisher, Springfield, Ill., 1965

Roberts WC: Coronary arteries in fatal acute myocardial infarction. Circulation 45:215, 1972

Roberts WC: Relationship between coronary thrombosis and myocardial infarction. Mod Concepts Cardiovasc Dis 41:7, 1972

CHAPTER 19

Brown MS, Dana SE, Goldstein JL: Regulation of 3-hydroxy-3-methylglutaryl coenzyme A reductase activity in human fibroblasts by lipoproteins. Proc Natl Acad Sci USA 70:2162, 1973

Fredrickson DS, Levy RI: Familial hyperlipoproteinemias. The Metabolic Basis of Inherited Disease, 3rd ed. Stanbury JB, Wyngaarden JB, Fredrickson DS, Eds. McGraw-Hill, Inc., New York, 1972, p 545

Goldstein JL, Hazzard WR, Schrott HG, Bierman EL, Motulsky AG: Genetics of hyperlipidemia in coronary heart disease. Trans Assoc Am Physicians 85:120, 1972

Goldstein JL, Hazzard WR, Schrott HG, Bierman EL, Motulsky AG: Hyperlipidemia in coronary heart disease. I. Lipid levels in 500 survivors of myocardial infarction. J Clin Invest 52:1533, 1973

Goldstein JL, Schrott HG, Hazzard WR, Bierman EL, Motulsky AG: Hyperlipidemia in coronary heart disease. II. Genetic analysis of lipid levels in 176 families and delineation of a new inherited disorder, combined hyperlipidemia. J Clin Invest 52:1544, 1973

Hazzard WR, Goldstein JL, Schrott HG, Motulsky AG, Bierman EL: Hyperlipidemia in coronary heart disease. III. Evaluation of lipoprotein phenotypes of 156 genetically defined survivors of myocardial infarction. J Clin Invest 52:1569, 1973

Nikkila EA, Antti A: Family study of serum lipids and lipoproteins in coronary heart disease. Lancet 1:954, 1973

Slack J: Risks of ischaemic heart disease in familial hyperlipoproteinaemic states. Lancet 2:1380, 1969

CHAPTER 20

Katz LN, Stamler J, Pick RP: Nutrition and Atherosclerosis. Lea & Febiger, Philadelphia, 1958

Stamler J: Lectures on Preventive Cardiology. Grune and Stratton, New York, 1967

Inter-Society Commission for Heart Disease Resources, Atherosclerosis Study Group and Epidemiology Study Group: Primary Prevention of the Atherosclerotic Diseases. Circulation, 42:A55, 1970

Geographic Pathology of Atherosclerosis. McGill HC Jr, Ed. The Williams & Wilkins Company, Baltimore, 1968

Arteriosclerosis – Report by National Heart and Lung Institute Task Force on Arteriosclerosis, Vol. I. U.S. Department of Health, Education and Welfare, Public Health Service. DHEW Publication Number (NIH) 72-137, Washington, D.C., 1971

Pathogenesis of Atherosclerosis. Wissler RW, Geer JC, Eds. The Williams & Wilkins Company, Baltimore, 1972

Stamler J: Epidemiology of coronary heart disease. Med Clin North Am 57:1:5, 1973

Coronary heart disease in seven countries. Keys A, Ed. Circulation 41:Suppl 1, 1970

Stamler J, Stamler R, Shekelle RB: Regional differences in prevalence, incidence and mortality from atherosclerotic coronary heart idsease. Ischaemic Heart Disease. deHaas JH, Hemker HC, Snellen HA, Eds. The Williams & Wilkins Company, Baltimore, 1970

Stamler J: Prevention of atherosclerotic coronary heart disease by change of diet and mode of life. Ischaemic Heart Disease. deHaas JH, Hemker HC, Snellen HA, Eds. The Williams & Wilkins Company, Baltimore, 1970

Stamler J: Acute myocardial infarction – progress in primary prevention. Br Heart J 33:Suppl 145, 1971

Atherosclerosis – Proceedings of the Second International Symposium on Atherosclerosis. Jones RJ, Ed. Springer-Verlag, New York, 1970

American Heart Association committee on reduction of risk of heart attack and stroke: Handbook of Coronary Risk Probability. American Heart Association, New York, EM590B, 1972 (currently out of print)

Implementation of fat-modified selective cycle menus in hospital food service. Hospitals 46: Jan. 1, 16, Feb. 1, 16, 1972

Preventive Cardiology. Tibblin G, Keys A, Werkö L, Eds. Almqvist and Wiksell, Halsted Printer, Stockholm, 1972

The Minnesota symposium on prevention in cardiology – reducing the risk of coronary and hypertensive disease. Blackburn H, Willis J, Eds. Reprinted from Minnesota Medicine, 52:8:1183, 1969

Stamler J, Berkson DM, Lindberg HA: Risk factors: their role in the etiology and pathogenesis of the atherosclerotic diseases. Pathogenesis of Atherosclerosis. Wissler RW, Geer JC, Eds. The Williams & Wilkins Company, Baltimore, 1972, p 41

Stamler J, Epstein FH: Coronary heart disease: risk factors as guides to preventive action. Preventive Medicine 1:27, 1972

Inter-Society Commission for Heart Disease Resources, Hypertension Group Study: Guidelines for the detection, diagnosis and management of hypertensive populations. Circulation 44: A263, 1971

Miettinen M, Turpeinen O, Karvonen MJ, Elosuo R, Paavilainen E: Effect of cholesterol-lowering diet on mortality from coronary heart disease and other causes. A twelve-year clinical trial in men and women. Lancet 2:835, 1972

Stamler J: High blood pressure in the United States – an overview of the problem and the challenge. National Conference on High Blood Pressure Education – Report of Proceedings. U.S. Department of Health, Education, and Welfare, Public Health Service, National Institutes of Health, DHEW Publication No. (NIH) 73-486, 11, 1973

Coronary Drug Project Research Group: The prognostic importance of the electrocardiogram after myocardial infarction. Experience in the coronary drug project. Ann Intern Med 77:677, 1972

Stamler J: An epidemiologist looks at sudden death. Med Com, Inc., New York (in press)

Lew EA, Seltzer F: Uses of the life table in public health. Milbank Mem Fund Q 48: (Suppl 1): 15, 1970

Katz LN, Stamler J: Experimental Atherosclerosis. Charles C Thomas, Publisher, Springfield, Ill., 1953

Cowdry's Arteriosclerosis: A Survey of the Problem, 2nd ed. Blumenthal HT, Ed. Charles C Thomas, Publisher, Springfield, Ill., 1967

Constantinides P: Experimental Atherosclerosis. Elsevier, Amsterdam, 1965

Friedman M: Pathogenesis of Coronary Artery Disease. McGraw-Hill, Inc. New York, 1969

The National Diet – Heart Study Final Report. Circulation 37:Suppl 1, 1968

Hammond EC: Smoking in relation to the death rates of one million men and women. National Cancer Institute Monograph No. 19. U.S. Public Health Service, Bethesda, 1966, p 127

Smoking and Health: Report of the Advisory Committee to the Surgeon General of the Public Health Service. U.S. Department of Health, Education, and Welfare, Public Health Service Publication No. 1103, Superintendent of Documents, U.S. Government Printing Office, Washington, D.C., 1964

Chapter 21

Friedman M, Byers SO: The induction of neurogenic hypercholesterolemia. Proc Soc Exp Biol Med 131:759, 1969

Friedman M, Byers SO, Rosenman RH: Plasma ACTH and cortisol concentration of coronary-prone subjects. Proc Soc Exp Biol Med 140:681, 1972

Friedman M, Byers SO, Rosenman RH, Li CH: Hypocholesterolemic effect of human growth hormone in coronary-prone (Type A) hypercholesterolemic subjects. Proc Soc Exp Biol Med 141:76, 1972

Friedman M, Rosenman RH: Association of a specific overt behavior pattern with blood and cardiovascular findings – blood cholesterol level, blood clotting time, incidence of arcus senilis and clinical coronary artery disease. JAMA 169:1286, 1959

Friedman M, Rosenman RH, Carroll V: Changes in the serum cholesterol and blood clotting time in men subjected to cyclic variation of occupational stress. Circulation 17:852, 1958

Friedman M, Rosenman RH, Straus R, Wurm M, Kositchek R: The relationship of behavior pattern A to the state of the coronary vasculature. A study of 51 autopsy subjects. Am J Med 44:525, 1968

Friedman M, St. George S, Byers SO, Rosenman RH: Excretion of catecholamines, 17-ketosteroids, 17-hydroxycorticoids and 5-hydroxyindole in men exhibiting a particular behavior pattern (A) associated with high incidence of clinical coronary artery disease. J Clin Invest 39:758, 1960

Rosenman RH, Friedman M, Jenkins CD, Straus R, Wurm M, Kositchek R: The prediction of immunity to coronary heart disease. JAMA 198:1159, 1966

Rosenman RH, Friedman M, Straus R, Jenkins CD, Zyzanski SJ, Wurm M: Coronary heart disease in the Western Collaborative Group Study. A follow-up experience of 4½ years. J Chronic Dis 23:173, 1970

Rosenman RH, Friedman M, Straus R, Wurm M, Kositchek R, Hahn W, Werthessen NT: A predictive study of coronary heart disease. JAMA 189:15, 1964

Chapter 22

Braasch W, Gudbjarnason S, Puri PS, Ravens KG, Bing RJ: Early changes in energy metabolism in the myocardium following acute coronary artery occlusion in anesthetized dogs. Circ Res 23:429, 1968

Brachfeld N: Maintenance of cell viability. Circulation 39, 40:Suppl 4:202, 1969

Herdson PB, Sommers HM, Jennings RB: A comparative study of the fine structure of normal and ischemic dog myocardium with special reference to early changes following temporary occlusion of a coronary artery. Am J Pathol 46:367, 1965

Jennings RB, Baum JH, Herdson PB: Fine structural changes in myocardial ischemic injury. Arch Pathol 79:135, 1965

Kübler W, Spieckermann PG: Regulation of glycolysis in the ischemic and anoxic myocardium. J Mol Cell Cardiol 1:351, 1970

Neely JR, Whitfield CF, Morgan HE: Regulation of glycogenolysis in hearts: effects of pressure development, glucose, and FFA. Am J Physiol 219:1083, 1970

Shell WE, Kjekshus JK, Sobel BE: Quantitative assessment of the extent of myocardial infarction in the conscious dog by means of analysis of serial changes in serum creatine phosphokinase (CPK) activity. J Clin Invest 50:2614, 1971

Shnitka TK, Nachlas MM: Histochemical alterations in ischemic heart muscle and early myocardial infarction. Am J Pathol 42:507, 1963

Sobel BE, Bresnahan GF, Shell WE, Yoder RD: Estimation of infarct size in man and its relation to prognosis. Circulation 46:640, 1972

Chapter 23

Braunwald E: Control of myocardial oxygen consumption. Am J Cardiol 27:416, 1971

Forrester JS, Diamond G, McHugh TJ, Swan HJC: Filling pressures in the right and left sides of the heart in acute myocardial infarction. A reappraisal of central venous pressure monitoring. N Engl J Med 285:190, 1971

Ganz WW, Forrester JS, Chonette D, Donoso R, Swan HJC: A new flow-directed catheter technique for measurement of pulmonary artery and capillary wedge pressure without fluoroscopy. Am J Cardiol 25:96, 1970

Hamosh P, Khatri IM, Cohn JN: Left ventricular function in acute myocardial infarction. J Clin Invest 50:523, 1971

Karliner JS, Ross J Jr: Left ventricular performance after acute myocardial infarction. Prog Cardiovasc Dis 13:374, 1971

Kazamias TM, Gander MP, Gault JH, Kostuk WJ, Ross J Jr: Roentgenographic assessment of left ventricular size in man: a standardized method. J Appl Physiol 32:881, 1972

Kazamias TM, Gander MP, Ross J Jr, Braunwald E: Detection of left ventricular wall motion disorders in coronary artery disease by radarkymography. N Engl J Med 285:63, 1971

Kostuk WJ, Ehsani AA, Karliner JS, Ashburn WL, Peterson KL, Ross J Jr, Sobel BE: Left ventricular performance after myocardial infarction assessed by radioisotope angiocardiography. Circulation 47:242, 1973

Kostuk WJ, Kazamias TM, Gander MP, Simon AL, Ross J Jr: Left ventricular size after acute myocardial infarction: serial changes and their prognostic significance. Circulation 47:1174, 1973

Mundth ED, Yurchak PM, Buckley MJ, Leinebach RC, Kantrowitz A, Austen WG: Circulatory assistance and emergency direct coronary artery surgery for shock complicating acute myocardial infarction. N Engl J Med 283:1382, 1970

Ross J Jr: The assessment of myocardial performance in man by hemodynamic and cineangiographic technics. Am J Cardiol 23:511, 1969

Ross J Jr, Sobel BE: Regulation of cardiac contraction. Annu Rev Physiol 34:47, 1972

Chapter 24

Anderson TW, Le Riche WH, MacKay JS: Sudden death and ischemic heart disease. Correlation with hardness of local water supply. N Engl J Med 280:805, 1969

Atkins JM, Leshin SJ, Blomqvist G, Mullins CB: Ventricular conduction blocks and sudden death in acute myocardial infarction. Potential indications for pacing. N Engl J Med 228:281, 1973

Epstein SE, Goldstein RE, Redwood DR, Kent KM, Smith ER: The early phase of acute myocardial infarction: pharmacologic aspects of therapy. Ann Intern Med 78:918, 1973

Friedman M, Manwaring JH, Rosenman RH, Donlon MD, Ortega P, Grube SM: Instantaneous and sudden deaths: clinical and pathological differentiation in coronary artery disease. JAMA 225:1319, 1973

Gevers W: The stimulus to hypertorphy in the heart (editorial). J Mol Cell Cardiol 4:537, 1972

Greene WA, Goldstein S, Moss AJ: Psychosocial aspects of sudden death. A preliminary report. Arch Intern Med 129:725, 1972

Kuller L, Cooper M, Perper J: Epidemiology of sudden death. Arch Intern Med 129:714, 1972

Lown B, Wolf M: Approaches to sudden death from coronary heart disease. Circulation 44:130, 1971

McNeilly RH, Pemberton J: Duration of last attack in 998 fatal cases of coronary artery disease and its relation to possible cardiac resuscitation. Br Med J 3:139, 1968

Paul O, Schatz M: On sudden death (editorial). Circulation 43:7, 1971

Roberts WC, Buja LM: The frequency and significance of coronary arterial thrombi and other observations in fatal acute myocardial infarction: a study of 107 necropsy patients. Am J Med 52:425, 1972

Spain DM, Bradess VA: Sudden death from coronary heart disease: survival time, frequency of thrombi, and cigarette smoking. Chest 58:107, 1970

Thompson P, Sloman G: Sudden death in hospital after discharge from coronary care unit. Br Med J 4:136, 1971

Chapter 25

Acute Myocardial Infarction & Coronary Care Units. Freidberg CK, Ed. Grune, New York, 1969

Klein MS, Shell WE, Sobel BE: Serum creatine phosphokinase (CPK) isoenzymes following intramuscular injections, surgery, and myocardial infarction: experimental and clinical studies. Cardiovasc Res (in press)

Lown B, Wolf M: Approaches to sudden death from coronary heart disease. Circulation 44:130, 1971

Myocardial Infarction 1972. Friedberg CK, Ed. American Heart Association Monograph No. 36, New York, 1972

Shell WE, Kjekshus JK, Sobel BE: Quantitative assessment of the extent of myocardial infarction in the conscious dog by means of analysis of serial changes in serum creatine phosphokinase (CPK) activity. J Clin Invest 50:2614, 1971

Shell WE, Lavelle JF, Covell JW, Sobel BE: Early estimation of myocardial damage in conscious dogs and patients with evolving acute myocardial infarction. J Clin Invest 52:2579, 1973

Sobel BE: Reducing the toll from sudden death. Calif Med 117:54, 1972

Sobel BE, Shell WE: Serum enzyme determinations in the diagnosis and assessment of myocardial infarction. Circulation 45:471, 1972

Chapter 26

Adgey AJA, Allen JD, Gettes JS, James RGG, Webb SW, Zaidi SA, Pantridge JF: Acute phase of myocardial infarction. Lancet 2:501, 1971

Bassett AL, Bigger JT Jr, Hoffman BF: "Protective" action of diphenylhydantoin on canine Purkinje fibers during hypoxia. J Pharmacol Exp Ther 173:336, 1970

Bassett AL, Hoffman BF: Antiarrhythmic drugs: electrophysiological actions. Annu Rev Pharmacol 11:143, 1971

Bigger JT Jr: Arrhythmias and antiarrhythmic drugs. Adv Intern Med 18:251, 1972

Bigger JT Jr: Electrical properties of cardiac muscle and possible causes of cardiac arrhythmias. Cardiac Arrhythmias. Dreifus LS, Likoff W, Eds. Hahnemann Symposiums 25, Grune & Stratton Inc., New York, 1973, pp 11-23

Bigger JT Jr, Jaffe CC: The effect of bretylium tosylate on the electrophysiologic properties of ventricular muscle and Purkinje fibers. Am J Cardiol 27:82, 1971

Carmeliet E, Vereecke J: Adrenaline and the plateau phase of the cardiac action potential: importance of Ca^{++}, Na^+ and K^+ conductance. Pfluegers Arch 313:300, 1969

Hinkle LE Jr, Carver ST, Stevens M: The frequency of asymptomatic disturbances of cardiac rhythm and conduction in middle-aged men. Am J Cardiol 24:629, 1969

Hoffman BF, Bigger JT Jr: Antiarrhythmic drugs. Drill's Pharmacology in Medicine, 4th ed. Di Palma JR, Ed. McGraw-Hill, Inc. New York, 1971, p 824

Koch-Weser J, Klein SW, Foo-Canto LL, Kastor JA, DeSanctis RW: Antiarrhythmic prophylaxis with procainamide in acute myocardial infarction. N Engl J Med 281:1253, 1969

Weidmann S: Effect of cardiac membrane potential on rapid availability of the sodium-carrying system. J Physiol (Lond) 127:213, 1955

Wit AL, Cranefield PF, Hoffman BF: Slow conduction and reentry in the ventricular conducting system. II. Single and sustained circus movement in networks of canine and bovine Purkinje fibers. Circ Res 30:11, 1972

CHAPTER 27

Adgey AAJ, Geddes JS, Mulholland HC, Keegan DAJ, Pantridge JF: Incidence, significance and management of early bradyarrhythmia complicating acute myocardial infarction. Lancet 2:1097, 1968

Bloom BS, Peterson OL: End results, cost and productivity of coronary-care units. N Engl J Med 288:72, 1973

Damato AN, Lau SH: Clinical value of the electrogram of the conduction system. Prog Cardiovasc Dis 13:119, 1970

Godman MJ, Lassers BW, Julian DG: Complete bundle branch block complicating acute myocardial infarction. N Engl J Med 282:237, 1970

Kent KM, Smith ER, Redwood DR, Epstein SE: Electrical stability of acutely ischemic myocardium. Influence of heart rate and vagal stimulation. Circulation 48:291, 1973

Killip T, Kimball JT: Treatment of myocardial infarction in a coronary care unit. A two-year experience with 250 patients. Am J Cardiol 20:457, 1967

Kimball JT, Killip T: Aggressive treatment of arrhythmias in acute myocardial infarction: procedures and results. Prog Cardiovasc Dis 10:483, 1968

Koch-Weser J, Klein SW, Foo-Canto LL, Kastor JA, DeSanctis RW: Antiarrhythmic prophylaxis with procainamide in acute myocardial infarction. N Engl J Med 281:1253, 1969

Scheidt S, Killip T: Bundle branch block complicating acute myocardial infarction. JAMA 222:919, 1972

Symposium on Current Concepts of Cardiac Pacing and Cardioversion. Meltzer LE, Kitchell JR, Eds. The Charles Press, Philadelphia, 1971

Webb SW, Adgey AJA, Pantridge JF: Autonomic disturbance at onset of acute myocardial infarction. Br Med J 3:89, 1972

CHAPTER 28

Alkjaersig N, Fletcher AP, Sherry S: The mechanism of clot dissolution by plasmin, and the maintenance of a sustained thrombolytic state in man. I. Induction and effects. II. Clinical observations on patients with myocardial infarction and other thromboembolic disorders. J Clin Invest 38:1086, 1959

Bett JHN, Biggs JC, Castaldi PA, Chesterman CN, Hale GS, Hirsh J, Isbister JP, McDonald IG, McLean KH, Morgan JJ, O'Sullivan EF, Rosenbaum M: Australian multicentre trial of streptokinase in acute myocardial infarction. Lancet 1:57, 1973

Fletcher AP, Alkjaersig N, Sherry S, Genton E, Hirsh J, Bachman F: The development of urokinase as a thrombolytic agent. Maintenance of a substantial thrombolytic state in man by its intravenous infusion. J Lab Clin Med 65:713, 1965

Sherry S: Fibrinolysis. Annu Rev Med 19:247, 1968

Symposium on Thrombolytic Therapy with Streptokinase at University of Melbourne. Australasian Annals of Medicine 19:Suppl 1:1, 1970

The Urokinase Pulmonary Embolism Trial. A national cooperative study. Circulation 47, Suppl 2:1, 1973

CHAPTER 29

Braunwald E: Control of myocardial oxygen consumption: physiologic and clinical considerations. Am J Cardiol 27:416, 1971

Cox JL, McLaughlin VW, Flowers NC, Moran LG: The ischemic zone surrounding acute myocardial infarction: its morphology as detected by dehydrogenase staining. Am Heart J 76:650, 1968

Ginks WR, Sybers HD, Maroko PR, Covell JW, Sobel BE, Ross J Jr: Coronary artery reperfusion. II. Reduction of myocardial infarct size at one week after coronary occlusion. J Clin Invest 51:2717, 1972

Libby P, Maroko PR, Bloor CM, Sobel BE, Braunwald E: Reduction of experimental myocardial infarct size by corticosteroid administration. J Clin Invest 52:599, 1973

Maroko PR, Bernstein EF, Libby P, DeLaria GA, Covell JW, Ross J Jr, Braunwald E: Effects of intraaortic balloon counterpulsation on the severity of myocardial ischemic injury following acute coronary occlusion. Counterpulsation and myocardial injury. Circulation 45:1150, 1972

Maroko PR, Kjekshus JK, Sobel BE, Watanabe T, Covell JW, Ross J Jr, Braunwald E: Factors influencing infarct size following coronary artery occlusions. Circulation 43:67, 1971

Maroko PR, Libby P, Bloor CM, Sobel BE, Braunwald E: Reduction by hyaluronidase of myocardial necrosis following coronary artery occlusion. Circulation 46:430, 1972

Maroko PR, Libby P, Covell JW, Sobel BE, Ross J Jr, Braunwald E: Precordial S-T segment elevation mapping: an atraumatic method for assessing alternations in the extent of myocardial ischemic injury following acute coronary occlusion. The effects of pharmacologic and hemodynamic interventions. Am J Cardiol 29:223, 1972

Maroko PR, Libby P, Ginks WR, Bloor CM, Shell WE, Sobel BE, Ross J Jr: Coronary artery reperfusion. I. Early effects on local myocardial function and the extent of myocardial necrosis. J Clin Invest 51:2710, 1972

Maroko PR, Libby P, Sobel BE, Bloor CM, Sybers HD, Shell WE, Covell JW, Braunwald E: Effect of glucose-insulin-potassium infusion on myocardial infarction following experimental coronary artery occlusion. Circulation 45:1160, 1972

Redwood DR, Smith ER, Epstein SE: Coronary artery occlusion in the conscious dog. Effects of alterations in heart rate and arterial pressure on the degree of myocardial ischemia. Circulation 46:323, 1972

Watanabe T, Covell JW, Maroko PR, Braunwald E, Ross J Jr: Effects of increased arterial pressure and positive inotropic agents on the severity of myocardial ischemia in the acutely depressed heart. Am J Cardiol 30:371, 1972

Chapter 31

Favaloro RG, Effler DB, Cheanvechai C, Quint RA, Sones FM: Acute coronary insufficiency (impending myocardial infarction and myocardial infarction): surgical treatment by the saphenous vein graft technique. Am J Cardiol 28:598, 1971

Fowler NO: "Preinfarctional" angina. A need for an objective definition and for a controlled clinical trial of its management. Circulation 44:755, 1971

Fulton M, Lutz W, Donald KW, Morrison SL, Kirby BJ, Duncan B, Kerr F, Julian DG, Oliver MF: Natural history of unstable angina. Lancet 1:860, 1972

Lambert CJ, Adam M, Geisler GF, Verzosa E, et al: Emergency myocardial revascularization for impending infarctions and arrhythmias. J Thorac Cardiovasc Surg 62:522, 1971

Miller DC, Cannom DS, Fogarty TJ, Schroeder JS, Daly PO, Harrison DC: Saphenous vein coronary artery bypass in patients with "preinfarction angina." Circulation 47:234, 1973

Ross RS: Surgery in ischemic heart disease—angina pectoris and myocardial infarction. Disease-A-Month, July 1972

Vakil RJ: Preinfarctional syndrome—management and follow-up. Am J Cardiol 14:55, 1964

Chapter 32

Banas JS, Brilla A, Soroff HS, Levine H: Evaluation of external counterpulsation for the treatment of severe angina pectoris. 45th Scientific Sessions of the American Heart Association. Circulation Suppl 2:46:74, 1972

Birtwell WC, Giron F, Ruiz U, Norton RL, Soroff HS: The regional hemodynamic response to synchronous external pressure assist. Trans Am Soc Artif Intern Organs 16:462, 1970

Birtwell WC, Giron F, Soroff HS, Ruiz U, Collins JA, Deterling RA Jr: Support of the systemic circulation and left ventricular assist by synchronous pulsation of extramural pressure. Trans Am Soc Artif Intern Organs 11:43, 1965

Birtwell WC, Ruiz U, Soroff HS, Deterling RA Jr: Technical considerations in the design of a clinical system for external left ventricular assist. Trans Am Soc Artif Intern Organs 14:304, 1968

Birtwell WC, Soroff HS, Giron F, Thrower WB, Ruiz U, Deterling RA Jr: Synchronous assisted circulation. J Can Med Assoc J 95:652, 1966

Messer JV, McDowell JW, Bing OHL, Soroff HS: Hemodynamic evaluation of external counterpulsation in human cardiogenic shock. Clinical Research 21:438, 1973

Nishimura A, Giron F, Birtwell WC, Soroff HS: Evaluation of collateral blood supply by direct measurement of the performance of ischemic myocardial muscle. Trans Am Soc Artif Intern Organs 16:450, 1970

Soroff HS, Birtwell WC, Giron F, Ruiz U, Nishimura A, Many MEL, Zawahry M, Deterling RA Jr: Treatment of power failure by means of mechanical assistance. Circulation Suppl 4:39, 40:292, 1969

Soroff HS, Birtwell WC, Norton RL, Cloutier CT, Kataoka K, Giron F: Experimental and clinical studies in assisted circulation. Transplant Proc 3:1483, 1971

Soroff HS, Levine HJ, Sachs BF, Birtwell WC, Deterling RA Jr: Assisted circulation. II. Effect of counterpulsation on left ventricular oxygen consumption and hemodynamics. Circulation 27:722, 1963

Chapter 33

Cox JL, McLaughlin VW, Flowers NC, Moran LG: The ischemic zone surrounding acute myocardial infarction: its morphology as detected by dehydrogenase staining. Am Heart J 76:650, 1968

Maroko PR, Bernstein FF, Libby P, DeLaria GA, Covell JW, Ross J Jr, Braunwald E: Effects of intraaortic balloon counterpulsation on the severity of myocardial ischemic injury following acute coronary occlusion: counterpulsation and myocardial injury. Circulation 45:1150, 1972

Mundth ED, Buckley MJ, Leinbach RC, DeSanctis RW, Sanders CA, Kantrowitz A, Austen WG: Myocardial revascularization for the treatment of cardiogenic shock complicating acute myocardial infarction. Surgery 70:78, 1971

Mundth ED, Yurchak PM, Buckley MJ, Leinbach RC, Kantrowitz A, Austen WG: Circulatory assistance and emergency direct coronary artery surgery for shock complicating acute myocardial infarction. N Engl J Med 283:1382, 1970

Page DL, Caulfield JB, Kastor JA, DeSanctis RW: Myocardial changes associated with cardiogenic shock. N Engl J Med 285:133, 1971

Sanders CA, Buckley MJ, Leinbach RC, Mundth ED, Austen WG: Mechanical circulatory assistance. Current status and experience with combining circulatory assistance, emergency coronary angiography, and acute myocardial revascularization. Circulation 45:1292, 1972

Chapter 34

Hellerstein HK: Exercise therapy in coronary disease. Bull NY Acad Med 44:1028, 1968

Hellerstein HK, Friedman EH: Sexual activity and the post-coronary patient. Arch Intern Med 125:987, 1970

Salzman SH, Hellerstein HK, Radke JD, Maistelman HM, Ricklin R: The quantitative effects of physical conditioning on the exercise electrocardiogram of middle-aged subjects with arteriosclerotic heart disease. Measurement in Exercise Electrocardiography. Ernest Simonson Conference. Blackburn H, Ed. Charles C Thomas, Publisher, Springfield, Ill., 1969

Index

denotes illustration or table

*denotes illustration or table

*denotes illustration or table

*denotes illustration or table

denotes illustration or table

W

X

Z

Illustration Credits

CHAPTER 1: 4 Bunji Tagawa; 6 Albert Miller; 7 Tagawa; 8, 9, 11, 12 Miller.

CHAPTER 2: 16-19 Gaetano Di Palma; 21 Albert Miller; 22, 23 Di Palma; 24 Miller; 25 Di Palma; 26 Miller; 27 Di Palma.

CHAPTER 3: 30-35 Bunji Tagawa.

CHAPTER 4: 39, 40 Bunji Tagawa; 41-43 Albert Miller; 45 Tagawa; 46, 47 Miller.

CHAPTER 5: 51-55 Albert Miller.

CHAPTER 6: 60 Bunji Tagawa; 61, 62 Tagawa with Albert Miller; 63 Miller; 64, 67 Tagawa with Miller; 68 Gaetano Di Palma.

CHAPTER 7: 71 Bunji Tagawa with Albert Miller; 72-75 Miller; 76, 77 Tagawa with Miller; 78 Miller.

CHAPTER 8: 81 Robin Ingle with Joan Dworkin; 82 Enid Kotschnig; 83 Albert Miller; 84 Adele Spiegler; 85 Miller; 88 Ingle.

CHAPTER 9: 94, 96 Bunji Tagawa with Robin Ingle; 97 Ingle.

CHAPTER 10: 103-105, 107 Carol Woike.

CHAPTER 11: 112-114 (top) Bunji Tagawa; 115, 116 Albert Miller.

CHAPTER 12: 120 (top) Albert Miller; 120 (bottom) Bunji Tagawa; 121 Miller; 122 Tagawa; 123, 124 (top) Miller; 124 (bottom) Tagawa; 126-128 Miller; 129 Tagawa; 130 Miller.

CHAPTER 13: 136-140 Bunji Tagawa.

CHAPTER 14: 144-147 Bunji Tagawa with Alan D. Iselin; 148-150 Albert Miller.

CHAPTER 15: 160 Albert Miller.

CHAPTER 16: 171-175 (photographs) Dan Bernstein.

CHAPTER 17: 178 Alan D. Iselin; 181 Albert Miller; 184 Iselin; 188 Miller.

CHAPTER 18: 197 Bunji Tagawa; 198 Albert Miller; 199 Tagawa; 200-202 Miller; 203 Tagawa; 204 Irwin Kuperberg.

CHAPTER 19: 207-213, 215, 216 Albert Miller.

CHAPTER 20: 220-222, 224-227, 229-233, 235 Albert Miller.

CHAPTER 21: 238-243 Albert Miller.

CHAPTER 22: 248, 249 (top) Bunji Tagawa; 250 Albert Miller; 252 Miller with Tagawa; 253-260 Miller.

CHAPTER 23: 262 (top) Bunji Tagawa with Irwin Kuperberg; 262 (bottom), 264-266, 269, 270 Tagawa.

CHAPTER 24: 274-280 Irwin Kuperberg.

CHAPTER 25: 286, 287 Jon Brenneis; 288 Albert Miller; 290 (top and middle) Brenneis; 290 (bottom), 291 Miller.

CHAPTER 26: 296, 297, 299, 300, 302, 303, 305 Bunji Tagawa.

CHAPTER 27: 308, 309 (top) Albert Miller; 309 (bottom) Bunji Tagawa; 314 Miller.

CHAPTER 28: 318-320, 322, 323 (top) Bunji Tagawa; 323 (bottom)-326 Albert Miller.

CHAPTER 29: 330 Robin Ingle; 331 Albert Miller; 333 (left), 334 (right) Ingle; 333 (right), 334 (left) Miller; 335-337 (right) Miller; 337 (left) Ingle; 341 Miller.

CHAPTER 30: 343, 344, 346, 347, 348, 349, 350 (photographs) Lester Bergman; 345, 346, 347, 348, 349, 350, 351 (drawings) Carol Woike.

CHAPTER 31: 354, 356-357 Albert Miller; 360 Carol Woike; 361, 362 Miller.

CHAPTER 32: 364, 366-368 Bunji Tagawa; 369 (photographs) Dan Bernstein.

CHAPTER 33: 372-374 (photographs) James B. Caulfield, M.D. (see Data Sources); 375, 376, 378, 380 Albert Miller.

CHAPTER 34: 383 Albert Miller (based on Blomqvist and Mitchell; see Data Sources), 385, 386-387 (bottom) Miller (386-387 (bottom) based on Clausen et al; see Data Sources), 387 (top) Miller (based on Frick et al; see Data Sources); 388 (photographs) Arthur Leipzig.

Data and Photo Sources

CHAPTER 4: 399 Drawing from J Cell Biol 42:22 and 24, 1969

CHAPTER 6: 62, 66 Photographs from studies by Dr. David Jacobowitz, University of Pennsylvania

CHAPTER 8: 88 Drawing from Circ Res 20:1, 1967

CHAPTER 11: 114 Photomicrographs from Annals of New York Academy of Sciences 156:140, 141, 1969

CHAPTER 12: 128 Graph data from Mellins et al, Pediatrics 41:560, 1968

CHAPTER 15: 156 Photomicrographs from Exp Mol Pathol 4:465, 1965 and Arch Pathol 84:118, © 1967, American Medical Association; 160 Charts based on diagrams by Dr. Yecheskiel Stein and Dr. Angelo Scanu derived from Biochim Biophys Acta 265:491, 1972; Schumacher VN, Adams GH: Annu Rev Biochem 38:113, 1969; and Lindren FT, Nichols AV in The Plasma Proteins, Putnam FW, Ed. Vol 2, Academic Press, New York, 1960

CHAPTER 16: 167-170 Photomicrographs from Am J Pathol, © 1965

CHAPTER 20: 225 Graph data from International Study on Epidemiology of Cardiovascular Disease, Keys A, Ed., Coronary Heart Disease in Seven Countries. Circulation 41:Suppl 1, 1970

CHAPTER 22: 248 Micrographs from Am J Pathol 57:553, 1969; 249 Micrographs from Arch Pathol 79:138, 140, © 1965, American Medical Association; 250 Micrographs from Lab Invest 20:551, 1969

CHAPTER 34: 383 Graph data based on Blomqvist and Mitchell, Coronary Heart Disease and Physical Fitness, Larsen OA, Malmborg BO, Eds., University Park Press, Baltimore, 1971, p 30; 386-387 Graph data based on studies by Clausen et al, ibid p 27; 387 (top) Graph data based on studies by Frick and Katila, ibid p 47